The Complete Advanced Pilot

A Combined Commercial & Instrument Course

Third Edition

Bob Gardner

Aviation Supplies & Academics, Inc.
Newcastle, Washington

ASA-CAP-3

The Complete Advanced Pilot: A Combined Commercial & Instrument Course
Third Edition
by Bob Gardner

Aviation Supplies & Academics, Inc.
7005 132nd Place SE
Newcastle, Washington 98059-3153

Visit the ASA website often, as any updates due to FAA regulatory and procdural changes
will be posted there: www.asa2fly.com

Printed in the United States of America

05   04   03   02   9   8   7   6   5   4   3   2   1

ISBN 1-56027-459-X
ASA-CAP-3

Library of Congress Cataloging-in-Publication data:

Gardner, Robert E., 1928–
    The complete advanced pilot / Bob Gardner.
            p.   cm.
        Includes index.
        ISBN 1-56027-174-4
        1. Airplanes—Piloting   2. Instrument flying.   3. Air pilots—
        Licenses—United States.   4. Aeronautics—Examinations,
        questions, etc. I. Title.
    TL 710.G278 1994   94-36384
    629.132'52'076—dc20   CIP

Original illustrations: Dick Bringloe and Don Szymanski

Photo credits: p. x—Jim Fagiolo; p. 1-13—King; p. 3-15—Cessna Corporation; p. 4-6—
King; p. 4-11—Narco; p. 5-1—Boeing Company; p. 5-36—Cessna Corporation; p. 5-39—
Dennis Newton; p. 5-41—Bendix Corporation; p. 8-14—Arnav; p. 8-26—Bob Gardner;
p. 10-15—King; p. 11-3, 11-4—Narco; p. 12-9—Bob Gardner; p. 13-1—General Aviation
News & Flyer; p. 13-13—Bob Gardner. Charts on p. 9-14 provided courtesy E. Allan
Englehardt, FAA Accident Prevention Program. Chapter 5 illustrations (satellite and weather
forecast products) on the following pages are from the website of the National Weather
Service and National Oceanic and Atmospheric Administration, and as such are in the public
domain and not subject to copyright protection: p. 5-4, 5-5, 5-6, 5-15, 5-25, 5-26, 5-27, 5-29,
and 5-37.

Contents

Continued

Continued

Foreword

to the Third Edition

As an aviation educator and journalist, I receive an abundance of e-mail asking aviation questions, often-complex ones. My answers are always prompt and wonderfully informational because an airline Captain knows everything. I confess: Two things I know readily are what bookshelf Bob Gardner's books are located on for easy reference, and I know Bob Gardner's phone number. Together with my own 35 years of experience that encompasses "knowing just about everything."

In reading the Foreword written seven years ago complimenting Bob's *The Complete Advanced Pilot*, I'm tempted to underline many comments, but not alter anything. The latest edition amplifies in some areas, updates to current procedures, corrects a couple minor errors and is another outstanding exhibit of Bob's mastery of aviation academics.

Therefore, from seven years ago, I repeat with utmost sincerity:

In a long and rewarding friendship, Bob Gardner has always delighted me with his multitude of talents. Foremost in my inventory, he is a total gentleman, a giving and caring person who is driven to share all the knowledge he's accumulated throughout a diverse and impressive career.

His aviation experience is abundant: a flight instructor, charter pilot, corporate and freight Captain, ground school instructor, splendid speaker and dedicated educator. He has again documented decades of accumulated knowledge in another brilliantly organized instructional adventure: *The Complete Advanced Pilot*. As with all of his books, Bob's organized mind carves a route for you to reach complex destinations of understanding through simple road maps of educational travel.

To make the complex simple is the accomplishment of the capable teacher. The need to share and give and uplift are attributes of a person of quality. I find Bob's book exceptionally readable, splendidly sectioned for ready reference for virtually any topic, and supplemented with the caliber of personal experience that integrates "technique" into "procedure" with mastery.

Someone once defined for me the specifics of the "good" and the "bad" teacher. The latter always held back, denied to others some ingredient of his personal knowledge, retained and guarded some educational asset that set him above the bunch. Bob Gardner has always met the "good" definition, wanting you to know *everything* he's learned, in ways you can employ it, and to gain the confidence that you have become an enlightened and safe pilot by having absorbed all that this good man can give to you.

I'm grateful for the opportunity to review and comment upon the latest educational achievement by Bob Gardner. As my peer, friend and fellow educator, Bob never fails to earn my applause and endorsement.

Capt. Dave Gwinn, TWA-Retired
November 2001

About the Author

Bob Gardner has long been an admired member of the aviation community. He began his flying career in Alaska in 1960 while in the U.S. Coast Guard. By 1966, Bob accomplished his Private land and sea, Commercial, Instrument, Instructor, CFII and MEL. Over the next 16 years he was an instructor, charter pilot, designated examiner, freight dog and Director of ASA Ground Schools.

Currently, Bob holds an Airline Transport Pilot Certificate with single- and multi-engine land ratings; a CFI certificate with instrument and multi-engine ratings, and a Ground Instructor's Certificate with advanced and instrument ratings. In addition, Bob is a Gold Seal Flight Instructor and has been instructing since 1968. He received the Flight Instructor of the Year Award for Washington State. To top off this impressive list of accomplishments, Bob is also a well-known author, journalist and airshow lecturer.

Books by Bob Gardner

The Complete Private Pilot

The Complete Multi-Engine Pilot

The Complete Advanced Pilot: A Combined Commercial/Instrument Course

Say Again Please: Guide to Radio Communications

Introduction

Just what is "an advanced pilot"? My definition is a pilot with a commercial certificate and an instrument rating. This certificate and rating will allow you to have a long and enjoyable career in aviation. Sure, a multi-engine rating is valuable, but thousands of pilots have flown thousands of revenue hours without ever flying a twin. And if the Airline Transport Pilot Certificate is the Ph.D. of aviation, the commercial and instrument tickets represent the bachelor's and master's degrees.

Most private pilots aim for the instrument rating first, knowing they can get started right away while their brains are used to studying. They also know that the ability to fly in the clouds will speed up the progress of acquiring the 250-hour minimum for the commercial pilot certificate (Part 61). Many pilots have no interest in getting a commercial certificate but want the instrument rating so they can free themselves of VFR restrictions.

All of these pilots face knowledge examinations—one in the case of the noncommercial aviator, two for the pilot who wants to fly for money. Some of the required information overlaps; for example, both examinations test your knowledge of weather, weight and balance, and regulations. I'm going to handle that by having two sets of review questions where appropriate—read all of the text and then check your understanding by doing the review questions for the proper knowledge test. All review questions for this edition have been taken from FAA test databases.

Where information is unique to instrument flight or to commercial operations I will make that clear, and of course there will be whole chapters that apply to only one of your immediate goals. I will lead off with the instrument rating information because that applies to all of you, and finish with what you need to fly for hire.

Some of the information may seem basic. There are two reasons for this: Many prospective commercial pilots earned the private certificate many years ago, so some review is helpful; also, the commercial knowledge exam explores some operational areas in more depth than did the private pilot knowledge exam. However, I am not going to cover all of the private pilot information that you have needed to know in order to fly safely up to this point. If it has been a long time since you reviewed the knowledge requirements of a Private ticket, it might benefit you to review *The Complete Private Pilot*.

This introduction has implied a heavy emphasis on knowledge exams, but that is not my style as an instructor. What you need to know for the knowledge test represents less than half of the text—the rest is solid information you must have but the FAA doesn't ask about. To ace the test, use the appropriate ASA test preparation book.

You will also note an emphasis on computers, the internet, and the worldwide web. Most pilots are to some extent technically oriented, and it is estimated that well over half of all pilots use home computers for flight planning, acquiring weather information, maintaining their logbooks, etc. Accordingly, I have included access information wherever it is appropriate. As web surfers know, if you can find one webpage you will find links to dozens of other pages ready to be accessed with the click of a mouse button. A good place to start is www.asa2fly.com. You can reach me at bobmrg@attbi.com; I am also active in several internet newsgroups such as rec.aviation.ifr, rec.aviation.piloting, and rec.aviation.students.

One final word: I am a flight instructor, and flight instructors love to talk. You should hear my voice in your ear as you read. Also, I know that it aids in understanding if some information is presented in different contexts—so if you see the same material in more than one section it is not due to poor editing but is intended to carry out an instructional purpose.

The Flight Instruments

You and Your Flight Instruments

The FAA will test your knowledge of the flight instruments on both the commercial and instrument knowledge examinations. The material in this chapter applies to both.

When you begin training for the instrument rating you must make a mental commitment to believe the indications of the flight instruments and to ignore physical clues to flight attitude. The days of instrument flight by "the seat of your pants" never existed. It takes commitment and concentration to sit in a cockpit with nothing to look at but a collection of gauges and to feel comfortable and confident in your ability to control the airplane, to know its position in space, and to guide it safely to your destination. It's an ego trip. Pilots are a special group, and instrument pilots are the cream of the crop.

It's difficult to place your faith in an instrument unless you know how it works, where it gets its information, and how to use its indications to control the airplane. We'll begin with how the flight instruments work and then examine the systems that allow them to function. In the next chapter, we will discuss how to develop the most efficient method of scanning the instruments.

The six basic flight instruments are divided into two groups by source of power or input: pitot-static and

gyroscopic. Your knowledge of how each instrument derives its input will help you troubleshoot any erratic indications and isolate the instrument or system which has failed.

Pitot-Static Instruments

The pitot-static system consists of a pitot (pressure-sensing) tube, a static (zero pressure) source, and related plumbing and filters. The pitot-static instruments are the airspeed indicator, the altimeter, and the vertical speed indicator; they measure changes in air pressure caused by the airplane's vertical and horizontal movements in the atmosphere (*see* Figure 1-1).

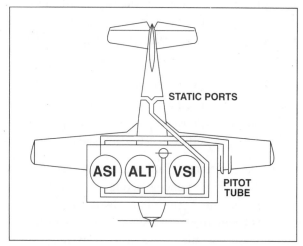

Figure 1-1. Pitot-static system

Airplanes equipped for instrument flight have pitot tube heaters, virtually identical to the resistance elements in your kitchen toaster, and they soak up a prodigious amount of electricity. Airplanes approved for instrument flight in commuter or on-demand operations must have pitot tube heaters. The pitot heat should be turned on before you fly into visible moisture, so that ice has no opportunity to form on the pitot tube. If water gets into the pitot plumbing it will cause erratic indications or worse. When the tubing connecting the pitot head to the airspeed indicator is blocked by ice, the air trapped between the point of blockage and the diaphragm in the instrument will expand as the airplane climbs, and the airspeed indicator will react as an altimeter, indicating higher airspeeds as altitude increases. A cross-check of the other instruments (especially the altimeter and VSI) will quickly pinpoint the ASI as having failed.

As a professional pilot or as a private pilot with a professional attitude, you should know what air-speed will result from a given pitch attitude and power setting; that is, you should be able to fly the airplane without an airspeed indicator if that becomes necessary in an emergency.

The static port is located where the airplane's motion through the air will create no pressure at all: on the side (or both sides) of the fuselage or on the back of the pitot tube. The airspeed indicator is calibrated to read the difference in pressure between impact air and still (static) air—both inputs are required.

If either the pitot tube or the static port is blocked the system will be useless, much like trying to get electricity from only one side of an electrical outlet. Blockage of the static system would disable the airspeed indicator, the altimeter, and the vertical speed indicator because no pressure differential would exist.

Depending on the location of the static source or sources, structural icing might cause such a blockage, and many all-weather airplanes are equipped with electrical static port heaters to eliminate this hazard.

Although an alternate static source is not required by 14 CFR 91.205 for noncommercial instrument flight, most IFR airplanes are equipped with one. (Part 135 requires an alternate static source for passenger-carrying flights operating under instrument flight rules.)

The alternate static source is a small valve or petcock at the pilot station which, when opened, vents the static system to the cockpit. When it is in use, the altimeter and airspeed indicator read slightly high; the vertical speed indicator will indicate correctly after momentarily reading in reverse. Opening the cabin vents will affect the readings of pitot-static instruments by slightly pressurizing the cabin when the alternate static source is being used.

If you are flying in icing conditions and your airplane does not have an alternate static source, water freezing in the static plumbing will put the pitot-static instruments out of commission. Your only option is to open the system to cabin pressure by breaking the glass on the vertical speed indicator. That will render the VSI pretty much useless (it would read backwards anyway) but save the day for the airspeed indicator and altimeter. The VSI isn't a required instrument anyway.

Situation	Airspeed	Altimeter	VSI
1. Blocked pitot.	zero	works	works
2. Blocked pitot and drain hole. Open static.	**high** in climb **low** in descent	works	works
3. Blocked static — open pitot.	**low** in climb **high** in descent	frozen	frozen
4. Using alternate cockpit static air.	reads high	reads high	momentarily shows a climb
5. Broken VSI glass.	reads high	reads high	reverses

Table 1-1. Pitot-static system failures

The Federal Aviation Regulations require that the altimeter and static system of any airplane used for instrument flight be inspected every 24 months, and that the logbook endorsement indicate the maximum altitude to which the system has been tested. For unpressurized airplanes this altitude will far exceed the service ceiling of the airplane.

Airspeed Indicator

The airspeed indicator requires input from both the pitot (pressure) and static (unchanging) sources. Air from the static port fills the airspeed instrument case, while air from the pitot tube is led to a diaphragm. As airspeed changes, the pressure exerted on the diaphragm also changes and the movement of the diaphragm in response to these changes is transmitted to the indicator needle. The designer tries to locate the pitot tube so that it registers pressure in free air and is not affected by local airflow around the supporting structure. The airspeed indicator is the only instrument that uses air pressure from the pitot tube.

At the start of the takeoff roll there is no difference in pressure between the pitot and static inputs, and the airspeed indicator will read zero. As the airplane accelerates, the pressure in the pitot tube increases and that pressure is transmitted to the airspeed indicator needle. The designer cannot completely isolate the pitot and static inputs from the effects of airflow around the wing or fuselage, so an airspeed correction table is provided. The needle on the airspeed indicator reads indicated airspeed (IAS); when corrected for installation or position error, it becomes calibrated airspeed (CAS). Note in Figure 1-2 that the greatest difference between indicated and calibrated airspeed occurs at low speeds which require high angles of attack, and that as the angle of attack is reduced and speed increases the difference between IAS and CAS becomes negligible. The colored arcs on the airspeed indicator are usually based on calibrated airspeed; other operating speeds may be based on indicated airspeed. Check the operator's handbook to be sure.

FLAPS UP												
KIAS	50	60	70	80	90	100	110	120	130	140	150	160
KCAS	55	63	71	80	89	99	108	118	128	138	147	157
FLAPS 10°												
KIAS	40	50	60	70	80	90	100	110	120	130	---	---
KCAS	50	54	62	71	81	91	100	110	120	130	---	---
FLAPS 30°												
KIAS	40	50	60	70	80	90	100	---	---	---	---	---
KCAS	47	54	62	71	81	90	101	---	---	---	---	---

Figure 1-2. Airspeed calibration

It takes a pressure of about 34 pounds per square foot on the pitot side of the airspeed indicator's diaphragm to make the airspeed needle register 100 knots at sea level—that's how the instrument shop calibrates your ASI. As the airplane climbs to altitude, the air becomes less dense. The airplane will have to move much faster through the less dense air at altitude to develop a pressure of 34 psf in the pitot tube, so the true airspeed will be faster than 100 knots when the airspeed indicator shows 100 knots. Your flight computer will allow you to make accurate calculations of true airspeed using IAS, pressure altitude, and temperature, but as a rule of thumb true airspeed increases by 2 percent per 1,000 feet of altitude. At sea level, under standard conditions, indicated and true airspeed will be equal; at 10,000 feet MSL, at the standard temperature for that altitude, an indicated 100 knots means a true airspeed of approximately 120 knots. When the ambient temperature rises above standard while indicated altitude is constant, pressure levels rise and both true airspeed and true altitude will increase.

At airspeeds in excess of 240 knots, heating caused by the compression of the air in the pitot tube must be taken into consideration in calculating true airspeed. Equivalent airspeed is calibrated airspeed corrected for the compressibility of the air, and should be of no concern at speeds less than 240 knots. Equivalent airspeed and calibrated airspeed are equal at sea level on a standard day—it is at high altitude and high airspeed that they differ.

You will use true airspeed in flight planning, but most airspeeds that you will use in actual flight are indicated airspeeds. You will always use the same indicated airspeeds, regardless of altitude. For example, if you are taking your flight training at a sea level airport and find that 110 knots indicated is the correct final approach speed, you will use 110 knots indicated airspeed on final when you fly to an airport at 5,000 feet above sea level as well. Your true airspeed will be 121 knots (2 percent times 5 = 10 percent, 1.1 times 110 = 121). Because the airplane approaching the airport at 5,000 feet is moving faster through the air to have an indicated airspeed of 110 knots, its ground speed will be higher and landing roll will be longer. A pilot who adds a few knots "just in case" while on final approach at a high altitude airport may have difficulty getting stopped on the available runway, especially if it is wet. Flying at the manufacturer's recommended airspeed will have predictable results.

A useful memory aid for the various airspeed corrections is "Ice Tea upside down." That is,

T rue (equivalent corrected for nonstandard temperature)

E quivalent (calibrated corrected for compressibility)

C alibrated (indicated corrected for installation or position error)

I ndicated

Pilots of light aircraft can safely ignore equivalent airspeed.

Figure 1-3. *Airspeed indicator with TAS window*

Figure 1-4. *Angle of attack indicator*

Most modern IFR airplanes are equipped with an airspeed indicator capable of being set to indicate true airspeed when the outside air temperature and pressure altitude are set in a window at the top of the instrument. True airspeed is read within the white arc at the bottom of the instrument. The inside calibrations on this type of instrument will still be indicated airspeeds, one in miles per hour and one in knots. *See* Figure 1-3.

Every airplane has a design maneuvering speed (V_A), which is the optimum speed in turbulence at maximum gross weight. Maneuvering speed is reduced as weight is reduced; get rid of ten percent of your payload weight and maneuvering speed will be reduced by five percent. Flight at or below maneuvering speed ensures that the airplane will stall before damaging aerodynamic loads are imposed on the wing structure.

The manufacturer may designate other speeds, which you will find in the Pilot's Operating Handbook and possibly placarded on the instrument panel. Landing gear extension and retraction speeds, maneuvering speed, and speeds for partial flap extension will be found in the operating handbook and not on the airspeed indicator.

You will be asked to interpret a velocity/G-load diagram, used to determine V-speeds, on the commercial pilot FAA knowledge examination. That subject will be covered in Chapter 2.

Angle of Attack Indicators

The airspeed indicator can be considered a form of angle of attack indicator, since indicated airspeed is dependent on both angle of attack and power setting. Several manufacturers provide actual angle of attack indicators, however, which are calibrated to measure the actual angle between the chord line and the relative wind and provide you with angle of attack information by some form of "safe-unsafe" or "fast-slow" instrument reading. One such instrument compares air pressure changes both vertically and horizontally and measures sink rate. *See* Figure 1-4.

In every case, you need only keep the instrument's needle in the "safe" area and no interpretation is required.

Altitude and Altimeters

You may recall Figure 1-5 from your private pilot training. Absolute altitude is your airplane's height above the ground as it might be measured by a radar altimeter. True altitude is your airplane's height above sea level; that's what it reads when you set the Kollsman window to the local altimeter setting. If you set it on the ground, indicated altitude should be within 75 feet of the published airport elevation; if it isn't, the altimeter needs work. Before you enrich the instrument shop, however, make sure that your airplane is not parked at a spot higher or lower than the airport reference point. Pressure altitude is measured above the standard datum plane of 29.92" Hg and is used at all times above 18,000 feet (Flight Level 180). You also use pressure altitude extensively in making performance calculations.

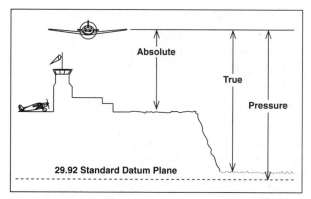

Figure 1-5. Altitude definitions

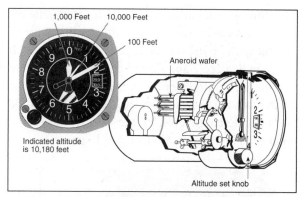

Figure 1-6. 3-Needle altimeter

Aircraft altimeters are aneroid (dry) barometers calibrated to read in feet above sea level (true altitude). The altimeter gets its input from the static port, which is unaffected by the airplane's movement through the air. An aneroid barometer contains several sealed wafers with a partial internal vacuum, so as the airplane moves vertically and the outside pressure changes, the wafers expand and contract much like an accordion. This expansion and contraction is transmitted through a linkage to the altimeter needles.

Barometers provide a means of weighing the earth's atmosphere at a specific location. At a flight service station or National Weather Service office, an actual mercury barometer may be used, and on a standard day the weight of the atmosphere will support a column of mercury (Hg) 29.92 inches high at sea level. Inches of mercury are the units of measure for barometric pressure and altimeter settings. The equivalent metric measure is 1013.2 millibars.

Up to 18,000 feet, altitude is measured above sea level, and sea level pressure will normally vary between 28.50" to 30.50" Hg. The *Aeronautical Information Manual* contains specific procedures to be followed if cold weather causes an altimeter setting of 31.00" or more. If the barometric pressure is less than 28.50", both you and your airplane should be protected from hurricane-force winds.

Your altimeter has an adjustment knob and an altimeter setting window, and you must enter the sea level barometric pressure (altimeter setting) at your location as received from a nearby flight service station or air traffic control facility (each time you are handed off from one ATC controller to another, you should receive an altimeter setting). You can only use field elevation

when nothing else is available, and even then you must get an altimeter setting as soon as possible. The altimeter will, when properly set, read altitude above mean sea level (MSL). *See* Figure 1-6.

As you increase the numbers in the altimeter setting window, the hands on the altimeter also show an increase: each .01 increase in the window is equal to 10 feet of altitude, each .1 is 100 feet, etc.

Misreading of altimeters has caused several accidents. The indication of the 3-needle altimeter found in many aircraft can be misinterpreted by 10,000 feet if the needle on the outside rim of the instrument is ignored or misread. In Figure 1-7, which instrument depicts 10,000 feet? Instrument R is correct. The 10,000-foot needle reads one, and the 1,000-foot and 100-foot needles read zero. What are the readings of instruments Q, S, and T? Check the bottom of the page for the answers.*

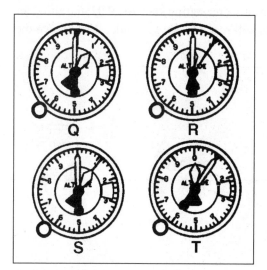

Figure 1-7. Reading 3-needle altimeter

---

* Q=1,000 feet; S=11,000 feet; T= 10,100 feet.

The drum-pointer altimeter is encountered quite often in light aircraft and is the altimeter of choice as you move up to more expensive flying machines. It has a single needle and a drum counter similar to an automobile's odometer. As the needle rotates, the drum reads the altitude directly in easily understood numbers. Each rotation of the needle causes the counter to increase 1,000 feet. *See* Figure 1-8.

Figure 1-8. Drum-pointer altimeter

Pressure Altitude

You will need to determine pressure altitude to convert indicated airspeed to true airspeed or to calculate density altitude using your flight computer.

There are two ways of accomplishing this: first, note your indicated altitude and altimeter setting, then turn the altimeter setting knob to 29.92; the altimeter needles will read pressure altitude. Write down the pressure altitude and return the altimeter setting knob to its original position. The second method requires some mental gymnastics: determine the difference between your present altimeter setting and 29.92 and add a zero. This will give you the difference in feet between your indicated altitude and the pressure altitude. Then add or subtract this value to (or from) the indicated altitude to get pressure altitude, remembering that the altimeter needles always move in the same direction as the numbers in the setting window.

For example, assume that you are cruising at an indicated altitude of 7,000 feet with the altimeter set to 30.15, and you need to know pressure altitude for a flight computer calculation.

The difference between 29.92 and 30.15 is .23, or 230 feet. If you turned the altimeter setting knob to lower its setting to 29.92, the needles would move counterclockwise 230 feet, so the pressure altitude is 6,770 feet. The advantage of this method is that there is no danger of resetting the altimeter incorrectly.

Above 18,000 feet the altimeter must be set to 29.92" Hg; you will be reading your altitude above the standard datum plane. By international agreement, a standard day at sea level is defined as having a barometric pressure of 29.92 (with the temperature 15°C), and by setting your altimeter to 29.92 it will read altitude above that standard level. Below 18,000 feet, having the correct altimeter setting will keep you out of the trees, while above 18,000 feet (where there are no trees or mountains in this part of the

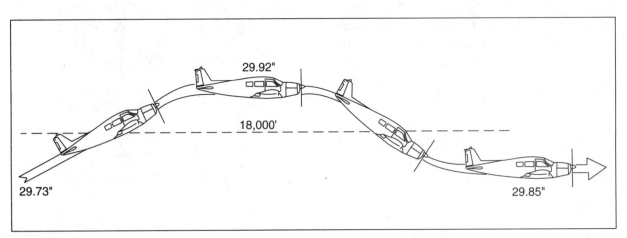

Figure 1-9. Change to pressure levels above 18,000 feet MSL

world), the common altimeter setting of 29.92 provides altitude separation for IFR flights. Pressure altitudes of 18,000 feet and above are referred to as Flight Levels: "I'd like to file for flight level 220." *See* Figure 1-9.

14 CFR 91.121 establishes minimum allowable IFR altitudes when surface barometric pressure is 29.91" or lower. The intent is to avoid conflict between IFR airplanes operating in Class A airspace and VFR or IFR airplanes operating at an indicated altitude of 17,500 feet (or below, depending on how low the surface pressure is). Assume that you set your altimeter to the reported surface setting of 28.92" before takeoff and maintain that setting as you climb. When you climb through an indicated 18,000 feet, you reset the altimeter to 29.92", changing its reading to 19,000 feet. If you then descend to an indicated 18,000 feet with that altimeter setting, you will be below airplanes flying at 17,500 feet with the surface altimeter setting. The FAA guards against this by not clearing any airplane to a flight level below 190 when the surface altimeter setting is 28.92" or below, and you guard against being assigned an altitude you didn't file for by checking 14 CFR 91.121 when the surface pressure is low. *See* Figure 1-10.

Current altimeter setting	Lowest usable flight level
29.92 (or higher)	180
29.91 through 29.42	185
29.41 through 28.92	190
28.91 through 28.42	195
28.41 through 27.92	200
27.91 through 27.42	205
27.41 through 26.92	210

(c) To convert minimum altitude prescribed under §§ 91.119 and 91.177 to the minimum flight level, the pilot shall take the flight level equivalent of the minimum altitude in feet and add the appropriate number of feet specified below, according to the current reported altimeter setting:

Current altimeter setting	Adjustment factor
29.92 (or higher)	None
29.91 through 29.42	500
29.41 through 28.92	1,000
28.91 through 28.42	1,500
28.41 through 27.92	2,000
27.91 through 27.42	2,500
27.41 through 26.92	3,000

Figure 1-10. *14 CFR 91.121 excerpt*

Effects of Temperature and Pressure on Altimeter Indications

When you fly into an area of lower barometric pressure (while maintaining a constant altimeter setting) your true altitude will be lower than your indicated altitude, and that can be dangerous.

Avoid this by frequently checking with ground stations to use an altimeter setting received from a station within 100 miles. If you fly into an area of colder temperatures, where air density is increased, indicated altitude will again be higher than true altitude. "From High to Low, Look Out Below" applies to both pressure and temperature. You have no means of adjusting for temperature changes, so remember that pressure levels rise on warm days and descend on cold days, and if you are flying a constant pressure level (altimeter setting), you may be dangerously low on a cold day.

Bernoulli's Theorem, which states that air pressure decreases when its velocity increases, comes into play when strong winds blow over mountain ranges. Barometric pressure can change rapidly and drastically under these conditions, so don't trust your altimeter when in turbulence near a ridge line.

Encoding Altimeter

The Federal Aviation Regulations require that an airplane be equipped with an altitude reporting transponder (Mode C) when operating within 30 nautical miles of Class B airspace from the surface up to 10,000 feet MSL, when in Class E airspace above 10,000 feet MSL, and when in Class C airspace or above its horizontal boundaries up to 10,000 feet MSL. Selecting "ALT" on your transponder will not do a bit of good unless your airplane has an altitude encoding altimeter or a blind encoder, however.

An encoding altimeter sends information to your transponder which enables it to transmit altitude information to the ground when interrogated by ATC radar. It reports altitude above the standard datum plane (29.92" Hg.) and is unaffected by any change in the altimeter setting. Encoding altimeters are usually identified as such on the face of the instrument.

A blind encoder is located remotely and has its own internal altimeter; the airplane you are flying may have a blind encoder and you won't be aware of it unless you check the airplane's logs—and you should. The blind encoder is also set to report altitude in relation to the standard datum plane, and equipment on the ground makes the necessary correction based on the local sea level pressure. There is nothing you can do in the cockpit that will affect the altitude readout seen by the controller.

Because these encoding devices are occasionally inaccurate or defective, the ATC controller may ask you to verify your altitude as indicated by the altimeter and, if the error is excessive, may ask you to turn off the Mode C. Do not change altitude unless directed to do so by the controller. It is not uncommon for one controller to tell a pilot that his or her encoder is reading incorrectly and should be checked, while controllers in adjacent sectors report no problem.

Vertical Speed Indicator

The vertical speed indicator (Figure 1-11) is a static-pressure instrument which reflects rate of climb or descent by detecting rate of change in air pressure. Its internal construction is similar to that of the altimeter, but the aneroid wafer in the vertical speed indicator has a calibrated leak which allows its internal pressure to stabilize when altitude is not changing. During changes, there is a pressure differential between the air in the wafer and the air surrounding it, and the instrument indicates the change in this differential as climb or descent rate in feet per minute.

Figure 1-11. Vertical speed indicator

The needle will lag actual changes in altitude until the rate of change stabilizes. However, if your instrument is marked "IVSI", it is an Instantaneous Vertical Speed Indicator and the lag has been eliminated. The VSI is not required for either VFR or IFR flight, but you won't find many airplanes without one. If the static port is clogged or frozen the VSI will be unusable—select the alternate static source if one is available.

Gyroscopic Instruments

The attitude indicator, the turn indicator, and the directional gyro or heading indicator operate on the principle of gyroscopic rigidity in space. A spinning body, such as a bicycle wheel, will maintain its position in space as long as a rotational force is applied—riding your bike "no hands" is an example of this.

Precession, or turning, occurs when any external force is applied to the spinning body, which will react as though the force has been applied at a point 90° away from the point of application in the direction of rotation.

When you lean your bicycle to the right, the top of the rotating wheel moves to the right; the resultant turning force is as though pressure has been applied to the left front of the wheel—90° in the direction of rotation—and the bike turns to the right. Actually turning the wheel to the right instead of leaning may cause the bicycle to topple over to the left, again the result of gyroscopic precession.

Turn and Slip Indicator

Your airplane may have either a turn needle or a turn coordinator, but in either case a ball instrument will be included. Both the turn needle and the turn coordinator indicate the rate of turn of the aircraft: when a turn needle is deflected a single needle-width, or when the turn coordinator's airplane wing is on the index, the airplane is turning at the rate of 3° per second, and a complete circle will take 2 minutes. NOTE: If a turn needle instrument is marked "4 MIN TURN," a single needlewidth turn is one-half standard rate and it will take 4 minutes to complete a 360° circle; these are found in high speed airplanes. *See* Figure 1-12.

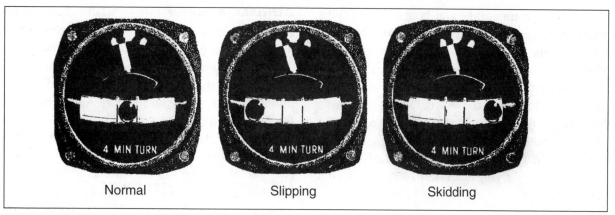

Figure 1-12. Turn and slip indicator; half-standard rate turn

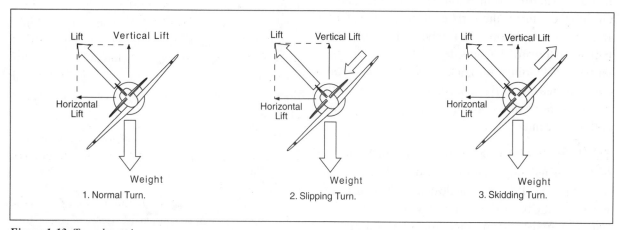

Figure 1-13. Turn dynamics

The turn indicator (needle) only shows rotation around the yaw axis, while the turn coordinator, with its gyro tilted 45 degrees from the vertical, reacts to both roll and yaw forces. That is, it shows both turn rate and roll rate.

Either instrument will deflect during turns while taxiing, because the airplane is rotating around the yaw axis. You can force the turn coordinator to give misleading indications in flight: push one rudder pedal while holding the wings level with aileron and the turn coordinator will obediently indicate a turn; bank the wings while maintaining a constant heading with rudder and it will indicate a turn while you are rolling into the bank. When the bank is established and you have stopped rolling, the TC will return to a wings-level indication. You are neither rolling nor yawing at that point. Note that the turn coordinator doesn't lie in normal, coordinated flight—you have to work at it. In either of the situations described the ball would be deflected well out of the center. *See* Figure 1-13.

Neither instrument indicates bank angle directly, although bank angle can be inferred if you understand the relationship between airspeed and rate of turn.

Consider a light trainer and a jet, both banked 20°: the trainer would complete a 360° turn in a much shorter time than the jet and with a much smaller radius. Conversely, if both airplanes maintained a 3° per second turn rate they would both complete the circle at the same time—but the jet would be at an extreme bank angle. The bank angle for a 3° per second turn is approximately 10 percent of the true airspeed plus 5, so the trainer at a TAS of 80 knots would bank only 13°, while the jet flying at a TAS of 400 knots would have to bank 45°.

The ball indicates the quality of the turn, with respect to rudder-aileron coordination. The force that causes an airplane to turn is the horizontal component of lift. If the rate of turn is too great for the angle of bank, the ball rolls toward the outside of the turn. This is termed a "skidding" turn, and either a steeper bank angle (increasing horizontal component) or less rudder pressure on the inside of the turn will return the ball to the center.

The reverse situation has the ball falling to the inside of the turn in a "slip," caused by too much horizontal lift component. Less bank angle or more inside rudder will return the ball to the center. A rule of thumb is to "step on the ball"—apply pressure to the rudder pedal on the side of the instrument that the ball is deflected toward. Turn needles or turn coordinators are almost always electrically driven, but you may find a turn needle driven by vacuum from an engine-driven vacuum pump or a venturi. Be sure that you know what makes your turn indicator operate.

If you are flying an airplane equipped with an autopilot, it is especially important that you know whether its roll input comes from the attitude indicator or the turn coordinator. If the vacuum pump fails, will you lose the autopilot as well? Will the electric turn coordinator work with the autopilot to keep the airplane rightside up while you sort the situation out?

The turn coordinator or turn needle should indicate turn direction correctly during taxi turns, and checking for proper operation should be a part of your IFR preflight check. The ball should move to the outside of any turns while taxiing.

Attitude Indicator

The attitude indicator is the only instrument on the panel that reacts instantaneously to pitch and roll inputs. The gyroscope and its linkage cause the horizon disc to move in both pitch and roll behind the miniature airplane. If you compare the movement of the horizon line in the attitude indicator with the movement of the natural horizon, you will see that the instrument instantly and accurately reflects changes in the pitch and roll attitude of the airplane. It is this instantaneous representation that makes the attitude indicator the most valuable instrument on the panel when reference to the natural horizon is lost. The bank angle markings at the top of the instrument are 10°, 20°, 30°, 45° (some instruments), 60° and 90°. Your instrument may or may not have pitch markings—those that do have them in increments of 5° above the horizon. If your instrument does not have pitch markings you can estimate pitch attitude by "bar widths"; the bar which represents the wings of your airplane is 2° thick. *See* Figure 1-14.

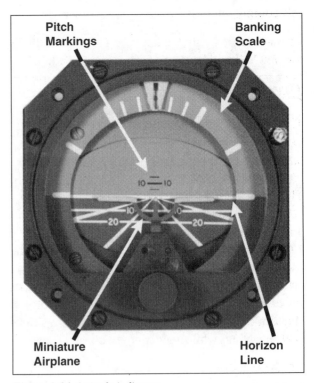

Figure 1-14. Attitude indicator

In most light airplanes, the gyroscopes in the attitude indicator and heading indicator are vacuum operated. An engine-driven vacuum pump draws air into the instrument case, and as the air passes over turbine wheels it imparts a rotational force. When the gyroscope rotors are up to speed, they become fixed in the plane of rotation and the airplane moves around them. The instrument presentations are so designed that the pilot has an accurate indication of airplane attitude and heading. Not all gyro installations are entirely vacuum operated—you may find that your heading indicator is electric and the attitude indicator is vacuum, or both may be electrically operated. Check the power source for each instrument in your airplane so that you can better deal with failures.

The attitude indicator has two types of error that are of interest to instrument pilots. The first is acceleration error: when you apply takeoff power the horizon line tilts down, giving you the misleading impression that your climb attitude is too steep. If you react to this with forward stick pressure you may find yourself coming out of the overcast nose down.

Cross-checking with the altimeter, airspeed indicator, and VSI will keep you from being fooled. When your vertical speed has stabilized the error disappears.

The second error develops in vacuum-operated attitude indicators during steep turns. The flow of air passing over the rotor is controlled by pendulous vanes which normally act to keep the gyro erect. They are affected by centrifugal force in steep turns, however, and introduce an error which reaches its maximum value after 180° of turn. If you turn exactly 180° and roll the wings level solely by reference to the attitude indicator's horizon bar, you will be in error by 3°–5°, and there will be a slight pitch up indication — this error corrects itself quickly, but a check of the turn coordinator to confirm wings level will help.

The error cancels itself out if the turn is a full 360°. If the turn is a skidding turn, the attitude indicator will show a slight bank in the opposite direction when the wings are levelled by visual reference or by checking the turn coordinator.

The attitude indicator should be fully erect within 5 minutes after engine start. Any tendency of the horizon line to tilt during taxi turns indicates that the instrument is not up to speed and may not be reliable.

Heading Indicator

You shouldn't always trust your heading indicator (directional gyro—see Figure 1-15) to tell you which way you are heading. The heading indicator is not a very smart instrument: it only repeats the heading that has been set into it. For that reason, it has an adjustment knob, and must be set to correspond to the magnetic compass (or to the runway heading) before it can be used for navigation. If you fail to set the heading indicator properly before takeoff and do not notice that it disagrees with the magnetic compass, you can be many miles off course in a surprisingly short time. Jeppesen approach plates give actual magnetic runway headings, while government plates use only the runway number.

Because the gyro's rotor spins at a velocity of about 18,000 rpm, its bearings must have a minimum of friction. As the bearings wear, or as dirt and contaminants (such as tobacco tar) collect at these critical points, the gyro will begin to slowly precess (drift) away from the heading you have set. You should check the heading indicator against the magnetic compass at least every 15 minutes, and more often if the instrument is showing signs of age such as

Figure 1-15. Heading indicator

grinding noises or rapid precession. You can learn a lot about the condition of your gyro instruments if you sit in the cockpit and listen to them spin down after shutting down the engine.

Reset the heading indicator to the magnetic compass only when the airplane is in straight and level, unaccelerated flight. The magnetic compass develops errors during banks, climbs, and descents, and you do not want to set these errors into your heading indicator.

Pilots have lined up for takeoff on the wrong runway in extremely poor visibility conditions, so you should check both the magnetic compass and heading indicator to ensure that you are in position on the correct runway for takeoff.

Magnetic Compass

The only instrument in your airplane that does not depend on some source of external power is the magnetic compass. All navigational procedures are based on magnetic information.

Unfortunately, the magnetic compass is subject to more errors than any other instrument. The "wet" magnetic compass consists of a card floating in a liquid, pivoted on a needle point, and having affixed to it small permanent magnets that align themselves (and therefore the card) with the earth's magnetic field. The magnetic compass is subject to several errors: oscillation error, acceleration error, and northerly turning error. Because of the single-point suspension, the compass card swings in even the slightest turbulence, and you must average its swings to approximate a constant heading. If your compass does not swing when the air gets rough, check to be sure that the fluid hasn't leaked out!

Northerly turning error is caused by the fact that the lines of force of the earth's magnetic field are parallel to the earth's surface at the equator, but bend downward toward the surface as latitude increases and are almost vertical at the magnetic poles.

This force, which pulls the ends of the compass magnets downward, is called "magnetic dip": when the airplane banks and the compass card tilts, the compass magnets, affected by dip, introduce a compass error. When you turn from a generally northerly

heading, the compass will momentarily turn in the opposite direction, slow to a stop, and then follow the progress of the turn—but lagging the actual heading change. The amount of lag diminishes as the heading approaches east or west. Conversely, when you turn from a southerly heading the compass jumps out ahead of the turn, and leads the heading change, with the amount of lead again diminishing as east or west is approached. The amount of lead or lag which is attributable to northerly turning error is approximately equal to the airplane's latitude.

Acceleration error is evident on headings of east or west. If the airplane is accelerated, without changing heading, the compass will indicate a turn to the north, while deceleration on an east or west heading will cause the compass to indicate a turn to the south. Don't trust your wet compass during departure climbs or descents into the terminal area. Use this memory aid: A N D S—Accelerate North, Decelerate South. *See* Figure 1-16.

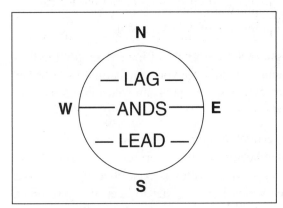

Figure 1-16. Magnetic compass errors

It is because of northerly turning error and acceleration error that you must set the heading indicator to agree with the magnetic compass only in straight and level, unaccelerated flight.

If you must rely solely on your magnetic compass for navigation, the most effective way to change heading is the timed turn. Note the magnetic compass heading, determine how many degrees you want to turn, and turn at 3° per second (using the index on the turn coordinator or turn needle) for the appropriate number of seconds. If you complete the turn within 5° or 10° of your target heading, you are within acceptable limits.

You may read about compass turns in other texts. A compass turn is one in which the pilot attempts to outsmart the lead and lag errors and factors latitude into the calculation. The FAA does not require instrument pilots to demonstrate the ability to perform compass turns because the concept defies reality. Visualize yourself flying in the clouds, in darkness, turbulence and rain, relying solely on the magnetic compass because your vacuum-operated heading indicator and attitude indicator have failed. Do you think that you would have the presence of mind to deal with things like latitude and applying one-half the bank angle to the lead or lag to figure out when to stop a turn? Unlikely. Use the turn instrument and sweep second hand for timed turns instead.

External forces that affect magnetic compass accuracy are variation and deviation. Variation, as you recall from your private pilot training, changes with geographic location and is independent of heading. Deviation is caused by the interaction of magnetic fields within the airplane itself and the earth's magnetic lines of force. Because deviation is affected by the airplane's heading, a compass correction card must be used. It is especially important that you refer to the compass correction card when using the automatic direction finder (ADF) for navigation.

Vertical Card Magnetic Compasses

You may find an airplane with a vertical card magnetic compass. These relatively new devices contain no liquid, and have little or no oscillation error. Their stability approaches that of the directional gyro. Acceleration error and northerly turning error are present, but are quickly damped by internal electrical currents. Variation and deviation must still be accounted for. Vertical card compasses are considerably more expensive (but easier to use) than liquid-filled compasses. If you own your own airplane and plan to fly instruments seriously, have a vertical card compass installed. *See* Figure 1-17.

Figure 1-17. *Vertical card compass*

Slaved Gyro Systems

If your airplane has a horizontal situation indicator (HSI) as a heading indicator, it may derive its directional information from a remote magnetic compass called a flux detector mounted in the tail or wing tip, away from electrical influences. Like the liquid-filled compass in the cockpit, it derives information from the earth's magnetic field (flux); unlike the "wet" compass, it does not have oscillation error and is *relatively* unaffected by magnetic dip. The detector does not rotate but develops a variable error signal as the airplane's relation to the lines of magnetic flux changes. The weak electrical signals from the magnetic flux detector must be amplified before being transmitted to the heading indicator, which then rotates or "slaves" into agreement with the directional information from the remote source.

Your system may provide two amplifiers, with a selector switch to allow you to change amplifiers if you suspect that one has failed.

The system includes compensating devices to minimize or eliminate any deviation error. The exact location of the amplifier(s) and compensating devices varies between manufacturers, and the location of the magnetic flux detector is determined by the installer. Figure 1-18 illustrates a possible installation with optional flux detector locations.

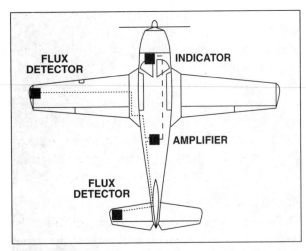

Figure 1-18. *Slaved compass system*

Figure 1-19. *Slaving control*

These installations include a slaving meter and buttons used to bring the directional gyro card into agreement with the magnetic compass in the cabin, just as you set your heading indicator to agree with the wet compass. The SLAVE-IN button is a toggle — push it in to activate slaving, push it again and it pops out to the FREE GYRO position. The slaving meter indicates the amount and direction of any difference between the heading displayed on the heading indicator and the actual magnetic heading, and it will deflect to one side or the other while the airplane is in a turn, just as the wet compass does. Accordingly, you should never attempt to adjust the slaved gyro unless the airplane is in straight and level flight or on the ground.

When you are in an airplane with a vacuum-operated heading indicator, you note any difference between the reading of the heading indicator and the indication of the wet compass, then use the heading indicator's adjustment knob to rotate its dial into agreement with the wet compass. The slaved gyro system is electric, and operates only when the airplane's electrical system is activated with the master switch. If the airplane has been moved since the master switch was turned off, there will probably be a difference between the slaved gyro heading indicator's reading and that of the wet compass, and the slaving meter's needle (slightly left of zero in Figure 1-19) will be deflected in the direction of the error. Numbers are really not important: Toggle the SLAVE-IN button to the popped-out FREE GYRO position, and if the slaving needle is deflected to the left, push the clock-

wise button on the left to zero it; if the needle is deflected to the right, use the counterclockwise button. The heading indicator dial will rotate accordingly. Then push the SLAVE-IN button in.

FAA knowledge test writers thrive on numbers, so their questions about slaved gyro systems will not simply let you look at a deflected slaving meter needle; for their purposes, you need to know what makes the needle deflect as it does.

When you turn on the master switch in your sophisticated airplane, you note that the magnetic compass reads 110° but the heading indicator reads 125° as in Figure 1-15 — ignore the slaving meter for the moment. Which way must the heading indicator card be rotated to bring 110° under the index? Clockwise, correct? You would put the slaving system in FREE GYRO mode and push the clockwise button on the left in Figure 1-19 to rotate the heading indicator card into agreement with the magnetic compass, then activate the slaving system by toggling the SLAVE-IN button to its IN position. The slaving meter needle? Oh, it was deflected to the left, because the desired heading was to the left of 125°; that's left compass error.

Systems

Your flight and navigation instruments will rely on the airplane's vacuum and electrical systems for power, and you need an understanding of how these systems operate to assess and correct failures.

Vacuum Systems

In some airplanes, the use of the term "vacuum system" is inaccurate, because their pumps provide a positive pressure instead of a vacuum. The gyroscope in the flight instrument will operate in exactly the same way in either case, so this discussion will deal with vacuum pumps as though they are all the same.

Vacuum pumps can be either "wet" or "dry." A wet pump is lubricated with engine oil, and is known for leaving black streaks on the bottom of the fuselage. This is the price the pilot pays for the relatively long service life of a wet vacuum pump. A dry vacuum pump consists of carbon vanes rotating in an aluminum housing, and therein lies the seeds of its destruction.

If the vanes were made of metal and a failure occurred which stopped rotation, damage to the gearing in the accessory case which drives not only the vacuum pump but the magnetos might result. The pump manufacturer avoids this by using the relatively soft carbon material for vanes and also by purposely weakening the pump's drive shaft so that it will shear, just like an outboard motor's shear pin.

If the shaft shears, your vacuum operated gyro instruments will gradually spin down and stop, giving you misleading information as their gyros slow. The suction gauge on the panel will give no warning of impending failure.

If the carbon vanes wear away at their outer edges, you may notice a gradual drop in the indication of the panel vacuum gauge. Small carbon granules wearing off of the vanes will not destroy the pump. Clearances are quite small, however, and if a large piece detaches itself from a carbon vane it will be a matter of moments before the rest of the vanes have chewed themselves up. WARNING: Turning the propeller backward to "loosen the engine up" or "spread some oil around before starting" may harm the vacuum pump, according to Lycoming.

Unlike buying accessories for an automobile, you can only install what the FAA has approved for your airplane. Depending on your airplane, you may not have a choice between a wet or dry vacuum pump.

Because the gyroscopic attitude indicator plays a major role in instrument flight, there are several after-market systems available to take over if the vacuum pump fails. They range from a separate electrically powered attitude indicator, to electric vacuum pumps, to backup vacuum systems operated from the intake manifold. There is a proposal before the FAA to allow the substitution of a battery-operated backup attitude indicator with a ball indicator for the turn instrument in light airplanes.

Electrical System

The basic electrical source in your airplane is the battery, but after it has provided power to the starter motor to start the engine it plays a secondary role. Most modern airplanes derive electrical power from an alternator, either directly driven by the engine through the accessory case or through a belt drive. If your alternator is belt driven, your preflight inspection must include a check of belt tension and condition.

An alternator requires an excitation current through its field windings before it can develop any output, and if your airplane's battery is completely drained the alternator will not be able to recharge it. A quick check of condition can be made when you turn on the master switch: you should be able to hear the solenoid close and the turn coordinator's gyro should begin to spin up. If neither of these events occurs, the battery should be recharged or replaced or a start with external power attempted. If you start the engine by "hand propping," there will be no excitation current and therefore no output from the alternator, and the battery will not be recharged in flight.

If your airplane has a split master switch, one half provides current to the alternator field windings and that side can be turned off during engine start to reduce the load on the battery. Once the engine is running, the alternator field side of the master switch can be turned back on to provide electricity to the rest of the electrical system. This procedure will not be found in the Pilot's Operating Handbook. *See* Figure 1-20.

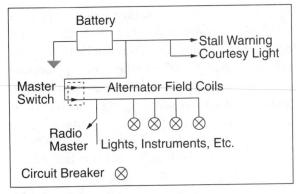

Figure 1-20. Electrical systems

The electric system will also have one or more voltage regulators, selectable by a switch. While emergency checklists vary between airplanes, most procedures involve reducing the load on the alternator by turning off unnecessary lights and radios and switching voltage regulators. Because almost all navigation instruments require electricity, you should know the emergency procedures that apply to your airplane. When the alternator fails, the airplane's battery will continue to supply the electrical needs of the airplane until it becomes discharged.

Failure of the electrical system can be insidious, because if you do not include the ammeter in your scan of the panel instruments and the alternator has failed you may have been dependent on battery power for an unknown length of time. Some airplanes have annunciator panels which signal alternator failure, but in others the dimming of the panel lights, the slow movement of the fuel gauges toward EMPTY, and a loss of communication will alert you to the existence of a problem. If you took off an hour ago with full tanks and the gauges now read empty, you are probably out of electricity, not out of fuel.

Circuit breakers protect individual elements of the electrical system such as the flap motor, radios, landing lights, etc. If the circuit breakers in your airplane are the type that can be pulled, you can use that capability to isolate a fault in the system. If the circuit breakers cannot be pulled individually and one should "pop," allow it to cool and make one attempt to re-set it. If it fails a second time, make no further effort.

Flight Instrument Failures

You can identify a failed instrument or system through your knowledge of how the instruments are powered or where they derive their inputs. When you are faced with a possible instrument malfunction you should look for a triangle of agreement. For example, a climbing right turn can be confirmed by the attitude and heading indicators (gyro, usually vacuum powered), the altimeter (pitot-static), the turn coordinator (gyro, usually electric), and the vertical speed indicator (static).

In Figure 1-21, one system has failed. Which is it? The attitude indicator shows a bank to the right but the heading indicator shows a turn to the left. The pitot-static instruments and turn coordinator all indicate level flight. The vacuum pump which powers the attitude indicator and heading indicator has failed.

One instrument has failed in Figure 1-22. Which one? The turn coordinator and heading indicator agree on a right turn, and the airspeed, altimeter, and VSI agree on a climb. The attitude indicator says diving left turn—but it has failed. Look for a triangle of agreement. If two out of three instruments agree, the third instrument must be suspect.

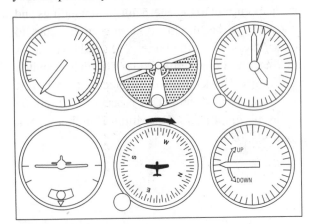

Figure 1-21. System failure

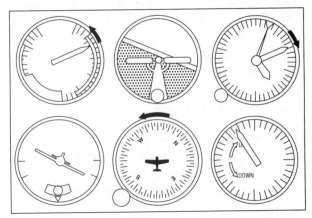

Figure 1-22. Instrument failure

In Figure 1-23, a system has failed. Which system? All three gyro instruments indicate a descending turn to the right, but the pitot-static instruments disagree. Because the turn coordinator is electrically driven while the attitude and heading indicators are vacuum driven, the gyro instruments have to be correct. The pitot-static system has failed.

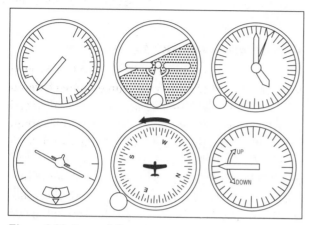

Figure 1-23. System failure

Autopilots, Flight Directors, and Flight Control Systems

During training for the instrument rating you will be in full control of the airplane, but after you are rated you may have an opportunity to fly one with some mechanical aid.

The simplest "autopilot" is a wing-leveler. It gives you a chance to read charts or do paperwork without the airplane turning upside down, and in my opinion one should be installed in every airplane used for serious IFR flying. It gets its input from either the directional gyro or the turn coordinator—you should know what the power source is in any autopilot-equipped airplane you fly. Many pilots have experienced vacuum pump failure with its accompanying control problems, unaware that they could have used their autopilot which derived its input from the electrically driven turn coordinator.

The next step up adds heading hold, which takes its input from the directional gyro. It is no smarter than the DG, however, so if you fail to keep the DG in agreement with the magnetic compass the heading hold will lead you astray. With heading hold you can track radials and localizers manually by making small adjustments to the heading "bug."

The last addition to a simple autopilot is the ability to track a navigation signal without any pilot input. These either have a "LOC REV" position for flying back course approaches or have a reversing switch to accomplish the same thing. They cannot track the signal from a nondirectional beacon.

An autopilot with altitude hold derives its information barometrically; it not only holds a desired altitude but allows you to control the rate of climb or descent. A "three-axis" autopilot includes a yaw damper.

All of the tracking devices described so far use raw data—the same needle indications you would follow if you were flying the airplane manually. A flight director provides a new set of visual clues for you to follow. Figure 1-24 shows command bars which provide attitude information and a delta which you maneuver to keep in relation to the command bars. Another form of display is the familiar cross needles of the instrument landing system, except that in a flight director they move in response to pitch and roll commands.

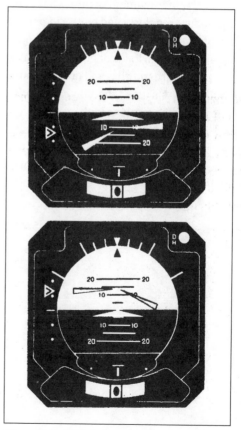

Figure 1-24. Flight director

The illustration shows flying straight and level (the delta); but a turn is commanded by the heading bug or by a navigation signal so the command bars bank accordingly, and by flying the delta into the vee of the command bars you would establish the required bank. A climb or descent is commanded by selecting a new altitude or by intercepting a glideslope and causes the command bars to pitch up or down, as shown. They will anticipate the level-off for you. The command bars react to many inputs too subtle for you to pick up: rate of turn, rate of needle movement, etc. By following the command bars you fly the airplane much more smoothly than you could with raw data. You do fly the airplane, though—it is not flown for you.

The last step ties the flight director and the autopilot together in a flight control system. Now the autopilot follows the movements of the command bars, and it is your job to monitor the procedure to ensure that a system failure won't cause the airplane to diverge from the desired path.

Recent studies have indicated that sophisticated systems may hamper, rather than aid, a pilot who does not use the equipment regularly and have a thorough understanding of its operation. If you have an opportunity to fly an airplane with loads of goodies, be sure that you read the manual carefully, and don't use any more of the bells and whistles than you can handle comfortably. If you fly an airplane with an autopilot, insist that your instructor allow you to use it during your training for the instrument rating. Not all of the time, of course, but often enough that you are comfortable using it.

There will be a flight manual supplement with operational checks to be performed before takeoff, and it will be in the back of the manual—out of sight, out of mind. It is your responsibility to ensure that these pretakeoff operational checks are performed. A sudden autopilot malfunction will throw the airplane out of control in a split second. For that reason, you also have to be sure that you know all of the ways that it can be disengaged or shut off entirely.

Computer-Based Training Devices

You can familiarize yourself not only with the basic instrumentation found in the average trainer, but also with the sophisticated navigation and approach aids used in airline and corporate cockpits through use of computer-based training devices such as ASA's *On Top* or *IP Trainer*. These software packages allow you to investigate the operation of all kinds of cockpit navigational displays and become comfortable with them before you get into the airplane and start the Hobbs meter running.

Chapter 1
Flight Instruments Review Questions

You should be able to answer all of these questions, regardless of whether you are studying for the instrument or commercial FAA Knowledge Exams. However, the questions below have been chosen from the respective FAA question database.

Instrument Student Questions

1. Under what condition will true altitude be lower than indicated altitude with an altimeter setting of 29.92" Hg?

   A—In warmer than standard air temperature.
   B—In colder than standard air temperature.
   C—When density altitude is higher than indicated altitude.

2. If the outside air temperature increases during a flight at constant power and at a constant indicated altitude, the true airspeed will

   A—decrease and true altitude will increase.
   B—increase and true altitude will decrease.
   C—increase and true altitude will increase.

3. En route at FL290, the altimeter is set correctly, but not reset to the local altimeter setting of 30.57" Hg during descent. If the field elevation is 650 feet and the altimeter is functioning properly, what is the approximate indication upon landing?

   A—715 feet
   B—1,300 feet
   C—Sea level

4. If both the ram air input and drain hole of the pitot system are blocked, what airspeed indication can be expected?

   A—No variation of indicated airspeed in level flight even if large power changes are made.
   B—Decrease of indicated airspeed during a climb.
   C—Constant indicated airspeed during a descent.

5. (Refer to Figure Q1-1.) What is the flight attitude? One instrument has malfunctioned.

   A—Climbing turn to the right.
   B—Climbing turn to the left.
   C—Descending turn to the right.

6. What should be the indication on the magnetic compass as you roll into a standard rate turn to the right from a south heading in the Northern Hemisphere?

   A—The compass will indicate a turn to the right, but at a faster rate than is actually occurring.
   B—The compass will initially indicate a turn to the left.
   C—The compass will remain on south for a short time, then gradually catch up to the magnetic heading of the aircraft.

7. Which condition during taxi is an indication that an attitude indicator is unreliable?

   A—The horizon bar tilts more than 5° while making taxi turns.
   B—The horizon bar does not align itself with the miniature airplane after warmup.
   C—The horizon bar vibrates during warmup.

Figure Q1-1. Instrument interpretation (instrument malfunction)

8. What pretakeoff check should be made of the attitude indicator in preparation for an IFR flight?

   A—The horizon bar does not vibrate during warmup.

   B—The miniature airplane should erect and become stable within 5 minutes.

   C—The horizon bar should erect and become stable within 5 minutes.

9. Errors in both pitch and bank indication on an attitude indicator are usually at a maximum as the aircraft rolls out of a

   A—180° turn.

   B—270° turn.

   C—360° turn.

10. What indications should you observe on the turn-and-slip indicator during taxi?

   A—The ball moves freely opposite the turn, and the needle deflects in the direction of the turn.

   B—The needle deflects in the direction of the turn, but the ball remains centered.

   C—The ball deflects opposite the turn, but the needle remains centered.

11. (Refer to Figure Q1-2.) The heading on a remote indicating compass is 120°, and the magnetic compass indicates 110°. What action is required to correctly align the heading indicator with the magnetic compass?

A—Select the free gyro mode and depress the counterclockwise heading drive button.
B—Select the slaved gyro mode and depress the clockwise heading drive button.
C—Select the free gyro mode and depress the clockwise heading drive button.

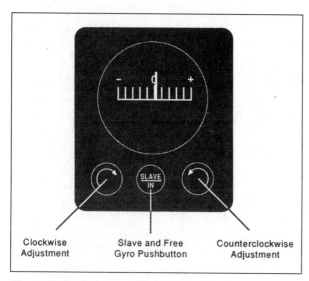

Figure Q1-2. Slaved gyro illustration

12. (Refer to Figure Q1-3.) Which illustration indicates a slipping turn?

A—1
B—3
C—2

Commercial Student Questions

13. Which airspeed would a pilot be unable to identify by the color coding of an airspeed indicator?

A—The never-exceed speed.
B—The power-off stall speed.
C—The maneuvering speed.

14. If severe turbulence is encountered during flight, the pilot should reduce the airspeed to

A—minimum control speed.
B—design-maneuvering speed.
C—maximum structural cruising speed.

15. Which statement is true about magnetic deviation of a compass? Deviation

A—varies over time as the agonic line shifts.
B—varies for different headings of the same aircraft.
C—is the same for all aircraft in the same locality.

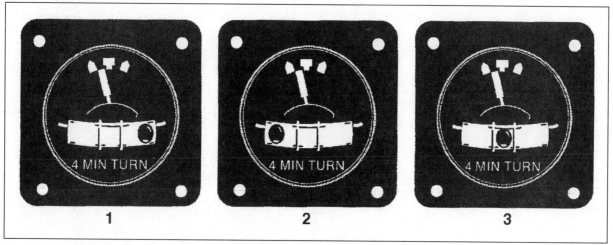

Figure Q1-3. Turn-and-slip indicator

16. What is an operational difference between the turn coordinator and the turn-and-slip indicator? The turn coordinator

A—is always electric; the turn-and-slip indicator is always vacuum-driven.

B—indicates bank angle only; the turn-and-slip indicator indicates rate of turn and coordination.

C—indicates roll rate, rate of turn, and coordination; the turn-and-slip indicator indicates rate of turn and coordination.

17. What is an advantage of an electric turn coordinator if the airplane has a vacuum system for other gyroscopic instruments?

A—It is a backup in case of vacuum system failure.

B—It is more reliable than the vacuum-driven indicators.

C—It will not tumble as will vacuum-driven turn indicators.

Aerodynamics

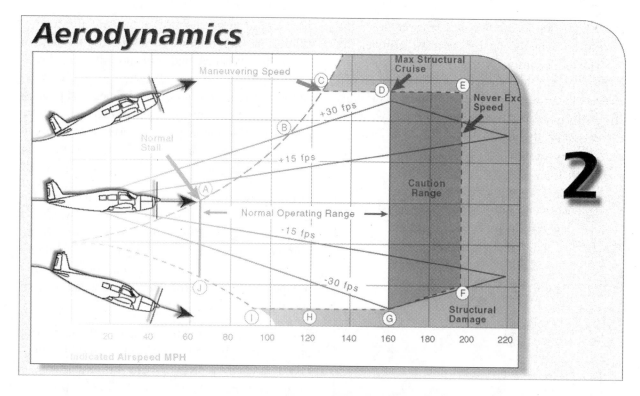

Our discussion of aerodynamics will start with those subjects of interest to instrument students only. It seems backwards to read about how to fly instruments followed by how to fly airplanes, but that's the way the two knowledge exams are laid out.

During your pilot training you learned many terms that were new; for example: induced drag, relative wind, angle of attack. You memorized many of these terms for the knowledge test and then forgot them, because you were learning to control the airplane by visual references. For instance, as soon as you could see the result of a change in angle of attack, you filed that information away in your mental data bank and no longer gave it conscious attention. Your goal was (and is) to make the act of flying smooth and natural, and not the result of mechanical control movements.

Now you are a more experienced pilot, comfortable in the air and secure in the knowledge of your ability. You can go back and analyze those once-strange terms and apply them to flying by reference to the flight instruments. To become a skilled instrument pilot, you must understand the aerodynamic effect of control inputs, so that when you cross-check and interpret the instrument readings you will know what control movements are required, and what the effect of those control movements will be.

Pitch, Power, and Trim Relationship

The fundamental rule of attitude instrument flight is "attitude plus power equals performance." To achieve consistent performance, any change in attitude will require a power change, and any power change will require a change in attitude.

The basis for that attitude/power relationship lies in the fact that induced drag varies as angle of attack is changed. If you lose 100 feet of altitude inadvertently, and attempt to regain your assigned altitude simply by raising the nose, the increased angle of attack will cause an increase in induced drag. *See* Figure 2-1.

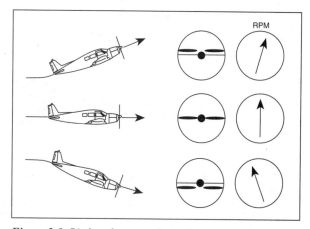

Figure 2-1. *Pitch and power relationship*

Drag — any kind of drag — can be overcome only with power, so raising the nose without adding power will result in an airspeed loss. Knowing this, if you desire to maintain a constant airspeed you will increase the power slightly every time you raise the nose, and you will reduce the power setting when you return to level flight. *See* Figure 2-2.

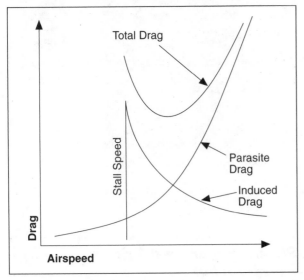

Figure 2-2. Drag vs. airspeed

When they attempt to regain lost altitude by simply pulling back on the control yoke, many pilots react to the increased back pressure by reaching for the trim wheel. This is a mistake. It requires the expenditure of energy to gain altitude, and you have only two types of energy at your disposal: kinetic energy (a function of airspeed), and fuel. You can attempt to regain altitude by abruptly pulling back on the control yoke and zooming upward; this method utilizes kinetic energy, sacrifices airspeed, and upsets your instructor.

The second source of energy, of course, is the throttle. Adding power will increase the airflow over the horizontal stabilizer and will blow the tail down, relieving stick pressure. The trim wheel adds no energy and cannot be considered a means of gaining altitude. You can cure yourself of this tendency by going back to a student pilot exercise: try to maintain either an altitude or an airspeed with trim alone—it can't be done.

Follow these rules when using elevator trim: in level flight, trim off any remaining pressure when the airspeed and altitude are at the desired values. When climbing or descending, trim off any remaining pressure when the vertical speed is correct. Do not use the trim as a means of changing airspeed, vertical speed, or altitude.

Lowering the nose reduces the angle of attack, with an accompanying reduction in induced drag. Maintaining a constant airspeed after lowering the nose means a power reduction—you are trading potential energy (based on altitude) for kinetic energy, and no added energy from fuel is required. Lowering the nose to initiate a descent will result in an increase in airspeed, and in most instances you will accept this bonus gladly; an exception might be on a non-precision approach where you are maintaining a constant airspeed so that you can estimate the time to the missed approach point more accurately.

Turn Dynamics

You know that when you bank the wings the total lift is made up of horizontal and vertical components, and it is the horizontal component of lift that determines the rate of turn. *See* Figure 2-3.

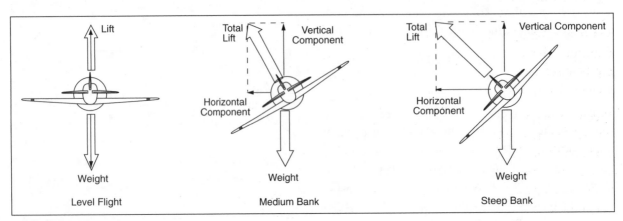

Figure 2-3. Forces in turns

You also know in order to avoid losing altitude you must increase the angle of attack to regain the amount of vertical lift that was available before you entered the turn. That increased angle of attack brings with it the usual increase in induced drag, but now the figures become alarming.

When you bank only 15° and add back pressure to maintain altitude, induced drag increases by an almost negligible 7 percent. In a protracted turn this will result in a small airspeed loss; a power increase of 50 rpm or ½ inch of manifold pressure should be sufficient to maintain a constant airspeed.

Inadvertently allowing the bank angle to increase to 30° will increase induced drag by 33 percent—now we're getting into big numbers. If you bank the wings 45° and attempt to maintain altitude with back pressure, induced drag will increase by 100 percent! When drag increases, the amount of power required to overcome that drag increases dramatically. *See* Figure 2-4.

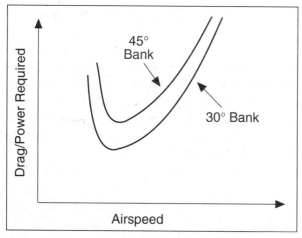

Figure 2-4. *Drag increases as bank angle increases*

You must remember two things about entering banked flight under instrument conditions. First, if maintaining a constant airspeed is your goal, power must be increased to overcome the added drag.

Second, every degree of bank beyond approximately 20° will exact a penalty of lost altitude unless you are quick and assertive with the throttle. The primary power instrument in level flight (including level turns) is the airspeed indicator, not the tachometer or manifold pressure gauge, and you should not let your eyes stray to those instruments when they should be concentrating on bank angle, altitude, and airspeed. With experience, you will know how much throttle movement is required; if your trainer has a fixed-pitch propeller, your ears will help, too, as you learn to recognize the change in engine sound.

What Controls What?

There is a continuing controversy over whether angle of attack or throttle controls airspeed. Here are quotes from two authorities:

"...angle of attack is the primary control of airspeed in steady flight."—*Aerodynamics for Naval Aviators.*

"Maintaining a desired altitude requires the ability to maintain a specific pitch attitude......maintaining an airspeed is accomplished...by adjusting the power..."—*Air Force Instrument Flying Manual.*

You can see that even the authorities disagree on the pitch/power relationship.

The truth lies in balancing kinetic energy, potential energy, and the energy derived from burning fuel, and you will find yourself using the elevator control and throttle interchangeably for pitch and speed control in different situations. As you look beyond your instrument trainer to more sophisticated airplanes, however, you may be interested to learn how the pitch/power relationship is handled. On a modern jet, flight guidance systems control the airplane's altitude and path over the ground while the autothrottle system controls airspeed. Every time the autopilot raises the airplane's nose the throttles move forward automatically to maintain airspeed, and every time the nose pitches down the throttles move aft to reduce power. There is no question that pitch controls altitude and throttle controls airspeed when the flight control systems are in command.

When power is fixed, airspeed is controlled with pitch changes. For example, your fixed-pitch propeller airplane probably uses full throttle for climb power, and in that case power is definitely fixed. The manufacturer of a turbocharged airplane with a constant speed propeller might recommend a power setting of 38" of manifold pressure and 2,400 rpm for climb power, and you must accept that as a fixed power setting although the throttle may not be fully open. In either of these situations you would establish climb airspeed by control of pitch attitude.

When power is variable, airspeed is controlled with the throttle. If you are told to maintain 4,000 feet and slow to 120 knots, you obviously cannot slow the airplane by raising the nose without also raising the controller's blood pressure. As you make power changes in level flight you will have to make compensating pitch changes. An increase in power setting will cause the nose to pitch up if you take no action; forward stick pressure and trim will hold altitude and convert the increased power into airspeed. A reduction in power setting calls for back pressure and trim to maintain altitude as the airplane slows.

When changing speed from cruise to approach speed, or when entering or recovering from a climb or descent, the power instrument(s) are primary, and they should get your attention only during those changes.

You should learn the power settings for climb, descent, cruise, and approach speeds, so that you can glance at the power instruments just long enough to make the appropriate setting: know what you are looking for before you move your eyes to the power instruments. Do not watch the needles on the power instruments as they move! After that initial setting, the airspeed indicator is primary for power, and you should make small throttle changes to achieve the desired airspeed. Taking your attention away from the flight instruments to "fine tune" the power setting will result in heading or altitude errors.

When you want to increase speed without changing altitude, expedite the change by adding more power than required; if you know that 20" of manifold pressure will result in an airspeed of 140 knots, and your target speed is 140, look at the MAP gauge and run it up to 24". As the airspeed indication approaches 140 knots, refer to the power instrument again and set the manifold pressure to 20". Use the same technique for slowing: use less power initially than is necessary to maintain the new lower airspeed and, as the ASI nears the target airspeed, increase the power.

Changing the power setting will result in subtle changes in pitch attitude and rudder pressure, and you should anticipate and react to these changes. A power increase, for example, will result in a pitch-up attitude and the requirement for right rudder pressure, while a power decrease will cause the nose to drop, and cause the heading indicator to indicate the need for less right rudder. If you do not anticipate these changes, you will constantly be surprised at the airplane's reactions to power changes, and you will be continually behind the airplane.

Spatial Disorientation

"I can fly by the seat of my pants" is often a fatal illusion. The human body was designed to live on the surface of the earth, not to maneuver in the air, and when we break the bonds of gravity to move in three dimensions our bodies send misleading messages to our brains. Any disagreement between what the body senses through the balance mechanism in the inner ear or that discredited seat-of-the-pants and the information sent to the brain from the sense of sight will cause confusion, disorientation, and sometimes nausea—it's not nice to fool Mother Nature. The word we use to describe this feeling is "vertigo."

A two-dimensional example of vertigo occurs when you are stopped at a traffic signal and the car beside you begins to move. Do you step on your brakes? For a split second your eyes tell your brain that *your* car is moving while your body tells your brain that it isn't. That's vertigo.

Accumulating flight hours is no guarantee against vertigo—the most grizzled old big-iron pilots can experience it. The only defense against vertigo is to concentrate on the flight instruments, interpret them correctly, and believe what they are telling you while ignoring the messages your body is sending to your brain.

A good example is "somatogravic illusion," two words you can forget as soon as you have read this paragraph. Picture this: You are taking off on a night that is pitch black, with no visual references other than the runway lights. The force of acceleration pushes you back against your seat and, sensing that you are in a nose-up attitude, you push forward on the stick and dive into the ground. Establishing a normal climb attitude using the flight instruments would have prevented this.

A rapid pushover from climb attitude to straight and level flight (often occasioned by a pilot noticing too late that the airplane is about to climb through its assigned altitude) might lead a pilot to feel that he is tumbling over backwards; again, use of the flight instruments would save the day.

A pilot can avoid spatial disorientation by limiting head movement—I'll bet that you can see every instrument on the panel with very little head movement. A typical instructor/examiner trick is to have the pilot pick a pencil or other item off of the floor while the nasty right-seater puts the airplane into an unusual attitude. When the pilot sits up, a mixed bag of messages is transmitted from the body to the brain, and the only way to recover is to lock onto the attitude indicator and resume straight and level flight.

A rapid crosscheck of the instruments is not as effective as a deliberate scan, getting required information from each instrument and responding accordingly.

Scanning

There are three inseparable elements involved in flying an airplane solely by reference to instruments: cross-checking, interpreting the instruments, and controlling the airplane in response to the instrument indications. You can progress into the use of navigational aids only after you have mastered these fundamental skills. If you brush over the fundamentals and rush into practicing instrument approaches, you will probably pass your instrument checkride and become a mediocre instrument pilot, capable of meeting the minimum requirements of safety but always playing catch-up. If you learn to control the airplane through application of good scanning techniques, you will be able to devote your attention to precision and will become an ulcer-free instrument pilot. (*See* Figure 2-5.) Rod Machado, psychologist, instrument instructor, and author, researched the logbooks of a number of instrument pilots and learned that those whose instructors had given them at least ten hours of instruction in attitude instrument flying received their ratings in fewer total hours than those whose instructors rushed past attitude flying and began training on approaches.

Figure 2-5. *Three elements of instrument flight*

I strongly recommend that you seek out a good instrument ground trainer and an instructor who appreciates the value of simulator time (simulator is the generic term; the FAA prefers "ground training device"). The very fact that there is no motion and thus no kinesthetic feedback forces you to rely solely on the instruments and not on the "seat of your pants." Simulators are more sensitive and thus more demanding than airplanes—if you can fly the simulator well, the airplane will be a piece of cake. Practice with a Personal Computer-based Aviation Training Device (PCATD) will speed the development of an efficient scan. ASA's *On Top* is ideal for this purpose, and ten hours logged using the device and endorsed by an instrument instructor count toward checkride requirements. If you want to work on your own, the *IP Trainer* by ASA will do the trick.

Control and Performance Instruments

The flight instruments and power instruments are divided into two groups: control instruments and performance instruments. Which group a particular instrument falls into depends on whether it reflects changes directly or indirectly. As you might imagine, you refer to the control instruments when changing the power or attitude necessary for maintaining or changing airplane performance, while the performance instruments are used to measure the effects of those changes. I refer to the performance instruments as the "How am I doing?" instruments because that is exactly how they are used. *See* Figure 2-6.

The attitude indicator gives an instantaneous and correct indication of changes in the airplane's attitude in relation to the natural horizon—it is a control instrument. The tachometer or the tachometer and manifold pressure gauge give direct indications of changes in available power—the power instruments are also control instruments. You will look to the control instruments when you want to change something. For instance, if your altitude is incorrect, you must refer to the attitude indicator to make the change. Or, if you want to transition from level flight to a climb, you must refer to the power instruments to set climb power. You then look at the performance instruments to assess the effect of the changes you have made.

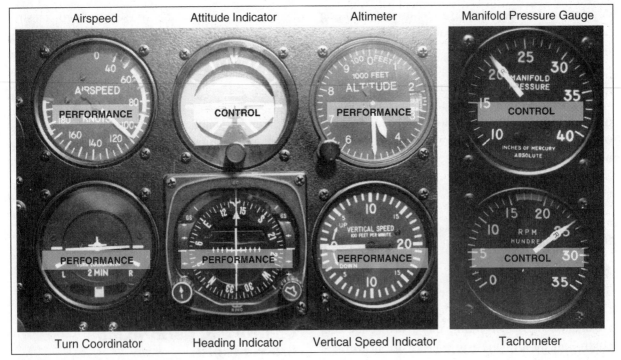

Airspeed	Attitude Indicator	Altimeter	Manifold Pressure Gauge

PERFORMANCE — CONTROL — PERFORMANCE — CONTROL

PERFORMANCE — PERFORMANCE — PERFORMANCE — CONTROL

Turn Coordinator	Heading Indicator	Vertical Speed Indicator	Tachometer

Figure 2-6. *Control and performance instruments*

The airspeed indicator, altimeter, turn coordinator, heading indicator, and vertical speed indicator reflect changes indirectly, so they are the performance instruments. The performance instruments measure the effect of the changes made with the control instruments.

Many instrument students attempt to scan all the flight instruments with the intention of somehow sorting out what is important from that which is unimportant. This method is inefficient because it assumes that the information provided by each of the instruments is of equal value. A more efficient method is to reduce the scan to only those instruments which provide information important to the maneuver being performed.

The attitude indicator should be the focus of your scan (until it fails; partial panel will be discussed later). Your eyes should be on the attitude indicator 80 percent of the time, leaving it only to check a performance instrument. Aviation physiologists tell us that a pilot's scan can be categorized as quick looks, reads, dwells, and stares. A quick look takes about two tenths of a second, a read lasts from three tenths of a second to one second, a dwell lasts from one to five seconds, and a stare lasts from five to ten seconds. *See* Figure 2-7.

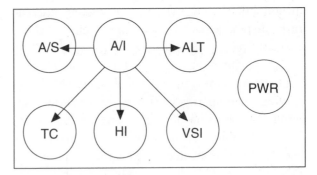

Figure 2-7. *Scan pattern*

You should be able to get the information you need from a performance instrument in two seconds, and with the cooperation of your instructor (and another person in the airplane to watch for traffic) you can prove it to yourself. Ask the instructor to cover the altimeter or heading indicator with a free hand and uncover it for two seconds at your command. You should be able to glance at the uncovered instrument and register its indication before it is covered again.

You can train yourself to move your eyes by saying the instrument reading out loud: "Four thousand, level, two three zero, level," etc. This training period will not take very long, because you will learn quickly that silence is not golden.

That is the secret of smooth instrument flight: glance at a performance instrument and note its indication—if it is incorrect, apply control pressure to start it moving in the correct direction and move your eyes to the attitude indicator, followed by a check of the other performance instruments (as required).

Check the errant instrument the next time it is due for a glance, but do not stare at it while the correction is in progress. That is the hardest lesson we have to learn as instrument pilots—you have to tear your eyes away from an instrument that is indicating a wrong altitude, heading, or airspeed. This takes mental effort and concentration.

Pilots are achievement oriented—they like to stick to a task until it is completed. That orientation may make it difficult for you to take your eyes away from an instrument until you have corrected a deviation, but you must learn to do so. That is where the control/performance concept comes in: when you notice (during a quick look) that you have deviated from your desired heading or altitude, you must shift your attention to the control instrument while applying control pressure to correct the error. Additional quick looks will tell you when the corrective action is complete.

Believe me, if you look at the altimeter for ten seconds during an altitude change, the airplane's heading will change dramatically while you are ignoring the heading indicator.

The Selected Radial Scan

The most efficient method of scanning the flight instruments is the selected radial scan, using the attitude indicator as the hub of a wheel with the spokes extending to the other instruments. *See* Figure 2-8.

Figure 2-8. Selected radial scan pattern

Thinking of the instrument panel as a wheel has another advantage—there is no way to get from one spoke to another on a wheel without going by way of the hub, and so it is with the instrument scan. Your eyes move outward from the attitude indicator to the other flight instruments selectively, depending on the maneuver in progress, while ignoring those instruments with no useful information to contribute to the successful completion of the maneuver. You do not move your eyes from one performance instrument to another, but always move them via the attitude indicator or hub.

Efficiency means that your scanning time is devoted only to the attitude indicator and one or two performance instruments, with no attempt being made to look at all six instruments.

It is important to keep your control inputs small and smooth, fighting the impulse to make a large control input when a discrepancy is noted. Don't let the instrument indications change so fast that your eyes can't keep up with the changes. The airplane's heading may change slowly when you have banked only 5°, but you won't overshoot the desired heading.

Primary/Supporting Instruments

In this system, the flight instruments are divided into primary and supporting instruments. The examiner may ask you to name the primary and secondary instruments for each phase of flight, but in my opinion you will find the control/performance method easier to learn. The instrument with the indication you want to keep steady or unchanging will be designated as the primary instrument.

Pitch Instruments

The altimeter, airspeed, and vertical speed indicator are the pitch performance instruments. The indication of each of these instruments will lag elevator inputs, either because of the design of the instrument or because of the airplane's inertia. *See* Figure 2-9.

The attitude indicator is the pitch control instrument, reacting instantaneously and correctly to pitch inputs, and it should be the focus of your scan.

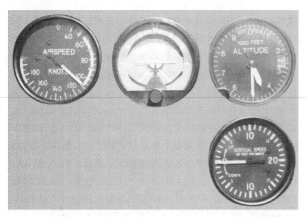

Figure 2-9. Pitch instruments

The attitude indicator consists of a representation of a miniature airplane fixed in the middle of the instrument and a disc with a horizon line which moves behind the miniature airplane in reaction to attitude changes. The thickness of the little airplane's wings or of the dot that represents the airplane's centerline is approximately 2°. Some manufacturers of attitude indicators provide pitch markings on the horizon disc so that you can determine the pitch attitude above or below the horizon precisely; others provide no pitch markings and you must rely on "bar widths" to change the airplane's attitude accurately. *See* Figure 2-10.

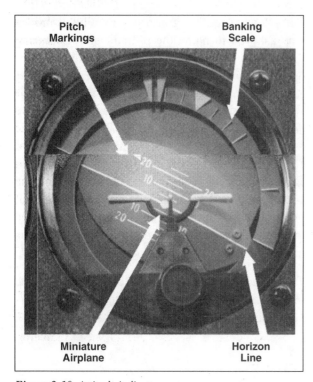

Figure 2-10. Attitude indicator

As part of your preflight instrument check, set the attitude indicator so that it reads correctly when you are seated in your normal position. The miniature airplane can be adjusted up and down, and you should adjust it so that the horizon line bisects the center dot. (This setting will have to be checked in flight; if the nosewheel strut of your airplane is over- or under-inflated the longitudinal axis may not be perfectly horizontal on the ground.) With the horizon line splitting the center dot, placing the bottom of the miniature airplane "bar" directly on the horizon line results in a 1° nose up attitude, and lowering the nose 1° is accomplished by placing the "bar" directly below the horizon line. *See* Figure 2-11.

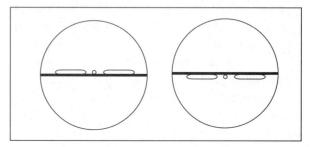

Figure 2-11. One degree pitch change

Initial Climb

A useful rule of thumb is that vertical speed in hundreds of feet per minute is equal to airspeed in miles per minute times degrees of pitch change. For ease of calculation, assume that your airplane's initial climb speed is 60 knots, or one mile per minute. To climb at 500 feet per minute, when the airplane has accelerated to rotation speed apply back pressure to pitch up 5° (or 2½ bar widths). This is your initial pitch target, and in the first few seconds after liftoff your priorities should be keeping the wings level and maintaining the target pitch attitude.

During the first few seconds of TRANSITION from the takeoff roll to the initial climb the primary instruments are:

For pitch control .... attitude indicator

For bank control .... attitude indicator

For power control .... power instruments

The manufacturer will suggest the best rate of climb speed or a cruise climb speed, and you will determine which applies in any IFR takeoff situation. When the initial climb has been established, quickly glance at the airspeed indicator to determine how close you are to the recommended airspeed, and apply another rule of thumb: each degree of pitch change should equal 5 knots of airspeed change.

Return your attention to the attitude indicator (the control instrument) and change the pitch attitude accordingly. You are now in a CONSTANT AIR-SPEED climb, and in this stabilized condition the airspeed indicator becomes primary for pitch. When the airspeed indicator shows the desired airspeed, look at the relation of the miniature airplane to the horizon; if power is unchanged and you maintain that pitch attitude the airspeed will not change. You have just increased the efficiency of your scan because you can maintain airspeed using the attitude indicator alone—you only have to look at the airspeed indicator occasionally to see how you are doing.

Constant Airspeed Climb

In a constant airspeed climb, the primary instruments are:

For pitch control .... airspeed indicator
For bank control .... heading indicator
Supporting pitch and bank .... attitude indicator

See Figure 2-12.

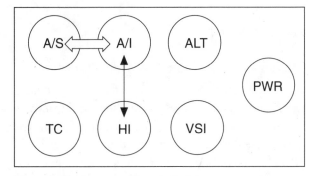

Figure 2-12. *Constant airspeed climb*

Bank control will be discussed later, but it should be apparent that if the heading does not change the wings must be level, so the heading indicator is designated as primary bank control during a constant airspeed climb. How do you keep the wings level? With the attitude indicator, by using the banking scale at the top of the instrument. Again, you control the airplane with the attitude indicator, while glancing at the airspeed and heading indicators occasionally to see how you are doing.

Enroute Climbs and Descents

The most efficient climb speed is usually slower than cruise speed. In transitioning from level cruise flight to a constant airspeed climb at the recommended climb airspeed, your scan is:

For pitch control .... attitude indicator
For bank control .... attitude indicator
For power control .... power instruments

Raise the miniature aircraft on the attitude indicator to the approximate nose-high pitch attitude for the desired airspeed; simultaneously, advance the throttle to the climb power setting. When the airspeed indicator stabilizes on the desired climb speed, your scan is:

For pitch control .... airspeed indicator
For bank control .... heading indicator
For power control .... fixed at climb setting

Constant Rate Climb

The *Aeronautical Information Manual* recommends that you climb or descend at an optimum rate to within 1,000 feet of an assigned altitude, and that the last 1,000 feet of vertical change be made at a rate of between 500 and 1,500 feet per minute to avoid inadvertently climbing or descending through the new altitude. During that last 1,000 feet you will enter a constant rate climb or descent.

During a stabilized constant RATE climb the primary instruments are:

For pitch control .... vertical speed indicator
For bank control .... heading indicator
For power control .... airspeed indicator

See Figure 2-13.

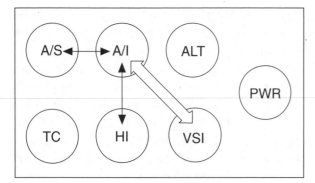

Figure 2-13. Constant rate and airspeed climb

When you establish a pitch attitude that results in a constant rate of change, note where the miniature airplane is in relation to the horizon line and hold that attitude. Without looking at the power instruments, control airspeed with the throttle. The only time you will look at the power instruments is during changes: from a climb to level flight, starting a descent, leveling off, etc.

When your airplane is stabilized in a constant rate climb the relationship of the attitude indicator's bar to the horizon line will govern rate of climb, the throttle will govern airspeed, and a zero-degree bank angle at the top of the attitude indicator will keep the heading constant. Your instructor should be able to cover the performance instruments for two to three minutes while you concentrate on the attitude indicator, and you should find the heading, airspeed, and rate of climb unchanged when the instruments are uncovered.

Leveling Off

The attitude indicator is the primary pitch reference during the TRANSITION from a climb or descent to level flight, and as you approach the desired altitude the attitude indicator should get your attention as you bring the miniature airplane to the horizon. Leveling off from a climb, lead by approximately 10 percent of the vertical speed (50 feet for a 500 fpm climb).

Leveling off from a constant-speed descent to maintain that speed in level flight, you have to contend with the airplane's inertia and must begin to add back pressure about 50 feet early for every 500 feet of descent rate. Simultaneously, set the power to the predetermined setting to maintain that airspeed in level flight.

To level off at a higher than descent speed, begin adding power 100 to 150 feet before reaching the new altitude; use the power setting that will maintain the desired airspeed in level flight. The airplane will want to pitch up when the power is added—don't let it. Hold the rate of descent constant until you are only 50 feet above the target altitude, then let it pitch up to level flight attitude.

As you transition to level flight, the movement of the altimeter needle will slow and the vertical speed indication will approach zero. At that point the altimeter becomes primary for pitch control—the transition is over.

You should know what power setting is needed to provide a given airspeed in level flight, and the power should be adjusted accordingly. The power instrument(s) is primary for power during the change, but when cruise power is set the airspeed indicator becomes the primary power reference. The heading indicator remains primary for bank during straight climbs, descents, and level flight. Figure 2-14 illustrates the level flight scan.

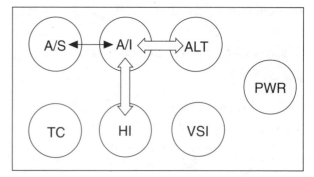

Figure 2-14. Level flight scan

Pitch Control on Partial Panel

If a failure in the vacuum or electrical system renders the attitude indicator useless, or if the attitude indicator tumbles because its bank limits have been exceeded while the airplane is in an unusual flight attitude (possibly because of the power source failure!), the altimeter and airspeed indicator can be used to establish a level flight pitch attitude. Whether the airplane is diving or climbing, apply elevator pressure to stop the altimeter and airspeed indicator needles; when the needles of those two instruments are stopped, the airplane is in level flight (this assumes that you have leveled the wings through use of the turn coordinator or needle).

Maneuver	Primary pitch	Primary bank	Primary power
Takeoff roll to initial climb	A/I	H/I	ENG
Constant airspeed climb	ASI	H/I	ENG
Constant rate climb	VSI	H/I	ASI
Transition to level off	A/I	H/I	ENG
Straight and level cruise (constant speed)	ALT	H/I	ASI
Transition to descent	A/I	H/I	ENG
Descent (constant speed)	ASI	H/I	ENG
Descent (constant rate)	VSI	H/I	ASI
Level turns (constant speed)	ALT	T/C	ENG
Climbing or descending turns (constant speed)	ASI	T/C	ENG
Climbing or descending turns (constant rate)	VSI	T/C	ASI

ASI = Airspeed indicator   **H/I** = Heading indicator   **VSI** = Vertical speed indicator
ALT = Altimeter   **T/C** = Turn coordinator   **ENG** = Manifold pressure and/or TACH

Note that the attitude indicator is primary only during *transitions*. Constant rate maneuvers assume constant airspeed, so two of the pitch instruments are involved; the ASI is always the power instrument under these conditions.

Table 2-1. Instrument scan pattern

Using the Vertical Speed Indicator

Although a standard vertical speed indicator exhibits a slight lag in reflecting pitch changes, it provides an accurate indication of vertical speed trends. If you notice it beginning to trend up, for instance, apply slight pressure to stop its movement while moving your eyes to the attitude indicator to lower its pitch indication fractionally. Look back at the VSI—its trend should be reversing. When the VSI indication is zero, check the attitude indicator closely and maintain its pitch indication while trimming off control pressures.

A vertical speed change of 200 feet per minute equals an airspeed change of approximately 5 knots if power is left constant. If you want to keep the airspeed needle from moving while making a vertical change of 200 fpm, try a throttle change of 100 rpm (fixed pitch propeller) or 2" of manifold pressure (constant speed propeller).

Use of Trim

Misuse of the trim control can cause more trouble than it is worth. The trim wheel is not a flight control and you should not be tempted to trim the airplane to a given airspeed or altitude.

If the airspeed or altitude are incorrect they should be changed by use of the throttle or elevator control as appropriate. Any stick pressure remaining after the altitude and airspeed are correct should be trimmed off.

Let's say that your airplane is maintaining level flight at 120 knots using 20" of manifold pressure and that all pressures have been trimmed off. Cockpit duties take your attention away from the flight instruments for a minute or two (this shouldn't happen, of course), and when you return to your normal scan you see that the altitude is 300 feet low. Don't touch the trim. Add pitch and power to regain the lost altitude (recover at 600 feet per minute, 3° pitch up at 2 miles per minute) and, when the altimeter again indicates the desired altitude, reduce the throttle to 20"—you should return to the stabilized condition that existed before you let your attention wander. If you had used the trim to relieve control pressures during the climb, you would have to go through the whole process of finding the correct trim setting for that airspeed and pitch attitude again.

During the first few hours of instrument training you should record pitch and power settings that result in predictable performance. An approach speed of 90 knots might be a comfortable speed in your airplane—what power setting and pitch attitude will result in level flight at 90 knots? What pitch attitude and power setting will result in a 500-foot-per-minute descent at an airspeed of 90 knots? (The pitch change should be just over 3° at 1.5 miles per minute). Can you transition from level flight at an altitude of 2,000 feet to a 500 fpm descent and then level off at 1,500 feet, maintaining 90 knots continuously? You can if you know the attitudes and power settings required. *See* Figure 2-15.

There is nothing magic about a vertical speed of 500 fpm, by the way, although it is a good ballpark figure. There will be instances when you will need to descend at 700 fpm or 900 fpm while keeping the airspeed constant. You can only develop this skill through practice. The climbing turn described in the FAA's *Instrument Flying Handbook* is an excellent exercise for this purpose.

Bank Instruments

The bank instruments are the attitude indicator, the turn coordinator, and the heading indicator. As was the case with pitch control, the attitude indicator is a primary instrument only while rolling into and recovering from banks, and yet it will get 80 percent of your scan time. The heading indicator is the primary bank instrument in straight and level flight, and the turn coordinator (or needle) is the primary bank instrument during turns; they are performance instruments, while the attitude indicator is a control instrument. *See* Figure 2-16.

Think of anything bad associated with flight—spins, diving spirals, structural overloads—and you will find that banked flight is involved in some way. When you bank the wings, you give up some vertical lift which then becomes horizontal lift to begin a change in heading. If you want to maintain altitude in banked flight, you must increase the angle of attack with back pressure to replace the vertical lift, and any increase in angle of attack means an accompanying increase in induced drag; the only thing you have available in the cockpit to overcome increased drag of any kind is the throttle.

Figure 2-16. *Bank instruments*

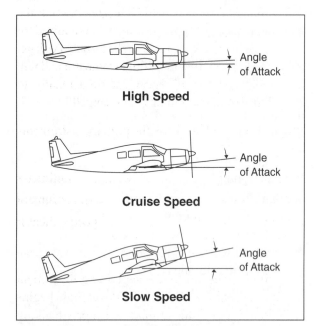

Figure 2-15. *Level flight pitch attitude*

Transition to Banked Flight

The FAA's *Instrument Flying Handbook* and the *Aeronautical Information Manual* define a heading change of 3° per second as a standard rate turn, and some IFR procedures (such as holding) are predicated on standard rate turns. Must you make all your turns at that rate? Of course not. Never bank any more steeply than you have to—10° is a useful figure and it is conveniently the first marking on the banking scale. Because of the penalties in lift and airspeed that overbanking exacts, think of the bank angle that results in a standard rate turn as the maximum bank angle that you will use, and approach that bank angle cautiously by using the 10° mark as a warning to begin neutralizing the ailerons. *See* Figure 2-17.

As with any transition, the change from wings level to banked flight begins with your eyes on the attitude indicator and its banking scale at the top. The bank angle required for a 3° per second turn can be approximated by dividing the true airspeed by ten and adding five degrees; it will differ in banks to the left and right due to torque forces. At a true airspeed of 100 knots, the bank angle for a standard rate turn is approximately 15°, and as you roll into the bank with your eyes on the banking scale that will be your target after passing the 10° checkpoint.

Figure 2-17. *Avoid overbanking!*

During the entry to or recovery from a turn the primary instruments are:

For pitch control .... altimeter

For bank control .... attitude indicator

For power control .... airspeed indicator

See Figure 2-18.

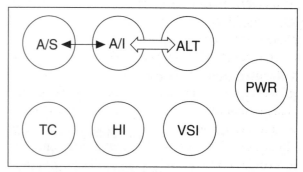

Figure 2-18. *Entering level turn*

Maintaining a Level Turn

When you have rolled to the target bank angle, your eyes should shift to the turn coordinator (or turn needle) which becomes the primary bank instrument. The primary instrument, you will recall, is that instrument with the indication which must remain constant. When you have assured yourself that the turn instrument is exactly on the standard rate turn index, glance up at the attitude indicator to see what bank angle is doing the job. You will find that the bank angle for a left turn is less than that required for a right turn. For the remainder of the turn you will get bank information from the attitude indicator and will only look at the turn instrument occasionally to ensure that its indication has not changed.

While established in a bank the primary instruments are:

For pitch control .... altimeter

For bank control .... turn instrument

For power control .... airspeed indicator

See Figure 2-19 on the next page.

The attitude indicator is the supporting instrument for pitch and bank. Rolling back to level flight begins with your eyes on the attitude indicator's banking scale. When it shows that the wings are level you must look at the turn instrument for confirmation.

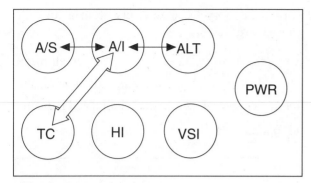

Figure 2-19. Maintaining level turn

The Efficient Scan

When you have used the attitude indicator to establish a bank angle that results in a 3° per second rate of turn, and a pitch attitude that results in level flight, you can safely ignore the turn instrument and altimeter, can't you? And if you have adjusted the power so that the desired airspeed is maintained with that attitude you can ignore the airspeed indicator, can't you? That is the efficient scan we have been discussing: all of the desired information is on the attitude indicator, and you need only glance at the performance instruments occasionally to assure yourself that the proper values are being maintained.

Heading Indicator

The heading indicator was named as a bank instrument and hasn't even been mentioned. The reason is that it need not be included in your scan until the turn is almost complete. If the goal of an efficient instrument scan is to direct attention only to those instruments with useful information, the heading indicator fails the test while a turn is in progress. A turn of 90°, for instance, will take thirty seconds; why devote any scanning time to it until at least 20 seconds have gone by? You will develop a sense of timing with experience, but while in training an occasional glance at the heading indicator will tell you how the turn is progressing. As the airplane approaches the new heading, of course, the heading indicator gets more scanning time to correctly lead the roll-out. A lead of about one-half the bank angle is a good starting point until you learn your own reaction time; every pilot ultimately gets a feel for the appropriate lead.

When only a small heading change is required, you should limit the bank angle to no more than the number of degrees to be turned. A 5°-turn deserves no more than a 5°-bank angle; if you bank more steeply you will surely overshoot the new heading. It is easy to limit the bank angle to 5° if you are looking at the banking scale as you apply aileron. Some instructors advocate "mini-banks," suggesting that you practice rolling into and out of a 5° bank without stopping as a means of making small heading changes. Rolling into and immediately out of a 10° bank will result in approximately a 10° change in heading.

Focus on the Attitude Indicator

In summary, the attitude indicator will be the focus of your eyes when entering, maintaining, and recovering from turns. You will use it to establish a pitch attitude that maintains level flight and a bank angle that results in a standard rate turn (or less).

Do not allow yourself to become distracted while the airplane is in a bank—that is no time to tune radios or look at charts. Maintenance of an exact bank angle deserves all your attention.

Straight and Level Flight Scan

In straight and level flight, the primary instruments are:

For pitch control .... altimeter
For bank control .... heading indicator
For power control .... airspeed indicator

See Figure 2-20.

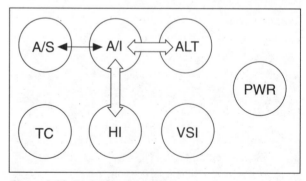

Figure 2-20. Straight and level scan

The attitude indicator is the supporting pitch and bank instrument in straight and level flight (remember that the altimeter is primary for pitch and the heading indicator is primary for bank).

Partial Panel

I have emphasized that the attitude indicator reacts instantaneously to pitch and bank control inputs. When it does not react instantaneously, you must assume that it has failed, and refer to the turn instrument for bank control while you sort the situation out. Coping with an instrument power source failure requires that you recognize the failure and then take action; if you fail to recognize what has happened, there will be little time to take action before a truly hazardous situation develops. *See* Figure 2-21.

Figure 2-21. Partial panel

It is unfortunate that pilots must have instrument failure simulated by covering the instruments and do not have the opportunity to experience an actual failure under controlled conditions, because a real-life failure will result in the attitude indicator slowly rolling over, and your only clue will be the realization that opposite aileron has no effect. Spend some time in an instrument ground training device where the instructor can fail the instruments without warning There are several PC-based simulator programs that do an admirable job of this.

Early recognition of instrument power source failure is essential, because either a turn coordinator or a turn needle will reach full deflection and come up against mechanical stops when you have rolled far enough. Beyond that point, you can be rolling into inverted flight and you will get no clue from the turn instrument. Be suspicious if objects begin to move from the floor of the airplane to the headliner.

If your attitude and heading indicators fail, you will have to rely on the magnetic compass, the turn instrument and the clock for turn information. When you have to operate with the emergency panel (needle, ball, airspeed, altimeter, and clock), you must make small control inputs and make them smoothly; the potential for overcontrolling is greater on partial panel because the performance instruments all lag to some extent.

Recovery from Unusual Attitudes on Partial Panel

The altimeter is the primary pitch reference when the attitude indicator has failed. If the altimeter needle is not moving, the airplane is in level flight. If you momentarily lose control of the airplane and enter an unusual flight attitude while operating on partial panel, the airplane's nose will be on or close to the horizon when the altimeter needle's movement stops.

The airspeed indicator may also be used to determine when the airplane is in level flight although its indication lags somewhat more than the altimeter. If you make inadvertent throttle movements during recovery from an unusual attitude the ASI may be misleading as a level flight indicator.

The turn instrument is the primary bank reference when you are limited to a partial panel. If your attitude and heading indicators fail and you enter an unusual attitude, you must level the wings using the turn coordinator. As you know, the turn coordinator reacts to both roll and yaw forces, and will deflect in the direction of yaw. Accordingly, you would level the turn coordinator's "wings" with rudder, not aileron, in a partial panel unusual attitude recovery. If the airplane enters a dive while on partial panel, you must level the wings before applying back pressure to avoid damaging G-forces.

Using the Power Instruments

The tachometer or manifold pressure gauge is a necessary distraction. As discussed under pitch control, you should know the power setting required for each condition of flight and be able to adjust the throttle with a minimum scan time devoted to looking at the power gauges. As you become familiar with your airplane, you may be able to make rough power adjustments by sound alone, without looking at the gauges. The deadliest sin is looking at the power instruments during the entire power change; this time with your attention diverted from the flight instruments is totally wasted.

The airspeed indicator is the primary power instrument when you are established in level flight or in a constant rate climb or descent. If you notice an airspeed discrepancy, check the pitch instruments before reaching for the throttle—that extra 5 knots may be the result of a momentary nose-down pitch attitude. If the pitch instruments tell you that all is well, the throttle has to be the answer. If the airspeed is lower than desired, add just enough power to start the airspeed needle moving in the right direction and quickly check the other flight instruments.

When your eyes make it back to the ASI again, pull off enough power to slow the movement of the needle and on the next scan make a further reduction to stop the needle where you want it. Do not make these changes by reference to the tachometer or manifold pressure gauge.

When the MAP gauge or tachometer is the primary instrument for power control—that is, during changes in the condition of flight—these are the general rules: don't reach for the throttle unless you know what the new setting will be, and don't stare at the instrument during the change. Ballpark the control movement based on sound and on your knowledge of the airplane, then glance at the power instrument(s) and complete the setting.

Learning the Numbers for Your Airplane

During the first few hours of training for the instrument rating you should become familiar with "the numbers" for your airplane so that you can combine attitude changes with known power settings for predictable performance. You will determine enroute cruise power settings by reference to the performance charts for your airplane, but power settings for maneuvering in the terminal area should be determined by experiment. Figure 2-22 suggests a format.

When you have decided on an approach speed, you should take your airplane up and learn how much power is required to maintain level flight at cruise speed and what it takes to slow to approach speed in level flight. Then record the power setting for a 500 fpm climb at recommended climb speed. At the same time, you should note the pitch picture on the attitude indicator for each evolution—the relationship of the dot to the horizon line.

With those numbers recorded you should be able to transition from level flight at cruise to approach speed to a 500 fpm descent and level off at a specified altitude by simply establishing known pitch attitudes and making appropriate power settings.

A 3° glide slope descends at approximately 600 feet per minute if your ground speed is 120 knots and 450 feet per minute if the speed is 90 knots; record the power setting required to maintain that airspeed and descent rate for use during precision approaches. When descending on a nonprecision approach a vertical speed of 700 to 1,000 feet per minute may be required, so make a note of the power required to descend at 1,000 feet per minute at the selected approach speed. (You'll learn about glide slopes and instrument approaches later).

If you fly an airplane with retractable landing gear, you should learn how much speed is lost if you extend the gear while maintaining altitude and what rate of descent results when you extend the gear and maintain airspeed. Record the power setting required to maintain level flight at approach speed with the gear up or down.

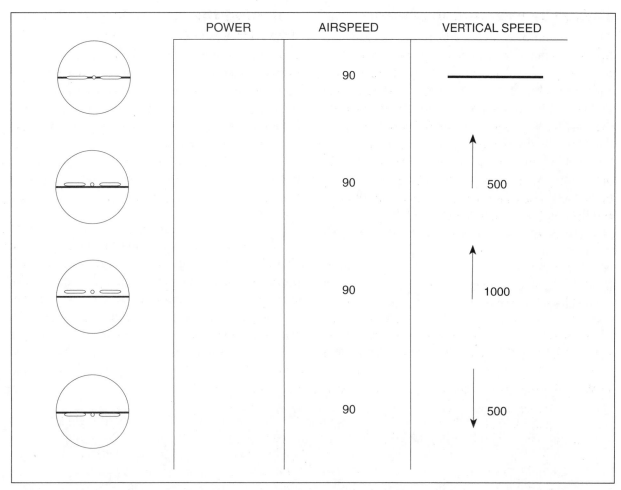

	POWER	AIRSPEED	VERTICAL SPEED
		90	
		90	500
		90	1000
		90	500

Figure 2-22. *Sample attitude and power setting worksheet*

As a general rule, a change of one inch in manifold pressure (with a constant speed propeller) or a change of 50 rpm (with a fixed pitch propeller) will result in a 100 fpm change in vertical speed. This is a ballpark figure, subject to small adjustments caused by changes in weight or density altitude, but it is quite useful. If extending the landing gear while maintaining airspeed results in a 300 fpm descent, a power reduction of two inches of MAP should cause the vertical speed to stabilize on 500 fpm with no change in airspeed. If your landing gear is welded down, a five-inch reduction or a change of 250 rpm should accomplish the same thing.

Use of the Throttle in Recovery from Unusual Attitudes

What you do with the throttle when you realize that the airplane is in an unusual attitude depends on the airplane's pitch attitude, and the best place to look for that information in a hurry is the airspeed indicator.

If the airspeed is low and decaying, full power is called for as you simultaneously lower the nose. A nose low unusual attitude is indicated by increasing airspeed, and the throttle setting must be reduced as the wings are rolled level.

Aerodynamics for Commercial Pilot Students

The flying public expects a commercial pilot to have a fuller understanding of aerodynamics than a private pilot. Remember the old saying that the private certificate is a license to learn? Now, as you prepare for the commercial pilot knowledge test and checkride, the chips are down—you must demonstrate that you have learned.

When you were a student pilot, your instructor probably stayed away from the theoretical aspects of aerodynamics for fear of overloading you with information. By now, you have flown enough to have developed a feel for how to make the airplane do what you want it to do, and converting that intuitive feel into numbers will come more easily.

Lift, Drag, and Angle of Attack

Figure 2-23 contains a lot of information about lift and drag, separately and in combination. You won't find this graph in your Pilot's Operating Handbook, but you should find a best glide speed in the emergency operations section. You can see that angle of attack is plotted against coefficient of lift, coefficient of drag, and the ratio of lift to drag. Note how the coefficient of lift is greatest just before the stall—that's why so much emphasis is placed on slow flight. Pilots should be comfortable at the low end of the airspeed range, instead of adding ten knots to the recommended approach speed for the spouse and kiddies.

The angle of attack at which the ratio of lift to drag is greatest also provides the best glide ratio. In fact, the glide ratio is equal to the L/D ratio. Figure 2-23

shows the best L/D as 12.5, so you can expect to glide 12.5 feet forward for every foot of lost altitude; for each mile traveled, you would lose 5,280 ÷ 12.5 or 422.4 feet. However, you would only achieve this performance at an angle of attack of 6 degrees. Increasing or decreasing the angle of attack would reduce the glide ratio. Note that at any angle of attack other than that which produces the maximum lift to drag ratio, there are two angles of attack for a given L/D ratio. For example, a ratio of 10 to 1 is achieved at both 3 and 12.4 degrees.

On the commercial knowledge test you will be asked to calculate the amount of altitude that would be lost per mile when gliding at a given angle of attack. This is a simple matter of ratios. If an airplane has a lift to drag ratio of 11 to 1 at a 10° angle of attack, you need only to divide 5,280 (the questions are based on statute miles) by 11 to get the answer: 480 feet per mile. At an 8° angle of attack (L/D ratio 12 to 1), you would lose 5,280 ÷ 12 or 440 feet per mile. At the

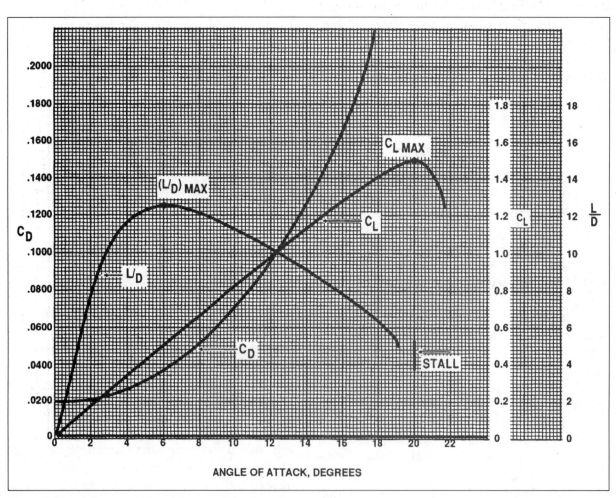

Figure 2-23. Coefficients of lift and drag vs. angle of attack

maximum L/D shown in Figure 2-23 you would lose 422 feet per mile. You can see that to cover the most ground before hitting it, you must fly at the optimum angle of attack. You can also see the impossibility of "stretching" a glide by increasing angle of attack.

Figure 2-23 does not consider either airspeed or weight. The angle of attack for maximum L/D is a function of wing design and is not affected by weight. Two airplanes with the same wing design, one heavy and one light, gliding from the same altitude, will land at the same distance from the starting point. However, their airspeeds will be different on the way down. The best glide speed varies directly with weight: a heavier airplane must fly faster and a lighter airplane must fly more slowly if the angle of attack is to remain at its optimum value. Unless you are fortunate enough to have an angle of attack indicator on board, you must rely on the airspeed indicator.

If your powered airplane turns into a glider you must consider the effect of wind on gliding distance. Gliding with the wind will always get you farther; with the wind behind you, use a glide speed slightly slower than normal to extend gliding range.

L/D and Range

When you begin planning cross-country flights, among the many factors to be taken into consideration is the question of range versus time — do you want to get to your destination in a hurry or would you rather get there a little more slowly and avoid a stop for fuel? The question is one of specific range: nautical miles of flying distance per pound of fuel. Since we measure speed in nautical miles per hour, the equation becomes knots divided by fuel flow in pounds per hour; maximum range means optimum airspeed and minimum fuel flow. (Maximum *endurance* is a matter of staying in the air for the maximum amount of time — pilots call it "time in the tanks.")

When the goal is maximum range, the optimum airspeed decreases as fuel is burned and the weight of the airplane decreases; the optimum specific range increases. If you do not reduce the throttle setting as fuel is consumed, airspeed will increase and fuel economy will suffer.

Lift, Stalls, and Load Factor

You have seen a graph similar to Figure 2-24 before. It is meant to impress on you the relationship between load factor and stalling. Load factor, as you may

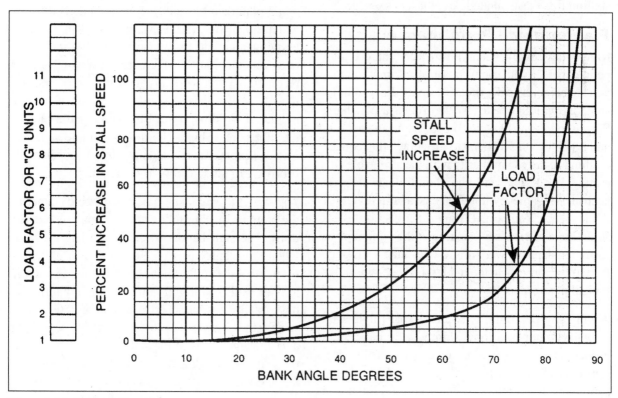

Figure 2-24. Stall speed/load factor

recall, is the ratio between the lift being developed by the wing and the weight of the airplane: at a load factor of two, the wing is supporting twice the weight of the airplane, and you, the pilot, are sinking into your seat with a force of 2 Gs. Load factor increases with bank angle, because in a bank the total lift developed by the wing is divided into vertical and horizontal components. If the airplane is to maintain altitude, the vertical component will equal the airplane's weight; the horizontal component of lift adds to the total load on the wing. As you can see from the graph, at a 60 degree bank angle the horizontal component of lift is equal to weight and the load on the wing has doubled. Note that the load factor remains constant if a constant bank angle is maintained.

Your job as a pilot is to fly the wing. You control angle of attack with the elevator, and by varying the angle of attack you control airspeed, lift, and drag. Check Figure 2-23 again to see how the coefficients of lift and drag are affected by angle of attack. You can make the airplane do pretty much anything you want it to by flying the wing, subject to one very real limitation: the critical angle of attack at which the airplane stalls. Although power can delay the onset of a stall, no amount of power can keep the wing from stalling if the critical angle of attack is exceeded.

Planform and Performance

Rightly or wrongly, when you are a commercial pilot people expect you to have a lot of information that you never received in primary training. For example, someone will ask you to take them out in a Whizbang Six, although you have never been in one in your life, and it will be very difficult to turn down the request. Nothing replaces familiarity with the airplane's Operating Handbook, and you should never take on such an assignment without at least a brief review of the airspeeds. You can get a rough idea of an airplane's flight characteristics by looking at the wing's planform (its shape, viewed from above) and the distance from the pilot seats to the rudder. Figure 2-25 shows typical planforms.

A wing's "aspect ratio" is its length (span) divided by its width (chord); a long, skinny wing has a high aspect ratio. Such a wing develops high lift proportional to drag, which is why you see them on sailplanes. It is pretty difficult to put fuel in a thin

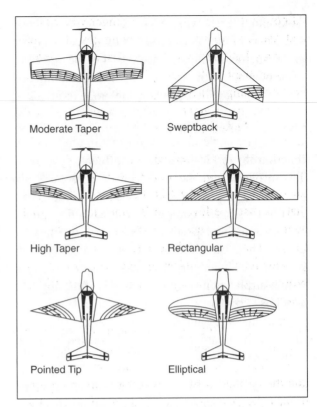

Figure 2-25. *Stall patterns of various wing shapes*

wing, which is why powered airplanes have relatively fat wings.

Wing planform plays a role in stall characteristics. You probably trained in an airplane with a rectangular wing, and your first experiences with stalls were relatively benign. That's because a wing with a rectangular planform stalls at the wing root first, and then the stall moves outward as the angle of attack is increased. Aileron control is maintained almost to the bitter end. This is the most desirable situation. You can expect fat, rectangular wings to be relatively forgiving of small errors in pitch control.

The designer gains some performance by tapering the wing or by combining straight and tapered sections. The stall begins further out along the wing when the planform is tapered, and it is logical to expect that the stall will progress out to the ailerons fairly rapidly. You will notice that many airplanes have "stall strips" attached to the leading edges of the wings; their purpose is to force airflow separation and the beginnings of the stalled condition close to the wing root while retaining the advantages of tapered wing construction. Thin, tapered wings will require more attention to pitch control.

Although it is unlikely that a stranger will walk up and ask you to fly a swept-wing jet, it's worth knowing that swept wings stall first at the wingtips and that their stall characteristics are sufficiently unusual compared to trainer type airplanes. Their designers go to great lengths to provide high lift devices for use at high angles of attack.

An airplane with a relatively short distance between the pilot station (approximate center of gravity) and the rudder is said to be "short coupled." This means that because the lever arm is short, it takes quick, aggressive rudder use to develop corrective yawing forces when the airplane decides to run off the runway during takeoff or landing. This is more of a problem with taildraggers than it is with tricycle geared airplanes.

Other clues to the performance of an unfamiliar airplane can be found in the wing loading (maximum gross weight divided by wing area in square feet), and the airplane's power loading (maximum gross divided by horsepower). An airplane with a light wing loading, for example, 11 pounds per square foot, will provide a rougher ride in turbulence than one with a ratio of 20:1. Low wing loading means (relatively) low stall speed, and that in turn affects approach and landing speeds. High power loading simply means more bang for the buck...er, horsepower: better climb performance, higher cruise speed.

V-Speeds and the G-Force Envelope

The graph of velocity versus G-forces, Figure 2-26, tells you, among other things, how the green and yellow arcs on the airspeed indicator are determined. The envelope that begins with a zero load factor is called the maneuvering envelope; the envelope beginning at +1 G is the gust envelope. The arc curving upward from zero load factor to point C is the stall line (maximum lift capability). A normal stall places a load of one G on the wing, so the stall speed is at point A. Speeds above point A on the arc are accelerated stall speeds. Point C, where the accelerated stall arc meets the 3.8 G limit load, represents maneuvering speed.

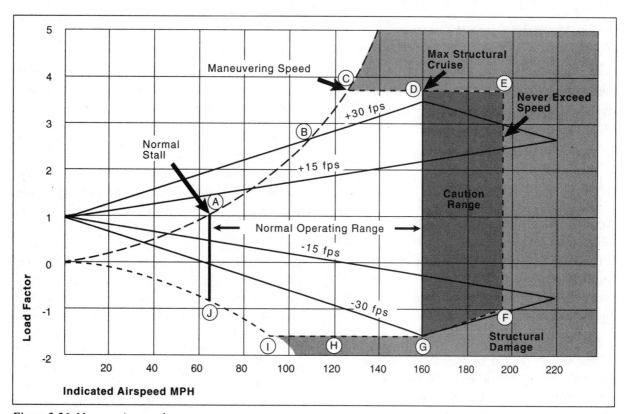

Figure 2-26. Maneuvering envelope

You know that an airplane certified in the Normal category is built to handle a maximum positive load of 3.8 Gs and a negative load of 1.5 Gs; note that in Figure 2-26 any force greater than those limits is labeled "Structural Damage." The lines labeled plus or minus 15 and 30 feet per second (fps) represent gust factors; you can see that at speeds lower than Point B, an encounter with a 30 fps gust will result in a stall, not structural damage, while hitting the same gust at a higher airspeed will result in forces approaching the load limit. The designer must consider gusts of up to 50 fps when designing the airplane.

The normal operating range, or green arc, extends from the normal stall line A-J to the maximum structural cruise line D-G. You can see that the G-forces imposed by gusts increase as airspeed increases toward line D-G.

The yellow arc, or caution range, exists between line D-G, where a gust of over 30 fps meets the limit load line and the E-F line. This is experimentally determined by a factory test pilot by diving the airplane until control surface flutter is experienced.

Drag Versus Speed Curves

You saw graphs like Figure 2-27 earlier in this chapter and when you were studying for your private pilot knowledge examination, but they are probably more meaningful now that you have more flight experience. Points A and B both represent minimum drag, which means maximum lift to drag ratio. This coincides with the speed for maximum glide range. It is important that you recognize the relationship between airspeed and the two types of drag.

Parasite drag, caused by the aircraft's structure, is minimal at low speeds and increases with speed until it equals the maximum thrust available from the engine; this is what determines maximum speed. The greatest contribution to parasite drag comes from the engine cooling intakes.

Induced drag is the price you pay for lift. It is greatest at low speeds, and decreases as speed increases. Induced drag is also affected by bank angle/load factor; when you bank the wings and divert part of the wing's lift to a horizontal force, the angle of attack must be increased to maintain altitude. That means more induced drag, which in turn means more

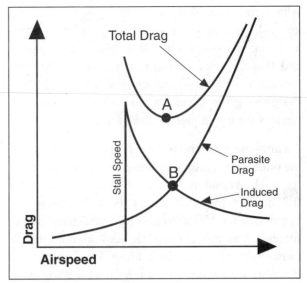

Figure 2-27. Drag vs. speed

power to maintain a constant airspeed. You can't have a drag increase without an accompanying increase in thrust if constant airspeed is a factor.

Ground effect, which is not accounted for in Figure 2-27 because it occurs only within one wingspan of the ground, changes the rules a bit. Because the proximity of the wing to the surface changes the airflow pattern around the airplane, induced drag is reduced and the wing can either develop the same amount of lift at a lower angle of attack, or at a constant angle of attack, develop more lift.

The reduction in induced drag, hardly noticeable when you are a wingspan above the runway, is 23 percent when one-fourth of the wingspan high and almost 50 percent when the wing is one-tenth of its span from the surface (about three feet for most general aviation airplanes). Getting a high wing within three feet of the surface is quite an accomplishment, so you can expect ground effect to be a more useful tool in low-wing airplanes. In any event, thrust must be reduced (reduced drag, remember?) or you will float down the runway.

Balanced Forces

One of the most difficult concepts to get across to a student is the concept of balanced forces. Do you understand it yet? You will be questioned on your knowledge of this subject and you need remember only one thing: in unaccelerated level flight or in a steady-state climb or descent, the sum of all upward forces is equal to the sum of all downward forces, and the sum of all forward forces is equal to the sum of all rearward forces. Simplistically, lift equals weight, thrust equals drag. In a climb or descent, however, the forces of lift, thrust, weight, and drag must be broken into horizontal and vertical components, which complicates matters. As long as you understand that constant airspeed means balanced forces you will be all right.

Stability

When your airplane is loaded so that the center of gravity falls within the design envelope, you experience stick forces that you have come to expect as normal: when you apply back pressure without trimming, the airplane feels nose heavy, and if you push forward on the stick and hold it you can feel the nose trying to rise. That's positive static stability. When the airplane is misloaded, you will get some unpleasant surprises.

If you apply back pressure and the airplane pitches up and maintains that nose-high attitude, it is demonstrating neutral longitudinal static stability—neutral, because the airplane no longer tries to regain a stable flight condition. Longitudinal dynamic instability would be indicated when you apply a little stick pressure, forward or aft, and the airplane doesn't stop at the desired pitch attitude but overshoots it, and the oscillations get worse and worse. Note that this discussion of longitudinal instability involves the lateral axis—a line from wingtip to wingtip—not the longitudinal axis.

The frightening thing about the stability problems just described is that they don't become apparent until you are airborne, and it's too late to do anything about it. Passengers can be asked to move back and forth in the airplane to help with an out-of-CG condition, but packages don't pay much attention to your pleas for help. Yet it is in cargo operations that this type of misloading can occur.

As a commercial pilot you need to understand longitudinal stability. When you are standing on the ramp at two o'clock in the morning with a truck full of packages that you would like to fit into the airplane, you have to understand the consequences of misloading. When the airplane leaps off the ground and you have to hold forward pressure to keep from stalling, it's too late to think about the location of the center of gravity and its effect on stability. When you have loaded the airplane so that the CG is so close to the aft limit that you're really not sure, and you feel the yoke "floating" in your hand, don't engage the autopilot—you might get a demonstration of divergent pitch oscillations. As a practical matter, stick "feel" is a function of the download on the horizontal stabilizer, and if the center of gravity is so far aft that little download is needed, there will be little stick pressure and the autopilot will hunt for a stable condition.

Anticipation

As you recall from your private pilot training, the rudder and wings are rigged to counteract the effects of "torque," that all-encompassing word that means P-factor, equal-and-opposite reaction to engine rotation, and the corkscrewing slipstream of propeller discharge air. And you learned in flight training that the corrective forces are good at a narrow band of cruise airspeeds—it takes a lot of right rudder at takeoff time, and it takes a lot of left rudder when diving power-off. As a commercial pilot with an instrument rating, you have to know when to add a little manual assistance.

The discharge air from the propeller corkscrews beneath the fuselage, emerges on the left side of the airplane, and exerts a force on the vertical fin and rudder that yaws the nose of the airplane to the left, causing a left-rolling tendency because it impinges on the vertical fin above the center of gravity. The manufacturer helps with the yaw by offsetting the vertical fin a few degrees from the longitudinal axis, and increases the angle of incidence of the left wing to offset the roll. When adding power, then, you must anticipate the need for right rudder—the amount depends on airspeed and the degree of change. You must understand these forces and anticipate the changes in control pressure.

Commercial Versus Instrument

There's not a single word in these last few sections that does not apply to you as an instrument pilot—you just won't find questions about aerodynamics or performance on the instrument examination.

Chapter 2
Aerodynamics Review Questions

The instrument knowledge exam is not big on aerodynamics as such, but does explore your knowledge of how the flight instruments reflect the aerodynamic facts of life. The commercial exam looks into your knowledge of the nuts and bolts of aerodynamics.

Instrument Student Questions

1. The gyroscopic heading indicator is inoperative. What is the primary bank instrument in unaccelerated straight-and-level flight?

   A—Magnetic compass
   B—Attitude indicator
   C—Miniature aircraft of turn coordinator

2. What instruments are considered supporting bank instruments during a straight, stabilized climb at a constant rate?

   A—Attitude indicator and turn coordinator
   B—Heading indicator and attitude indicator
   C—Heading indicator and turn coordinator

3. What is the primary bank instrument once a standard rate turn is established?

   A—Attitude indicator
   B—Turn coordinator
   C—Heading indicator

4. As power is increased to enter a 500 feet per minute rate of climb in straight flight, which instruments are primary for pitch, bank, and power respectively?

   A—Airspeed indicator, heading indicator, and manifold pressure gauge or tachometer.
   B—VSI, attitude indicator, and airspeed indicator.
   C—Airspeed indicator, attitude indicator, and manifold pressure gauge or tachometer.

5. What is the primary pitch instrument when establishing a constant altitude standard rate turn?

   A—Altimeter
   B—VSI
   C—Airspeed indicator

6. What instrument(s) is(are) supporting bank instrument when entering a constant airspeed climb from straight-and-level flight?

   A—Heading indicator.
   B—Attitude indicator and turn coordinator.
   C—Turn coordinator and heading indicator.

7. Which instruments are considered to be supporting instruments for pitch during change of airspeed in a level turn?

   A—Airspeed indicator and VSI.
   B—Altimeter and attitude indicator.
   C—Attitude indicator and VSI.

8. Which instruments should be used to make a pitch correction when you have deviated from your assigned altitude?

   A—Altimeter and VSI.
   B—Manifold pressure gauge and VSI.
   C—Attitude indicator, altimeter, and VSI.

9. To level off from a descent to a specific altitude, the pilot should lead the level-off by approximately

   A—10 percent of the vertical speed.
   B—30 percent of the vertical speed.
   C—50 percent of the vertical speed.

10. To enter a constant-airspeed descent from level-cruising flight, and maintain cruising airspeed, the pilot should

   A—first adjust the pitch attitude to a descent using the attitude indicator as a reference, then adjust the power to maintain the cruising airspeed.

   B—first reduce power, then adjust the pitch using the attitude indicator as a reference to establish a specific rate on the VSI.

   C—simultaneously reduce power and adjust the pitch using the attitude indicator as a reference to maintain the cruising airspeed.

11. What is the correct sequence in which to use the three skills used in instrument flying?

   A—Aircraft control, cross-check, and instrument interpretation.

   B—Instrument interpretation, cross-check, and aircraft control.

   C—Cross-check, instrument interpretation, and aircraft control.

12. (Refer to Figure Q2-1.) What is the flight attitude? One system which transmits information to the instruments has malfunctioned.

   A—Level turn to the right.
   B—Level turn to the left.
   C—Straight-and-level flight.

Commercial Student Questions

13. (Refer to Figure 2-26 on Page 2-21.) The vertical line from point D to point G is represented on the airspeed indicator by the maximum speed limit of the

   A—green arc.
   B—yellow arc.
   C—white arc.

14. To produce the same lift while in ground effect as when out of ground effect, the airplane requires

   A—a lower angle of attack.
   B—the same angle of attack.
   C—a greater angle of attack.

Figure Q2-1. Instrument interpretation (instrument malfunction)

15. Which maximum range factor decreases as weight decreases?

    A—Altitude
    B—Airspeed
    C—Angle of attack

16. Which is true regarding the forces acting on an aircraft in a steady-state descent? The sum of all

    A—upward forces is less than the sum of all downward forces.
    B—rearward forces is greater than the sum of all forward forces.
    C—forward forces is equal to the sum of all rearward forces.

17. Why is it necessary to increase back elevator pressure to maintain altitude during a turn? To compensate for the

    A—loss of the vertical component of lift.
    B—loss of the horizontal component of lift and the increase in centrifugal force.
    C—rudder deflection and slight opposite aileron throughout the turn.

18. While maintaining a constant angle of bank and altitude in a coordinated turn, an increase in airspeed will

    A—decrease the rate of turn resulting in a decreased load factor.
    B—decrease the rate of turn resulting in no change in load factor.
    C—increase the rate of turn resulting in no change in load factor.

19. A propeller rotating clockwise as seen from the rear, creates a spiraling slipstream that tends to rotate the airplane to the

    A—right around the vertical axis, and to the left around the longitudinal axis.
    B—left around the vertical axis, and to the right around the longitudinal axis.
    C—left around the vertical axis, and to the left around the longitudinal axis.

20. If the airplane attitude remains in a new position after the elevator control is pressed forward and released, the airplane displays

    A—neutral longitudinal static stability.
    B—positive longitudinal static stability.
    C—neutral longitudinal dynamic stability.

21. In small airplanes, normal recovery from spins may become difficult if the

    A—CG is too far rearward and rotation is around the longitudinal axis.
    B—CG is too far rearward and rotation is around the CG.
    C—spin is entered before the stall is fully developed.

Performance

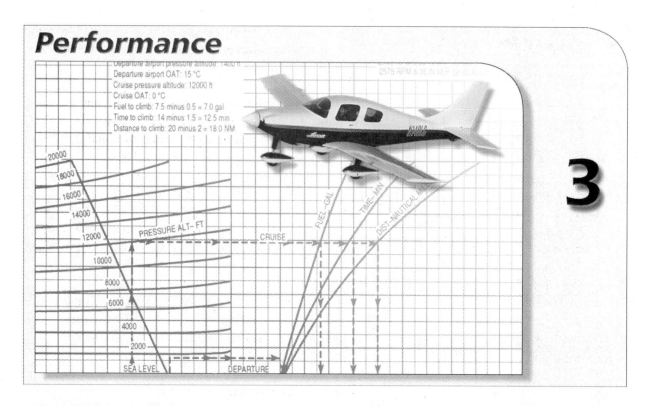

Departure airport pressure altitude: 1400 ft
Departure airport OAT: 15 °C
Cruise pressure altitude: 12000 ft
Cruise OAT: 0 °C
Fuel to climb: 7.5 minus 0.5 = 7.0 gal
Time to climb: 14 minus 1.5 = 12.5 min
Distance to climb: 20 minus 2 = 18.0 NM

2575 RPM & 36 IN M.P. (2-BLAD...

"Can We Get Off the Ground Safely?"

The first element in planning a flight in any kind of weather is determining whether your airplane is capable of carrying out your plans. This means that you must perform weight and balance calculations, check the performance data in the Pilot's Operating Handbook, and check the weather. There is obviously no difference between commercial and instrument pilots (or instrument-rated commercial pilots) where these factors are involved. The review questions will be based on the individual knowledge exams.

Weight and Balance Calculations

As I stated earlier, there are no weight and balance or performance problems in the instrument pilot exam. In keeping with the title of this book, however, I will include a "complete" discussion. As an instrument pilot, you will be more concerned about proper loading than you have been as a VFR pilot, because when you are on the gauges you do not want problems with the airplane's handling characteristics to interfere with your concentration on the navigation and communication requirements of instrument flight. Also, if the airplane is loaded so that it is close to gross weight or near a center of gravity limit, the addition of structural ice may exceed those limits.

Loading information can be found in the approved airplane flight manual in a number of forms, but manufacturers always make it possible to calculate the center of gravity position by adding the weights and their moments. The presentation in Table 3-1 on the following page is typical. Basic empty weight includes unusable fuel and full oil.

Note that the arm for each seat, baggage compartment, and fuel tank is given. The airplane's empty weight and Moment/100 are provided. When doing a weight and balance calculation, be sure to use the most current information. This should be in the airframe log or on an FAA Form 337. For each item of added weight the arm (distance from datum) is given, and the table provides moments (weight times arm) for selected weights. When the weight of an item or passenger falls between tabulated values you must interpolate. Total all of the weights and moments and divide the total moment by the total weight to provide the distance of the CG from the datum.

To make some airplanes more useful, their manufacturers have provided alternative passenger seating arrangements such as seats which can be swiveled to face either forward or aft or seats which convert to bench seating. Because moving a seat changes its distance from the datum, the loading tables include

Weight and Moment Tables

Baggage

Weight (Pounds)	Nose Compartment Arm = -31"	Wing Locker Arm = 63"	Cabin Compartments Arm = 96"	Arm = 124"	Arm = 126"
			Moment/100		
10	-3	6	10	12	13
20	-6	13	19	25	25
30	-9	19	29	37	38
40	-12	25	38	50	50
50	-16	32	48	62	63
60	-19	38	58	74	76
70	-22	44	67	87	88
80	-25	50	77	99	101
90	-28	57	86	112	113
100	-31	63	96	124	126
110	-34	69	106	136	139
120	-37	76	115	149	151
130	-40	82	125	161	164
140	-43	88	134	174	176
150	-46	94	144	186	189
160	-50	101	154	198	202
170	-53	107	163		
180	-56	113	173		
190	-59	120	182		
200	-62	126	192		
210	-65	132			
220	-68	139			
230	-71	145			
240	-74	151			
250	-78				
260	-81				
270	-84				
280	-87				
290	-90				
300	-93				
310	-96				
320	-99				
330	-102				
340	-105				
350	-108				

Crew and Passengers

Weight (Pounds)	1st or 2nd Seats Arm = 37"	3rd or 4th Seats Bench Seat Arm = 71"	Individual Seat Arm = 68"	5th or 6th Seat Arm = 102"
		Moment/100		
10	4	7	7	10
20	7	14	14	20
30	11	21	20	31
40	15	28	27	41
50	18	36	34	51
60	22	43	41	61
70	26	50	48	71
80	30	57	54	82
90	33	64	61	92
100	37	71	68	102
110	41	78	75	112
120	44	85	82	122
130	48	92	88	133
140	52	99	95	143
150	56	106	102	153
160	59	114	109	163
170	63	121	116	173
180	67	128	122	184
190	70	135	129	194
200	74	142	136	204
210	78	149	143	214
220	81	156	150	224
230	85	163	156	235
240	89	170	163	245
250	92	178	170	255
260	96	185	177	265
270	100	192	184	275
280	104	199	190	286
290	107	206	197	296
300	111	213	204	306

Fuel

Gallons	Weight (Pounds)	Main Wing Tanks Arm = 35"	Auxiliary Wing Tanks Arm = 47"	Wing Locker Tanks Arm = 49"
		Moment/100		
5	30	10	14	15
10	60	21	28	29
15	90	32	42	44
20	120	42	56	59
25	150	52	70	74
30	180	63	85	88
35	210	74	99	103
40	240	84	113	118
45	270	94	127	
50	300	105	141	
55	330	116	155	
60	360	126	169	
63	378	132	178	
65	390	136		
70	420	147		
75	450	158		
80	480	168		
85	510	178		
90	540	189		
95	570	200		
100	600	210		

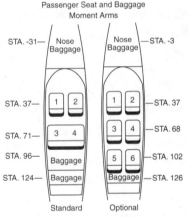

Passenger Seat and Baggage Moment Arms

Standard — Optional

Operating Weights and Moments

Operating Weights	Pounds	Mom/100
Maximum Takeoff Weight	5500	
Maximum Landing Weight	5400	
Maximum Zero Fuel Weight	4900	
Basic Empty Weight	3472	1220

Center of Gravity Limits (Reference = 0.00 Inches)

C.G. Limit @ Weight		Inches Aft Datum	% MAC
Forward	5500	38.67 Inches	26.69
	4500 or less	32.00 Inches	15.84
AFT	5500	43.10 Inches	33.90
	5100 or less	43.60 Inches	34.71

Table 3-1. Weights and moments

arms and moments for all possible arrangements. Be sure that your calculations are based on the actual positions of the seats for each flight.

	Weight	Moment/100
Passenger, seat 1	170 lbs	63
Passenger, seat 2	160 lbs	59
Passenger, seat 3 (individual)	100 lbs	68
Passenger, seat 4 (individual)	120 lbs	82
Baggage, wing locker	50 lbs	32
Baggage, cabin compartment (126")	65 lbs	82
Fuel, main wing tanks	100 gal*	210
Fuel, aux wing tanks	63 gal*	178
Fuel, wing locker tanks	20 gal*	59

*(Convert the fuel from gallons to pounds.) Total all weights and moments, and don't forget the empty weight and moment of the airplane. The totals should be 5,235 pounds and 2,053.

The moments for each weight item, except the cabin baggage, are taken directly from the table; the cabin baggage moment must be interpolated between the moments for 60 and 70 pounds.

Divide 2,053 by 5,235: the answer is .3922. The moments are in inches/100, however, so you must multiply by 100 to get the CG location in inches: 39.22" aft of datum. According to the information provided, the CG limits for this weight are 38.67" and 43.10", and the loading is well within limits. The CG will move forward as fuel is burned off, but note that the forward CG limit changes for weights under 4,500 pounds.

As you have seen, you can do any weight and balance problem with the Pilot's Operating Handbook and a 4-function calculator. It is time-consuming, and until you have completed all of the calculations you cannot be sure that the airplane is loaded within the envelope.

With ASA's CX-2 Pathfinder calculator you get constantly updated information on the total weight and CG position.

Zero Fuel Weight

In referring to Table 3-1 you saw the term "zero fuel weight," which may be an unfamiliar term. It is the maximum weight that can be concentrated in the fuselage (passengers, cargo, and baggage), and it is based on the ability of the wing to accept bending stresses. The wing is what holds the airplane up, and the cabin sits right in the middle of it; add enough weight in the center and the wing will fold up around your ears.

All weight over and above the zero fuel weight must be in the form of fuel in the wings or baggage in wing lockers. This restriction is common when an airplane has a wide range of loading options.

Graphic Solutions

Some manufacturers provide the weight/arm/moment information in graphic form, and also present the operating envelope graphically. Some Piper models use a plastic slide device for loading calculations. Other manufacturers use the tabular form for determining moments and present the envelope graphically. You will find problems using both of these presentations in the review section.

As a practical matter, you will be calculating weight and balance and checking performance figures at the same time, because the fuel portion of the weight and balance problem depends on such performance data as true airspeed and fuel flow.

Many flight planning programs for personal computers include the ability to store the airplane's basic weight/moment and center of gravity limits, add the figures for a proposed trip, and display the CG with its relationship to those limits.

Weight and Balance for Commercial Pilots

When you start charging for your services, the FAA takes a closer look at how you handle weight and balance. If you operate under Part 135, you may have to prepare a manifest listing the weight of all passengers or cargo and the center of gravity position you calculated. You will have to add a bathroom scale to your flight equipment, too, because your weight and balance data must be based on actual, not average, weights. Also, Part 135 requires that all multi-engine airplanes be weighed every 36 months to make sure that your basis for calculations is accurate. Remember that the empty weight includes unusable fuel, hydraulic fluid, and undrainable oil (for some aircraft, it includes all of the oil—check the Pilot's Operating Handbook).

The Commercial Pilot Knowledge Exam goes beyond the simple CG location problems you did for your private exam and gets into weight shifting. First, however, it explores your knowledge of fundamentals. Try this:

- Weight A is 120 pounds, and is located 15 inches aft of datum.
- Weight B is 200 pounds, and is located 117 inches aft of datum.
- Weight C is 75 pounds, and is located 195 inches aft of datum.

(If any of the distances were negative numbers, that weight would be located ahead of the datum).

What is the center of gravity location aft of datum?

It's the old weight, arm, and moment game. Multiply the weight by the arm to get moment; for weight A it is 1,800 inch-pounds, for weight B the moment is 23,400 inch-pounds, and for weight C it is 14,625 inch-pounds. Total the moments and you get 39,825. The total weight on board is 395 pounds. Divide moment by weight to get center of gravity location aft of datum: 100.8 inches. I like to think of moment over weight as a spider standing on a mirror—you may have your own memory aid.

Some problems refer to the weight location as a station number rather than inches aft of datum—it's the same thing. Here's a very practical problem:

- Total weight is 4,037 pounds at takeoff.
- Center of gravity is at station 67.8 at takeoff.
- Fuel burn is 14.7 gallons per hour.
- Fuel weight is located at station 68.0

Where will the center of gravity be after 1+45 hours in flight?

You can't deal with changes in moment without knowing what they were originally, so you must first multiply 4,037 by 67.8 to get the total moment at takeoff: 273,708.6 inch-pounds.

After 1+45 flight time you have burned 14.7 x 1.75 = 25.7 gallons of fuel at 6 pounds per gallon or 154.2 pounds. That weight reduction has occurred at station 68.0, reducing the total moment by 68 x 154.2 or 10,485.6 inch-pounds, making the new total moment 273,708.6 – 10,485.6, or 263,223.0. The airplane now weighs 4,037 – 154.2 = 3,882.8 pounds, making your moment-over-weight problem 263,223.0 ÷ 3,882.8, or 67.79 inches aft of datum.

Almost all general aviation airplanes are designed so that the change in center of gravity as fuel is consumed will not affect controllability. You might want to do some calculations for the airplane you fly so that you can anticipate CG movement as fuel is burned off.

You may find that you have to shuffle people or bags around in order to get the center of gravity into the safe range. Let's say that you have your airplane loaded and calculate its weight at 3,550 pounds and the center of gravity at 95.0 inches aft of datum. That's fine—except the aft limit is 92.0. The airplane will never fly under those conditions. The aft baggage compartment is at station 179 and the forward baggage compartment is at station 42. It doesn't take a rocket scientist to realize that something must be taken out of the aft baggage compartment and moved forward. But how much? If the forward baggage compartment has a maximum weight limit, you can't move too much.

The formula is:

$$\frac{\text{weight to be moved}}{\text{total weight}} = \frac{\text{change in CG}}{\text{distance moved}}$$

Using your pocket calculator, cross-multiply and divide. The unknown is weight to be moved, so multiply total weight times the desired change in CG: 3,550 x 3 inches = 10,650, and divide by the other known factor, distance moved (179 – 42 = 137 inches), to get 77.7 pounds to be moved forward. Piece of cake. Not quite so easy when Mom and Pop want to sit together and you need to move one of them forward to solve a CG problem. There's a lot to be said for flying cargo instead of passengers.

Weight and Balance Data

The airplane's basic weight and balance information—the location of weights and their moment arms—will be in your Pilot's Operating Handbook or Approved Flight Manual. You will probably also find figures for empty weight and total moment in the same location, but unless the airplane is new you should take this information with a grain of salt. Installation and removal of equipment, typically electronic equipment, will change the empty weight and moment from the factory values. The latest information should be on a Form 337 but may be found in the airframe log. When the change is made on a Form 337, all previous 337s should be marked "superseded" by the person doing the work. Check the date of any logbook entry against the latest 337 to be sure that you are dealing with the newest information.

Predicting Performance

Airplanes are manufactured and fly all over the world, and pilots everywhere rely on consistent performance in accordance with their airplane's Operating Handbook. Would you expect an airplane manufacturer to provide a different handbook to a Peruvian mountain pilot than the manual provided to a miner in Death Valley? Obviously, the operating conditions vary widely in altitude and temperature. Of course, manufacturers need print only one manual, and the reason lies in the term "International Standard Atmosphere (ISA)." At airplane manufacturing sites, engineering test flights go on—rain or shine, summer or winter. All of the airspeeds, rates of climb, fuel burns, and takeoff and landing distances determined by test pilots are reduced to what they would be on a standard day at sea level.

By internationally accepted standards, a standard day has a barometric pressure of 29.92" Hg and a temperature of 15°C at sea level. The standard atmospheric temperature lapse rate (decrease in temperature with increasing altitude) is assumed to be 2°C per 1,000 feet of altitude above sea level—these conditions represent the International Standard Atmosphere.

Density Altitude

The basis for predicting performance is density altitude—pressure altitude corrected for non-standard temperature. When you are planning your IFR flight you must calculate the effect that existing or forecast weather conditions will have on your takeoff and climb performance from a departure airport. You must also consider the true airspeed and fuel consumption rate at your chosen cruise altitude, and compare the predicted landing distance to the amount of runway available at the destination airport (and any enroute airports you might have to use in an emergency). You will have to compute the density altitude for the different airports, consult your airplane's performance charts, and get the numbers for the expected conditions.

The charts, tables, computers, etc., that are used in calculating the effect of density altitude on performance take into account only pressure altitude and temperature—no provision is made for the effects of humidity on performance. A conservative approach is to add 1,000 feet to any density altitude you arrive at by use of pressure altitude and temperature, and then calculate the performance figures based on that altitude.

You can read air temperature directly from the outside air temperature gauge (OAT); pressure altitude, however, must be calculated or determined indirectly.

The quickest way to determine pressure altitude when you are in the airplane is to note the setting in the Kollsman window and then set it to 29.92; the altimeter will then indicate pressure altitude. (Return the altimeter setting to its previous setting before you forget it!) If you are determining density altitude for a distant airport and have gotten its temperature and altimeter setting from the hourly weather sequence reports, determine the difference between 29.92 and the reported altimeter setting and apply the difference to the field elevation:

Altimeter setting:
$$
\begin{array}{r}
30.20 \\
- 29.92 \\
\hline
.28 \quad = 280 \text{ feet}
\end{array}
$$

Continued

Field elevation: 2,348
                   − 280
Pressure altitude = 2,068

(1.0" = 1,000 feet, .1" = 100 feet, .01" = 10 feet)

To be sure that you apply the pressure difference correctly, ask yourself which way the altimeter needles will move as the altimeter setting is changed from 30.20 to 29.92. In the example, they will move counterclockwise, and the pressure difference must be subtracted from the field elevation to derive pressure altitude at that airport.

Another method is to use the slide rule side of your flight computer by setting the pressure altitude (29.92 reading of the altimeter) in the window opposite the temperature and read density altitude at the index. You can use the reading of your airplane's outside air temperature (OAT) gauge without correction.

Pressure altitude, density altitude, and true altitude are all equal at sea level on a standard day, a condition which does not often occur. Pressure altitude is equal to density altitude only when the temperature is standard for that pressure altitude. If the air mass is warmer than standard, density altitude will be higher than pressure altitude, and if the air mass is colder than standard, density altitude will be lower than pressure altitude. You will read performance figures in the aviation press which refer to "ISA +10°" or "ISA -5°." These figures show performance at temperatures differing from the International Standard Atmosphere.

To determine the standard temperature for a given pressure altitude, double the altitude and subtract 15, remembering that the standard temperature at sea level is 15°C and that above 7,500 feet the temperature will be a negative number. For example, the standard temperature at 27,000 feet is -39°C (54 − 15 = 39).

A reference to International Standard Atmosphere temperatures can be confusing if you don't know the rules. ISA + 5 at 27,000 feet is -34°, so adding degrees makes the temperature warmer. ISA − 10° means a temperature colder than standard. This distinction is important because you can inadvertently exceed your engine's operating pressures when using handbook power settings at temperatures colder than standard.

Because true altitude is the actual altitude above mean sea level, when you are on the ground your altimeter should read the published airport elevation when you set the altimeter to the current local altimeter setting.

Takeoff Performance Charts

As an instrument-rated commercial pilot you must be certain that your airplane can accelerate to liftoff speed and climb to clear obstacles given the existing conditions. For IFR operations, many departure procedures require specific climb performance, and you must be sure that your airplane will be off the ground and climbing as early as is safely possible. Note: Take all performance charts with a grain of salt—it is unlikely that you will be able to match the performance of a factory pilot in a brand-new airplane.

Table 3-2 is a takeoff distance chart. It takes into consideration weight, pressure altitude, wind, and runway surface. Figure 3-1 is a crosswind component chart, to be used in conjunction with Table 3-2. Use of this type of table may require interpolation.

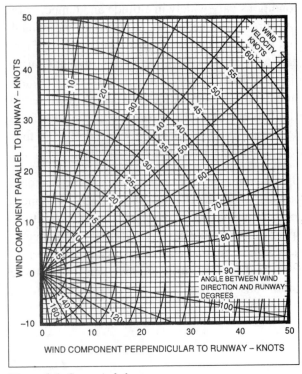

Figure 3-1. *Crosswind chart*

Weight .... 5,500 lbs

Departure runway 36

Runway surface .... concrete

Wind direction/speed .... 055°/18 knots

Temperature .... 23°F

Pressure altitude .... 3,000 feet

What is the normal takeoff distance (not the ground roll)?

NORMAL TAKEOFF DISTANCE

CONDITIONS:
1. Power - FULL THROTTLE and 2700 RPM Before Brake Release
2. Mixtures - LEAN For Field Elevation
3. Wing Flaps - UP
4. Cowl Flaps - OPEN
5. Level, Hard Surface, Dry Runway

NOTE:
1. If Full Power is applied without brakes set, distances apply from point where full power is applied.
2. Decrease all distances 7% for each 10 knots headwind.
3. Increase all distances 5% for each 2 knots tailwind.
4. Increase all distances 7.9% for operation on firm dry sod runway.

WEIGHT POUNDS	TAKEOFF TO 50' OBSTACLE SPEED-KIAS	PRESSURE ALTITUDE FEET	-20°C (-4°F)		-10°C (14°F)		0°C (32°F)		10°C (50°F)	
			GROUND ROLL FEET	TOTAL DISTANCE TO CLEAR 50'	GROUND ROLL FEET	TOTAL DISTANCE TO CLEAR 50'	GROUND ROLL FEET	TOTAL DISTANCE TO CLEAR 50'	GROUND ROLL FEET	TOTAL DISTANCE TO CLEAR 50'
5500	92	Sea Level	1330	1650	1440	1760	1550	1890	1660	2020
		1000	1470	1810	1580	1940	1700	2080	1830	2240
		2000	1610	1990	1740	2140	1880	2300	2020	2470
		3000	1780	2200	1920	2360	2070	2540	2300	2800
		4000	1970	2430	2130	2620	2370	2900	2550	3120
		5000	2180	2700	2430	2980	2620	3220	2820	3470
		6000	2490	3080	2690	3320	2900	3590	3130	3880
		7000	2790	3440	2990	3730	3240	4040	3500	4380
		8000	3090	3880	3350	4220	3620	4590	3920	5000
		9000	3470	4420	3760	4830	4080	5290	4420	5800
		10,000	3880	5050	4220	5550	4580	6130	4980	6810
5100	88	Sea Level	1110	1380	1200	1480	1290	1590	1380	1690
		1000	1220	1510	1320	1620	1420	1740	1520	1860
		2000	1340	1660	1450	1780	1560	1910	1680	2040
		3000	1480	1820	1600	1960	1720	2100	1850	2250
		4000	1630	2010	1760	2160	1900	2330	2050	2500
		5000	1800	2220	1940	2390	2100	2570	2330	2840
		6000	1990	2460	2150	2650	2400	2930	2580	3160
		7000	2210	2730	2470	3030	2660	3270	2870	3530
		8000	2540	3140	2750	3400	2970	3680	3210	3980
		9000	2840	3540	3080	3840	3330	4170	3610	4530
		10,000	3170	3990	3440	4340	3730	4730	4040	5160
4700	85	Sea Level	920	1140	990	1220	1060	1300	1140	1390
		1000	1010	1250	1080	1340	1170	1430	1250	1530
		2000	1100	1360	1190	1460	1280	1570	1370	1670
		3000	1210	1500	1310	1600	1410	1720	1510	1840
		4000	1340	1650	1440	1770	1550	1900	1670	2030
		5000	1470	1810	1590	1940	1710	2090	1840	2240
		6000	1620	2000	1750	2150	1890	2310	2030	2480
		7000	1800	2210	1940	2380	2090	2560	2260	2760
		8000	1990	2460	2160	2650	2330	2860	2600	3170
		9000	2230	2750	2490	3060	2690	3300	2900	3560
		10,000	2560	3160	2770	3420	3000	3700	3240	4010
4300	81	Sea Level	750	930	800	1000	860	1060	920	1130
		1000	820	1020	880	1090	940	1160	1010	1240
		2000	890	1110	960	1190	1030	1270	1110	1360
		3000	980	1210	1050	1300	1130	1390	1220	1490
		4000	1080	1330	1160	1430	1250	1530	1340	1630
		5000	1180	1460	1270	1560	1370	1680	1470	1790
		6000	1300	1600	1400	1720	1510	1840	1620	1980
		7000	1440	1770	1550	1900	1670	2040	1800	2190
		8000	1590	1960	1720	2100	1850	2260	2000	2430
		9000	1770	2180	1910	2340	2060	2530	2230	2720
		10,000	1960	2420	2120	2610	2290	2810	2560	3120

Table 3-2. Takeoff distance chart

The table does not include data for 23°F, so you must interpolate between the distances given for 14° and 32°. At a pressure altitude of 3,000 feet and a gross weight of 5,500 pounds, the distances given for the two temperatures are 2,360 and 2,540. Add them together and divide by 2: the takeoff distance at 23° is 2,450 feet. Now apply the wind correction. The table says that 7 percent must be subtracted for each 10 knots of headwind. The angle between the runway and the reported wind is 55°; enter Figure 3-1 at 55° and follow that line to its intersection with the arc representing 18 knots; from that point move left to the headwind scale to read 10.5 knots. 2,450 feet reduced by 7 percent (2,450 times .93) is 2,278 feet.

Some situations require that you interpolate for several values.

Weight .... 4,500 lbs

Departure runway 27

Runway surface .... sod

Wind direction/speed .... 010°/10 knots

Temperature .... 41°F

Pressure altitude .... 1,000 feet

What is the normal takeoff distance?

The table provides no information for a gross weight of 4,500 pounds or for 41°F. Select the values for 4,300 and 4,700 pounds and for 32° and 50°; add the four values and divide by 4:

1430 + 1530 + 1160 + 1240 ÷ 4 = 1,340 feet

The wind angle is 100°, resulting in a 2-knot tailwind component. The table requires that the takeoff distance be increased by 5 percent for each 2 knots of tailwind and by 7.9 percent for operation on a sod runway. To derive the total distance add .05 (for the tailwind) and .079 (for the sod runway) for an increase of .129 or 12.9 percent. Multiply the runway length (1,340) by 1.129 to get 1,513 feet as the total distance required for takeoff.

Standing water on the runway can retard acceleration, and as little as ½ inch of slush can make a takeoff impossible. As a rule of thumb, you should attain 75 percent of rotation speed in the first one-half of the available runway. If your airplane fails to accelerate that quickly there is something wrong. Taxi back and think it over.

Figure 3-2 provides a graphic solution to the takeoff distance problem. This presentation of operating parameters is found in many operating handbooks and the method of solution is the same in each case.

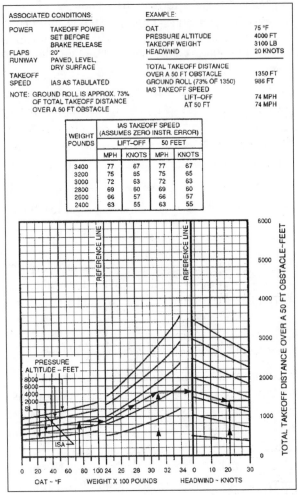

Figure 3-2. *Obstacle takeoff chart*

Because it combines pressure altitude and temperature, the left-hand segment of the chart determines density altitude. The point at which a line drawn vertically from the temperature scale intersects the arc representing pressure altitude represents density altitude. Having found that point, draw a line horizontally to the right to the first reference line.

If you are lucky, one of the arcs in the weight section will begin right there—but chances are that your density altitude reference point will fall between the printed arcs and you will have to interpolate. Draw a vertical line from the airplane's weight to a real or imaginary arc in the weight section and from that intersection go horizontally to the right to the second reference line. I'm sure that by now you know what to do in the wind section to solve any problem. Some charts have sections for runway gradient in addition to those in Figure 3-2. Note that this chart gives the distance to clear a 50-foot obstacle. You might come across a similar takeoff distance chart with a separate section for obstacle height.

See how the sample problem is solved in the figure and then try this one:

Temperature .... 30°F
Pressure altitude .... 6,000 feet
Weight .... 3,300 lbs
Headwind component .... 20 knots

My answer is 1,500 feet. *See* Figure 3-3.

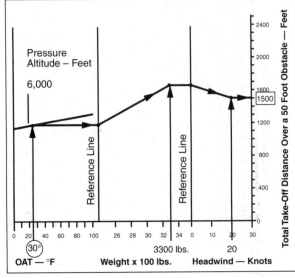

Figure 3-3. *Takeoff distance graph*

Rate-of-Climb/Maximum Climb Charts

Restrictions on departure procedure charts are given in feet per mile: "Climb of 250 ft/nm required." To convert this to feet per minute, multiply by your ground speed in miles per minute: at 120 knots, the quoted departure would require a climb rate of 500 feet per minute. The rate-of-climb/maximum climb chart (Figure 3-4) enables you to predict your airplane's performance at a given weight and density altitude. The line marked ISA represents the International Standard Atmosphere; as a general rule, if the density altitude falls on the left side of the ISA line you can expect better than normal performance, while poorer than normal performance should be expected if the density altitude is to the right of the ISA line. Note that the indicated airspeed for best rate of climb decreases as density altitude increases.

Weight .... 4,700 lbs

Pressure altitude .... 5,000 feet

Outside air temperature .... 32°F

What is the maximum rate of climb under these conditions?

Draw a line vertically from 32°F to intercept a line which is your best estimate of where the arc for 5,000 feet would be. From that point, draw a horizontal line to intersect the vertical line marked 5,500 pounds. This will be called a reference line on other similar performance charts. Draw a line paralleling the heavy slanting lines which crosses a line drawn upward from the point representing 4,700 pounds. From this final point of intersection draw a horizontal line to the rate-of-climb scale. In this example the answer is 1,700 feet per minute.

Climb Gradient

Use the feet-per-mile calculation when the load is heavy, the temperature is warm, the airport elevation is high, or the relative humidity is greater than 50 percent. Feet-per-minute is great, but when there are obstacles to be overcome, and they are some distance away, you need feet-per-mile to determine whether you will clear them. And remember — if you take off into the wind and the obstacles are downwind, your climb rate will suffer because of the tailwind.

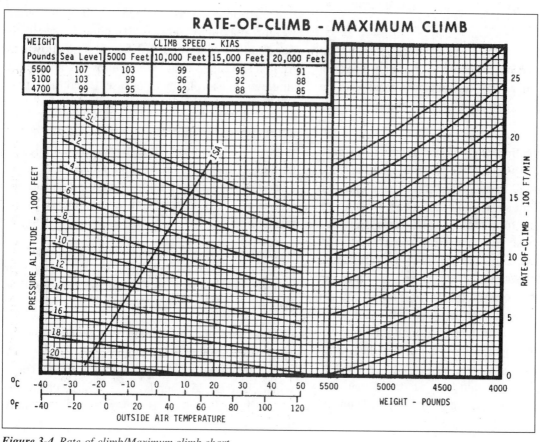

Figure 3-4. *Rate-of-climb/Maximum climb chart*

Single-Engine Rate of Climb

Multi-engine pilots must know how their airplanes will climb with a propeller feathered, and the single-engine rate-of-climb chart is another density altitude and weight related chart which is used in exactly the same way as was the maximum rate of climb chart.

Weight .... 5,300 lbs

Pressure altitude .... 1,000 feet

Temperature .... 80°F

Again, draw a vertical line from 80°F on the temperature scale to intersect the line representing 1,000 feet. From this point of intersection draw a horizontal line to the 5,500-pound reference line; from this point, follow the slanting lines to meet a line drawn vertically from 5,300 pounds on the weight scale. Now draw a line horizontally to the single-engine rate of climb scale. I get 330 feet per minute…what do you get?

Time, Fuel, and Distance to Climb

You are expected to do a better job of planning as a commercial pilot, because you must juggle payload and fuel to meet a paying customers needs, rather than just winging it as a private pilot. Unplanned fuel stops don't impress the customers.

You know that your airplane is going to burn fuel at a greater rate during the climb to cruise altitude than it will burn after level-off, but how much will be used? There are two methods of presenting this information.

The graphic method (Figure 3-5) asks you to figure the fuel burn from sea level to cruise altitude and from sea level to the departure field elevation. The sample problem shows how it is done. Outside air temperature at cruise altitude is 0° (from the winds aloft forecast), so you draw a line from 0° vertically to the line representing pressure altitude at cruise and then straight across to the curves for fuel, time, and distance. In the example, pressure altitude is 12,000 feet and lines dropped vertically to the fuel, time, and distance scale show values of 7.5 gallons, 14 minutes, and 18 nautical miles. That means that if you took off from a sea level airport and climbed to 12,000 feet, those would be your fuel, time, and distance figures. But you're not taking off from sea

level, you're taking off from an airport 1,400 feet above sea level.

So you go through the exercise again (although, just between you and me, I wouldn't bother if I was that close to sea level—but this is an FAA exam, right?). Outside air temperature at 1,400 feet is 15°, so you start there and draw a vertical line to a line representing a pressure altitude of 1,400 feet and again, horizontally to the Fuel, Time, Distance arcs. Clustered together at that low altitude and hard to read, aren't they? But with the help of the example, we'll give it our best shot. Fuel at .5 gallon is a good guess, time at 1.5 minutes is a little easier to see, and distance at 2 miles is fairly evident. Now that you know what it takes to go from sea level to 12,000 feet and from sea level to 1,400 feet, you subtract the values for the climb to field elevation and you are in business—7 gallons, 12.5 minutes, and 18 miles down the road. That puts you at what the "big boys" call "top of climb" (TOC). You know how much fuel was in the tanks at takeoff, so you begin your cruise calculations by subtracting 7 gallons from full tanks (assuming that you filled them).

Don't forget to look at the conditions under which that performance was obtained: 3,600 pounds gross weight, maximum power, 90 knots indicated, no flaps and no wind. Figure 3-5 makes no allowance for taxi and runup fuel; I would allow 3 gallons for a single-engine airplane just in case. Be conservative.

The second method is tabular (Figure 3-6). Check the notes: standard temperature, 30 inches and 2,500 rpm, and a mixture setting based on altitude; 16 pounds of fuel for starting, taxi, and takeoff are to be added to your calculations. There is no example, so I'll take a problem from the commercial pilot written.

Aircraft weight is 3,700 pounds, departure airport pressure altitude is 4,000 feet, and the outside air temperature (OAT) is 21°C. How much fuel will be used in a climb to 12,000 feet?

Pick out the value for 4,000 feet (12 pounds) and the value for 12,000 feet (37 pounds) at 3,700 pounds gross. Because you are starting out at 4,000 feet, it will only take 25 pounds (37 − 12) to climb the remaining 8,000 feet. But now you must apply the notes.

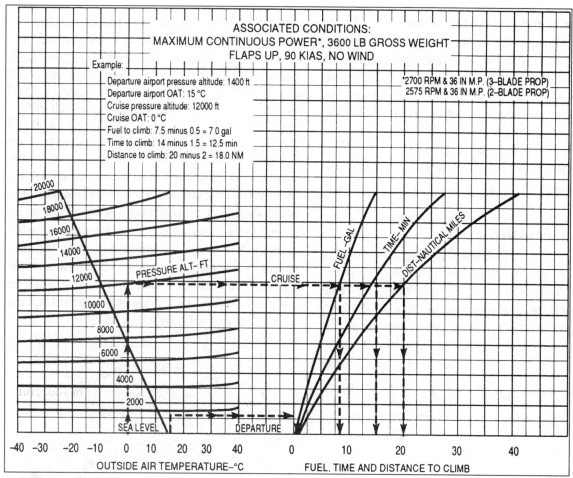

ASSOCIATED CONDITIONS:
MAXIMUM CONTINUOUS POWER*, 3600 LB GROSS WEIGHT
FLAPS UP, 90 KIAS, NO WIND

Example:
Departure airport pressure altitude: 1400 ft
Departure airport OAT: 15 °C
Cruise pressure altitude: 12000 ft
Cruise OAT: 0 °C
Fuel to climb: 7.5 minus 0.5 = 7.0 gal
Time to climb: 14 minus 1.5 = 12.5 min
Distance to climb: 20 minus 2 = 18.0 NM

*2700 RPM & 36 IN M.P. (3–BLADE PROP)
2575 RPM & 36 IN M.P. (2–BLADE PROP)

Figure 3-5. *Time, fuel, and distance to climb*

NORMAL CLIMB - 110 KIAS

CONDITIONS:
Flaps Up
Gear Up
2500 RPM
30 inches Hg
120 PPH Fuel Flow
Cowl Flaps Open
Standard Temperature

NOTES:
1. Add 16 pounds of fuel for engine start, taxi, and takeoff allowance.
2. Increase time, fuel, and distance by 10% for each 7°C above standard temperature.
3. Distance shown are based on zero wind.

WEIGHT LBS	PRESS ALT FT	RATE OF CLIMB FPM	FROM SEA LEVEL		
			TIME MIN	FUEL USED POUNDS	DISTANCE NM
4000	S.L.	605	0	0	0
	4000	570	7	14	13
	8000	530	14	28	27
	12,000	485	22	44	43
	16,000	430	31	62	63
	20,000	365	41	82	87
3700	S.L.	700	0	0	0
	4000	665	6	12	11
	8000	625	12	24	23
	12,000	580	19	37	37
	16,000	525	26	52	53
	20,000	460	34	68	72
3400	S.L.	810	0	0	0
	4000	775	5	10	9
	8000	735	10	21	20
	12,000	690	16	32	31
	16,000	635	22	44	45
	20,000	565	29	57	61

Figure 3-6

The standard temperature at 4,000 feet is 7°C (double the altitude and subtract the result from 15°C), so the OAT of 21°C is 14° warmer than standard. You are to increase the time, fuel, and distance by 10 percent for every 7° above standard, so multiply 25 pounds by 1.2 to reflect the 20 percent difference: 30 pounds. You're not through, though. Don't forget the 16-pound allowance for startup and taxiing. At the top of climb, then, you will have burned 46 pounds if you followed the procedure of reducing the fuel flow as directed.

Cruise Performance

Unless you fly at altitudes below approximately 7,000 feet, the throttle of your fixed-pitch propeller airplane will be full forward at cruise altitude, and the cruise performance charts in the Pilot's Operating Handbook will tell you what true airspeed to expect at different pressure altitudes. Performance charts for airplanes with constant-speed propellers recognize that different combinations of manifold pressure and rpm can deliver the same power output, and allow you to choose between speed and economy. They also provide projected true airspeed figures for different pressure altitudes.

You should investigate the fuel burn at different power settings during the planning process. If your airplane has 64 gallons of usable fuel and burns 12 gallons per hour (gph) at the proposed power setting, the endurance is 5:20 excluding taxi and climb fuel (5 hours to be conservative). If you choose a power setting at which the fuel burn is 10 gph, what will the endurance be? An additional hour, approximately. Will that make a fuel stop unnecessary? If so, the loss of true airspeed will be worthwhile. Check the winds aloft forecast—maybe the wind at a different altitude will make up for the power reduction. The CX-2 Pathfinder has both fuel burn and endurance functions.

There are many flight planning programs available for personal computers, and more than one will choose the most efficient altitude when you provide the wind and fuel burn data.

If your planning is based on handbook true airspeed figures, you should make occasional inflight checks to be sure that you are making good the planned true airspeed (TAS) and, because the book figures are

based on pressure altitude, you must crank that into your calculations. Your flight computer makes it easy, because it has a window into which you can set pressure altitude and outside air temperature and convert indicated airspeed to true airspeed. Don't be deterred by references to calibrated airspeed (CAS); at cruise speeds the difference between CAS and indicated airspeed (IAS) are negligible.

Figure 3-7 shows a flight computer set up to make the IAS to TAS conversion. The pressure altitude has been determined to be 7,000 feet by momentarily setting the altimeter's Kollsman window to 29.92, and the OAT gauge reading is -5°C. Find the indicated airspeed on the inner scale; the true airspeed is opposite it on the outer scale. In the illustration, an indicated airspeed of 145 knots is found to equal a true airspeed of 159 knots.

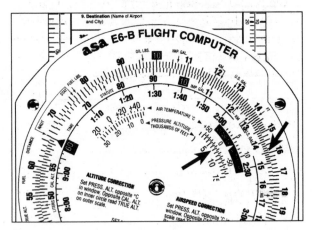

Figure 3-7. Speed conversion

You can work the problem backwards, of course, if you want to know the indicated airspeed that will give the desired true airspeed. The computer setup is exactly the same, and you find the required IAS on the inside, opposite the desired TAS on the outside.

When pressure altitude and air temperature are known, the CX-2 will allow you to convert CAS to TAS, or to determine the CAS necessary to make good a specific true airspeed.

All of this is moot if you have a DME, LORAN, or GPS groundspeed readout. With any of those black boxes available, you should establish a minimum ground speed which must be made good if you are going to arrive at the destination with fuel in reserve.

When the groundspeed digits flash a number below that minimum, start thinking about an unplanned fuel stop.

Normal Landing Distance

Good instrument pilots include an examination of the airport diagram on the destination airport's approach plate as part of their preflight planning. How long is the runway that is aligned with the approach course? How wide is it (important to visualization for night landings)? What type of approach and runway light system is installed? Will I be able to turn off at a midfield intersection, have to taxi to the end to leave the runway, or have to taxi back on the active? Know before you go.

The landing distance chart will help you determine how much runway will be required at the destination at the predicted landing weight, considering the reported wind conditions. This calculation can probably wait until you get an up-to-date report on the destination airport's winds from ATIS or Flight Watch. Use Figure 3-8 and the following information:

Weight	4,600 lbs
Pressure altitude of airport	1,500 feet
Runway in use	36
Runway surface	concrete
Wind direction/speed	030°/23 knots
Surface temperature	32°F
Flap setting	35°

What is the ground roll distance?

As there is no distance information for a pressure altitude of 1,500 feet, you must interpolate between the figures for 1,000 feet and 2,000 feet, using the box for 4,600 pounds and the column under 32°F. The figures are 450 feet and 460 feet, making the distance for a pressure altitude of 1,500 feet equal 455 feet. Referring to the wind component chart (Figure 3-1) determine the headwind component by following the line for an angle between the runway and the wind of 30° in to its point of intersection with the arc representing 23 knots: the headwind component is 20 knots. Note 3 tells you to decrease the calculated distance by 3 percent for each 4 knots of headwind. A decrease of 15 percent makes the ground roll distance 387 feet.

NORMAL LANDING DISTANCE

CONDITIONS:
1. Throttles - IDLE
2. Landing Gear - DOWN
3. Wing Flaps - 35°
4. Cowl Flaps - CLOSE
5. Level, Hard Surface Runway
6. Maximum Braking Effort

NOTE:
1. Increase all distances by 25% of ground run for operation on firm sod runway.
2. When landing with flaps UP, increase the normal approach speed by 12 knots. Expect total landing distance to increase by 35%.
3. Decrease all distances by 3% for each 4 knots headwind. For operations with tailwinds up to 10 knots, increase all distances by 5% for each 2 knots of wind.

WEIGHT POUNDS	SPEED AT 50' OBSTACLE - KIAS	PRESSURE ALTITUDE FEET	-20°C (-4°F)		-10°C (14°F)		0°C (32°F)		10°C (50°F)	
			GROUND ROLL FEET	TOTAL DISTANCE TO CLEAR 50' OBSTACLE	GROUND ROLL FEET	TOTAL DISTANCE TO CLEAR 50' OBSTACLE	GROUND ROLL FEET	TOTAL DISTANCE TO CLEAR 50' OBSTACLE	GROUND ROLL FEET	TOTAL DISTANCE TO CLEAR 50' OBSTACLE
5400	93	Sea Level	570	1720	590	1740	610	1760	630	1780
		1000	590	1740	610	1760	630	1780	660	1810
		2000	610	1760	630	1780	660	1810	680	1830
		3000	630	1780	660	1810	680	1830	710	1860
		4000	660	1810	680	1830	710	1860	730	1880
		5000	680	1830	710	1860	730	1880	760	1910
		6000	710	1860	730	1880	760	1910	790	1940
		7000	730	1880	760	1910	790	1940	820	1970
		8000	760	1910	790	1940	820	1970	850	2000
		9000	790	1940	820	1970	850	2000	880	2030
		10,000	820	1970	850	2000	890	2040	920	2070
5000	89	Sea Level	480	1630	500	1650	520	1670	540	1690
		1000	500	1650	520	1670	540	1690	560	1710
		2000	520	1670	540	1690	560	1710	580	1730
		3000	530	1680	560	1710	580	1730	600	1750
		4000	550	1700	580	1730	600	1750	620	1770
		5000	580	1730	600	1750	620	1770	640	1790
		6000	600	1750	620	1770	640	1790	670	1820
		7000	620	1770	640	1790	670	1820	690	1840
		8000	640	1790	670	1820	690	1840	720	1870
		9000	670	1820	700	1850	720	1870	750	1900
		10,000	700	1850	720	1870	750	1900	780	1930
4600	86	Sea Level	400	1550	420	1570	430	1580	450	1600
		1000	410	1560	430	1580	450	1600	460	1610
		2000	430	1580	450	1600	460	1610	480	1630
		3000	450	1600	460	1610	480	1630	500	1650
		4000	460	1610	480	1630	500	1650	520	1670
		5000	480	1630	500	1650	520	1670	540	1690
		6000	500	1650	520	1670	540	1690	560	1710
		7000	520	1670	540	1690	560	1710	580	1730
		8000	540	1690	560	1710	580	1730	600	1750
		9000	560	1710	580	1730	600	1750	620	1770
		10,000	580	1730	600	1750	620	1770	650	1800
4200	82	Sea Level	330	1480	340	1490	350	1500	370	1520
		1000	340	1490	350	1500	370	1520	380	1530
		2000	350	1500	370	1520	380	1530	390	1540
		3000	370	1520	380	1530	390	1540	410	1560
		4000	380	1530	390	1540	410	1560	420	1570
		5000	390	1540	410	1560	420	1570	440	1590
		6000	410	1560	420	1570	440	1590	460	1610
		7000	420	1570	440	1590	460	1610	470	1620
		8000	440	1590	460	1610	470	1620	490	1640
		9000	460	1610	480	1630	490	1640	510	1660
		10,000	480	1630	490	1640	510	1660	530	1680

Figure 3-8. Normal landing distance

If the runway was sod, the ground roll would be 484 feet, and if you landed with the flaps up it would be 522 feet. By referring to the Airport/Facility Directory, you will know what the runway surface is in advance, but you won't know in advance that the flap actuating system will decide to go on strike. Base your calculations on the worst-case situation. Remember that a glide slope or VASI intersects the runway surface about 1,000 feet from the threshold, and that there are optical illusions during night approaches that may cause you to be mistaken when estimating your altitude and distance from the threshold. Although you should be able to calculate the ground roll distance alone, a more conservative approach would be to calculate the total distance to land, which includes both the runway left behind during a descent over a 50-foot obstacle and the ground roll distance.

As an instrument pilot, you know that you will be landing on runways which are wet, icy, covered with slush, etc. Airplane tires will hydroplane at or above the airspeed which is 9 times the square root of the tire pressure; compute this value for your airplane and be sure that you touch down below hydroplaning speed.

Instrument Pilots: Ice Adds Weight

Go through the performance charts and check the effect of added weight on takeoff distance, climb performance, and landing distance. In each case, added weight is bad news. The cruise charts you have used show only the change in airspeed that accompanies a weight difference, but you must consider that it takes power to support that weight at a constant altitude, and that increasing the power setting will add to the fuel flow and reduce the airplane's range and endurance. If ice is a possibility, allow a healthy cushion between your takeoff weight and the airplane's maximum gross weight.

Your airframe/engine combination is rated at a given number of pounds per horsepower, derived by dividing maximum gross weight by engine horsepower. If the added weight of structural ice takes the airplane beyond maximum gross weight, the engine will be overtaxed even if it is operating at peak efficiency—and it won't be.

Clear ice (the type which is encountered when water droplets are large), and freezing rain (which coats the entire airplane in a sheet of ice) are the greatest villains when weight alone is considered.

Ice Also Adds Drag

Any discussion of the effect of icing on an airplane's performance has to begin with what is, to the eye of the uninitiated, its most innocuous form: frost. What possible harm could those tiny white crystals cause, after all? (*See* Figure 3-9.) They closely follow the contours of the airfoil, and they obviously don't weigh much. What that velvety white coating does is cover the airplane with an uncountable number of

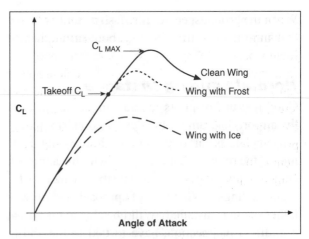

Figure 3-9. Effect of ice and frost on lift

drag producing crystals, creating enough parasitic drag to make it impossible for the airplane to accelerate to takeoff speed. Ideally, frost should be completely removed from the airplane before takeoff. Practically, frost should be polished smooth on the surfaces of the wings, horizontal stabilizer/elevator, rudder, and propeller. You will experience a gain in performance for every square foot of fuselage surface that is polished well.

Rime ice (which has the same milky white appearance as frost) is an in-flight drag producer. It develops when small water droplets freeze on contact with the airplane, and you will see it begin to form on the leading edge of any collecting surface with a small radius: the outside air temperature probe, struts, protruding gas caps, and of course the leading edges of the wings. It collects much more rapidly on the smaller radius leading edges of the horizontal stabilizer and vertical fin than it does on the wings, but they are not as readily seen from the pilot's seat—and what you can't see can hurt you.

Disruption of Lift Development

Mixed icing, which combines the worst features of rime and clear ice, is the greatest hazard to lift development. If you attempt to hold altitude by increasing the angle of attack, the ice will begin to form below and behind the leading edge of the wing. This changes the aerodynamic characteristics of the wing in unpredictable ways—none of the changes are improvements.

Some airplanes which are certificated for flight into known icing have a minimum airspeed limitation for just this reason. Figure 3-10 shows a "ram's horn" ice formation between the fuselage and deicing boot caused by mixed ice. When mixed icing is encountered, take immediate action to get out of the icing environment and keep the angle of attack as small as possible by establishing a descent attitude and sacrificing altitude. Never attempt to maintain altitude in icing conditions by adding back pressure.

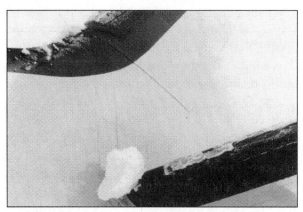

Figure 3-10. Structural ice buildup

If the controller insists that you maintain the assigned altitude, make sure that you have mentioned the icing problem. Controllers react to the word "ice." If you have to, declare an emergency in order to get out of the icing conditions.

Always hand-fly the airplane in icing conditions if your airplane is equipped with an autopilot, because you can detect subtle degradations in performance that the autopilot would cover up.

Effects on Engine Performance

You can't see ice form on the propeller, but it does, and anything that changes the profile of the propeller blade will decrease its efficiency. The outer two-thirds (approximately) of the propeller blade flex enough to shed most ice, but the inner third's relatively slow movement and thick profile make it a candidate for a load of ice. This is why electric deice boots are located only on the inner one-third of the propeller.

Another power-related effect of icing is the reduction in intake air that results when the openings into the engine cowling behind the prop spinner are reduced in size by ice accumulation. Your engine needs air to live, just as you do. You can bypass iced-over air filters and provide the engine with air by pulling the carburetor heat knob or by opening the alternate air doors on your fuel-injected engine.

Effect of Ice on Landing Performance

Accident statistics tell us that the typical structural icing accident happens on short final, because the pilot expects the airplane to react normally to control inputs.

An accumulation of ice on its lifting surfaces will make the landing performance of your airplane completely unpredictable. Because the manufacturer does not publish data for landing with a coat of ice, you become a test pilot. You can be certain that the stall speeds in the Pilot's Operating Handbook do not apply, and that changes in configuration such as extension of flaps will have unexpected results.

You can also be sure that using the flaps as though the ice isn't there is a mistake. The best place to experiment with these effects is at altitude, slowing the airplane to approach speed and changing configuration to see what will happen. You can't go wrong by adding several knots to your normal approach speed and making configuration changes in small increments (if that is possible). Use the test pilot's technique of only changing one thing at a time and evaluating the effect of each change before experimenting further.

Tailplane Stall

I mentioned earlier that ice collects first on things with a small radius like antennas and the horizontal stabilizer, and that you should be cautious about changing configuration with ice on the airplane. Let me combine those two warnings: If you add flaps during an approach and there is ice on the horizontal stabilizer, that surface can stall and cause the airplane to pitch down uncontrollably with little or no altitude for recovery. Figure 3-11 shows how the horizontal stabilizer's angle of attack is affected when the downwash from the upper surface of the wing increases due to flap extension. The illustration shows a T-tail configuration, but the same hazard exists with a conventional empennage.

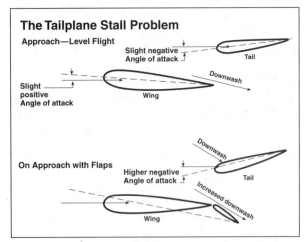

Figure 3-11. *Changing configuration can be hazardous with ice on the airplane.*

Online Icing Information

Now you know that structural ice adds drag, affects lift performance, and cuts into your engine's lung-power. That means that if you are collecting ice with a constant power setting you can expect to lose airspeed, altitude, or both. Naturally, you would add power to overcome the drag, assuming that your engine has any power left to offer.

A National Weather Service experimental website at www.awc-kc.noaa.gov/awc/vvice.html offers a color display of just how much power you would have to add (in percentage terms) if you just sat there and did nothing for 15 minutes. The page is divided into 2,000-foot slices of altitude and time periods from one to twelve hours in the future. You are to look along your flight path at the altitude ranges you expect to use, and interpret the color code (the usual sequence of green, yellow, red, purple, magenta in order of increasing severity) to determine/guess whether your airplane could handle it. A normally aspirated piston engine above about 7,000 feet with the throttle fully open could not handle a requirement for an extra ten percent, for instance. Keep in mind that this is an experimental site, not to be considered official.

Turbulence and Maneuvering Speed

As a VFR pilot, you stayed away from the danger of severe turbulence by avoiding thunderstorms and by staying on the ground when the weather was grungy. As an IFR pilot, you still must avoid thunderstorms, but flying among the clouds can and will expose you and your airplane to turbulence.

The Pilot's Operating Handbook for your airplane lists a maneuvering speed for maximum gross weight, but it probably doesn't give any speeds for lighter weights. This is an important omission, because maneuvering speed decreases as weight decreases, and if you fly at the book number when your airplane is light you may overstress the airframe (and your frame).

A useful rule of thumb is to reduce maneuvering speed by one-half the percentage decrease in weight. That is, if your airplane is 20 percent below maximum gross, reduce maneuvering speed by 10 percent. Make a table of maneuvering speed versus various operating weights and include it with your flight planning material. You can use the same method to adjust the best-angle and best-rate of climb speeds for lighter-than-gross weights.

Chapter 3
Performance Review Questions

The good news is that there are no weight-and-balance or performance chart questions on the instrument test. The bad news is that the examiner will expect you to demonstrate knowledge in these areas. Look over the questions for commercial students.

Commercial Student Questions

After it checks your knowledge of the basics of weight and balance, the commercial test gets into some practical applications.

1. GIVEN:
   Weight A—155 pounds at 45 inches aft of datum
   Weight B—165 pounds at 145 inches aft of datum
   Weight C—95 pounds at 185 inches aft of datum

   Based on this information, where would the CG be located aft of datum?

   A—86.0 inches
   B—116.8 inches
   C—125.0 inches

2. (Refer to Figure Q3-1.) GIVEN:
   Empty weight (oil is included) .... 1,271 lbs
   Empty weight moment (in-lbs/1,000) ... 102.04
   Pilot and copilot .... 400 lbs
   Rear seat passenger .... 140 lbs
   Cargo .... 100 lbs
   Fuel .... 37 gal

   Is the airplane loaded within limits?

   A—Yes, the weight and CG are within limits.
   B—No, the weight exceeds the maximum allowable.
   C—No, the weight is acceptable, but the CG is aft of the aft limit.

3. GIVEN:
   Total weight .... 4,137 lbs
   CG location .... station 67.8
   Fuel consumption .... 13.7 gph
   Fuel CG .... station 68.0

   After 1 hour 30 minutes of flight time, the CG would be located at station

   A—67.79.
   B—68.79.
   C—70.78.

4. An aircraft is loaded with a ramp weight of 3,650 pounds and having a CG of 94.0, approximately how much baggage would have to be moved from the rear baggage area at station 180 to the forward baggage area at station 40 in order to move the CG to 92.0?

   A—52.14 pounds
   B—62.24 pounds
   C—78.14 pounds

5. (Refer to Figure 3-2 on Page 3-7.) GIVEN:
   Temperature .... 75°F
   Pressure altitude .... 6,000 feet
   Weight .... 2,900 lbs
   Headwind .... 20 knots

   To safely take off over a 50-foot obstacle in 1,000 feet, what weight reduction is necessary?

   A—50 pounds
   B—100 pounds
   C—300 pounds

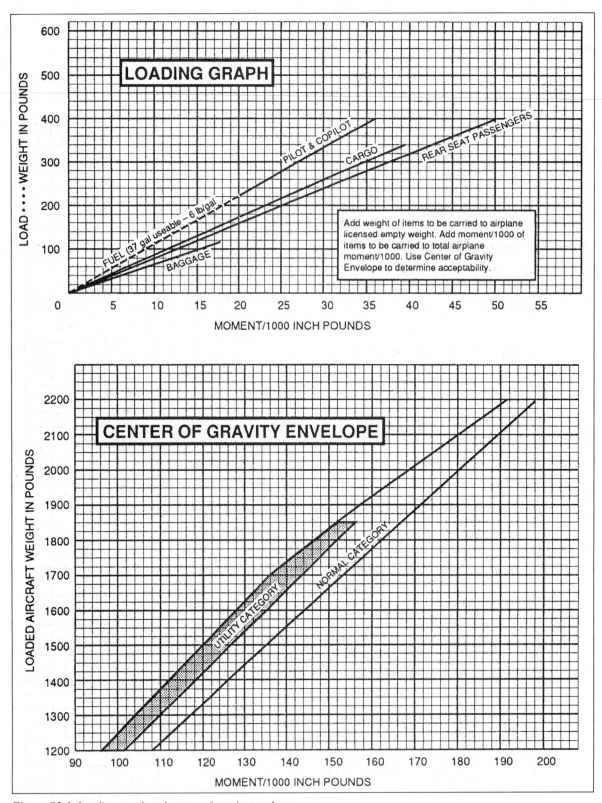

Figure Q3-1. *Loading graph and center-of-gravity envelope*

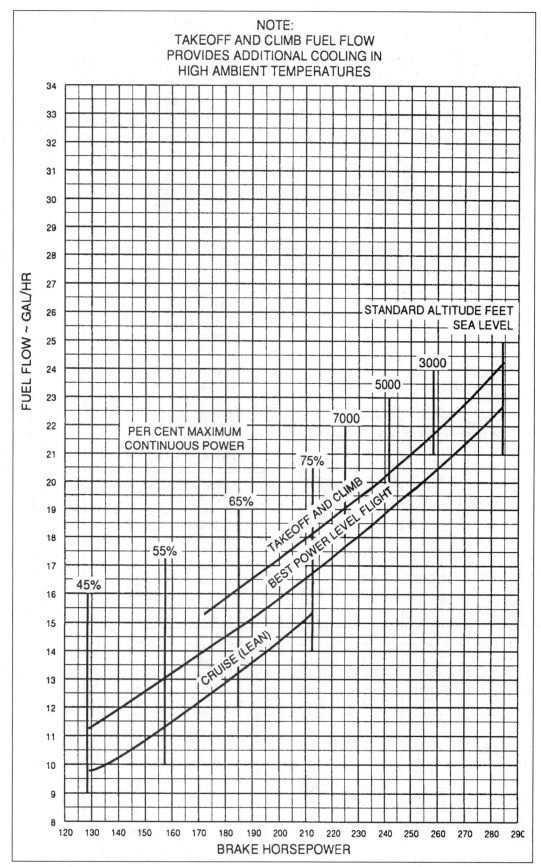

Figure Q3-2. Fuel consumption vs. brake horsepower

6. (Refer to Figure Q3-2.) GIVEN:

Fuel quantity .... 47 gal
Power-cruise (lean) .... 55 percent

Approximately how much flight time would be available with a night VFR fuel reserve remaining?

A—3 hours, 8 minutes
B—3 hours, 22 minutes
C—3 hours, 43 minutes

7. (Refer to Figure Q3-3.) GIVEN:

Aircraft weight .... 3,400 lbs
Airport pressure altitude................... 6,000 feet
Temperature at 6,000 feet .... 10°C

Using a maximum rate of climb under the given conditions, how much fuel would be used from engine start to a pressure altitude of 16,000 feet?

A—43 pounds
B—45 pounds
C—49 pounds

MAXIMUM RATE OF CLIMB

CONDITIONS:
Flaps Up
Gear Up
2600 RPM
Cowl Flaps Open
Standard Temperature

PRESS ALT	MP	PPH
S.L. TO 17,000	35	162
18,000	34	156
20,000	32	144
22,000	30	132
24,000	28	120

NOTES:
1. Add 16 pounds of fuel for engine start, taxi and takeoff allowance.
2. Increase time, fuel and distance by 10% for each 10 °C above standard temperature.
3. Distances shown are based on zero wind.

WEIGHT LBS	PRESS ALT FT	CLIMB SPEED KIAS	RATE OF CLIMB FPM	FROM SEA LEVEL		
				TIME MIN	FUEL USED POUNDS	DISTANCE NM
4000	S.L.	100	930	0	0	0
	4000	100	890	4	12	7
	8000	100	845	9	24	16
	12,000	100	790	14	38	25
	16,000	100	720	19	52	36
	20,000	99	515	26	69	50
	24,000	97	270	37	92	74
3700	S.L.	99	1060	0	0	0
	4000	99	1020	4	10	6
	8000	99	975	8	21	13
	12,000	99	915	12	33	21
	16,000	99	845	17	45	30
	20,000	97	630	22	59	42
	24,000	95	370	30	77	60
3400	S.L.	97	1205	0	0	0
	4000	97	1165	3	9	5
	8000	97	1120	7	19	12
	12,000	97	1060	11	29	18
	16,000	97	985	15	39	26
	20,000	96	760	19	51	36
	24,000	94	485	26	65	50

Figure Q3-3. Fuel, time, and distance to climb

8. (Refer to Figure 3-5 on Page 3-11.) GIVEN:

Airport pressure altitude.................. 4,000 feet
Airport temperature............................... 12°C
Cruise pressure altitude .... 9,000 feet
Cruise temperature .... -4°C

What will be the distance required to climb to cruise altitude under the given conditions?

A—6 miles
B—8.5 miles
C—11 miles

9. (Refer to Figure Q3-4.) If the cruise altitude is 7,500 feet, using 64 percent power at 2,500 RPM, what would be the range with 48 gallons of usable fuel?

A—635 miles
B—645 miles
C—810 miles

10. Which is the best technique for minimizing the wing-load factor when flying in severe turbulence?

A—Change power settings, as necessary, to maintain constant airspeed.
B—Control airspeed with power, maintain wings level, and accept variations of altitude.
C—Set power and trim to obtain an airspeed at or below maneuvering speed, maintain wings level, and accept variations of airspeed and altitude.

Gross Weight- 2300 Lbs.
Standard Conditions
Zero Wind Lean Mixture

NOTE: Maximum cruise is normally limited to 75% power.

ALT.	RPM	% BHP	TAS MPH	GAL/ HOUR	38 GAL (NO RESERVE)		48 GAL (NO RESERVE)	
					ENDR. HOURS	RANGE MILES	ENDR. HOURS	RANGE MILES
2500	2700	86	134	9.7	3.9	525	4.9	660
	2600	79	129	8.6	4.4	570	5.6	720
	2500	72	123	7.8	4.9	600	6.2	760
	2400	65	117	7.2	5.3	620	6.7	780
	2300	58	111	6.7	5.7	630	7.2	795
	2200	52	103	6.3	6.1	625	7.7	790
5000	2700	82	134	9.0	4.2	565	5.3	710
	2600	75	128	8.1	4.7	600	5.9	760
	2500	68	122	7.4	5.1	625	6.4	790
	2400	61	116	6.9	5.5	635	6.9	805
	2300	55	108	6.5	5.9	635	7.4	805
	2200	49	100	6.0	6.3	630	7.9	795
7500	2700	78	133	8.4	4.5	600	5.7	755
	2600	71	127	7.7	4.9	625	6.2	790
	2500	64	121	7.1	5.3	645	6.7	810
	2400	58	113	6.7	5.7	645	7.2	820
	2300	52	105	6.2	6.1	640	7.7	810
10,000	2650	70	129	7.6	5.0	640	6.3	810
	2600	67	125	7.3	5.2	650	6.5	820
	2500	61	118	6.9	5.5	655	7.0	830
	2400	55	110	6.4	5.9	650	7.5	825
	2300	49	100	6.0	6.3	635	8.0	800

Figure Q3-4. Cruise and range performance

Navigation

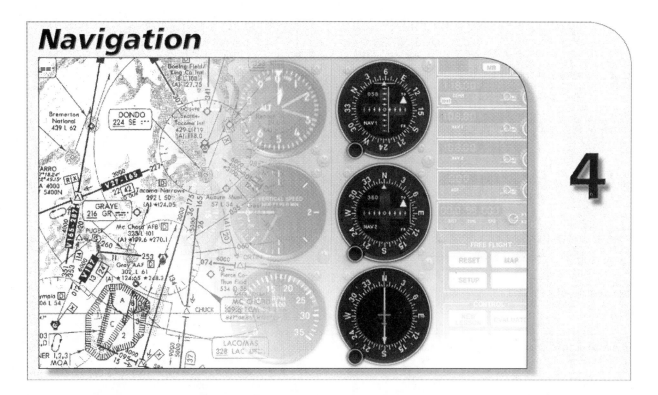

4

You will be asked about the basics of radio navigation on the Commercial Pilot Knowledge Exam and, as you might imagine, grilled on them during the instrument test. This chapter will prepare you for both. A note of caution: If you pick up a question-and-answer book for the commercial test and see instrument approach plates, ignore them. Questions referring to those plates are for lighter-than-air pilots.

Basic VOR Navigation

You may use VOR navigation as an integral part of VFR cross-country flying, or you may have sworn off electronic aids the day after your private pilot checkride and now navigate strictly by pilotage. I don't know for sure, so a brief review is in order.

The VOR (VHF Omni-directional Range) system uses frequencies in the 108.000 MHz to 117.950 MHz range. Each station transmits a 3-letter identifier in Morse code, and some stations also use a voice identifier. When the transmitter is off the air or undergoing maintenance or adjustment, the identifier is removed entirely or the Morse code for TEST (– · ··· –) is substituted.

Omni-directional means that the VOR (or omni, the terms are interchangeable) transmits in all directions—360° around the compass. You use the VOR

indicator in the instrument panel to determine your airplane's position in relation to the station. As you rotate the omnibearing selector (OBS) a full 360°, the course deviation indicator needle (CDI) will center twice: once when it indicates your direction FROM the station and again when it indicates the direction TO the station from your location. A TO-FROM flag, or ambiguity indicator, is provided so that you can tell which is which. The VOR indication is entirely independent of the heading of the airplane, a fact that you can readily prove to yourself by going out and flying a complete circle with the CDI centered. *See* Figure 4-1 on the next page.

Full-scale deflection on an omni indicator is 10°, and you should check the sensitivity of yours by occasionally rotating the OBS 10° to see if the needle moves from the center to the last dot on either side.

When the heading of your airplane and the OBS setting are in general agreement, you must fly toward the needle to intercept the selected radial. If your heading is 300°, the OBS is set to 270°, and you are north of the radial, the needle will be deflected to the left. To cause the needle to move toward the center, you will have to turn to a heading to the left of 270°, not simply "turn left." *See* Figure 4-2 on the next page. You will fly toward the needle almost all the time—there are only

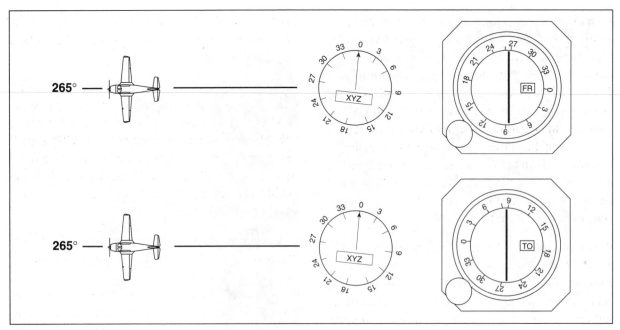

Figure 4-1. *VOR orientation on the 265° radial*

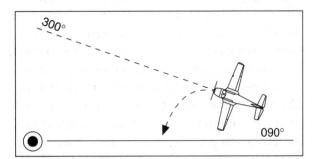

Figure 4-2. *Fly toward the needle to intercept the selected radial.*

two situations (involving localizers, which will be discussed later) when you will turn to a heading opposite to the needle deflection. A VFR pilot who pays strict attention to the VOR and thoroughly understands it is not only a rarity but may not be looking out the window frequently enough. A typical instrument student has a good understanding of the VOR airway system but has never had to rely on it exclusively, and has seldom, if ever, had a controller give instructions to intercept and follow a certain radial or airway.

Using the Victor airways to navigate requires the ability to maintain a constantly updated mental picture of your position, so that you can respond to an ATC vector or react to a direction change on an enroute chart quickly and easily.

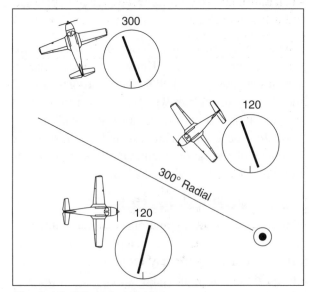

Figure 4-3. *Orientation problem*

"Intercept the 300° radial and proceed inbound." Which do you set the OBS to, 300° or 120°? When the needle centers, which way do you turn, southeast or northwest? The answer to those questions lies in the fact that (in radio navigation) the term radial means FROM. If you are proceeding inbound, or TO the station, you must set the OBS to the reciprocal of the designated radial or 120°. When the needle centers you should turn to the southeast and track the radial inbound. *See* Figure 4-3.

As an instrument pilot, you should never be in any doubt; if the VOR station is southeast of your position there should be little hesitation and wasted motion in turning the omnibearing selector to 120°. The same is true when the controller says, "Cleared present position direct to the Denver VORTAC..." You should be certain enough of your present position to turn the OBS to the general direction of Denver, confirm a "to" indication, and then fine-tune it to center the needle. If you have no idea where Denver is in relation to your position you should mail your pilot certificate to the FAA.

When you are directed to intercept a radial and fly toward the station, keep in mind that the radials converge on the VOR station. The interception will occur more quickly when you are closer to the station. As you pass over a VOR station to intercept a radial outbound, the radials diverge—spread out—and it may take a few extra degrees of intercept angle and a few more seconds before the intercept takes place, the further you are out. *See* Figure 4-4.

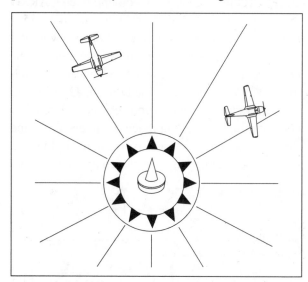

Figure 4-4. Radials converge and diverge

The first step in intercepting a radial is to turn to a parallel heading and set the omnibearing selector to agree with that heading. Then the VOR needle tells you what to do. If you are to intercept the 120° radial outbound, for example, turn the airplane to 120° first and then turn the OBS to 120°. If the needle is deflected to the right, it is saying, "Select a heading to the right of 120°." It is not saying "Turn right." You have a choice of intercept headings between 121° (which would take forever), and 210°, a 90° angle of

interception. Unless you are directly over the VOR transmitter, your initial intercept angle should be a 30° "cut," or 150°.

Consider the effect of the wind on the intercept, remembering that the needle always moves into the wind. In this example, a wind from the left (090°?) will blow your airplane toward the 120° radial, speeding up the interception, while a wind from the right (250°?) will drift the airplane away from the radial and delay the intercept, requiring an increased angle of interception.

Unless you are flying on a transition (*see* Chapter 9) or the controller says, "Maintain your present heading to intercept....", you will determine the angle of interception, and a "cut" of 30° is a good starting point, even as close to the station as 3 miles. If the intercept isn't proceeding as rapidly as you would like (keep centering the needle to monitor your progress), determine the angular difference between where you are (with the needle centered) and where you want to be (the desired radial). If you are on a heading of 120° to intercept the 150° radial outbound and it seems to be taking forever, use the OBS to center the needle and see how close to the 150° radial you are. For example, if the needle centers on 170°, there is a 20° difference between where you are and where you want to be: double that difference to establish a new intercept angle. In this example you would turn to 110°, a 40° intercept (45° is the largest intercept angle you should use until you have more experience.) *See* Figure 4-5.

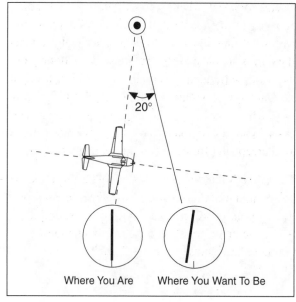

Figure 4-5. Estimating intercept angle

When you are on an intercept heading, be patient. Not so patient that you are reluctant to add 10° to your cut to speed things up, but patient enough so that you don't add 10° every 30 seconds until you are intercepting at a 60° angle and the needle moves across the face of the instrument like a windshield wiper.

When you are within 10° of intercepting the desired radial, the needle will come alive (this is called "case break") and begin to move toward the center. Its rate of movement will be affected by your angle of interception, the wind, and your distance from the station. The rule is this: if the needle is moving, you should be turning; when the needle stops, stop your turn. With a standard omni presentation it is difficult to adjust your rate of turn to match the rate of needle movement, but you must give it your best shot. If you are intercepting the 120° radial and the needle is just beginning to move, it is a waste of time to turn immediately to 120° and then have to backtrack.

Glance (do not stare) at the VOR indicator as you are turning, and be ready to level the wings when the needle movement slows. If there is any wind at all, one of your goals is to establish the reference heading which stops the needle by offsetting wind drift, so a needle which you have stopped a dot or two off center is more valuable than a momentarily centered needle. Each dot equals 2°, so half-scale deflection a mile from the station represents an off-course error of only 500 feet. *See* Figure 4-6.

Generally speaking, if you are within 10 nautical miles of the VOR and have the OBS set to the final approach course, the width of the airspace protected from obstacles and terrain is greater than full-scale needle deflection. Do not use this knowledge as a license to take chances, however; the fact that errors may exist both in the VOR transmission and in your receiver-indicator dictates that you must be very close to the centerline before descending.

Identifying an intersection is easy if the omnibearing selectors of both VORs are set to the radials (FROM) that form the intersection. Then the rule is: if the needle is on the same side as the station, you're not there yet. If you are supposed to turn at the intersection, first turn to the desired heading and then rotate the OBS to agree with your direction of flight The OBS should always agree with your direction of flight.

In Figure 4-7 you are flying southwestbound with your #1 VOR set to the Seattle 227° radial, with the intention of turning south on the Olympia 351° radial at CARRO intersection. As you approach CARRO the needle on your #2 VOR (which is set to the 351° radial) is pegged to the left: the station is on your left and you have not yet reached the intersection. As the needle swings toward the center, you turn to a heading of 171° and then reset the OBS on #2 to 171° to track the radial inbound. If you become distracted by cockpit duties as you approach the intersection and the #2 VOR needle is moving toward the right when you next look at it, you have passed the intersection.

Figure 4-6. *Two-dot deflection*

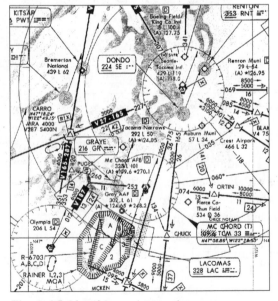

Figure 4-7. *Identifying an intersection*

Distance Measuring Equipment (DME)

What is the difference between a VOR and a VORTAC? A VORTAC is a VOR colocated with TACAN (Tactical Air Navigation), a military transmitter which provides distance information in nautical miles on an ultra-high frequency (UHF). Your aeronautical chart might also include a VOR-DME, which is non-military. As far as you are concerned, there is no difference—when you select the VOR-DME or VORTAC frequency the DME is tuned in automatically.

UHF is subject to even greater line-of-sight restrictions than the VHF signal from a VOR, so don't be surprised if you are flying at a relatively low altitude and can receive the VOR signal but get no distance readout. If the DME is actually out of service, you will notice that the Morse code identification on the VOR signal has gaps in it. In normal operation, the DME sends the identifier every 30 seconds.

The distance (range) indicated by your DME is slant range, not distance as measured along the ground. When your DME indicates 10.0 NM, for example, your linear distance from the DME antenna is less than 10 miles. The difference becomes less noticeable as distance increases, but increases as you approach the VORTAC, which is least accurate at high altitudes close to the VORTAC or VOR-DME. You can rely on DME indications if you are at least 1 mile away for each 1,000 feet above the facility.

Because the DME keeps track of distance from the antenna as you fly, its readout includes ground speed as well as distance—a very useful capability.

Intercepting and Tracking with a Horizontal Situation Indicator

The horizontal situation indicator makes visualizing your position in relation to a radial easy, and also helps in establishing a turn rate that will not outrun the needle as it moves toward the center. *See* Figure 4-8.

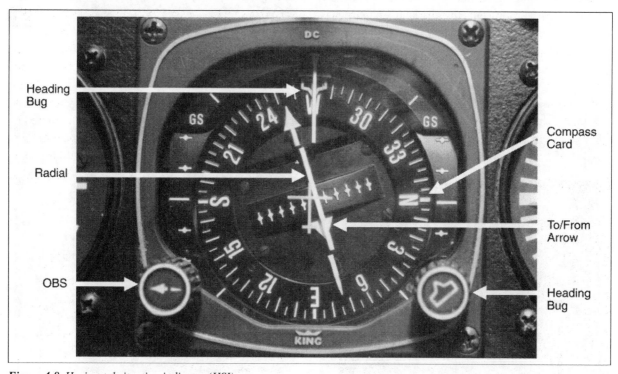

Figure 4-8. Horizontal situation indicator (HSI)

The course deviation indicator (or needle) portion of an HSI is the movable segment in the center. The omnibearing selector indicator is the arrowhead, and the TO-FROM indicator is the white triangle which always points toward the station. Your position is represented by the little airplane in the center of the instrument. The heading indicator provides the background. It is called a horizontal situation indicator because it permits you to view your airplane's position and its heading in relation to a radial. It is a bird's-eye view.

When you use an HSI to navigate on VOR airways or radials, you get proper sensing (fly toward the needle) whether you use the head or the tail of the needle to point to the desired radial. The TO-FROM will not change, because it always points to the station, but needle deflection will be the same. This is illustrated in Figure 4-9. It is a great time saver when you are flying in instrument conditions.

When the lubber line (the line at the top of the instrument that represents the airplane's heading) is aligned with the top of the offset segment when it is fully deflected, you have an automatic 45° angle of interception.

This is often called the Poor Man's Flight Director. When the needle comes alive and begins to move toward the center, adjust your rate of turn to keep the lubber line touching the needle, as shown in Figure 4-10. By doing this, when the needle stops its movement you will stop turning automatically.

Figure 4-10. Note lubber line touching radial

Figure 4-9. No reverse sensing

The heading that stops the needle's movement is the reference heading, and the angle between the reference heading and the selected radial is the wind correction angle.

When you have established the reference heading, turn into the wind until the needle moves to the center—then return to the reference heading to keep it there.

Figure 4-11 illustrates the comparison between an HSI and a conventional VOR indicator. The TO-FROM indicator of NAV 1 points to 170°, so the airplane is located approximately North of the VOR station. The omnibearing selector (arrowhead) points to 350°, but the needle is deflected 5° to the left (each dot is equal to 2°); if you turned the OBS to rotate the needle counterclockwise, the needle would center after 5° of rotation, so the airplane is presently located on the 345° radial. At a distance of 60 nautical miles from the station, a 5° deflection represents an off-course error of five miles.

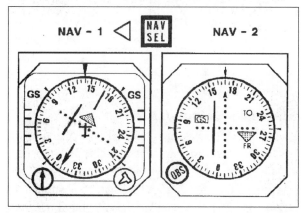

Figure 4-11. *NAV display comparison*

As stated earlier, if you reversed the arrowhead of NAV 1 to 170°, the needle deflection would still be to the left; when you are using an HSI with a VOR signal you never get reverse sensing.

NAV 2 is a conventional VOR indicator, set to the 170° radial of a second VOR station. You are north of the station selected on NAV 1 and south of the station selected on NAV 2. NAV 2's needle is deflected 4° to the left, so turning the OBS to 166° would center the needle. If you turned the OBS to 346°, the TO-FROM flag would switch to TO, and you would get reverse sensing.

The Localizer

You will get a full description of the Instrument Landing System (ILS) in Chapter 10, but a discussion of its localizer (left-right) function fits in here. The omnibearing selector (OBS) has no effect when a localizer frequency is selected (it will end in an odd decimal: .1, .3, .5 etc.). The localizer transmits a "fly left/fly right" signal that is usually, but not always, aligned with the runway, and when you are inbound to the runway you will fly toward the needle—but very carefully, like porcupines make love. Localizers are much more sensitive than VORs.

Every localizer transmits both a "front course" and a "back course" signal, although in most cases the FAA does not authorize the use of the back course signal. At an airport where runway 6 is the main instrument runway, an airplane approaching from the southwest would be in the front course area and would fly toward the CDI needle to stay on the runway centerline. If it overflew the runway and departed to the northeast it would be in the back course area, but in most cases it would probably not be using the back course signal for navigation.

Some airports have a published back-course localizer approach. If this was the case at the airport described above, an airplane approaching from the northeast would be in the back course area and would fly *away from* the CDI needle indications (reverse sensing) if a standard omni head was in use. If the pilot of that airplane had an HSI, he would set the head of the OBS needle to 060° (the front course), and would fly *toward* the deflected CDI, or normal sensing. Another advantage of the HSI.

Tracking and Intercepting with a Radio Magnetic Indicator

A radio magnetic indicator (RMI) has a compass card that is either coupled to the airplane's compass system or has its own internal gyro and accurately reflects the airplane's heading. It can have two needles—each can be either an ADF indicator or a VOR indicator—or it can have a single switchable needle. In Figure 4-12 (on next page) the single needle displays ADF information and the double needle displays VOR information. Unlike a standard omni indicator or HSI, the head of the VOR needle of an RMI points to the station continuously, and your magnetic bearing from the station (or radial) is indicated at the tail of the needle.

Figure 4-12. Radio magnetic indicator (RMI)

To track directly to a VOR, turn until the needle points directly ahead (0° relative) and note the magnetic bearing to the station.

If the needle points straight ahead and the heading is 090°, your position is on the 270° radial as indicated by the tail of the needle. If the wind blows you away from the direct course, correct into the wind and wait for the head of the needle to fall to 090°, indicating that you have re-intercepted the radial, then establish a correction into the wind to avoid drifting off course again. You may find that a heading of 098° keeps the RMI needle pointing 8° to the left of 090° until you pass over the station. This relationship, tracking inbound by holding a heading into the wind while the needle is deflected an equal amount away from the wind, will be important when we compare ADF tracking to homing.

Figure 4-13 illustrates the use of an RMI in four situations. Instrument 1 shows the airplane on a heading of 055° with the VOR station directly ahead; the airplane is located on the 235° radial, southwest of the station, and is proceeding inbound. The heading of instrument 2 is also 055°, but the needle is pointing to 235°. In this situation, the airplane is located on the 055° radial proceeding outbound.

Instrument 3's situation is similar. It is located on the 235° radial proceeding outbound. The airplane in instrument 4 is crossing a radial. Which one? The tail of the needle represents the airplane's position FROM the station, so it must be crossing the 235° radial and would have to turn to 055° to fly to the station.

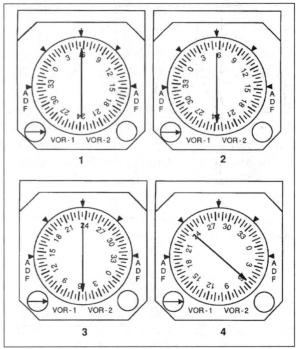

Figure 4-13. RMI intercepts

Intercepts Using an RMI

Another situation in which an RMI is very helpful is with a clearance to intercept a radial and proceed inbound. Figure 4-14 shows the RMI indications with the airplane on a heading of 090° with a clearance to intercept the 240° radial and proceed inbound. The tail of the needle indicates that the airplane is located on the 300° radial. Visualize the need to "pull" the tail of the needle from 300° to 240° by turning right. How much to the right? Look 30° from the head of the needle on the same side as the desired radial. In this case the intercept heading is 150°.

Memory aid: B-N-C.

Look from the desired bearing to the head of the needle plus 30° on the same side as the radial: Bearing, Needle, Correction.

Look at Figure 4-13 and visualize a pilot with indicator 1 "cleared to intercept the 360° bearing to the station (180° radial) and proceed inbound"; move your eyes from the desired Bearing (360°) to the Needle (055°), plus a 30° Correction on the same side as the desired radial (180°); 085° is the intercept heading.

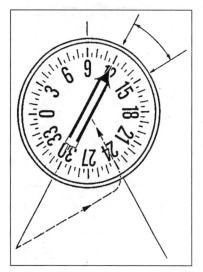

Figure 4-14. Inbound intercept with an RMI

A similar situation is a clearance to intercept a radial and proceed outbound. Figure 4-15 shows the airplane located on the 030° radial, heading 240°, with a clearance to intercept the 060° radial and track it outbound. Again, think of "pulling" the tail of the needle from 030° to 060°; this time, however, you must select an intercept heading 30° on the other side of the desired radial, or 090°.

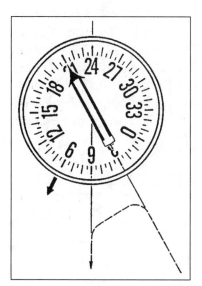

Figure 4-15. Outbound intercept with an RMI

Memory aid: N-B-C.

(Since you are working with the tail of the needle, television fans, think of the NBC peacock's tail). Look from the tail of the needle to the desired bearing from, plus 30°: Needle, Bearing, Correction.

To illustrate, take another look at Figure 4-13. A pilot with indication 4 is cleared to intercept the 150° radial and proceed outbound. Move your eyes from the Needle's tail (235°) to the desired Bearing FROM (150°), plus a 30° Correction.

The intercept heading to pull the tail from 235° to 150° is 120°.

ADF Orientation

The needle on your ADF indicator always points toward the transmitter antenna, and indicates the station's bearing relative to the nose of the airplane. If the needle is pointing 90° to the right, or directly off the right wingtip, the relative bearing is 090°; similarly, the tail of the airplane is 180° relative and the left wingtip is 270° relative to the nose of the airplane. The ADF indicator has tick marks at the cardinal points and may have tick marks at the 45°, 135°, 225°, and 315° points as well. The ADF card itself has calibrations 5° apart.

The key to all ADF orientation is this: magnetic heading, plus or minus relative bearing, equals magnetic bearing to the station. The ADF indicator and the RMI simply provide a mechanical means of solving the equation.

Figure 4-16 (on the next page) will give you some practice at ADF orientation. Airplane 7 is on a heading of 270°; which ADF indicator shows that it is on the 120° magnetic bearing FROM the station? If the airplane is southeast of the station and is heading west, the ADF needle should point between the nose and the right wing. Indicator 5 looks right to me.

Airplane 2's heading is 045°; which indicator shows that airplane 2 is on the 255° magnetic bearing TO the station? 255° TO the station is 075° FROM the station, so airplane 2 is east-northeast, of the station heading northeast. The ADF needle should point 30° to the left of the tail, and indicator 4 meets that test.

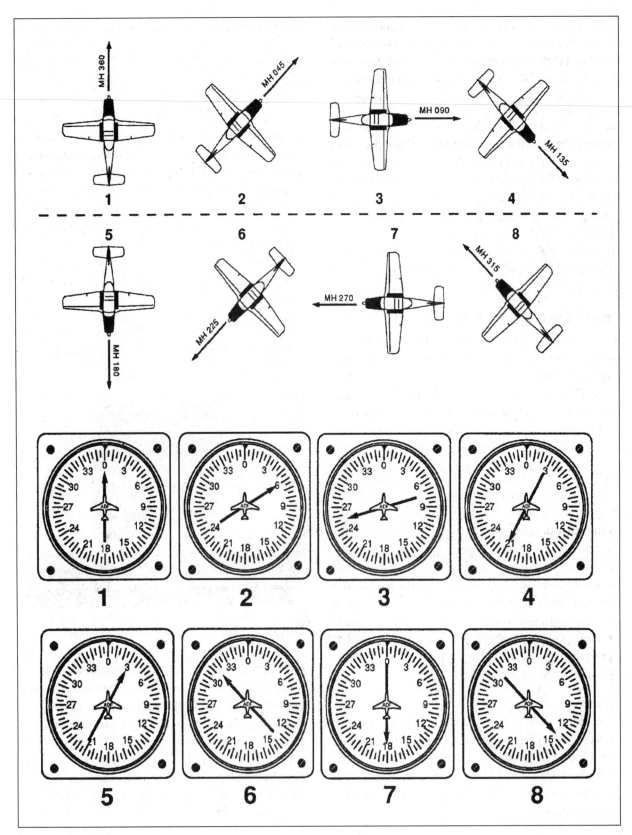

Figure 4-16. *ADF orientation problem*

Let's try one more. Airplane 5 is heading 180°. Which indicator shows that number 5 is on the 240° bearing TO the station? It is 060° FROM the station heading south; the needle should point 60° to the right of the nose. Indicator 2 would be correct.

In each of these situations the pilot knew what bearing the airplane was located on. Consider a pilot trying to determine the airplane's position from ADF bearings. The pilot of airplane 8 is looking at indicator 8; where is the airplane located in relation to the station? The airplane's position is indicated by the tail of the ADF needle, and it is deflected 45° to the left of the nose; the airplane is heading 315°, and 45° to the left of 315° is 270°. Airplane 8 is due west of the station.

Intercepting ADF Bearings

First, a definition: the Pilot/Controller Glossary in the *Aeronautical Information Manual* defines "bearing" as the magnetic direction "to or from" any point; controllers are supposed to say "course to" or "bearing from." If you don't understand a controller's instructions regarding ADF bearings be sure to ask for a clarification.

Use of the automatic direction finder in the airplane with nondirectional beacons on the ground has an undeserved reputation for difficulty. Admittedly, it is the least precise method of electronic navigation available in the cockpit; its accuracy suffers if you neglect to keep the heading indicator in agreement with the magnetic compass, and it can be confused by electrical storms. Installing an NDB is an inexpensive means of establishing an instrument procedure at an airport, however, and that should keep NDB approaches in use until the FAA begins to shut them down after the turn of the century.

Instrument approach procedures using the automatic direction finder require that you intercept and track bearings to or from a nondirectional radio beacon. A nondirectional radio beacon shares one characteristic with a VOR—it gets less accurate as you fly away from the transmitting antenna and more accurate as you approach it.

The automatic direction finder in your airplane probably has a rotatable azimuth card (turn the knob on the lower left in Figure 4-17). By rotating the azimuth card so that its indication always agrees with your heading indicator you get the same capability as an RMI at a fraction of the cost. Some instrument instructors will discourage you from using the rotatable azimuth and insist that you perform the mental gymnastics necessary to convert relative bearings to magnetic bearings. Believe me, anything that can make NDB tracking easier is worth the trouble it takes. You know the heading you are supposed to be maintaining, either as a vector or for wind correction, so set the rotatable azimuth to that heading—don't reach up to change it every time you drift off a few degrees. When the heading indicator shows you are steering the correct heading, glance up at the ADF indicator to check how you are doing. Re-set the azimuth only when you decide that another heading would be better for wind correction.

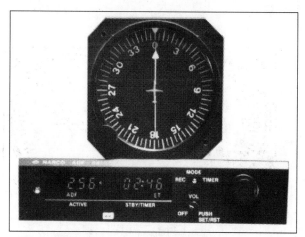

Figure 4-17. Automatic direction finder (ADF)

Although reaching to reset the azimuth card can be a distraction, using it in this way is the easiest method of ADF navigation. Note: Some instructors also discourage the use of the rotatable azimuth "because the examiner won't let you use it." There is nothing in the Practical Test Standards that either encourages or discourages its use. Show the examiner that you know how to use it intelligently, and you will have no problems.

Let's look at two situations where you are required to intercept a bearing. First, assume that you are over the Plattsburgh VORTAC and have been cleared for the NDB approach to runway 23 at Saranac Lake, New York (Figure 4-18). Turn the airplane to a heading of 274° and then rotate the azimuth card until 274 falls under the index. The head of the ADF needle is deflected to the left and, under no-wind conditions, will move counterclockwise toward 227° as you proceed toward the final approach course. If you make any heading changes you must reset the azimuth card to agree with the new heading.

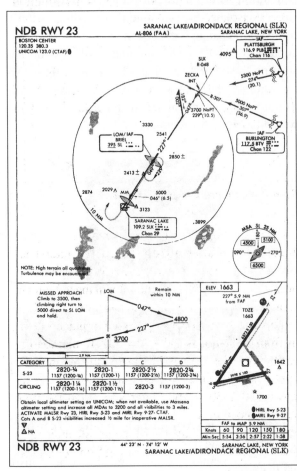

Figure 4-18. *NDB approach at Saranac Lake, New York*

As the ADF needle approaches 232° (a 5° lead) you initiate a turn to 227° and roll out on course. If you are momentarily distracted and look back at the ADF indicator to find that the head of the needle has moved past 227°, start turning inbound immediately. Once the needle has passed the inbound course it will not move back, no matter how devoutly you wish it would (no-wind conditions, remember).

Now assume that your instructor is one of those that insists that you leave the rotatable azimuth alone, leaving north (or zero degrees) set under the index and working with relative bearings only. This requires some mental arithmetic. Again referring to Figure 4-18, assume that you call Boston Center over the Burlington VORTAC and hear, "Fly heading 250° to intercept the NDB final approach course to runway 23 at Saranac Lake." You must subtract 227 from 250 to determine that the needle will be deflected 23° to the left when you intercept the final approach course, and that you must maintain a heading of 250° until the needle deflection nears 23° before turning inbound.

When intercepting an ADF bearing don't wait until the needle indicates the desired course exactly. Allow a lead of 3 to 5 degrees to avoid flying through the approach course. Remember that at 90 knots the airplane's turn radius is approximately one-half mile, and that if you wait too long to turn you will overshoot by that amount.

Tracking Inbound to a Radio Beacon

"Tracking" means following a straight line over the ground by crabbing into the wind, and the ability to track a bearing is essential to successful NDB approaches. Whether the radio beacon is on the airport or located at a distance, you will have to track a published bearing.

The preceding section covered intercepting NDB bearings in no-wind conditions. Unfortunately for pilots, such conditions seldom exist. Figure 4-19 illustrates a typical tracking problem using the rotatable azimuth card. Assume that the beacon shown is the BRIEL outer compass locator in Figure 4-18.

"Swiftwing 23Z, cleared present position direct to the BRIEL outer compass locator." The first thing you must do as the pilot of Swiftwing 23Z is to determine the track to the station. Turn until the ADF needle points straight ahead (0° relative)—the magnetic heading is the direct course to the beacon. For example, if the heading with the ADF needle at 0° relative is 220°, turn the rotatable azimuth card to 220°: that will be the direct track to the station (*see* Figure 4-19, position A). In no-wind conditions, the ADF needle will point directly over the nose until

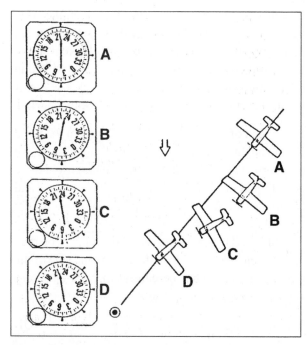

Figure 4-19. Typical tracking problem

you pass over the beacon. With a wind from the right, however, the ADF needle will gradually move to the right, into the wind (position B). When it has moved 10°, change heading twice that amount (20°) into the wind and reset the azimuth card to 240°. The head of the needle will now be deflected to the left of straight ahead (position C). When you are tracking toward a beacon the needle should always be deflected to the side of the nose opposite the wind.

The head of the needle falls toward the bottom of the instrument as you maintain a correction into the wind; it rotates from the nose position down either side to the tail position. As you maintain a heading of 240°, the needle will fall to an indication of 220°, and you will be back on the direct course (position D) — but not for long. You should retain a small correction into the wind to avoid being drifted off course again. Turn to 230° and rotate the ADF azimuth card to 230°; you are steering 10° into the wind and the ADF needle is deflected 10° to the left of the nose to 220°. If the needle moves into the wind (to the right) you do not have enough wind correction; try adding another 5° to a new heading of 235°. If the needle moves away from the wind and toward the nose you have too much correction and should halve it to a heading of 225°. If the needle remains steady your wind correction is just right.

Tracking a Bearing Outbound

Intercepting a bearing from a station is accomplished in much the same way. This example will not use the rotatable azimuth card but will illustrate a new concept in the use of the ADF. When you use this method the position of the azimuth card is irrelevant; you could perform the procedure with no markings other than the five-degree calibrations on the card. Figure 4-20 shows the top of the ADF indicator divided into plus and minus quadrants. When the head or tail of the needle is in the minus quadrant its deflection is subtracted from the airplane's heading; when the head or tail is in the plus quadrant its deflection is added to the airplane's heading.

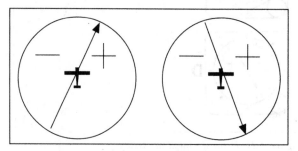

Figure 4-20. The plus and minus quadrants

Position A in Figure 4-21 (on next page) shows your airplane shortly after crossing the BRIEL radio beacon, having turned left to track the 150° bearing from the station. This time the wind is from the left, and in position B the tail of the needle has moved 10° into the plus quadrant. Accordingly, your airplane's bearing from the station is 150 + 10 = 160°. Remembering that the head of the needle always moves into the wind, you turn 20° to the left; the tail of the needle shows 130 + 30 = 160° after you reach the new heading (position C). Position D shows that with a heading of 130° and the tail of the needle indicating plus 20° you are on the 150° bearing from the station and tracking it.

The magnetic heading of the airplane plus or minus the needle deflection (head or tail) should equal the published course. Thinking this way will allow you to ignore minor heading changes. For example, assume that a published procedure turn course is 060° to intercept the 015° bearing to the station. If you concentrate on steering exactly 060°, you may fly through the final approach course without realizing it. Interception of the 015° bearing occurs when the

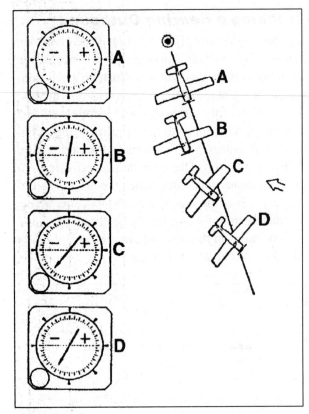

Figure 4-21. *Using the quadrant system*

If your wind correction heading is correct, the ADF needle will be straight up and down when you are steering the published course. If you have undercorrected, the head of the ADF needle will point toward the wind and you will have to choose a new wind correction heading which is more into the wind.

If the head of the needle points away from the wind when you turn back to the published course you have overcorrected. If the wind is strong enough and there is sufficient time, maintain the published course and let the wind drift your airplane back onto the courseline. Sometimes the smartest thing to do is to do nothing. If time or wind is in short supply you may have to select a heading on the downwind side of the published course, but be careful to make it a very small downwind correction.

It is tempting to overcorrect when tracking NDB bearings. A common error is maintaining a drift correction long after it has accomplished the task of getting you on course. One knot of crosswind component will drift your airplane sideways 100 feet per minute—if you will be tracking for only a minute or so you can't get hurt badly at that rate. At approach speeds of 60-120 knots you can offset the effect of each knot of crosswind component with a correction of one degree or less, so your maximum crab angle in degrees should be no greater than the crosswind component.

Important: Do not delude yourself that all is well if the needle is pointing either straight ahead or straight behind the airplane. The only time that situation should exist is when you are exactly on the desired course in a dead calm. If there is any wind at all, you should be steering a wind correction heading and the needle should be deflected away from the up-and-down position. Therefore, if the needle is straight up and down you are probably doing something wrong—like forgetting to allow for wind drift.

magnetic heading is 060° and the head of the needle is deflected 45° into the minus quadrant; if you let the heading slip to 055° the intercept becomes 055° minus 40°, and if your heading error takes you to 065°, the intercept becomes 065° minus 50°. Don't get hung up on a specific number.

That is not the end of the story on tracking outbound, because bearings diverge as they radiate away from the antenna. Five miles from the antenna, a 3° error will displace your airplane one-quarter mile off course. The only way to be sure of your position in relation to the final approach course when tracking away from the radio beacon is to turn back to the published course every 30 to 45 seconds; when you do, the head of the ADF needle will point to the courseline so that you can start correcting back to it.

Service Volume

Both VORs and NDBs have service volume restrictions, which basically tell you how reliable their signals are at various distances. The listing in the Airport/Facility Directory for a given navaid will indicate in which class a given navaid is included. For example, VOR/DME/TACAN classes are:

(T) Terminal, good for up to 25 NM from 1,000' to 12,000'

(U) Low Altitude, good for up to 40 NM from 1,000' to 18,000'

(V) High Altitude,
  good for up to 40 NM from 1,000' to 14,500'
        "   100 NM from 14,500' to 18,000'
        "   130 NM from 18,000' to 45,000'
        "   100 NM from 45,000' to 60,000'

(All altitudes measured above the elevation of the facility.)

This means that when you are planning a flight using Victor airways at 17,000 feet you should select only Class H VORs not more than 200 NM apart. A flight at 12,000 feet could use Class L facilities not more than 80 NM apart or a mixture of L and H facilities meeting the service volume restrictions.

Nondirectional beacons listed as Class LOM or LMM are good for not more than 15 NM, Class H beacons are good out to 50 NM, and Class HH beacons are good out to 75 NM. Altitude is not involved in NDB service volumes.

It is not unusual to see an instrument student attempting to tune in and use a Class LOM beacon when 25 miles or more away. What a waste of time.

Global Positioning System (GPS)

The navigation systems discussed thus far are ground-based; their transmitters take up real estate and electrical power, and they must be maintained and calibrated by FAA technicians. The future of aerial navigation lies in space — and the future is now.

Chapter 8 discusses the details of how GPS is used by VFR and IFR pilots. Suffice it to say that GPS navigation requires none of the interpretive skills needed for VOR or NDB navigation — turn it on, tell it where you want to go, and you will be deluged with information to a degree of accuracy never before achieved. The downside is that GPS navigators, with their moving maps and pages of data, are the opposite of the "heads up" displays used by sophisticated military and some civil aircraft — GPS can become a "heads down" display, keeping pilots from scanning for traffic conflicts when in visual meteorological conditions.

The FAA's goal is to have GPS replace all ground-based navigation aids by 2010; LORAN (also discussed in Chapter 8) will be the only backup system available.

A Final Word on the Use of Navaids

When applying techniques for tracking radials and bearings you must keep in mind that flying IFR is much like crossing a stream by stepping on the rocks: each fix or navaid is a rock, and if you pass directly over the fix at the published altitude you will not get wet. You may become disoriented or confused, but if you return directly to the navaid you will get a fresh start; all of the errors you committed in getting there will be erased. Never let your concentration on procedure or technique take precedence over your goal of passing over the fix — which is a fancy way of saying that if your carefully calculated wind correction heading makes you miss the navaid by a mile, you haven't gained anything.

As long as the VOR system and NDBs exist, you will be able to use them as your primary navaids while using your hand-held GPS as a backup. You won't be fooling anyone — GPS is far more accurate than either system, and you will have these old fashioned navaids tuned in just to give yourself legal cover.

Use Your Computer

In Chapter 1, I suggested that you use a computer-based training aid to become familiar with the flight instruments and how they operate. Now I am suggesting you continue to use the magic of the microprocessor to experiment with radio navigational aids, so they will be old friends by the time you get into the airplane.

Chapter 4
Navigation Review Questions

Instrument Student Questions

1. As a rule of thumb, to minimize DME slant range error, how far from the facility should you be to consider the reading as accurate?

   A—Two miles or more for each 1,000 feet of altitude above the facility.

   B—One or more miles for each 1,000 feet of altitude above the facility.

   C—No specific distance is specified since the reception is line-of-sight.

2. (Refer to Figure Q4-1.) Which restriction to the use of the OED VORTAC would be applicable to the (GNATSI1.MOURN) departure?

   A—R-333 beyond 30 NM below 6,500 feet.

   B—R-210 beyond 35 NM below 8,500 feet.

   C—R-251 within 15 NM below 6,100 feet.

3. (Refer to Figures Q4-2 and Q4-3.) To which aircraft position(s) does HSI presentation "B" correspond?

   A—11

   B—5 and 13

   C—7 and 11

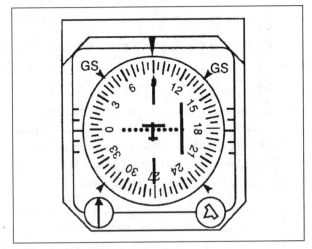

Figure Q4-3. HSI presentation "B"

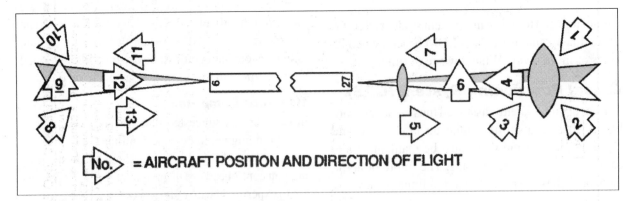

Figure Q4-2. Aircraft position and direction of flight

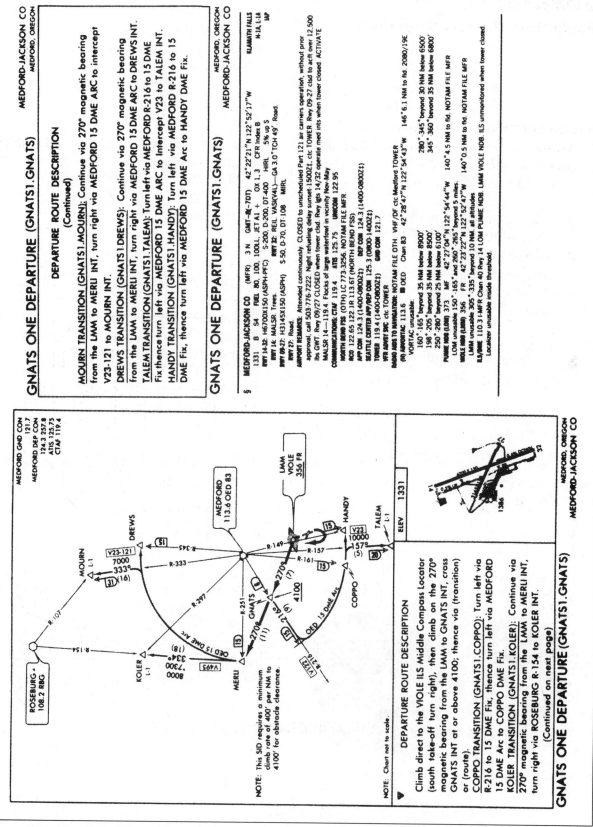

Figure Q4-1. GNATS One Departure and excerpt from Airport/Facility Directory

4. Which of the following should be considered as station passage when using VOR?

   A—The first flickering of the TO-FROM indicator and CDI as the station is approached.
   B—The first full-scale deflection of the CDI.
   C—The first complete reversal of the TO-FROM indicator.

5. When should your transponder be on Mode C while on an IFR flight?

   A—Only when ATC requests Mode C.
   B—At all times if the equipment has been calibrated, unless requested otherwise by ATC.
   C—When passing 12,500 feet MSL.

6. For operations off established airways at 17,000 feet MSL in the contiguous U.S., (H) Class VORTAC facilities used to define a direct route of flight should be no farther apart than

   A—75 NM.
   B—100 NM.
   C—200 NM.

7. (Refer to instruments in Figure Q4-4.) On the basis of this information, the magnetic bearing FROM the station would be

   A—175°.
   B—255°.
   C—355°.

8. (Refer to Figure 4-16 on Page 4-10.) If the magnetic heading shown for airplane 8 is maintained, which ADF illustration would indicate the airplane is on the 090° magnetic bearing FROM the station?

   A—3
   B—4
   C—6

9. (Refer to Figure Q4-5.) If the radio magnetic indicator is tuned to a VOR, which illustration indicates the aircraft is on the 315° radial?

   A—2
   B—3
   C—4

10. (Refer to Figure Q4-6.) Which OBS selection on the No. 1 NAV would center the CDI and change the ambiguity indication to a TO?

    A—175°
    B—165°
    C—345°

11. (Refer to Figure Q4-7.) In which general direction from the VORTAC is the aircraft located?

    A—Northeast
    B—Southeast
    C—Northwest

12. In which publication can the VOR receiver ground checkpoint(s) for a particular airport be found?

    A—*Aeronautical Information Manual.*
    B—En Route Low Altitude Chart.
    C—Airport/Facility Directory.

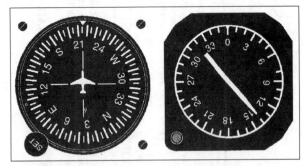

Figure Q4-4. *Directional gyro and ADF indicator*

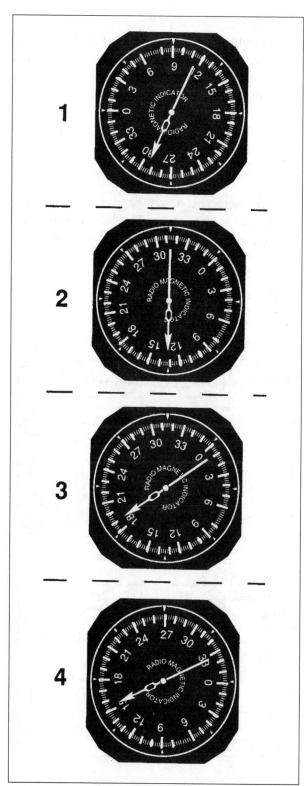

Figure Q4-5. *Radio magnetic indicator*

FREQ	N.M.	KNOTS	MIN
115.0	60.0	180	20.0

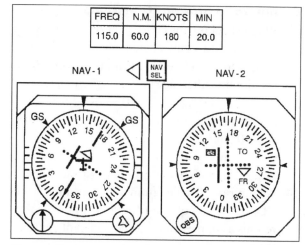

Figure Q4-6. *No. 1 and No. 2 NAV presentation*

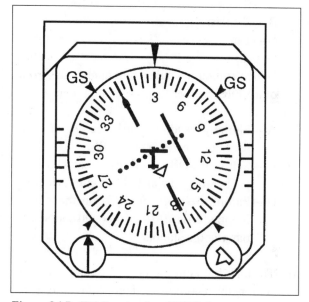

Figure Q4-7. *CDI direction from VORTAC*

13. When checking the course sensitivity of a VOR receiver, how many degrees should the OBS be rotated to move the CDI from the center to the last dot on either side?

    A—5° to 10°
    B—10° to 12°
    C—18° to 20°

14. An aircraft 60 miles from a VOR station has a CDI indication of one-fifth deflection, this represents a course centerline deviation of approximately

    A—6 miles.
    B—2 miles.
    C—1 mile.

15. Which situation would result in reverse sensing of a VOR receiver?

    A—Flying a heading that is reciprocal to the bearing selected on the OBS.
    B—Setting the OBS to a bearing that is 90° from the bearing on which the aircraft is located.
    C—Failing to change the OBS from the selected inbound course to the outbound course after passing the station.

16. To track inbound on the 215 radial of a VOR station, the recommended procedure is to set the OBS to

    A—215° and make heading corrections toward the CDI needle.
    B—215° and make heading corrections away from the CDI needle.
    C—035° and make heading corrections toward the CDI needle.

17. (Refer to Figure Q4-8.) Which instrument shows the aircraft in a position where a 180° turn would result in the aircraft intercepting the 150 radial at a 30° angle?

    A—2
    B—3
    C—4

18. What is the maximum bearing error (+ or −) allowed for an operational VOR equipment check when using an FAA-approved ground test signal?

    A—4 degrees
    B—6 degrees
    C—8 degrees

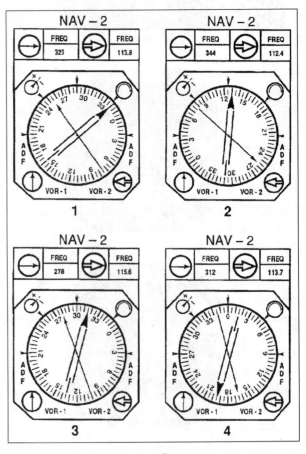

Figure Q4-8. *Radio magnetic indicator*

Weather

5

To prepare for the instrument and commercial pilot Knowledge Exams you must review much of the material you studied when you were working toward the private pilot certificate. This chapter will repeat a considerable amount of that information but will relate it to commercial operations or those on instrument flight plans.

As an instrument-rated pilot, the mere existence of clouds will no longer concern you; in fact, you will feel safest on a day when you can climb through an overcast and fly in the sunshine while the VFR pilots are stuck on the ground. This does not mean that your weather concerns are over, however. When you do your preflight check of weather conditions you will be looking for areas of turbulence or icing and planning ways to avoid those hazards. Destination weather forecast to be at or below IFR minimums will affect your planning, of course, forcing you to look for either a suitable alternate or a different destination.

Assuming that the weather at your destination at your ETA is acceptable, you should choose a route of flight with minimum enroute altitudes that do not require the last ounce of performance from your airplane. When you are operating in the clouds and ice or turbulence makes your present altitude untenable, you cannot always simply descend to avoid the hazard. It is better to choose a route where your cruise altitude will be above the MEA so that you can descend to that level if necessary for comfort or safety.

All pilots, not just instrument pilots, will benefit from technological advances being implemented by the National Weather Service (NWS) during this decade. Weather reports and forecasts will become more accurate and more timely as the new equipment comes on line.

Textual Information

You can get weather reports and forecasts in textual form through DUAT, PanAm Weathermation, or one of the many online services. DUAT is paid for by the FAA, and many states provide PanAm services free of charge. There is no question that textual weather is the absolute minimum you should have when planning a flight.

Requesting a standard briefing from DUAT makes the following available:

Aviation Area Forecast (FA)
Aviation Routine Weather Report (METAR)
Terminal Area Forecast (TAF)
Winds Aloft Forecast (FD)
Severe Weather Forecast Alert (AWW)
SIGMETs and AIRMETs
Convective Sigmet (WST)
Center Weather Advisory (CWA)
Notices to Airmen (NOTAMs)
Pilot Reports (PIREPs)

Weather information is so widely disseminated to pilots and is available through so many outlets that "I didn't know" is not considered an excuse for flying into bad weather. If you fail to ask, the fault is yours alone—you can't blame the briefer or anyone else. Because of this, the courts have interpreted "forecast" to mean "known."

Detailed information on weather reports and forecasts is contained in the *Aeronautical Information Manual*.

Area Forecasts

The best place to look for a broad-brush treatment of cloud cover and thunderstorms is the aviation area forecast (FA), Figure 5-1. As stated in the forecast, "Thunderstorms imply severe or greater turbulence, severe icing, low-level wind shear, and IFR conditions." More specific forecasts of IFR conditions, mountain obscuration, icing, and turbulence are found in AIRMETs. This precautionary statement is included in all area forecasts:

"SEE AIRMET SIERRA FOR IFR CONDS AND MTN OBSC."

Note that except for the outlook portion, the area forecast itself does not mention the existence of instrument meteorological conditions.

Always take the initiative to look for AIRMET TANGO for turbulence, strong surface winds, and low-level wind shear, and AIRMET ZULU for icing and the freezing level. Figures 5-2 through 5-4 (on

the next three pages) show the text of all three AIRMETs together with their graphic representations available through the Aviation Weather Center (AWC) web page at http://aviationweather.noaa.gov. Click on "Standard Briefing," then on "AIRMETs" and all three graphics will be there. Looking at graphics is a lot easier than trying to make sense of the geographic references in the textual presentation. As a bonus, the graphics are in color.

The National Weather Service textual products are written by forecasters to be used by other forecasters, and they are not user-friendly. Technology has overtaken the NWS insofar as public access to weather information is concerned, and the agency is adjusting to the change through the use of the worldwide web.

There are six Aviation Area Forecasts, each for a specific geographic area: Boston, Miami, Chicago, Dallas/Fort Worth, Salt Lake City, and San Francisco.

New area forecasts are issued three times a day and are valid for 18 hours, plus a 6-hour outlook.

METARs (Hourly Observations)

Every reporting weather station issues an hourly observation called an aviation routine weather report, or METAR, which includes cloud cover and visibility, wind direction and velocity, altimeter setting, and remarks. Figure 5-5 (on Page 5-7) is the key to interpreting METARs. Note: This key will not be available to you for your FAA Knowledge Exam, so learn to read and understand the information without the key.

The general format is: Identifier, date-time group, wind, visibility, weather (obstructions to visibility), sky condition, temperature and dew point, altimeter setting, and remarks.

Figure 5-6 (on Page 5-8) contains hourly METARs for several stations: Omaha, NE (KOMA); Pittsburgh, PA (KPIT); Dallas-Fort Worth, TX (KDFW); and Chicago, IL (KORD). It should be apparent that you will never see a report with observations from such widely scattered sites, but each example contains something of interest.

Continued on Page 5-8

```
ZCZC MKCFA1W
FAUS6 KBOS 211845
BOSC FA 211845
SYNOPSIS AND VFR CLDS/WX
SYNOPSIS VALID UNTIL 221300
CLDS/WX VALID UNTIL 220700...OTLK VALID 220700-221300
ME NH VT MA RI CT NY LO NJ PA OH LE WV MD DC DE VA AND CSTL WTRS
.
SEE AIRMET SIERRA FOR IFR CONDS AND MTN OBSCN.
TS IMPLY SEV OR GTR TURB SEV ICE LLWS AND IFR CONDS.
NON MSL HGTS DENOTED BY AGL OR CIG.
.
SYNOPSIS...AT 18Z STG SFC LOW WAS OVER SERN VA WITH CDFNT CURVG
OFF S ATLC CST. TROF XTNDD FROM LOW TO OH. BY 13Z LOW WILL MOV TO
JUST CST OF LONG ISLAND.
.
ME NH VT
NRN ME...BKN080. 19-21Z BKN030 OVC080. OCNL SN. 22-02Z OVC010-
020. VIS 3-5SM SN. TOPS FL200. OTLK...IFR CIG SN.
ELSW...OVC010-020. VIS 3-5SM SN. TOPS FL200. OTLK...IFR CIG SN.
.
MA RI CT
OVC010-020. VIS 3-5SM BR. OCNL RA SRN CSTL SXNS. OCNL FZRA SN PE
ELSW. SFC WND 06020G30KT. TOPS FL200 LWRG TO 150 AFT 00Z.
OTLK...IFR CIG SN.
.
NY LO
LO WRN AND NERN NY...OVC020-030. VIS 3-5SM SN. OCNL PE SRN PTN.
TOPS FL200. OTLK...IFR CIG SN.
SERN NY...OVC010-020. VIS 3-5SM BR. OCNL SN PE INTR SXNS. OCNL RA
PE CSTL SXNS AND LONG ISLAND. SFC WND 06020G30KT. TOPS 150.
OTLK...IFR CIG SHSN.
.
PA NJ
WRN AND NRN PA...OVC025. VIS 3-5SM SN. TOPS FL200. OTLK...IFR CIG
SN.
NJ AND SERN PA...OVC010-020. VIS 3-5SM RA SN BR. SFC WND
06020G30KT. TOPS 150. OTLK...IFR CIG SHSN.
.
OH LE
WRN OH...OVC020-030. VIS 3-5SM SN. TOPS FL200. 00-03Z OVC020-030.
OCNL VIS 3-5SM SHSN. TOPS 100. OTLK...MVFR CIG.
LE AND ERN OH...OVC020-030. VIS 3-5SM SN. OCNL RA SRN PTN TIL
00Z. TOPS FL200. OTLK...IFR CIG SHSN.
.
WV MD DC DE VA
APLCNS WWD...OVC025-040. VIS 3-5SM RA SN. TOPS FL200. OTLK...IFR
CIG SHSN.
E OF APLCNS AND N OF LYH-SBY LN...OVC010-020. VIS 3-5SM BR. WDLY
SCT SHRA. TOPS 150. OTLK...MVFR CIG SHRA.
E OF APLCNS AND S OF LYH-SBY LN...OVC010-020. VIS 3-5SM BR. WDLY
SCT SHRA. 02-05Z BKN-OVC030. ISOL SHRA. TOPS 100. OTLK...VFR.
.
CSTL WTRS
E OF 71W AND N OF ACK...OVC010-020. VIS 3-5SM RA SN. TOPS FL200.
OTLK...IFR CIG RA SN.
E OF 71W AND S OF ACK...OVC010-020. VIS 3-5SM BR. SCT SHRA TSRA.
TOPS FL200. CB TOPS FL400. OTLK...MVFR CIG SHRA.
W OF 71W...OVC010-020. ISOL SHRA N OF ACK. 00Z OVC010-020. WDLY
SCT SHRA. TOPS 150. OTLK...MVFR CIG SHRA.
....

NNNN
```

Figure 5-1. Area forecast (FA)—for Boston (from Aviation Weather Center web page)

```
ZCZC MKCWA1S
WAUS1 KBOS 212045
BOSS WA 212045
AIRMET SIERRA UPDT 3 FOR IFR AND MTN OBSCN VALID UNTIL 220300

.
AIRMET IFR...ME NH VT MA RI CT NY NJ PA OH LE LO WV MD DC DE VA
AND CSTL WTRS
FROM 50NW CAR TO YSJ TO 200SE ACK TO ORF TO TRI TO HNN TO CVG TO
FWA TO DTW TO 50NW CAR
OCNL CIG BLW 010 VIS BLW 3SM PCPN. CONDS CONTG SPRDG NWD OVER NEW
ENG DURG PD...CONTG ELSW...ENDG SERN VA AND WRN OH BY 03Z...CONTG
ELSW THRU 09Z.

.
AIRMET MTN OBSCN...ME NH VT MA NY PA WV MD VA NC SC GA
FROM CAR TO MLT TO CON TO HAR TO CHO TO AND TO ATL TO CHA TO TRI
TO HNN TO PIT TO BUF TO SYR TO 40N SLK TO CAR
MTNS OBSC IN CLDS AND PCPN. CONDS CONTG BYD 03Z THRU 09Z.
....=

NNNN
```

Figure 5-2. Boston AIRMET SIERRA—IFR and mountain obscuration

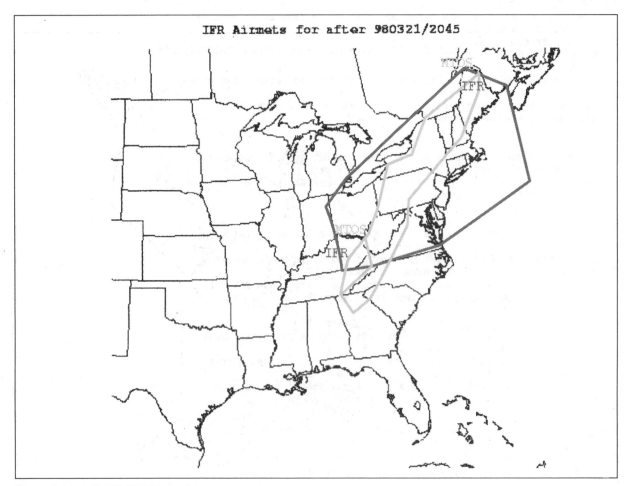

Figure 5-2A. AIRMET SIERRA graphic representation

```
ZCZC MKCWA1T
WAUS1 KBOS 212045
BOST WA 212045
AIRMET TANGO UPDT 5 FOR TURB AND LLWS VALID UNTIL 220300
.
AIRMET TURB...ME NH VT MA RI CT NY NJ PA OH LE LO WX MD DC DE VA
AND CSTL WTRS
FROM 50NW CAR TO YSJ TO 200SE ACK TO 80E ECG TO TRI TO HNN TO CVG
TO FWA TO DTW TO 50NW CAR
MOD TO ISOL SEV TURB BLW 080. CONDS CONTG BYD 03Z THRU 09Z.
.
AIRMET TURB...ME NH VT MA RI CT NY NJ PA OH LE LO WV AND CSTL
WTRS
FROM 50NW CAR TO YSJ TO 200SE ACK TO 160ESE SBY TO ACY TO HAR TO
HNN TO CVG TO FWA TO DTW TO 50NW CAR
OCNL MOD TURB BTN FL200 AND FL350. CONDS CONTG BYD 03Z THRU 09Z.
.
LLWS POTENTIAL OVER MA RI CT NY NJ PA LO MD DE THRUT PD.
....=

NNNN
```

Figure 5-3. Boston AIRMET TANGO—*turbulence, low-level wind shear and strong surface winds.*

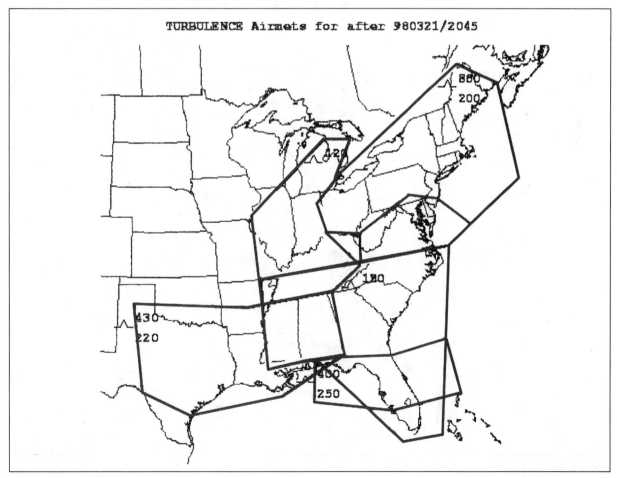

Figure 5-3A. AIRMET TANGO *graphic representation*

```
ZCZC MKCWA1Z
WAUS1 KBOS 212045
BOSZ WA 212045
AIRMET ZULU UPDT 4 FOR ICE AND FRZLVL VALID UNTIL 220300
.
.....SEE SIGMET QUEBEC SERIES FOR AREA OF SEV ICE.....
.
AIRMET ICE...ME NH VT MA RI CT NY NJ PA OH LE LO WV MD DC DE VA
AND CSTL WTRS
FROM 50NW CAR TO YSJ TO 200SE ACK TO 160E ORF TO TRI TO HNN TO
CVG TO FWA TO DTW TO 50NW CAR
MOD TO ISOL SEV RIME/MXD ICGICIP ABV FRZLVL TO FL200. FRZLVL SFC-
040 WRN AND NRN PTNS...SLPG TO 080 SERN PTN. CONDS CONTG BYD 03Z
THRU 09Z.
.
FRZLVL...SFC-040 N OF RWI-HAR-ACK LN.
         040-060 S OF RWI-HAR-ACK LN.
....=

NNNN
```

Figure 5-4. Boston AIRMET ZULU—icing and freezing levels

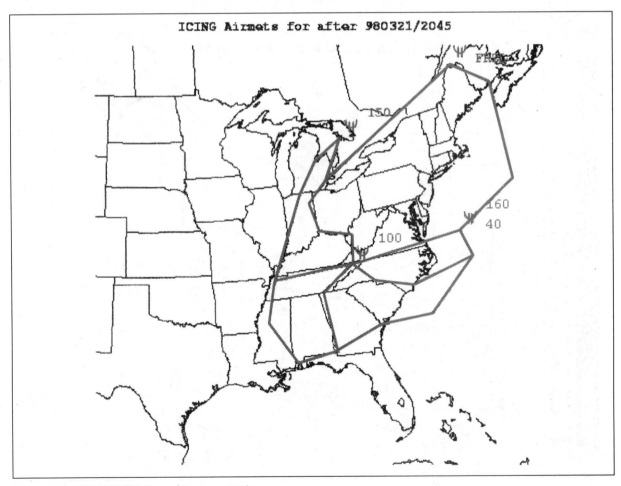

Figure 5-4A. AIRMET ZULU graphic representation

Key to Aerodrome Forecast (TAF) and Aviation Routine Weather Report (METAR)

TAF KPIT 091730Z 091818 15005KT 5SM HZ FEW020 WS010/31022KT
FM1930 30015G25KT 3SM SHRA OVC015 TEMPO 2022 1/2SM + TSRA OVC008CB
FM0100 27008KT 5SM SHRA BKN020 OVC040 PROB40 0407 1SM -RA BR
FM1015 18005KT 6SM -SHRA OVC020 BECMG 1315 P6SM NSW SKC

METAR KPIT 091955Z COR 22015G25KT 3/4SM R28L/2600FT TSRA OVC010CB
18/16 A2992 RMK SLP045 T01820159

Forecast	Explanation	Report
TAF	Message type: TAF-routine or TAF AMD-amended forecast, METAR-hourly, SPECI-special or TESTM-non-commissioned ASOS report	METAR
KPIT	ICAO location indicator	KPIT
091730Z	Issuance time: ALL times in UTC "Z", 2-digit date, 4-digit time	091955Z
091818	Valid period: 2-digit date, 2-digit beginning, 2-digit ending times	COR
	In U.S. METAR: CORrected ob; or AUTOmated ob for automated report with no human intervention; omitted when observer logs on	
15005KT	Wind: 3 digit true-north direction, nearest 10 degrees (or VaRiaBle); next 2-3 digits for speed and unit, KT (KMH or MPS); as needed, Gust and maximum speed; 00000KT for calm; for METAR, if direction varies 60 degrees or more, Variability appended, e.g. 180V260	22015G25KT
5SM	Prevailing visibility: in U.S., Statute Miles & fractions; above 6 miles in TAF Plus6SM. (Or, 4-digit minimum visibility in meters and as required, lowest value with direction)	3/4SM
	Runway Visual Range: R; 2-digit runway designator Left, Center, or Right as needed: "/"; Minus or Plus in U.S., 4-digit value, FeeT in U.S., (usually meters elsewhere); 4-digit value Variability 4-digit value (and tendency Down, Up or No change)	R28L/2600FT
HZ	Significant present, forecast and recent weather: see table (on back)	TSRA
FEW020	Cloud amount, height and type: Sky Clear 0/8, FEW >0/8-2/8, SCaTtered 3/8-4/8, BroKeN 5/8-7/8, OVerCast 8/8; 3-digit height in hundreds of ft; Towering CUmulus or CumulonimBus in METAR; in TAF, only CB. Vertical Visibility for obscured sky and height "VV004." More than 1 layer may be reported or forecast. In automated METAR reports only, CLeaR for "clear below 12,000 feet"	OVC010CB
	Temperature: degrees Celsius; first 2 digits, temperature "/" last 2 digits, dew-point temperature; Minus for below zero, e.g., M06	18/16
	Altimeter setting: indicator and 4 digits; in U.S., A-inches and hundredths; (Q-hectoPascals, e.g., Q1013)	A2992
		Continued

Key to Aerodrome Forecast (TAF) and Aviation Routine Weather Report (METAR) *Continued*

Forecast	Explanation	Report
WS010/3 1022KT	In U.S. TAF, non-convective low-level (≤ 2,000 ft) Wind Shear; 3-digit height (hundreds of ft); "/"; 3-digit wind direction and 2-3 digit wind speed above the indicated height, and unit, KT	
	In METAR, ReMarK indicator & remarks. For example: Sea-Level Pressure in hectoPascals & tenths, as shown: 1004.5 hPa; Temp/dew-point in tenths °C, as shown: temp. 18.2°C, dew-point 15.9°C	RMK SLP045 T01820159
FM1930	FroM and 2-digit hour and 2-digit minute beginning time: indicates significant change. Each FM starts on new line, indented 5 spaces.	
TEMPO 2022	TEMPOrary: changes expected for < 1 hour and in total, < half of 2-digit hour beginning and 2-digit hour ending time period	
PROB40 0407	PROBability and 2-digit percent (30 or 40): probable condition during 2-digit hour beginning and 2-digit hour ending time period	
BECMG 1315	BECoMinG: change expected during 2-digit hour beginning and 2-digit hour ending time period	

Table of Significant Present, Forecast and Recent Weather – Grouped in categories and used in the order listed below; or as needed in TAF, No Significant Weather.

QUALIFIER

Intensity or Proximity

'-' Light   "no sign" Moderate   '+' Heavy

VC Vicinity: but not at aerodrome; in U.S. METAR, between 5 and 10SM of the point(s) of observation; in U.S. TAF, 5 to 10SM from center of runway complex (elsewhere within 8000m)

Descriptor

MI Shallow	BC Patches	PR Partial	TS Thunderstorm
BL Blowing	SH Showers	DR Drifting	FZ Freezing

WEATHER PHENOMENA

Precipitation

DZ Drizzle	RA Rain	SN Snow	SG Snow grains
IC Ice crystals	PL Ice pellets	GR Hail	GS Small hail/snow pellets
UP Unknown precipitation in automated observations			

Obscuration

BR Mist (≥ 5/8SM)	FG Fog (< 5/8SM)	FU Smoke	VA Volcanic ash
SA Sand	HZ Haze	PY Spray	DU Widespread dust

Other

SQ Squall	SS Sandstorm	DS Duststorm	PO Well developed
FC Funnel cloud	+FC Tornado/waterspout		dust/sand whirls

– Explanation in parentheses "( )" indicate different worldwide practices.
– Ceiling is not specified; defined as the lowest broken or overcast layer, or the vertical visibility.
– NWS TAFs exclude turbulence, icing & temperature forecasts; NWS METARs exclude trend forecasts

January 1999
Aviation Weather Directorate

Department of Transportation
FEDERAL AVIATION ADMINISTRATION

Figure 5-5. METAR and TAF key

```
METAR KOMA 232151Z 13010KT 12SM SCT030TCU SCT080 SCT250 34/20 A2982 RMK
TCU SW-W SLP101

METAR KPIT 232250Z 24010KT 10SM VCSH SCT030 BKN 100 29/26 A2986 RMK SCT V
BKN SLP 121

METAR KDFW 232050Z 06006KT 1/4SM R17LM1000FT FG-DZ VV003 06/06 A2969 RMK
DZB28 SLP058

SPECI  KORD 230452Z 020452Z 02029G49KT 1 1/2SM TSRAGR OVC005CB 22/17
A2982 RMK LTGICCG GRB12 TS OHD MOV NE GR 3/4 SLP059
```

Figure 5-6. METAR examples

Each report begins with METAR (or SPECI, for a special report), followed by K and the airport's 3-letter identifier. Reports from Alaska begin with PA, while reports from Hawaiian stations begin with PH. The six-digit date-time group is the time of observation in Coordinated Universal Time (UTC), also known as ZULU time or Greenwich Mean Time. All four examples are for the 23rd day of the month. If the report is from an automatic observing station such as AWOS or ASOS, "AUTO" will follow the date-time group.

Before METAR became effective, pilots had to remember some arcane rules when reading weather sequences: "Gee, the altimeter setting and sea-level pressure come before and after the wind and temperature group—which one is which? Which is in inches and which is in millibars? And do I add 30 or subtract 29? Is the wind in knots or statute miles per hour?" Now the reports deliver the goods in a straightforward manner.

The first group after the date-time group is for wind; the true direction is given in three digits and the velocity is given in two digits: At Omaha, the wind at the time of observation was from 130 degrees at 10 knots, at Pittsburgh it was from 240 degrees at 10 knots, and at Dallas-Fort Worth it was from 060 at 6 knots. At Chicago-O'Hare, however, the wind was gusty, blowing from 020 at 29 knots with gusts to 49 knots. You probably would stay away from O'Hare anyway, but this wind gives you an additional excuse.

A calm wind is reported as 00000KT and a variable wind as VRB. If the wind direction is varying 60 degrees or more at a speed greater than 6 knots, this will be shown as 180V260.

The wind group (easily identifiable by "KT" for knots) is followed by the visibility group—which always ends in "SM" for statute miles. Omaha and Pittsburgh look pretty good for VFR, but the reports for KDFW and KORD wave a red flag at VFR pilots. Down in Texas, the visibility is only one-quarter mile, while in the Windy City the visibility is "1½ miles" (when the visibility element contains whole numbers and fractions, they are separated by a space).

If there is any restriction to visibility, the next group tells you what is causing it. At Pittsburgh, there are SHowers in the ViCinity (within ten miles). "SHVC" seems backward to me, but that's the way it is. At Dallas-Fort Worth, the visibility on runway 17L (R17L) is less than 1,000 feet (M for minus—if it was over 1,000 feet it would be P1000; the P stands for plus). The restriction to visibility at DFW is fog (FG) and drizzle (DZ). As a VFR pilot, you don't really care about the details—you're not going there anyway. There is something tricky about low visibility readings, however; FG is used only when the visibility is between zero and ⅝ of a mile. From ⅝ to six miles, BR (from the French BRume, "mist") is used.

At O'Hare, things are really nasty: a thunderstorm (TS), rain (RA), and hail (GR). The METAR format is used internationally, and GRaupel is French for hail. The report uses "+" to indicate "heavy" and "–" to indicate "light." This applies only to the *first* type of precipitation listed, so +RASNSH means heavy rain showers, not heavy snow showers.

A nice addition to weather observations is an indication of what is going on in the vicinity (VC, 5 to 10 miles). VCRA means that it is raining in the vicinity, but not at the airport. If the prevailing visibility noted by the official observer differs from the tower visibility, the lower of the two readings is included in the body of the METAR, and the other is placed in "Remarks."

Now that you know what the wind and visibility are, the question becomes "What is the cloud cover?" The observer divides the sky into eight sections, or octas. FEW is used if the clouds cover less than ¼ of the sky; SCT still means scattered clouds covering ⅜ to ½ of the sky, while BKN still means a broken layer covering ⅝ to ⅞ of the sky. OVC still means an unbroken overcast layer. "Sky clear," (SKC) has replaced "clear" (CLR).

There is no such thing as a "thin" layer anymore, and the METAR will not tell you the official ceiling: FEW and SCT do not constitute a ceiling, while BKN and OVC are ceiling reports.

The height of each cloud layer is given in hundreds of feet, but with three digits. Omaha, where the wind and visibility are fairly benign, reports a scattered layer at 3,000 feet and towering cumulus—not a good sign. The inclusion of TCU in the body of the report means that the towering cumulus is within 10 miles of the station. Omaha also has a scattered layer at 8,000 feet and another scattered layer at 25,000 feet. Pittsburgh reports a scattered layer at 3,000 feet and a broken layer at 10,000 feet. Dallas-Fort Worth (a quarter of a mile in fog and drizzle, remember) is reporting VV003, meaning that the observer estimated the vertical visibility into the cloud layer to be 300 feet; VV/// means essentially that the vertical visibility is zero. You won't be surprised to learn that O'Hare is reporting an overcast at 500 feet with cumulonimbus clouds (CB).

Right after the cloud cover comes the temperature and dew point—in Celsius. (Before you complain, remember that the Europeans wanted us to use meters instead of feet for both visibility and cloud height.) If either the temperature or the dew point is below zero degrees Celsius, the letter M for minus will be used. At OMA, the temperature-dewpoint spread is 14 degrees; at PIT the spread is only 3°, which makes you wonder how long that ten-mile visibility will last; at DFW the temperature and dew point are equal, so the air is saturated with moisture. That explains the fog and drizzle. ORD has a 5° spread, getting close to saturation. You should be more interested in the difference between temperature and dew point — the spread — than you are about the actual temperature.

The altimeter setting is always given in four digits preceded by A. Nothing hard about that. Jumping ahead a bit, SLP is always in "Remarks"; it means Sea Level Pressure.

Remarks (RMK) expands on the body of the report. At Omaha, the towering cumulus is reported to be southwest through west; the wind is out of the southeast, so it is *possible* that they are moving away. But maybe not. Check further. At Pittsburgh, the scattered layer at 3,000 feet is variable to broken. If you are flying at 6,500 feet and it turns into a broken layer at 3,000 feet, will you be able get down while staying the legal minimum distance from clouds? At DFW, the drizzle began at 28 minutes past the hour and was obviously still present when the observation was made. At O'Hare there is a light show in progress: lightning in clouds and cloud-to-ground, the hail began at 12 minutes past the hour, the thunderstorm is overhead (OHD) but moving northeast. The hailstones are ¾-inch in diameter. What a great day to be somewhere else!

A full discussion of the criteria used in these reports and a full list of abbreviations can be found in *Aviation Weather Services* (FAA Advisory Circular 00-45E), or Chapter 7 of the *Aeronautical Information Manual*.

An important part of your flight planning is to look at or ask for the most recent METAR for your destination airport and several enroute reporting stations, so that you can see whether the weather is good enough for VFR operations at your destination.

Check those reports against the TAF (explanation coming right up) to see if the forecast is holding up. You should also be sure that you can make an enroute stop if you need to. Check the METAR for the previous hour (if available) to see if there are trends you can detect. Is the spread between temperature and dew point increasing or decreasing? Is the barometric pressure rising or falling? (Check the altimeter setting.) Are the cloud layers rising or lowering? Wind picking up? Shifting? Which runway will probably be in use at the destination when you get there? Any Notices to Airmen? Remember, you are *required* to inform yourself about anything that could affect the safety of your flight.

A METAR from a sensor with no nearby human observer (unaugmented) will have AUTO following the date-time group. If the METAR from an automated site is fed to an observer for modification or augmentation, you will never know it because the METAR from that station won't give you a clue.

Terminal Aerodrome Forecasts (TAFs)

Terminal aerodrome forecasts, or TAFs, are prepared four times daily: 0000Z, 0600Z, 1200Z, and 1800Z for selected reporting stations. TAFs predict conditions for a 5-mile area surrounding the airport. Each forecast (with the exception of special forecasts) is valid for 24 hours. Figure 5-7 contains a TAF for Oklahoma City.

Those stations that prepare TAFs issue their first report of the day only after two METAR observations have been made. This means that you could be well on your way before a TAF for your destination airport is available.

TAFs use the same abbreviations as METARs, with a few additions based on the fact that they are forecasts, not observation reports (*see* the TAF code key in Figure 5-5).

The station identifier and date-time group are interpreted the same as METARs. The six-digit group following the date-time group is the valid period for the forecast—routinely 24 hours. Thus 051212 means that the forecast is valid from 1200Z on the 5th to 1200Z on the 6th, while 110024 means that the forecast is valid from 0000Z on the 11th to 0000Z on the 12th. In this situation, the end of the period is read as 2400Z. An amended forecast, identified up front as TAF AMD, is necessarily valid for less than 24 hours. If you see 010524 on an amended forecast, you know that the TAF is valid from 0500Z on the 1st (the time that the amendment is issued) until 2400Z on the 2nd day of the month.

The format for the body of the forecast is wind-visibility-weather-sky condition-optional data, followed by forecasts for specific time slots when applicable.

Wind is read exactly the same as a METAR: 18010KT means that the wind is forecast to be from 180 degrees true at 10 knots, while 35012G20KT tells you that the wind is forecast to be from 350 degrees at 12 knots gusting to 20 knots. Calm is coded as 0000KT and variable winds are forecast as VRB.

Visibility is read using the same qualifiers and contractions used in METAR reports. When the visibility is expected to be better than six statute miles, however, it will be coded as P6SM (the P stands for plus). Expected weather phenomena that affect visibility are coded the same as METAR; when the forecast visibility is P6SM, there will be no weather group.

Sky condition uses the same format as METAR; CB is the only cloud type used in TAF forecasts.

TAFKOKC 051130Z 051212 14008KT 5SM BR BKN030 TEMPO 1316 1 1/2SM BR
      FM1600 16010KT P6SM SKC BECMG 2224 200013G20KT 4SM SHRA OVC020 PROB40
      0006 2SM TSRA OVC008CB BECMG 0608 21015KT P6SM NSW SCT040

Figure 5-7. TAF example

"Optional data" is a wind shear forecast for the first 2,000 feet of the atmosphere over the station. WS010/ 18040KT means that a wind shear at 1,000 feet above the ground is expected, with the wind from 180 degrees at 40 knots. Compare this with the surface wind forecast to see how the shear will affect your flight.

PROB40 is used when the probability of thunderstorms or other events occurring is in the range of 30 percent to less than 50 percent, and is followed by a four-digit group giving the beginning and ending hours of the period during which the change is expected. PROB40 will not be used in the first six hours of the forecast period.

Assume that the body of the forecast called for "4SM SHRA OVC020." You would expect to have four miles visibility in rain showers with a 2,000-foot overcast during the valid period of the forecast. However, if you saw PROB40 2102 1/2SM +TSRA, you would know that there is about a forty percent chance that sometime between 2100Z and 0200Z the visibility will drop to one-half statute mile in a heavy thunderstorm with rain. Not a sure thing, and the timing might be off, but you have been alerted to the possibility.

Change indicators are FM (from), TEMPO (temporarily), and BECMG (becoming).

FM is used when a rapid change, usually occurring in less than one hour, in prevailing conditions is expected. If the valid period of a TAF is 051212 and you see "FM1600 16010KT P6SM SKC" you will know that the forecaster anticipates that at 1600Z the wind will become 160 at 10 knots, the visibility will increase to over six statute miles, and the sky will be clear. A FM group will always mark the beginning of a new line in a TAF, and will include all of the required elements— wind, visibility, weather, and sky condition.

BECMG is used when the change is expected to occur over a longer period, usually two hours. The time period is given as a four-digit group marking the beginning and end of the change period—the change will occur *sometime* during this period, so don't expect perfect timing.

OVC012 BECMG 1416 BKN020 means that the forecast ceiling is a 1,200-foot overcast, becoming 2,000 broken between 1400Z and 1600Z. This is what you like to see—a forecast of improving weather.

TEMPO is used when a change is expected to last less than an hour, and only the changed elements are included. Any unchanged elements are carried forward. SCT030 TEMPO 1923 BKN030 is a forecast for a 3,000-foot scattered layer with the ceiling occasionally worsening to a 3,000-foot broken layer between 1900Z and 2300Z. The forecast wind and visibility aren't expected to change, because they are not mentioned in the TEMPO group. This might be a suitable forecast for a flight from A to B, but how about the return flight a couple of hours later?

NSW in the BECMG and TEMPO groups means "no significant weather."

This is how you would interpret the TAF in Figure 5-7: It is the TAF for Oklahoma City issued at 1130Z on the fifth day of the month and valid from 1200Z until 1200Z on the sixth.

The wind at the beginning of the period is forecast to be from 140 degrees at 8 knots, and the visibility is forecast to be 5 statute miles in mist. Sky cover is forecast to be a broken layer at 3,000 feet. Temporarily, between 1300Z and 1600Z, the visibility is expected to drop to 1½ statute miles in mist. From 1600Z, expect the wind to be from 160 at 10 knots with visibility greater than 6 statute miles with sky clear, becoming (between 2200Z and 2400Z) wind from 200 at 13 gusting to 20 knots with visibility 4 statute miles in rain showers and an overcast layer at 2,000 feet. There is a 40 to 60 percent chance that between 0000Z and 0600Z the visibility will drop to 2 statute miles in a thunderstorm and rain with an overcast layer at 800 feet with cumulonimbus clouds becoming, between 0600Z and 0800Z, wind from 210 at 15 knots, visibility better than 6 statute miles, and no significant weather with a scattered layer at 4,000 feet.

Don't try to absorb it all at once; break it down into time periods. What will be happening at the beginning of the period? What change will occur at 1300Z? What should you expect after 1600Z? How about 2200Z? Midnight? After all, you should be able to estimate your time of arrival within an hour, shouldn't you? Find the time slot that fits your ETA and then check the time periods on either side—because predicting the weather is an art, not a science.

Convective Outlook (AC)

The convective outlook is a textual description of the prospects for general and severe thunderstorm activity in the next 24 hours. They are transmitted twice a day, at 0700Z and 1500Z, and are valid until 1200Z the next day. Forecasters use the convective outlook to update the severe weather outlook charts. Because afternoon is air-mass thunderstorm time, use the AC for planning flights late in the day.

Severe Weather Forecast Alert (AWW)

Severe weather forecast alerts are usually combined with severe weather bulletins (WW) and define areas of possible severe thunderstorms or tornado activity. These advisories are unscheduled and are issued as required by the NWS Forecast Center in Kansas City, MO.

AIRMETs and SIGMETs

SIGMETs and AIRMETs (other than AIRMETs Sierra, Tango, and Zulu) are issued for the six areas corresponding to the FA areas. The maximum forecast period is four hours for SIGMETs and six hours for AIRMETs. They are issued only when the area affected or forecast to be effective exceeds 3,000 square miles—so don't be surprised if localized conditions don't show up in one of these warnings.

When the following weather phenomena potentially hazardous to light aircraft are forecast, AIRMETs are broadcast every six hours with unscheduled amendments issued as needed.

1. Moderate icing.
2. Moderate turbulence.
3. Sustained winds of 30 knots or more at the surface.
4. Extensive mountain obscurement.
5. Widespread areas where ceilings of less than 1,000 feet AGL and/or visibility less than 3 miles.

A SIGMET is broadcast upon receipt at the FSS and at 15 and 45 minutes past the hour when the following phenomena hazardous to all aircraft is forecast:

1. Severe and extreme turbulence not associated with TRWs.
2. Severe icing not associated with TRWs.
3. Widespread dust storms, sandstorms, or volcanic ash lowering visibility to below 3 miles.

Three convective SIGMET bulletins are published at 55 minutes past each hour; each covers a specific area: from the East Coast to 87°W, from 87° to 107°W, and from 107°W to the Pacific Coast. They are issued for the following phenomena:

1. Tornadoes.
2. Lines of thunderstorms.
3. Embedded thunderstorms.
4. Thunderstorm areas where more than 40 percent of the area will be covered with Level 4 storms (see Radar Summary Chart section for description of levels)
5. ¾-inch or larger hail and/or wind gusts of 50 knots or greater.

If a convective SIGMET applies to an area within 150 miles of a flight service station (FSS) it will be broadcast upon receipt, on the hour, and at 15, 30, and 45 minutes past the hour.

If the threatening appearance of the weather has not given you enough cause for concern to voluntarily check with the FSS for inflight warnings, ARTCC controllers will broadcast an alert message on their frequencies when a SIGMET is received.

Transcribed Weather Broadcasts

Transcribed Weather Broadcasts (TWEBs) are available on selected VORs and NDBs across the country, although the number of such outlets is decreasing. A TWEB is similar to an area forecast in content, but with more specific information contained in a route format which might match your planned trip. Figure 5-8 shows how both chart suppliers show the availability of TWEB on VOR frequencies. The Airport/Facility Directory is your best source of information on which navaids have TWEB—check the "Radio Aids to Navigation" listing.

A continuous recording of meteorological and aeronautical information is available from automated flight service stations; this service is called "Telephone Information Briefing Service (TIBS)," 1-800-WX-BRIEF. TWEBs are also available online through the Aviation Weather Center web page. Because they are route-specific, TWEBs are not included in standard briefings.

Where the Hazardous Inflight Weather Advisory Service (HIWAS) is available, information regarding severe weather is broadcast on specified VORs and NDBs and there are no separate broadcasts of AIRMETs, SIGMETs, or Convective SIGMETs. The same type of symbology is used for HIWAS as is used for TWEB, except that the letter "H" is used. When a HIWAS broadcast is made, Center controllers and FSS personnel will announce it on all except emergency frequencies, advising all aircraft to monitor the nearest HIWAS broadcast or to contact Flight Service.

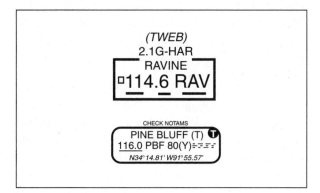

Figure 5-8. *TWEB symbology*

Center Weather Advisory (CWA)

Center Weather Advisories are unscheduled, and are a forecast of conditions beginning within the next two hours. They are an excellent argument in favor of getting flight following or monitoring the appropriate Center frequency when VFR. They are issued:

1. As a supplement to an existing SIGMET, AIRMET, area forecast or convective SIGMET.

2. When an inflight advisory has not been issued, but observed or expected conditions meet the criteria for a SIGMET/AIRMET based on pilot reports and other sources.

3. When observed or developing weather does not meet the criteria for a SIGMET, AIRMET, or convective SIGMET but pilot reports indicate the weather will adversely affect traffic flow in the Center's airspace.

Winds and Temperature Aloft Forecast (FD)

You can gain insight into potential turbulence and icing in addition to flight planning information by reading the winds and temperature aloft forecast (FD). *See* Figure 5-9. This forecast tabulates computer generated wind and temperature predictions for 9 standard altitude levels. No wind prediction is made for an altitude within 1,500 feet of station elevation and no temperature prediction is made for a level within 2,500 feet of station elevation. For the lower six levels, the first two digits represent the forecast true wind direction ±10°, the second two digits represent the forecast wind velocity in knots, and the last two digits represent the temperature. The code for calm winds is 0000, while 9900 is used to represent a forecast of light and variable winds.

Above 24,000 feet all temperatures are negative and no sign is shown. At high altitudes the wind speed may exceed 100 knots, and the report is coded to reflect that. When the reported wind speed exceeds 100 knots, the coded wind direction will be increased by 50: a wind from 210° will be coded as 71. The code group for a wind of 125 knots from that direction will be 7125. If the wind is forecast to exceed 200 knots the wind velocity is coded as 99: a wind from 150° at 250 knots will be coded as 6599.

```
VALID 141200Z  FOR USE 0900-1500Z.  TEMPS NEG ABV 24000

FT  3000    6000    9000    12000    18000    24000    30000    34000    39000

EMI 2807  2715-07  2728-10  2842-13  2867-21  2891-30  751041  771150  780855
ALB 0210  9900-07  2714-09  2728-12  2656-19  2777-28  781842  760150  269658
PSB       1509+04  2119+01  2233-04  2262-14  2368-26  781939  760850  780456
STL 2308  2613+02  2422-03  2431-08  2446-19  2461-30  760142  782650  760559
```

Figure 5-9. *Winds and temperature aloft forecast*

By comparing wind direction at different altitudes you can anticipate wind shear, and by examining temperatures you can determine whether the air will be cold enough to minimize the possibility of structural icing. If you find that the wind velocity is forecast to change by 3 to 5 knots for each 1,000 feet of altitude change, anticipate light turbulence; a change of 6 to 9 knots presages moderate turbulence. If the FD indicates that wind velocity will change more than 10 knots for every 1,000 feet of altitude change, stay on the ground.

The cruise performance charts for your airplane may require you to compare forecast (or existing) conditions to the International Standard Atmosphere when determining fuel consumption or power output. You can determine the standard temperature for any altitude by doubling the altitude, subtracting 15, and changing the sign. The standard temperature for 10,000 feet is -5°C (20 – 15). The standard temperature for 30,000 feet is -45°C (60 – 15). If the temperature at 30,000 feet in a winds aloft forecast is predicted to be -40°, engine performance will not be as good as book figures because the air is warmer than standard. The converse is true when the air is colder than standard.

Weather Charts

If there is an automated flight service station that you can drive or taxi to, you are indeed fortunate. Flight service stations are an endangered species, and the National Weather Service has quit the pilot briefing business. The odds are that the only way you will be able to see and analyze weather charts is through a DUAT vendor, web page, or a private sector weather provider. Of course, the FAA wants you to demonstrate your ability to decipher different kinds of charts.

Surface Analysis Charts

No trees will die to repeat information about the surface analysis charts you have been using since you were a student pilot. You know that they are where to find highs, lows, troughs, ridges, and fronts. Because they are old when you see them, surface charts are not the best source of information on runway winds and airport cloud cover. You can, however, derive useful wind information from noting how closely together the isobars are packed.

Radar Summary Charts

The radar summary chart shows you where storm cells were and the direction in which they were moving at the time the chart was produced; it also shows the altitude of the tops of cells in hundreds of feet as observed on radar. *See* Figure 5-10. Because this chart shows the vertical extent of rain-filled clouds it can be used together with the weather depiction chart to give a three-dimensional picture of clouds and precipitation.

You should be aware that older weather radars reflect only precipitation, not clouds, and that the clouds may extend considerably higher than the tops shown on the radar summary chart. The type of precipitation is shown as well as + and – signs indicating the trend since the last chart was issued. The Doppler WSR-88 radar (NEXRAD, covered later) does indicate the presence of hail.

An isolated cell is plotted on the radar summary chart as an echo 20 miles in diameter and its direction and speed of movement are indicated by an arrow labeled with the speed. A group of similar echoes is plotted as an area of echoes, with all of the hatched area inside the contours on the chart considered to be covered by echoes; the direction and velocity of movement of a group of echoes is indicated as a

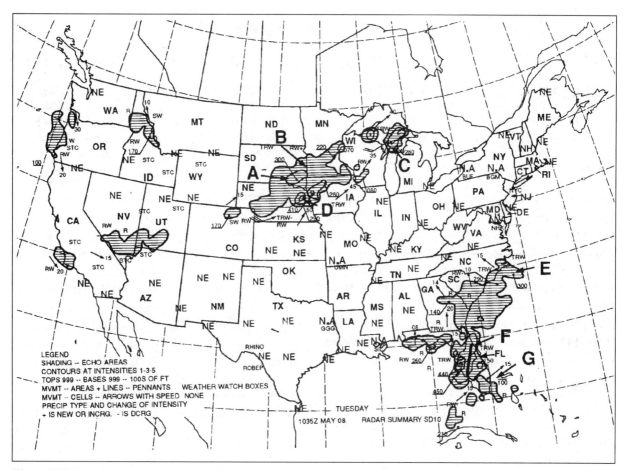

Figure 5-10. *Radar summary chart*

flagged arrow with one feather of the arrow representing 10 knots, a half-feather indicating 5 knots, and a pennant indicating a speed of 50 knots.

To be depicted as a line of echoes (a solid black bar), the echoes must form a line at least 30 miles long and at least 5 times as long as it is wide; if radar shows no apparent breaks between the echoes the line will be labeled SLD (solid). You should never attempt to penetrate a solid line of echoes.

Three contour lines represent six levels of storm intensity: the outside contour line represents levels 1 and 2, with weak to moderate echoes, and light to moderate precipitation and turbulence; the second contour line encloses levels 3 and 4, with strong to very strong echoes, heavy to very heavy precipitation, and the possibility of severe turbulence; the inner contour represents levels 5 and 6, where echoes and precipitation are intense to extreme and severe turbulence is possible. Inside the third contour line hail is likely and lightning must be expected.

While the plotted cells may not be in the same location when you arrive, you should plan to pass upwind from the direction of movement of cells or areas. Hail damage is a possibility in clear air downwind from storm cells. Graphic representations of cells, color-coded for intensity and labeled with the elevation of their tops are available through the AWC website.

Convective Outlook Chart

The convective outlook chart, Figure 5-11 (on next page), is a preliminary outlook for thunderstorm activity. The Day One panel is issued five times daily, beginning at 0600Z, and forecasts conditions for 1200Z until 1200Z the following day. The Day Two panel is issued twice daily, and forecasts conditions from 1200Z the following day until 1200Z the next day. Confused? If today is Monday, use the Day One chart to see what is expected from 1200Z today until 1200Z tomorrow. Look at the Day Two chart to see what is expected from 1200Z Tuesday until 1200Z Wednesday.

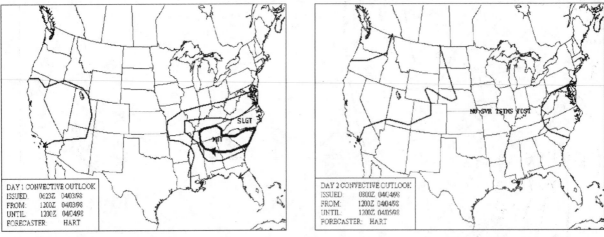

NOTATION	EXPLANATION
SEE TEXT	Used for those situations where a SLGT risk was considered but at the time of the forecast, was not warranted.
SLGT (Slight risk)	A high probability of 5 to 29 reports of 1 inch or larger hail, and/or 3-5 tornadoes, and/or 5 to 29 wind events,...or...a low/moderate probability of moderate to high risk being issued later if some conditions come together.
MDT (Moderate risk)	A high probability of at least 30 reports of hail 1 inch or larger; or 6-19 tornadoes; or numerous wind events (30).
HIGH (High risk)	A high probability of at least 20 tornadoes with at least two of them rated F3 (or higher), or an extreme derecho causing widespread (50 or more) wind events with numerous higher-end wind (80 mph or higher) and structural damage reports.

Figure 5-11. *Convective outlook charts*

The SLGT, MDT, and HIGH levels of risk are detailed in the table shown under the charts in Figure 5-11. An outline with no level of risk indicates general thunderstorms are expected.

Radar Reports (SDs)

When conditions are changing rapidly, reports from radar stations may be more valuable than the radar summary chart, although visualization is easier with the chart. Radar stations report each hour with special reports as required, and these reports are available on the computer screens at the flight service station. SDs report the location of precipitation along with type, intensity, and trend. This is a typical radar report:

LZK 1133 AREA 4TRW+/+ 22/100 88/170 196/180 220/115 C2425 MT 310 AT 162/110

The first portion of this report tells you that it is the Little Rock radar station 1133 GMT observation, reporting an area with four-tenths coverage containing thunderstorms and heavy rain showers increasing in intensity (4TRW+/+). The number groups represent bearings and distances from the radar station which, when plotted and connected, outline the area of echoes. Cells are reported to be moving from 240° at 25 knots (C2425). Finally, the maximum tops (MT) are at 31,000 feet located 110° and 162 NM from the reporting station.

The usual + and – signs are used to report intensity, with ++ indicating very heavy, X indicating intense, and XX indicating extreme. Where dimensions of an echo are available they are reported as "15W" (15 miles wide).

Significant Weather Prognostic Charts

Significant weather prognostic charts, shown in Figures 5-12 and 5-13, are intended to be used for advance planning. Each chart includes the time for which it is valid. These charts show you where turbulence is to be expected, at what altitude the freezing level is forecast to be, the type and extent of precipitation anticipated; and for the high level chart, the type and extent of clouds you may encounter in flight.

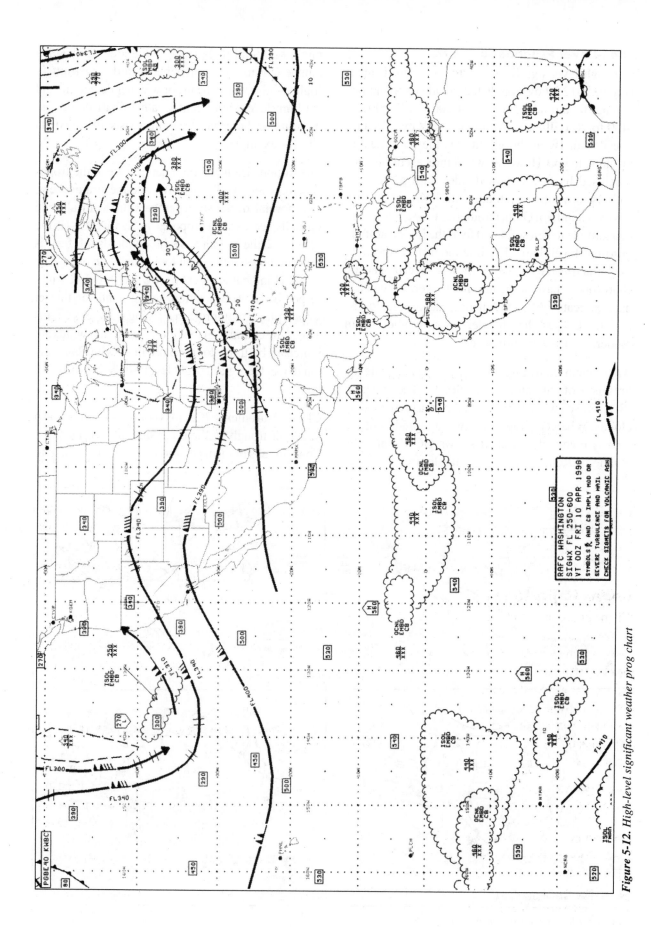

Figure 5-12. High-level significant weather prog chart

High-Level Prognostic Charts

The high-level significant weather prognostic chart (Figure 5-12) shows predicted cloud cover and turbulence for altitudes between 24,000 and 63,000 feet (400 to 70 millibars). You may think that because you do not fly at those altitudes the chart has no meaning to you. However, when forecast turbulence (enclosed by heavy dashed lines with a "witches hat") is shown by an altitude with XXX under it, as it is over southern Ohio, turbulence may extend from that altitude to below 24,000 feet (the lowest altitude on a high-level chart). That line should have meaning for you and lead you to look at the low-level prognostic chart for the base of the turbulent layer. A "witches hat" indicates light turbulence...according to the legend, CB or the thunderstorm symbol mean moderate to severe turbulence.

Areas enclosed by large scalloped lines indicate the presence of cumulonimbus clouds. The notation ISOL is used when ⅛ or less of the area is covered by clouds. When coverage of between ⅛ and ⅘ of the area is involved, the chart shows OCNL, and the notation FRQ is a sign that cumulonimbus clouds

might be found in ⅝ to ⅞ of the area. Embedded thunderstorms are an invisible hazard to instrument flights without any means of weather detection, and the high level significant weather chart points out those areas where that possibility exists: FRQ EMBD CB, for example.

The tropopause is the boundary between the troposphere, where we live and fly, and the stratosphere. The normal decrease in temperature with altitude virtually ceases at the tropopause. In Figure 5-12, the height of the tropopause in hundreds of feet is indicated by symbols that look like home plate. The L and H indicate centers of low and high pressure, respectively. The position and strength of the jet stream play a major role in steering weather systems across the country. In the figure, jet stream winds are indicated by those long, snaky lines with flags; the wind over Georgia at flight level 340 is shown as 130 knots.

Clear air turbulence (CAT) is commonly found in an upper air trough on the polar side of the jet stream. Long streaks of cirrus clouds can sometimes help to

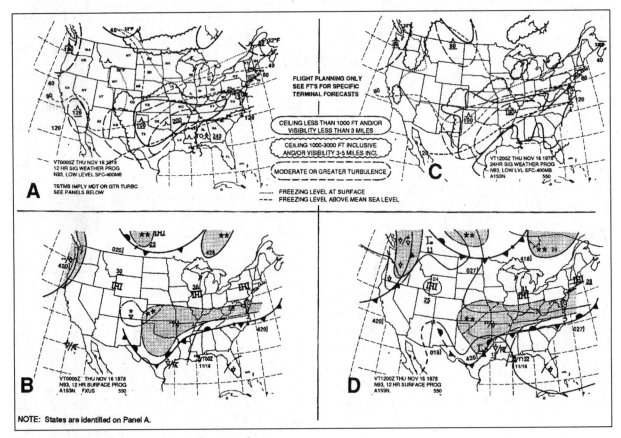

Figure 5-13. Low-level significant weather prog chart

visually identify the jet stream and associated clear air turbulence. Just like an experienced tourist, the jet stream goes south in the winter and north in the summer; its strength diminishes in the summer.

Low-Level Charts

The low-level significant weather prognostic chart, Figure 5-13, is presented as four panels—the two on the left predict conditions that are expected to exist in twelve hours and the two on the right forecast conditions 24 hours in advance. The valid time is given on the chart. "Low level" means that conditions between the surface and 24,000 feet are predicted.

The two top charts predict ceiling, visibility, turbulence, and freezing level. The legend for ceiling and visibility is printed on the charts and the symbols for turbulence are the same as those used in the high level charts. Moderate or greater turbulence is shown on prog charts as an underlined number in an area defined by dashed lines. The line represents the surface and the number above the line is the top of the expected turbulent layer. Areas where IFR weather is forecast to occur are enclosed by a smooth line, and a scalloped line is used to enclose areas where marginal VFR conditions are forecast.

The lower two charts outline areas of predicted precipitation and/or thunderstorms. The smooth lines enclose areas where continuous or intermittent precipitation is expected, and the dash-dot lines enclose areas where showers and thunderstorms are predicted to occur. The shading indicates where one-half or more of the enclosed area can expect the forecast precipitation. Table 5-1 shows the symbols used for various types of precipitation.

Constant Pressure Charts

Constant pressure charts (Figure 5-14 on Page 5-21) are drawn from measured data, not forecast conditions. There are 5 levels for which charts are produced: 850 millibars (mb) (5,000 feet), 700 mb (10,000 feet), 500 mb (18,000 feet), 300 mb (30,000 feet) and 200 mb (39,000 feet). The 200 mb chart is primarily of interest to jet pilots; pilots of turboprops and pressurized piston-powered airplanes will find information of value in all constant pressure charts.

Symbol	Meaning	Symbol	Meaning
⋀	Moderate Turbulence	▽	Rain Shower
⋀	Severe Turbulence	⁎▽	Snow Shower
⋔	Moderate Icing	↳	Thunderstorm
⋔	Severe Icing	⌒	Freezing Rain
●	Rain	)	Tropical Storm
⁎	Snow	)	Hurricane (typhoon)
)	Drizzle		

Examples:	Intermittent	Continuous
Rain	●	● ●
Drizzle	)	))
Snow	⁎	⁎ ⁎

Table 5-1. *Standard weather symbols*

When you are planning your flight, look at the 850, 700, and 500 mb charts to determine temperatures, temperature-dewpoint spreads, and winds along your route. At the upper left of each station symbol you will find the measured temperature, and directly beneath it the temperature-dewpoint spread in degrees. The station symbol is shaded if the spread is less than 5°. If the temperature is near or below freezing and the spread is small you must consider the possibility of encountering structural icing. Because of the lack of moisture (and the extremely cold temperatures) at high altitudes, no temperature-dewpoint figure is given on the 300 and 200 mb charts.

To aid you in determining whether your flight will take you toward warmer or colder air, points of equal temperature are connected by lines called isotherms at 5°C intervals. Wind direction and velocity are shown by arrows with barbs: a pennant indicates 50 knots, a full barb indicates 10 knots, and a half-barb indicates 5 knots.

Relate the positions of low pressure areas on each of the constant pressure charts to each other and to the surface analysis chart; widespread cloudiness and precipitation often develop in advance of an upper air low which is not evident at the surface. A low pressure system that exists in much the same location on both the surface and upper air charts is associated with generally adverse flying weather.

If there is a low pressure center or trough on the 500 mb chart (approximately 18,000 feet) located to the west of your route of flight, conditions are ideal for the development of thunderstorms. They will probably be located to the southeast of the low pressure center's surface position.

The 300 and 200 mb constant pressure charts give the jet pilot additional information. These charts include isotachs, which are lines of equal wind speed; knowing the position of the airplane's flight path in relation to the jet stream gives the pilot maximum advantage of favorable winds. Also, areas where clear air turbulence may be encountered are related to the position of the jet stream. Areas where wind speeds of 70 to 110 knots are expected are hatched on the chart, and clear areas inside the hatched areas show where wind speeds more than 110 knots are expected.

In Figure 5-15, the constant pressure chart for 300 mb or 30,000 feet, you can see the jet stream because wind velocities from 70 to 110 knots are hatched. Clear areas within the hatched areas indicate wind velocities of 110 to 150 knots. A hatched area within a clear area within a hatched area (kind of like a knothole) would represent 150 to 190 knots and so on. You can see that things are forecast to be exciting at altitudes near 30,000 feet off the east coast. Even if you do not have access to the charts, the briefer can give you jet stream locations and wind velocities.

Freezing Level Data

Current information on the height of the freezing level and relative humidity is critical to your ability to avoid structural icing. When the National Weather Service makes an upper air sounding with a weather balloon, it reports the freezing level and the relative humidity at the point of crossing. This measurement is the basis for the freezing level chart discussed later.

The days of weather balloons are numbered, to some extent. When they come on-line, new radars and wind profilers will make it possible to detect icing conditions with a greater degree of accuracy than ever before.

Four-Panel Chart

The National Weather Service produces a chart showing forecast stability, freezing level, precipitable water, and relative humidity. Their name for it is the composite moisture stability chart, but because it consists of four panels on one chart it is commonly referred to as the four-panel chart (Figure 5-16 on Page 5-22).

The upper left panel is the stability chart. As an instrument pilot you must be aware of areas of instability because they indicate the possibility of turbulence, icing, or both. The lifted index (top number) is derived by subtracting the temperature of a parcel of air theoretically lifted from the surface to the 500-mb level and cooled at the standard lapse rate to the actual temperature at that level. A stable condition is indicated when the index is positive, while a zero index indicates neutral stability. A negative number indicates instability, with increasing instability shown by larger numbers. Unstable air means that convective currents are possible, and that means turbulence. A lifted index of -2 is enough to make tornadoes possible, and a lifted index of -4 has been identified in many general aviation thunderstorm accidents.

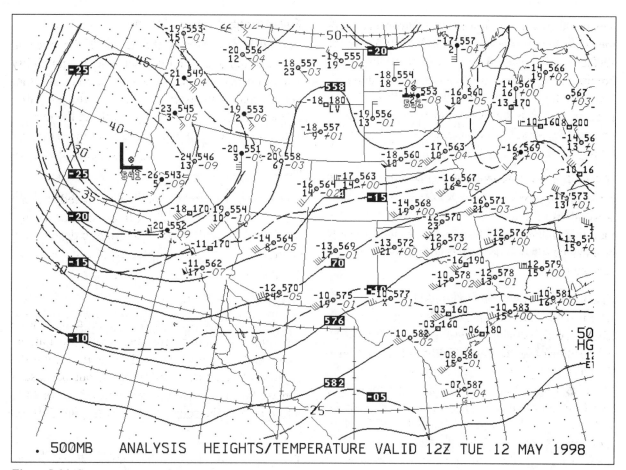

Figure 5-14. *Constant pressure chart*

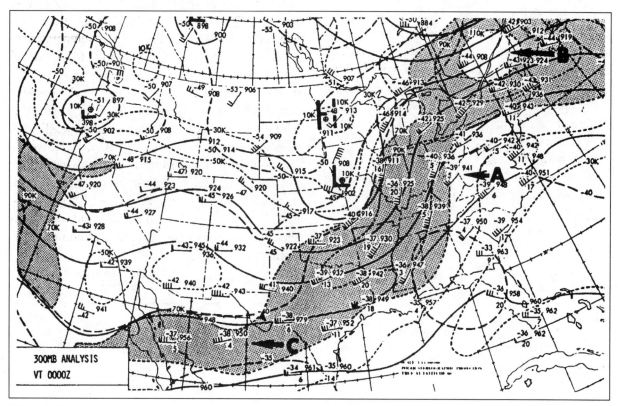

Figure 5-15. *300 MB analysis*

The K index is of interest to meteorologists, but for pilot use it is enough to say that a large number supports cloudiness and precipitation. When instability and large amounts of moisture are found together violent weather can result.

The National Weather Service will outline areas of instability on the lifted index/K index chart, and will darken in the station circle when the lifted index is zero or minus. On the upper right panel (precipitable water) the station circle will be darkened if the value will be one inch or more, and on the average relative humidity chart (lower right) the station circle will be darkened if the relative humidity is forecast to be 50 percent or more.

The upper right panel shows precipitable water from the surface to 500 millibar (18,000 feet). The amount shown is the amount of liquid precipitation that would result if all of the water vapor were condensed.

You obviously want to avoid wet air. Unfortunately, no information about droplet size is available.

The lower left panel shows observed freezing level data from upper air soundings. The lower right panel is a plot of an analysis of the average relative humidity, again from the surface to 500 millibar. An average relative humidity of 70 percent or greater usually means extensive clouds and possible precipitation. An average of 70 percent over 18,000 feet of altitude means that there has to be one or more layers with 100 percent relative humidity.

When you look at the four panel chart and overlay your planned route of flight, look for areas where you will be flying in unstable air above the freezing level with high relative humidity and a large amount of precipitable water. The worst combination of turbulence and potential icing will be in those areas.

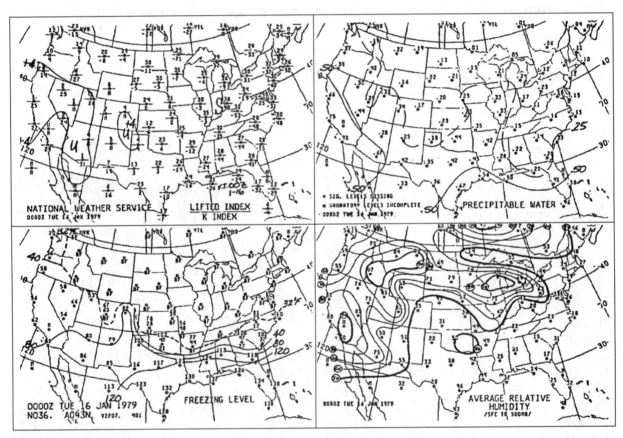

Figure 5-16. *Four-panel chart*

Weather Depiction Chart

The weather depiction chart (Figure 5-17 on next page) tells you more about what to expect at your destination than what to expect en route, although fronts which might affect enroute weather are shown on the chart. The chart legend is given in Table 5-2. The number below the station symbol represents the ceiling, if the lowest cloud layer is broken or overcast. If cloud cover is few or scattered, the number represents the lowest cloud layer in hundreds of feet. To the left of the station symbol, visibility and the character of any obstruction to visibility are shown. The weather depiction chart is a great planning device, but must be followed up by study of hourly sequences which will provide more current information.

All of these "old fashioned" charts (radar summary, surface plot, constant pressure, 4-panel, significant prognostics, etc.) are available to computer users at the AWC website, http://aviationweather.noaa.gov.

Satellite Images

Your weather briefer can call up satellite images on the screen at the flight service station, but it is far better if you can see the images themselves. You can find them in television weather reports and on newspaper weather pages, but the best source is the worldwide web on your computer.

There are three basic types of satellite pictures: visual, infrared, and water vapor. Each has something of value for you as a pilot, but you must remember that you are looking at pictures that are not current — the date and time at which the image was made is on the image itself. They are frequently updated, however, and weather systems do not move at the speed of airplanes, so the information is valuable in planning a flight that will take place in a matter of hours after you view the images.

Figures 5-18, 5-19, and 5-20 (on Pages 5-25 through 5-27) were downloaded from the http://www.goes.noaa.gov/index.html website at 1730Z on 18 June 1998 and are from the GOES-9 satellite; the GOES-8 satellite provides similar images for the east coast. The visual image (Figure 5-18) is based on

Plotted	Interpreted
8	Few clouds, base 800 feet, visibility more than 6.
12	Broken sky cover, ceiling 1,200 feet, rain shower, visibility more than 6.
5∞	Thin overcast with breaks, visibility 5 in haze.
30	Scattered at 3,000 feet, clouds topping ridges, visibility more than 6.
2=	Sky clear, visibility 2, ground fog or fog.
1/2	Sky partially obscured, visibility 1/2, blowing snow, no cloud layers observed.
2= 200	Sky partially obscured, visibility 2, fog, cloud layer at 20,000 feet. Assume sky is partially obscured since 20,000 feet cannot be vertical visibility into fog. It is questionable if 20,000 feet is lowest scattered layer or ceiling.*
1/4 5	Sky obscured, ceiling 500, visibility 1/4, snow
1 12	Overcast, ceiling 1,200 feet thunderstorm, rain shower, visibility 1.
M	Data missing.

* Note: Since a partial and a total obscuration (x) is entered as total sky cover, it can be difficult to determine if a height entry is a cloud layer above a partial obscuration or vertical visibility into a total obscuration. Check the METAR.

Table 5-2. *Examples of plotted data on the weather depiction chart*

reflectivity — how well the clouds or other surfaces reflect sunlight. The brightest white clouds are cumulus buildups, and generally, the brighter they are the higher they are. Satellite images cannot show cloud layers, however, so you can't tell the elevation of cloud bases by looking at satellite images. Tall clouds almost always mean nasty weather, though, and you might want to think twice before flying beneath them. Thick stratocumulus clouds will not look as bright as cumulonimbus. Thin stratus clouds just look like milky veils. Don't be misled by the reflection from snowy areas — they can be almost as bright as tall clouds; but you should be aware of snow-covered areas from other weather sources.

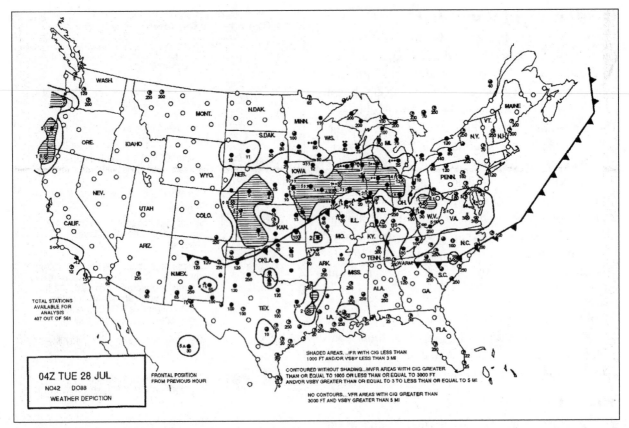

Figure 5-17. *Weather depiction chart*

Infrared images (Figure 5-19) measure temperature, so the highest clouds are the coldest and the brightest on the satellite image—lower clouds are darker. Infrared images can be taken at night, of course, but because cloud and ground temperatures are low at night their interpretation is tricky for those who are not meteorologists.

Water vapor images (Figure 5-20) are not as directly applicable to flight planning as the visual and infrared images, but they do show mid-level storms. You know that when moisture is added to the atmosphere the dew point goes down, and that when the temperature/dewpoint spread gets low enough there is a potential for clouds and fog, so it's nice to be able to see where moist air is coming from. Just as with the other images, lighter means more water vapor and darker means less, with black indicating areas where the air is very dry.

On this same web page you can get more detailed visual, infrared, and water vapor images for the Great Lakes area, the Southeast United States and the Caribbean, the Northeast United States, the Mid-Atlantic states, and the Gulf of Mexico. You can also get satellite winds for 10,000 feet and 10,000 to 23,000 feet; images for 23,000-52,000 feet are also available, but I doubt that many readers of this book will be flying at those altitudes. The three levels are color-coded, but this is a black-and-white book.

Satellite images are available at http://adds. aviationweather.noaa.gov. The satellite pictures overlay with colored circles indicating airports that are reporting IFR, MVFR, or VFR conditions (*see*

Continued on Page 5-28

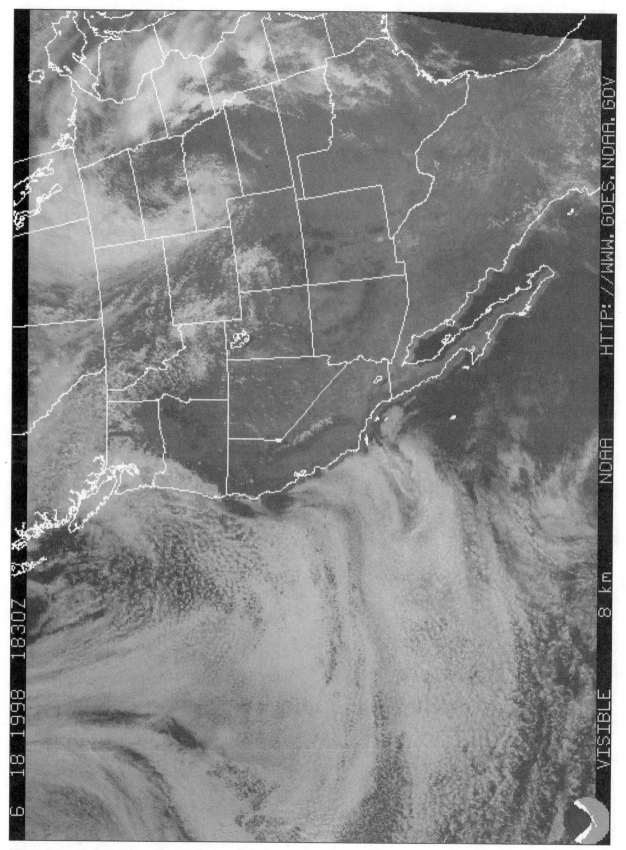

Figure 5-18. GOES 9 Western U.S. (visible image)

Figure 5-19. GOES 9 Western U.S. (infrared)

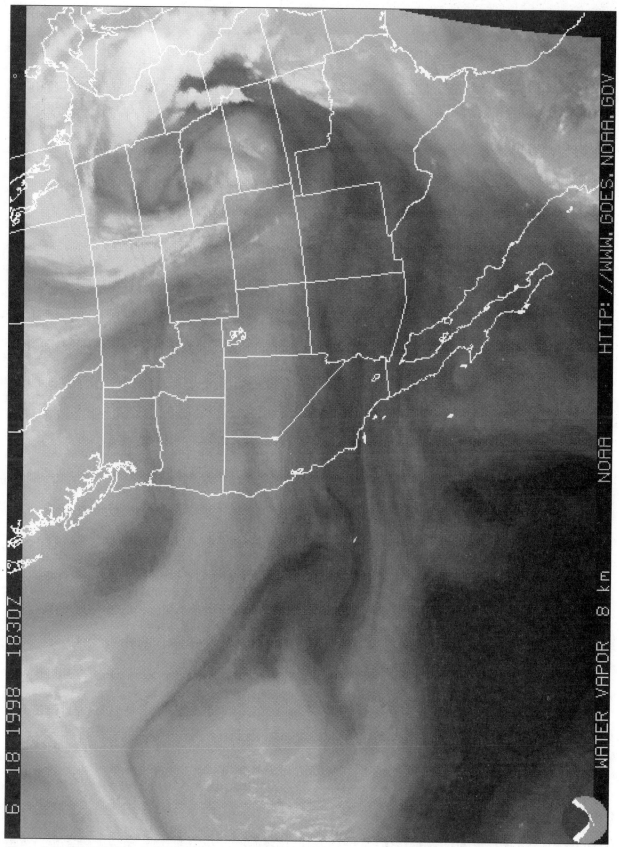

Figure 5-20. GOES 9 Western U.S. (water vapor image)

Figure 5-21), and use the same symbology for cloud coverage as does the weather depiction chart. Unlike the weather depiction chart, you do not get restrictions to visibility or the height of cloud bases, but the ability to see the satellite picture backed up with how it looks to a ground observer is quite valuable. Satellite images can also be found in other varieties at the GOES website, www.goes.noaa.gov.

Inflight Weather Advisories

Your IFR planning must be based on the weather information gathered before takeoff, but the conduct of the flight must be based on information acquired as the flight progresses.

The FAA has little sympathy for a pilot who flies into unforecast deteriorating weather if information about the change was available through inflight broadcasts.

The Enroute Flight Advisory Service (EFAS, also known as Flight Watch) is available on 122.0 between the hours of 0600 and 2200 local time across the country. Flight Watch is a dedicated position at a flight service station with no responsibility other than the transmission of weather information to pilots who call and request it.

There are discrete frequencies for flights above Flight Level 180. The Flight Watch remote network is depicted on the inside back cover of the Airport/Facility Directory and on the reverse side of Jeppesen's Low Altitude Enroute Planning Chart.

Some large flight service stations have weather radar which can give real-time location of storm cells. If you don't know the name of the nearest EFAS station, a call to "Flight Watch" on 122.0 with your approximate position will probably get a reply.

Data Link

The cutting edge of technology, insofar as getting weather information while en route, is Data Link. Already tested in Alaska by the FAA and well-received by the pilot community, Data Link puts weather radar data, METAR text, or both, on a five-inch screen in your cockpit. This is not big-iron stuff—it is designed for cross-country capable planes from the Bonanza/Skylane class on up. A fixed-frequency receiver gets the data that you want from ground stations and puts it right on your panel. The display can also be linked to a GPS and used as a moving map.

Some states, such as Virginia, are subsidizing the cost of the transmitting stations; until other states climb on the bandwagon, monthly cost will be about $50 after the initial $8,000 for the equipment and installation. The manufacturer anticipates nationwide coverage above 3,000 feet AGL by the end of 2002.

"Center, Are You Showing Any Weather on My Route?"

Radars at air route traffic control centers (ARTCCs) are designed to keep airplanes from running into one another, not to keep airplanes from running into weather, and many controllers will tell you that they are unable to display weather. This is a half-truth—they are unable to display weather very well and will not volunteer any weather information. Ask the controller to push the WX-3 key on the keypad; the display will show slashes for precipitation falling at a little over .1 inch per hour and H's where the rain is falling out of the sky at between .2 and .3 inches per hour. You don't want to be anywhere near the H's.

Airborne weather radar is much better than ATC weather for showing bad stuff, but if you don't have airborne radar, the controller's WX-3 key is a great help. Airborne radar will be discussed later.

Every air route traffic control center has a Center Weather Service Unit manned by meteorologists, not air traffic controllers. You can't talk directly to the CWSU, but you can be sure that if there is any hazardous weather along your route the CWSU has so informed the controller for that sector. On the other hand, a terminal facility (approach/departure control) with the new ASR-9 radar not only sees weather returns but can classify their intensity.

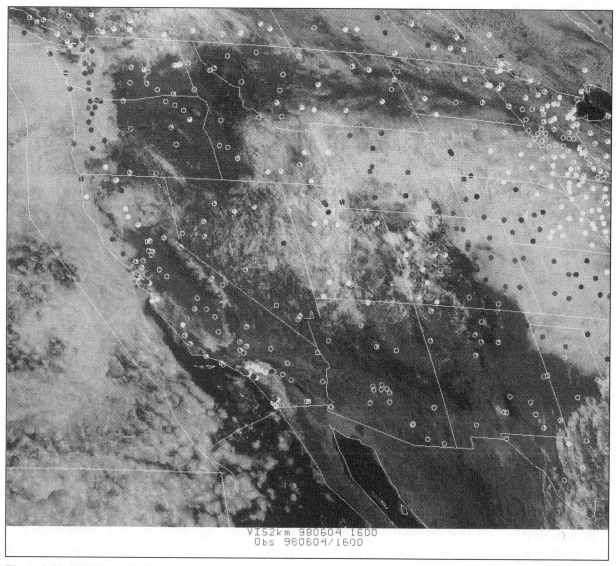

Figure 5-21. GOES 9 visible/fog image with sky cover and aviation flight conditions

NEXRAD, the newest and most sophisticated weather radar, has the capability of providing to the CWSU information not previously available from any source such as gust front movement, downbursts, and rotation of the wind within an air mass. It reaches out as far as 200 miles, and promises to revolutionize aviation weather reporting and forecasting.

A useful enroute ploy is to take advantage of the pilot who is ahead of you on the airway. Ask Center if the planes ahead of you reported any icing or turbulence, or if you hear a pilot reporting something meteorologically unpleasant ask the controller where that airplane is. After all, if the other plane is on the same sector frequency that you are on, it can't be too far away.

"Approach, Are You Painting Any Weather...?"

Center radars and terminal radars are two totally different breeds. There is no employee of the National Weather Service at a terminal radar facility, just an overworked controller. If you want weather information from an approach or departure controller, your first question must be "Do you have ASR-9 radar?" If the answer is no, and the controller's scope is showing any weather at all, it is severe weather. Older terminal radars had several layers of weather suppression circuitry, and anything bad enough to fight its way through all that suppression is really nasty.

If your controller is fortunate enough to have ASR-9 radar (and they are being installed at a rapid pace), he or she can call up six different levels of precipitation. You don't want to get close to anything worse than level 2. The controller can limit the display to level 2 echoes and tell you where they are in relation to your flight path. Steer clear, because the associated turbulence may extend beyond the precipitation echoes. Levels 3 through 6, of course, should be avoided by at least 20 miles.

Automated Observations

The Automatic Meteorological Observing Station (AMOS), Automatic Weather Observing Station (AWOS), and Automatic Surface Observation System (ASOS) are, as their names indicate, devices that measure different weather parameters and make them available to pilots. AMOS information is not broadcast, but is available at flight service stations with other METAR information.

There are four different types of AWOS; you can determine the type of unit at a given reporting point by referring to the A/FD. AWOS-A reports only altimeter setting. An AWOS-1 reports wind speed and direction, temperature, dew point, altimeter setting, and density altitude when it is at least 1,000 feet above field elevation. AWOS-2 adds visibility, and AWOS-3 adds visibility and ceiling/cloud cover. The observations, broadcast on a discrete frequency, are updated each minute.

An ASOS observes parameters that an AWOS can't measure. In fact, it can make a fairly accurate hourly sequence report containing all of the required elements. However, it can't see clouds higher than 12,000 feet MSL or distant clouds, it can't see lightning or hear thunder, and it only looks in one direction (the NWS has separate automated lightning-strike detection capability). Looking in only one direction means that an ASOS cannot report prevailing visibility, but its sensors are sufficiently advanced in technology that there is strong correlation between an ASOS and a human report of visibility.

At locations where visibility changes rapidly and might adversely affect flight operations, multiple sensors are installed. A joint effort of the FAA and National Weather Service, the ASOS is now the primary surface weather observing system. Over 1,700 systems will be installed nationwide.

There are human observers at some AWOS and ASOS installations to provide weather and visibility information when the reported visibility falls below 3 miles; for the most part, however, automated observing stations are unmanned.

You can get the latest reading from an AWOS or ASOS in plain language (no interpretation required) using your computer. The address is www.faa.gov/asos/asos.htm. The radio frequency and telephone number for each observing station is included.

As wonderful as these automated observers are, you should never accept their readings uncritically. Base your planning on the weather being worse than reported and you'll always be ready.

Pilot Reports

Pilot reports, or PIREPs, are invaluable: they represent weather as experienced by another pilot flying along your route. You should contribute a pilot report whenever unforecast weather is encountered, whenever any weather phenomenon of interest to pilots is seen, and whenever you have a spare moment and want to help other pilots. Figure 5-22 is a rough sketch that I prepare while climbing out so that I can give cloud bases and tops, temperatures, and the distance from a VORTAC when I made the notation. A PIREP based on this sketch would be invaluable to a pilot planning a flight at 6,000 feet.

Be aware that if you expect ATC to write down your report and pass it along to other pilots you must use the words "pilot report" or PIREP. ATC has no responsibility to record casual comments. Ideally, you should leave Center frequency and make your pilot report to Flight Watch.

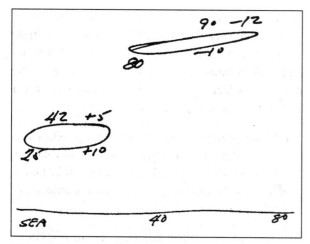

Figure 5-22. Pilot's cloud base and temperature log

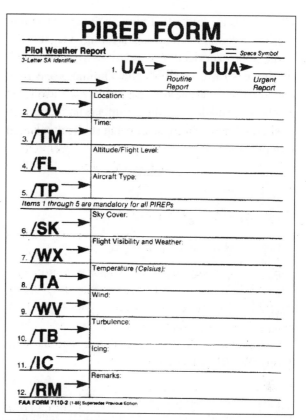

Figure 5-23. PIREP form

As you stand at the weather briefer's desk, what would you ask a pilot in flight if you were able to? What are the tops? What is the temperature at your altitude? Is the cloud cover broken or overcast? If there are cloud layers, what are their bases and tops? These are the types of questions that you can answer with a pilot report when you are enroute. Figure 5-23 shows a PIREP form; pads of them are available at flight service stations.

You should be aware of the fact that the National Transportation Safety Board attaches no *legal* importance to pilot reports. If you get into trouble because you relied on a PIREP that was in conflict with an official forecast you will get no sympathy from the judge.

Other Sources of Weather Information

Telephone briefings (1-800-WX-BRIEF) have replaced in-person contact. Automated Flight Service Station briefers have dozens of full-color weather maps and charts available on their computer monitors at the touch of a button, but it is unlikely that your briefer will call up something like the 750 mb constant pressure chart or the composite moisture stability chart unless you ask for it. Without prompting from you, your briefing will probably be limited to information available in text form. Cell phone users should realize that when you use 1-800-WX-BRIEF you will be connected to the AFSS nearest to where the phone is registered—which might not be where you are. *See* Appendix B for a list of direct toll-free telephone numbers.

The FAA has recognized the increasing use of personal computers by contracting with GTE Federal Systems and Data Transformation Corporation to provide textual weather information through use of the Direct User Access Terminal (DUAT) program. Both companies make available to the user the same weather reports and forecasts that appear on the computer screens at Flight Service Stations; the ability to file a flight plan directly with the FAA using a home computer is part of the free service. Both companies make their access software available to pilots free of charge.

GTE and DTC know that pilots like to see weather maps and charts to aid in self-briefing, and each has value-added services such as color charts and satellite images for a small charge. The types of value-added services are constantly being expanded, and you should call the telephone numbers in Figure 5-24 to get the free software and the latest information on other services.

```
GTE DUAT
1-800-345-DUAT
Basic service free

Data Transformation Corp. (DTC)
1-800-AID-DUAT
Basic service free

JeppFax
1-800-677-JEPP
(charge to credit card)
```

Figure 5-24. *DUAT vendors*

Jeppesen Sanderson, although not a DUAT contractor, also provides weather information by facsimile. Use the phone number in Figure 5-24 and pay by credit card. Jeppesen also has a page on the worldwide web.

Several states contract with PanAm Weather Services to provide computer-based weather information to pilots at home or at selected fixed-base operators.

The newest source of weather information for pilots is from vendors who transmit textual weather information and weather charts via facsimile (fax). This makes it possible for pilots to receive the information they need for planning right in their office or hotel room. The scope of information available and the cost varies widely. These services advertise in aviation magazines and newspapers.

Online Weather

Table 5-3 lists online sources of aviation weather. Computer users know that worldwide web addresses come and go without fanfare, so be warned. There is sufficient overlap and duplication to ensure that what you are looking for is available online. Use a search engine to look for weather-cams and road-cams along your route of flight; with luck, you may be able to see the weather en route and at your destination — but check the forecasts, because what you see is not necessarily what you will find when you arrive. Members of the Aircraft Owners and Pilots Association have access to an excellent series of weather pages on the web.

Icing

There is no question that structural icing should be the greatest concern of all instrument pilots. An encounter with ice can leave you with an overloaded airplane, requiring a greater angle of attack to lift the increased load (which in turn increases stall speed), and can erase any excess power you might need to climb out of the icing environment. The best rule is to learn how to identify potential icing situations and avoid them; if you do have an inadvertent encounter with an ice-bearing cloud, you should take immediate action to get out of it. A common mistake is to fly mile after mile into icing clouds in the hope that you will penetrate them and fly into the clear. When you finally realize you are in over your head, you must backtrack through those same icy clouds—not good.

In the section of this chapter on sources of weather information, you learned that the inflight hazards portion of an area forecast contains an icing section, that the radar summary chart shows the location of storm cells which imply the possibility of icing, that the constant pressure charts show you the measured temperature and dew point at various altitudes, and that the four-panel chart predicts instability, freezing level, relative humidity, and water content. None of these sources report droplet size, and the shape of an ice formation is a function of droplet size. Droplets big enough to splash on the windshield should be a warning of moderate to severe icing ahead.

The best source of information on icing, of course, is a PIREP from a pilot who has flown along your projected course at your proposed altitude; although you must accept the fact that ice may show up where none was reported and vice versa, and remember that a pilot report does not give you a free pass into an area where the NWS has forecast icing. Pods of icing conditions can move horizontally, coating one airplane with a sheet of ice and leaving the next one unaffected.

Unless your airplane is certificated for flight into known icing conditions (only a few non-transport category airplanes are), you must take seriously any

Main AWC page: http://aviationweather.noaa.gov

AWC weather products: aviationweather.noaa.gov/awc/Aviation_Weather_Center.html

GOES East: aviationweather.noaa.gov/awc/goes8e.html

GOES West: aviationweather.noaa.gov/awc/goes9w.html

Visfog Data: aviationweather.noaa.gov/awc/visfog.html

NCAR: www.rap.ucar.edu/weather/aviation.html

   "   www.rap.ucar.edu/index.html

NCAR Icing: www.rap.ucar.edu/largedrop/

Icing: aviationweather.noaa.gov/awc/nnice.html

   "   aviationweather.noaa.gov/awc/vvice.html

Mountain waves: aviationweather.noaa.gov/awc/mwave.html

Convective activity forecast: aviationweather.noaa.gov/awc/vvstorm.html

More:

http://adds.aviationweathercenter.noaa.gov   (Excellent flight planning tool.)

http://www.faa.gov/asos/asos.htm   (AWOS-ASOS website, with easy links to TAF/METAR info (by station).

http://iwin.nws.noaa.gov/iwin/iwdspg1.html   (NWS "Interactive Weather Information Network")

http://wxp.atms.purdue.edu/quick.html

http://www-frd.fsl.noaa.gov/mab/microburst/Welcome.html   (Microburst information article with weather photos, from FSL—the NOAA's Forecast Systems Laboratory.)

http://www.goes.noaa.gov/index.html   (GOES Satellite Server.)

http://maps.fsl.noaa.gov   (Rapid Update Cycle (RUC) forecasts from NCEP.)

http://www.intellicast.com/LocalWeather/World/UnitedStates/RadarSummary/

http://www.rap.ucar.edu/largedrop/integrated/index.html

http://www.rap.ucar.edu/largedrop/integrated/regional_new.html

http://nic.fb4.noaa.gov

http://www.avwx.com   ("Pacific Northwest Aviation Weather")

General weather forecast sites:

http://weather.unisys.com/aviation.index.html

http://www.wunderground.com

http://www.accuweather.com

(Note: The weather observing and forecasting agencies combine and overlap to some extent, and some of these URLs might change. Better too much information than not enough.)

Table 5-3. Weather URLs

forecast of conditions conducive to icing: moisture and a temperature below freezing. According to the findings of a National Transportation Safety Board administrative law judge, the term "known icing conditions" does not mean that a pilot has reported ice but that conditions conducive to ice formation have been forecast.

Online Sources of Icing Information

Computer users with access to the worldwide web can check out icing potential by using these *experimental* sites:

www.awc-kc.noaa.gov/awc/nnice.html
www.awc-kc.noaa.gov/awc/vvice.html
www.rap.ucar.edu/largedrop/integrated/index.html

The National Weather Service and universities with atmospheric research departments are working to improve the delivery of icing information to pilots, and these programs are constantly changing. Use them for background, but remember that the data you see is not official and that you must get the official word from a briefer.

Icing in Stratus Clouds

Stratiform clouds imply that any ice you encounter will be rime ice, the milky white, granular form of icing which adds little in weight but a lot in drag. The reason for the increased drag is that stratus clouds form when moist air is cooled slowly in a stable air mass; the water droplets are small and freeze instantaneously on impact, creating a rough, uneven surface. Icing is a possibility in stratus clouds when the outside air temperature is between +2°C and -10°C; there will be a temperature drop wherever airflow over a curved surface or discontinuity increases in speed. The greatest potential for ice accumulation exists in the top one-third of the cloud layer, and a climb or descent of a few thousand feet should get you out of the icing layer. Stratiform cloud systems and their associated icing potential can be horizontally extensive.

One of the joys of being instrument rated is the ability to fly on top of the clouds, and a major uncertainty associated with flight "on top" is deciding when to leave the clear air and sunshine and descend into the murk. If there is liquid water in the clouds below, and the temperature is below freezing, you will want to delay the descent as long as possible. On the other hand, if the clouds are comprised of ice crystals you should not be reluctant to sink into them. How can you tell?

Look at the photo at the beginning of the chapter. When you look toward the sun and see a bright spot, that spot is the sun's reflection from ice crystals; you can safely assume that a descent into the clouds will not turn your airplane into an ice sculpture. If there is no spot on the cloud tops on the side toward the sun, check the down-sun side. If you see a circular rainbow (called a "glory") surrounding your airplane's shadow, that rainbow is created by sunlight being refracted by liquid water. Stay out of it as long as you can, and plan to descend through the cloud layer quickly.

Icing in Cumulus Clouds

Cumuliform clouds are a sign of vertical development in unstable air, and water droplets caught in the updrafts can rise well above the freezing level and remain in liquid form. When these large water droplets strike your airplane, they form a clear, thick coating which adds weight. Clear ice is a possibility in cumulus clouds when the air temperature is between 0°C and 15°C, although it is possible to accumulate clear ice at much colder temperatures in clouds with extensive vertical development. *See* Figure 5-25.

Icing conditions within a single cumulus cloud may exist for several thousand feet vertically, but the horizontal extent is dictated by the size of the cloud itself. Because these lozenge-shaped areas of icing move as the clouds move, you may experience ice where a pilot collected none only a few minutes earlier, or you may fly ice free along an airway where other pilots have reported ice. Unless you are abso-

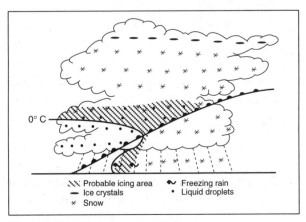

Figure 5-25. Icing in cumulus clouds

lutely sure that there is clear or warmer air a short distance above you, your escape route from clear icing must be horizontal or down.

A common error by general aviation pilots is penetrating the fluffy white top of a cumulus cloud while thinking that it will only be a few seconds until the airplane emerges into sunshine on the other side. This carries the potential of coating the whole airplane with ice and should be avoided.

As you scan the weather maps, charts, and forecasts for signs of icing conditions, be alert to instability and a source of lifting. A frontal surface where moist air is being pushed aloft is a sign of potential icing. These conditions will usually move with the front. When moist air is blowing across mountain tops, a pocket of icing conditions may exist on the upwind side, and it will stay essentially stationary; on the lee side, the air will warm and dry as it descends, affording a momentary haven before the next ridgeline's row of moisture-filled cumulus. *See* Figure 5-26.

Mixed ice, a combination of rime and clear, is the worst you can get from flight into clouds. It combines the rough, drag producing texture of the rime with the tenacious grip of clear ice to form unpredictable shapes on airplane surfaces. NASA wind tunnel experiments have shown that under certain conditions a "ram's horn" ice structure can form on the leading edge of a wing and create drag that cannot be overcome with full power.

Do not try to maintain altitude while accumulating structural ice. As the airplane gets heavier and the angle of attack is increased to overcome the loss of lift, ice will begin to form on the lower surface of the leading edge. Tell the controller that you are accumulating ice, it will make a difference in the way your flight is handled. If you have to, declare an emergency to get out of icing conditions. Do not attempt to maintain your assigned altitude when you are collecting ice and your airspeed is diminishing. (*See* Table 5-4, for an explanation of icing intensities.)

Ice Accretion

The rate of ice accumulation is affected by the size of the water droplets, the radius of the collecting surface, the amount of water in the air and the airspeed. Because small radius objects collect ice first, you should look at

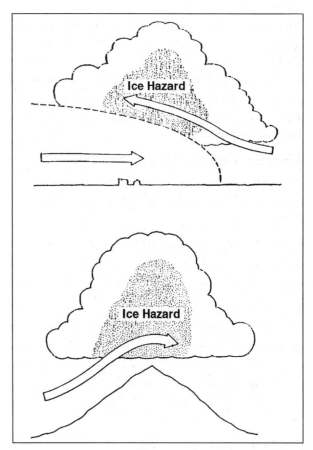

Figure 5-26. *Sources of lifting*

the outside air temperature probe, the leading edge of a wing strut, a protruding gas cap, or something similar when you are in potential icing conditions. You may even see the first traces in the corners of the windshield where the air must change direction rapidly and both pressure and temperature drop due to Bernoulli effect. Keep in mind that the horizontal stabilizer has a much smaller leading edge radius than the wing, so when you can see ice on the leading edge of the wing there may be three times as much on the leading edge of the horizontal stabilizer. *See* Figure 5-27 (on next page).

If the ice on the horizontal stabilizer disrupts the airflow sufficiently, that control surface may stall and put the airplane into an uncontrollable dive. Most icing accidents occur on short final for just that reason.

Freezing Rain

Freezing rain is the most hazardous type of icing condition that you can encounter, since the ice forms all over the airplane and not just on the leading edges. You do not have to be in clouds to be exposed to

Intensity	Airframe ice accumulation	Pilot report
Trace	Ice becomes perceptible. Rate of accumulation slightly greater than rate of sublimation. It is not hazardous even though deicing/anti-icing equipment is not used unless encountered for an extended period of time (over one hour).	Aircraft indentification, location, time UTC, intensity and type of icing*, altitude/FL, aircraft type, IAS
Light	The rate of accumulation may create a problem if flight is prolonged in this environment (over one hour). Occasional use of deicing/anti-icing equipment removes/prevents accumulation. It does not present a problem if the deicing/anti-icing equipment is used.	
Moderate	The rate of accumulation is such that even short encounters become potentially hazardous and use of deicing/anti-icing equipment or diversion is necessary.	
Severe	The rate of accumulation is such that deicing/anti-icing equipment fails to reduce or control the hazard. Immediate diversion is necessary.	

*Icing may be rime, clear and mixed.

Rime ice: Rough milky opaque ice formed by the instantaneous freezing of small supercooled water droplets.

Clear ice: A glossy, clear or translucent ice formed by the relatively slow freezing of large supercooled water droplets.

Mixed ice: A combination of rime and clear ice.

Table 5-4. *Icing intensities*

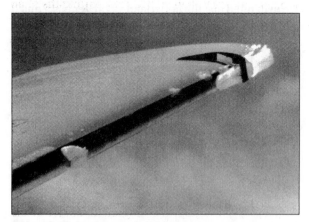

Figure 5-27. *Airplane surface icing*

freezing rain. If the rain is freezing at your altitude, it must exist in liquid form at some higher altitude, but don't let that lure you into climbing unless you have virtually unlimited power available. The weight of the ice will degrade the climb performance of your airplane, and ice on the propeller will reduce it to a useless club. Land as soon as practicable or head for known VFR conditions as fast as you can.

If there is anything good about freezing rain it is that the conditions conducive to freezing rain are readily forecast; you should never have a surprise meeting with freezing rain if you get a good weather briefing and stay in touch with changes in the weather by using TWEBs and Flight Watch.

Figure 5-28 shows the product of an experimental program at the Aviation Weather Center. Icing severity is indicated by increasing numbers within the contours. Download an example at aviation-weather.noaa.gov/awc/nnice.html.

Anti- and Deicing Systems

Anti-icing systems are designed to prevent ice from forming. Turbine-powered airplanes have heated engine inlets and leading edges for just that purpose. Some propeller airplanes have electrically heated boots on their propellers which are turned on before entering icing conditions to keep the props free from ice. If the boots are turned on after ice has accumulated, there will be momentary vibration as one blade sheds its ice before the other. The sound of ice striking the fuselage after being slung from the propeller does nothing for your peace of mind.

Some older airplanes have alcohol anti-icing systems that sling alcohol out along the propeller surface through centrifugal force. The pilot of such an airplane must realize that the supply of alcohol is limited and divert immediately.

Deicing systems get rid of ice after it has accumulated, and the most common form of deicing system is the carburetor heat control. If your airplane has the proper instrumentation, you can also use the carburetor heat as an anti-icing system.

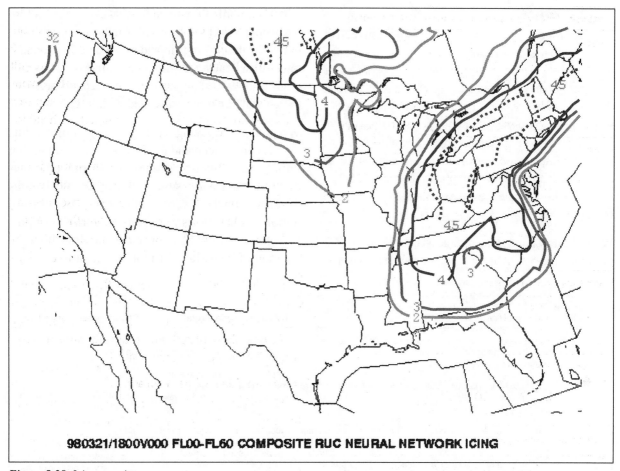

Figure 5-28. *Icing severity*

Inflatable boots on the leading edges of the wings are deicing systems that should be activated at the first sign of ice. Your manual may tell you to let some ice accumulate before activation—that is old information that has been proven false by Goodrich, the manufacturer of the boots.

A "weeping wing" may be in your future if you fly a Bonanza, Cessna 207, or the right model of Mooney. The TKS system, which forces a viscous fluid through millions of holes drilled in the leading edge of the wing and lets the airflow over the wing distribute it over the entire surface, has been approved for a limited number of models.

Many pilots say that the most effective weapon against ice is a turbocharger, asserting that the ability to get above the clouds quickly or to have climb power in reserve is better than boots.

Icing Certification

Airplanes certificated for flight into icing conditions have proven only that they can fly for 17.4 NM in a stratus layer or 3.8 NM in cumulus clouds, with droplets no larger than 40 microns (millionths of an inch) in diameter, and are able to get rid of the accreted ice. Flight continued beyond those distances or with larger droplet sizes is outside of the certification envelope—which makes you a test pilot because the manufacturer has no data on how the airplane will fly under such conditions.

Meteorologists now know that liquid droplets as large as 1,000 microns can be encountered above the freezing level, although conditions that severe are highly localized and difficult to predict. The pilot, of course, has no way of knowing the diameter of the droplets the airplane is encountering. Icing conditions are not repeatable—what you flew in last week might cause you to lose control tomorrow.

Turbulence

The significant weather prognostic and convective outlook charts are tools for avoiding turbulence forecast to exist in 12 or 24 hours, and the radar summary chart allows you to see where cells were at the time of observation. To afford your passengers a smooth ride, you want to avoid areas of convective activity; if the synopsis calls for an unstable air mass, surface temperatures are warm, and temperatures aloft are colder than standard, the chances of experiencing turbulence are excellent. *See* Table 5-5 for an explanation of turbulence reporting criteria.

When the dew point at the surface is reported to be 50°F or higher, the potential for severe turbulence exists.

Virga is a shaft of precipitation that evaporates before it reaches the surface; it is a visual indicator of a column of rapidly descending air, and you should fly around it rather than beneath it. Microbursts, those narrow columns of downrushing air that can force airliners into the ground, are often associated with virga.

When you are flying in the clear, cumulonimbus clouds can be seen and avoided—keep in mind that turbulence exists on all sides of a storm cell, however, and skirt a visible cell by 10 to 20 miles depending on the severity of the storm. At night, the lightning characteristic of thunderstorms will provide you with a light show and a warning about the location of cells. It is far more difficult to estimate

Turbulence Intensity	Aircraft reaction	Reaction inside aircraft	Reporting term definition
Light	Turbulence that momentarily causes slight, erratic changes in altitude and/or attitude (pitch, roll, yaw). Report as *Light Turbulence;** or Turbulence that causes slight, rapid and somewhat rhythmic bumpiness without appreciable changes in altitude or attitude. Report as *Light Chop.*	Occupants may feel a slight strain against belts or shoulder straps. Unsecured objects may be displaced slightly. Food service may be conducted and little or no difficulty is encountered in walking.	Occasional – less than 1/3 of the time. Intermittent – 1/3 to 2/3 of the time. Continuous – More than 2/3 of the time.
Moderate	Turbulence that is similar to Light Turbulence but of greater intensity. Changes in altitude and/or attitude occur but the aircraft remains in positive control at all times. It usually causes variations in indicated airspeed. Report as *Moderate Turbulence;** or Turbulence that is similar to Light Chop but of greater intensity. It causes rapid bumps or jolts without appreciable changes in aircraft altitude or attitude. Report as *Moderate Chop.*	Occupants feel definite strains against seat belts or shoulder straps. Unsecured objects are dislodged. Food service and walking are difficult.	Note: 1. Pilots should report location(s), time (UTC), intensity, whether in or near clouds, altitude, type of aircraft and, when applicable, duration of turbulence. 2. Duration may be based on time between two locations or over a single location. All locations should be readily identifiable.
Severe	Turbulence that causes large, abrupt changes in altitude and/or attitude. It usually causes large variations in indicated airspeed. Aircraft may be momentarily out of control. Report as *Severe Turbulence.**	Occupants are forced violently against seat belts or shoulder straps. Unsecured objects are tossed about. Food service and walking are impossible.	
Extreme	Turbulence in which the aircraft is violently tossed about and is practically impossible to control. It may cause structural damage. Report as *Extreme Turbulence.**		

* High level turbulence (normally above 15,000 feet AGL) that is not associated with cumuliform cloudiness, including thunderstorms, should be reported as CAT (clear air turbulence) preceded by the appropriate intensity, or light or moderate chop.

Table 5-5. Turbulence intensities and reporting criteria

your distance from a cell at night, however. Airborne radar or a weather mapping system are invaluable in avoiding storm-related turbulence. Never use radar exclusively as a means of picking your way through a line of storm cells—radar is a storm avoidance aid. What looks like a thin spot might be the worst part of a cell with its ferocity masked by attenuation of the radar signal. Interpretation of weather radar requires training. More on weather radar later.

When a storm cell reaches the mature stage, precipitation begins at the surface and the downdrafts increase in intensity. When these downdrafts strike the ground, a "gust front" is developed which may move across the ground at 40 to 80 mph and contain winds strong enough to damage aircraft on the ground. The gust front may exist as far as 15 miles from the storm cell's location and may contain winds up to 70 mph. It will be invisible except as dust and debris are kicked up by its passage. Exercise extreme caution when thunderstorm activity is reported near your area of operations. A useful numerical relationship is this: The strength of a downdraft is equal to windspeed ahead of the storm minus the speed at which the storm is moving over the surface. If the wind ahead of a thunderstorm is 25 knots and the storm front is moving over the ground at 15 knots, the downdraft is 10 knots or 1,000 feet per minute. Can you outclimb that downdraft at full power?

An air mass thunderstorm (one begun by surface heating) may rise vertically (Figure 5-29), and in an upright storm cloud the precipitation-induced downdrafts will ultimately overcome the updrafts and end the life of that storm cell. If the winds aloft cause the cumulonimbus cloud to tilt, however, the rain will fall downwind from the cell and the rising air currents that keep the storm alive will continue unabated. This is a steady-state thunderstorm. If the lifted index in the area is -2 or a larger negative number (refer to Figure 5-16), treat any thunderstorm as a steady-state storm, and give it a wider berth when navigating to avoid it.

Figure 5-29. *Air mass thunderstorm*

Intense, localized downdrafts known as microbursts may be strong enough to force an airplane to the ground and have been responsible for many accidents. Any storm cell contains the ingredients for wind shear, which is defined as a change in wind direction or velocity, either vertical or horizontal, anywhere in the atmosphere. Although light airplanes have less inertia than transport category airplanes and can react more quickly to change, you should be alert for any sudden change in airspeed which might signal a shear zone when taking off or landing.

Another signpost of turbulence is the standing lenticular cloud which develops downwind from a mountain or ridgeline when winds exceed 50 knots. These clouds form when there is sufficient moisture available above the condensation level, but there is invisible turbulence below and downwind from these clouds which you should be aware of and avoid. In Figure 5-30, standing lenticulars can be seen above altocumulus clouds.

Figure 5-30. *Standing lenticular*

When you encounter turbulence—and this advice is equally applicable to an inadvertent brush with the outskirts of a thunderstorm—maintain attitude, do not chase altitude, adjust the power settings to those which will maintain maneuvering speed in level flight and don't chase the airspeed (the airspeed indicator will lie to you in turbulence anyway). If you are flying a retractable, extending the gear will improve stability.

Fog

At the beginning of this chapter, I said that as an instrument pilot the mere existence of clouds will no longer concern you, and that is true—unless the clouds are stratus clouds based at the surface. If fog is going to blanket your destination airport at your ETA, it is hardly worthwhile taking off in the first place.

Ground fog (or radiation fog) can ruin a perfectly beautiful night IFR flight. It forms over land on clear, calm nights when the land radiates its heat into the air and the warm, moist air condenses over the cooled surface, forming a low-level temperature inversion. Ground fog can be so shallow that you will be able to see the runway environment clearly as you approach the airport (Figure 5-31), and yet the surface visibility will be reported in fractions of a mile. On the ground, an observer (or the runway visual range transmissometer) looks horizontally at a fog layer that might only be 20 feet thick vertically and sees only a few hundred feet. Your planning clues are high pressure, a terminal forecast with no wind or cloud cover predicted, and a source of moisture such as a lake, a river, or even a recent rainfall.

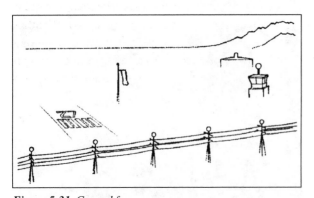

Figure 5-31. *Ground fog*

Advection fog is largely a coastal phenomenon, caused by a moist air mass moving over colder land or water, but it can extend deep into the land area when southerly winds blow moist air over a cold continental surface. This type of fog is called sea fog or steam fog when it is the result of warm moist air blowing from the land to the sea. An advection fog layer may be deepened and intensified by wind, up to about 15 knots. Winds above 15 knots lift the layer into a low ceiling. Your planning clues are wind blowing from a source of moisture and a relatively cool surface temperature with a small temperature/dewpoint spread. *See* Figure 5-32.

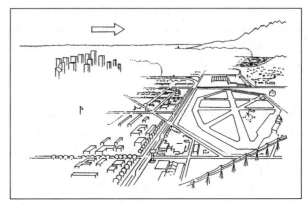

Figure 5-32. *Advection fog*

Upslope fog develops when moist, stable air is cooled as it moves up sloping terrain, and is common on the eastern slopes of the Rocky Mountains. Depending on the depth of the stable air mass, upslope fog may extend several thousand feet in altitude. If your destination airport is on the windward side of a mountain range or ridgeline, your planning clues are a wind blowing toward the airport from a lower elevation, a moist stable air mass reported in the synopsis to the area forecast, and a low temperature/dewpoint spread.

Precipitation-induced fog can bring a disappointing end to a miserable instrument flight. You have been fighting ice and turbulence all the way, keeping abreast of the weather at the destination, only to learn that precipitation-induced fog has reduced the visibility below landing minimums when you arrive.

Precipitation-induced fog develops when warm rain or drizzle fall into cooler air and evaporate, saturating the cool air. It is associated with warm fronts (warm air over cold) but can occur with a stationary front. Planning should include checking the surface map to locate and identify fronts, looking at sequences at several airports between your destination and the frontal surface for a temperature/dewpoint trend, and monitoring the destination's temperature/dewpoint en route.

Weather Detection

The best way to avoid hazardous weather is to detect its presence visually, and that may be possible when you are flying on top of the clouds in the daytime. At night, or when you are enveloped in clouds, you might encounter weather conditions which will make your flight uncomfortable at best and downright hazardous at worst.

Weather radar or weather mapping systems that react to and display electrical discharges have strengths and weaknesses, and those pilots who can do so often have both on board. Panel space, electrical power limitations, or structural considerations may dictate which system is chosen if only one can be accommodated. *See* Figure 5-33.

Weather radar beams energy ahead of the airplane and displays any reflected signals on a cathode ray tube in the instrument panel.

Radar signals bounce off of wet precipitation; clouds, ice, and snow will not show up on radar unless they are accompanied by considerable moisture. The level of precipitation (which implies severity) can be shown by shading on monochrome screens and by different colors on a color radar. Where the precipitation is especially severe, either type of CRT uses a display called "contouring" as a warning. Radar cannot detect turbulence, although you can safely assume that an area of heavy precipitation will be turbulent.

Radar's strong point is its ability to display the range and azimuth of precipitation with some degree of accuracy. This allows you to detect a suspicious area while some distance away and to divert around it.

Figure 5-33. *Airborne weather radar*

Radar's weak point is signal attenuation. Only a very small portion of the transmitted signal is reflected because the precipitation weakens or attenuates it, and this can have misleading effects. If there is a lot of water falling out of the sky the radar signal may be severely attenuated, and the CRT display will show only a small return, just the reverse of reality. Also, a large, ugly storm may be hiding behind the one on the radar screen but you don't see it because the radar signal doesn't get past the nearer downpour. Weather radar is to be used as a weather avoidance tool, not a weather penetration tool, because its indications can be misleading. Fly around, not between, the blips on the radar screen.

The mere existence of a weather radar display on an instrument panel is not the solution to all weather problems. It is easy for a pilot to misinterpret what the radar is indicating and to fly into destructive weather when it looks as if it is clear sailing ahead. There are several sources of radar training; contact the Aircraft Owners and Pilots Association or National Business Aircraft Association for information.

Weather mapping systems such as the 3M StormScope or Insight's StrikeFinder display electrical discharges caused by vertical air currents. This would, of course, include the cloud-to-cloud or cloud-to-ground lightning strokes associated with a thunderstorm. When masses of air brush past one another, differences in electrical potential are developed which culminate in electrical discharges.

These systems display such discharges on a CRT in the panel, in different ways and with different degrees of sophistication depending on cost. Each system has its strengths and weaknesses. Azimuth information is correct, but the strength of the discharge may cause misleading range information: a weak, nearby discharge may be displayed at the same range as a strong, distant stroke. It does show in which direction the activity is taking place, day or night, and you should divert around a cluster of discharges just as you would around a heavy radar return.

Weather mapping systems let you look at a horizon full of dark, threatening-looking clouds and be sure that they contain no convective activity. Just as was the case with weather radar, proper use of weather mapping systems requires training.

Wind Shear and Turbulence for the Commercial Pilot

Passengers like a smooth ride, but you can't always guarantee one. You can, however, warn your passengers that portions of the flight will be uncomfortable due to turbulence, and you can fly the airplane to minimize that discomfort.

Area forecasts always say that the term "thunderstorm" implies icing, turbulence, and low level wind shear. Now that people are going to give you money to take them places, you may be tempted to treat warnings of thunderstorms more casually than you

did as a private pilot, thinking that if you deliver your passengers to their destination in spite of the TRW they will applaud your airmanship. Quite the contrary. Between dives into the airsickness bag, they will be mentally composing letters to their representatives in Congress and your boss, questioning how you could have let them in for such a rough ride without warning. Let me suggest that you approach each situation with this in mind: "How will this decision look during the investigation?"

You can expect turbulence when penetrating a temperature inversion, either departing or when approaching to land, and you should be alert to airspeed changes when passing through the inversion zone. You should be able to learn about potential inversions from area forecasts (FA) as well as from winds and temperatures aloft forecasts (FD).

Virga is another sign of possible turbulence. When you see a shaft of rain falling from a cloud and evaporating after falling a few thousand feet, you can be sure that there is still a column of descending air for you to detour around if you are going to miss the elevator ride. Virga is an excellent indicator for a dry microburst.

Although the term "wind shear" applies to a change in wind speed and direction that can occur at any altitude, the written test questions concentrate on the hazardous shears associated with strong inversions and thunderstorms and how you should react to them.

As far as you are concerned, it doesn't matter if a wind shear results in a shift from a headwind to a tailwind, a decreased headwind component, or from a headwind to no wind at all—in either case you would experience a loss of airspeed equal to the decrease in wind velocity over the control surfaces. The airplane will pitch down to regain its trim speed and you must respond with takeoff power (maximum available power, if close to the ground), and pitch up to an attitude close to that you would use for minimum controllable airspeed. If you get a stall warning, that's just fine—hold that attitude. Until the microburst phenomenon (severe downdraft) was understood, airplanes were lost because pilots were conditioned by training to reduce the angle of attack when a stall warning was received.

Note that this decreasing headwind component situation will occur only if you have ignored readily available weather information or the evidence of your own eyes. A likely scenario is taking off to beat a thunderstorm approaching the airport from a direction opposite to the takeoff path; when it reaches your position, the gust front that precedes the storm will create a strong tailwind and may reduce the headwind component below that necessary to sustain flight. But you knew the storm was coming, didn't you? Remember, it's better to be on the ground wishing you were in the air than the other way around.

If the storm is chasing you toward the airport, you might experience that loss of lift while on the approach, when altitude to recover is in short supply. If you monitor the power and airspeed necessary to stay on an appropriate descent path and find that more power and a greater pitch attitude is required, go somewhere else until the storm has passed. Another clue is available by comparing indicated airspeed and groundspeed information provided by DME, RNAV, LORAN, or GPS. If the groundspeed readout is greater than the indicated airspeed, you should think about aborting.

The opposite situation, encountering an increasing headwind component, is less hazardous unless you are on short final. The airplane will pitch up and the airspeed will momentarily increase. Your normal reaction will be to push the nose over and reduce power, but if that gust of wind is brief you may find the whole windshield full of unyielding terrain. Any power reduction should be small—keep your hand on the throttle.

A more benign situation is a calm-wind takeoff when the wind at 2,000 feet or so above the ground is strong—a typical temperature inversion situation. As you pass through the inversion level you will experience either a gain or a loss of airspeed, depending on whether you are climbing into the wind or against it, and the airplane will react just as it does close to the ground. With plenty of altitude for recovery, this should be more of an annoyance than a hazard.

Microbursts

Intense, localized downdrafts known as microbursts may be strong enough to force an airplane to the ground and have been responsible for many accidents. Vertical downdrafts can be as strong as 6,000 feet per minute, far in excess of the climb rate of most aircraft, and an individual microburst can last as long as 15 minutes. A 45-knot headwind can shear to a 45-knot tailwind (90 knots total) in less than two miles.

A microburst has been compared to a firehose shooting water downward onto a flat surface; like the water from the firehose, the downrushing air from the microburst moves outward in all directions, creating gust fronts with accompanying wind shear. Procedures to be followed when flying in or near a severe downdraft are discussed in Chapter 10.

Estimating Cloud Bases

Flying a single-engine airplane under Part 135 carries some restrictions, the most onerous being that you must be able to descend under VFR in case of engine failure. If the air mass is even a little unstable, that means flying either beneath the clouds, where the air is bumpy because of rising air currents, or above a scattered cloud layer. To choose a comfortable cruise altitude, then, you should be able to estimate the height of cumulus cloud bases. The temperature lapse rate is approximately 2.5°C per thousand feet, and if you know the temperature and dew point at field elevation you can come up with a fair estimate of the bases. For example, if the hourly sequence report says that the temperature is 10° and the dew point is 1°, the spread is 9°. Dividing 9 by 2.5 gives you 3.6 (thousand) feet above field elevation, so if the field is 2,000 feet above sea level the cloud bases are approximately 5,600 feet above sea level.

Summary of Weather Reports and Forecasts

The worst mistake a newly fledged commercial/instrument pilot can make is to assume that the rating makes it possible to fly in any kind of weather. Very few light airplanes can challenge the weather gods with impunity. It is better to disappoint family, friends, and business associates by canceling a trip than to subject them to the hazards of icing and turbulence just because you have been given a piece of paper that makes it legal to do so.

Part 135's strict equipment requirements on IFR flight for single-engine airplanes will make you a keener student of weather reports and forecasts. You won't be able to file to an airport that doesn't have an approved source of weather information, and (unless the FAA issues operations specifications which allow it) you won't be able to operate under IFR in uncontrolled airspace.

At an on-demand charter operation, passengers can ask to be taken to places where you simply can't go, and they won't be happy when you tell them so. Don't let yourself be pressured into doing anything you don't want to do—it is your pilot certificate and livelihood that is on the line.

A Review of Weather Basics

Did you take your private pilot knowledge test some time ago? Do you remember only enough to stay VFR? Let's go back and review the basics.

In The Beginning...

The uneven heating of the earth's surface by the sun drives all weather systems; land absorbs more heat than water, deserts get hotter than forests, parking lots get hotter than golf courses—not a difficult concept to understand. For all practical purposes, weather that affects us as pilots exists in the troposphere, which varies in height but averages 25,000 feet above sea level in the mid-latitudes where we live. Separating the troposphere from the stratosphere is the thin layer of the tropopause, where the gradual decrease in temperature with altitude (lapse rate) stabilizes. Above the tropopause the temperature is relatively stable.

The rotation of the earth causes the general wind direction in the latitudes of North America to be westerly (*see* Figure 5-34), and these westerlies are strongest near the tropopause—these are the jet streams that you see on television weather maps. To be classified as a jet stream, wind velocity must be 50 knots or greater. Like a tourist, the jet stream moves north in the summer and south in the winter, gaining strength during its winter visit to the southland.

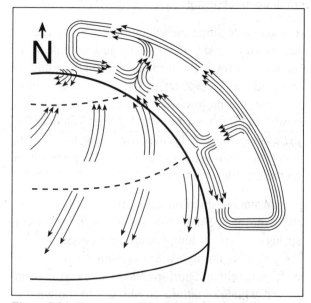

Figure 5-34. The rotation of the Earth causes cell-like circulation patterns and influences prevailing winds.

Fronts

Weather systems generally move from west to east, steered by the westerly winds aloft. The basic building block of a weather system is the air mass, which takes on the characteristics of the surface over which it is moving. For example, an air mass over water might be cool and moist until it moves over land and becomes warm and dry through evaporation. A "front" is where air masses with different characteristics meet; a *cold front* (Figure 5-35) exists where cooler air moves in to displace warmer air (because the cooler air is heavier), and a *warm front* (Figure 5-36) exists where a moving mass of warm air slides up the back of a cooler air mass because the warmer air isn't heavy enough to shoulder the cool air out of the way. By the way, temperatures are relative—when an air mass with a surface temperature of 10°C overtakes an air mass with a surface temperature of -20°C, that is a warm front—even if it is not bathing suit weather.

Figure 5-35. *Cross-section of a typical cold front*

Figure 5-36. *Cross-section of a typical warm front*

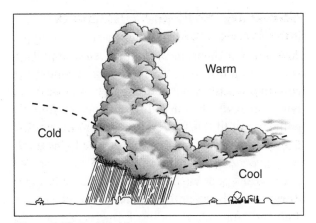

Figure 5-37. *Occluded fronts*

As you might expect, a *stationary front* is one that isn't going anywhere, so any associated bad weather will be around for awhile. An *occluded front* (Figure 5-37) occurs when an encroaching air mass lifts an air mass with different characteristics clear of the surface—a cold air mass overtaking a cool air mass might lift warm air, for example. There are both warm and cold occlusions, depending on relative temperatures, but you can count on fairly miserable weather in any case.

Your outside air temperature gauge will tell you when you have crossed a frontal boundary, but an even better clue is a heading change—you will always change heading to the right when crossing a frontal boundary because the wind changes direction abruptly.

Stability

The standard temperature at sea level is 15°C, and the standard rate of decrease is 2° per 1,000 feet of altitude increase. Knowing that makes it possible for you to make an informed guess as to the stability of the atmosphere. For example, if the winds and temperatures aloft forecast expects the temperature at 9,000 feet to be -10°C, is that warmer or colder than standard, and what does that mean? Using the standard lapse rate of 2° per 1,000, the temperature should decrease 18° from the standard sea level value of 15°C to a value of -3° at 9,000 feet—but the weather folks expect it to be -10°, or 7° colder. A basic rule for pilots is that cold air over warm air is bad news, so you can expect some cloud buildups if there is sufficient moisture in the air (and if the forecast is accurate). This is an unstable air mass: convective clouds, showers, a bumpy ride, and good visibility.

If an air mass is colder at the surface than at altitude, it would just sit there, making it a stable air mass. Automobile exhaust, heat from industrial activities, and warm air from other sources will rise through the cold air until its temperature equals that of the overlying warm air; then it will stop rising and trap the pollutants at the surface. When the air temperature does not decrease with altitude it is called a *temperature inversion*, the father of smog. So a stable air mass means poor visibility, stratus clouds (because warm air will rise until its temperature equals the ambient temperature and no further), drizzle, and smooth flying conditions.

The cold air does not have to move into an area to create a temperature inversion; on a clear, calm night the earth radiates its heat into the atmosphere, leaving behind a cool surface with warmer temperatures above. When we discussed ground fog earlier in this chapter you saw this effect.

Highs and Lows

When the sun heats an air mass, it rises—and cooler air rushes in to replace it. Air, like water, runs downhill, so a region of rising air is a low-pressure center. Conversely, as an air mass cools it descends, creating downward (high) pressure. The earth's rotation, in combination with Coriolis effect, causes the air rushing toward a low-pressure area to circulate counter-clockwise, and the air rushing outward from a high-pressure area to rotate clockwise (*see* Figures 5-38 and 5-39). Remember those two facts and add in a little water vapor and you can become your own forecaster.

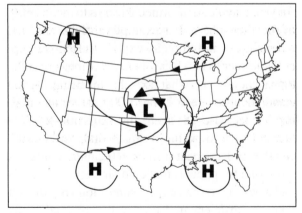

Figure 5-38. *Circulation around pressure centers*

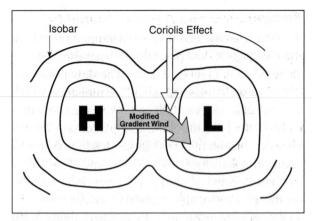

Figure 5-39. *Coriolis effect*

The moisture contained in that rising hot air is going to condense and become clouds, and when there is enough moisture up there that moisture is going to fall on your head. Whether it is drizzle, sleet, hail, or snow depends on surface temperature. If you are flying along in cold air and note that your airplane is turning into an ice sculpture, you know that there is warmer air above, where that water is still in liquid form. Wet snow is the other side of the coin—temperatures are colder above you and precip in solid form is beginning to melt at your altitude.

Wind

Knowing that the wind direction at the tropopause is generally westerly doesn't explain why the wind at Hometown Municipal is usually out of the south. Below 2,000 feet above the surface, wind direction is greatly affected by local terrain, while above that altitude the wind generally parallels the isobars (lines of equal barometric pressure). Wind speed also increases with altitude as the effect of terrain diminishes.

These local effects make it hard to know what the wind will be at a nontower airport by reading the weather forecasts. It might not hurt to call ahead and get a weather report from someone at your destination.

Temperature and Relative Humidity

You don't need a lecture on what temperature is, but the meaning of dew point might have escaped you since you last cracked a book. The dew point of a parcel of air is reached when the moisture within that parcel is 100% saturated; relative humidity tells us how close to saturation that parcel is. There is always moisture in the air. Prove this to yourself by taking a cold soft drink out of a cooler on a hot summer day and watching the water droplets form on the outside of the container. Where does the water come from? It sure doesn't leak through the side of the can or bottle.

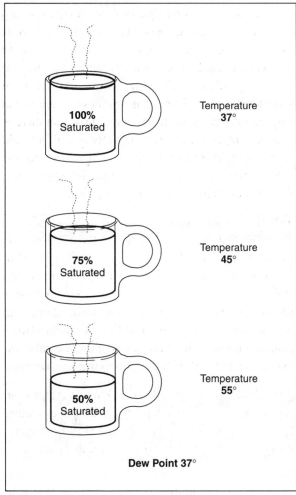

Figure 5-40. Temperature vs. saturation

Dew point is always lower than temperature—when they are equal, the relative humidity is 100 percent. When the "spread" between temperature and dew point is less than 5°, investigate further—if the air is being cooled (sun is setting, for example), or if moisture is being added to the air mass (wind blowing over a body of water, for example), there is an excellent chance that something—fog, rain, drizzle, smog—is going to complicate your life. On the other hand, an increasing spread means improving visibility. Never fly toward an area where the temperature-dewpoint spread is decreasing or is less than 3° (5° is a caution flag, 3° is a red flag).

Clouds

You can tell a lot about the weather by just looking at the clouds. A cloud forms when the temperature of rising air equals its dew point. Clouds come in families—low, middle, high, and "extensive vertical development." Stratus clouds are flat, like pancakes, and cover large areas; cumulus clouds are puffy, isolated, and indicate columns of rising air. The high clouds are composed of ice crystals and present no hazard to pilots. Cumulonimbus clouds, or "CBs," tower thousands of feet into the air and must be avoided at all cost—the word "nimbus" means raincloud, with the potential of becoming a thunderstorm.

Isolated puffy clouds are called fair weather cumulus, and you will find smoother flying conditions above them than below them—each cloud marks the top of a column of rising air.

In mountainous areas, lens-shaped clouds called "standing lenticulars" can be observed downwind of peaks when the wind exceeds 40 knots and the air is stable. They are called "standing" because they appear to be stationary, but in fact what you see is the top of a wave, with air flowing in, being carried upward to the condensation level, and then descending. They are indicators of extreme turbulence. Unseen below them and further downwind, "roll clouds" can tear an airplane to pieces in seconds.

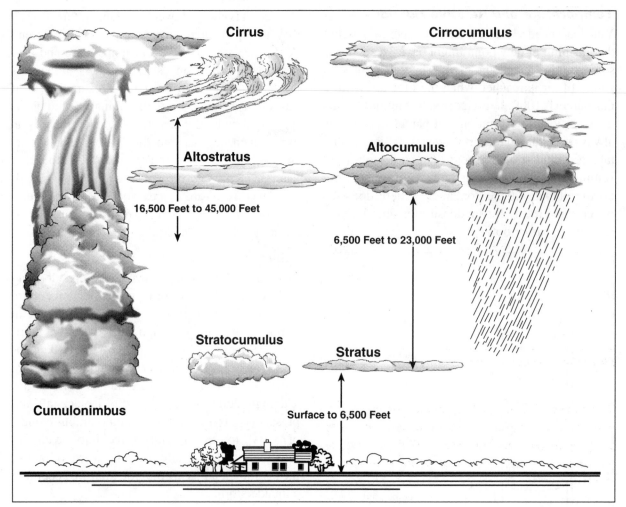

Figure 5-41. *Typical cloud formations*

Thunderstorms

Strange as it might seem, an official weather observer must see lightning before the word "thunderstorm" can be used in a weather report. That's because lightning is always associated with a thunderstorm—up to that point it is just a severe storm with gusty winds, turbulence, icing, and hail.

The recipe for a thunderstorm includes just three ingredients: air that is moist, air that is unstable, and a source of lifting. Consider an asphalt parking lot in Kansas being heated by the sun with an unstable air mass over the state. The column of heated air rises faster and faster because it is encountering colder-than-standard air as it rises (cold over warm, remember?). The updraft gathers strength as cooler air rushes toward it. When the rising air reaches its condensation level it releases heat (the latent heat of condensation, for you physicists), forms a cumulus cloud, and rises even faster. Soon there is so much moisture at the top of the cloud that it begins to fall back through the rising air as rain—the friction between the rising and descending air creates an electrical charge and lightning strikes begin. Rain at the surface marks the mature stage of the storm; soon the downdrafts overcome the updrafts and the thunderstorm dies. But what if the cloud is made to lean downwind by winds aloft? The rain will fall outside of the rising air—this is a steady-state thunderstorm.

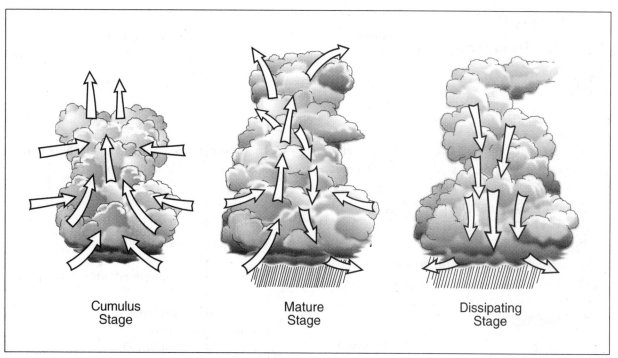

Figure 5-42. Life cycle of a thunderstorm

When the words "unstable air mass" are included in your weather briefing, look for sources of lifting along your route. Rising terrain will do the trick as the air mass hits the slopes and is forced upward. A frontal boundary is also a good source of lifting—a fast moving cold front can spawn squall lines and tornadoes.

Paradoxically, when you are experiencing a smooth flight with increasing ground speed, you may be caught in air that is moving toward the center of a strong thunderstorm, and you won't be congratulating yourself on the smooth, fast flight when you get closer. Watch for ground station reports of dew points warmer than 50°F...they are a sure indicator of strong convection.

A thunderstorm that has risen through a heavy stratus layer will be invisible to a pilot flying in that layer without weather detection equipment on board—that is an "embedded" thunderstorm, and if you encounter one there are a few basic rules to follow: cinch down your seat belt, turn up the cockpit lighting, turn off the autopilot, maintain attitude with the wings level and don't chase either airspeed or altitude. Don't try to turn around—the shortest way out is straight ahead. And don't worry about calling ATC because you probably won't be able to grab the mike or push the push-to-talk button. Just ride it out.

That should bring you up to speed on weather basics—now in the following review, let's put that knowledge to practice along with the previous study of aviation weather reports and forecasts.

Chapter 5
Weather Review Questions

There's no such thing as "instrument pilot" weather as opposed to "commercial pilot" weather, except that a VFR-only commercial pilot isn't going to fly very much. These questions are taken from the respective exams, but you should be able to answer all of them.

Instrument Student Questions

1. If the air temperature is +8 °C at an elevation of 1,350 feet and a standard (average) temperature lapse rate exists, what will be the approximate freezing level?

    A—3,350 feet MSL
    B—5,350 feet MSL
    C—9,350 feet MSL

2. Which is true regarding the use of airborne weather-avoidance radar for the recognition of certain weather conditions?

    A—The radarscope provides no assurance of avoiding instrument weather conditions.
    B—The avoidance of hail is assured when flying between and just clear of the most intense echoes.
    C—The clear area between intense echoes indicates that visual sighting of storms can be maintained when flying between the echoes.

3. What determines the structure or type of clouds which form as a result of air being forced to ascend?

    A—The method by which the air is lifted.
    B—The stability of the air before lifting occurs.
    C—The amount of condensation nuclei present after lifting occurs.

4. The presence of standing lenticular altocumulus clouds is a good indication of

    A—a jetstream.
    B—very strong turbulence.
    C—heavy icing conditions.

5. Where do squall lines most often develop?

    A—In an occluded front.
    B—In a cold air mass.
    C—Ahead of a cold front.

6. What is an operational consideration if you fly into rain which freezes on impact?

    A—You have flown into an area of thunderstorms.
    B—Temperatures are above freezing at some higher altitude.
    C—You have flown through a cold front.

7. Which conditions are favorable for the formation of radiation fog?

    A—Moist air moving over colder ground or water.
    B—Cloudy sky and a light wind moving saturated warm air over a cool surface.
    C—Clear sky, little or no wind, small temperature/dewpoint spread, and over a land surface.

8. (Refer to Figure Q5-1.) The aircraft in position 3 will experience which effect in a microburst encounter?

   A—Decreasing headwind
   B—Increasing tailwind
   C—Strong downdraft

9. The reporting station originating this Aviation Routine Weather Report has a field elevation of 620 feet. If the reported sky cover is one continuous layer, what is its thickness? (Tops of OVC are reported at 6,500 feet.)

   METAR KMDW 121856Z AUTO 32005KT 1 1/2SM +RABR OVC007 17/16 A2980

   A—5,180 feet
   B—5,800 feet
   C—5,880 feet

10. Area forecasts generally include a forecast period of 18 hours and cover a geographical

    A—terminal area.
    B—area less than 3,000 square miles.
    C—area the size of several states.

11. (Refer to Figure Q5-2.) The Weather Depiction Chart in the area of northwestern Wyoming, indicates

    A—overcast with scattered rain showers.
    B—1,000-foot ceilings and visibility 3 miles or more.
    C—500-foot ceilings and continuous rain, less than 3 miles visibility.

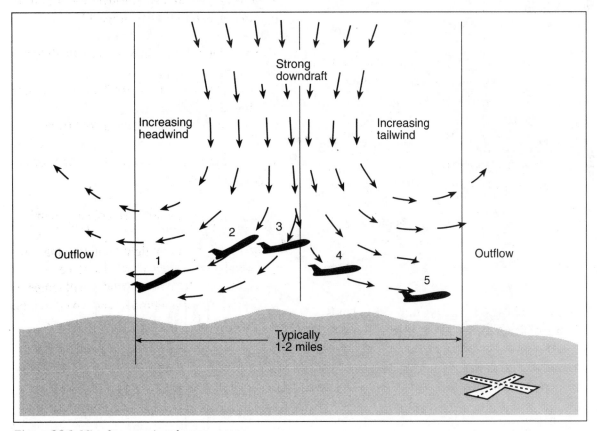

Figure Q5-1. Microburst section chart

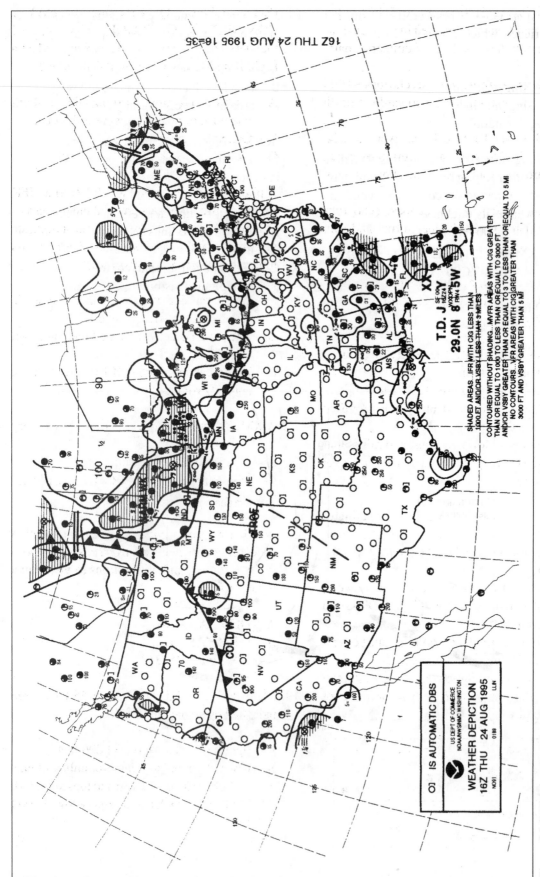

Figure Q5-2. Weather depiction chart

12. (Refer to Figure 5-10 on Page 5-15.) What weather conditions are depicted in the area indicated by arrow A on the Radar Summary Chart?

A—Moderate to strong echoes; echo tops 30,000 feet MSL; line movement toward the north west.

B—Weak to moderate echoes; average echo bases 30,000 feet MSL; cell movement toward the southeast; rain showers with thunder.

C—Strong to very strong echoes; echo tops 30,000 feet MSL; thunderstorms and rain showers.

13. What conclusion(s) can be drawn from a 500-millibar Constant Pressure Chart for a planned flight at FL180?

A—Winds aloft at FL180 generally flow across the height contours.

B—Observed temperature, wind, and temperature/dewpoint spread along the proposed route can be approximated.

C—Upper highs, lows, troughs, and ridges will be depicted by the use of lines of equal pressure.

14. (Refer to Figure Q5-3.) What is the meaning of the symbol depicted as used on the U.S. Low-Level Significant Weather Prognostic Chart?

A—Showery precipitation (e.g. rain showers) embedded in an area of continuous rain covering half or more of the area.

B—Continuous precipitation (e.g. rain) covering half or more of the area.

C—Showery precipitation (e.g. thunderstorms/rain showers) covering half or more of the area.

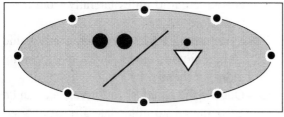

Figure Q5-3

15. (Refer to Figure Q5-4.) Using the DAY 2 CONVECTIVE OUTLOOK, what type of thunderstorms, if any, may be encountered on a flight from Montana to central California?

A—Moderate risk area, surrounded by a slight risk area, of possible severe turbulence.

B—General.

C—None.

16. A pilot planning to depart at 1100Z on an IFR flight is particularly concerned about the hazard of icing. What sources reflect the most accurate information on icing conditions (current and forecast) at the time of departure?

A—Low-Level Significant Weather Prognostic Chart, and the Area Forecast.

B—The Area Forecast, and the Freezing Level Chart.

C—Pilot weather reports (PIREPs), AIRMETs, and SIGMETs.

17. AIRMETs are issued on a scheduled basis every

A—15 minutes after the hour only.

B—15 minutes until the AIRMET is canceled.

C—six hours.

18. Which forecast provides specific information concerning expected sky cover, cloud tops, visibility, weather, and obstructions to vision in a route format?

A—DFW FA 131240

B—MEM TAF 132222

C—249 TWEB 252317

19. (Refer to Figure Q5-5 on Page 5-56.) The area indicated by arrow H indicates

A—light turbulence below 34,000 feet.

B—isolated embedded cumulonimbus clouds with bases below FL180 and tops at FL340.

C—moderate turbulence at and below 34,000 feet.

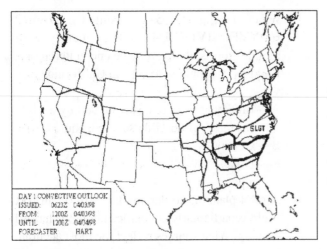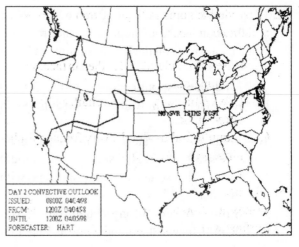

Figure Q5-4. Convective outlook charts

Commercial Student Questions

20. Which is true with respect to a high- or low-pressure system?

    A—A high-pressure area or ridge is an area of rising air.
    B—A low-pressure area or trough is an area of descending air.
    C—A high-pressure area or ridge is an area of descending air.

21. During the winter months in the middle latitudes, the jet stream shifts toward the

    A—north and speed decreases.
    B—south and speed increases.
    C—north and speed increases.

22. Moisture is added to a parcel of air by

    A—sublimation and condensation.
    B—evaporation and condensation.
    C—evaporation and sublimation.

23. Which would decrease the stability of an air mass?

    A—Warming from below.
    B—Cooling from below.
    C—Decrease in water vapor.

24. What is the approximate base of the cumulus clouds if the temperature at 2,000 feet MSL is 10°C and the dewpoint is 1°C?

    A—3,000 feet MSL
    B—4,000 feet MSL
    C—6,000 feet MSL

25. The conditions most favorable to wave formation over mountainous areas are a layer of

    A—stable air at mountaintop altitude and a wind of at least 20 knots blowing across the ridge.
    B—unstable air at mountaintop altitude and a wind of at least 20 knots blowing across the ridge.
    C—moist, unstable air at mountaintop altitude and a wind of less than 5 knots blowing across the ridge.

26. Of the following, which is accurate regarding turbulence associated with thunderstorms?

    A—Outside the cloud, shear turbulence can be encountered 50 miles laterally from a severe storm.
    B—Shear turbulence is encountered only inside cumulonimbus clouds or within a 5-mile radius of them.
    C—Outside the cloud, shear turbulence can be encountered 20 miles laterally from a severe storm.

27. What visible signs indicate extreme turbulence in thunderstorms?

   A—Base of the clouds near the surface, heavy rain, and hail.
   B—Low ceiling and visibility, hail, and precipitation static.
   C—Cumulonimbus clouds, very frequent lightning, and roll clouds.

28. GIVEN:

   Winds at 3,000 feet AGL .... 30 kts
   Surface winds .... Calm

   While approaching for landing under clear skies a few hours after sunrise, one should

   A—increase approach airspeed slightly above normal to avoid stalling.
   B—keep the approach airspeed at or slightly below normal to compensate for floating.
   C—not alter the approach airspeed, these conditions are nearly ideal.

29. Which in-flight hazard is most commonly associated with warm fronts?

   A—Advection fog
   B—Radiation fog
   C—Precipitation-induced fog

30. The remarks section of the Aviation Routine Weather Report (METAR) contains the following coded information. What does it mean?

   RMK FZDZB42 WSHFT 30 FROPA

   A—Freezing drizzle with cloud bases below 4,200 feet.
   B—Freezing drizzle below 4,200 feet and wind shear.
   C—Wind shift at three zero due to frontal passage.

31. When total sky cover is few or scattered, the height shown on the Weather Depiction Chart is the

   A—top of the lowest layer.
   B—base of the lowest layer.
   C—base of the highest layer.

32. Which is true concerning the radar weather report (SD) for KOKC?

   KOKC 1934 LN 8TRW++/+ 86/40 164/60
   199/115 15W L2425 MT 570 AT 159/65
   2 INCH HAIL RPRTD THIS CELL

   A—There are three cells with tops at 11,500, 40,000, and 60,000 feet.
   B—The line of cells is moving 060° with winds reported up to 40 knots.
   C—The maximum tops of the cells is 57,000 feet located 65 NM southeast of the station.

33. A freezing level panel of the composite moisture stability chart is an analysis of

   A—forecast freezing level data from surface observations.
   B—forecast freezing level data from upper air observations.
   C—observed freezing level data from upper air observations.

34. The minimum vertical wind shear value critical for probable moderate or greater turbulence is

   A—4 knots per 1,000 feet.
   B—6 knots per 1,000 feet.
   C—8 knots per 1,000 feet.

35. From which of the following can the observed temperature, wind, and temperature/ dew point spread be determined at a specified altitude?

   A—Stability Charts
   B—Winds Aloft Forecasts
   C—Constant Pressure Analysis Charts

36. Which weather chart depicts conditions forecast to exist at a specific time in the future?

   A—Freezing Level Chart
   B—Weather Depiction Chart
   C—12-Hour Significant Weather Prognostic Chart

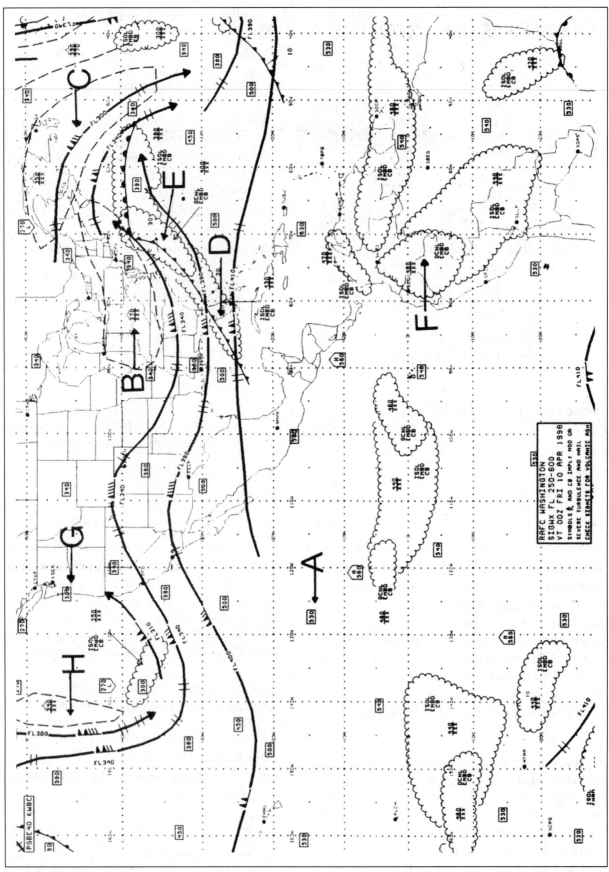

Figure Q5-5.

Charts and Publications

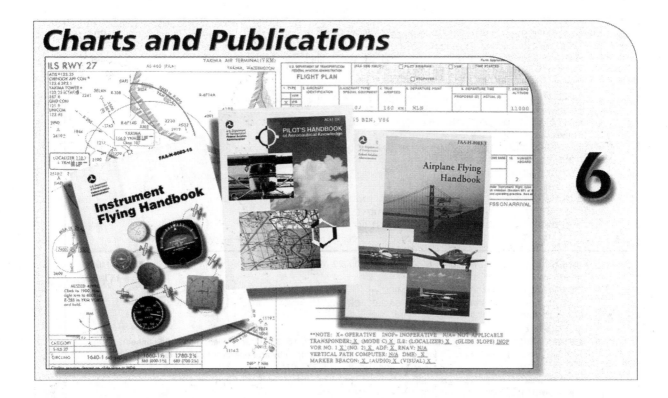

6

Airport/Facility Directory

Commercial pilot applicants can skip to the end of this chapter, because it is almost entirely about instrument charts. Trust me—almost everything you learned about VFR charts during your private pilot training still applies. There are some navigation-type questions on the commercial exam, however, and they will be discussed at the end of the chapter.

As you learned in Chapter 3, planning any type of flight requires the use of performance tables and weight and balance data in the Pilot's Operating Handbook, making that publication number one on your list of what to refer to in planning an IFR flight. You should approach that portion of the planning task conservatively, because if you make a mistake in calculating your fuel requirements, or load the airplane out of CG, the consequences can be devastating.

Your next source of information should be the Airport/Facility Directory (A/FD). In the listing for your destination airport you will find all the information you might possibly need, such as communication and navaid frequencies, runway lengths and widths, special local procedures, and fuel and maintenance availability.

In the back of the A/FD you will find Center frequencies, tower enroute-control (TEC) city pairs, and IFR preferred routes. The A/FD also includes telephone numbers for getting weather briefings and filing flight plans. If your airplane has a LORAN or GPS installation, you will find the listing of latitude and longitude of each airport and navaids useful for designating waypoints.

The A/FD lists ground and airborne VOR checkpoints as well as locations of VOTs to test your navigation equipment, and you will find restrictions to enroute navigational aid (such as unusable radials) listed for each VOR/VORTAC. Figure 6-1 (on the next page) is excerpted from the Airport/Facility Directory. Can you answer these questions?

1. In Figure 6-1A, on what frequency and during what time period can you receive a continuous broadcast of inflight weather advisories at Omak, WA?

2. In Figure 6-1B, which frequency should you use to request flight following service when in the vicinity of Prineville, OR?

3. In Figure 6-1C, how would you close your flight plan at Plains, MT?

Continued on Page 6-3

OMAK (OMK)   3 N   UTC−8(−7DT)   N48°27.86' W119°31.08'   SEATTLE
  1301   B   S4   **FUEL** 100LL, JET A   L−9A
    RWY 17−35: H4654X150 (ASPH)   S−75, D−200, DT−400   MIRL   IAP
      RWY 17: REIL. VASI(V2L)—GA 3.0° TCH 43'.
      RWY 35: REIL. VASI(V2L)—GA 3.0° TCH 46'.
    AIRPORT REMARKS: Attended Mon−Fri 1600−0100Z‡. Fuel avbl 24
      hrs−credit card. ACTIVATE MIRL Rwy 17−35—CTAF.
    WEATHER DATA SOURCES: ASOS 118.325 (509) 826−2655.
    COMMUNICATIONS: CTAF/UNICOM 122.8
      SEATTLE FSS (SEA) TF 1−800−WX−BRIEF. NOTAM FILE OMK.
      RCO 122.2 (SEATTLE FSS)
      SEATTLE CENTER APP/DEP CON 126.1
    RADIO AIDS TO NAVIGATION: NOTAM FILE GEG.
      SPOKANE (H) VORTACW 115.5   GEG   Chan 102   N47°33.90'
        W117°37.61'   285° 93.4 NM to fld. 2760/21E. **HIWAS.**
      NDB (MHW) 219   OMK   N48°27.21' W119°31.00'   at fld.
        NOTAM FILE OMK. Unusable byd 15 NM.
A

PRINEVILLE (S39)   3 SW   UTC−8(−7DT)   N44°17.22' W120°54.23'   KLAMATH FALLS
  3250   B   S4   **FUEL** 100LL, JET A   H−1A, L−1B
    RWY 10−28: H5000X60 (ASPH)   S−30   MIRL   IAP
      RWY 10: Tree.   RWY 28: VASI(V2L)—GA 3.0° TCH 34'.
    RWY 15−33: H4000X40 (ASPH)   S−5   LIRL
      RWY 33: Trees.
    AIRPORT REMARKS: Attended dalgt hours. Deer on and invof arpt. Rwy 15−33 surface rough, many large unsealed
      cracks, weeds growing on rwy, loose grvl on rwy. Rwy 15−33 limited by arpt operator to 5000 lbs max weight.
      ACTIVATE MIRL Rwy 10−28, VASI Rwy 28, and LIRL Rwy 15−33—CTAF.
    COMMUNICATIONS: CTAF/UNICOM 122.8
      MCMINNVILLE FSS (MMV) TF 1−800−WX−BRIEF. NOTAM FILE MMV.
      SEATTLE CENTER APP/DEP CON 128.15
    RADIO AIDS TO NAVIGATION: NOTAM FILE RDM.
      DESCHUTES (H) VORTACW 117.6   DSD   Chan 123   N44°15.17' W121°18.21'   065° 17.4 NM to fld. 4100/18E.
        HIWAS.
      BODEY NDB (HW/LOM) 411   RD   N44°18.48' W121°01.14'   086° 5.1 NM to fld. NDB unusable 091°−111° byd
        25 NM blo 14,000'.
B

PLAINS (S34)   1 NW   UTC−7(−6DT)   N47°28.35' W114°54.01'   GREAT FALLS
  2462   B   L−9B
    RWY 12−30: H3060X50 (ASPH)   MIRL
      RWY 12: P−line.   RWY 30: P−line.
    RWY 07−25: 1750X100 (TURF)
      RWY 07: Fence.   RWY 25: Hill.
    AIRPORT REMARKS: Unattended. Rwy 07−25 CLOSED indef. Rwy 07−25
      gopher holes and dirt mounds on rwy surface. Rwy 12−30
      markings NSTD size, numbers small, white cones lgtd next to
      each rwy lgt mark entire rwy length.
    COMMUNICATIONS: CTAF 122.9
      GREAT FALLS FSS (GTF) TF 1−800−WX−BRIEF. NOTAM FILE GTF.
    RADIO AIDS TO NAVIGATION: NOTAM FILE BOI.
      MULLAN PASS (H) VOR/DME 117.8   MLP   Chan 125   N47°27.42'
        W115°38.76'   068° 30.4 NM to fld. 6100/20E.
C

CODY   N44°37.23' W108°57.88'   NOTAM FILE COD.   GREAT FALLS
  (L) VORW/DME 111.8   COD   Chan 55   189° 6.5 NM to Yellowstone Regional. 4790/14E.   L−9C
    VOR portion unusable: 043°−113° byd 10 NM below 9,500'.
    DME unusable: 043°−113° byd 10 NM blo 9,500'
                  113°−138° byd 22 NM blo 10,000'
                  138°−183° byd 32 NM blo 11,000'
                  183°−343° byd 30 NM blo 17,000'
  RCO 122.3 (CASPER FSS)
D

Figure 6-1. *Excerpts from A/FD*

4. In Figure 6-1D, between which radials of the COD VOR/DME is the VOR considered unusable beyond 10 nautical miles below 9,500 feet MSL? Where can't the DME be trusted?

The answers to questions like these can be found in the A/FD, and also at websites like www.airnav.com and www.landings.com.

There are two major sources of IFR charts: the Jeppesen Company and the FAA National Aeronautical Charting Office (NACO, formerly NOS). All government publications on the subject of instrument flight use NACO charts, and they are used on all knowledge examinations where knowledge of IFR procedures is required. Each source has both advantages and disadvantages, and I have included enough information to allow you to make an informed choice.

When comparing approach charts, keep in mind that when the FAA designs an instrument procedure it is in textual form, i.e., "Intermediate segment 160°, procedure turn east within 10 NM." The two chart providers take this textual information and convert it to graphic form. The FAA procedures designer does not tell Jeppesen or NACO how the information is to be presented to the user.

As you begin your instrument training you will probably use NACO charts and approach plate books. Most instrument students do, because materials printed by the NACO may be purchased as needed. Also, most instrument students want to develop familiarity with NACO charts and approach plates in preparation for the FAA Knowledge Exam.

These are the major differences between NACO and Jeppesen:

• NACO prints a table of glide slope descent rate versus ground speed and a tabulation of changes in IFR minimums due to inoperative components at the back of each approach plate book where it is not easily accessible, while Jeppesen includes this information on every plate to which it applies. Similarly, information on non-standard takeoff and alternate minimums is provided in the chart coverage of each airport by Jeppesen but is listed separately by NACO.

• RNAV approach plates are included in the NACO chart booklet; RNAV coverage is a separate subscription service from Jeppesen.

• Jeppesen now offers approach plates in 18 regional booklets similar to those that the NACO has used for years. New booklets are issued every 56 days. An interim 28-day update is also available. NACO charts are available in loose-leaf and bound chart booklets, and are published every 56 days; a booklet of changes and revisions is published 28 days after each issue of the chart booklet.

• Jeppesen is phasing in the use of color to emphasize terrain contours on its approach plates.

• NACO is phasing in the use of brown tint to depict terrain within the plan view (10 NM) when it exceeds 4,000 feet above airport elevation, or when terrain within a 6 NM radius of the airport reference point rises to at least 2,000 feet above airport elevation.

Those are the major differences; as specific items of information are discussed, the presentation of that information by NACO and Jeppesen will be discussed and the differences pointed out. The illustrations used in this book are for reference only, as they are out-of-date charts; the procedure for a given airport may be different as you read this book than it was when the illustrations were chosen for the book.

Enroute Low-Altitude Charts

The National Aeronautical Charting Office covers the continental United States with 12 four-color enroute low-altitude charts, while Jeppesen uses 16 blue-and-green charts to cover the same area. Instrument departure procedures will get you into the enroute system and approach procedures will get you out of it, but most of your instrument flying will require reference to enroute charts. The enroute low-altitude structure extends from the surface to 18,000 feet above sea level, where the enroute high-altitude charts take over.

NACO enroute low-altitude charts will have a small boxed "C" or "D" next to the airport symbol to remind you of the communications requirement at tower-controlled airports ("D*" if it is a part-time tower).

Enroute charts show the magnetic courses of the airways you will fly and provide distance information along the airways not only between VORs but also between intersections. This not only aids in flight planning but makes inflight ground speed checks easier. There is no appreciable difference in presentation between the NACO and Jeppesen.

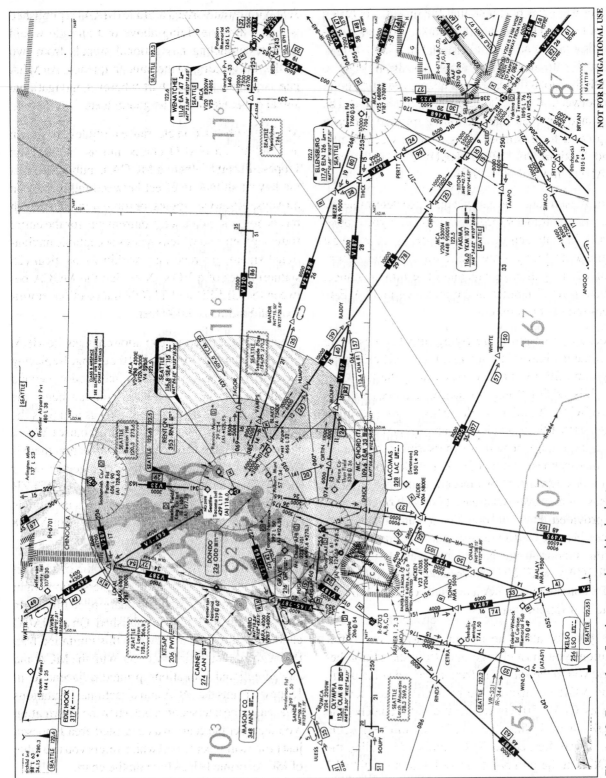

Figure 6-2. Excerpt from Seattle enroute low-altitude chart

Refer to Figure 6-2; note that the distance between Seattle and TITON intersection (a compulsory reporting point) on V-4 is enclosed in a box: 78 NM. (Usually the distance in the box is from VOR to VOR, but not if there is a compulsory reporting point in between. Check the total mileage closely.) The distance between intersections is printed for each segment; for example, along V-4 between Seattle and Yakima, HUMPP to RADDY is 15 NM and RADDY to CHINS is 29 NM.

You must refer to the enroute charts to determine the minimum altitudes for the segments on your route. The minimum enroute altitude (MEA) is the lowest altitude at which you are assured of acceptable reception of navigation signals and of terrain clearance. There is no difference in the presentation of MEAs between the two sources.

Because more pilots are flying direct routes using area navigation devices such as the Global Positioning System (GPS; to be discussed later), the FAA has established Off-Route Obstacle Clearance Altitudes (OROCA). Similar to the Maximum Elevation Figures (MEFs) on sectional charts, they are presented as a large number with a superscript in rectangles formed by lines of latitude and longitude. An OROCA provides 1,000 feet of obstacle clearance in most areas; in mountainous areas, 2,000 feet of clearance is provided. For example, if you want to fly direct from Ellensburg to the Snohomish County airport using random-route navigation such as GPS, the OROCA would be 11,600 feet. *Note:* Do not expect GPS courses and VOR airways to coincide; they are totally different systems.

As you fly along an airway between two VOR stations you must change over from the station behind you to the station in front of you at some point. The VOR changeover point (COP) takes several forms. On V-120 between Seattle and Wenatchee the COP is at the Z-shaped mark, 51 NM from Seattle. On the airway formed by the Olympia 176° radial, the COP is at the turn point marked with a small "x" 2 miles south of WINLO intersection. On V-204 between Olympia and Yakima it would be at WHYTE intersection, and where there is no obvious COP it is the halfway point: 40 miles out on V-2 between Seattle and Ellensburg.

A maximum authorized altitude (MAA) is published when an airplane flying above that altitude would receive conflicting navigational signals from two VORs transmitting on the same frequency. An MEA gap is printed on the chart wherever navigational signal coverage cannot be guaranteed.

Minimum obstruction clearance altitudes are shown as "*4200" on NACO charts and as "4200T" on Jeppesen charts. Where a MOCA is published, it is the lowest altitude in effect between radio fixes on airways, off-airway routes, or route segments which meets obstacle clearance requirements for the entire route segment and which ensures acceptable navigational signal coverage only within 22 nautical (25 statute) miles of a VOR. Note that the MOCA between the GLEED and TITON intersections northwest of Yakima is 5,000 feet.

When a change in terrain elevation changes the MEA, both Jeppesen and NACO signal the change by placing a crossbar on the airway at the intersection beyond which the change is effective. You can begin the climb or descent to the new altitude as you pass the intersection (with Center's approval, of course). Where there is no change in MEA at an intersection there is no crossbar. There is no MEA change for either airway forming RADDY intersection. At BEEZR intersection, west of Ellensburg, there is no altitude change on V-2, but there is an MEA change on V-298 flying northwest from Yakima as it joins V-2.

If the terrain rises so steeply that a climb of 152 feet per nautical mile after passing the intersection might not clear it by an adequate margin, a minimum crossing altitude (MCA) is published. On an NACO chart, your attention is drawn to this limitation by a flag with an X at the intersection, with the MCA and any directional limitations printed adjacent to it. Jeppesen prints the MCA and directional limitations adjacent to the intersection, but when the information would clutter the chart in a congested area Jeppesen just prints a numbered ball which refers you to a table of MCAs printed elsewhere on the chart.

Refer to Figure 6-2 again. A pilot flying up V-298 from Yakima has an MEA of 6,500 feet to PERTT intersection, and the MEA steps up to 9,000 feet at that point. No minimum crossing altitude is published and the pilot can begin the climb at PERTT. A

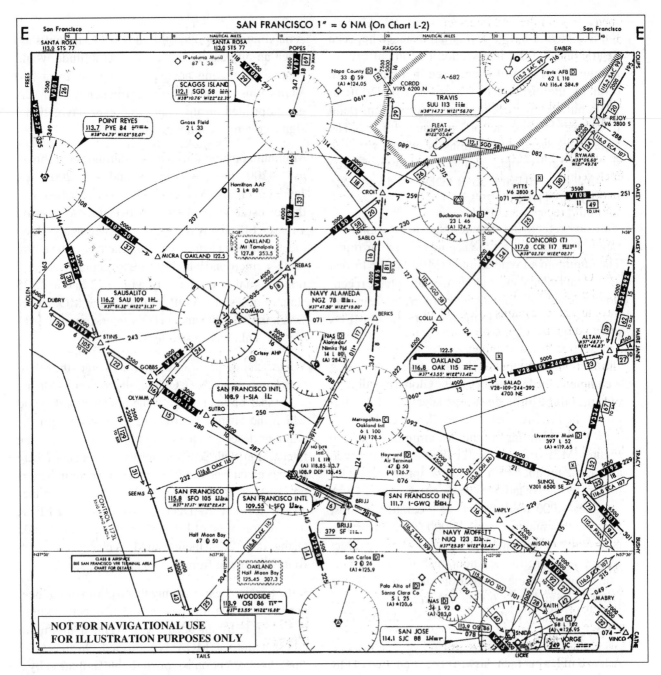

Figure 6-3. *NACO area chart excerpt*

pilot flying from Olympia to Yakima on V-204 cannot cross MCKEN intersection unless the minimum crossing altitude of 5,000 feet has been attained before reaching the intersection.

When you must identify an airway intersection through use of an off-course VOR and intervening terrain may interfere with its reception, a minimum reception altitude (MRA) is published. NACO uses a flag with an R in it (and the altitude) at the intersection to call your attention to this limitation; Jeppesen prints MRA and the altitude adjacent to the

intersection. In Figure 6-2 a pilot flying south from Olympia on V-287 must fly at an altitude of at least 9,500 feet to receive the off-course radial that forms MALAY intersection.

If your airplane is equipped with distance measuring equipment, some intersections can be identified by DME distances. Jeppesen identifies these intersections with the letter D with an arrow pointing from the VORTAC for the first intersection along the airway or with an arrow, the letter D, and the DME distance for subsequent intersections. NACO uses an open arrow for the first intersection and the distance enclosed in a large letter D for subsequent intersections.

A pilot flying south from Olympia on V-287 with DME aboard can identify TONNO intersection by DME distance because it has an open arrow and the segment distance is 17 NM; MALAY intersection can be identified at 5,000 feet using the DME distance enclosed in the large letter D: 33 NM. With distance measuring equipment you may be able to ignore minimum reception altitudes.

There are minor differences in symbology between NACO and Jeppesen enroute charts. Jeppesen and NACO indicate locations where transcribed weather broadcasts (TWEBs) are available. Every NACO enroute chart contains a legend of chart symbols, while you must refer to the Jepp manual's introduction section for a detailed explanation of legend information. Both Jeppesen and NACO charts include a complete listing of communication frequencies and special use airspace restrictions.

Note: NACO is phasing in computer navigation fixes (CNFs) for use by pilots using database navigation (GPS, INS, etc.). These lat./long. figures will initially appear at airway turning points marked with an "x." They have no relevance for pilots not using database navigation and are not to be referred to in filing flight plans or requesting clearances.

Area Charts

Area charts show congested areas in more detail, and they are printed on a larger scale than are enroute low-altitude charts. NACO prints a single A1/A2 chart that includes 13 area charts, scaled from 5 miles per inch to 8 miles per inch. Figure 6-3 is a portion of the San Francisco area chart. The legend for the enroute chart applies to the area chart. Jeppesen prints area charts separately, and there are over 30. The only major difference between the two is that terrain contours are printed on certain Jepp area charts.

Departure Procedures and STARs

Jeppesen includes departure procedures (DPs) and Standard Terminal Arrival Route (STAR) charts as a part of its airway manual service. NACO includes DPs and STARs in their chart booklets. Figure 6-4 is a typical DP chart. Note that because of the terrain around Reno there is a required minimum climb rate

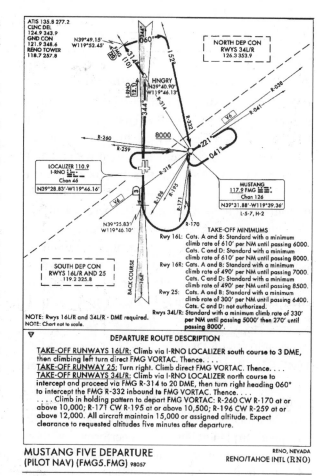

Figure 6-4. DP for Reno, NV

of 610 feet per nautical mile on Runway 16L. To convert this to feet per minute, multiply 610 feet by your airspeed (ground speed, if available) in miles per minute. At 120 knots, for instance, the required climb rate would be 2.0 x 610 feet = 1,220 feet per minute.

Instrument Approach Procedure Charts

Instrument approach procedure charts are referred to as either charts or plates, and I will use the two terms interchangeably. NACO publishes approach charts for the continental United States in 24 packets, and a new complete packet is issued every 56 days. You simply recycle the old book when the new one comes out. (*See* Figure 6-5 on Page 6-9.) Information on NACO products (including updates) is available at http://naco.faa.gov. Jeppesen sends out revised charts to its subscribers every two weeks, and you must go through your airway manual and replace individual pages to keep your manual current. If a specific approach has not changed, its plate may stay in your Jeppesen manual for years. Jeppesen has specific subscription procedures for pilots with special requirements.

Chart and Procedure Identification

Procedures with straight-in minimums are identified by runway number: NDB RUNWAY 10; VOR RUNWAY 23. When only circling minimums are published, the procedure is identified with a letter: NDB-A; VOR-C. NACO prints the procedure identification, city, and airport name at both top and bottom of each approach plate. Jeppesen prints the city, airport name, and procedure identification in the upper right corner of each plate; the date of issuance and the effective date are printed on each plate. The Julian date of effectiveness is printed on each NACO plate: "90347" means that the plate became effective on the 347th day of 1990.

A procedure with DME in the identification (LOC/DME RUNWAY 13; VOR/DME-A) cannot be performed without operative distance measuring equipment on board. There are many nonprecision approaches that provide lower minimums for DME-equipped airplanes but can be performed without that equipment on board; in those cases DME is not included in the procedure identification. In Figure 6-6, note that pilots with DME on board have a 240-foot advantage over those without DME.

An approach plate identified as "VOR or GPS" or "NDB or GPS" is called an overlay approach, and can be flown using either the underlying ground-based navaid, or an approved GPS installation. Stand-alone GPS approaches are simply identified as "GPS RWY 6" and can only be flown using GPS; as new plates are issued, the designations will be changed to "RNAV RWY 6."

Communication and Navigation Frequencies

NACO approach plates include all applicable communication frequencies for an arriving aircraft near the top of each plate. The notation "ASR" means that radar is available for surveillance approaches. NACO charts list frequencies for approach and departure control facilities but do not indicate whether or not those facilities have radar; you must look in the front of the approach plate booklet to make that determination. Jeppesen places (R) after frequencies of approach and departure control facilities which have

radar available. If you relied on NACO approach plate alone, you would not know that Kennedy Approach has radar available (Figure 6-7). The same is true at Boeing Field (Figure 6-8). Note that there are such things as non-radar approach control facilities that plot your position reports with grease pencil on plastic; if you get lost, don't ask them for help.

Jeppesen prints communication frequencies in the normal order of use for IFR arrival as a "briefing strip" at the top of the first approach chart in each airport series (except where the airport diagram is on a separate page). Frequencies to be used upon departure are printed on the back of the chart, again in order of use.

NACO has also switched to the "briefing strip" presentation and uses symbology to depict missed approach instructions.

Both NACO and Jeppesen print navigation frequencies and Morse code identifiers on the plan view portion of each plate.

Plan View

The plan view portion of an instrument approach plate shows the procedure as seen from above so that you can visualize the path you will follow in flying the approach. The entire plan view portion of a Jeppesen plate is drawn to scale, and the scale is identified along the left margin. NACO plates are drawn to scale only within the 10 mile circle; navigation facilities in the enroute structure can be shown on NACO plates. Both Jepp and NACO use shades of brown to depict terrain that exceeds 4,000 feet above airport elevation or rises to at least 2,000 feet above the airport within six miles of the airport reference point. *Do not assume that the positions of terrain features and/or obstacles are depicted accurately.*

Approach plates are printed so that the top of the sheet is true north. Courses and headings on the plates are printed in relation to magnetic north. Knowing this can help you "eyeball" directional information from the approach plate, because you can estimate a direction from a nearby printed course. For example, in Seattle the magnetic variation is approximately 20°E, so a horizontal line across the approach plate is oriented 070°-250° magnetic, and an airplane flying straight up the chart is making good a track of 340° magnetic.

Figure 6-5. *NACO chart services*

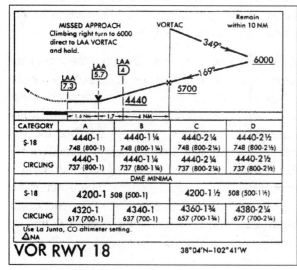

Figure 6-6. *The DME advantage*

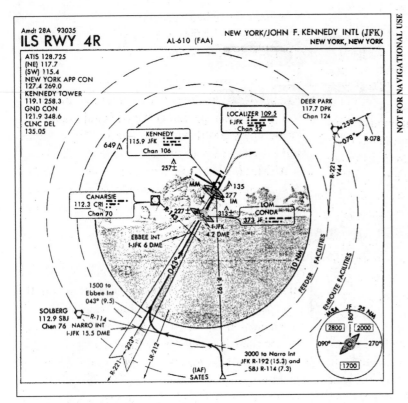

Figure 6-7. *Kennedy approach*

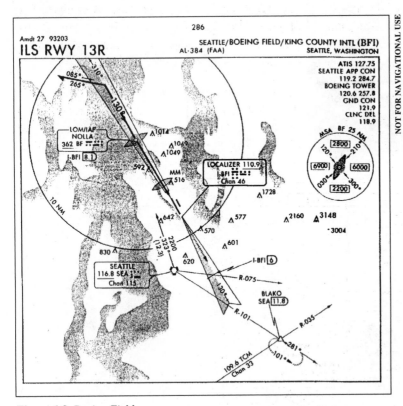

Figure 6-8. *Boeing Field*

Profile View

The profile view shows the altitudes you are to observe during the approach, with headings provided where they are applicable. Note that when a course reversal is required the line descending from procedure turn altitude to the MDA or glide slope intercept altitude is labeled with the inbound course. The profile view also shows the fix from which the procedure turn distance limit is measured; Jeppesen names the fix, while NACO simply identifies it as VOR, NDB, etc. Both use a Maltese cross to identify the final approach fix for a nonprecision approach.

Don't assume that a steeply sloped line means a rapid descent—both Jeppesen and NACO use cartographic conventions. On the approach plate for Telluride, Colorado, the angle of the printed descent line is quite steep, but the altitude changes only 20 feet in 5 miles.

If your glideslope receiver fails, or if the glideslope transmitter on the ground is inoperative, almost all ILS approaches are usable as nonprecision localizer approaches. The profile view on a Jeppesen chart shows the nonprecision profile as a dashed line with altitude designations; NACO plates do not provide this information. Both services print the minimum MSL altitude at which the course reversal is to be performed and the altitude at which the glideslope crosses the final approach fix; Jeppesen also prints the altitude above the ground at these locations. Only Jeppesen prints the MSL and AGL altitudes at which the glideslope crosses the nonprecision final approach fix (FAF) and the middle marker. *Note:* The

FAA has established a program of decommissioning middle markers (MM). You may not find an MM on the ILS you are shooting.

The final approach segment for an ILS approach begins where the glideslope intercept altitude intersects the glideslope, not at the final approach fix as shown on the profile view; the Maltese cross applies to the localizer-only approach or circling approach. NACO indicates the point of glideslope interception with a lightning arrow and Jeppesen simply shows the glideslope line beginning its downward slope.

Although most glideslopes cross the final approach fix almost immediately after interception, you will occasionally intercept the glideslope (GS) several miles from the FAF. When you refer to an ILS approach plate you can calculate the distance between the point at which you intercept the glideslope and the final approach fix by subtracting the altitude at which the GS crosses the fix from the glideslope intercept altitude and dividing by the glideslope angle x 100. For example, you intercept the glideslope at Dutchess County Airport in Poughkeepsie, NY, at 2,200 feet and lose 600 feet before crossing the FAF at 1,600 feet. The glideslope angle is 3°, or 300 feet per mile, so the glideslope is intercepted 2 miles outside the marker (Figure 6-9).

Both services show the distance from the runway threshold to fixes along the final approach path; it is often instructive to make a comparison between the distance from the middle marker to the threshold and

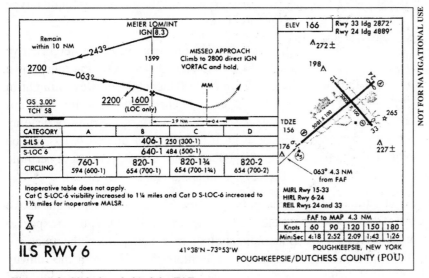

Figure 6-9. Glideslope behind the FAF

the required visibility. If the MM is one-half mile from the threshold and one-half mile visibility is required for the approach, you should be able to see the threshold from the middle marker (when there is one). At Dutchess County Airport (Figure 6-9) the required visibility is one mile and the middle marker is only .4 mile from the threshold. If the visibility is below minimums, you will begin the missed approach long before you get to the middle marker when shooting the ILS at POU. Compare this with Figure 6-8; at Boeing Field, the middle marker is crossed before the airplane reaches the missed approach point. Missed approach instructions are printed with the profile view. Jeppesen has begun a program of printing a capital M on the profile view to indicate the missed approach point.

Minimums

No single piece of information available on an instrument approach plate is more important to you than the minimum descent altitude (DA) or decision height (DH), and you should be able to get that information at a glance. The chart makers are no longer using DH, but you might find it on older charts or in older texts. Jeppesen prints the lowest minimums at the left side of the minimums table, with the altitude above mean sea level followed by the height above the touchdown zone elevation or airport elevation in parentheses. The minimums increase across the page as facilities are reported inoperative or when altimeter settings must be received from remote locations. Circling minimums are on the right side of the table. In Figure 6-10, the lowest authorized decision height is 765 feet, (200 feet AGL) increasing to 980 feet if the glide slope is out of service. The increase in circling minimums as you step up in category is based on the larger turning radius of faster airplanes.

NACO prints minimums from top to bottom, but the lowest minimums are not always at the top. If an approach has two sets of minimums based on equipment—such as with or without DME—the lowest minimums authorized using the additional equipment are printed at the bottom.

Figure 6-11 shows a minimum descent altitude of 3,440 feet (428 feet AGL) without DME at the top and an MDA of 3,320 feet (308 feet AGL) at the bottom. This emphasis on how minimums are presented is intentional. You will be getting information from the

← 0.5 → ← 7.3 NM →				
CATEGORY	A	B	C	D
S-ILS 16R	765/24 200 (200-½)			
S-LOC 16R	980/24 415 (400-½)		980/40 415 (400-¾)	
CIRCLING	1040-1 434 (500-1)	1060-1 454 (500-1)	1060-1½ 454 (500-1½)	1160-2 554 (600-2)
BOEING FIELD/KING COUNTY INTL ALTIMETER SETTING MINIMUMS				
S-ILS 16R	858-½ 293 (300-½)			858-¾ 293 (300-¾)
S-LOC 16R	1060-½ 495 (500-½)		1060-¾ 495 (500-¾)	1060-1 495 (500-1)
CIRCLING	1140-1 534 (600-1)		1140-1½ 534 (600-1½)	1180-2 574 (600-2)

Figure 6-10. NACO minimums

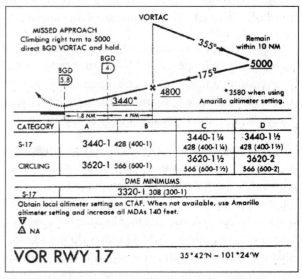

Figure 6-11. Review the minimums carefully.

approach plates in quick glances, and it is not uncommon for a pilot to misread the plate and start a missed approach from circling instead of straight-in minimums. Know where the information is located before you look at the plate. Many pilots use colored pens or markers to make the minimums for their type of operation more visible.

Straight-in minimums are published as height above touchdown zone elevation (HAT); the touchdown zone is the first 3,000 feet of the runway. Straight-in minimums are published only when the final approach course is within 30° of the runway heading and descent from the final approach fix can be accomplished at a rate of 300 feet or less per mile (400 feet per mile in some special cases).

Circling minimums are published as height above the elevation of the airport (HAA). You can expect to find only circling minimums when the final approach course is more than 30° from the runway heading, or when a steep descent would be required to pass over the final approach fix at the published altitude and land on the numbers. An approach with only circling minimums will have a letter instead of a runway number: NDB-A, VOR-C, etc.

The FAA charting office prints heights above ground level using a smaller, lighter type face; the minimums in parentheses apply only to military operations and you can ignore them (*see* Figure 6-11). The minimum descent altitude for the straight-in VOR approach places the airplane 428 feet above the runway threshold. Although decision height and minimum descent altitude govern how close to the ground you can descend on an instrument approach, it is the visibility minimum that counts. Each approach has a required minimum flight visibility, and if the reported visibility is less than the published figure you are not supposed to attempt the approach.

That last sentence sounded wishy-washy, didn't it? For good reason. Part 91 says that you are required to have a certain amount of flight visibility to land, and what you get from the tower, the ATIS, or the weather observer is ground visibility. If the required visibility is $\frac{1}{2}$ mile and the tower controllers say that they can only see things $\frac{1}{4}$ mile away, you can continue the approach and land if, in your opinion, you had the runway in sight from $\frac{1}{2}$ mile out. The tower may file a violation against you, however, and it will be your word against the controller's (plus any instrumentally derived visibility data).

Down the road a few hundred hours, when you are flying for an air taxi or air carrier, you will be bound by the reported visibility and will not be able to substitute your own judgment, if the report is received prior to the FAF.

On an ILS approach plate you may see something like this in the minimums area: 273/24. The 273 is decision height in feet above mean sea level; the 24 means that a runway visual range (RVR) of 2,400 feet is required; RVR is a figure reported by a transmissometer—a light source with a receiving device located at a distance down the runway. The tower controller gets a readout of runway visual range based on the amount of light that makes it from the light source to the receiver. Major airports may have more than one transmissometer; typical loca-

tions would be at the touchdown zone, midfield, and the rollout end of the runway.

If RVR is required for your proposed approach and the data is not available, use this table of equivalents:

Required RVR	Substitute
1,600	$\frac{1}{4}$ SM
2,400	$\frac{1}{2}$ SM
3,200	$\frac{5}{8}$ SM
4,000	$\frac{3}{4}$ SM
4,500	$\frac{7}{8}$ SM
5,000	1 SM
6,000	$1\frac{1}{4}$ SM

If a required element of an instrument approach system such as a lighting system is inoperative, you must look in the front of the NACO booklet for the "Inoperative Components Table" to determine the adjustments to be made to the published minimums. Jeppesen includes the minimums for inoperative components on each approach plate. Typically, if an approach lighting system is inoperative the required visibility will be increased.

Different minimums usually, but not always, apply to different aircraft categories. The FAA categorizes aircraft based on an approach speed of 1.3 times the stalling speed of the aircraft in the landing configuration at maximum certificated gross landing weight:

Category A: Speed less than 91 knots.

Category B: Speed 91 knots or more but less than 121 knots.

Category C: Speed 121 knots or more but less than 141 knots.

Category D: Speed 141 knots or more but less than 166 knots.

Category E: Speed 166 knots or more.

An aircraft can fit into only one category. However, if it is necessary to maneuver at speeds over the upper airspeed limit of the category for your airplane, you should observe the minimums for the next higher category. For example, assume that 1.3 times your airplane's V_{SO} is 85 knots but you are circling to land at 115 knots; in this situation you would observe the category B circling minimums for the approach because of the increase in radius of turn at the higher speed.

Minimum Sector Altitudes

Minimum sector altitudes are sometimes called minimum safe altitudes, and that is not a bad way of viewing them. Wherever an instrument approach has a VOR or an NDB close by, the FAA establishes sectors with a 25 mile radius defined by bearings or radials from that facility and publishes sector altitudes which provide 1,000 feet of terrain clearance. Both Jeppesen and NACO print the MSA circle on each approach plate to which it applies.

Where an approach has no navaid from which azimuths can be measured, such as a localizer approach with no low frequency aids or a GPS approach, no MSA circle is published.

The MSA circle with its associated altitudes has nothing whatsoever to do with the instrument approach itself—the altitudes shown are for emergency use only. Many pilots and instructors try to include the MSA circle altitudes in flying the approach, and for that reason Jeppesen and NACO are considering removal of the MSA circle from approach charts.

Ground Speed/Time Table

For nonprecision approaches, when the final approach fix is not on the airport, a ground speed/time table is provided to enable you to estimate the time from the FAF to the missed approach point based on your ground speed. The missed approach point is identified adjacent to the ground speed/time table. NACO provides a table in the back of each approach plate booklet that lets you convert ground speed and descent angle to rate of descent in feet per minute; Jeppesen provides this information on each ILS approach plate.

Using your flight computer to calculate the time en route for a distance as short as 2.3 miles is easy—but the method differs from normal practice. In place of the normal speed reference use 36 (for 3,600 seconds), and read the time scale in minutes and seconds instead of hours and minutes. In Figure 6-12, the 36-speed reference is set at 110 knots, and the example shows that a distance of 1.5 miles will be flown in 49 seconds.

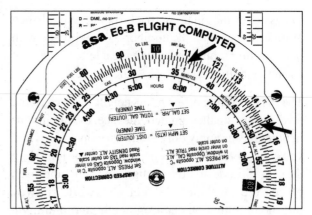

Figure 6-12. *Short distance*

If you have left your flight computer at home but have a four-function calculator available, multiply the distance by 3,600 and divide by the ground speed to get the time in seconds.

Although you are to initiate a missed approach from an ILS when you reach decision height and do not have the runway in sight, a ground speed table is provided on ILS plates. You might need it to determine the missed approach point if the glideslope cannot be used and the approach reverts to a LOC approach. You will find a ground speed/time table on the plate for some approaches where a straight-in localizer-only approach is not authorized—the ILS Runway 27 at Yakima, Washington is an example. In this situation, illustrated in Figure 6-13, the ground speed/time table is provided so that you can identify the missed approach point by timing if you drift off of the localizer.

Airport Diagram

NACO provides an airport diagram on every approach plate, with the airport elevation, runway width and length, lighting systems, and touchdown zone elevation included, as shown in Figure 6-13. Note that the type of lighting system is indicated and the presence of VASI is shown. For a description of the various lighting systems you must go to the Legend pages in the NACO approach chart booklet (a copy of this is shown in Figure 6-14).

Jeppesen prints a separate chart for each airport, including the airport diagram, information on lighting systems, takeoff and alternate minimums, and the instrument departure procedure. Where they are installed, the airport diagram shows the locations of

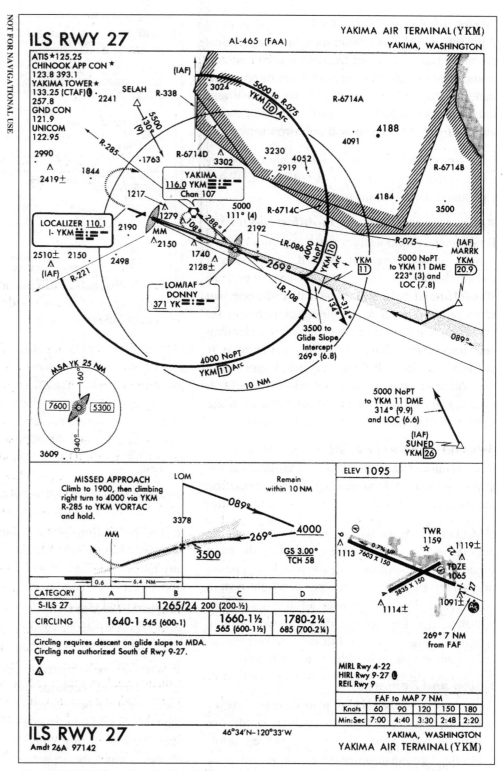

ILS RWY 27

AL-465 (FAA)

YAKIMA AIR TERMINAL (YKM)
YAKIMA, WASHINGTON

ATIS ★125.25
CHINOOK APP CON ★
123.8 393.1
YAKIMA TOWER ★
133.25 (CTAF) ⓒ
257.8
GND CON
121.9
UNICOM
122.95

YAKIMA
116.0 YKM
Chan 107

LOCALIZER 110.1
I- YKM

LOM/IAF
DONNY
371 YK

MSA YK 25 NM
7600   5300

ELEV 1095

MISSED APPROACH
Climb to 1900, then climbing
right turn to 4000 via YKM
R-285 to YKM VORTAC
and hold.

LOM
Remain
within 10 NM

089°
3378
269°   4000
3500
GS 3.00°
TCH 58
MM
0.6   6.4 NM

TWR
1159
1119±
1113   7603 X 150
TDZE
1065
1114±
1091±
A5

269° 7 NM
from FAF

CATEGORY	A	B	C	D
S-ILS 27	1265/24 200 (200-½)			
CIRCLING	1640-1 545 (600-1)		1660-1½ 565 (600-1½)	1780-2¼ 685 (700-2¼)

Circling requires descent on glide slope to MDA.
Circling not authorized South of Rwy 9-27.

MIRL Rwy 4-22
HIRL Rwy 9-27 ⓒ
REIL Rwy 9

FAF to MAP 7 NM					
Knots	60	90	120	150	180
Min:Sec	7:00	4:40	3:30	2:48	2:20

ILS RWY 27
Amdt 26A 97142

46°34'N–120°33'W

YAKIMA, WASHINGTON
YAKIMA AIR TERMINAL (YKM)

Figure 6-13. ILS Rwy 27 at Yakima, WA

low-level windshear detectors around the airport. Jeppesen provides information on each airport diagram plate which a user of NOS plates must research in the Airport/Facility Directory. This information includes magnetic variation and the distance and radial from the nearest VORTAC, useful for establishing an RNAV waypoint on the airport.

Both services provide the latitude-longitude coordinates of the airport for users of GPS and LORAN equipment without databases.

Approach and Runway Lighting Systems

If you intend to shoot an approach to minimums at a strange airport at night, studying the approach and runway lighting system ahead of time will prepare you for the visual picture you will see when you break out of the clouds. The approach lights are on the list of visual clues you must have before leaving decision height or the minimum descent altitude. If an ALSF-2 approach lighting system is your only visual clue, you must not descend below 100 feet AGL until you have passed the horizontal row of white lights which is 1,000 feet from the threshold.

A practice that works every time is to add 50 feet to the touchdown zone elevation and ensure that the altimeter reads at least that high as you cross the threshold.

NACO identifies the type of lighting system on the airport diagram and prints the information shown in Figure 6-14 in each approach plate booklet. Jeppesen prints a representation of the approach light system on the plan view and includes a fuller description with the airport diagram. The Jeppesen airway manual contains a large, detailed, full-color illustration of each lighting system in addition to the legend.

Notes and Remarks

At the bottom of each NACO plate there is a box for notes such as restrictions to circling, conditions under which the approach is not authorized, pilot-controlled lighting information, etc. Pilot-controlled lighting systems are indicated by white-on-black symbols.

When takeoff minimums are other than standard (operators other than Part 91) the letter T in an inverted triangle is printed in this box to alert you to refer to the "IFR Takeoff and Departure Procedures"

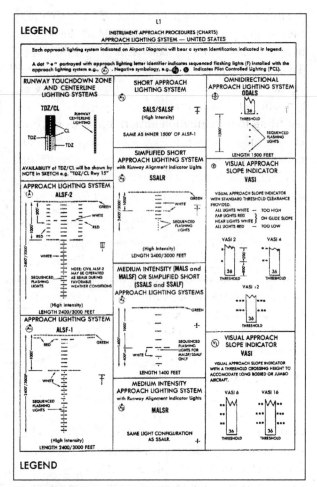

Figure 6-14. Excerpt from NACO legend

section in the front of the book. As a Part 91 pilot (neither air taxi nor air carrier), you need not observe any takeoff visibility restrictions, and can take off under zero-zero conditions; this is not a wise or recommended procedure, however. As you gain experience, you will learn that a procedure that is legal is not necessarily a safe one.

You will not be expected to perform an instrument takeoff on your checkride and should question your instructor if the procedure is asked for during training. You should refer to this section for your departure procedure in any event, because the terrain and obstacles which the departure procedure is designed to avoid do not care whether you are operating under Part 91 or 135—they are just as hard and unyielding whether you get paid for running into them or not.

Unless the weather at your destination airport is forecast to be 2,000 feet and 3 miles or better from one hour before until one hour after your ETA, you must designate an alternate airport and carry enough fuel to get you to the destination and then to the alternate plus 45 minutes fuel at normal cruise speed. To determine if a prospective alternate is legally adequate you *must* check its weather forecast and the types of instrument procedures provided for it. If you are filing to a destination airport that does not have an instrument approach you must file an alternate, and if you intend to use a GPS approach at your filed destination, the alternate must have an instrument approach that is not dependent upon the Global Positioning System.

The standard alternate minimums for a precision approach are 600 feet and 2 miles visibility; for a nonprecision approach the standard alternate minimums are an 800-foot ceiling and 2 miles visibility. Some airports have special requirements due to terrain or obstructions which dictate higher alternate minimums.

If the weather conditions required to designate the airport as an alternate are other than standard, the letter A is printed in an triangle in the remarks box of NACO plates to alert you to refer to the "IFR Alternate Minimums" section in the front of the book. (Note in Figure 6-11 that the airport is not authorized as an alternate.) Jeppesen prints the alternate minimums (standard or nonstandard) and the takeoff minimums beneath the airport diagram; runway lengths, widths and details of lighting systems are also printed beneath the airport diagram. Notes are printed with the profile view.

When you check the weather and the approaches available at the alternate you are simply qualifying the alternate as legal under the regulations. If you decide that you can't make it into the destination airport and proceed to the alternate, you are to observe the published minimums for the approach you use when you get there. At that point, forget about 600-2 and 800-2 — they are only qualifying factors.

If the words OCNL, OCNLY, or TEMPO appear in the forecast for the time period you use to qualify an alternate, you must assume the worst—whatever nasty weather *might* occur must be treated as a sure thing, and you can't use that airport as an alternate.

You may be surprised to find that an airport you would like to designate as an alternate has one or more instrument approaches marked NA (not authorized) for use as an alternate. In these situations, some portion of the navigation equipment is not monitored by the FAA and could be inoperative at your time of arrival—but you would have no way of knowing that. So the decision is taken out of your hands by declaring the approach NA.

You do not have to actually go to your filed alternate if you miss the approach at your destination; the ATC controller does not even know what your filed alternate is (that information is retained by the FSS at which you filed). It is a good idea to have a "planning alternate" in mind—one that might not have an instrument approach but which you expect to find VFR conditions if you must divert.

IFR Departure Procedure

When an IFR departure procedure is published, you will find it in the front of the NACO approach plate booklet. Jeppesen prints the departure procedure on the back of the first approach plate for each airport. No departure procedure is published if a 152 feet per mile rate of climb would clear all obstructions. In this situation it is a good idea to check the sectional chart to familiarize yourself with the surrounding terrain. Departures are discussed in detail in Chapter 7.

Notices To Airmen

There are three categories of Notices to Airmen; all three are available at flight service stations. The briefer has access to all three, although you may have to probe a little to get everything you need.

NOTAM (D) information concerns all navigational facilities which are a part of the National Airspace System, all IFR airports, and VFR airports shown with a "§" in the A/FD. The FSS briefer has access to NOTAM (D) information for the entire country, although it may be necessary to request information about a distant airport by teletype. Navaid outages, runway closures, and problems with approach lighting systems qualify for NOTAM (D) handling. NOTAM (D)'s are appended to the hourly weather reports and remain available while they are valid or until published. When a NOTAM is published in the Class II Notices to Airmen (Figure 6-15), which is issued every 28 days, it disappears from the briefer's ready reference and you must ask specifically if there are any published NOTAMs which might affect your flight.

NOTAM (L) information has to do with such things as taxiway closures, men and equipment working on or near the runway, and minor lighting outages that do not affect instrument approach procedures. NOTAM (L) information is distributed locally and is not attached to hourly weather reports. Your briefer can ask the FSS at your destination if any NOTAM (L) are effective, and if your flight will cover much distance you should request this information. Breaking out of an overcast to find a work crew with a backhoe digging a ditch near the runway is hard on the nerves.

No NOTAM will be as effective as a phone call to an operator at the destination airport. They might have information about the airport that is not yet available through the NOTAM system.

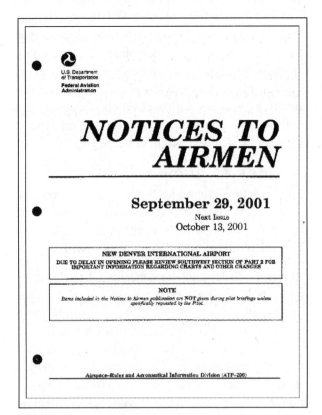

Figure 6-15. *Published NOTAMs*

FDC NOTAMs contain such things as amendments to instrument approach procedures and are obviously of interest to a pilot planning an instrument flight. They are transmitted with the hourly weather only once, and are kept on file at the FSS until canceled or published. Each FSS will keep on file any FDC NOTAMs involving conditions within 400 miles of its location. Information on conditions more than 400 miles distant or which has been published must be requested by the pilot. It is embarrassing to ask a controller for an approach which has been NOTAMed out of service if the information was available in published form and you failed to ask for it during your preflight briefing.

Aeronautical Information Manual

The AIM comes at the end of the list of publications not because it is the least important, but because you should not have to refer to it in planning a specific trip. Keeping up with changes in the *Aeronautical Information Manual* should form a part of your continuing education in aviation, because each new issue of the AIM (published semiannually) might contain a procedural change with an impact on your proposed flight. Don't fall into the trap of thinking that the AIM is only advisory, not regulatory, and that you need not follow its recommendations: ATC controllers assume that pilots are going to follow the procedures laid out in the AIM and their instructions to you are based on that assumption.

The Pilot/Controller Glossary portion of the AIM (which is also included in the Jeppesen J-Aid, and much of it is in Appendix A of this book) is your source of information on the meaning of a specific word or phrase used by a controller. Before you ask "what does procedure turn inbound mean?" or "are bearings measured to or from the station?"—check the glossary. You can't communicate if you don't understand the language.

For Commercial Students Only

The commercial pilot knowledge exam will test your ability to perform some calculations that were not included when you prepared for the private pilot test.

Multiple Elements

You will be asked to combine several performance figures in a problem such as this:

Airport elevation .... 1,000 feet
Cruise altitude .... 9,500 feet
Rate of climb .... 500 ft/min
Average true airspeed .... 135 knots
True course .... 215°
Average wind velocity .... 290° at 20 kts
Variation ....3°W
Deviation .... -2°
Average fuel consumption .... 13 gal/hr

Determine the approximate time, compass heading, distance, and fuel consumed during the climb. Nothing there you have never done before, right? You just haven't been asked to come up with all of those numbers in one bunch.

The first thing you need is time to climb. At 500 feet per minute it will take 17 minutes (or .28 hour) to climb from field elevation to 9,500 feet. At 13 gallons per hour that is 3.64 gallons. On a multiple choice test you might be able to stop right there, if one of the choices combines 17 minutes with 3.6 or 3.7 gallons an hour. Come back and refine the answer if you have time.

But that's test-taking strategy, and you want methodology. With the true course, true airspeed, wind direction and wind velocity, you should be able to come up with a ground speed and wind correction angle using either a manual or electronic flight computer. Using a CX-2 Pathfinder, I get a true course of 223° and a ground speed of 128 knots. Applying variation and deviation results in a compass course of 224°. How does that match with the multiple choice selection you based on time and fuel burn?

To pin down the correct answer selection you need distance. Climbing at a ground speed of 128 knots for .28 hour will take you just over 36 nautical miles. See an answer choice that says 17 minutes, 224°, 36 NM and 3.7 gallons? That's the one.

Unknown Wind

This is one of the reasons why pilots buy LORAN and GPS sets—to figure out the actual wind direction and velocity and make pilot reports when things get boring. You didn't get these problems on the private test because at that time flight computers were new to you.

I am not going to show you how to use your flight computer to do unknown wind problems; read the instruction manual that came with it.

Off-Course Problems

This is another subject that was covered in the instruction book for your flight computer, but it deserves some discussion here.

You have flown 48 miles from the departure airport and suddenly realize that you are 4 miles off course. You need to know how many degrees into the wind you must turn in order to regain the courseline at the destination, which is 120 miles away.

With a manual flight computer, set the distance off course (4) over the distance flown (48) and read the number of degrees of course change required to parallel the courseline over the arrow (60). I get 5°. Now set the distance off course (4) over the distance to go (120) to get the additional course change needed to return to the courseline at the destination. I get 2°, for a total of 7°. If it was me, I would change course 10° so that I would return to the courseline before I reached the destination—but this is an exam, not real life.

You could do the same thing, faster, with a four-function calculator. Distance off course times 60 divided by distance flown to get degrees to parallel, distance off times 60 divided by distance to go to get degrees to converge. Add the two answers to get total correction.

Chapter 6

Charts and Publications Review Questions

Instrument Student Questions

1. (Refer to Figure Q6-1.) At which minimum altitude should you cross the STAKK intersection?

   A—6,500 feet MSL
   B—1,400 feet MSL
   C—10,200 feet MSL

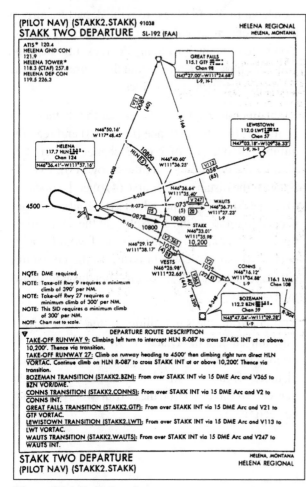

Figure Q6-1. *Stakk Two departure*

2. (Refer to Figure Q6-2.) Using an average ground speed of 140 knots, what minimum rate of climb would meet the required minimum climb rate per NM as specified on the instrument departure procedure?

   A—350 feet per minute
   B—475 feet per minute
   C—700 feet per minute

3. (Refer to Figure Q6-3.) When en route on V448 from YKM VORTAC to BTG VORTAC, what minimum navigation equipment is required to identify ANGOO intersection?

   A—One VOR receiver.
   B—One VOR receiver and DME.
   C—Two VOR receivers.

4. What is the definition of MEA?

   A—The lowest published altitude which meets obstacle clearance requirements and assures acceptable navigational signal coverage.
   B—The horizontal distance a pilot should see when looking down the runway from a moving aircraft.
   C—An altitude which meets obstacle clearance requirements, assures acceptable navigation signal coverage, two-way radio communications, adequate radar coverage, and accurate DME mileage.

5. ATC may assign the MOCA when certain special conditions exist, and when within

   A—22 NM of a VOR.
   B—25 NM of a VOR.
   C—30 NM of a VOR.

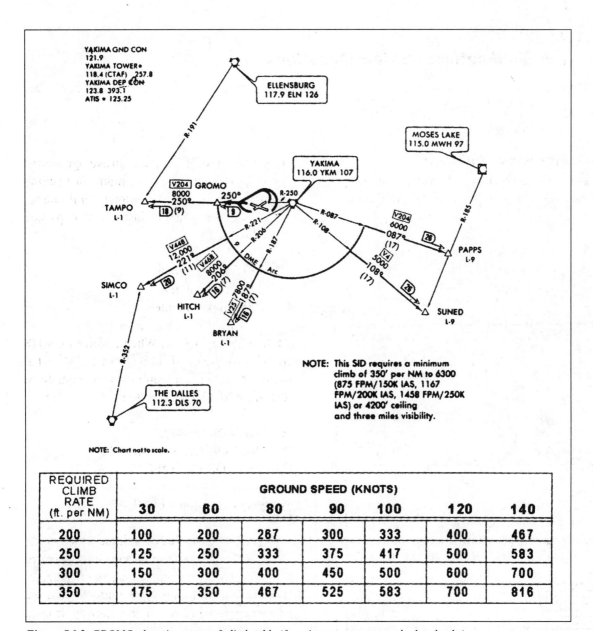

NOTE: This SID requires a minimum climb of 350' per NM to 6300 (875 FPM/150K IAS, 1167 FPM/200K IAS, 1458 FPM/250K IAS) or 4200' ceiling and three miles visibility.

NOTE: Chart not to scale.

REQUIRED CLIMB RATE (ft. per NM)	GROUND SPEED (KNOTS)						
	30	60	80	90	100	120	140
200	100	200	267	300	333	400	467
250	125	250	333	375	417	500	583
300	150	300	400	450	500	600	700
350	175	350	467	525	583	700	816

Figure Q6-2. GROMO plan view; rate-of-climb table (from instrument approach plate books)

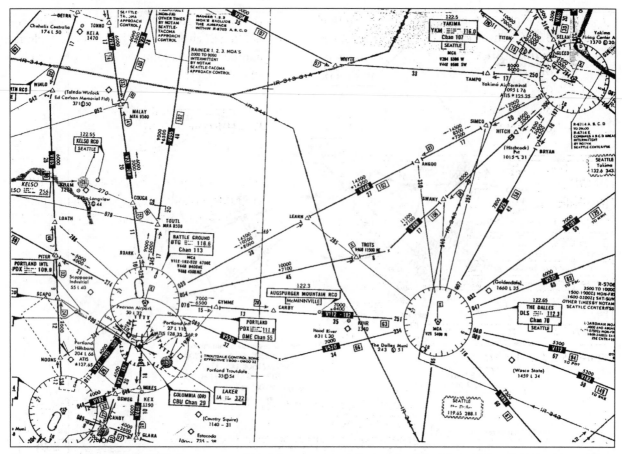

Figure Q6-3. *Enroute chart segment*

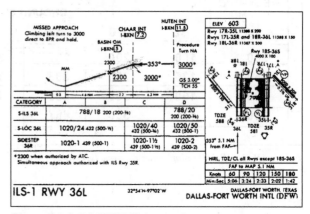

Figure Q6-4. *ILS RWY 36L (excerpt)*

6. (Refer to Figures Q6-4 and Q6-5.) What is the difference in elevation (in feet MSL) be-tween the airport elevation and the TDZE for RWY 36L?

A— 15 feet
B— 18 feet
C— 22 feet

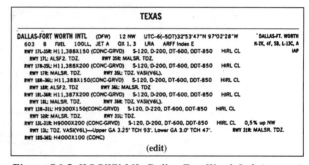

Figure Q6-5. *ILS RWY 36L, Dallas-Fort Worth Intl. (excerpt)*

7. (Refer to Figure Q6-6.) What is the minimum altitude at which you should intercept the glide slope on the ILS RWY 6 approach procedure?

A—3,000 feet MSL
B—1,800 feet MSL
C—1,690 feet MSL

8. (Refer to Figure Q6-6.) Which runway and landing environment lighting is available for approach and landing on RWY 6 at Bradley International?

A—HIRL, REIL, and VASI
B—HIRL and VASI
C—ALSF2 and HIRL

9. (Refer to Figures Q6-7 and Q6-8.) Which aircraft approach category should be used for a circling approach for a landing on RWY 27?

A—A
B—B
C—C

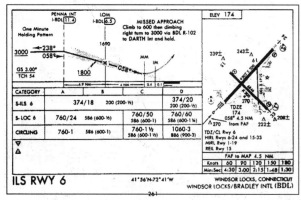

Figure Q6-6. *ILS RWY 6 (BDL)*

		AIRCRAFT INFORMATION	
MAKE Cessna		MODEL 310R	
N 242T		Vso 72	

AIRCRAFT EQUIPMENT/STATUS**

**NOTE: X= OPERATIVE   INOP= INOPERATIVE   N/A= NOT APPLICABLE
TRANSPONDER: X (MODE C) X ILS: (LOCALIZER) X (GLIDE SLOPE) INOP
VOR NO. 1 X (NO. 2) X ADF: X RNAV: N/A
VERTICAL PATH COMPUTER: N/A DME: X
MARKER BEACON: X (AUDIO) X (VISUAL) X

Figure Q6-7. *Flight plan aircraft and information*

AIRCRAFT APPROACH CATEGORIES

Speeds are based on 1.3 times the stall speed in the landing configuration at maximum gross landing weight. An aircraft shall fit in only one category. If it is necessary to maneuver at speeds in excess of the upper limit of a speed range for a category, the minimums for the next higher category should be used. For example, an aircraft which falls in Category A, but is circling to land at a speed in excess of 91 knots, should use the approach Category B minimums when circling to land. See following category limits:

MANEUVERING TABLE

Approach Category	A	B	C	D	E
Speed (Knots)	0-90	91-120	121-140	141-165	Abv 165

Figure Q6-8. *Excerpt from Instrument Approach Procedures—legend*

10. What obstacle clearance and navigation signal coverage is a pilot assured with the Minimum Sector Altitudes depicted on the IAP charts?

    A—1,000 feet and acceptable navigation signal coverage within a 25 NM radius of the navigation facility.
    B—1,000 feet within a 25 NM radius of the navigation facility but not acceptable navigation signal coverage.
    C—500 feet and acceptable navigation signal coverage within a 10 NM radius of the navigation facility.

11. (Refer to Figure Q6-9.) What is the minimum altitude descent procedure if cleared for the S-ILS 9 approach from Seal Beach VORTAC?

    A—Descend and maintain 3,000 to JASER INT, descend to and maintain 2,500 until crossing SWAN LAKE, descend and maintain 1,260 until crossing AGNES, and to 991 (DH) after passing AGNES.
    B—Descend and maintain 3,000 to JASER INT, descend to 2,800 when established on the LOC course, intercept and maintain the GS to 991 (DH).
    C—Descend and maintain 3,000 to JASER INT, descend to 2,500 while established on the LOC course inbound, intercept and maintain the GS to 991 (DH).

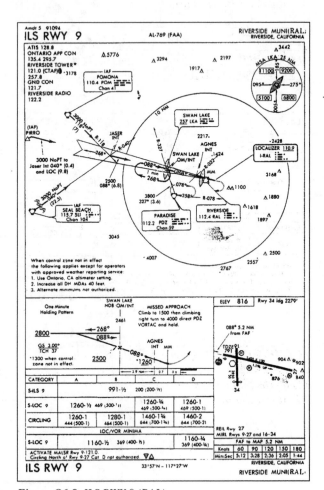

Figure Q6-9. *ILS RWY 9 (RAL)*

12. Aircraft approach categories are based on

A—certificated approach speed at maximum gross weight.
B—1.3 times the stall speed in landing configuration at maximum gross landing weight.
C—1.3 times the stall speed at maximum gross weight.

13. (Refer to Figure Q6-10.) What would be the approach minimums if you must use the Moisant Field altimeter settings?

A—440-1.
B—480 and 1/2.
C—580 and 1/2.

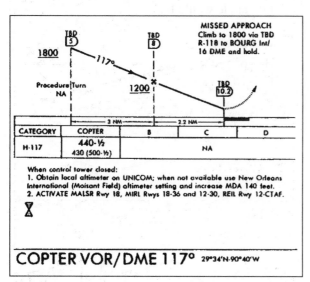

Figure Q6-10. *COPTER VOR DME—117 degrees (HUM)—(excerpt)*

14. What does the Runway Visual Range (RVR) value, depicted on certain straight-in IAP Charts, represent?

A—The slant range distance the pilot can see down the runway while crossing the threshold on glide slope.
B—The horizontal distance a pilot should see when looking down the runway from a moving aircraft.
C—The slant visual range a pilot should see down the final approach and during landing.

15. If the RVR is not reported, what meteorological value should you substitute for 2,400 RVR?

A—A ground visibility of 1/2 NM.
B—A slant range visibility of 2,400 feet for the final approach segment of the published approach procedure.
C—A ground visibility of 1/2 SM.

Continued

Commercial Student Questions

As stated at the beginning of the chapter, there are no chart questions on the commercial pilot exam. But there are a few basic navigation questions, and some of them are included here so that the commercial students will not feel left out.

16. If fuel consumption is 80 pounds per hour and ground speed is 180 knots, how much fuel is required for an airplane to travel 460 NM?

    A—205 pounds
    B—212 pounds
    C—460 pounds

17. GIVEN:

    Wind .... 175° at 20 kts
    Distance .... 135 NM
    True course .... 075°
    True airspeed .... 80 kts
    Fuel consumption .... 105 lb/hr

    Determine the time en route and fuel consumption.

    A—1 hour 28 minutes and 73.2 pounds.
    B—1 hour 38 minutes and 158 pounds.
    C—1 hour 40 minutes and 175 pounds.

18. GIVEN:

    True course .... 105°
    True heading .... 085°
    True airspeed .... 95 kts
    Ground speed .... 87 kts

    Determine the wind direction and speed.

    A—020° and 32 knots.
    B—030° and 38 knots.
    C—200° and 32 knots.

19. GIVEN:

    Distance off course .... 9 mi
    Distance flown .... 95 mi
    Distance to fly .... 125 mi

    To converge at the destination, the total correction angle would be

    A—4°
    B—6°
    C—10°

The IFR System and Departures

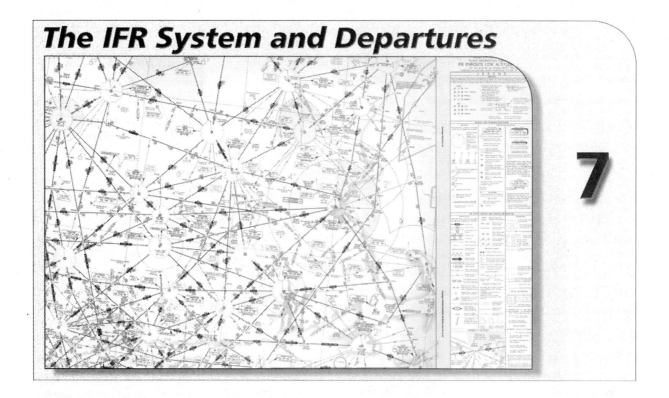

Understanding the System

When instrument pilots talk about the IFR system they use the word "system" advisedly. It is a system, and fitting smoothly into it is 90% of instrument flying. As you and your instructor fly on IFR training trips you will notice that the departure follows a predetermined path, that hand-offs from one controlling facility to another occur at the same point on each flight, and that the frequencies you use follow a pattern. As the enroute phase of each trip blends into the approach phase, you will pass over readily identified points at predictable altitudes. Very little happens by chance. One of your goals as an instrument pilot will be to develop the ability to anticipate what the system will require of you next and to be ready for it.

Every enroute low-altitude chart has a panel listing the ground control, tower, and approach/departure control frequencies for the airports on that chart (Figure 7-1). Where approach and departure control airspace is divided into sectors, the communications panel lists the radials which form the sector boundaries. Air route traffic control center (ARTCC) frequencies are shown on the chart; the name of the Center remote transmitter site is included in the box. Figure 7-2 shows the NACO and Jeppesen symbol-

Figure 7-1. Enroute chart communication panel

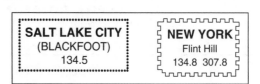

Figure 7-2. Center symbology

ogy for Center frequencies. Boundaries between Centers use the same symbology: castellations ("postage stamps") on NACO charts and dotted lines on Jeppesen charts. Center frequencies are also listed in the Airport/Facility Directory.

By using the A/FD, enroute low-altitude charts, and approach plates, you should be able to list every frequency you will use from the ATIS at the departure airport to the ground control frequency at your destination. There should be no surprises. However, you will find it useful to write new frequencies on your enroute charts close to where a changeover occurs. On the next trip over the same route you will be ready. You will find this to be especially valuable at boundaries between Center and approach control airspace, where the handling of your flight is covered by "letters of agreement" (LOA) between the facilities.

An LOA between a Center and a terminal facility might say something like this: "Arriving propeller flights being handed off from Sector 24 and destined for Podunk, Bigburg, or Acme Metro will cross WHIZZ intersection at 5,000 feet, descending to 4,000 feet." Or, "Propeller flights (except turbo-props) departing Acme Metro during west flow operations with destination airports to the south and southeast will cross the XYZ VORTAC at or above 6,000 feet; turboprops and jets will cross XYZ VORTAC at or above 14,000 feet cleared to Flight Level 230."

When the heading and altitude assigned to your flight don't really agree with what the *Aeronautical Information Manual* would lead you to expect, the reason is almost always a letter of agreement that is not readily available to the public. Just keep track of how you are handled and expect the same thing next time.

The Flight Plan Form

As a VFR pilot, you knew that filing a flight plan with a flight service station was not mandatory but was strongly recommended. As an IFR pilot, that exercise of discretion is no longer available; you can't get into the IFR system without telling the air traffic control people what you have in mind.

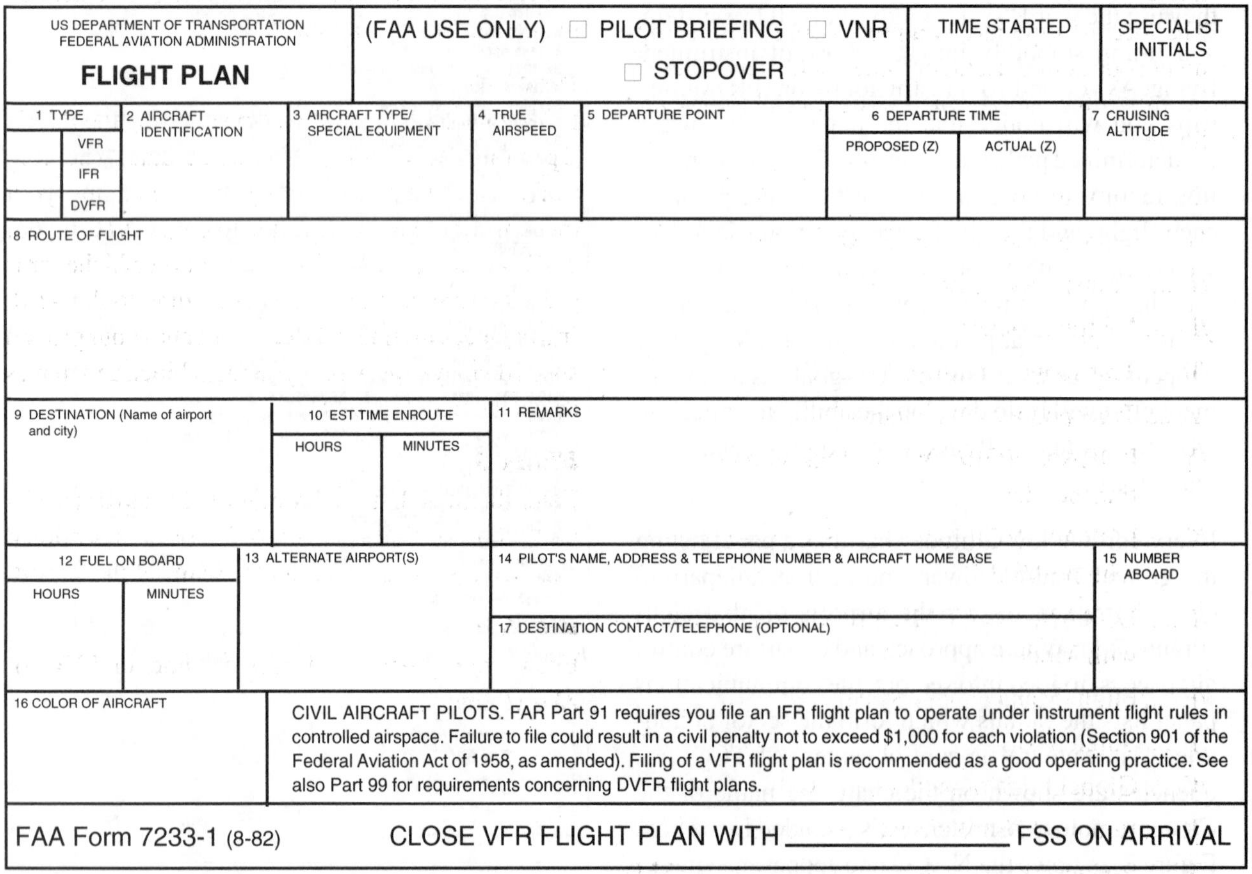

US DEPARTMENT OF TRANSPORTATION FEDERAL AVIATION ADMINISTRATION **FLIGHT PLAN**	(FAA USE ONLY) ☐ PILOT BRIEFING ☐ VNR ☐ STOPOVER			TIME STARTED	SPECIALIST INITIALS

1 TYPE	2 AIRCRAFT IDENTIFICATION	3 AIRCRAFT TYPE/ SPECIAL EQUIPMENT	4 TRUE AIRSPEED	5 DEPARTURE POINT	6 DEPARTURE TIME		7 CRUISING ALTITUDE
VFR					PROPOSED (Z)	ACTUAL (Z)	
IFR							
DVFR							

8 ROUTE OF FLIGHT

9 DESTINATION (Name of airport and city)	10 EST TIME ENROUTE		11 REMARKS
	HOURS	MINUTES	

12 FUEL ON BOARD		13 ALTERNATE AIRPORT(S)	14 PILOT'S NAME, ADDRESS & TELEPHONE NUMBER & AIRCRAFT HOME BASE	15 NUMBER ABOARD
HOURS	MINUTES			
			17 DESTINATION CONTACT/TELEPHONE (OPTIONAL)	

16 COLOR OF AIRCRAFT	CIVIL AIRCRAFT PILOTS. FAR Part 91 requires you file an IFR flight plan to operate under instrument flight rules in controlled airspace. Failure to file could result in a civil penalty not to exceed $1,000 for each violation (Section 901 of the Federal Aviation Act of 1958, as amended). Filing of a VFR flight plan is recommended as a good operating practice. See also Part 99 for requirements concerning DVFR flight plans.

FAA Form 7233-1 (8-82)   CLOSE VFR FLIGHT PLAN WITH _____ FSS ON ARRIVAL

Figure 7-3. Flight plan form

Even if you file with a Direct User Access Terminal (DUAT) provider, you will use the format of the familiar FAA Form 7233-1, and you will be using more of its blocks for your IFR operation than you did for VFR flights. Refer to Figure 7-3.

Block 1

Most of the time, you will simply check the "IFR" box, but there may be times when you will want to file a composite VFR/IFR flight plan. The most common composite flight is a VFR departure, changing to an IFR flight plan at an enroute fix. In this situation, check both the VFR and IFR blocks, and insert the time and point at which you expect to switch to IFR in Block 8; you have to close the VFR portion with an FSS. If you propose to depart IFR and switch to VFR en route, you will have to note the point at which you intend to cancel your IFR clearance and activate the VFR portion. The ATC controller does not get a copy of your flight plan form, so making the necessary notifications is your responsibility.

Block 2

The aircraft N number.

Block 3

The aircraft type and equipment code. The equipment code is important; enroute controllers will rely on this information when assigning altitudes and holding fixes.

/X .... No transponder

/T ..... Transponder with no Mode C

/U .... Transponder with Mode C

/D .... No transponder

/B .... Transponder with no Mode C

/A .... Transponder with Mode C

/Y .... LORAN, VOR/DME, or INS with no transponder

/C .... LORAN, VOR/DME, or INS, transponder with no Mode C

/I ...... LORAN, VOR/DME, or INS, transponder with Mode C

/E ..... Flight Management System (FMS)

/F ..... Single FMS

/G .... Global Positioning System (GPS)

/R .... Required Navigational Performance

/W ... Reduced Vertical Separation Minima (RVSM)

The definition of area navigation (RNAV) includes LORAN and GPS, if your LORAN has been approved for IFR en route. GPS sets manufactured under TSO C-129 (ask the dealer) can be used for enroute navigation, but not as the sole source of navigational data. Equipment that uses ground-based navaids (VOR, NDB, RNAV) must be installed and operational. If your airplane is RNAV-equipped, file /C, /I, or /W even if you have not filed a random route. Use /W, of course, if you have an approved GPS installation. ATC may take advantage of your ability to navigate point-to-point to expedite your trip.

Many non-pilot controllers have not yet caught on to the capabilities of LORAN and GPS, however, and to them "slant India" or "slant Whiskey" means that you can navigate direct only to a point identified by a radial and distance from a VOR or VORTAC. If you have a LORAN or GPS with a database you might have to tell a controller that you can go direct to an intersection or other point in space. You can't go wrong by using a latitude-longitude description of that point in space; the computer at one Center might not recognize the name of an airport or intersection in another Center's airspace.

Block 4

Enter your computed true airspeed, using the Pilot's Operating Handbook performance data. The controller may use this information in planning your movements. You are expected to notify ATC if your TAS varies more than 5% or 10 knots (whichever is greater) from the filed value, according to the AIM. In a radar environment the controller has your ground speed displayed as part of your data block and makes decisions based on that.

Block 5

Enter the three letter identifier of the departure airport; you can find it in the A/FD or on a sectional chart. If it is unknown, enter the name of the airport.

Block 6

Enter your proposed departure time in UTC or ZULU time.

Block 7

Enter your initial desired altitude or the highest altitude you plan to fly en route. If you plan to fly tower-enroute (TEC) or on an IFR preferred route, check the A/FD. The TEC listing will have a maximum authorized altitude and the preferred routes may have altitudes specified. Both TEC and preferred routes will be discussed later.

Block 8

Define the route of flight using navaid identifiers, airway numbers, and intersection names if you plan to leave an airway at an intersection or use an initial approach fix as a clearance limit. When filing VOR/DME RNAV, define the route using waypoints (navaid identifiers with radial and distance—MIA 235022 is the Miami 235° radial at 22 nautical miles). Using LORAN or GPS and filing a direct route, file a latitude-longitude waypoint (for example, 4715/12215—four figures for latitude in degrees and minutes, slant, longitude in degrees and minutes) in the next Center's airspace if your flight will cross a Center boundary. Also, you must file a waypoint within 200 NM of the boundary in the airspace of the Center you are leaving.

If any portion of your flight is to be off-airways you must consider the Standard Service Volume of the navaids to be used (AIM 1-1-8) and select navaids to define the off-airways segment no further apart than the distance specified for your cruise altitude in the AIM. In a radar environment, ATC may initiate direct routes that exceed service volume limits; in such cases ATC will provide radar monitoring and navigational assistance. When off-airways you must also choose an altitude that will provide 1,000 feet of clearance from terrain and obstructions within 5 miles of your track (2,000 feet in mountainous terrain).

Block 9

Enter the three letter identifier of the destination airport, including the name of the city and state if necessary for clarity. Vancouver, Washington, and Vancouver, B.C., are not that far apart. Portland, Maine, and Portland, Oregon do not present the same problem.

Block 10

Enter your estimated time en route based on the latest forecast winds. This exercise will take you back to your student pilot days, but accuracy will be much more important than it was for those VFR flights. En route flight planning will be explored in detail later in this chapter. Calculate the ETA to the destination airport, not to an initial approach fix—that's the way the system wants you to do it.

Block 11

This is the place for "No DP," "No oxygen on board," "One hour layover at Kansas City," "No overwater," etc. Remarks are not passed along to all controllers, so when you arrive at a point in your flight where something in this block becomes important, make sure that the controller knows about it. Don't ever assume that a controller knows every detail about your flight or that the last controller passed on a request to your current controller. Be assertive.

Block 12

Enter the total fuel on board at the departure point, not just what your computations indicate you will need. You must carry sufficient fuel to reach your destination, fly from there to your alternate, and have a 45 minute reserve on board when you land. Make it a point of pride to never eat into your reserve fuel. Do not hesitate to declare "minimum fuel" if that becomes a possibility.

Block 13

Unless the weather at your point of first intended landing is forecast to have a ceiling of at least 2,000 feet AGL with a visibility of 3 miles or better from one hour before until one hour after your estimated time of arrival, you must file an alternate airport. The weather at the alternate must be forecast to meet the alternate minimums specified at your ETA. If your destination is an airport without an approved instrument approach, you must file an alternate.

Blocks 14, 15 and 16 entries are the same as VFR flights.

Blocks 2 through 11 will be transmitted to the ARTCC; the remainder will be kept on file at the FSS. In the event of lost communication, this means that the controller at your destination will not necessarily know what your alternate is.

Special Planning Considerations

There are a very small number of airports that require extra planning consideration. At the very busiest airports, you will have to have a reservation on file. Those airports are JFK, LaGuardia, and Newark in the New York area, Washington National airport, and O'Hare in Chicago. The AIM contains details on making reservations (4-1-21). You will not be asked about High Density Airport Operations on your knowledge examination.

As a newly fledged instrument pilot you are much more likely to be affected by AIM 5-1-8 "IFR Operations to High Altitude Destinations." There are eleven airports (Chadron, Nebraska is the easternmost) with minimum descent altitudes (MDAs) higher than 2,000 feet AGL and/or which have visibility minimums greater than 3 miles. If one of these airports is your destination and you are deciding whether or not to file an alternate (Block 13 on the flight plan form), a forecast of 2,000 and 3 or better would lead you to believe that no alternate is required. However, if you do your fuel planning on that basis and find out upon arrival that even 2,000 and 3 is below landing minimums you are going to be in a world of hurt. If you fly in the west, or if you plan to do a lot of transcontinental IFR flying, check this out.

Departure Procedures (DPs)

The first step in using the system is learning how to enter it. The IFR departure procedure gets you from the runway to the en route structure, and whether it is simple or complex depends on the terrain and obstructions around the departure airport, the status of the departure airport (controlled or uncontrolled), and the nature of the overlying airspace.

There is one rule governing departures that you ignore at your peril: You are responsible for terrain and obstacle clearance until ATC not only has you in radar contact but can give you vectors. Simply hearing "radar contact" or being in radio communication does not relieve you of this responsibility. A momentary lapse on the part of ATC cannot cause you to collide with a mountain if you know where you are, and you *must* know where the mountains are — always carry sectional charts on IFR flights.

If you are departing from an airport that has a published instrument approach procedure, you will find the instrument departure procedure for that airport printed in the front of the NACO approach plate book or on the back of the first Jeppesen plate for that city. These procedures include headings and altitudes to fly to enable you to climb to your first assigned altitude (or to your filed altitude), and to join the airway while staying safely clear of terrain and obstructions.

The FAA provides departure procedures only for airports with instrument approach procedures. If you are departing an airport that has no published departure procedure, you must plan a departure path that keeps you well clear of all obstacles while climbing to join the enroute structure (use that sectional again). In this situation you will most likely be cleared direct to the nearest VOR or airway, with instructions to contact Center as you reach a certain altitude.

This type of departure puts more responsibility on your shoulders than any other, because the ATC controllers cannot provide any type of service until you are in controlled airspace and are at or above the Minimum Instrument Altitude (MIA) as dictated by §91.177, or are on an airway. It is especially foolhardy for you to assume that a radar controller can provide terrain clearance information during your climb. Terrain clearance is your responsibility. If I seem to be placing a lot of emphasis on this point it is because accident statistics indicate that some pilots are more than willing to place their lives and the lives of their passengers in the hands of ATC.

If the first controller you talk to after getting airborne is a departure controller, surveillance radar and a display of terrain and obstacles at the controller's position should keep you clear of things to hit. On the other hand, Center controllers aren't allowed to give you vectors until you reach the minimum instrument altitude—while you are climbing toward that altitude you had better know where the hard things are. Listen for the word "vector"; it has significant meaning to you.

A common clearance is "When able, proceed direct to PODUNK VOR; climb and maintain…." That clearance does not mean to head for the VOR as soon as you have climbed 400 feet or as soon as you can receive a good signal from PODUNK. It means that you are to proceed to PODUNK when you can do so without hitting anything; reception of a good signal from the navaid is understood.

If you receive an abbreviated clearance it will always contain the name of the destination airport (or a specific fix) and an altitude; if a procedure departure is to be flown its name will be included in an abbreviated clearance: "Cleared to PODUNK airport via WHOMP-6 departure, then as filed, climb and maintain 8,000 feet…" Do not hesitate to ask for a full-route clearance if you feel uncomfortable with an abbreviated clearance.

Figure 7-4 is an excerpt from an enroute low-altitude chart covering the central California coast. The departure procedure for the Santa Ynez airport, near the bottom center of the chart, calls for pilots departing on runway 8 to turn left and climb to 6,000 feet on a heading of 260° to intercept V-27, thence to ORCUT, and for pilots departing runway 26 to climb to 6,000 feet via the RZS 275° radial and V-27 to ORCUT. There is higher terrain both north and south of Santa Ynez, thus the emphasis on climbing westbound. Please note that although radar contact might be established with the Vandenberg AFB controller at a lower altitude, the responsibility for terrain separation rests wholly on the shoulders of the pilot until the minimum instrument altitude is reached. This is the type of clearance you are going to receive 90 percent of the time, and you cannot expect the controller to keep you out of the trees.

What if the only published procedure is for runway 27 and your destination lies east of the departure airport? If you are sure that you can remain VFR while climbing to the MEA, file your IFR flight plan with a fix east of the airport as your departure point, using your best estimate of your ETA over that fix as departure time. When your flight strip shows up at Center, there will be no doubt that you will call from over that fix to pick up your IFR clearance from Center.

You don't have to follow the published departure procedure—but it sure is a good idea to do so unless you are satisfied that you can stay clear of terrain and obstructions visually during your climb. My suggestion is that you always follow the published procedure if one exists. If you decide to "roll your own" and it doesn't work out, your insurer will use your failure to follow a published procedure as a reason to deny coverage. Where no departure procedure is published, you are authorized to "climb on course"; the fact that there is no procedure in the book means that there are no obstacles which you could not clear with a climb rate of 152 feet per mile between the airport and the point at which you join the enroute airway.

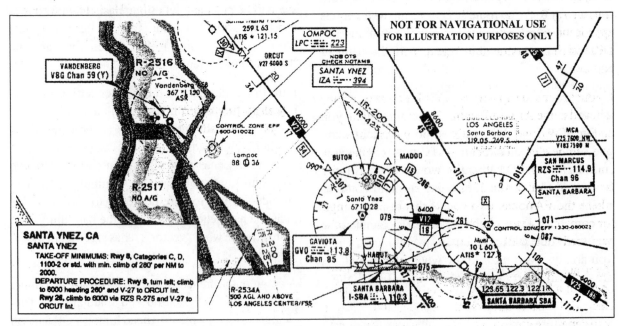

Figure 7-4. Enroute chart excerpt, with departure procedure from approach plate book

▼ **TAKE-OFF MINIMUMS AND (OBSTACLE) DEPARTURE PROCEDURES** ▼

99084

BENNINGTON, VT
WILLIAM H. MORSE STATE
    TAKE-OFF MINIMUMS: **Rwy 13,** 2200-3, restricted to
    CAT A and B only, CAT C NA. **Rwy 31,** 500-2 or std.
    with a min. climb of 240' per NM to 1400.
    DEPARTURE PROCEDURE: **Rwy 13,** climbing left
    turn direct to CAM VORTAC, continue climb in
    hold to 3500 before proceeding on course. **Rwy
    31,** climbing right turn direct CAM VORTAC,
    continue climb in hold to 3500 before proceeding
    on course.

BERLIN, NH
BERLIN MUNI
    TAKE-OFF MINIMUMS: **Rwys 18, 36,** 1000-2.
    DEPARTURE PROCEDURE: **Rwys 18, 36,** climb
    visually over the airport to 2100, continue climb to
    3000 via BML R-192, then climbing right turn to
    4400 direct BML VOR/DME and hold. Climb in
    holding pattern (N, left turns, 192° inbound) to
    MEA before proceeding on course.

BRIDGEPORT, CT
IGOR I. SIKORSKY MEMORIAL
    TAKE-OFF MINIMUMS: **Rwy 11,** 300-1.
    Rwy 29, 500-1.

BURLINGTON, VT
BURLINGTON INTL
    TAKE-OFF MINIMUMS: **Rwy 15,** 1000-2 or std. with
    a min. climb of 260' per NM to 1600. **Rwy 19,** 700-2 or
    std. with a min. climb of 220' per NM to 1200.
    DEPARTURE PROCEDURE: **Rwy 1,** climb runway
    heading to 800, then climbing left turn direct
    BTV VORTAC before proceeding on course.
    Rwys 15,19, climbing right turn direct
    BTV VORTAC, climb in holding pattern (SW, left
    turns, 036° inbound) to 4100 before proceeding on
    course. **Rwy 33,** climbing left turn direct
    BTV VORTAC, climb in holding pattern (SW, left
    turns, 036° inbound) to 4100 before proceeding on
    course.

Figure 7-5A. *Excerpt from Northeast 1 approach plates packet, IFR departures*

A sectional chart comes in handy when planning your departure path; when in doubt, climb directly over the airport until you are at a safe altitude or are in radar contact. You must be in at least Class E airspace before ATC can control you, but this should be no problem in most areas—there are few airports with instrument approaches left where Class E airspace does not extend to the surface. Figure 7-5A, a listing of departure procedures taken from the Northeast 1 packet of approach charts indicates no specific instructions for IFR departures from Bridgeport, CT, while a complex procedure must be followed at Burlington, VT. Note that in the listing of approaches for Bridgeport (Figure 7-5B) there is a DP, which is illustrated in Figure 7-5C on the next page.

If your proposed trip will use an IFR preferred route, as listed in the Airport/Facility Directory (Figure 7-6 on Page 7-9), and the listing begins with an airway, you will be cleared direct to that airway and then on course. If the A/FD listing shows a fix first, you will be cleared to that fix. If you fly on the east coast, where the FAA has designated preferred routings for many city pairs, checking for the existence of a preferred route will save planning time.

If you are fairly certain that you will be able to climb on top of a layer of haze or an overcast and be in the clear while still in airspace that belongs to the tower or to departure control, you can save time by request-ing a climb to VFR conditions on top (put OTP in Block 7), where you will be expected to cancel this local IFR clearance. At some airports you can bypass the whole IFR flight-planning procedure and address this request to the ground controller, but your departure will usually have to be coordinated with the ATC facility governing your area.

That doesn't eliminate the time saving possibilities, however. Ask the tower controller for a climb to VFR on top when you get on the tower frequency, and you may hear, "Amend your clearance. Cleared to Hometown VOR [you are departing Hometown airport],

Continued on Page 7-11

Figure 7-5B. *Bridgeport, CT approach and departure listings in index*

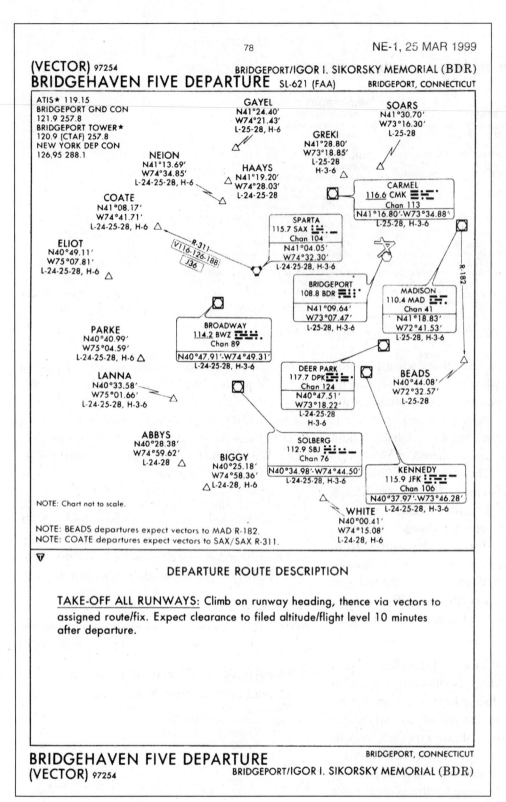

(VECTOR) 97254
BRIDGEHAVEN FIVE DEPARTURE SL-621 (FAA)

BRIDGEPORT/IGOR I. SIKORSKY MEMORIAL (BDR)

BRIDGEPORT, CONNECTICUT

ATIS★ 119.15
BRIDGEPORT GND CON
121.9 257.8
BRIDGEPORT TOWER★
120.9 (CTAF) 257.8
NEW YORK DEP CON
126.95 288.1

GAYEL
N41°24.40'
W74°21.43'
L-25-28, H-6

SOARS
N41°30.70'
W73°16.30'
L-25-28

GREKI
N41°28.80'
W73°18.85'
L-25-28
H-3-6

NEION
N41°13.69'
W74°34.85'
L-24-25-28, H-6

HAAYS
N41°19.20'
W74°28.03'
L-24-25-28

CARMEL
116.6 CMK
Chan 113
N41°16.80'-W73°34.88'
L-25-28, H-3-6

COATE
N41°08.17'
W74°41.71'
L-24-25-28, H-6

SPARTA
115.7 SAX
Chan 104
N41°04.05'
W74°32.30'
L-24-25-28, H-3-6

ELIOT
N40°49.11'
W75°07.81'
L-24-25-28, H-6

R-311
V116-126-188
J36

R-182

BRIDGEPORT
108.8 BDR
N41°09.64'
W73°07.47'
L-25-28, H-3-6

MADISON
110.4 MAD
Chan 41
N41°18.83'
W72°41.53'
L-25-28, H-3-6

PARKE
N40°40.99'
W75°04.59'
L-24-25-28, H-6

BROADWAY
114.2 BWZ
Chan 89
N40°47.91'-W74°49.31'
L-24-25-28, H-3-6

DEER PARK
117.7 DPK
Chan 124
N40°47.51'
W73°18.22'
L-24-25-28
H-3-6

BEADS
N40°44.08'
W72°32.57'
L-25-28

LANNA
N40°33.58'
W75°01.66'
L-24-25-28, H-3-6

ABBYS
N40°28.38'
W74°59.62'
L-24-28

SOLBERG
112.9 SBJ
Chan 76
N40°34.98'-W74°44.50'
L-24-25-28, H-3-6

BIGGY
N40°25.18'
W74°58.36'
L-24-28, H-6

KENNEDY
115.9 JFK
Chan 106
N40°37.97'-W73°46.28'
L-24-25-28, H-3-6

WHITE
N40°00.41'
W74°15.08'
L-24-28, H-6

NOTE: Chart not to scale.

NOTE: BEADS departures expect vectors to MAD R-182.
NOTE: COATE departures expect vectors to SAX/SAX R-311.

DEPARTURE ROUTE DESCRIPTION

<u>TAKE-OFF ALL RUNWAYS:</u> Climb on runway heading, thence via vectors to assigned route/fix. Expect clearance to filed altitude/flight level 10 minutes after departure.

BRIDGEHAVEN FIVE DEPARTURE
(VECTOR) 97254

BRIDGEPORT, CONNECTICUT
BRIDGEPORT/IGOR I. SIKORSKY MEMORIAL (BDR)

Figure 7-5C. Bridgeport Departure plate

A system of preferred routes has been established to guide pilots in planning their route of flight, to minimize route changes during the operational phase of flight, and to aid in the efficient orderly management of the air traffic using federal airways. The preferred IFR routes which follow are designed to serve the needs of airspace users and to provide for a systematic flow of air traffic in the major terminal and en route flight environments. Cooperation by all pilots in filing preferred routes will result in fewer traffic delays and will better provide for efficient departure, en route and arrival air traffic service.

The following lists contain preferred IFR routes for the low altitude stratum and the high altitude stratum. The high altitude list is in two sections; the first section showing terminal to terminal routes and the second section showing single direction route segments. Also, on some high altitude routes low altitude airways are included as transition routes.

The following will explain the terms/abbreviations used in the listing:

1. Preferred routes beginning/ending with an airway number indicate that the airway essentially overlies the airport and flight are normally cleared directly on the airway.

2. Preferred IFR routes beginning/ending with a fix indicate that aircraft may be routed to/from these fixes via a Standard Instrument Departure (SID) route, radar vectors (RV), or a Standard Terminal Arrival Route (STAR).

3. Preferred IFR routes for major terminals selected are listed alphabetically under the name of the departure airport. Where several airports are in proximity they are listed under the principal airport and categorized as a metropolitan area; e.g., New York Metro Area.

4. Preferred IFR routes used in one direction only for selected segments, irrespective of point of departure or destination, are listed numerically showing the segment fixes and the direction and times effective.

5. Where more than one route is listed the routes have equal priority for use.

6. Official location identifiers are used in the route description for VOR/VORTAC navaids.

7. Intersection names are spelled out.

8. Navaid radial and distance fixes (e.g., ARD201113) have been used in the route description in an expediency and intersection names will be assigned as soon as routine processing can be accomplished. Navaid radial (no distance stated) may be used to describe a route to intercept a specified airway (e.g., MIV MIV101 V39); another navaid radial (e.g., UIM UIM255 GSW081); or an intersection (e.g., GSW081 FITCH).

9. Where two navaids, an intersection and a navaid, a navaid and a navaid radial and distance point, or any navigable combination of these route descriptions follow in succession, the route is direct.

10. The effective times for the routes are in UTC. During periods of daylight savings time effective times will be one hour earlier than indicated. All states observe daylight savings time except Arizona, that portion of Indiana in the eastern time zone, Puerto Rico, and the Virgin Islands. Pilots planning flight between the terminals or route segments listed should file for the appropriate preferred IFR route.

11. (90–170 incl) altitude flight level assignment in hundred of feet.

12. The notations "pressurized" and "unpressurized" for certain low altitude preferred routes to Kennedy Airport indicate the preferred route based on aircraft performance.

13. High Altitude Preferred IFR Routes are in effect during the following time periods unless otherwise noted.

Sun .... 1300–2259 local time.
Mon thru Fri .... 0701–2259 local time.
Sat .... 0701–1459 local time.

14. Use current SIDs and STARs for flight planning.

15. For high altitude routes, the portion of the routes contained in brackets [ ] is suggested but optional. The portion of the route outside the brackets will likely be required by the facilities involved.

LOW ALTITUDE

SPECIAL LOW ALTITUDE DIRECTIONAL ROUTES

	Route	Effective Times (UTC)
Low altitude IFR traffic 13000 feet and below overflying the Portland, OR Area:		
Southbound/southwestbound	OLM V165 UBG	1400–0700
Northbound	UBG V165 OLM	1400–0700
Low Altitude IFR traffic 15000 feet and below overflying the Seattle, WA Area:		
Southbound/Southwestbound	LOFAL V287 OLM V165 UBG	1400–0700
Northbound	UBG V165 OLM V287 LOFAL	1400–0700
Low Altitude IFR traffic 9000 feet and below terminating/departing airports in the Seattle, WA Area:		
Northbound	UBG V165 CARRO	1400–0700
Southbound	OLM V165 UBG	1400–0700
Low Altitude IFR traffic from the Seattle, WA Area landing Paine:		
Northbound	direct PAE at 4000 feet	1400–0700
Low Altitude IFR traffic from the North terminating at McMinnville, OR, Aurora State, OR, or Hillsboro, OR:		
Southbound	V165 UBG	1400–0700

Figure 7-6. IFR preferred routes from the A/FD

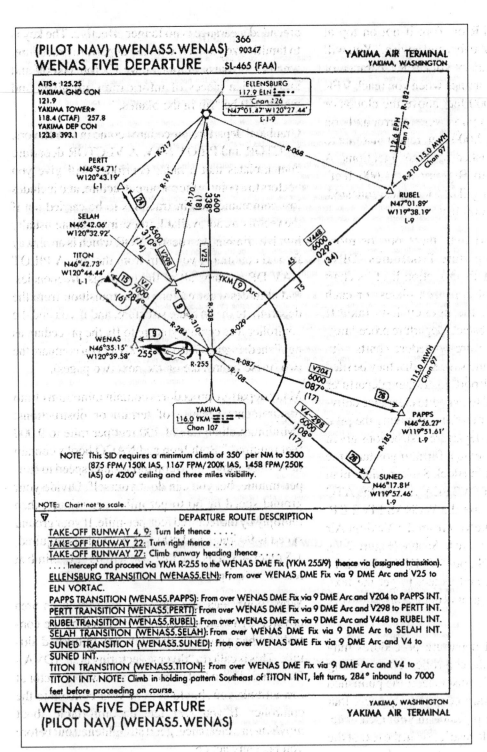

(PILOT NAV) (WENAS5.WENAS)   366
WENAS FIVE DEPARTURE   90347
    SL-465 (FAA)

YAKIMA AIR TERMINAL
YAKIMA, WASHINGTON

ATIS* 125.25
YAKIMA GND CON
121.9
YAKIMA TOWER*
118.4 (CTAF) 257.8
YAKIMA DEP CON
123.8 393.1

ELLENSBURG
117.9 ELN ● ●
Chan 126
N47°01.47'W120°27.44'
L-1-9

PERTT
N46°54.71'
W120°43.19'
L-1

SELAH
N46°42.06'
W120°32.92'

TITON
N46°42.73'
W120°44.44'
L-1

WENAS
N46°35.15'
W120°39.58'

RUBEL
N47°01.89'
W119°38.19'
L-9

PAPPS
N46°26.27'
W119°51.61'
L-9

SUNED
N46°17.8↑
W119°57.46'
L-9

YAKIMA
116.0 YKM
Chan 107

NOTE: This SID requires a minimum climb of 350' per NM to 5500
(875 FPM/150K IAS, 1167 FPM/200K IAS, 1458 FPM/250K
IAS) or 4200' ceiling and three miles visibility.

NOTE: Chart not to scale.

DEPARTURE ROUTE DESCRIPTION

TAKE-OFF RUNWAY 4, 9: Turn left thence . . . .
TAKE-OFF RUNWAY 22: Turn right thence . . . .
TAKE-OFF RUNWAY 27: Climb runway heading thence . . . .
. . . . Intercept and proceed via YKM R-255 to the WENAS DME Fix (YKM 255/9) thence via (assigned transition).
ELLENSBURG TRANSITION (WENAS5.ELN): From over WENAS DME Fix via 9 DME Arc and V25 to
ELN VORTAC.
PAPPS TRANSITION (WENAS5.PAPPS): From over WENAS DME Fix via 9 DME Arc and V204 to PAPPS INT.
PERTT TRANSITION (WENAS5.PERTT): From over WENAS DME Fix via 9 DME Arc and V298 to PERTT INT.
RUBEL TRANSITION (WENAS5.RUBEL): From over WENAS DME Fix via 9 DME Arc and V448 to RUBEL INT.
SELAH TRANSITION (WENAS5.SELAH): From over WENAS DME Fix via 9 DME Arc to SELAH INT.
SUNED TRANSITION (WENAS5.SUNED): From over WENAS DME Fix via 9 DME Arc and V4 to
SUNED INT.
TITON TRANSITION (WENAS5.TITON): From over WENAS DME Fix via 9 DME Arc and V4 to
TITON INT. NOTE: Climb in holding pattern Southeast of TITON INT, left turns, 284° inbound to 7000
feet before proceeding on course.

WENAS FIVE DEPARTURE
(PILOT NAV) (WENAS5.WENAS)

YAKIMA, WASHINGTON
YAKIMA AIR TERMINAL

Figure 7-7. Yakima Air Terminal

climb and maintain VFR on Top; if not on top at 7,000 feet, maintain 7,000 feet and advise." You will be expected to either cancel your IFR clearance or ask for a VFR on top clearance when you reach VFR conditions (at least 1,000 feet above the clouds or haze layer). If the tops reports were in error and you are still in the clouds at 7,000 feet, report that fact to ATC and you will be asked for your intentions. A reply of "Victor 206 to Bigburg at 11,000 feet" should result in something like "Cleared as requested, climb and maintain 11,000 feet."

Your departure airport may have one or more published obstacle Departure Procedures (DPs). NACO lists graphical DPs in section B of its chart packets with the list of approach plates for each airport; in section C, the agency lists takeoff minimums and textual obstacle departure procedures. Jeppesen includes departure procedure charts with its subscription service and suggests that they be filed with the plates for the airport. Instrument departures procedures are intended to expedite clearance delivery and shorten communications by giving the pilot one plate with complex departure instructions given both graphically and in textual form. If you have the DP available, include it in Block 8 of the flight plan form: "WENAS5.PERTT V2 SEA…" tells the ATC system that you plan to use the WENAS FIVE DP, PERTT transition to take you from the Yakima Air Terminal to Victor 2 en route to Seattle (Figure 7-7). If you do not have the DP, put "No DP" in Block 11 of the flight plan form and expect to get the text, word for word, from the ground or clearance delivery controller.

Use of some graphical departure procedures may leave you wondering if the controller left something out of your clearance. For instance, if the published DP includes the departure control frequency, that information may not be repeated in your clearance. Also, if there is an altitude restriction in the text of the DP such as: "Maintain runway heading for vectors, stay at or below 2,000 feet, expect clearance to filed altitude within 6 nautical miles of the airport…" the controller need not specifically mention the altitude restriction in your clearance. However, if the tower controller says "Cleared for takeoff, climb and maintain 4,000 feet," the 2,000-foot restriction is thereby canceled; any restriction that is not restated in an amended clearance is no longer effective. The key is to familiarize yourself with the departure procedure, whether textual or graphical, well before takeoff and know which pieces of information are given and which will be "fill in the blanks."

Graphical departure procedures come in two flavors, VECTOR and PILOT NAV. A VECTOR departure contemplates that a radar controller will give you vectors to a point in the enroute structure, and includes lost communication instructions to be carried out if the vectors are not available; these instructions usually involve climbing to a nearby VOR which is an airway fix and continuing your trip from that fix. A PILOT NAV DP contains all of the headings, frequencies, and altitudes required for you to transition from the departure to the en route structure, and if you and the controller lose contact you are to fly the procedure as published. Figures 7-8A and 7-8B let you compare the two (these figures are on the next two pages).

Many departure procedures contain minimum climb requirements because of terrain or obstructions: "Minimum climb rate of 400 feet per mile to 9,000 feet required." Both Jepp and NACO books contain tables that allow you to convert ground speed to feet-per-minute, but you can do it yourself. Divide your ground speed by 60 to get miles per minute, then multiply by the required feet-per-mile. If your ground speed is 90 knots and 400 feet per mile is required, 1.5 times 400 tells you that you will have to climb at least 600 feet per minute.

When your departure path lies entirely in an area covered by radar, you may be vectored by the controller when you are well below any published altitude. This is called a "diverse vectoring area" (DVA). Of course, if you feel uncomfortable with a vector at low altitude you should convey your concern to the controller. If you *ever* feel uncomfortable about *anything* in a clearance, get it straightened out before you take any action.

Tower Enroute Control (TEC) can be used when a short IFR flight will stay in the airspace of adjoining approach control facilities and no coordination with a Center is required. City pairs where TEC is available (and the maximum enroute altitudes) are listed

Continued on Page 7-14

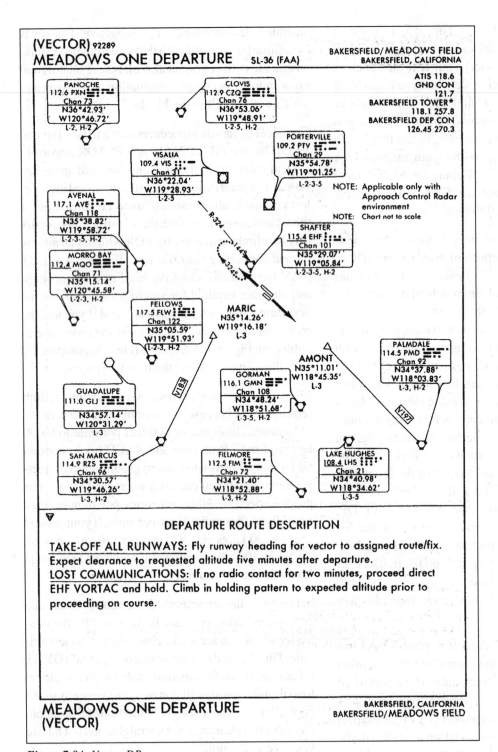

(VECTOR) 92289
MEADOWS ONE DEPARTURE   SL-36 (FAA)

BAKERSFIELD/MEADOWS FIELD
BAKERSFIELD, CALIFORNIA

ATIS 118.6
GND CON
121.7
BAKERSFIELD TOWER*
118.1 257.8
BAKERSFIELD DEP CON
126.45 270.3

PANOCHE
112.6 PXN
Chan 73
N36°42.93'
W120°46.72'
L-2, H-2

CLOVIS
112.9 CZQ
Chan 76
N36°53.06'
W119°48.91'
L-2-5, H-2

PORTERVILLE
109.2 PTV
Chan 29
N35°54.78'
W119°01.25'
L-2-3-5

VISALIA
109.4 VIS
Chan 31
N36°22.04'
W119°28.93'
L-2-5

AVENAL
117.1 AVE
Chan 118
N35°38.82'
W119°58.72'
L-2-3-5, H-2

R-324

144°

324°

SHAFTER
115.4 EHF
Chan 101
N35°29.07'
W119°05.84'
L-2-3-5, H-2

NOTE: Applicable only with
Approach Control Radar
environment

NOTE: Chart not to scale

MORRO BAY
112.4 MQO
Chan 71
N35°15.14'
W120°45.58'
L-2-3, H-2

FELLOWS
117.5 FLW
Chan 122
N35°05.59'
W119°51.93'
L-2-3, H-2

MARIC
N35°14.26'
W119°16.18'
L-3

V183

PALMDALE
114.5 PMD
Chan 92
N34°37.88'
W118°03.83'
L-3, H-2

AMONT
N35°11.01'
W118°45.35'
L-3

GUADALUPE
111.0 GLJ
N34°57.14'
W120°31.29'
L-3

GORMAN
116.1 GMN
Chan 108
N34°48.24'
W118°51.68'
L-3-5, H-2

V197

SAN MARCUS
114.9 RZS
Chan 96
N34°30.57'
W119°46.26'
L-3, H-2

FILLMORE
112.5 FIM
Chan 72
N34°21.40'
W118°52.88'
L-3, H-2

LAKE HUGHES
108.4 LHS
Chan 21
N34°40.98'
W118°34.62'
L-3-5

DEPARTURE ROUTE DESCRIPTION

TAKE-OFF ALL RUNWAYS: Fly runway heading for vector to assigned route/fix.
Expect clearance to requested altitude five minutes after departure.
LOST COMMUNICATIONS: If no radio contact for two minutes, proceed direct
EHF VORTAC and hold. Climb in holding pattern to expected altitude prior to
proceeding on course.

MEADOWS ONE DEPARTURE
(VECTOR)

BAKERSFIELD, CALIFORNIA
BAKERSFIELD/MEADOWS FIELD

Figure 7-8A. Vector DP

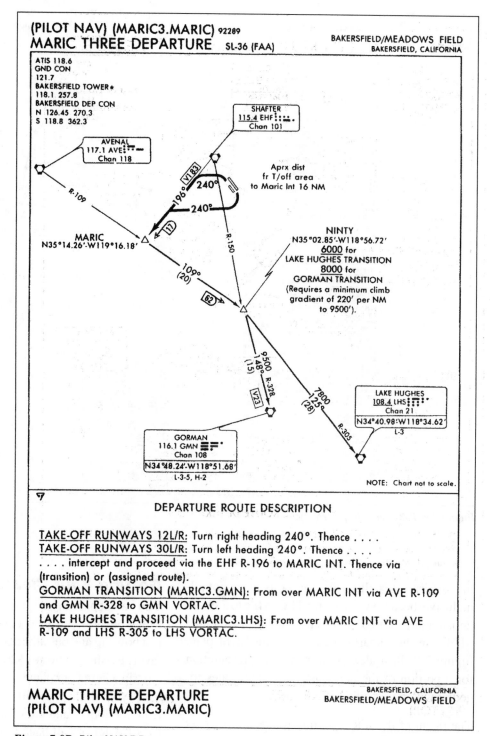

(PILOT NAV) (MARIC3.MARIC) 92289
MARIC THREE DEPARTURE   SL-36 (FAA)

BAKERSFIELD/MEADOWS FIELD
BAKERSFIELD, CALIFORNIA

ATIS 118.6
GND CON
121.7
BAKERSFIELD TOWER★
118.1 257.8
BAKERSFIELD DEP CON
N 126.45 270.3
S 118.8 362.3

AVENAL
117.1 AVE
Chan 118

SHAFTER
115.4 EHF
Chan 101

Aprx dist
fr T/off area
to Maric Int 16 NM

R-109

240°

240°

196°

VT83

MARIC
N35°14.26'-W119°16.18'

109°
(20)

62

NINTY
N35°02.85'-W118°56.72'
6000 for
LAKE HUGHES TRANSITION
8000 for
GORMAN TRANSITION
(Requires a minimum climb
gradient of 220' per NM
to 9500').

R-150

9500 R-328
148°
(15)

7800
125°
(28)

Y23

LAKE HUGHES
108.4 LHS
Chan 21
N34°40.98'-W118°34.62'
L-3

R-305

GORMAN
116.1 GMN
Chan 108
N34°48.24'-W118°51.68'
L-3-5, H-2

NOTE: Chart not to scale.

DEPARTURE ROUTE DESCRIPTION

TAKE-OFF RUNWAYS 12L/R: Turn right heading 240°. Thence . . . .
TAKE-OFF RUNWAYS 30L/R: Turn left heading 240°. Thence . . . .
. . . . intercept and proceed via the EHF R-196 to MARIC INT. Thence via
(transition) or (assigned route).
GORMAN TRANSITION (MARIC3.GMN): From over MARIC INT via AVE R-109
and GMN R-328 to GMN VORTAC.
LAKE HUGHES TRANSITION (MARIC3.LHS): From over MARIC INT via AVE
R-109 and LHS R-305 to LHS VORTAC.

MARIC THREE DEPARTURE
(PILOT NAV) (MARIC3.MARIC)

BAKERSFIELD, CALIFORNIA
BAKERSFIELD/MEADOWS FIELD

Figure 7-8B. Pilot NAV DP

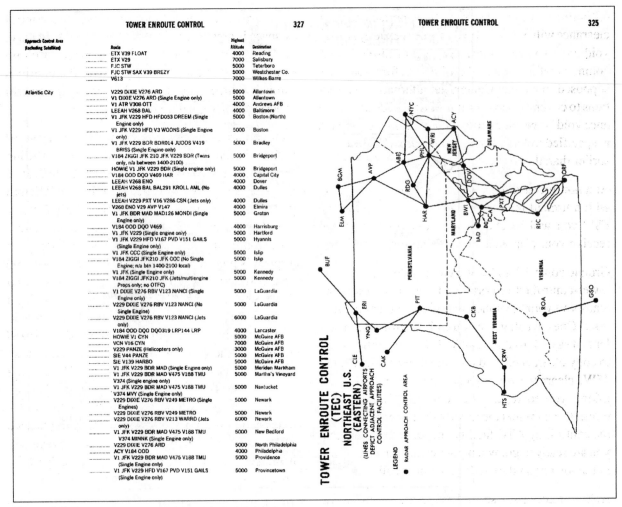

Approach Control Area (Including Satellites)	Route	Highest Altitude	Destination
	ETX V39 FLOAT	4000	Reading
	ETX V29	7000	Salisbury
	FJC STW	5000	Teterboro
	FJC STW SAX V39 BREZY	5000	Westchester Co.
	V613	7000	Wilkes Barre
Atlantic City	V229 DIXIE V276 ARD	5000	Allentown
	V1 DIXIE V276 ARD (Single Engine only)	5000	Allentown
	V1 ATR V308 OTT	4000	Andrews AFB
	LEEAH V268 BAL	4000	Baltimore
	V1 JFK V229 HFD HFD053 DREEM (Single Engine only)	5000	Boston (North)
	V1 JFK V229 HFD V3 WOONS (Single Engine only)	5000	Boston
	V1 JFK V229 BDR BDR014 JUDDS V419 BRISS (Single Engine only)	5000	Bradley
	V184 ZIGGI JFK 210 JFK V229 BOR (Twins only, n/a between 1400-2100)	5000	Bridgeport
	HOWIE V1 JFK V229 BDR (Single engine only)	5000	Bridgeport
	V184 OOD DQO V469 HAR	4000	Capital City
	LEEAH V268 ENO	4000	Dover
	LEEAH V268 BAL BAL291 KROLL AML (No jets)	4000	Dulles
	LEEAH V229 PXT V16 V286 CSN (Jets only)	4000	Dulles
	V268 ENO V29 AVP V147	4000	Elmira
	V1 JFK BDR MAD MAD126 MONDI (Single Engine only)	5000	Groton
	V184 OOD DQO V469	4000	Harrisburg
	V1 JFK V229 (Single engine only)	5000	Hartford
	V1 JFK V229 HFD V167 PVD V151 GAILS (Single Engine only)	5000	Hyannis
	V1 JFK CCC (Single Engine only)	5000	Islip
	V184 ZIGGI JFK210 JFK OCC (No Single Engine; n/a btn 1400-2100 local)	5000	Islip
	V1 JFK (Single Engine only)	5000	Kennedy
	V184 ZIGGI JFK210 JFK (Jets/multiengine Props only; no OTFC)	5000	Kennedy
	V1 DIXIE V276 RBV V123 NANCI (Single Engine only)	5000	LaGuardia
	V229 DIXIE V276 RBV V123 NANCI (No Single Engine)	5000	LaGuardia
	V229 DIXIE V276 RBV V123 NANCI (Jets only)	6000	LaGuardia
	V184 OOD DQO DQO319 LRP144 LRP	4000	Lancaster
	HOWIE V1 CYN	5000	McGuire AFB
	VCN V16 CYN	7000	McGuire AFB
	V229 PANZE (Helicopters only)	3000	McGuire AFB
	SIE V44 PANZE	5000	McGuire AFB
	SIE V139 HARBO	5000	McGuire AFB
	V1 JFK V229 BDR MAD (Single Engine only)	5000	Meriden Markham
	V1 JFK V229 BDR MAD V475 V188 TMU V374 (Single engine only)	5000	Martha's Vineyard
	V1 JFK V229 BDR MAD V475 V188 TMU V374 MVY (Single Engine only)	5000	Nantucket
	V229 DIXIE V276 RBV V249 METRO (Single Engines)	5000	Newark
	V229 DIXIE V276 RBV V249 METRO	5000	Newark
	V229 DIXIE V276 RBV V213 WARRD (Jets only)	6000	Newark
	V1 JFK V229 BDR MAD V475 V188 TMU V374 MINNK (Single Engine only)	5000	New Bedford
	V229 DIXIE V276 ARD	5000	North Philadelphia
	ACY V184 OOD	4000	Philadelphia
	V1 V229 BDR MAD V475 V188 TMU (Single Engine only)	5000	Providence
	V1 JFK V229 HFD V167 PVD V151 GAILS (Single Engine only)	5000	Provincetown

Figure 7-9. Tower-enroute presentation

Continued from Page 7-11

in the Airport/Facility Directory; this list is not all-inclusive, because you can use TEC to file to a small, unlisted airport in a larger city's area. Just include "TEC" in the remarks section of your flight plan. Figure 7-9 illustrates a tower-enroute presentation for a portion of the northeastern United States together with a partial list of city pairs.

The intent of the IFR departure procedure is to get you out of the terminal area at the departure airport and to guide you smoothly into the IFR enroute system. When you look at the departure procedure you will find a fix that appears in both the departure instructions and on the enroute low-altitude chart. It may be a navaid or an intersection or it may be as simple as intercepting a radial, but you will be able to tie the departure directly to the enroute chart.

Getting Your Clearance

You can depart any airport under Instrument Flight Rules, but how you get your clearance will depend on just how big and busy the departure airport is. If your favorite fishing hole is a $20 taxi ride from the small airstrip where your plane is tied down, you may have to file your flight plan with a long distance phone call from the lodge, and either wait while the FSS contacts Center or call back to the FSS for your clearance. (I'm assuming that your favorite fishing hole is too far out in the boonies for cellular coverage.) Be sure to tell the briefer how long it will take to get to the airplane and get it into the air, or ask for a specific time. When you receive your clearance it will contain a **clearance void** time. The ATC system is reserving a slot in the enroute structure for you based on the timetable you gave the briefer, and if you don't get off before that time the slot will evaporate and your clearance will be void. (If you take off exactly at your void time, you have blown it.) Just in case you lose communications after takeoff and before you were supposed to contact Center, get alternative instructions to cover that possibility. The flip side of "clearance void" is **release time**; if your clearance contains a specified release time, you cannot depart any earlier than that time.

At a non-tower airport with an FSS on the field, or with a limited remote communication outlet to the FSS, you will be able to file your flight plan and receive your clearance through those channels.

Ground control doubles as clearance delivery at most tower-controlled airports, and the same voice that reads you your clearance will give you taxi instructions. One caveat: when you call the ground controller and say, "FastWing 345W IFR to Bigville, ready to copy clearance," and the controller says, "Roger, 45W, clearance on request," the controller is not asking you to repeat the request. "Clearance on request" means that the folks in the tower have called the controlling ATC facility and have told them that you are ready to go; when your clearance is received in the tower cab they will give you a call.

At busier airports, a special frequency is designated for clearance delivery, and you must call that controller for your clearance. You can ask for your clearance either before taxiing or after you have completed your runup; my suggestion is to take the clearance in the parking area so that you can study anything unexpected, rather than create a traffic jam in the runup area while you try to locate some obscure intersection. If you have a handheld receiver, eavesdropping on the clearance delivery frequency while still in the planning area will give you an idea of the departure procedure in use and allow time to study it. At really busy airports, pre-taxi clearance is required, and you are to call for your clearance no more than ten minutes before you are ready to depart. On Jeppesen charts this is indicated by "Cpt" preceding the frequency. NACO advises you of this requirement in the A/FD but not on their approach plates.

The vertical extent of approach/departure control airspace is greater than that of Class C or D airspace, and you may be able to get a clearance to climb through an overcast or haze layer to VFR conditions through a direct request to such a facility if you will cancel IFR while still in their airspace.

You should file your IFR flight plan at least 30 minutes before your planned departure time. During that 30 minutes the computer at the Air Route Traffic Control Center is ensuring that your flight will fit into its traffic flow and is printing out "flight strips" at any tower, approach/departure facility, and Center along your route of flight. These strips include your airplane's type, its call letters, its filed airspeed, and your destination. It is important for you to know that these controllers have this information on your flight so that when you contact them you need not repeat it. The only thing that controllers like to be reassured about is altitude—when you make an initial contact with any controller, be sure to mention the altitude you are maintaining or the altitude to which you are climbing or descending. They don't even trust altitude encoding altimeters—until a controller hears a pilot make a verbal altitude report, that airplane will be called out to other pilots as "altitude 7,500—unverified."

To eliminate any possibility of confusion, avoid using the words "to" or "for" when talking to ATC about altitudes. "Leaving four thousand, climbing six thousand" gets the message across without giving the controller the impression you are on the way to 26,000 feet ("climbing to six thousand").

From the Terminal Area to the Enroute Structure

If you are departing a controlled airport with no radar approach or departure facility, the first person you will talk to after leaving tower frequency is the Center controller. Where there is a radar approach control (RAPCON) facility, you will talk to one or more of its controllers before being handed off to Center. Remember, each controller has a flight strip on your flight. You only have to say, "Houston Center (or Miami Departure Control), this is Fleetwing 2345X at 1,800 feet climbing 7,000"; you do not have to tell the controller that you are IFR or include your destination.

While you are IFR in controlled airspace, the controller can allow you to provide your own visual separation from other IFR or VFR aircraft. "Flightbird 23X, traffic your 2 o'clock at 4,000 feet—do you have visual contact with that traffic?" Hearing an affirmative, the controller will say something like "Maintain visual separation, turn right heading 340 degrees, climb and maintain 6,000 feet." Visual separation can be used in either terminal or enroute airspace up to 17,000 feet MSL. Visual separation is not authorized in Class A airspace.

An ARTCC has several sectors, each with a team of controllers and one or more discrete frequencies. As you fly from sector to sector, each controller in turn will give you the frequency for the next sector, and it would seem unnecessary for you to look up these frequencies. If, however, you always keep one step ahead and select the frequency for the next controller well in advance and at your leisure, you won't be faced with the possibility of having to tune a radio when it is not convenient to do so.

A single controller might have several transmitter sites available. If this is the case, you might hear "Contact me on my frequency 128.5." You are leaving the coverage area for the frequency you are using and are entering the coverage area for 128.5. After making the switch, all you have to do is say "45X on 128.5" or "45X level at 11,000" to assure the controller that you are now on the correct frequency for your area. Make a note of this on your low-altitude enroute chart so that you will be ready for the changeover the next time you fly in this area.

Try to stay ahead of the system. You can have everything running smoothly and on schedule, and hear, "San Diego ATIS information MIKE is current—do you have it?" By the time you have tuned the ATIS frequency, noted the information, and reported back on the ATC frequency, your well-laid plans may be in ruins. When the air gets turbulent it is sometimes hard to put your hand on the tuning knob, much less turn it accurately. Do as many tasks as possible when your workload is low.

There are many ways for you to use the system to your advantage without compromising safety. Although you have filed your flight plan via airways, once you are in Center airspace and in radar contact you can ask the controller for a vector to your destination or to a point along a straight-line route to your destination. Don't be bashful; if your GPS gives you a heading to your destination or to a fix many miles away, tell the controller that you can navigate direct. The controller may ask you to climb to a higher altitude before giving you the vector, but when you are on a direct route you are accepting responsibility for your own navigation (and your own terrain clearance). You do not have to file via airways, of course. If you will remain in a radar environment for the duration of the flight you can file "direct." Before you do so, however, consider what you would do in the event of lost communications.

When selecting navaids to define off-airways or random routes, you must check the A/FD to see what class each navaid fits into, and you must be sure that the length of your direct segments does not exceed the standard service volume. For example, the Waco, Texas VORTAC is listed as an (H) class facility. The A/FD says that an H class VOR is good for 40 miles at altitudes from 1,000 feet AGL up to 14,500 feet AGL, for 100 miles at altitudes between 14,500 feet AGL and 60,000 feet AGL, and for 130 miles at altitudes between 18,000 feet and 45,000 feet AGL. Because you know your flight altitude, you can be sure to pick navaids that will provide acceptable service over the planned segment lengths. Since the advent of GPS, standard service volumes have diminished in importance—but you should understand them for the oral portion of your checkride.

A Center controller cannot allow you to fly at an altitude lower than the minimum enroute altitude if you are navigating via airways. However, if you are able to fly in visual conditions below the MEA and want to stay in the IFR system, just ask the controller for a clearance from your present position DIRECT to your destination, and ask for the lower altitude that will get you into the clear. Unless complying with your request will put you below the controller's minimum instrument altitude, and providing you remain in radar contact, you may be cleared as requested—but don't count on it. DIRECT and "radar contact" are the magic words. Don't expect solid reception of navigational signals when flying below the MEA—you will be relying on ATC radar for guidance.

Think long and hard before you give up the Air Traffic Control system's protection by canceling your IFR clearance. If the weather worsens unexpectedly and you need to reactivate your IFR status, you may find yourself at the bottom of the priority list, air-filing a flight plan with a flight service station. Why not stay in the system all the way to touchdown? You can ease the load on the controller by advising that you are in VFR conditions, and you will continue to receive traffic advisories. At your destination you can ask for a visual approach. There is little to gain by saying, "Cancel my IFR clearance" while en route.

If the weather at your destination is "clear and a million," however, don't hesitate to cancel IFR and proceed VFR. Until you do so, the controller is obliged to maintain IFR horizontal and vertical separation for you, and that might mean vectors far out of your way. Cancel IFR and you give yourself and the controller more alternatives.

IFR Flight Planning List

Materials Needed
- IFR charts
- VFR charts
- Plotter
- Computer/Calculator
- Aircraft manual
- Navigation log
- Flight plan form
- Pencils

Planning the Flight
Aircraft availability and maintenance status

Select route of flight

Call for weather briefing:
  Takeoff weather
  Enroute weather
    Check enroute airports
  Winds at altitude
  Temperatures at altitude
  Freezing level
  Cloud layers – bases – tops
  AIRMETs and SIGMETs
  PIREPs
  Destination and alternate forecast
  NOTAMs (FDC, L, D, published)

Departure leg planning, takeoff to top-of-climb:
  Taxiway and runway layout
  Frequencies for communication
  DP or IFR departure procedures
  Check sectional for departure terrain
  Transition to enroute structure
  Level-off altitude
  Climb data
    Speed/Leg times/Fuel burn

Enroute planning, top of climb to descent point:
  Airway planning
  MEAs
  Terrain awareness
  Cruise data
  Speed/Leg times/Fuel burn
  Transition to destination IAF
  Transition to alternate IAF
  Total time en route (for flight plan)
  Fuel planning
  Departure to destination to alternate plus 45
    minutes at normal cruise

Descent planning:
  Plan the most likely approach
  Use transition route to IAF
  If vectors anticipated, plan request-descent-
    point from cruise altitude
  Review approach plate for altitudes and times

Approach planning:
  File to an initial approach fix
  Use the MEAs on transition segments
  Know the missed approach procedure
  Review airport layout, taxiways and lighting

File flight plan:
  Complete weight and balance calculations
  Preflight carefully, especially fuel, gas caps and
    baggage compartment doors
  Load aircraft
  Call for clearance
  Record takeoff time

Remember this: if the success of your plan relies on a specific situation occurring (forecast tailwind must exist, destination weather must improve as forecast, etc.), don't go. A smooth instrument flight is like a Broadway play—it's all done at rehearsal, the rest is easy. Have a good flight!

Chapter 7
The IFR System and Departures Review Questions

This chapter is for instrument students only.

Instrument Student Questions

1. When departing from an airport located outside controlled airspace during IMC, you must file an IFR flight plan and receive a clearance before

   A—takeoff.
   B—entering IFR conditions.
   C—entering Class E airspace.

2. What are the minimum fuel requirements for airplanes in IFR conditions, if the first airport of intended landing is forecast to have a 1,500-foot ceiling and 3 miles visibility at flight-planned ETA? Fuel to fly to the first airport of intended landing,

   A—and fly thereafter for 45 minutes at normal cruising speed.
   B—fly to the alternate, and fly thereafter for 45 minutes at normal cruising speed.
   C—fly to the alternate, and fly thereafter for 30 minutes at normal cruising speed.

3. When filing a composite flight plan where the first portion of the flight is IFR, which fix(es) should be indicated on the flight plan form?

   A—All points of transition from one airway to another, fixes defining direct route segments, and the clearance limit fix.
   B—Only the fix where you plan to terminate the IFR portion of the flight.
   C—Only those compulsory reporting points on the IFR route segment.

4. (Refer to Figure 7-3 on Page 7-2.) What information should be entered in block 7 of an IFR flight plan if the flight has three legs, each at a different altitude?

   A—Altitude for first leg.
   B—Altitude for first leg and highest altitude.
   C—Highest altitude.

5. For aircraft other than helicopters, is an alternate airport required for an IFR flight to ATL (Atlanta Hartsfield) if the proposed ETA is 1930Z?

   TAF KATL 121720Z 121818 20012KT 5 SM HZ
     BKN030
     FM2000 3 SM TSRA OVC025CB
     FM2200 33015G20KT P6SM BKN015 OVC040
     BECMG 0608 02008KT BKN 040 BECMG 1012
     00000KT P6SM CLR=

   A—Yes, because the ceiling could fall below 2,000 feet within 2 hours before to 2 hours after the ETA.
   B—No, because the ceiling and visibility are forecast to remain at or above 1,000 feet and 3 miles, respectively.
   C—No, because the ceiling and visibility are forecast to be at or above 2,000 feet and 3 miles within 1 hour before to 1 hour after the ETA.

6. What does the symbol T within a black triangle in the minimums section of the IAP for a particular airport indicate?

   A—Takeoff minimums are 1 mile for aircraft having two engines or less and ½ mile for those with more than two engines.
   B—Instrument takeoffs are not authorized.
   C—Takeoff minimums are not standard and/or departure procedures are published.

7. What point at the destination should be used to compute estimated time en route on an IFR flight plan?

A—The final approach fix on the expected instrument approach.

B—The initial approach fix on the expected instrument approach.

C—The point of first intended landing.

8. When departing from an airport not served by a control tower, the issuance of a clearance containing a void time indicates that

A—ATC will assume the pilot has not departed if no transmission is received before the void time.

B—the pilot must advise ATC as soon as possible, but no later than 30 minutes, of their intentions if not off by the void time.

C—ATC will protect the airspace only to the void time.

9. (Refer to Figure Q7-1.) What route should you take if cleared for the Washoe Two Departure and your assigned route is V6?

A—Climb on the LOC south course to WAGGE where you will be vectored to V6.

B—Climb on the LOC south course to cross WAGGE at 9,000, turn left and fly direct to FMG VORTAC and cross at or above 10,000, and proceed on FMG R-241.

C—Climb on the LOC south course to WAGGE, turn left and fly direct to FMG VORTAC. If at 10,000 turn left and proceed on FMG R-241; if not at 10,000 enter depicted holding pattern and climb to 10,000 before proceeding on FMG R-241.

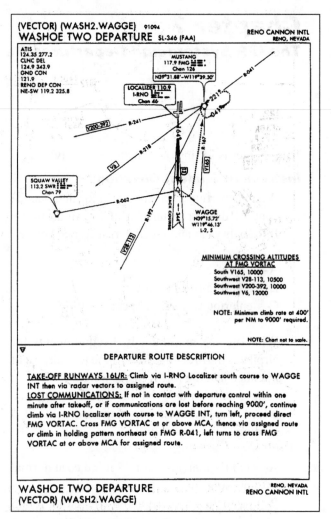

Figure Q7-1. WASHOE Two departure

10. (Refer to Figure Q7-1.) Of the following, which is the minimum acceptable rate of climb (feet per minute) to 9,000 feet required for the WASH2 WAGGE departure at a GS of 150 knots?

A—750 feet per minute
B—825 feet per minute
C—1,000 feet per minute

11. (Refer to Figure Q7-2.) What VHF frequencies are available for communications with Cedar City FSS?

A—123.6, 121.5, 108.6, and 112.8
B—122.2, 121.5, 122.6, and 112.1
C—122.2, 121.5, 122.0, and 123.6

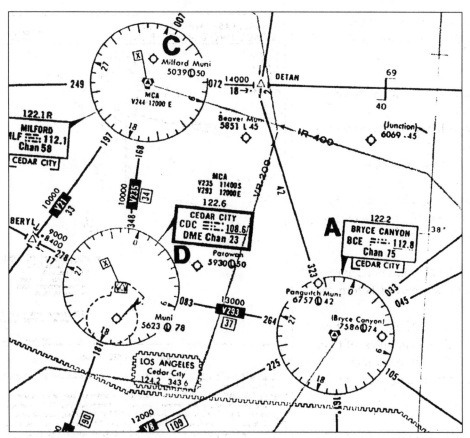

Figure Q7-2. *Enroute chart segment*

12. Which ATC clearance should instrument-rated pilots request in order to climb through a cloud layer or an area of reduced visibility and then continue the flight VFR?

A—To VFR-On-Top.
B—Special VFR to VFR Over-the-Top.
C—VFR Over-the-Top.

13. An airport without an authorized IAP may be included on an IFR flight plan as an alternate, if the current weather forecast indicates that the ceiling and visibility at the ETA will

A—be at least 300 feet and 2 miles.
B—be at least 1,000 feet and 1 mile.
C—allow for a descent from the MEA approach, and a landing under basic VFR.

En Route

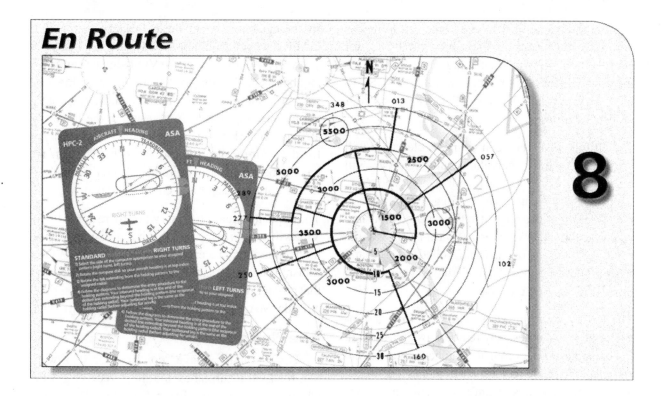

Enroute Operations

Chapter 7 explained how the ATC system works and covered departure procedures. This chapter picks up your flight as it enters the enroute environment and discusses the variables that might affect it, including a holding clearance or loss of communications. I'll also go over "random route navigation" systems such as area navigation, LORAN, and GPS again to place them in the enroute context.

Area navigation (RNAV) became popular in the 1970s; it used a course-line computer to define courses between fixes identified by radial and distance from a VORTAC or VOR-DME—points in space, rather than the radio facilities themselves. This "rho-theta" system has been referred to as RNAV since that time. LORAN and the Global Positioning System also allow pilots to navigate to points in space, so the FAA has designated all three systems as RNAV. In this text, RNAV will mean the rho-theta system using radials and distances.

Altitudes

Unless you have filed a direct random route (RNAV, GPS or LORAN), you will be flying VOR airways. One of the joys of being an instrument pilot is that the chart makers provide you with much of the informa-

tion you had to ferret out with a computer and plotter when you were a VFR pilot: outbound magnetic courses are shown where airways cross VORs, and the distance between fixes and the total distance between navaids is printed right on the chart. No more wondering if you used the Sectional or WAC side of the plotter or if you mistook statute miles for nautical miles.

Not only that—both NACO and Jeppesen print IFR planning charts that allow you to use one chart in planning a flight of hundreds of miles. These charts don't provide very much detail, but they do provide airway numbers and distances.

When you file your IFR flight plan, you should insert in block 7 of the flight plan form the altitude for the initial segment of the flight, according to the AIM. If you want to, put your desired flight altitude in "Remarks"; that decision will be dictated by winds and icing conditions. If you put your desired final altitude in block 7, the controller who "owns" that altitude might be well along your route, and the first enroute controller you talk to might not be able to clear you to that altitude because he or she does not know the traffic situation in a distant sector. It's better to file for the initial altitude on the flight plan form and then work out the details with the enroute controllers as you proceed on course. Allow ATC some time for coordination—if you want a higher altitude in 10 minutes, ask for it 20 minutes ahead of time. Similarly, if you want higher in 10 miles, make your request 20 miles early.

The altitude you receive in your IFR clearance will be dictated by traffic conditions, although ATC will make every effort to meet your needs. The ATC controller may clear you to a wrong-way altitude or may go along with a request to fly at an odd thousand when westbound or vice versa. You must observe the even-odd thousand rule in uncontrolled airspace, and the VFR "even-odd + 500 feet" rule when operating on a VFR-On-Top clearance.

The most recent altitude you receive from a controller governs, unless any restrictions are restated. For example, if your original clearance was to "climb and maintain 5,000 feet, expect higher in ten miles," and a controller says "Climb and maintain 10,000 feet," the 5,000-foot restriction is cancelled.

Minimum Enroute Altitude

Flight at the minimum enroute altitude (MEA) ensures that you will receive good navigational guidance from the VORs that define the airway and you will be at least 1,000 feet above the terrain within 4 NM either side of the centerline (2,000 feet in mountainous areas). The MEA is printed above the airway number. A T-bar at an intersection indicates an altitude change; if the line representing the airway does not have a T-bar the MEA is unchanged as you pass that intersection. Find SUZZY intersection west of Bozeman in Figure 8-1. The MEA on V-343 is 10,800 feet on both sides of the intersection. However, the MEA changes from 8,000 feet to 10,800 feet at THESE intersection as indicated by the T-bars.

There are areas in the western half of the country where VORs are so widely separated that navigational signal coverage cannot be guaranteed for a route segment, and in these instances an "MEA GAP" is shown along the airway. In most instances you will not actually lose the VOR signal at an MEA gap but its quality may be less than acceptable. The gaps are usually of short duration and simply maintaining heading will keep you within the protected airspace. If the FAA insisted on solid signal coverage for the entire route in these areas the MEA might have to be raised to an altitude beyond the capabilities of normally aspirated engines (or people).

The opposite situation exists when there are so many VORs in a geographic area that it is possible to climb high enough to receive signals from two VORs transmitting on the same frequency. The FAA covers that possibility by publishing a maximum authorized altitude (MAA) along airways that might be affected.

The Snitch

ARTCC computers have "conflict alert" software that tracks IFR airplanes and those receiving VFR advisory service. Its "Error Detection Program," also known as "the snitch," watches for altitude

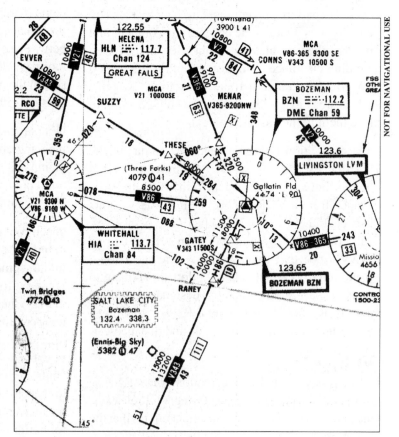

Figure 8-1. Enroute chart segment

mistakes that reduce separation below the minimum required for IFR (5 miles and 1,000 feet below 29,000 feet—Flight Level 290). If separation between two IFR airplanes is lost, a message is automatically printed at the Area Manager's desk—the controller can't do anything about it. Bogus alerts are common: quite frequently, one of the airplanes is VFR or operating VFR-On-Top (discussed later). Military planes climbing to join a formation will obviously set off an alert.

The Area Manager has to investigate and find out if a violation has occurred. If the controller can explain the situation to the AM's satisfaction all is forgotten. If pilot error is alleged, the airplane tail number and the circumstances will be forwarded to the Flight Standards District Office for action. Then you get a letter that you would really rather not receive.

The moral of this discussion is that you cannot relax on altitude control. The snitch is set at roughly 4.9 miles laterally and 700 feet vertically. If you drift 300 feet low and the airplane beneath you is right on its assigned altitude, the snitch will generate an alert. Be sure that you always have a current altimeter setting in your altimeter's Kollsman window and pay attention to your altitude. If you are experiencing convective activity that makes holding altitude difficult, don't hesitate to tell the controller; having that transmission on Center's audio tape might keep you from getting that letter from the FSDO.

Ask for a "block altitude" if you are riding a roller-coaster: "Center, Skybird 45X requests a block altitude from 7,000 to 9,000 feet." If that block of altitudes is free of traffic and the controller gives you the clearance, you own the airspace and can bounce up and down as much as you like within the block.

If there are no other airplanes around and you wander off an assigned altitude, no conflict will exist and nothing happens. You just don't know about all of the other traffic, however. If a controller asks for your altitude and you are a hundred feet or so away from where you should be, tell the controller that you are level *at the assigned altitude* and get back where you belong as fast as you can. The controller can use your verbal report in his discussion with the Area Manager. Don't lie yourself into a midair collision; if you are 500 feet off altitude and the controller asks about it, confess

and correct. You want to be alive to receive that letter from the FAA. When in doubt, file an Aviation Safety Reporting System form with NASA (*see* Chapter 11).

Minimum Obstruction Clearance Altitude

A minimum obstruction clearance altitude (MOCA) is published when an aircraft within 22 nautical miles of a VOR can safely descend to that altitude as part of an approach procedure. Descent to the MOCA is initiated at the fix beyond which the lower altitude applies. NACO indicates MOCAs with an asterisk, i.e. *2300; Jeppesen uses a T, i.e. 2300T. Figure 8-1 shows examples of MOCAs on an NACO chart as *13,200 feet southwest of BZN on V343, and *9,100 feet northwest of BZN on V365.

Minimum Crossing Altitude

When there is a change in the minimum enroute altitude at an intersection or VOR you should initiate the climb at that point. When there is an MEA change at an intersection the FAA assumes that you will be able to initiate a climb of at least 150 feet per nautical mile below 5,000 feet, 120 feet per mile between 5,000 feet and 10,000 feet, or 100 feet per mile above 10,000 feet, and still clear the terrain by 2,000 feet. Those requirements are not too demanding—150 feet per mile at 120 knots is only 300 feet per minute (*see* Table 8-1). When the high terrain is so close to the intersection that these climb rates would not clear the terrain, a minimum crossing altitude (MCA) is published, and you must be at or above the MCA before you reach the intersection. MCAs are usually directional; the restriction is imposed only as you approach the higher terrain. Both NACO and Jeppesen print the MCA adjacent to the intersection to which it applies. When putting it there would clutter the chart, Jeppesen prints a numbered ball at the intersection and provides a keyed MCA table elsewhere on the chart.

SL through 5,000 feet	150 ft./NM
5,000 feet through 10,000 feet	120 ft./NM
10,000 feet and over	100 ft./NM

Table 8-1. *Required climb rate when no MCA is published*

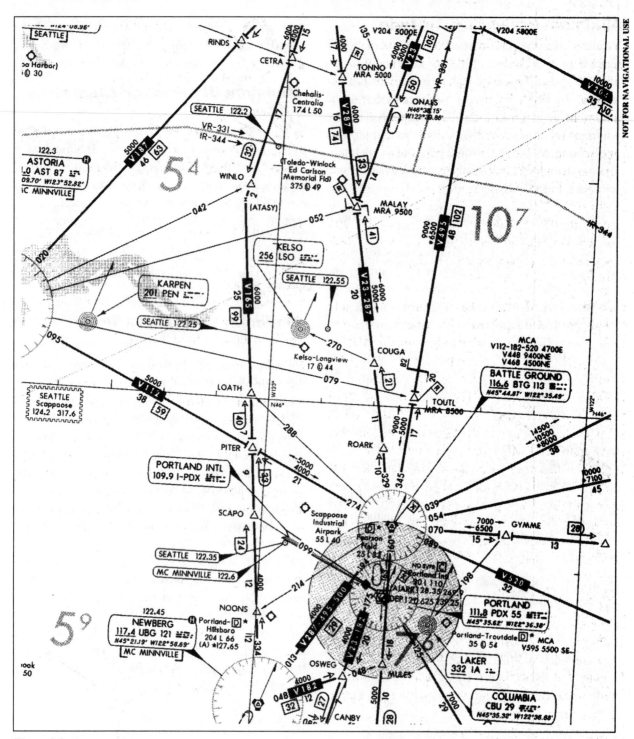

Figure 8-2. *Enroute chart segment*

Minimum Reception Altitude

You can't identify an intersection unless you can receive the VOR radials that form it. When it is not possible to receive a good signal from an off-course VOR at the MEA because of distance or terrain, a minimum reception altitude (MRA) is published and you must fly at or above that altitude to identify the intersection. MRAs are printed adjacent to the intersections to which they apply by both NACO and Jeppesen. In Figure 8-2, an airplane flying north on V-495 from BTG must be at least 8,500 feet MSL to receive the 079° radial from the off-course VOR and identify TOUTL intersection; the 9,000-foot MEA guarantees reception for the VORs defining the airway.

Is it necessary to receive the off-course VOR at all? If your airplane is equipped with distance measuring equipment, you may be able to ignore most MRAs. When a DME reading is available from the VORTAC that forms the airway, you can use that reading to identify the intersection. The open arrow south of TOUTL indicates that it is a usable DME fix on an NACO chart; Jeppesen identifies intersections that have approved DME distances with the letter D; i.e. D26. The distance figure enclosed in a large letter D on NACO charts is the total of two or more segment distances; for example, 41 NM at MALAY. If there is no open arrow or distance figure, the FAA has test flown that route and has determined that the DME information is not sufficiently accurate.

Keep in mind that DME distances are slant range distances, and that DME accuracy is greatest at low altitudes and long distances from the station, where slant range is almost equal to horizontal range. As you approach a VORTAC at higher altitudes, the accuracy of the on-board DME readout diminishes until the DME reads your altitude above the station as you pass directly overhead.

ATC may assign a DME-equipped aircraft a crossing altitude which is above the MEA, but below the MRA, for a fix that is formed using either DME or cross bearings. In this case, ATC will identify the fix as the "HOGGI DME fix" or by the radial-distance location ("the Crescent City 343° radial 42 mile DME fix").

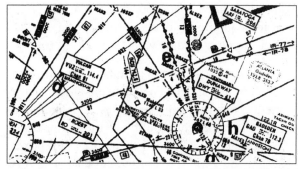

Figure 8-3. The "string of beads" on 316 and 331 radials (off the DWY VOR) indicates substitute route.

Although VOR airways are the primary means of navigation, there are a few intersections which are formed by a radial and a bearing from a low-frequency navaid. Figure 8-3 shows such an intersection used when a segment of a VOR airway is unusable and a low-frequency navaid is used with a VOR, forming a substitute route.

No matter what you request as an enroute altitude, the controller will be guided by the minimum instrument altitude or MIA (approach and departure controllers use minimum vectoring altitude or MVA). Just above the controller's radar scope is a display of the various MIAs for that sector. This information is not available to pilots. These charts look like mosaics or jigsaw puzzles, with oddly shaped sections of airspace having altitudes assigned based on high terrain or man-made obstructions (Figure 8-4). The

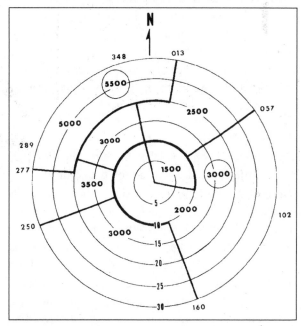

Figure 8-4. Minimum vectoring altitude chart

controller can compare your position and the route you are requesting with the restrictions on the chart and clear you accordingly.

As you fly the enroute portion of your trip, the controller may assign you a different altitude unexpectedly; this is usually caused by a potential airspace conflict. Each IFR airplane flies in the center of a "boxcar" of airspace, with the size of the boxcar determined by the speed of the airplane. The ATC radar computer not only tracks your airplane, but can predict when your boxcar might come too close to that of another IFR flight. When this potential exists the controller must move one or both of the airplanes to resolve the conflict. One mile is one twenty-eighth of an inch on the controller's scope, so don't expect hair-splitting accuracy.

Minimum Off-Route Clearance Altitude (OROCA)

This is an altitude that provides a 1,000-foot buffer in non-mountainous areas and a 2,000-foot buffer in mountainous areas within the United States. The increasing use of random-route navigation has prompted the FAA to add OROCA to the minimum altitudes discussed in the AIM (4-4-8 and Glossary).

Enroute Altitude Changes

When changing altitudes, ATC expects you to climb or descend at your airplane's most efficient rate until you reach an altitude 1,000 feet from the new altitude, and at 500 feet per minute for that final 1,000 feet. Pretend that you are your own copilot, and call out (or mutter) "A thousand to go" at the appropriate altitude; in the absence of an altitude alerting device, that should keep you from "busting" your altitude assignment.

VFR-On-Top

If you break out on top of the clouds during the climb to your filed altitude, you can tell the controller that you would like "VFR-On-Top." This is an IFR clearance that keeps you in the IFR system but gives you some latitude as well. While you are operating VFR-On-Top you are neither fish nor fowl—you must adhere to IFR regulations such as position reporting, following your assigned route, flying at or above the MEA, and carrying out ATC instructions, while enjoying the freedom to change altitude when you want to, if you climb or descend in VFR condi-

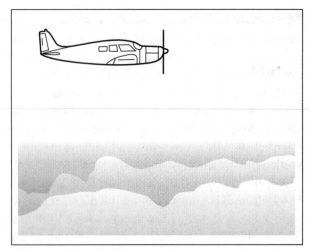

Figure 8-5. VFR-On-Top

tions. Of course, you should advise the controller before you change altitude. The altitude you choose when VFR-On-Top must be the correct VFR altitude for the direction of flight—an odd or even thousand plus 500 feet.

While you are flying VFR-On-Top you must maintain the same flight visibility and distance from clouds that you would observe if VFR, and you must keep a wary eye out for non-IFR pilots who are also flying on top of the clouds. The FAA calls that type of operation "VFR over-the-top." The controller will keep you advised of all IFR flights that might present a potential conflict and of all *known* VFR traffic.

Why ask for VFR-On-Top? It opens the door to a vector direct to your destination (or to an enroute fix), it gives you some latitude in choice of cruise altitude, and it keeps you in the system so that when the clouds ahead begin to build you don't have to go through the flight plan filing procedure but can just say "I'd like an IFR assigned altitude," (often referred to as a "hard" altitude).

If you are cruising along on an On-Top clearance at something-thousand-plus-500 feet and the controller says "Climb/descend and maintain something-thousand feet," without your asking for it, you are now back in the system and no longer subject to VFR rules.

Warning: The majority of air traffic controllers are not pilots, and, based on their experience with air carriers, they have difficulty understanding why a pilot would ask for VFR-On-Top. East of the Mississippi many controllers are not used to requests for

VFR-On-Top clearances. Be assertive—refer them to the Air Traffic Control Manual.

Cruise Clearances

You have to listen carefully when a controller gives you a clearance. For instance, "Maintain 12,000 feet" means exactly that; if you let the altitude vary more than 300 feet, causing a possible conflict with other traffic, you may set off the snitch. If the controller says, "Cruise 12,000 feet," however, you can descend at your discretion to any intermediate IFR altitude between 12,000 feet and the MEA at your discretion; that block of airspace belongs to you because the controller has determined that there is no IFR traffic between 12,000 feet and the MEA. You may, quite legally, descend a few thousand feet (while still above the minimum IFR altitude, of course) to see how the weather is down there, and then climb back up without saying a word to ATC. When you leave your last assigned altitude permanently, however, you are expected to advise the controller. Once you have reported leaving your assigned altitude you cannot return to that altitude without a specific clearance, so the controller can then assign that altitude to another aircraft.

If your destination is a non-tower airport, "Cleared to Smalltown Airport, cruise 5,000 feet" constitutes a clearance to fly any published approach at that airport without further clearance.

But what if your destination is a non-tower airport that does not have an instrument approach?—you can't descend below the MEA unless you can see the destination airport. The way to play this is to file to a nearby airport that has an approach procedure, using a route with a fix or intersection near the destination airport. That way, if you can see your destination when you reach that fix, you can just cancel IFR and begin your descent. If you can't see it you can just continue on your filed route to the nearby airport. If you encounter VFR conditions on your approach to your "safety valve" airport you can cancel IFR, break off the approach, and proceed to your original destination. However, if your safety-valve airport is below VFR minimums, you cannot simply make a low approach and continue to your original destination unless you have informed ATC of your intentions. Your IFR clearance got you to the safety-valve airport, which was your clearance limit, and in the absence of coordination it takes a Special VFR clearance to get out.

VFR Climb/Descent

When you are in Center or terminal airspace, the controller can allow you to provide your own visual separation when in VFR conditions (*see* Table 8-2). Let's say that you are cruising along at an assigned altitude of 6,000 feet and want to climb to 10,000 feet because of some icy-looking clouds ahead. You ask the controller for 10,000 feet and are told "unable due to traffic at 7,000 feet." All you have to do is say "I have that traffic in sight" and you are on your way. Or you could say "Request VFR climb to 10,000 feet," which would be met with "Cleared as requested, maintain visual separation, report level."

Warning: If you ask for a VFR descent and the controller not only approves it but says "IFR cancellation received, squawk 1200, change to advisory frequency approved, good day," the controller has dropped the ball and must be corrected. Asking for a VFR climb/descent while on an instrument flight plan is *not* the same as canceling IFR.

The second ploy is to ask the controller for a VFR-On-Top clearance. The reply would be "Maintain VFR conditions on top, report any altitude changes." Of course, you would tell the controller that you were climbing to a VFR altitude of 9,500 or 10,500, depending on the direction of flight. Again, ask for 10,000 feet as a hard altitude when you are above the traffic and it is convenient to do so.

Separation Standards by Airspace Type			
	En Route	Terminal	
	ARTCC	TRSA or Class B	Class C
IFR to IFR	5 miles 1,000 feet	3 miles 1,000 feet	3 miles 1,000 feet
IFR to VFR	No separation; traffic advisories and safety warnings	1.5 miles 500 feet	Conflict resolution; 500 feet
VFR to VFR	No separation	1.5 miles	No separation
Visual separation authorized	Yes below 18,000 feet	Yes	Yes
Diverging course separation	Yes	Yes	Yes

Table 8-2

Pilot's Discretion

Quite often a controller will preface an altitude change with "At pilot's discretion, climb/descend..." That means just what it says. The controller needs you at a different altitude, but not right now. You might even ask for PD if you were cleared to descend into some wet-looking clouds and would rather delay the transformation from an airplane to an ice cube: "Could 34X have discretion on that?" Be sure to pass along the PD restriction when being handed off from one sector controller to another: "34X is level at 14,000 with discretion to descend 8,000." If this doesn't match the new controller's plans, of course, expect to be cleared to 8,000 feet right away. This might very well be to meet a letter-of-agreement restriction at an ATC airspace boundary.

Operating in a Non-Radar Environment

If you take your instrument training in a busy metropolitan area in Class C or B airspace, you will learn to deal with busy controllers and develop the ability to screen those transmissions which are directed to you from a steady stream of communications—a valuable skill. Unless you leave the radar environment, however, you may not learn to navigate and shoot approaches on your own.

When you are out of radar contact the controller relies on you to provide position reports so that conflicts with other traffic may be avoided. On your enroute chart you will note that some intersections and many VOR symbols are marked with a solid triangle instead of an open triangle. These are mandatory reporting points, and the format of your report should be PTA-TEN:

P   Position: the name of the reporting point.

T   Time over the reporting point.

A   Altitude.

T   Type of flight plan; only for reports to a Flight Service Station. A Center or approach controller knows that you are operating IFR.

E   Estimate: your ETA at the next reporting point (and its name).

N   Next: the name of next succeeding reporting point.

If you were flying along V-348/316 west to east (Figure 8-6), your report over Sudbury VORTAC might be "FastWing 1234X over Sudbury at 23 past the hour, 10,000, estimating North Bay at 43, Killaloe."

This is a good place to discuss the difference between "radar contact lost," and "radar service terminated." An ATC controller can lose radar contact because of your altitude, because of your distance from the antenna, etc. In this situation, the controller cannot see your target or the targets of airplanes that might be in conflict with your flight path; separation and advisory service is not possible, but you are still on your IFR flight plan and radar contact might be regained at any time. The controller might say "Radar contact lost, contact Salt Lake Center in ten miles on 132.75," in which case things would return to normal as soon as you contacted SLC Center.

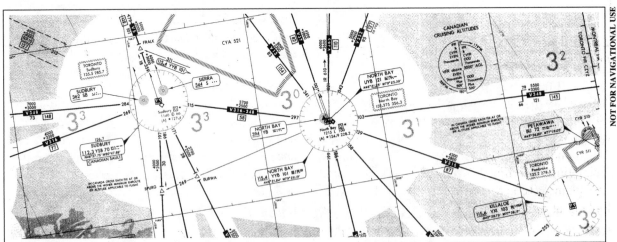

Figure 8-6. Position reporting

"Radar service terminated" is usually followed by "Squawk VFR, change to advisory approved"; or "Frequency change approved," leaving it up to you to decide which frequency to change to. You will hear this when you cancel IFR, or due to workload when you are receiving VFR traffic advisories. When you hear this transmission you are no longer on an instrument flight plan or receiving radar services. Don't be reluctant to ask the controller why you are being terminated if it is not at your request— sometimes they misunderstand a communication and assume that you want to cancel IFR. "Request VFR-On-Top" is such a misunderstanding.

Popping Up

The ideal situation, from the viewpoint of the ATC system, is for you to file an IFR flight plan, receive a clearance, and follow that clearance to your destination. That way there are no surprises for the ATC controllers. When you are en route on what was planned as a routine VFR flight, however, you may find the weather situation deteriorating and decide to make use of your instrument rating. It happens every day.

Figure 8-7. Popping up

Sad but true…every year, rated instrument pilots run into antenna towers and mountains while attempting to stay visual when the clouds are reaching toward the ground. It's hard to imagine why they do not use their ratings and climb to safety; very few are around to explain. Whether you are on top of a cloud deck, looking at buildups ahead, or less than 1,000 feet above the ground looking at a grey wall ahead, a pop-up clearance will solve your problem. It's not complicated…call Center, give them your aircraft identification, position, and altitude, and request an IFR clearance to your destination.

If you are on top of the clouds in VFR conditions (Controller: "What are your flight conditions?") you might be shuffled off to the FSS to air-file a flight plan if ATC is busy and entry into instrument meteorological conditions is not imminent. If you are flying beneath a cloud deck at an altitude lower than the minimum instrument altitude, you must start a climb toward that altitude. The controller will ask if you can maintain your own terrain and obstacle clearance during the climb because, after all, ATC has no responsibility for you at that point. If you can, fine; if you can't, and must climb into the clouds without being able to see any terrain or obstacles, the controller will consider this to be an emergency situation. The "E" word does not have to be said by the pilot. As soon as the controller has you on radar and can compare your position to the terrain map located over the radar scope, he can give you suggested headings. The word "vector" will not be used until you are above the minimum instrument altitude. Good argument for positional awareness and the use of sectional charts by instrument pilots.

Radio frequencies for ARTCCs are printed on low-altitude enroute charts and in the A/FD (*see* Figure 8-8), and you should be able to come up with the correct frequency for the area in which you are flying. When all else fails, call a nearby flight service station on 122.2, give your position, and ask for the Center frequency in your area. When you make contact with Center, the ATC controller has every right to tell you to remain VFR while you air-file through the FSS or, if the situation warrants, to have you proceed to and hold at a fix while awaiting a clearance.

However, depending on such variables as where you are and how busy the controller is at the moment, your request may be met with, "Say your type aircraft and filed true airspeed," followed by an IFR clearance that will take you from your present position into the en route structure to your destination. That is "popping up." Savvy instrument pilots try to get a foot in the door early by requesting radar flight following; if it is available, it puts them in touch with a controller while they are still VFR.

Flying Direct Routes

You don't have to fly via federal airways; there are other options, some depending on your on-board equipment and others on your location and altitude. You should be aware of your alternatives.

Direct: "Straight line flight between two navigational aids, fixes, points or any combination thereof."—*Pilot/Controller Glossary.*

Unless you plan to fly so far that the curvature of the earth becomes important, a straight line is the shortest distance between two points, and as an instrument pilot you can make good use of the word "direct."

When you are flying on the federal airways your flight path will seldom be a straight line between departure point and destination. Placement of VORs is dictated by a variety of considerations, so the VOR stations that define the airway probably aren't laid out in a straight line.

If an ARTCC has you in radar contact, relief may be as easy as saying, "Center, 45X requests a heading direct Salt Lake City." If your present altitude will keep you at least 1,000 feet above the terrain along the direct route (2,000 feet in mountainous terrain such as that around Salt Lake City), Center will probably give you a heading that will approximate a straight line. If diversions due to weather or a healthy wind drift angle cause you to depart from that straight line, you can expect corrective vectors as you proceed. Don't be surprised if you are cleared "direct Twin Falls, direct Salt Lake City" if Twin Falls is along the straight line route. Your mandatory report over Twin Falls (points defining a direct route become mandatory reporting points) will reassure the Center controller that your off-airways flight is proceeding as planned.

No one expects to pick up a usable signal from a VOR 200 miles away at low altitude, but requesting "…a heading until receiving PODUNK VOR suitable for navigation" can get you started in the right direction, with the admonition to inform Center when you are receiving a solid signal from PODUNK. This works especially well when your handheld GPS has given you the course and distance to PODUNK. You are not, of course, navigating with an unapproved GPS— it is just giving you a helping hand.

Figure 8-8 (A/FD Center Frequencies)

AIR ROUTE TRAFFIC CONTROL CENTERS — 191

Air Route Traffic Control Center frequencies and their remoted transmitter sites are listed below for the coverage of this volume. Bold face type indicates high altitude frequencies, light face type indicates low altitude frequencies. To insure unrestricted IFR operations within the high altitude enroute sectors, the use of 720 channel communications equipment (25 kHz channel spacing) is required.

®ALBUQUERQUE CENTER   H-2, L-4-5-6-13-15 (KZAB)
- Animas - 133.0 127.95
- Childs Peak - 135.15 132.45 126.45 125.25
- Globe (Site Nr 1) - 124.5
- Globe (Site Nr 2) - 135.15 133.85 132.35 132.35 125.4
- Prescott - 135.725 135.725 134.325 128.45
- Seligman - 135.325 128.45
- Tucson - 133.0 127.95
- Winslow - 132.9 128.45
- Zuni - 135.8 134.6 125.2

®DENVER CENTER - 125.9   H-1-2-3, L-5-6-7-8-9-10-11 (KZDV)
- Alamosa - 128.375
- Aspen - 132.85 128.5 119.85
- Brush - 133.95
- Cheyenne - 134.575 133.175 133.0 125.9
- Colby - 132.175 127.65
- Cortez - 133.425
- Denver - 133.4 132.85 128.65 126.875 126.5 125.95 119.85
- Durango - 133.425
- Eastonville - 134.975
- Farmington - 133.425 128.125 125.675
- Goodland - 132.5
- Grand Island West - 132.7
- Grand Mesa - 135.125 134.275 128.5 127.8 127.725
- Gunnison - 133.525 127.8
- Hanksville - 135.37
- Hayden - 128.5 128.325
- La Junta - 134.125 133.4 132.225
- Lusk - 135.6
- North Platte - 132.7
- Ogallala - 132.7 126.325
- Pueblo - 135.4 128.375 127.525
- Sterling - 125.95
- Tuba City - 133.425 128.125
- Walton Peak - 126.5

®LOS ANGELES CENTER - 132.5 128.2   H-2, L-2-3-4-5, A-2 (KZLA)
- Arr—Dep U.S. - 135.45 134.55 134.4 133.4 132.15 128.05 127.4 126.4 126.0 119.0
- Bakersfield - 135.3 133.05 127.1
- Baldwin Hills - 132.85 125.65 118.55
- Barstow - 135.575 134.65 133.55 132.5 132.3 126.35
- Blythe - 135.45 128.15
- Boron - 132.625
- Cedar City - 135.55 135.25 127.35 124.2
- Julian - 135.75 135.45 128.6 128.15 127.4 125.85 125.65
- Keeler - 132.625 127.9 127.9
- Nelson - 134.65 124.85 124.2
- Mount Potosi - 132.625 127.9 127.9
- Ontario - 125.85
- Riverside - 126.35
- Saddle Peak - 134.75 132.6 125.8
- San Luis Obispo - 124.15 119.05
- Santa Barbara - 135.5 134.425 132.15 119.05
- Santa Catalina - 134.575
- Seligman - 134.95 133.2 124.85
- Tonopah - 127.9
- Twentynine Palms - 133.2 128.15
- Yuma - 121.35

Figure 8-8. Center frequencies are listed in the A/FD

This usually works like a dream, especially west of the Mississippi, but there have been cases where pilots who popped up and subsequently had problems faced certificate action because they had not provided ATC with all of the elements of an IFR flight plan. To be safe, get it on Center's audio tape. Say "Just for the record, Center, 34X has 4 hours of fuel on board and our filed alternate is Boston Logan."

If you can't maintain VFR while getting a pop-up clearance, don't descend…terrain and manmade obstacles have caught many a scud-runner. Start climbing as soon as you lose VFR cloud clearance; there won't be any traffic below the minimum instrument altitude for your location, and there are a lot more mountains and antennas than there are airplanes flying in the clouds.

There is another use of "direct" that you may find of value. If you are en route along an airway with a minimum enroute altitude of 12,000 feet MSL and it looks as though you would be in the clear at 10,000 feet, tell the controller that you would like to proceed direct at 10,000 feet. The controller has a "minimum instrument altitude" chart at the radar position and may clear you as requested if your flight will be at or above the MIA. NOTE: The MIA chart at Center is drawn with 5 miles of separation from obstacles and high terrain, while MIA maps at terminal facilities are drawn with 3 mile separation. This means that Approach Control can do some things that Center can't.

In Center airspace, the minimum instrument altitude is the same as the Enroute-Minimum Safe Altitude Warning (E-MSAW) altitude. This system alerts the controller when you stray toward high terrain while under Center control. MIAs also give controllers information regarding off-airway minimum altitudes for IFR operations.

Under "direct" conditions, radar is your primary means of navigation. This clearance will allow you to descend below the MEA, but you must remain in radar contact; if the controller loses contact you will be directed to climb. If the reason for your descent below the MEA was to get below a potential icing situation, this may present a problem. Flight at the MEA always guarantees adequate reception of navigational signals, so if you want to fly direct below the MEA you may lose VOR guidance. Flying "direct" is an excellent method of staying in the IFR system while flying below the published minimum enroute altitude. Keep in mind, however, that this is not a sure thing. If the controller answers your request with "unable," there's nothing you can do—with the possible exception of canceling your instrument clearance and staying on Center frequency until you reach an enroute segment with a lower MEA.

This discussion of "direct" will not be of much use to those of you who live in the northeast corner of the country; at present, Johnstown, Pennsylvania, is probably as far east as direct routings are available because of the congested airspace.

Random Route Navigation

At present, there are several methods of flying direct routes while receiving navigational guidance: rho-theta area navigation, GPS, and LORAN. A brief caution: don't predicate your estimated fuel burn on getting a direct routing when you ask for one. ATC can always give you a routing far longer than you had planned on.

Area Navigation

An RNAV system consists of a VOR receiver, a DME receiver, and a computer (Figure 8-9). Almost all systems can operate in either the VOR/DME or RNAV modes, and in the VOR/DME mode you are able to stay constantly aware of your exact position. When the voice in your headphones asks for your position, you can say with confidence, "45X is 23.5 miles out on the Springfield 245° radial." Of course, that capability would exist if your VOR and DME receivers were in different black boxes—the RNAV installation just reduces the number of boxes.

An area navigation installation really shines in the RNAV mode, in which radial and distance information is processed by a computer, electronically relocating VORTAC stations to define your route of flight. These relocated VORTACs are called RNAV "waypoints," and the equipment in your airplane may enable you to program two or more waypoints to define a straight line flight. The only limitation is that you must be within reception distance of the VORTAC on which the waypoint is based. RNAV routes will be approved only when the entire flight will take place in a radar environment.

Establishing a waypoint is easy: for waypoint #1 you dial in the frequency of VORTAC and the radial and distance from that facility of the waypoint. Select #2 and repeat the process, using the same VORTAC or another.

Figure 8-9. *Typical RNAV display*

Figure 8-10 can be used to illustrate how RNAV would be used on a wholly imaginary flight from the Wharton Municipal Airport at the bottom of the chart to the Montgomery County Airport north of Houston International. There is no airway connecting these airports, and the entire route is covered by radar at Houston Center. (Jeppesen publishes RNAV charts, but you must still check enroute altitudes on a low-altitude enroute chart.)

The AIM says that when you file for a random route you must begin and end the random portion at a navaid or transition fix—something that Center's computer will recognize. The Wharton NDB (ARM) is on the field and will serve as the starting point, and the RILAY VOR/DME waypoint on the Montgomery County VOR/DME approach plate (which is an initial approach fix) will be the end of the RNAV route. For the purpose of this exercise, and to stay clear of the Houston Class B airspace as much as possible, draw a line from the ARM NDB to MARIT intersection southeast of the Navasota VORTAC (TNV). Just to make it interesting, though, let's establish an enroute waypoint off of the Eagle Lake VORTAC (ELA) It is most convenient to choose radials already on the enroute chart as waypoints, measuring the distance from the VORTAC to your courseline where required.

So far, the route portion of the flight plan form would be as follows: ARM > ELA083014 > TNV125007. The arrows mean "direct." Where did the distances come from? I just used a piece of paper and the scale at the bottom of the chart. For each waypoint you must list the VORTAC identifier followed by the radial and distance in a 6-digit format. For instance, ELA083014 is the Eagle Lake VORTAC 083° radial at 14 NM. You do not have to have multiple waypoint capability in your RNAV installation, although it is convenient. As you pass each waypoint you can always set up the next one.

From MARIT it is a straight shot to RILAY, so the rest of your filed route would be > IAH359016 > CXO.

This sample RNAV trip has more waypoints than it needs, simply to illustrate the use of RNAV. The typical RNAV set will accept at least four preset waypoints, so you could set the waypoint east of Eagle Lake as #1, MARIT as #2, RILAY as #3, and the MAP waypoint as #4, all before leaving the ramp

at Wharton Muni. Using RNAV mode, the CDI will indicate the course to #1 and the DME will count down from 20.0 (the initial distance from Wharton to the Eagle Lake 083 waypoint) to zero; as you pass over #1, select #2 and the set will display the course and distance to MARIT, then on to RILAY. You will be hitting RILAY at quite an angle, however, necessitating a holding pattern entry at RILAY to get aligned with the final approach course. Good thing that you are in contact with Houston Approach and can ask for vectors.

The missed approach point is always MAP (duh!). By the way, if on your knowledge exam you get a question referring to a LORAN/RNAV approach, ignore the LORAN part and answer based on your knowledge of RNAV.

This imaginary trip probably couldn't happen in real life, but it is illustrative of how RNAV is used.

Nothing has been said about what altitude to file for on the flight plan form. When you are flying in Class G airspace, terrain clearance is your responsibility; if you are off-airways but still in Class E airspace (as you would be in this example), ATC retains responsibility. You must select an altitude which provides 2,000 feet of terrain clearance in mountainous areas and 1,000 feet of terrain clearance in non-mountainous areas. Use the minimum enroute altitudes in the area as guides. In this example, 3,000 feet looks about right. You must be in constant radar contact while on a direct random route, and ATC may request altitude changes to ensure that contact.

When your random route flight will cross Center boundaries, you must include a waypoint within 200 NM of the boundary on the side of the Center whose area you are leaving. This affords the Center controller an opportunity to coordinate with the succeeding Center's controller.

Random route navigation adds another dimension to VFR-On-Top: you don't have to follow the airways. Just climb to an altitude 1,000 feet or more above the clouds and ask the controller for an RNAV clearance direct to your destination.

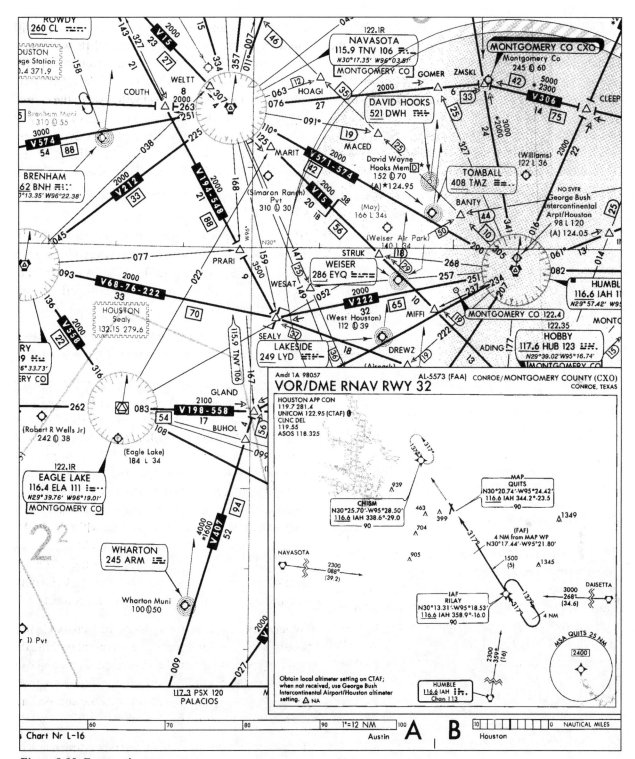

Figure 8-10. *Enroute chart segment*

Computer Navigation Fixes (CNF)

Because random route navigation involves flying TO waypoints, some intersections, DME fixes, and turn points contained in databases are not located on airways. To distinguish these CNFs from conventional reporting points, their names will be enclosed in parentheses on low altitude and approach charts (MABEE). The CNF name will not be used for any ATC application such as holding, radar vectors, or clearances.

LORAN

LORAN exploded onto the aviation electronics scene in the early 1980s. It had been used by mariners for years as a long-range navigation aid, but the large size and heavy weight of the receivers had kept them out of all but military airplanes. As solid-state electronics and the development of microprocessors began to shrink all types of electronic equipment, the airborne LORAN receiver became practical. LORAN (the "-C" will be dropped in this book because there is no other type of airborne LORAN) operates on the very low frequency of 100 kilohertz. Radio waves at that frequency are very long, and they travel great distances along the surface of the earth (ground waves). LORAN ground waves are usable 1,200 to 1,600 miles from the transmitters. A portion of the transmitted energy is propagated upward and is reflected from the ionosphere. These "sky waves"

complicate the LORAN navigation problem at night (when they are strongest), and at the extreme limits of the usable ground wave signal because, having traveled to the ionosphere and back, they arrive later than the ground wave and confuse the receiver. *See* Figure 8-11.

Unlike area navigation, which bases its navigational information on radials and distances from VORTACs, LORAN is an earth-referenced navigation system. Its navigational information is based on the latitude and longitude of the transmitting stations; your cockpit positional readout (and the position of waypoints) is also based on the latitude-longitude system.

The heart of the LORAN system is time and time delays. A LORAN chain consists of a master station and two or more secondary stations. Each chain operates on a unique group repetition rate (GRR); that is, the timing of the transmissions from the master and secondaries is different for every chain. As required during a flight, you can change from one chain to the next by selecting the GRR. LORAN equipment manufacturers have different ways of accomplishing this, but none of them are difficult.

If you enter the position of a navaid, an airport, or even your favorite fishing hole into the LORAN, it will read out the bearing and distance to that point plus your ground speed and ETA. Some units have

Figure 8-11. Typical LORAN display

databases which contain the positions of hundreds of airports and navaids which can be called up by using their 3-letter identifiers. Other features available (depending on the manufacturer) are warnings when your altitude is lower than the terrain ahead, warnings when entering Special Use Airspace such as Restricted Areas, and an emergency readout of one or more of the closest airports. The information available varies between manufacturers and is changing with bewildering speed, but most include:

- Present position and estimated position error.
- Track and ground speed.
- Distance and time to destination.
- Off course error in degrees and miles.
- Desired track.
- Bearing and distance to a waypoint.

Waypoints can be entered using latitude and longitude coordinates or range and bearing from a navaid. The lat-lon position of most navaids and airports can be found in the A/FD. Most LORAN manufacturers include databases that store the locations of all VORs or of all public use airports in the United States. Some warn you when there is higher terrain or Special Use Airspace ahead.

The line connecting the master station with each secondary is called the baseline; the best positional accuracy is found at right angles to the baseline, with accuracy decreasing as you approach either station. The baseline extension is that area "behind" a transmitting station, and the worst positional accuracy exists in that area. As an example, the master station for the U.S. west coast chain is located at Fallon, Nevada, and one of its secondaries is located at Searchlight, Nevada. The baseline extension passes near Phoenix and Tucson, Arizona, and accuracy is poor in that area.

Most LORAN units evaluate the strength and accuracy of the received signals and use only the most accurate in solving the navigational problem. At extreme distances and at night, the receiver may have difficulty in distinguishing between the ground wave from the transmitter and the skywave bounced from the ionosphere, and may "lock on" to the wrong signal.

Because LORAN positioning is based on lat-lon coordinates, its basic directional information is in relation to true north. You fly with magnetic information, of course, and each LORAN set either calculates magnetic variation automatically or requires that you enter it manually so that the tracks and bearings you derive from the LORAN are in relation to magnetic north.

The FAA permits some LORAN equipment to be connected to a VOR indicator so that you can select either VOR or LORAN for course guidance; other units have internal course deviation indicators for steering information.

The Coast Guard has informed Congress that it intends to shut down the LORAN system. The marine industry is fighting this decision, as are pilots who are reluctant to put all of their navigational eggs into the GPS basket. It is unlikely that the GPS constellation of satellites could become inoperative all at once—but it is almost certain that a single GPS receiver in an airplane will fail at some time. LORAN is a good backup; expect it to be around until at least 2008.

Whether a specific installation is approved for IFR en route (there are no LORAN approaches) can be determined only by checking the supplements in the Approved Flight Manual or a Form 337 prepared by an avionics shop.

Global Positioning System

The Global Positioning System (GPS) is a satellite-based system operated by the Department of Defense. The FAA has approved the use of FAA-approved panel-mounted installations for enroute navigation and nonprecision approaches. Handheld GPS receivers are not approved for any navigational purpose in instrument meteorological conditions, and it is likely that they will never be approved. With an approved installation, the FAA is sure of the antenna location, the integrity of the power source, and any interface between the GPS and the navigational instruments. The avionics industry has invested millions of dollars in the design and certification of panel-mounted installations and will oppose any attempt to approve handhelds for IFR use.

The Local Area Augmentation System (LAAS), which provides precision GPS approach capability, will become available on a limited basis in 2002. It will provide this capability not only at the airport where it is installed, but at nearby airports as well. Initial plans are for 31 Category I installations (same minimums as an ILS) and 112 Category III installations (very low minimums with special approval). Widespread use will depend on how quickly the FAA can design the approaches and distribute the approach plates.

Wide Area Augmentation System (WAAS) consists of two geostationary satellites in low earth orbit, and 25 ground reference stations (GRS's). The accurately-located GRS's receive GPS signals from the satellite constellation and transmit error correction signals to a wide-area master station (WMS). The WMS develops a correction message and uplinks it to one of the geostationary satellites, which in turn transmits the corrections to the receiver in your airplane. Approaches using WAAS will be nonprecision.

WAAS and LAAS will require new GPS receivers, but the GPS box in your airplane will still be usable—only the instrument minimums will be affected. (*See* Figures 8-12 and 8-13.) The WAAS satellites are expected to cover all of North America. If the WAAS program does not meet its schedule, two geostationary satellites operated by an international agency will be able to provide partial coverage of the continental United States.

Reception of four or more satellites provides a three-dimensional position fix, something LORAN is not capable of. *Note: Do not use GPS altitude for any operational purpose (AIM 1-1-21).* Unlike LORAN, which can provide false information due to skywave contamination or poor station geometry, an approved GPS either gives you an accurate position or nothing at all. A feature called receiver autonomous integrity monitoring (RAIM) that is present in all approved receivers detects any satellite failure or erroneous information and warns the user that the position information is faulty—RAIM requires a signal from a fifth satellite.

Note: If you get an "RAIM failure" error message, you must have a backup means of navigation available, and your chosen alternate must have a non-GPS approach.

All IFR-approved panel-mounted installations have databases which include the positions of navaids, intersections, airports, and any other information required to steer your airplane to the runway threshold with a high degree of accuracy. These databases must be kept up to date, just like a chart subscription service. For pilot convenience, the databases can also include information such as radio frequencies, fuel availability, runway orientation and length, and airport elevation. These databases cannot be edited by the user.

Most panel-mounts and high-end handhelds also have moving map displays, which show your airplane's position as it moves across the sky.

Until WAAS and LAAS become available, the weak spot of GPS is altitude accuracy. Horizontal accuracy can be as good as 100 feet under the most desirable conditions, but vertical accuracy can be off by as much as 600 feet. GPS does not measure altitude above ground level or sea level but above the "GPS sphere." That is why precision GPS approaches are still in the future—the near future.

Bells and Whistles

A GPS receiver is the heart of a "multifunction device" (MFD). With inputs from ground-based datalinks, the outside air temperature gauge, a fuel totalizer, a lightning detector, etc., you are able to see your path over the ground displayed on an enroute chart, approach plate, or geographical map together with distances, times, speeds, bearings, weather, special use airspace, terrain features, approach paths…all it takes is money and space in the panel. In a few years your MFD will also display the position and altitude of nearby aircraft. These are exciting times in electronic navigation.

Let's Get Practical

According to the regulations, if your instrument panel boasts only a single VOR receiver/indicator you can legally fly IFR anywhere in the United States. It wouldn't be easy, but it would be legal. With that single VOR as legal cover, it is possible for you to use your handheld GPS to fly in the National Airspace System under IFR if you know how to use that system. You cannot use a handheld GPS as your sole source of guidance without an operable VOR on

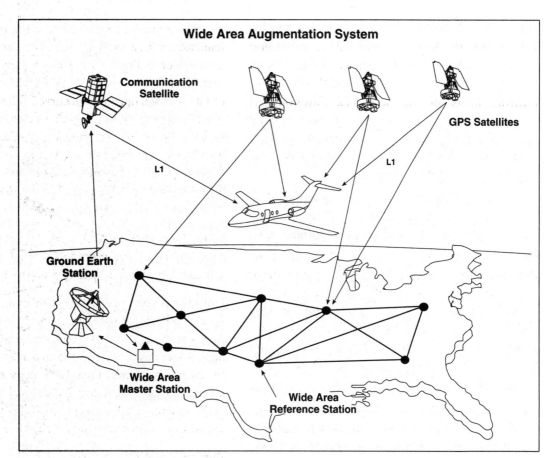

Figure 8-12. WAAS

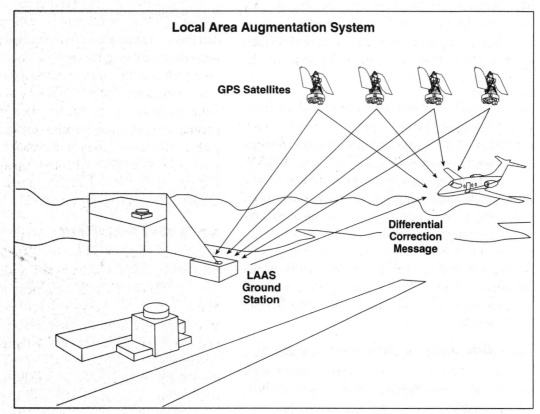

Figure 8-13. LAAS

board—it does not have to be on, but it has to be available if needed and, unless Center has given you a route outside of the service volume of the ground-based navaids to be used, you must be within that service volume.

First, the fact that you have a handheld GPS on board does not affect the equipment designation on your flight plan—you cannot file /G; use the appropriate designation for the equipment installed in the panel. Mention the GPS in the Remarks section of the flight plan, though—"GPS on board" is sufficient to give controllers some options that they might not otherwise consider.

Forget about airways; file departure airport-direct-destination airport. The most likely obstacle to doing this successfully is the failure of the ATC computer to have one or both of these airports in its memory—if it has a database, your handheld GPS probably has more memory than the computer at Center. There are two solutions to this problem: if your destination airport is relatively small, file to a large nearby airport; when you get into its terminal airspace, the controllers at that end will be familiar with all of the local airports and you can simply change your destination with them. The second ploy is to file to the latitude/longitude position of your destination. A flight from Arlington, Washington, to Hawthorne, California, would be filed KAWO..N3355/W11820..KHHR, where KAWO is Arlington and KHHR is Hawthorne. The Seattle ARTCC computer knows exactly where 33° 55' N 118° 20' W is, even if it never heard of Hawthorne. Put "Lat-lon is KHHR" in the Remarks section so that the humans who process your flight plan will understand. There is no need for intermediate waypoints. Pilots in the northeastern states can expect some problems with this because of the congested airspace, but it should work everywhere else.

What if your GPS fails? Well, what if your VOR fails?…you have to be in radar contact to get a "direct" clearance, so just advise ATC and follow instructions.

Lost Communication Procedures

The advent of small, portable VHF transmitter-receivers may spell the end of concerns about IFR procedures if two-way communications are lost, but until there is one in every airplane the FAA will make provision for that situation. You will be asked about lost communications procedures on the instrument pilot knowledge exam, and again during the oral. As a practical matter, ATC controllers want you on the ground as soon as possible, and will protect the airspace around all potential approach procedures you might use until you are on the ground. Your clearance will almost certainly be the destination airport, which may or may not have a navigation facility on the field, so rather than wander around trying to find the airport, go to any initial approach fix (all will be protected by ATC) and shoot the approach. Do not expect to find this advice in the regulations or AIM.

As the regulations are written, the FAA has provided for loss of two-way voice communications while the navigation radios somehow hum right along. This is unlikely. You may lose your ability to transmit and still be able to acknowledge instructions by either making identification turns or activating the IDENT feature of your transponder, or you may lose reception capability and broadcast your intentions in the blind on 121.5 MHz or an ATC frequency. In either case a form of communication exists, and you still have your navigation radios to get to your destination.

The event you must be prepared for—one that the regulations do not contemplate—is total electrical failure. That's why pilots are buying portable transceivers. The least expensive alternative is a preflight briefing that identifies the location of solid VFR weather within the range of the airplane.

There are many reasons why you might not be able to receive radio transmissions from the ground, but two are common enough to discuss here. If the cabin speaker fails and you do not have a headset on board, you are out of luck; the obvious solution is to buy some insurance in the form of an inexpensive set of earphones compatible with your radios. That is also the solution for the second common problem, the failure of an audio amplifier. In some installations the audio signals from all of the radios are fed through a single audio amplifier, and if that amplifier fails you have effectively lost all of your receivers. The headphone output does not depend on the audio amplifier, however, and your emergency headset will save the day.

Microphones do not fail nearly as often as do push-to-talk switches, but having a spare mike in the airplane is still an excellent idea. A stuck mike button will not only block out all of your receivers but will let listeners for miles around eavesdrop on your efforts to track down the reason for the sudden silence; exercise moderation in your use of language in this situation—the FCC frowns on broadcast expletives. If your airplane has a microphone button on the control yoke and it sticks in the ON position, you will have to shut off your radios and get the portable transceiver out of your flight bag.

In any event, when communications are interrupted and you want ATC to know that all is not well, squawk 7600 on your transponder for the rest of the flight. This is the procedure called for in the *Aeronautical Information Manual*, and it contemplates a flight in the clouds all the way to your destination. The AIM does not tell you to squawk VFR code 1200 if VFR conditions are encountered and the emergency is over, but I think it is an excellent idea. As long as you continue the 7600 squawk ATC will reserve airspace for you, and this may cause other flights to be rerouted unnecessarily if you are going to continue to a landing under VFR conditions.

The FAA breaks the lost-communication problem down into four elements: route, altitude, time, and when to descend. All bets are off if you encounter VFR conditions during the communication emergency, however—you are expected to stay VFR and land as soon as practicable. This obviously does not apply if you encounter a break in the overcast and find nothing beneath you but water or mountains.

Route

If ATC has cleared you to your destination via a specific routing and you subsequently lose communications, they will expect you to continue the flight in accordance with that clearance. If you are being vectored to a fix or to intercept an airway when everything goes silent, you should continue flying the vector heading until you reach the fix or airway and continue as before. Notice that controllers will always tell you the reason for a vector: "Turn right heading 200°, vector to intercept V-27." In each case you are to carry out the intent of the vector if communications fail. Vectors for spacing in traffic or for weather avoidance cannot be neatly categorized,

but it should be apparent that ATC does not intend that you fly away from the airway or approach course indefinitely, and that the prudent action when communications fail is to return to the course guidance you were following before the vector.

If you are not flying on an assigned route, but have been told to expect further clearance via an assigned route, proceed by the most direct means to the route you were told to expect and continue to your destination.

If you have no assigned route and have not been told to expect one (a difficult situation to imagine—how did you get into the IFR system in the first place?), fly to your destination via your flight planned route—this is an excellent reason to have a copy of your filed flight plan in the cockpit.

Altitude

The altitude to maintain in a lost-communications situation is easy to determine: the last assigned altitude, the MEA, or an altitude you have been told to expect, whichever is higher. If you are assigned 6,000 feet and encounter a route segment with an MEA of 9,000 feet you are expected to climb and maintain 9,000. If the following route segment has an MEA of 4,000, you are expected to descend to 6,000 (the last assigned), not the MEA. If ATC has told you to expect 11,000 feet in 5 miles (or 5 minutes), you are stuck at 11,000 feet for the rest of the flight if no higher MEA intervenes.

Time

When to leave the clearance limit is probably the most confusing of all lost communication situations. Ninety-nine and 44/100 percent of the time the clearance limit will be the destination airport. In this case, the FAA says that 14 CFR 91.185(c)(3) doesn't apply. "You just fly your route, complete the approach and land." Which approach? Your choice. When you have a clearance limit short of your destination airport, then 14 CFR 91.185(c)(3) takes hold and you must determine if the fix is an approach fix or not. If it isn't, proceed to one that is. When at a fix which an approach begins, calculate your ETA at that fix from the flight plan; i.e., total ETE minus approach time. Start your descent and approach as close as possible to this time.

If the smoke erupts from the radios while you are holding with an expect-further-clearance time, you are to leave the hold at that time and proceed as above, holding at the IAF until your calculated ETA if you arrive early. If you arrive late, of course, you are expected to descend and shoot the approach.

Descent

The last element of the lost communications problem is the one that pilots have the most difficulty in accepting: when do you start the descent from your enroute altitude? When altitude was discussed earlier in this section, I mentioned that if you were told to expect 11,000 feet then you would be stuck at that altitude unless a higher MEA intervened. If you interpret that to mean that you are going to show up over your destination airport in this example at 11,000 feet, you are exactly right. You may not leave the enroute altitude until your ETA. That may mean a 20 minute descent in a holding pattern and a landing 20 minutes after your ETA, but that is the way the rule is written. If no holding pattern is shown on the approach plate, you are to descend in a holding pattern on the final approach course and on the same side the procedure turn is depicted.

How much of all this did you include in your fuel planning? Probably none of it, since communication failures are not common. If fuel becomes a problem, you can use your emergency authority under 14 CFR 91.3 and descend whenever you want to.

The best solution to the loss of communications problem is still a battery-powered transceiver.

Holding Patterns

Because a clearance to hold at a fix is used as an enroute traffic metering method more often than not, a discussion of holding will close out this chapter on enroute procedures. In the terminal area, holding is associated with missed approaches; with reasonable proficiency and decent weather you will never miss an approach.

The most likely scenario is this: You are steaming down the airway when Center tells you to hold at a fix several miles ahead. You acknowledge, and when you arrive at the fix you turn right and start holding. Enroute holding is a no-brainer. Unfortunately, when you take your instrument checkride the examiner will make it a little harder on you.

Learning how to enter and fly holding patterns takes on an importance in the instrument training curriculum far out of proportion to how often these skills are exercised in everyday IFR flying; however, when you are unexpectedly directed to hold at some obscure fix on a dark and stormy night, you will understand why holding is emphasized in your training.

Holding is a time-killing procedure. ATC may need to delay you until a traffic conflict is resolved or until you can be funneled into a busy terminal area. You may have to hold until another pilot has completed the approach into your destination airport, or until the snowplows have cleared the runway. Or you may request a hold while waiting for improving weather. In any of these situations, you are going to fly around in circles at an economical power setting, waiting for further clearance.

A holding fix can be a VOR, an NDB, a DME fix along a radial, or an intersection of two VOR radials. Where low frequency airways exist, you might be directed to hold where two such airways intersect or where a VOR radial intersects a bearing from a nondirectional beacon. The amount of protected airspace set aside by the FAA for holding depends on how accurately the fix can be identified, and the altitude at which you are to hold.

When you are to hold at an NDB or VOR at a low altitude, the protected airspace will be relatively small; because the zone of ambiguity immediately above the transmitting antenna increases with altitude, the size of the holding airspace is similarly increased as holding altitudes go up. The intersection of two VOR radials several miles from the VOR stations may, because of signal spread, be difficult to identify accurately; you might fly for several seconds with no apparent needle movement and be unable to determine exactly when the needle was centered. In such a situation, the FAA will establish a holding pattern and altitude that provides obstacle and terrain clearance for several hundred square miles around the intersection.

Holding Instructions

Interpreting the controller's holding instructions will not be a problem if you will remember some simple rules:

1. A standard holding pattern is a racetrack with right turns at both ends. *See* Figure 8-14.

2. You will be told to hold in a compass direction (north, southwest, etc.) from the holding fix and that will be the general direction of your first turn when you reach the holding fix.

3. Your holding instructions will include the airway, radial, or bearing on which you are to hold.

4. You will always fly inbound on the holding course toward the holding fix; you will never turn your back on the holding fix and fly away from it along the holding course.

The holding instructions should also include the time at which you should expect a further clearance. If you are not issued an EFC time, ask for one.

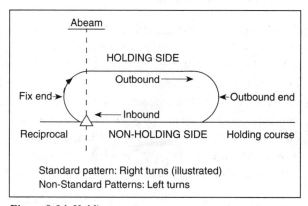

Figure 8-14. Holding pattern

ATC is supposed to give you holding instructions not less than 5 minutes before you arrive at the fix, and you are to slow to holding speed when 3 minutes from the fix. This is to give you time to figure out what to do when you get there and ensure that you don't scream over the fix at cruise speed.

Until you have become comfortable with visualizing holding pattern entries, it may be helpful for you to sketch the situation on a scratch pad or on the en route chart itself. As the controller reads the holding clearance, follow this procedure:

1. Draw a line toward the fix from the holding direction. In Figure 8-15, you are directed to

hold northwest of the fix. Write the holding radial or bearing next to the fix.

2. At the fix, continue the line for right turns or left turns as directed. Remember that right turns are standard and the controller will only specify left turns.

3. The holding course is the direction TO the fix; write it along the line, as in Figure 8-15.

4. If your airplane is DME equipped and you are assigned 5 mile legs, note that figure at the outer end of the line.

5. Always write EFC next to your drawing and ask the controller for a further clearance time if one is not included in the holding instructions. Note the holding altitude in the same place.

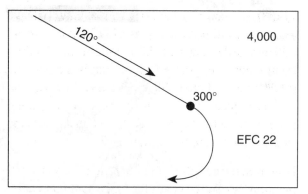

Figure 8-15. Holding notation

Let's try some examples to see how they would work:

"Cleared to the El Dorado VORTAC, hold north on the 350° radial, maintain 6,000 feet." When you arrive over the El Dorado VORTAC, your first turn will be in a northerly direction. When established in the holding pattern, you will be inbound on the 350° radial (OBS will read 170° TO) and you will turn right as you pass over the VORTAC. *See* Figure 8-16 on next page.

"Cleared to LOFAL intersection, hold east on V-287, left turns. Maintain 5,000 feet" (*see* Figure 8-17 on next page). LOFAL intersection is made up of two airways, V-4 and V-287. When you arrive at LOFAL, your first turn will be to the east. The inbound course of the holding pattern will be on the Paine Field 236° radial toward LOFAL, turning left when the Seattle 307° radial is intercepted. Some instrument students will insist that this pattern should

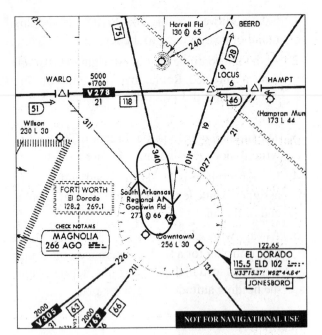

Figure 8-16. *"Hold north on the 350° radial"*

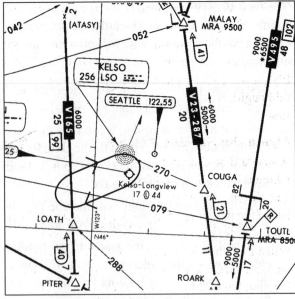

Figure 8-18. *"Hold west on the 250° bearing"*

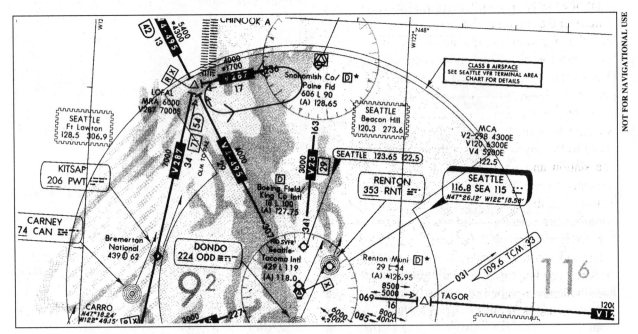

Figure 8-17. *"Hold east on V-287, left turns"*

be described as holding southeast of LOFAL, because the holding airspace is south of V-287 and east of LOFAL; this thinking is incorrect. The holding course is east of LOFAL as instructed by the controller; whether the holding airspace is north or south of the airway is determined by whether the pattern is standard or non-standard.

"Cleared to the KELSO radiobeacon, hold west on the 250° bearing, maintain 2,000 feet." *See* Figure 8-18. Your first turn when passing over the radiobeacon will be to the west (250°). After flying one minute outbound you will turn and fly eastbound toward the radiobeacon, turning right at station passage.

Your instruction on how to fly holding patterns will cover two areas: how to enter the hold as recommended by the *Aeronautical Information Manual*, and how to fly the pattern once you have entered it. Flying the pattern seems to be the easiest to learn (although not the easiest to do), so it will be discussed first.

Flying the Holding Pattern

A standard holding pattern consists of a one minute inbound leg (below 14,000 feet; 1½ minutes above that altitude), 180° standard rate right turns at each end of the pattern, and an outbound leg which, in no-wind conditions, would also be one minute long. When the wind is blowing—and it always is—you are to adjust the length of the outbound leg so that the inbound leg will be just one minute long.

The easiest possible holding situation occurs when you are approaching a fix along an airway and the controller tells you to hold in a standard holding pattern at the fix along the airway. (Note that this is also the procedure to use with lost communications or when no holding instructions have been received.) You simply fly to the fix and turn right. The AIM says that the initial outbound leg should be one minute in duration, so you need to know when to start your stopwatch. If the holding fix is a VOR station, the TO-FROM flag will flip to FROM as you pass over the station and begin your right turn, and it will continue to read FROM until you are abeam of the station on the outbound leg. Do not reset the omnibearing selector—you are not using the VOR for navigation on the outbound leg. Punch your stopwatch when the flag changes from FROM to TO, or when you level your wings when completing the turn, whichever comes later. You now have one full minute to reset the OBS to the inbound course.

At the end of one minute outbound, begin a standard rate turn to the right to intercept the inbound course; start the stopwatch as you level the wings. In no-wind conditions, the inbound leg will also be one minute long, but no-wind conditions are infrequent. If you arrive over the holding fix in more than one minute, there was a tailwind as you flew outbound. Divide the extra time by two and subtract it from the next outbound leg: for example, if the inbound leg took 80 seconds, fly the next outbound leg for 50 seconds. If the trip inbound is shorter than one minute, there was

a headwind during the outbound leg. Double the extra time and add it to the next outbound: If inbound was 50 seconds, make the next outbound 80 seconds.

When holding on a non-directional beacon, start timing the outbound leg when the ADF needle points 90° to the outbound course. In no-wind conditions that will be when the needle points directly at the wing tip.

If you are to hold at the intersection of two VOR radials, start timing the outbound leg when you level the wings at the completion of the turn to the outbound course, and time the inbound leg from wings level until the needle identifying the off-course radial centers, as closely as you can estimate it. There is plenty of protected airspace in this situation so don't be concerned if you cannot establish the fix precisely.

If you have distance measuring equipment on board, and are told to hold on a VORTAC radial at the 15 mile DME fix, ask the controller to assign 3 or 5 mile legs. That will eliminate the clock from your scan, because you will simply fly between two DME readings. If you are to hold in the direction away from the VORTAC on the 15 mile fix with 3 mile legs, you will shuttle back and forth between the 15 and 18 mile DME readings.

You will never receive a clearance to hold over a VORTAC with a DME leg distance limit. DME holding fixes are a minimum of 7 miles from the facility because of DME's inaccuracy close to the station.

Wind Drift Correction

The AIM says that the first outbound leg must always be one minute long, without allowing for wind, but when it comes to wind drift correction, the AIM says that you must allow for a known wind.

That is going to involve a certain amount of guesswork, aided by any wind drift information that you have developed during the enroute phase. If the wind is blowing from the holding side, you can't go wrong if you over-correct into the wind—when you turn inbound you will still be in protected airspace. If the wind is blowing from the non-holding side, however, too much correction might bring you too close to the holding course. Make your initial wind correction one-half of the reported wind and you will be close:

if the outbound course is 360°, and the wind is reported to be from the west at 20 knots, make your initial outbound heading 350°.

You will get the best wind correction information while flying inbound, because that is the only time that you will have a localizer, radial, or bearing to refer to. Determine how much wind correction angle is necessary to stay on course on the inbound leg, and triple that angle for the outbound correction. If your outbound wind correction angle is the same as the inbound correction, the effect of the wind on your radius of turn will ensure that you will not roll out on the inbound course.

Your turns in a holding pattern should always be standard rate, 3° per second turns, making no attempt to correct for wind drift in the turns. Because the airplane's radius of turn will decrease as you turn into the wind and increase as you turn downwind, the holding pattern as seen from the ground will be pear-shaped. Figure 8-19 illustrates the result of the inbound and outbound wind corrections, plus the effect of the wind on turn radius.

Watch the CDI or ADF needle as you turn to intercept the inbound leg; when your heading is within 30° of the inbound course, the localizer or VOR needle should be alive or the ADF needle should be within 30° of the nose of the airplane. If this is not the case, stop turning and retain that 30° intercept angle until you do intercept the inbound course. Start timing when wings are level even if 30° off.

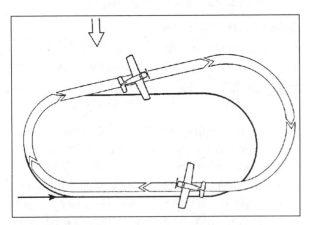

Figure 8-19. *The outbound correction should be triple the inbound correction*

Holding Pattern Entries

For most instrument pilots, flying a holding pattern is a piece of cake once they have made a successful entry; it is the entries that create uncertainty. The FAA's Instrument Rating Practical Test Standard says that the applicant shall use "an entry method that keeps the airplane within the holding pattern airspace"; it does not say that you must use the entry recommended by the AIM. You will find that most instructors push the AIM recommendations anyway, thinking that the examiner will be impressed, but in fact the examiners know what is allowed by the PTS and will accept anything that works.

Your decision on the "proper" method of entry should be made when you are heading directly toward the holding fix, and this should create no problem. Of the instances which require holding, 98 percent find the airplane on an airway or published course toward the fix. The other 2 percent arise when the pilot suddenly realizes the need for an IFR clearance and the ATC controller requires that the airplane hold at a fix while the computer fits it into the system.

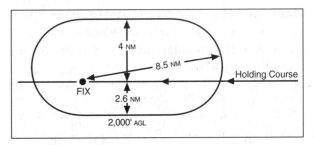

Figure 8-20. *Holding pattern template*

Procedures designers use templates when designating protected airspace for holding patterns. Figure 8-20 illustrates the smallest such area; it is for holding on a navaid such as a VOR or NDB at 2,000 feet AGL, at a maximum airspeed of 175 knots. Intersection holding patterns, or holding patterns at higher altitudes (or for faster airplanes) are larger. The overall size of the airspace reserved in the illustration is 6.7 NM wide (2.6 NM on the nonholding side) and 11.6 NM long, so you can see that staying inside the holding airspace should not be a problem.

The AIM recommends three types of holding pattern entry (a standard right-hand pattern is assumed in each case)—*see* Figure 8-21.

Direct: the holding airspace is on the side of the fix from which you are approaching; fly to the fix, turn right and fly the pattern.

Teardrop: the holding airspace is on the far side of the fix; upon arrival at the fix, turn left into the holding airspace 30° or less and hold this heading for one minute; turn right and intercept the inbound course.

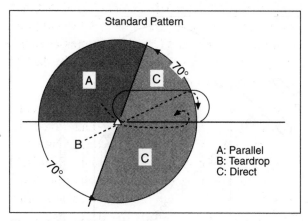

Figure 8-21. Holding pattern entry

Parallel: the holding airspace lies at an angle to the course on which you approach the fix; upon arrival at the fix turn to parallel the outbound holding course on the non-holding side, fly outbound for one minute and then turn into the holding airspace to intercept the inbound course.

Some pilots (and some instructors) do not turn onto the non-holding side when a parallel entry is indicated but fly outbound along the holding course for one minute and then turn 225° into the holding airspace to intercept the holding course. This is not covered in the AIM but is recommended in the Air Force *Instrument Flying Manual* and works very well.

There will be some holding situations where the descriptions above will not apply or where you have a choice of two types of entry; the wind will also figure into your decision on the method of entry to use.

With the airplane headed directly toward the holding fix, look at the directional gyro and mentally divide it into three segments: if you are to hold in a standard right hand pattern, the smallest segment will be the 70° to the right of the nose of the airplane, and it will be called the teardrop segment; the next largest segment will be the 110° to the left of the nose, and it will

be the parallel segment; the 180° left over will be the direct segment. Many instructors call this the "thumb rule," possibly the only thumb rule that actually uses a thumb (Figure 8-22). For a right hand pattern, place your right thumb on the heading indicator with the bottom edge of your thumb at the right wing tip position: the teardrop segment lies between the top edge of your thumb and the nose of the airplane. (Other instructors advocate using the HI adjustment knob: an imaginary diagonal line from the knob across the center of the instrument defines the three segments, with the teardrop and parallel segments to the right and left of the nose respectively and the direct segment below the line for a standard pattern.)

With the three segments identified, what next? Look for the outbound holding course on the heading indicator and determine which segment it is in. That will be the entry type. If you find that the outbound course is close to the dividing line between two types of entry, choose the entry that will keep you in the holding airspace, considering the effects of wind drift.

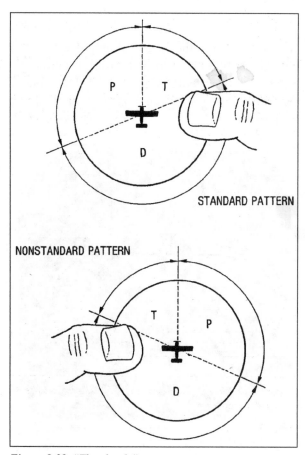

Figure 8-22. "Thumb rule"

Still another method of determining the type of entry requires that you visualize the fix as being at the center of the heading indicator and your airplane's position as being at the bottom of the heading indicator flying upward as shown in Figure 8-23.

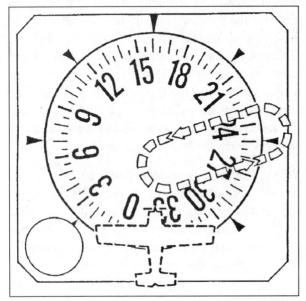

Figure 8-23. Holding pattern visualization

Figure 8-24 shows a device called a "Holdicator," designed to aid in the visualization process. In the illustration, the holding instructions are to hold northeast on the 025° radial, right turns. It looks like a teardrop entry to me. (If you want to buy one, contact the author through ASA or "bobmrg@halcyon.com".)

Figure 8-24. Holdicator

Then there is the "when all else fails" method, to be used when you are tired and confused and your brain has turned to pudding: fly to the fix and turn to the outbound course for one minute. During that minute, puzzle out which direction you must turn to enter the holding airspace and, when the time is up, turn into the holding airspace and return to the fix to hold as directed. (*See* Figure 8-25.)

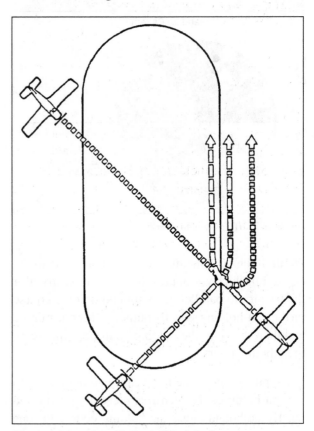

Figure 8-25. "When all else fails" method

The wind will affect your decision on the type of entry to use. In Figure 8-26, a teardrop entry would be appropriate in no-wind conditions, but with the wind as illustrated the airplane would be blown into the holding course and, when turning downwind toward the inbound course, would be blown onto the non-holding side. In this instance a parallel entry would be best; the airplane might be blown slightly toward the non-holding side (one knot of crosswind component drifts the airplane 100 feet per minute, and the airplane will only be outbound one minute), but, because of the reduced turn radius when turning into the wind, it will probably end up close to the inbound course.

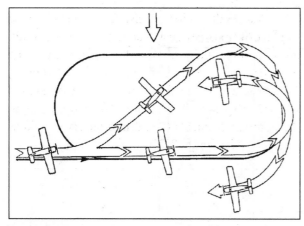

Figure 8-26. Effect of wind on entry method

Time and altitude reaching a clearance limit is a mandatory report in both radar and non-radar environments, and a holding fix is a clearance limit. If you are cleared to hold at MUCHO intersection or the RABID VOR, make that report when you reach the fix, not after you have begun the entry procedure. The recommended format is P-T-A: position, time of arrival, and altitude. Departing the holding fix is also a mandatory report.

Holding Speed

You are to begin slowing to holding speed when 3 minutes or less from the holding fix, and are to cross the fix at or below the maximum holding speed for your type of airplane:

For all aircraft between MHA (minimum holding altitude) and 6,000 feet MSL, holding speed is 200 KIAS. For all aircraft between 6,001 and 14,000 feet MSL, holding speed is 230 KIAS; for 14,000 feet MSL and above, holding speed is 265 KIAS. Exceptions to these speeds will be indicated by an icon.

Timed Approaches

You won't be doing timed approaches from a holding fix unless you do a lot of flying into major airports. You've heard about airliners being stacked up over an airport like O'Hare, waiting for approach clearance? That's what this is all about. As the airplane that is #1 to land gets cleared for the approach, #2 descends to become #1, and everyone else in the stack descends as well.

First, this only happens at controlled airports. Second, the pilot must maintain direct communications with the approach controller until instructed to contact the tower. Third, if there is more than one missed approach procedure, none must require a course reversal (who wants to fly in the face of inbound traffic?); and fourth, if only one missed approach procedure is available, the reported ceiling and visibility must be equal to or greater than the highest circling minimums for the approach.

If you find yourself in this situation, you must time your final turn in the holding pattern so as to leave the final approach fix inbound at the assigned time.

Standard Terminal Arrival Routes

The enroute portion of your flight might terminate in a standard terminal arrival route (STAR). Like DPs, STARs are published, formalized routings which reduce the complexity of clearances. Jeppesen includes STARs in their Airway Manual; NACO has a separate "STAR and Profile Descent Charts" section in each approach chart booklet. If you don't want to use a STAR, put "NO STARs" in the remarks section of your flight plan form.

The name of a STAR will tell you which intersection all of the transitions lead to. For example, the LYNXX SEVEN ARRIVAL into Burbank (*see* Figure 8-27 on next page); LYNXX intersection is the central point in the procedure.

Entering the Terminal Area

If the termination of your flight does not involve a STAR, the enroute portion will terminate at an initial approach fix, identified as IAF on the approach plate. When you look at the approach plates for your destination airport you may find several initial approach fixes, serving pilots arriving from different directions. Chapter 9 will take you the rest of the way.

Figure 8-27

Instrument Student Questions

1. Except when necessary for takeoff or landing or unless otherwise authorized by the Administrator, the minimum altitude for IFR flight is

   A— 3,000 feet over all terrain.

   B— 3,000 feet over designated mountainous terrain; 2,000 feet over terrain elsewhere.

   C— 2,000 feet above the highest obstacle over designated mountainous terrain; 1,000 feet above the highest obstacle over terrain elsewhere.

2. (Refer to Figure Q8-1.) Which point would be the appropriate VOR COP on V552 from the LFT to the TBD VORTACs?

   A— CLYNT intersection.

   B— HATCH intersection

   C— 33 DME from the LFT VORTAC.

3. (Refer to Figure Q8-2 on next page.) En route on V468 from BTG VORTAC to YKM VORTAC, the minimum altitude at TROTS intersection is

   A— 7,100 feet.

   B— 10,000 feet.

   C— 11,500 feet.

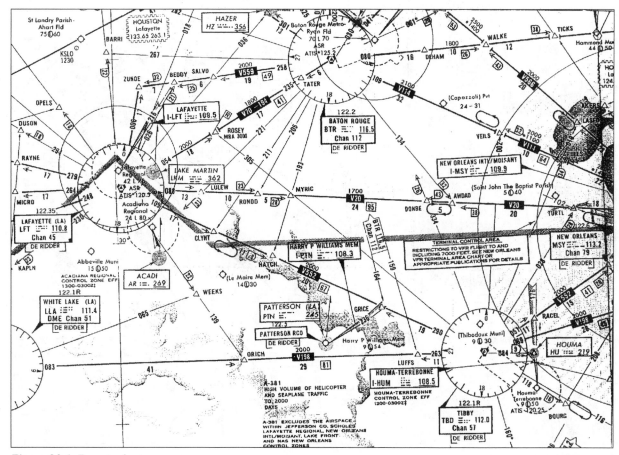

Figure Q8-1. Enroute chart segment

4. What is the recommended climb procedure when a nonradar departure control instructs a pilot to climb to the assigned altitude?

A— Maintain a continuous optimum climb until reaching assigned altitude and report passing each 1,000-foot level.

B— Climb at a maximum angle of climb to within 1,000 feet of the assigned altitude, then 500 feet per minute the last 1,000 feet.

C— Maintain an optimum climb on the centerline of the airway without intermediate level-offs until 1,000 feet below assigned altitude, then 500 feet per minute.

5. When is a pilot on an IFR flight plan responsible for avoiding other aircraft?

A— At all times when not in radar contact with ATC.

B— When weather conditions permit, regardless of whether operating under IFR or VFR.

C— Only when advised by ATC.

6. For which speed variation should you notify ATC?

A— When the ground speed changes more than 5 knots.

B— When the average true airspeed changes 5 percent or 10 knots, whichever is greater.

C— Any time the ground speed changes 10 mph.

7. What action should you take if your No. 1 VOR receiver malfunctions while operating in controlled airspace under IFR? Your aircraft is equipped with two VOR receivers. The No. 1 receiver has Omni/Localizer/Glide Slope capability, and the No. 2 has only Omni.

A— Report the malfunction immediately to ATC.

B— Continue the flight as cleared; no report is required.

C— Continue the approach and request a VOR or NDB approach.

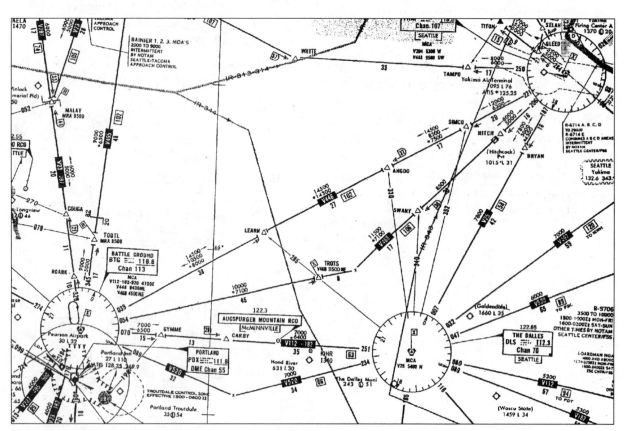

Figure Q8-2. Enroute chart segment

8. (Refer to Figure Q8-3.) You arrive at the 15 DME fix on a heading of 350°. Which holding pattern correctly complies with the ATC clearance below, and what is the recommended entry procedure?

   "...HOLD WEST OF THE ONE FIVE DME FIX ON THE ZERO EIGHT SIX RADIAL OF THE ABC VORTAC, FIVE MILE LEGS, LEFT TURNS..."

   A—1; teardrop entry.
   B—1; direct entry.
   C—2; direct entry.

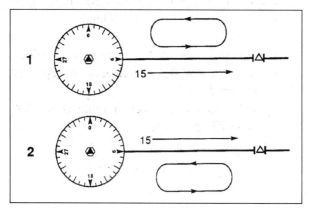

Figure Q8-3. Holding entry procedure

9. What timing procedure should be used when performing a holding pattern at a VOR?

   A—Timing for the outbound leg begins over or abeam the VOR, whichever occurs later.
   B—Timing for the inbound leg begins when initiating the turn inbound.
   C—Adjustments in timing of each pattern should be made on the inbound leg.

10. When holding at an NDB, at what point should the timing begin for the second leg outbound?

    A—When the wings are level and the wind drift correction angle is established after completing the turn to the outbound heading.
    B—When the wings are level after completing the turn to the outbound heading, or abeam the fix, whichever occurs first.
    C—When abeam the holding fix.

11. If only one missed approach procedure is available, which of the following conditions is required when conducting "timed approaches from a holding fix"?

    A—The pilot must contact the airport control tower prior to departing the holding fix inbound.
    B—The reported ceiling and visibility minimums must be equal to or greater than the highest prescribed circling minimums for the IAP.
    C—The reported ceiling and visibility minimums must be equal to or greater than the highest prescribed straight-in MDA minimums for the IAP.

12. During an IFR flight in IMC, you enter a holding pattern (at a fix that is not the same as the approach fix) with an EFC time of 1530. At 1520 you experience complete two-way communications failure. Which procedure should you follow to execute the approach to a landing?

A—Depart the holding fix to arrive at the approach fix as close as possible to the EFC time and complete the approach.

B—Depart the holding fix at the EFC time, and complete the approach.

C—Depart the holding fix at the earliest of the flight planned ETA or the EFC time, and complete the approach.

13. What altitude and route should be used if you are flying in IMC and have two-way radio communications failure?

A—Continue on the route specified in your clearance, fly at an altitude that is the highest of last assigned altitude, altitude ATC has informed you to expect, or the MEA.

B—Fly direct to an area that has been forecast to have VFR conditions, fly at an altitude that is at least 1,000 feet above the highest obstacles along the route.

C—Descend to MEA and, if clear of clouds, proceed to the nearest appropriate airport. If not clear of clouds, maintain the highest of the MEA's along the clearance route.

14. If Receiver Autonomous Integrity Monitoring (RAIM) is not available when setting up a GPS approach, the pilot should

A—select another type of navigation and approach system.

B—continue to the MAP and hold until the satellites are recaptured.

C—continue the approach, expecting to recapture the satellites before reaching the FAF.

Arrivals

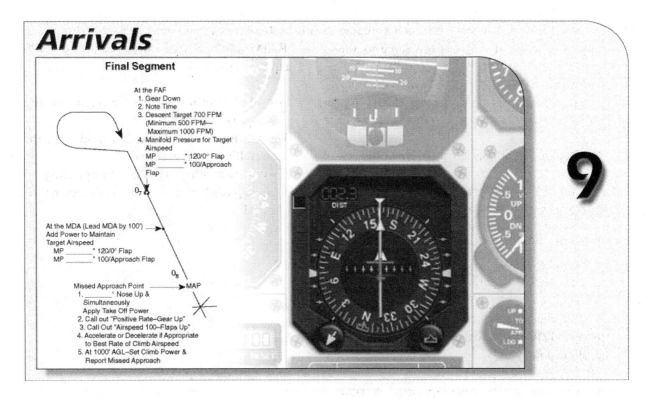

Final Segment

At the FAF
1. Gear Down
2. Note Time
3. Descent Target 700 FPM
   (Minimum 500 FPM—
   Maximum 1000 FPM)
4. Manifold Pressure for Target
   Airspeed
   MP _____ " 120/0° Flap
   MP _____ " 100/Approach
   Flap

At the MDA (Lead MDA by 100')
Add Power to Maintain
Target Airspeed
MP _____ " 120/0° Flap
MP _____ " 100/Approach Flap

Missed Approach Point ——▶ MAP
1. _____ " Nose Up &
   Simultaneously
   Apply Take Off Power
2. Call out "Positive Rate–Gear Up"
3. Call Out "Airspeed 100–Flaps Up"
4. Accelerate or Decelerate if Appropriate
   to Best Rate of Climb Airspeed
5. At 1000' AGL–Set Climb Power &
   Report Missed Approach

Destination

The destination end of the system is just the reverse of the departure end. The Center controller will clear you to a navaid or intersection that is the starting point for a transition or feeder route to an initial approach fix for the destination airport. Center will either clear you for the approach or hand you off to an approach controller. You will find that there is always at least one navaid or intersection which appears on both the enroute chart and the approach plate that ties the two together; it is at that point that you will leave the enroute structure and enter the terminal area. If it is not marked "IAF" (initial approach fix) on the approach plate, there will be a feeder route (transition) between that point and the IAF. Navaids which are part of the enroute structure are to be considered initial approach fixes even if not designated IAF on the approach plate.

Transitions play a major role in flight planning. Your destination airport may have several instrument approaches, some precision and some non-precision, and those approaches may serve more than one runway. During the preflight weather briefing, you should learn what wind conditions are expected at the destination at your ETA so that you can predict which approach will be in use, and then you should look at that approach plate to find an initial approach

fix in the direction from which you will be coming. A legal or flyable transition *always* has a course, distance, and altitude associated with it, and is depicted as a heavy black line.

When flying a transition, remember that you cannot descend to the altitude published for the transition unless you have heard "Cleared for the approach." Without an approach clearance you must maintain the last assigned altitude until you hear those magic words. Don't be reluctant to call the controller and "request lower" when a transition would allow you to descend—sometimes that request will generate an approach clearance.

To illustrate, look at Figure 9-1 on the next page. The Abilene Regional ILS RWY 35R is shown on both the approach plate and the enroute low-altitude chart, and there is a feeder route from TUSCOLA to the initial approach fix at the TOMHI outer compass locator. Without radar vectoring, you would fly via airways to TUSCOLA, direct to the TOMHI LOM, and then complete the approach as published. If the controller said "Cleared for the approach," you would descend to 3,900 feet after passing TUSCOLA; otherwise, you would stay at your last assigned altitude.

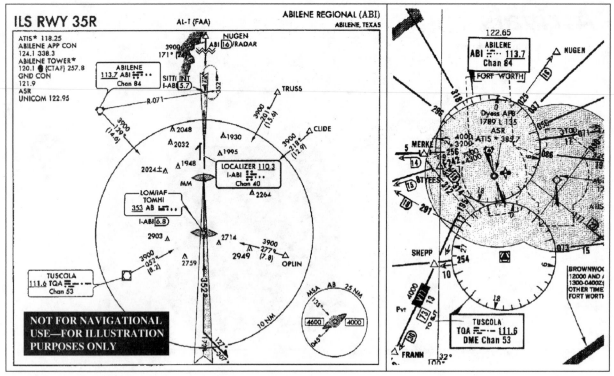

Figure 9-1. *Abilene ILS 35R, approach plate and enroute chart excerpt*

None of the transitions to the Abilene ILS 35R initial approach fix has "NoPT" printed next to it, so in the absence of radar vectoring every one of the transitions would require that the course reversal (procedure turn) be performed. Procedure turns will be discussed later.

Each approach plate, whether you use NACO or Jeppesen, identifies initial approach fixes (IAFs) and shows you how to get to the IAF from a navaid or intersection shown on an en route or area chart. *Warning:* some intersections exist only on an area chart or an approach plate and not on the associated enroute low-altitude chart. If your departure or destination airport is shown on an area chart, be sure to have that area chart readily available.

In looking at an approach chart you may find a radial that is a transition in disguise, and you must refer to the enroute low-altitude en route chart to unmask it. In Figure 9-2 there is apparently no way for a pilot cleared to the VORTAC to fly to the initial approach fixes on the DME arc segments. However, a check of the enroute low-altitude chart reveals that the 272° radial is V-182 and the 325° radial is V-357. The airway segments, of course, have bearings, distances, and altitudes assigned and have been flight checked.

You can pretty well accept that any radial that begins a DME arc is an airway. (Don't let the "GPS" in the chart title throw you—GPS approaches will be discussed later.)

Occasionally, space restrictions make it impossible for the chart printers to show a line with an arrow for a transition—the distance is just too short. In those cases, the bearing, altitude, and distance for the transition will be printed adjacent to the segment (*see* the NUGEN transition in Figure 9-1, or the outbound transition from the BKE VORTAC to the 4-mile DME fix in Figure 9-2).

Note: Procedure titles such as "GPS RWY 12" in Figure 9-2 will gradually change to "RNAV RWY 12," reflecting the FAA decision to include all random route navigation procedures under a single title. More on the new approach plates toward the end of Chapter 10.

If the transition includes the words "NoPT (No Procedure Turn)," you will not perform a course reversal but will continue the approach from the IAF; in fact, if for some reason you want to perform a

Continued on Page 9-5

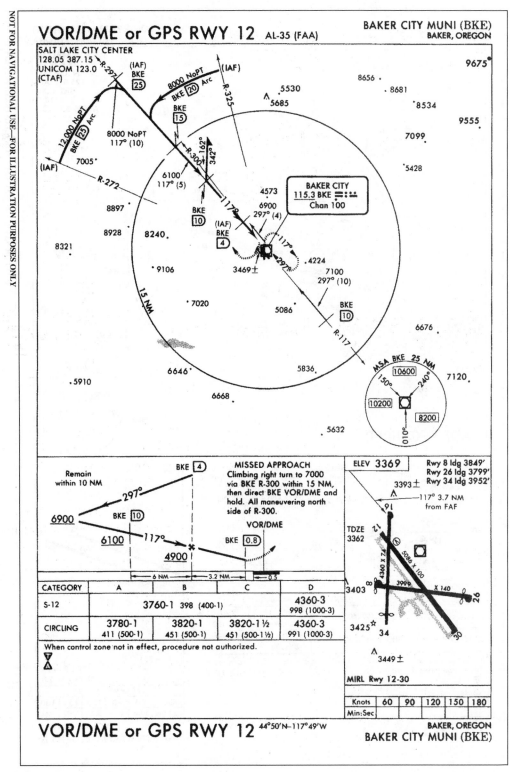

Figure 9-2. DME arcs

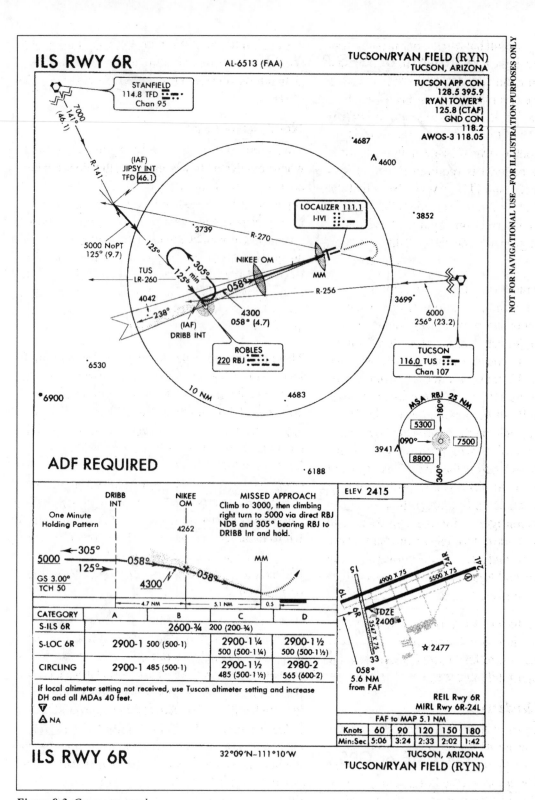

Figure 9-3. *Course reversal*

procedure turn, you will have to get permission from ATC beforehand. If the letters NoPT are not included in the transition identification, you are required to perform a course reversal. Figure 9-3 (on Page 9-4) illustrates this point. If you are inbound to DRIBB from the TFD VORTAC, no procedure turn is required, but a course reversal (the mandatory one-minute holding pattern) is required if you are inbound from the Tucson (TUS) VOR. Note that the TUS 270° radial is not a transition, but simply identifies JIPSY intersection. Again, a legal transition has a heading, an altitude, and a distance associated with it.

If you are being radar vectored, listen carefully to the controller: If the clearance is to a navaid, such as, "Cleared present position direct Gray radio beacon, cleared for the approach" and the procedure requires a course reversal, you are required to make that procedure turn. If, however, the controller says, "Turn right heading 110, *vector to the final approach course*," you will not be making a procedure turn, even if one is depicted on the approach plate. In this instance, the controller will position you on the approach course well before the FAF. The purpose of a procedure turn is to place you in position on the final approach course early enough to get the airplane properly configured for the approach with speed stabilized. If the controller can do that for you, why reverse course and terrorize the pilots following you on the approach? Again, procedure turns will be discussed in detail later.

Where radar vectoring is available, you might not have much occasion to use transitions, but where there is no radar controller to guide you across the skies you will definitely use them.

Altimeter Setting?

You can't begin an instrument approach procedure without a current altimeter setting. In some cases (Figure 9-3 again), there are higher minimums if the local altimeter is not available but a setting can be received from a remote source; the minimums go up in this situation. Ryan Field has an AWOS, and the procedures designers have made allowance for a remote altimeter from Tucson International. If your

destination has an AWOS or ASOS and there is no provision for a remote altimeter setting, you must abandon the approach if the AWOS or ASOS is out of service.

No Approach?

Transitions and "vectors to final" don't help much when your destination is an airport that does not have an instrument approach. Your best bet while the flight is still in the planning stage is to identify a nearby airport that does have an approach and file that airport as your destination. If weather conditions are good enough for you to see the destination airport from the MEA of the airway, cancel IFR and complete the trip VFR; if clouds make this impossible, you still have the approach at the nearby airport as an alternative.

There are two possible situations that you might be faced with in the shoot-the-approach-and-scud-run-to-the-destination scenario. If the ceiling and visibility are below VFR minimums and the airport with the approach has a combined tower/TRACON, getting a clearance to do a low approach followed by Special VFR out of the Class D airspace and onward is fairly easy. Tell the radar controller what you are planning to do well in advance, so any necessary coordination can be accomplished. If the tower is not associated with a radar facility (or if there is no tower, in which case you are dealing with the Class E boundary), you will have to land and pick up a Special VFR clearance on the ground.

In either case, the fact that you had to shoot an approach indicates that the weather is not VFR in the area, and you will be scooting along beneath a 1,200-foot or a 700-foot floor of controlled airspace. Will people on the ground report you for low flying, if you have to be 500 or 600 feet above the ground? What if the weather at the "VFR" airport is worse than expected...now you are below radar coverage, and in uncontrolled airspace where ATC can do nothing for you unless you declare an emergency, and even then there is not much they can do. Think long and hard before planning to shoot an approach and then scud run to a nearby airport.

Approach Segments

The "United States Standard for Terminal Instrument Procedures" (or TERPS) is the book used by the folks who design instrument approaches. You can get it from the Government Printing Office, or from one of the many suppliers of government publications on CD-ROM, when you become an instrument instructor—you won't need it before that happy day. It breaks an instrument approach into four segments: initial, intermediate, final, and missed approach. Surprisingly, the approach designer starts with the missed approach segment because if you can't miss the approach without hitting something it is madness to begin it. Obstructions in the missed approach segment frequently require higher visibility minimums for the approach than would be apparent from an examination of the terrain underlying the approach to the runway. A good example is South Lake Tahoe, California, an airport in a bowl, where the approach path is over the lake but there are mountains straight ahead; the missed approach point is 4.4 miles from the airport (the visibility minimum is 5 miles) and a climbing right turn to 11,000 feet is required.

The initial segment of an instrument approach procedure begins at the IAF, and is designed to allow a pilot to depart the enroute phase and maneuver to enter the intermediate segment. Some approaches do not have an initial segment. You will never need to know about the initial approach segment unless the controller says "Cleared for the approach to Bigtown Airport, report on initial." If you were not already aware that this controller does not have radar, a requirement that you report your position should alert you. That request tells you that you are going to fly over a navaid and perform a course reversal, and the controller wants to know when you have passed the facility outbound.

The intermediate segment blends the initial segment into the final approach segment, and it is intended that the pilot establish approach configuration and airspeed while on this segment. The terrain clearance provided by the designer gets a little tighter as you proceed from the initial to the intermediate segment. The procedure turn is part of the intermediate segment. This segment ends at the final approach fix.

The minimum altitude at which the procedure turn is to be accomplished is based on the "required obstacle clearance" in the procedures designer's manual. Because the airspace protected for the course reversal is so large, a man-made obstacle or terrain feature that appears to be well clear of the procedural track may be pushing the PT altitude higher than would appear to be necessary.

The final approach segment is where alignment and descent for landing are accomplished, and the obstacle and terrain clearance standards are tightest. It begins at the FAF and ends at the runway or missed approach point, whichever comes first. Some approaches (like South Lake Tahoe) have a visual segment—if you can't see the runway from the missed approach point (several miles out in these situations) you must initiate the missed-approach procedure. On approach plates, the FAF for a nonprecision approach is indicated by a Maltese cross. The final approach point (not fix) for a precision approach is shown with a lightning symbol on NACO plates and is a point where the procedural track starts down on Jeppesen plates.

When a controller says asks you to "report procedure turn inbound," you are to make that report when established on the intermediate segment heading toward the final approach fix, not while you are still performing the course reversal. The controller's reason for requiring this report is usually traffic between you and the airport; the controller wants to know when you start flying toward the airport so that proper spacing can be established.

As you might imagine, the missed approach segment begins at the missed approach point (MAP). For nonprecision approaches, this might be established by timing from the FAF, by a fix, or by a navaid. For precision approaches a missed approach is to be initiated when the airplane has descended to decision altitude (DA) and there is no visual contact with the approach lights or runway environment. The designer provides obstruction clearance beginning at the MAP on the assumption that you initiate a climb of at least 152 feet per nautical mile at that point; if you delay the missed approach in hopes of seeing something through the murk, you risk hitting something the designer intended you to miss.

Procedure Turns

"Procedure turn" is one of those phrases that separates IFR pilots from VFR pilots; it certainly isn't used during primary training. Once phrases such as "procedure turn" and "glide slope" enter your vocabulary, you know that you are taking a big step up in the aviation world.

A procedure turn is simply a course reversal. If your destination airport is served only by an approach to runway 18 and you are coming from the south, it is reasonably certain that you will have to fly to a position north of the airport and reverse course. The FAA doesn't really care just how you accomplish this course reversal, but it does insist that it be performed within a given distance (usually 10 nautical miles) of a navigational aid or intersection, and on the side of the final approach course depicted on the approach plate. There is a 200-knot speed limit, but that should be of minimal importance to you right now.

Subject to those restrictions, you can reverse course by using a racetrack pattern, a teardrop, a 90°-270° turn, or the published 45° turn. Only the prohibition against aerobatics in a Class B, C, D, or E airspace designated for an airport keeps you from doing an Immelmann turn or a Cuban Eight. Figure 9-4 illustrates several options that are available to you.

The two options at the top of Figure 9-4 are racetrack patterns. Do not confuse these course reversals with the holding pattern designated for the missed approach. Note that in Figure 9-6 (on Page 9-8) the missed approach holding pattern has an assigned altitude of 3,000 feet, while the course reversal is to be performed no lower than 1,900 feet—the airspace is protected for you at 1,900 feet from the facility for a distance of 10 nautical miles.

In fact, the airspace protected for a course reversal is much larger than you would imagine (Figure 9-5). There is no special airspace reserved for faster airplanes such as air carriers or military jets. If the airspace is large enough for them to reverse course safely it is more than enough so for you in your prop job, even under the most adverse wind conditions.

The minimum altitude at which the procedure turn is to be accomplished is based on the "required obstacle clearance" in the procedure designer's manual. Because the protected airspace for course reversal is so large, a man-made obstacle or terrain feature that appears to be well clear of the procedural track may be pushing the PT altitude higher than would appear to be necessary.

Both Jeppesen and NACO approach plates depict courses for a turn 45° away from the final approach course and its reciprocal. These published courses are useful in no-wind conditions, or when you are tired and not up to mental gymnastics—the 45°-180° procedure turn is neither required by the FAA nor recommended in preference to other methods, although many instructors refer to it as a "standard procedure turn." It is, however, an excellent starting method for instrument students.

In most cases, you have 10 miles in which to reverse course—where should you begin the procedure turn? After flying outbound one minute or two minutes is not the correct answer. The governing factors should be how much altitude you must lose after completing the course reversal and how much distance it will take to lose that altitude comfortably. A secondary consideration is that you want to allow yourself enough time to perform all pre-landing duties and get the airplane into approach configuration at approach speed before you begin the descent to DH or MDA. Two minutes is reasonable, three minutes is even better unless a strong tailwind might blow you past the distance limit.

Unless your instrument instructor has convinced you that the 45°-180° procedure turn ranks right up there with the flag, motherhood, and apple pie, the type of turn you use will depend on such variables as the direction from which you approach the fix and the wind direction. To make the right choice you must remember that your airplane's turn radius increases when you turn downwind and decreases as you turn into the wind.

The 90°-270° turn (Figure 9-6) is quick, takes up little room, and requires no mathematical skills whatsoever. It should only be performed if the initial turn is downwind. When you are ready to reverse course, turn 90° (30 seconds at 3° per second) in the direction shown on the approach plate for the course reversal; when you have turned 90°, roll smoothly into a standard rate turn in the other direction and hold it until you are established on the inbound course. No

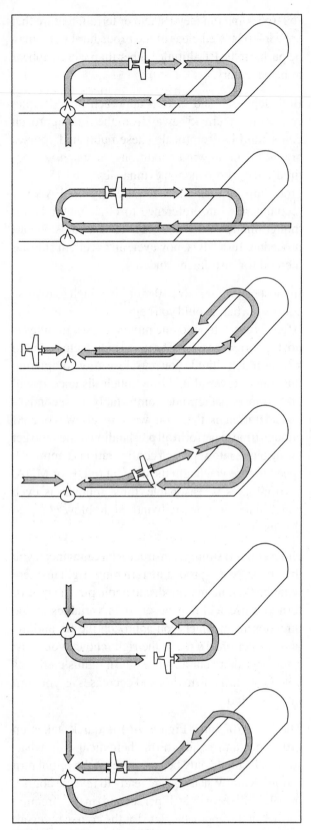

Figure 9-4. *Course reversal options*

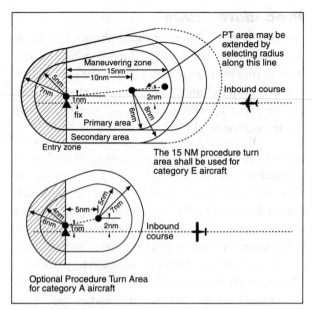

Figure 9-5. *Course reversal protected airspace*

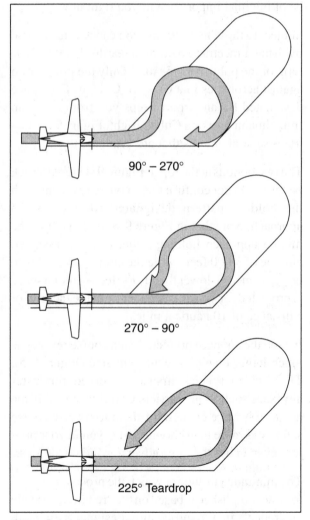

Figure 9-6. *Additional alternate methods*

timing, no math. If the initial turn is to be into the wind, make a 270°-90°. Turn 270° away from the outbound course and then 90° to align yourself with the inbound course. These are ideal course reversals if you are flying on partial panel. If you are nearing the 10-mile limit and are concerned that you will exceed it while accomplishing the course reversal, use a 270°-90° turn (Figure 9-6), but tell the controller what you are planning to do.

A teardrop maneuver should be familiar from your study of holding pattern entries, and requires only that you determine an initial heading and the time you will fly on that heading before you turn inbound. A turn of 30° away from the outbound course for one minute will work in no-wind conditions, but you should adjust both heading and time to allow for a known wind. The outbound time for this type of teardrop should be at least one minute, never less.

Another form of teardrop course reversal is the 45° turn for one minute — as illustrated in Chapter 5 of the FAA's *Instrument Flying Handbook*.

The Air Force *Instrument Flying Manual* suggests an easy method of course reversal: fly outbound on the inbound course for the desired amount of time (based on altitude to be lost inbound), then turn 225° to intercept the inbound course at a 45° angle (Figure 9-6). The drawback of this procedure is that it returns you to the final approach course closer to the airport than when you left it, while most other course reversal methods end up farther away from the airport.

Figure 9-7 shows how the 45° teardrop might be used in transitioning from a missed approach into a second approach: home back to the beacon while climbing to the missed approach altitude; crossing the beacon, turn immediately to the 45° outbound course (adjusted for wind), starting your watch as you cross the course line. Fly for at least a minute, again allowing for wind, and then roll back toward the course line. In situations like this, with both the missed-approach and procedure turn airspace on the same side of the final approach course, you have protection from obstacles all the way from the facility (NDB or VOR) to ten miles out. This is more than enough airspace to do any kind of course reversal you can dream up.

Mandatory Holding Pattern Course Reversal

There are many approaches across the country where a 1-minute holding pattern is depicted in lieu of a procedure turn, and when such a pattern is shown on the approach plate it must be flown (you must at least make an appropriate holding pattern entry). In almost every case, the airspace required for a "normal" course reversal would infringe on airspace reserved for another purpose—the 1-minute holding pattern airspace is much tighter.

You don't have to fly a complete pattern if altitude is not a problem, just cross the fix once as the initial approach fix and again as the final approach fix. In fact, if you decide to fly one or more complete racetracks to lose altitude you must inform ATC of your intentions.

The ILS approach to runway 33L at Wichita Falls, TX is an example (Figure 9-8). A pilot flying the transition from FLOPP intersection would make a direct entry and fly the holding pattern as depicted to intercept the localizer, while a pilot transitioning from the Wichita Falls VORTAC would perform a teardrop entry.

Can you use a racetrack pattern to reverse course when one is not depicted? Of course you can. In Figure 9-9, a pilot approaching the PINCK outer marker from the BOWIE VORTAC could perform a direct entry to the depicted missed approach holding pattern and extend that pattern a minute or so northbound to allow time to descend from 2,500 feet to 2,200 feet. Remember, on the west side of the localizer there's ten miles worth of airspace protected all the way up to 2,500 feet.

Figure 9-10 illustrates an unusual type of course reversal. When a procedure such as this is shown on the plate it must be flown as depicted.

When you are required to perform a course reversal to intercept an ILS final approach course, ignore the clock and fly outbound until the glide slope has come up to at least the centered position before beginning the course reversal; this should result in you being beneath the glide slope when you turn inbound. Reliance on flying outbound for a specified time might result in being above the glide slope as you intercept the localizer inbound.

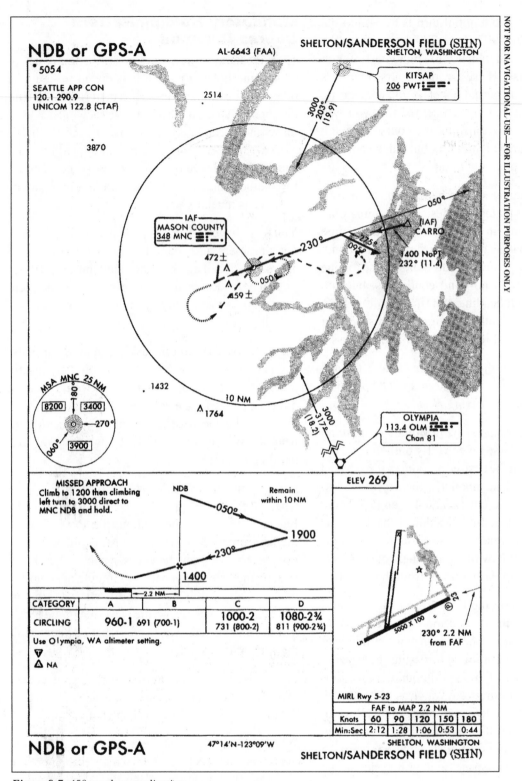

Figure 9-7. *45° teardrop application*

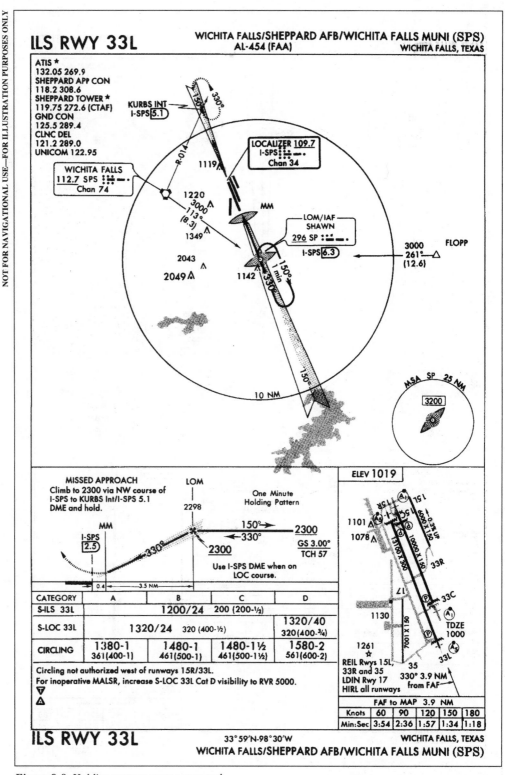

Figure 9-8. Holding pattern course reversal

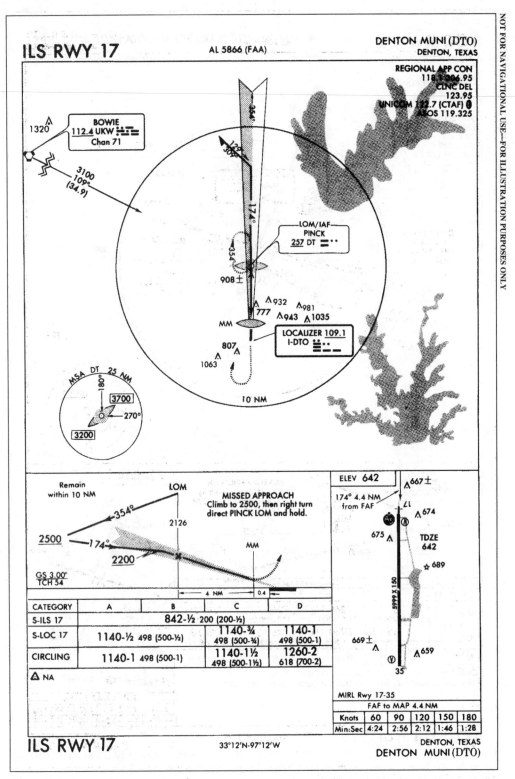

Figure 9-9. *Racetrack course reversal*

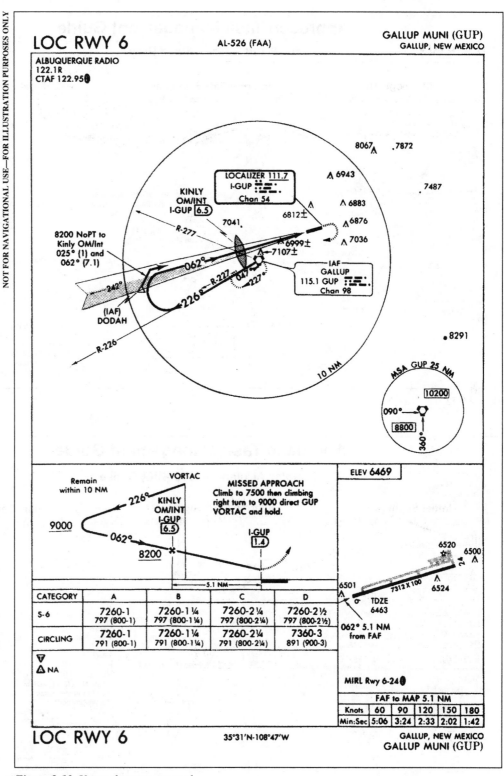

Figure 9-10. Unusual course reversal

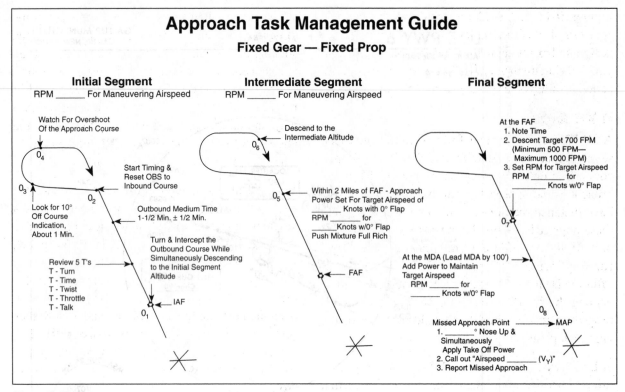

Figure 9-11

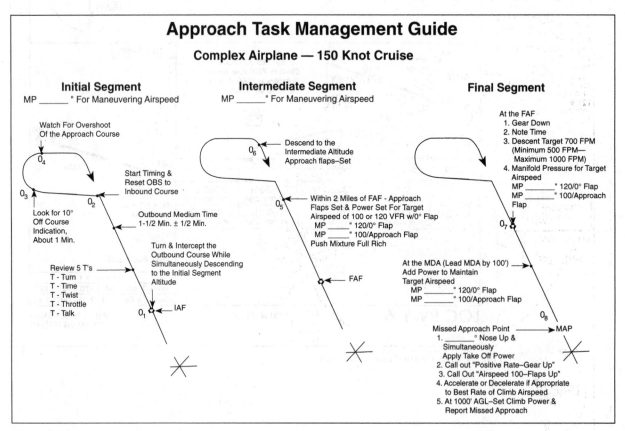

Figure 9-12

Figures 9-11 and 9-12 are provided through the courtesy of E. Allan Englehardt, an airline pilot and designated examiner in the Chicago area. I think that you will find them to be useful guides to appropriate actions while you are maneuvering for an approach.

DME Arcs

A DME arc is a special form of initial approach segment that leads smoothly into the final approach course for either a precision or nonprecision approach. Some approaches can be used only if you have distance measuring equipment on board, and these approaches have the abbreviation "DME" as part of the procedure identification: VOR-DME Runway 35, ILS-DME runway 27. Other approaches offer the DME arc as an alternative method of intercepting the final approach course. In these cases a procedure turn or a transition would be shown on the approach plate.

A DME arc has the same width as an airway: four miles either side of the centerline. Never assume that all the airspace between the arc and the DME transmitter is protected—there might be some real estate sticking up into the air between the transmitter and the inner edge of the protected airspace. Also, you are protected only when you fly at or above the designated altitude for the arc. In mountainous terrain, you may find an arc approach with stepdown fixes that allow you to descend to a lower altitude on the arc when you are safely past high terrain.

You will almost always approach an arc at a 90° angle; where a transition or airway meets the arc at anything other than a right angle, the approach plate will indicate a radial which is at a right angle to help you calculate your first heading on the arc. Some arcs are flown from the outside in, as an airway intersects the arc, as in Figure 9-13. V-25 brings you into the arc from the north on the 338° radial, and V-448 intercepts the arc from the southwest using the 221° radial. You must enter the arc at an initial approach fix (IAF); terrain clearance is not guaranteed if you "roll your own."

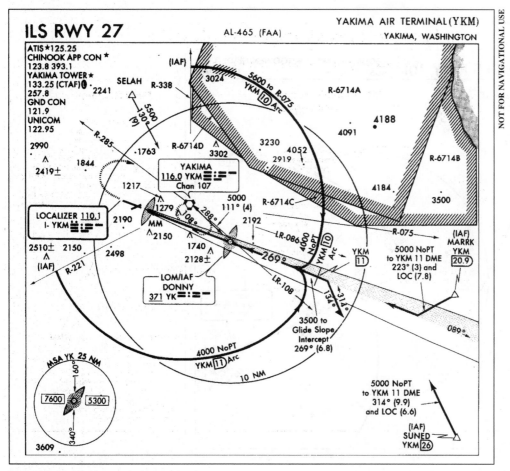

Figure 9-13. *Airway arc intercept*

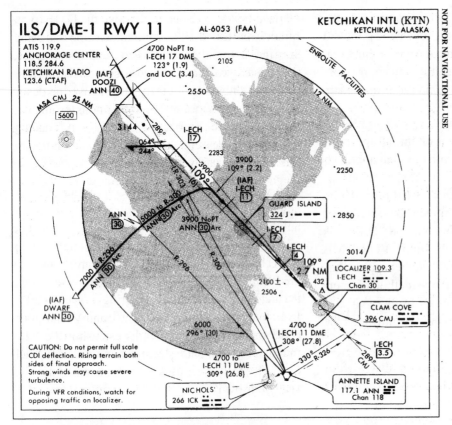

Figure 9-14. Transition from inside the arc

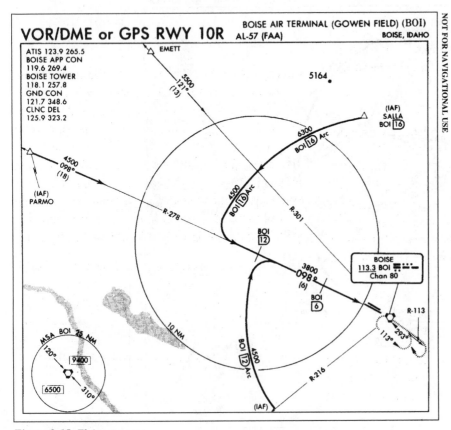

Figure 9-15. Flying an arc

In other situations you approach the arc from the inside on a transition route; the DME arc to the ILS/DME-1 at Ketchikan, Alaska is a good example (Figure 9-14). On most transitions, pilots must pass over the Annette Island VORTAC before transitioning to the arc. Note that there is no radar but lots of rocky terrain at Ketchikan (and in most of southeast Alaska, for that matter), and pilots are on their own.

In either case, you will turn 90° to get established on the arc. A ballpark lead at speeds up to 150 knots is .5 mile; start your turn when .5 mile from the arc and you should roll out right on the arc in no-wind conditions. Keep in mind that the protected airspace is 4 miles wide on either side of the arc; however, don't let it bother you if you roll out a few tenths of a mile off the arc. You can tell by inspecting the approach plate whether you are going to be circling clockwise or counterclockwise on the arc, and that is the key to flying it with precision. Refer to Figure 9-15 and assume that you are approaching on the 216° radial with your omnibearing selector set to 036°. You will be turning 90° to the left when your DME reads 12.5 nautical miles, and a look 90° to the left on your heading indicator tells you that the first heading will be 306°. When you arc clockwise, the omnibearings increase as you go: you approached on the 036° bearing TO the station and will cross the 046°, then the 056°, the 066° bearing to the station, and so forth as you arc to the right.

As you roll out on the new heading of 306° and begin your descent to 4,500 feet, turn the omnibearing selector to increase its reading to 046°. Look 90° to the left on the omni head to learn what your new no-wind heading should be: 316°. The needle will be off center initially, but will move into the center as you approach the radial. When the needle centers, advance the OBS to 056° and again look 90° to the left to find your new no-wind heading. In no-wind conditions, you will continue this procedure until your OBS reads 098°; when the needle moves toward the center on that setting you will turn inbound toward the airport.

Flying a counter-clockwise arc requires exactly the same procedure, except that the numbers will get smaller as you rotate the omnibearing selector to the left.

The wind always blows in the real world, and you will find that the DME reading will slowly drift away from its 12 mile indication. If the reading decreases, all you have to do is hold your last heading and you will fly back out to the arc; when the DME reads 12 again, crab into the wind a few degrees and add that wind correction to each subsequent no-wind heading reading from the face of the omni indicator. A 5° correction for each .5 mile inside the arc should be adequate. If you drift appreciably outside the arc, correct 10° back toward it for every .5 mile discrepancy; holding a heading insures that you will fly away from the arc toward the unseen obstacles that lurk out there.

Can GPS Substitute for DME?

A DME arc is centered on the VORTAC; the GPS location of the VORTAC is published in the Airport/Facility Directory (don't use the airport reference point—it might be in the parking lot). An IFR-approved GPS can be used to substitute for the DME to fly an arc if the VORTAC waypoint is included in the GPS database.

Flying Arcs Using a Radio Magnetic Indicator

Flying a DME arc with an RMI is easy. Because the needle of the RMI always points to the VOR antenna, when you turn 90° onto the arc the needle will point directly off the wing tip. To follow the arc, maintain the initial heading until the needle falls 5° to 10° behind the wing tip; this will cause the distance to increase slightly. Next, turn toward the facility to bring the RMI needle 5° to 10° ahead of the wing tip, and maintain that heading until the needle once again falls aft of the wing tip. Repeat this procedure until you intercept the final approach course. When flying arcs with an RMI, correct for wind drift by turning 10° to 20° into the wind for each .5 mile off the arc radius.

The wind's effect on your flight path will change continually as you turn, so be alert to remove any wind correction angle that is no longer needed. If you find that you are outside the arc you must take immediate action to turn toward it—maintaining your heading will just take you farther away from the arc.

Using a Horizontal Situation Indicator

Flying an arc with a horizontal situation indicator is simple because you don't have to look to see what heading is perpendicular to the radial that you are on. Just turn the airplane until the heading is perpendicular to the HSI's arrow and that takes care of it (Figure 9-16).

Because you never get reverse sensing from a VOR signal when using an HSI, it makes no difference whether you have the arrow's head or its tail set to the desired radial. Just as was the case with the standard VOR head, once you are on the arc just rotate the OBS clockwise or counterclockwise every 10° to agree with your movement around the station; with an HSI, the course deviation indicator will move out in front of the little airplane symbol and you will always be flying toward the needle.

When a DME arc is part of an instrument departure procedure you will set the OBS to a radial FROM the station. When you reach the arc radius and turn onto the arc, you will rotate the OBS as above, always flying toward the needle and advancing the OBS each time it centers until you reach the radial or airway which takes you toward your destination.

Lead Radials

Because almost all DME arcs cross the final approach course at a 90° angle, the FAA may provide a lead radial to warn you when interception is imminent; the lead radial (where provided) is designed to give at least two miles of warning before the final approach course is crossed. In Figure 9-13, the ANN 303 degree radial is the lead radial.

The turn radius of most light aircraft is much less than two miles, so if you begin the turn inbound as you cross the lead radial you will turn inside the final approach course. This can be a real problem if you need course guidance to descend to a lower altitude. You can calculate your own lead radial in most cases. Divide the arc radius into 60 to learn the number of nautical miles per degree; divide the answer by two for airspeeds of 150 knots or less to learn the number of degrees of lead which you should use in beginning the turn onto the final approach course. For an arc with a radius of 10 miles you would lead the turn inbound by 3°.

The GPS Terminal Arrival Area (TAA)

Figure 9-17 shows how pilots will navigate in the TAA when there is an RNAV (formerly GPS) approach plate for a designated runway. The "T" structure normally provides a "NoPT" segment for aircraft using the approach; however, a racetrack holding pattern may be provided at the straight-in IAF where necessary to meet a descent gradient requirement. Note that TURTL, TTURN, and FIRST are all initial approach fixes. Instead of the segmented Minimum Sector Altitude circle on old approach plates, each IAF has a 90° or 180° segment depicted on the plan view.

Two methods of approach procedure selection are available: channel number and menu, depending on the GPS equipment being used. Note the channel number in the upper left corner of Figure 9-17; this number would be entered into the GPS equipment by the pilot. Using the menu method, the pilot first selects the airport name and then selects the approach runway. In either case, the pilot then activates the procedure by selecting the appropriate IAF. When within 30 miles of the IAF, the pilot is expected to proceed directly to the fix.

The GPS will give an "arm" annunciation when your airplane is 30 miles from the airport reference point; arm the "approach" mode at this time (some equipment models do this for you). This will increase sensitivity from ±5 miles either side of the centerline

Figure 9-16. Crossing the 077° radial

to ±1 mile either side. Fly the initial approach leg using CDI or moving map guidance. When within 2 miles of the final approach waypoint the approach mode will switch to "active"; the RAIM will change to approach sensitivity and CDI sensitivity will increase to ±.3 mile, all automatically.

How a procedure turn is handled varies with equipment model. Different manufacturers have different ideas on how a pilot should accomplish procedure turns, holding, or anything else that varies from automatic, sequential waypoint selection.

Summary

We have made it from the enroute phase of flight through some kind of transition or vectoring to the approach itself, and that subject deserves a chapter of its own.

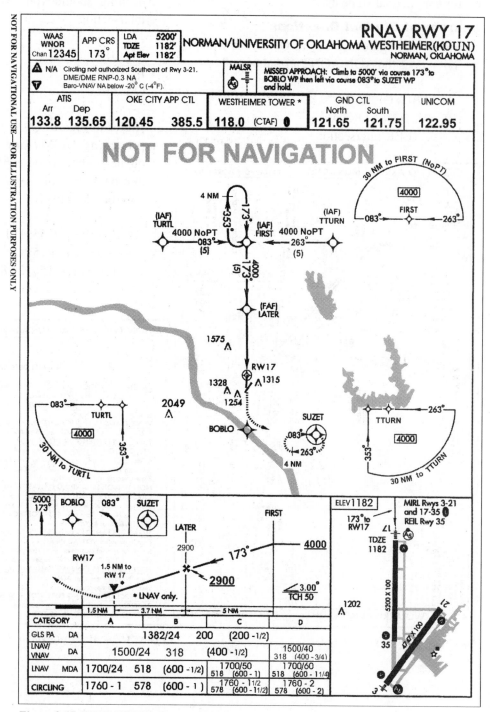

Figure 9-17. RNAV RWY 17, Norman, OK

This is another review section with nothing of interest for commercial students.

Instrument Student Questions

1. (Refer to Figures Q9-1 and Q9-2.) At which point does the AQN.AQN2 arrival begin?

   A—ABI VORTAC
   B—ACTON VORTAC
   C—CREEK intersection

2. (Refer to Figures Q9-1 and Q9-2.) On which heading should you plan to depart CREEK intersection?

   A—010°
   B—040°
   C—350°

3. (Refer to Figures Q9-1, Q9-3, and Q9-4.) Approaching DFW from Abilene, which frequencies should you expect to use for regional approach control, control tower, and ground control respectively?

   A—119.05; 126.55; 121.65.
   B—119.05; 124.15; 121.8.
   C—125.8; 124.15; 121.8.

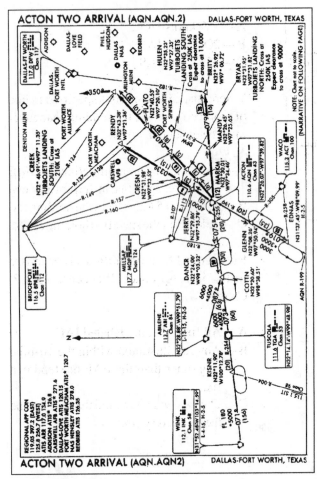

Figure Q9-1. *ACTON two arrival*

ACTON TWO ARRIVAL (AQN.AQN2)   DALLAS-FORT WORTH, TEXAS

ARRIVAL DESCRIPTION

ABILENE TRANSITION (ABI.AQN2): From over ABI VORTAC via ABI R-087 and AQN R-255 to AQN VORTAC. Thence . . . .

EDNAS TRANSITION (EDNAS.AQN2): From over EDNAS INT via AQN R-199 to AQN VORTAC. Thence . . . .

WINK TRANSITION (INK.AQN2): From over INK VORTAC via INK R-071, TQA R-254, TQA R-073 and AQN R-255 to AQN VORTAC. Thence . . . .

TURBOJETS LANDING DALLAS-FT. WORTH INTL, MEACHAM, CARSWELL AFB, DENTON, ALLIANCE: (Landing South): From over AQN VORTAC via AQN R-040 to CREEK INT, thence heading 350° for vector to final approach course. (Landing North): From over AQN VORTAC via AQN R-040 to CREEK INT. Expect vectors at BRYAR INT.

NON-TURBOJETS LANDING DALLAS-FT. WORTH INTL, MEACHAM, CARSWELL AFB, DENTON, ALLIANCE: (Landing South): From over AQN VORTAC via AQN R-033 to RENDY INT. Expect vectors to final approach course. (Landing North): From over AQN VORTAC via AQN R-040 to CREEK INT. Expect vector at BRYAR INT.

TURBOJETS LANDING DALLAS-LOVE FIELD and ADDISON: (Landing South): From over AQN VORTAC via AQN R-040 to CREEK INT, thence heading 350° for vector to final approach course. (Landing North): From over AQN VORTAC via AQN R-079 to BRITY INT. Expect vector to final approach course.

NON-TURBOJETS LANDING DALLAS-LOVE FIELD and ADDISON: (Landing South/North): From over AQN VORTAC via AQN R-079 to BRITY INT. Expect vector to final approach course.

ALL AIRCRAFT LANDING FORT WORTH SPINKS, ARLINGTON, NAS DALLAS, REDBIRD, and PHIL L. HUDSON: (Landing South/North): From over AQN VORTAC via AQN R-079 to BRITY INT. Expect vectors to final approach course.

Figure Q9-2. *ACTON two arrival description*

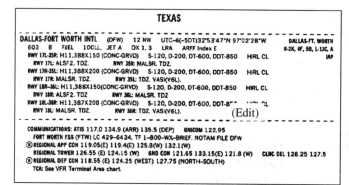

Figure Q9-3. *ILS-1 RWY 36L, Dallas-Fort Worth International*

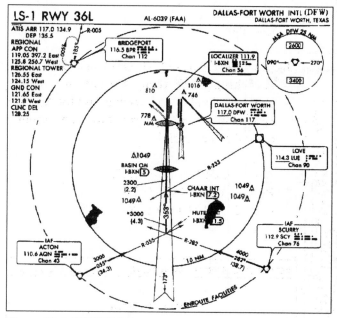

Figure Q9-4. *ILS RWY 36L*

4. When being radar vectored for an ILS approach, at what point may you start a descent from your last assigned altitude to a lower minimum altitude if cleared for the approach?

A—When established on a segment of a published route or IAP.

B— You may descend immediately to published glide slope interception altitude.

C—Only after you are established on the final approach unless informed otherwise by ATC.

5. You are being vectored to the ILS approach course, but have not been cleared for the approach. It becomes evident that you will pass through the localizer course. What action should be taken?

A—Turn outbound and make a procedure turn.

B—Continue on the assigned heading and query ATC.

C—Start a turn to the inbound heading and inquire if you are cleared for the approach.

6. When the approach procedure involves a procedure turn, the maximum speed should not be greater than

A—180 knots IAS.

B—200 knots IAS.

C—250 knots IAS.

7. Where a holding pattern is specified in lieu of a procedure turn, the holding maneuver must be executed within

A—the 1 minute time limitation or DME distance as specified in the profile view.

B—a radius of 5 miles from the holding fix.

C—10 knots of the specified holding speed.

8. How can an IAF be identified on a Standard Instrument Approach Procedure (SIAP) Chart?

A—All fixes that are labeled IAF.

B—Any fix illustrated within the 10-mile ring other than the FAF or stepdown fix.

C—The procedure turn and the fixes on the feeder facility ring.

9. (Refer to Figure Q9-5.) If cleared for NDB RWY 28 approach (Lancaster/Fairfield) over ZZV VOR, the flight would be expected to

Category A aircraft
Last assigned altitude 3,000 feet

A—proceed straight in from CRISY, descending to the MDA after CASER.
B—proceed to CRISY, then execute the teardrop procedure as depicted on the approach chart.
C—proceed direct to CASER, then straight in to S-28 minimums of 1620-1.

10. (Refer to Figure Q9-6.) If your aircraft was cleared for the ILS RWY 17R at Lincoln Municipal and crossed the Lincoln VOR at 5,000 feet MSL, at what point in the teardrop could a descent to 3,000 feet commence?

A—As soon as intercepting LOC inbound.
B—Immediately.
C—Only at the point authorized by ATC.

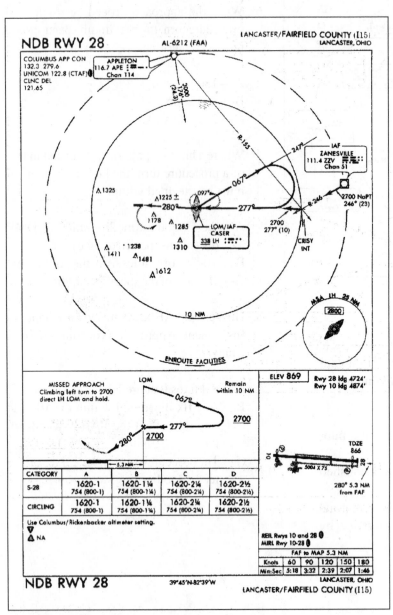

Figure Q9-5. NDB RWY 28, Lancaster/Fairfield County

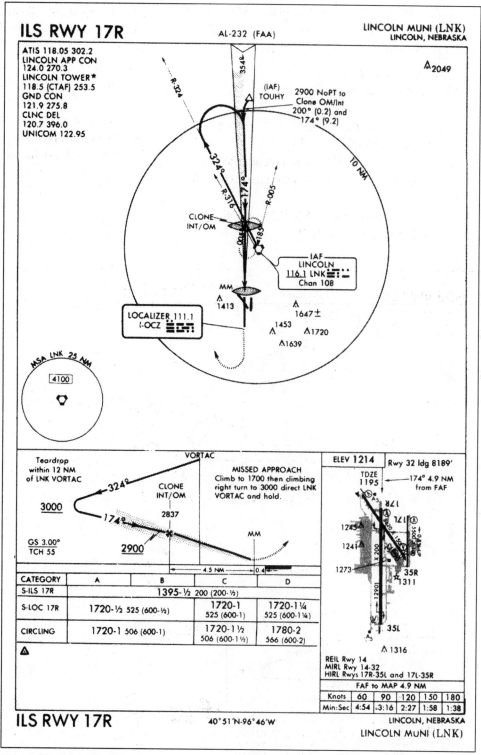

Figure Q9-6. *ILS RWY 17R, Lincoln, Nebraska*

Instrument Approaches

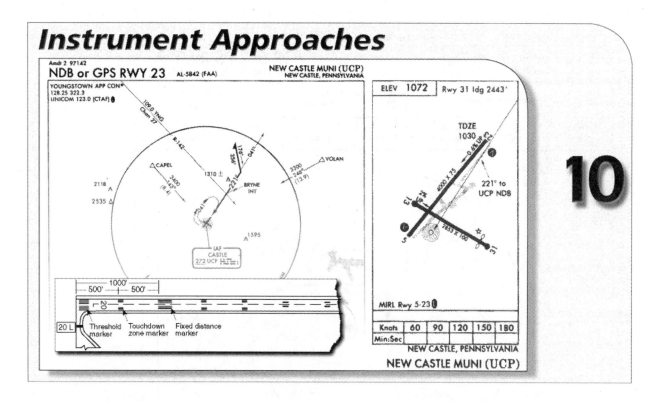

In the Terminal Area

Chapters 7 through 9 have taken you from the departure airport to an initial approach fix for the destination airport, making provision for a holding pattern along the way or a procedure turn to get lined up for the approach in use. This chapter will take you the rest of the way.

Nonprecision Approaches

The textbook distinction between precision and nonprecision approaches is that precision approaches have vertical guidance—some form of glide slope or descent information. My opinion is that precision approaches offer you more information than nonprecision approaches and are therefore easier to fly.

The latest available FAA statistics report that only about one-third of the approved instrument approaches in the U.S. are precision approaches. You can see right away that the study of nonprecision approaches will have a direct effect on your success as an instrument pilot. The FAA is designing approximately 5,000 GPS approaches and these will also be nonprecision. Precision approaches using GPS won't come until 2004 at the earliest.

Nonprecision approach procedures include VOR and VOR-DME, NDB, localizer (with some variants), GPS and GPS overlays, and surveillance radar. Radar procedures will be discussed separately. The VOR and NDB procedures can be further broken down into two types: those in which the facility is on the airport and those in which it is not. I'll discuss each situation; any nonprecision approach in the book should fall into one of these categories.

Note: The AIM permits the use of a VFR-only or handheld GPS receiver solely for purposes of situational awareness. All GPS overlay and stand-alone approaches are predicated upon the use of an IFR-approved GPS installation with a current database.

VOR On Airport with No Final Approach Fix

Figure 10-1 illustrates a typical VOR approach with the VOR located on the airport and no final approach fix. The final approach segment begins where the procedure turn intersects the final approach course ("procedure turn inbound"). The VOR is a part of the enroute system—it is on an airway on a low-altitude enroute chart—and, unless you are in a radar environment, you will approach it at or above the

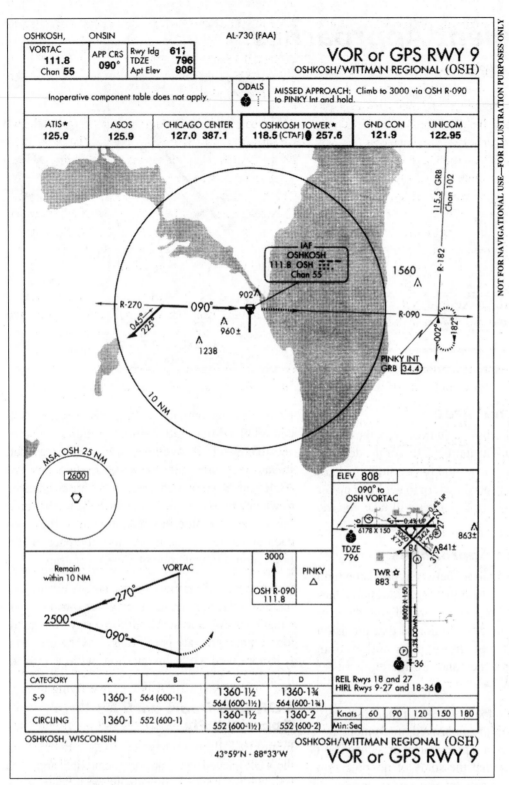

Figure 10-1. *Typical VOR approach*

altitude shown for the airway on the low-altitude enroute chart.

If you are in a radar environment the controller has the option to assign you the minimum vectoring altitude, which will be lower than that shown on the chart. The outbound heading for this approach is 270°; the protected airspace extends 1.25 miles either side of the VOR at right angles to the final approach course, and there is little chance that you will violate that limit as you turn at typical general aviation speeds. If you begin your turn as soon as rapid needle movement indicates that you are almost overhead, you will have an easier time of intercepting and tracking the outbound course. If your #2 VOR receiver is not needed to identify any points on the final approach course, setting it to the outbound course will aid you in making a smooth turn to intercept.

This is your first exposure to the famous five T's: turn, time, throttle, twist, and talk (Figure 10-2). Your instructor may have other ideas about the sequence, but the idea is to ingrain a habit pattern of Turning to an intercept heading, starting your Timer, reducing Throttle to descend, Twisting the omnibearing selector (or the ADF's rotatable azimuth), and finally, making any required report (Talk). All five T's will not apply in every situation, but by mentally reviewing them you will ensure that none are forgotten. There is a 6th T, Tires, for pilots of airplanes with retractable landing gear.

Figure 10-2. Memory aid

The outbound course is shown on both the profile and plan views of the approach; to allow for errors, the protected airspace gets wider as you fly away from the VOR, but you should expend every effort to keep the VOR needle centered.

This type of approach requires a course reversal, and it must be accomplished within the distance noted on the profile view. The manner in which you reverse course is entirely up to you (see "Procedure Turns" in Chapter 9), but the course reversal must be accomplished on the side of the final approach course shown on the plate. At Oshkosh/Wittman (Figure 10-1), the course reversal must be performed south of the final approach course.

Regardless of which type of course reversal you use, you will turn away from the radial which you have been tracking (or paralleling) outbound, and the VOR display will provide no useful information during the turn. Take advantage of that time to reset the omnibearing selector to the inbound course.

As you turn inbound to intercept the course to the airport, gauge your rate of turn to match the rate of needle movement: if the needle is moving, you should be turning, and when the needle stops you should stop the turn. If the course deviation indicator has not come off the peg by the time you are within 30° of the inbound course, stop the turn and retain that 30° intercept angle until the needle comes to life.

If you are asked to report "procedure turn inbound" to the tower or Center controller, make the report as soon as you turn onto the inbound course (270° radial). This is also where you would leave 2,500 feet for the minimum descent altitude (MDA).

Your rate of descent must be great enough to ensure that you reach the MDA before overflying the airport; don't be overly cautious about descent rate— it's better to descend 700-800 feet per minute and break out early than to descend slowly and pass over the VOR before you reach the MDA. To calculate the minimum descent rate on a nonprecision approach, assume that you are going to break out of the overcast well above the MDA and that you want to be in position to land on the numbers. For this calculation, ignore the published MDA—you are going to be in the clear before you reach that altitude.

Assume that you will be 5 miles from the threshold when you have completed the course reversal and rejoined the final approach course; that will probably require an outbound leg of more than one minute, maybe as long as three minutes in no-wind conditions. Approximately 1,700 feet must be lost in that 5 mile descent, a rate of about 340 feet per mile. If your ground speed is 90 knots, a minimum descent rate of 610 feet per minute will be required. Completing the procedure turn closer to the airport will require a steeper descent, of course, and you must consider how your passengers will react to diving at the runway. Using more of the 10-mile distance provided for course reversal will make for a more reasonable descent rate and give you more time to get ready for the landing or missed approach, and that is my recommendation.

Expect to miss every approach; have the radios set up as necessary and know the first heading and altitude of the missed approach procedure. If you are still in the clouds as you approach MDA, switch your thinking from a landing to a miss. Most of the time you will be pleasantly surprised by seeing the runway, but in those few situations where the weather doesn't cooperate you will be mentally prepared.

The term "control zone" disappeared from the regulations and AIM in September 1993. The FAA replaced this term on the approach plates with "When altimeter setting is available" or "surface area of Class E airspace."

If the VOR has a five-letter name in the GPS database you can select it as a waypoint. Make sure that its "direct track" coincides with the published final approach course. Don't mistake GPS distance to the waypoint for distance to the runway threshold.

VOR On Airport With Final Approach Fix

The final approach fix (FAF) can be a DME fix along the final approach course, an intersection formed by a radial from a distant VOR, or a fan marker. Where a fan marker is installed, it will light the white light on the panel and send the Morse code letter R (.-.), modulated at 3,000 Hz. These final approach fixes will usually be stepdown fixes which allow you to descend to a lower altitude once you have passed them. The FAF is marked by a Maltese cross.

VOR Off Airport With Final Approach Fix

When the VOR is not on the field, there will be a final approach fix. The VOR itself may not be the final approach fix, and a course reversal may or may not be required. The greatest difference between the two types of approaches is that in those situations where there is a final approach fix (and no DME), you must determine the missed approach point by timing.

At Northeast Philadelphia (Figure 10-3), you must lose 1,379 feet (1,500 – 121) in 5 miles (to the threshold, remember, not the VOR), a rate of 276 feet per mile. 552 fpm would do the trick when flying the approach at 120 knots, while 414 feet per minute would work at 90 knots. But you don't want to arrive at MDA just as you arrive at the threshold, do you? Give yourself time to prepare for a normal landing by descending at a greater rate. I like to see 700-1,000 fpm to the MDA with a constant airspeed.

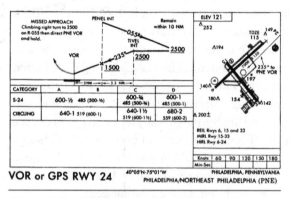

Figure 10-3. *VOR off airport*

Assume that you are shooting the VOR/DME or GPS-A into Wheeler, Texas, without an approved GPS on board—*see* Figure 10-4. (Why doesn't the title of the approach have a runway number in it? Because there are no straight-in minimums.) Crossing directly over the VOR shouldn't be a problem, but consider how radials spread out with distance from the facility—28.4 miles out times 100 feet of spread per mile equals 2,840 feet, or almost one-half mile per degree. Depending on the method of VOR checking you use, your VOR indicator could be as much as six degrees in error and still be legal—that would put you more than three miles away from the airport with a centered CDI needle. My point is that the farther the airport is from the facility, the sharper you have to be. If you have to be wrong, be sure that you make your mistakes into the wind.

Both Jeppesen and NACO approach plates provide tables giving the elapsed time from the final approach fix to the missed approach point at different *ground speeds;* interpolation is required if your ground speed differs from a tabulated amount. An easier method (which requires considerable faith in the accuracy of the wind report) is to fly at an indicated airspeed which equals the tabulated amount plus the estimated headwind component. For instance, if the table on the approach chart lists a time for a ground speed of 90 knots and you estimate the headwind component to be 11 knots, fly at an indicated airspeed of 101 knots to make the time valid.

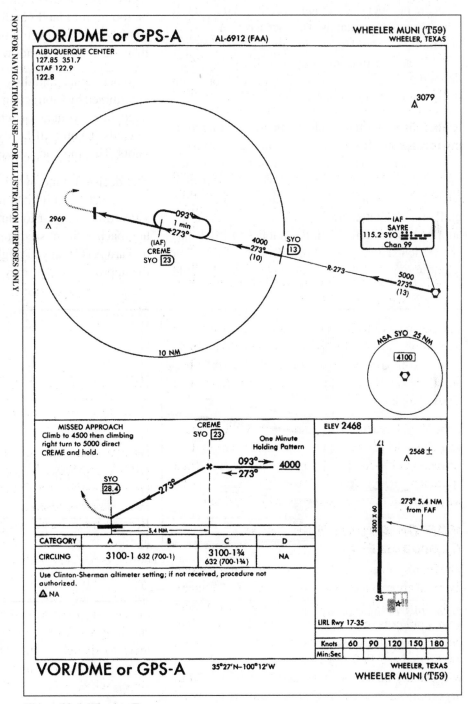

Figure 10-4. Wheeler, Texas

There is a subtle trap in the concept of flying at the MDA until the tabulated time expires on a straight in approach; if you break out of the clouds at the minimum descent altitude precisely as the clock runs out you will find yourself from 400 to 1,100 feet above the runway (632 feet at Wheeler, TX), and probably too high for a normal approach and landing.

Consider the least adverse situation: you are 400 feet over the numbers at a ground speed of 90 knots. If you descend immediately at a descent rate of 400 feet per minute, it will take one minute to reach the surface, and in that minute you will fly 1½ miles down the runway. This is not a prudent action, even if the runway is two miles long.

Rather than "fly out the clock" before making your missed approach decision, you should establish a decision window (Figure 10-5) on the final approach segment. This is a point at which you would decide whether a landing is probable and, if one seems unlikely, begin preparations to carry out the missed approach procedure when the published MAP has been reached. One method of calculating a decision window requires that you decide on a comfortable rate of descent and divide that figure into 60. As an example, most pilots feel comfortable descending at 500 feet per minute, and at that rate they will lose 100 feet every 12 seconds. If the height of the MDA above the touchdown zone is 400 feet it will take 4 x 12 or 48 seconds to descend from the decision window to the numbers, so the decision window is established by subtracting 48 seconds from the published time-to-MAP. The assumption is that you will be too high to land comfortably if you pick up the runway visually from a point closer to the runway than the decision window.

Another "quick and dirty" decision window can be determined by subtracting one minute from the tabulated time if your approach speed is 90 knots, and 40 seconds if you will be flying the approach at 120 knots. This method ignores variations in MDA.

The decision window eliminates the need for last-minute action to initiate the go-around, and it provides time for you to shift mental gears from the approach to the missed approach. It even allows you to warn ATC that you might not be able to complete the approach so that they can fit you back into the

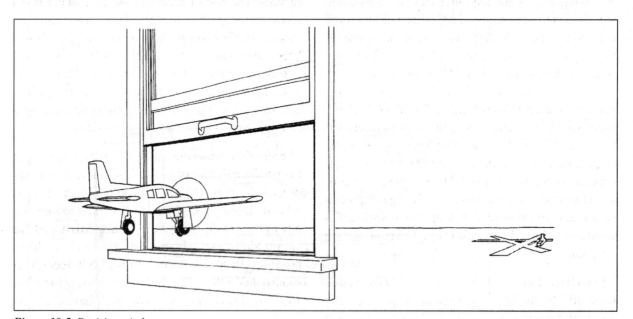

Figure 10-5. Decision window

system with minimum delay. They won't be upset if you land successfully, of course, but they will appreciate the warning.

Again, if the VOR is in the GPS database you can select it as a waypoint and use GPS guidance if your GPS installation is approved for IFR.

NDB Approach Without Final Approach Fix

When the nondirectional beacon is on the airport, there is no final approach fix, and timing to the missed approach point is not necessary. You must fly over the navaid and track outbound on (or parallel to) the published course while descending to procedure turn altitude and then inbound, just as in the VOR approach, but in the case of the NDB approach outbound tracking is more difficult. The comforting thing about this type of approach is that you can't fly to the beacon without finding the airport and no timing is required. The approach to Atlanta, Texas is an example (Figure 10-6 on next page). Note that a pilot flying any of the feeder routes to the ATLANTA NDB must perform a course reversal. This is another situation where a little innovation in reversing course would pay off: a pilot coming in from LASSA could simply turn to a heading of 230° (plus or minus wind correction) and make a racetrack reversal, descending to 2,000 feet in the turn, while a pilot coming from the Texarkana VORTAC could turn right to 230° over the beacon and make a 45-180° course reversal. Coming from BELCHER VORTAC my recommendation would be a half-standard-rate left turn to 230° over the beacon and a *l-o-o-o-ng* racetrack (inside of 10 miles, of course). Why re-intercept the outbound course? There's plenty of protected airspace on the west side of the final approach course and you'll have plenty of time to establish a wind correction inbound after completing the course reversal.

"If you have done one procedure turn you have done them all," as the saying goes, but determining the point of interception of an NDB final approach course after a course reversal requires some thought. Figure 10-7 indicates that a pilot completing a 45° procedure turn at New Castle, Pennsylvania, will be flying 176° to intercept the inbound, and that point will be reached when the ADF needle points 45° to

the right of the nose. Magnetic heading (176°) + relative bearing (45°) = bearing to the station (221°), right? 176° is the no-wind course, and if you are steering 180° to allow for a southwest wind, then 180° + 41° = 221°. If the wind blows where you live (as it does where I live), don't get hung up on no-wind courses just because they are printed on the approach plate.

Because of the wind, it's nice to have a trick or two up your sleeve when working with the ADF. Turning inbound from the course reversal at New Castle, check the progress of the 221° mark on the heading indicator as it rotates, and when it is directly off your right wing tip (as you pass through 131°), look at the ADF needle. If it is pointing to the right wing tip, don't stop the turn at 176°—both the airplane and the needle have 90° to go. If it is ahead of the wing tip, stop the turn at 176° (or your wind correction heading), because the airplane has 90° to go but the needle has more than 90° to go; this is the desired situation.

If, when 221° passes the 90° point the ADF needle is behind the wing tip, you are going to fly through the final approach course unless you steepen the bank to increase the rate of turn, a maneuver that I don't recommend. Just be forewarned that in this case you should not only forego the stop at 176°, but should keep right on turning to a heading to the right of 221° in order to intercept the final approach course. You will find that there is no shortage of people who will advise you to ignore needle indications during a turn—but try it my way once or twice.

The nice thing about this kind of NDB approach is that the needle indications get more sensitive as you approach the beacon and you can't find the beacon without finding the airport. As mentioned before, however, you do not want to reach MDA and the airport simultaneously, because you will not be in position to land. You want to leave 1,840 feet just as soon as the VOR needle shows you crossing the YNG 142° radial (I can't believe you don't have a VOR).

NDB With Final Approach Fix

All of the preceding discussion of ADF tracking applies when you must fly over a nondirectional beacon located on the airport, and then track back to

Continued on Page 10-10

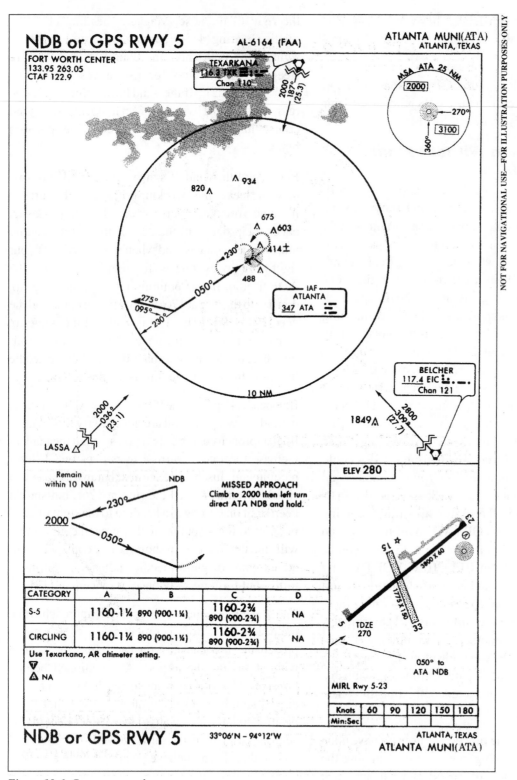

Figure 10-6. *Course reversal*

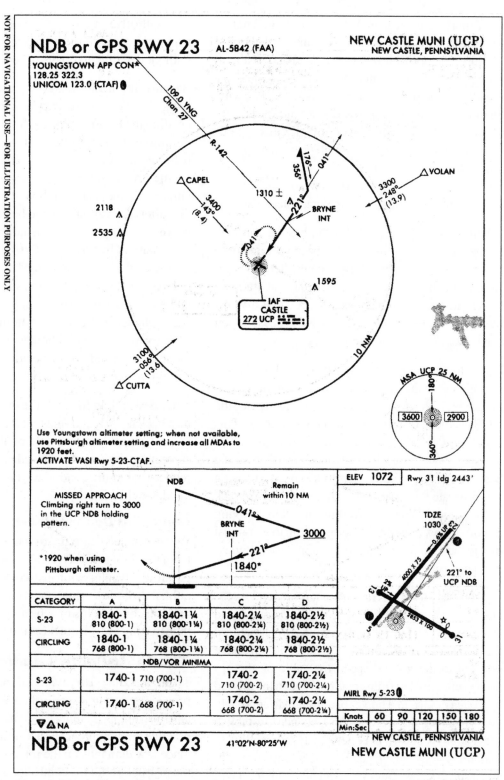

Figure 10-7. NDB final approach intercept

the airport on the beacon. When the beacon is not on the airport, you must use elapsed time to determine the missed approach point. The NDB approach at International Falls, Minnesota, is an example (Figure 10-8). The protected airspace is 1.25 miles wide on either side of the beacon and expands as you fly toward the field, an indication of why this type of approach is the least precise of all instrument procedures. If the weather is low and the obstacles are high, like that tower on short final, you should give serious consideration to going somewhere else.

Whether you have overflown the beacon and performed a procedure turn or have been vectored onto the intermediate segment by a controller, you will find yourself outside of the beacon and tracking toward it. This is simple when the navaid is a VOR, but a little more complex with an NDB because you can either home or track to a beacon.

Instructors quite properly insist on tracking, but if you are less than two minutes away from the beacon my advice is to home to it, simply turning to place the ADF needle at 0° relative and keeping it there. This suggestion might not meet with the approval of purists, but your objective is to pass directly over the beacon, and last-minute exercises in needle chasing can frustrate this goal if you are attempting to track to the station. When the ADF needle starts moving rapidly—how "rapidly" is defined is up to you—just turn to the inbound course plus or minus a wild-guess wind correction.

As you pass over the radio beacon inbound to the airport, turn to the published inbound course and start your timer. Do not apply a wind correction until the need for one becomes evident. You will have referred to the ground speed timetable on the approach chart to determine elapsed time to the missed approach point and, I hope, for a straight in approach, you will have subtracted 40 to 60 seconds to establish a decision window. It is here that your ability to maintain a constant airspeed (for accuracy in timing) and a specific descent rate (to get down in time) will come into play.

Be especially wary of overcorrecting—it is a common error. At a 90-knot ground speed, a 10° correc-tion will offset a direct 15-knot crosswind component; how often do you experience such a crosswind without deciding to go elsewhere?

Because the direction and velocity of the wind change with altitude, do not expect one wind correction heading to be correct during the entire descent to the minimum descent altitude. Turn back to the published course every 30 to 45 seconds; the head of the needle will point toward the course line. For example, assume that the inbound course is 270°, and that after a few moments the head of the needle has moved to the right of the tail, indicating a north wind. You respond by turning to 280° and the head of the needle settles down pointing 10° to the right of the tail. As you descend, the wind shifts to the northwest and its velocity decreases, but you do not notice the subtle change in needle position and continue to steer 280° (or worse, you blithely assume that the movement of the needle to a position pointing directly behind the airplane is a sign that you are on course).

After descending for a minute or two, however, you turn back to 270° and find that the head of the needle is now pointing to the left of the tail! Your 10° correction was more than adequate to offset the reduced wind drift and you were flying away from the desired course.

Don't Just Do Something, Sit There!

When any needle points to the left and the wind is from the right (or vice versa), you must consider the possible advantages of just continuing to steer the published course while the wind drifts the airplane back on course. This may be a more practical action than turning away from the wind to chase the needle.

The Instrument Landing System

There are only two types of precision approach procedures: ground controlled approaches (GCA) and instrument landing systems (ILS). It's fun to practice GCA approaches at military fields, but they place few demands on the pilot other than to follow the instructions of the controller. If you can maintain a heading and keep your airplane's vertical speed under reasonable control, you can complete a ground controlled approach successfully.

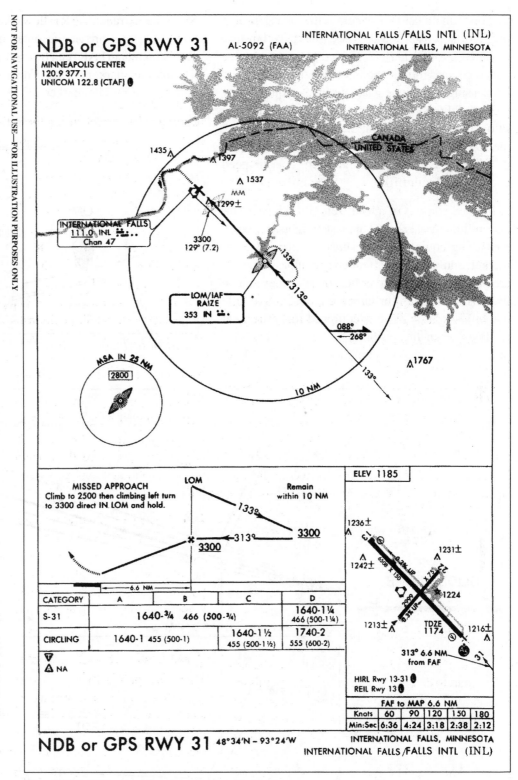

Figure 10-8. NDB not on the airport

The instrument landing system is the most common precision approach and also the easiest to fly because so much information is provided. Accurate course guidance and glide slope information are obtained from a single instrument and timing is required only when the glide slope is not available for some reason. Pilots who complain about having difficulty flying the ILS probably have not developed the fundamental piloting skills of heading, pitch, and airspeed control. *See* Figure 10-9.

A full ILS consists of a localizer, glide slope, outer and middle markers, and approach lights. Distance measuring equipment can substitute for the outer marker, and where low frequency compass locators are provided at the marker beacon sites they can be used as substitutes for either the outer or middle markers. At large airports equipped for instrument landings when the visibility is less than one-half mile, there is also an inner marker. *See* Figure 10-10.

Surveillance radar (ASR) allows the controller to tell you when you are at the outer marker, but only precision radar (PAR) can be used as a substitute for the middle marker. *Note:* The FAA is gradually phasing out middle markers.

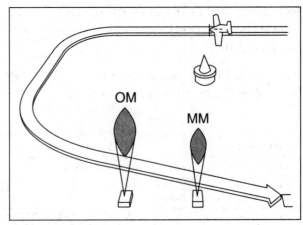

Figure 10-10. *Transition to final*

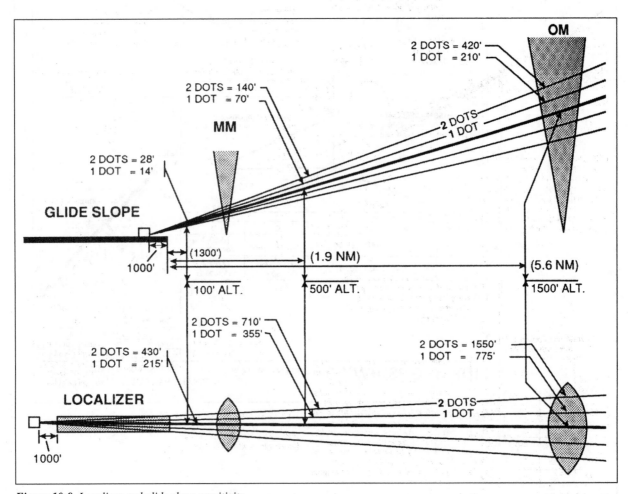

Figure 10-9. *Localizer and glide slope sensitivity*

The localizer is transmitted on a very high frequency (VHF) between 108.1 and 111.95 MHz (the decimal is always an odd number), and the beam width is adjusted so that full-scale deflection of the CDI needle from left to right represents a course width of approximately 700 feet at the runway threshold. The localizer is at the far end of the runway, so long runways have skinnier localizers than short runways. *See* Figure 10-11.

Beam width in degrees may vary from 3° to 6° but 5° is a typical figure and easy to work with.

When you select an ILS frequency on your navigation radio you will note three definite differences from the VOR signal: the coded identification will be preceded by two dots (the Morse code of the letter I), the omnibearing selector will have no effect on needle position, and the TO-FROM needle will always read TO, regardless of where you are in relation to the antenna. A VOR transmits in all directions, but the ILS signal is only usable 10° either side of the centerline within 18 miles of the antenna, widening to 35° either side of center within 10 miles of the antenna. Don't tune a localizer frequency when you

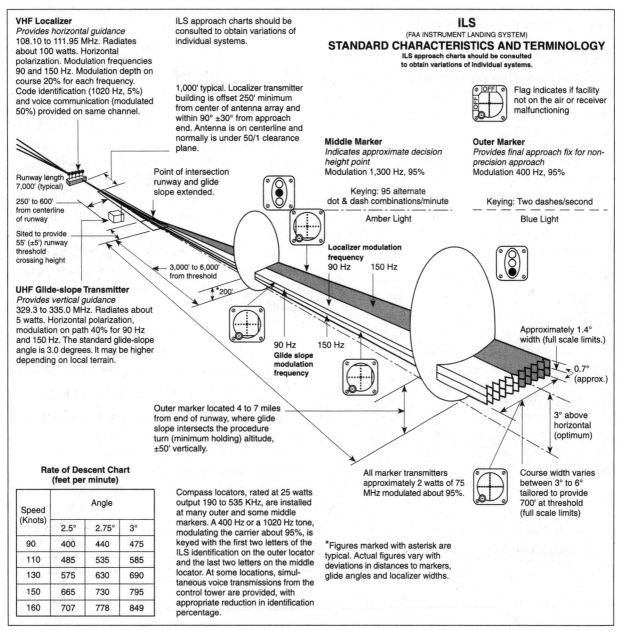

VHF Localizer
Provides horizontal guidance
108.10 to 111.95 MHz. Radiates about 100 watts. Horizontal polarization. Modulation frequencies 90 and 150 Hz. Modulation depth on course 20% for each frequency. Code identification (1020 Hz, 5%) and voice communication (modulated 50%) provided on same channel.

ILS approach charts should be consulted to obtain variations of individual systems.

1,000' typical. Localizer transmitter building is offset 250' minimum from center of antenna array and within 90° ±30° from approach end. Antenna is on centerline and normally is under 50/1 clearance plane.

Runway length 7,000' (typical)

250' to 600' from centerline of runway

Sited to provide 55' (±5') runway threshold crossing height

Point of intersection runway and glide slope extended.

3,000' to 6,000' from threshold

*200'

UHF Glide-slope Transmitter
Provides vertical guidance
329.3 to 335.0 MHz. Radiates about 5 watts. Horizontal polarization, modulation on path 40% for 90 Hz and 150 Hz. The standard glide-slope angle is 3.0 degrees. It may be higher depending on local terrain.

Outer marker located 4 to 7 miles from end of runway, where glide slope intersects the procedure turn (minimum holding) altitude, ±50' vertically.

ILS
(FAA INSTRUMENT LANDING SYSTEM)
STANDARD CHARACTERISTICS AND TERMINOLOGY
ILS approach charts should be consulted to obtain variations of individual systems.

Flag indicates if facility not on the air or receiver malfunctioning

Middle Marker
Indicates approximate decision height point
Modulation 1,300 Hz, 95%

Keying: 95 alternate dot & dash combinations/minute

Amber Light

Outer Marker
Provides final approach fix for non-precision approach
Modulation 400 Hz, 95%

Keying: Two dashes/second

Blue Light

Localizer modulation frequency
90 Hz   150 Hz

90 Hz   150 Hz
Glide slope modulation frequency

Approximately 1.4° width (full scale limits.)

0.7° (approx.)

3° above horizontal (optimum)

Course width varies between 3° to 6° tailored to provide 700' at threshold (full scale limits)

All marker transmitters approximately 2 watts of 75 MHz modulated about 95%.

Compass locators, rated at 25 watts output 190 to 535 KHz, are installed at many outer and some middle markers. A 400 Hz or a 1020 Hz tone, modulating the carrier about 95%, is keyed with the first two letters of the ILS identification on the outer locator and the last two letters on the middle locator. At some locations, simultaneous voice transmissions from the control tower are provided, with appropriate reduction in identification percentage.

*Figures marked with asterisk are typical. Actual figures vary with deviations in distances to markers, glide angles and localizer widths.

Rate of Descent Chart (feet per minute)

Speed (Knots)	Angle		
	2.5°	2.75°	3°
90	400	440	475
110	485	535	585
130	575	630	690
150	665	730	795
160	707	778	849

Figure 10-11. ILS standard characteristics and terminology

are 90° from the runway and expect to receive an identifier.

All marker beacons transmit on 75 MHz, so there is no tuning for you to do; in most airplanes the marker beacon receiver is turned by the master switch and there is no separate on-off control.

You distinguish between the outer, middle, and inner markers by the Morse code signal that each sends, its audio tone, and the color of the light that flashes on the instrument panel when you fly within range of the marker beacon.

Outer markers transmit a continuous string of two dashes per second (– – – –) modulated at 400 Hz, and flash the blue/purple light on the instrument panel. When you pass over a middle marker you will hear a string of alternating dots and dashes (– · – · – · –·) 95 times per minute at an audio tone of 1,300 Hz, and the orange light on the panel will flash in synchronization with the tone.

Inner markers flash the white light and send continuous dots (·····) at a 3,000 Hz tone. Inner markers are located between the middle marker and the threshold at major airports; unless you are flying for an air carrier you will be able to see the runway long before you pass over the inner marker.

Many outer markers are collocated with low frequency nondirectional beacons called compass locators, and the combination is called a locator-outer marker (LOM). There are considerably fewer locator-middle marker (LMM) combinations.

These low frequency aids, when used with your automatic direction finder, can help you anticipate the interception of the ILS localizer. The Morse code identifier of a locator-outer marker is the first two letters of the ILS identifier. At Texarkana, Texas, the ILS identifier is I-TXK and the LOM identifier is TX. The identifier for a locator-middle marker is the last two letters of the ILS identifier; if Texarkana had a locator-middle marker its identifier would be XK.

Tracking the Localizer

The key to flying the localizer successfully lies in heading control. The instrument approach plate give you the magnetic course of the localizer centerline, and once you have captured the localizer (in no-wind conditions), flying that magnetic heading will lead you directly to the threshold. Unfortunately, there are few times when the wind is dead calm, and you must select a heading which will correct for wind drift and keep the localizer needle centered.

There is an old recipe for rabbit stew that begins "First, catch a rabbit." The recipe for flying the ILS must begin with capturing the localizer. Because the localizer is approximately four times as sensitive as a VOR radial, it is easy to fly right through it; making sure that the intercept angle is not too great is a responsibility shared by you and the controller (if you are being vectored). The ideal intercept angle is no more than 30°, and controllers attempt to limit the intercept angle to that value or less when the airplane is within eight miles of the approach gate. As you can see in Figure 10-12, the gate is one mile outside of the final approach fix or five miles from the threshold, whichever is greatest. In a no-radar environment, when you are on your own, you must ensure that the angle at which you intercept the localizer is not too great.

When the approach controller gives you a vector to intercept the localizer, keep in mind that the vector is only the means to an end: getting the needle off of the peg and moving toward the center.

Don't let this scenario happen to you: The controller says "Turn right heading 100°, this is a vector to intercept the localizer and proceed inbound, cleared for the approach." As you pass 080° in your right turn, the needle comes alive and begins to move

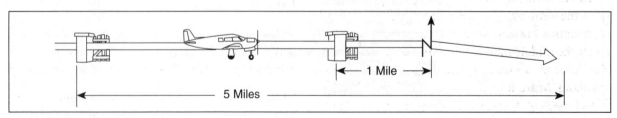

Figure 10-12. Approach gate

toward the center. Unfortunately, your head is up and locked and you are concentrating on turning to 100° as cleared; as you level the wings with the heading indicator precisely on 100°, you note with dismay that the needle has pegged on the other side. You were so anxious to comply with the clearance that you forgot what it was for. When the needle comes off the peg, the vector has served its purpose and is of no further importance—when the needle starts moving toward the center you should turn to the published heading (or a predetermined wind-correction heading) just as quickly as you can.

I need to make a brief digression at this point. When you are being vectored to a localizer the controller must say "Cleared for the approach" (or at least tell you to intercept and proceed inbound) if you are going to turn and follow the localizer to the runway. Without that verbiage, you are honor-bound to stay on the vector heading and fly right through the localizer. Nine times out of ten that is not what the controller wants—if ATC wants you to fly through the localizer they will tell you so and give the reason. Be assertive. Say "Is 34X cleared for the approach?" or "34X is intercepting!" to elicit an approach clearance from the controller.

The localizer signal spreads out 100 feet per nautical mile for every degree of course width; that is, at five miles from the antenna a 5° localizer signal would be 2,500 feet wide and at ten miles from the antenna it would be 5,000 feet wide (approximately one-half mile either side of the centerline). At a distance of ten miles from the localizer antenna and at an airspeed of 90 knots, approximately 20 seconds will elapse between the first movement of the localizer needle (called "case break" or "needle alive") and an on-course indications, in no-wind conditions.

One of the most important skills you must learn is how to prevent overcorrecting as you get close to the runway; the 5° heading change that is just right 10 miles out is far too much when you are but a mile from the runway. The indication in Figure 10-13 represents a horizontal error of approximately 100 feet at the middle marker, and can safely be ignored. You have to adjust your reactions as you near the threshold. Make it your goal to limit bank angles to 5° and heading changes to 2° when you are inside the outer marker.

Figure 10-13. *One degree error at the middle marker*

Quite often, the angle at which you intercept the localizer will be determined by a controller's vector or by a transition. When you have a choice in the matter, however, such as when a course reversal is required, limit the angle of interception to no more than 30°. Read the discussion on procedure turns in Chapter 9 for some options that are available.

When you are intercepting the localizer from a teardrop, racetrack, or 90-270° procedure turn, stop the turn 30° from the inbound heading if the needle is not alive and hold that heading until you detect needle movement. There is nothing to be gained by turning all the way to the published heading and then turning back to the intercept heading.

Once the needle is alive, the best rule is "if the needle is moving, you should be turning—if the needle stops, stop the turn." Initially, your goal is to stop the movement of the needle, not to center it. The heading that stops the needle (by offsetting wind drift) is called the reference heading, and once you have established the reference heading in your mind centering the needle is easy.

Tracking the localizer requires that you talk to yourself a lot. Unless you internalize the conversation, however, your passengers may question your sanity.

This kind of thinking is what I have in mind: You say to yourself, "The inbound course is 128° and the wind is from the right. When the needle comes alive

I'm going to turn to 135° and try it for a few seconds. I won't go any further left than 128° no matter what."

After intercepting the localizer (needle alive) and flying several seconds on a heading of 135° while ignoring the localizer needle you take a quick glance at it and say to yourself "It looks like 135° isn't enough to make the needle move toward the center. It must be the reference heading. I'll try 140° for a while."

You shift your eyes back to the flight instruments for just a few seconds to turn to a heading of 140°, then glance back at the localizer needle. "Ah, the needle is moving fairly quickly toward the center. I'll take off a couple of degrees and try 138°."

Again, you concentrate on the flight instruments to ensure that a heading of 138° and the proper position on the glide slope are being maintained, then glance back at the needle for a second or two: "Fine, the needle is moving more slowly. When it gets to the center I'll go back to 135° because when I tried 135° before, the needle hardly moved."

After several seconds of accurately maintaining 135° and ignoring the needle: "That seems to be too much. I'll try 134°."

Then: "Perfect. As long as the wind doesn't change I have the localizer under control, and if it does shift I know that a heading change of 1° or 2° will do the trick."

Back to reality—did you notice any heading changes of more than five or ten degrees in that little discussion? No way. Did you steer the airplane by watching the localizer needle? Nope. Heading control is the key.

You may consider flying to an accuracy of 1° an unattainable goal, and maybe it is. But should you use that as an excuse for sloppiness? Set your goals high and come as close to them as you can.

Never apply aileron in response to an off-center needle indication unless you know what heading you are turning to—don't just turn toward the needle and hope for the best. Again, saying the new heading out loud will help. Tracking a localizer requires precise heading control (is there an echo in here?). When you apply aileron pressure, do so with your eyes on the

attitude indicator so that you can limit the bank angle. Better yet, keep the wings level and just nudge the nose to a new heading with rudder pressure—that's the best way to make small heading changes.

Looking at the localizer needle for more than two seconds is a typical student mistake. The indicator can tell you where you are in relation to where you want to be, but it is useless when it comes to steering the airplane. All you want to know when you move your eyes to the localizer needle is whether it is stationary or moving, and if it is moving you need to know in which direction and how fast.

An excellent method of proving this to yourself (or having your instructor prove it to you) is to cover the omni head for five or ten seconds at a time and only uncover it for brief periods. When you have tracked a localizer from the outer marker to the runway by heading control alone, you will realize that the key to a successful ILS approach does not lie in staring at the omni indicator.

When you have captured the localizer and the needle swings to the side away from the wind, think before you act. Will the wind blow the airplane back onto the final approach course if you just steer the published course? If you go after the needle aggressively, will the heading change plus the wind drift cause an overcorrection? Make the wind work for you: One knot of crosswind component will move the airplane sideways 100 feet in one minute, and the localizer narrows as you approach the threshold.

Anticipating the Intercept

Where a nondirectional beacon is collocated with the outer marker, you can use its indication to anticipate localizer intercept. Figure 10-14 illustrates. If the controller has you on a heading of 100° to intercept a localizer with an approach course of 130°, glance at the needle on the ADF indicator occasionally; as its deflection approaches 27° or so to the right of the airplane's nose, you can expect the localizer needle to come alive momentarily. The ADF indicator will also help if the controller's vector will take you directly to or inside of the marker—if the airport is to the right and, when you roll out on the vector heading the ADF needle points straight ahead or to the left, ask for another vector that will allow you to intercept the localizer outside of the outer marker.

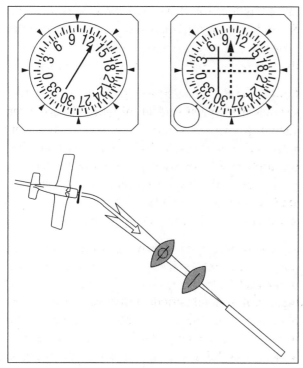

Figure 10-14. The ADF aids in localizer interception

Tracking the Glide Slope

Your approach plate will dictate a glideslope intercept altitude, and you must maintain that altitude until the glideslope needle comes down from the top of the indicator, centers, and begins to descend. You should be prepared to follow it down without changing airspeed. Do not wait until you reach the outer marker to begin your descent. The approach plate will also tell you the altitude at which the glide slope crosses the outer marker and in many cases you will descend hundreds of feet on the glide slope before reaching the outer marker. Note that at Port Angeles, Washington, the glide slope is intercepted over four miles from the outer marker. Glideslope intercept occurs at 3,800 feet MSL and the glide slope crosses the marker at 2,481 MSL; at 300 feet per mile (3°), the GS descends for 4.4 miles before reaching the outer marker (Figure 10-15 on next page).

The point at which the glide slope crosses the glideslope intercept altitude is called the "final approach *point*," and represents the final approach fix for the ILS; the Maltese cross marks the FAF for the nonprecision (no glide slope) approach. On Jepp plates, the heavy black line starts down at the final approach point, while on NACO plates that point is indicated by a lightning stroke.

It is good practice to check your altimeter when the glide slope crosses the outer marker to make sure that you are not tracking a false glide slope.

If either the wind or an inaccurate vector place you in a position where the glideslope needle comes alive before you intercept the localizer, you cannot follow the glide slope down—you must maintain altitude until the localizer comes alive. Even though the protected airspace is wider than full-scale localizer deflection, with the localizer needle pegged against the side of the instrument you have no sure way of knowing just how far off course you are.

Do not wait until the localizer needle is perfectly centered before beginning your descent on the glide slope. Why substitute the error of being too high for the error of being slightly off course? If the needle is alive you are in protected airspace. This does not mean that you shouldn't take action to center the needle, of course, just that you shouldn't concentrate on one problem to the exclusion of others.

A common question is, "When should I extend the gear when flying a retractable gear airplane?"

It never hurts to slow to approach speed early; doing so increases thinking time and helps you to stay ahead of the airplane. Some instructors advocate gear extension when the glideslope needle is one dot above center, asserting that the drag of the gear alone is sufficient to start a descent without a change in airspeed. That's good advice...but if you are falling behind the airplane, get the gear down early.

Both NACO and Jeppesen provide information on the rate of descent required to stay on the glide slope for different ground speeds (Figure 10-16). For a 3° glide slope you can ballpark the descent rate by adding a zero to your airspeed (ground speed is even better) and dividing the result in half: at 90 knots that works out to 450 feet per minute. The value of approximating the necessary descent rate is this: If you are clocking 120 knots over the ground and are above the glide slope, it will take a vertical speed greater than 600 feet per minute to recapture the glide slope. A descent rate less than 600 feet per minute will make the situation worse.

Another rule you can use in maintaining the glide slope is this: if your speed is higher than desired and

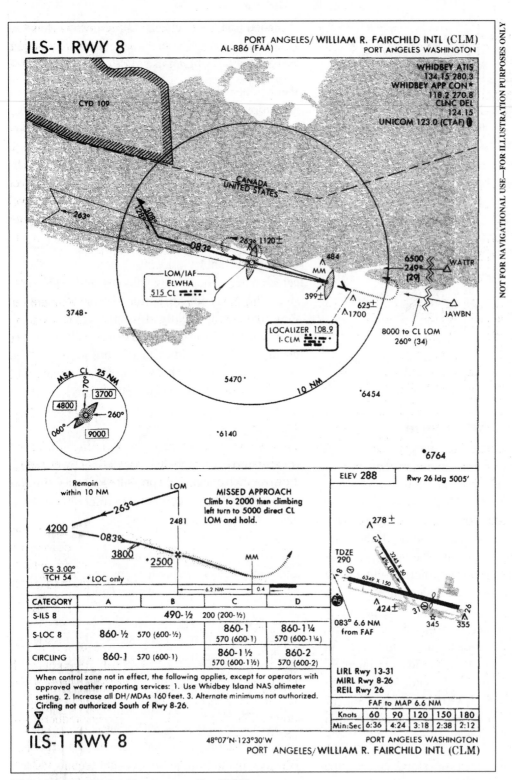

Figure 10-15. *Glideslope intercept outside of LOM*

INSTRUMENT APPROACH PROCEDURE CHARTS
RATE OF DESCENT TABLE
(ft. per min.)

A rate of descent table is provided for use in planning and executing precision descents under known or approximate ground speed conditions. It will be especially useful for approaches when the localizer only is used for course guidance. A best speed, power, attitude combination can be programmed which will result in a stable glide rate and attitude favorable for executing a landing if minimums exist upon breakout. Care should always be exercised so that the minimum descent altitude and missed approach point are not exceeded.

ANGLE OF DESCENT (degrees and tenths)	GROUND SPEED (knots)										
	30	45	60	75	90	105	120	135	150	165	180
2.0	105	160	210	265	320	370	425	475	530	585	635
2.5	130	200	265	330	395	465	530	595	665	730	795
3.0	160	240	320	395	480	555	635	715	795	875	955
3.5	185	280	370	465	555	650	740	835	925	1020	1110
4.0	210	315	425	530	635	740	845	955	1060	1165	1270
4.5	240	355	475	595	715	835	955	1075	1190	1310	1430
5.0	265	395	530	660	795	925	1060	1190	1325	1455	1590
5.5	290	435	580	730	875	1020	1165	1310	1455	1600	1745
6.0	315	475	635	795	955	1110	1270	1430	1590	1745	1905
6.5	345	515	690	860	1030	1205	1375	1550	1720	1890	2065
7.0	370	555	740	925	1110	1295	1480	1665	1850	2035	2220
7.5	395	595	795	990	1190	1390	1585	1785	1985	2180	2380
8.0	425	635	845	1055	1270	1480	1690	1905	2115	2325	2540
8.5	450	675	900	1120	1345	1570	1795	2020	2245	2470	2695
9.0	475	715	950	1190	1425	1665	1900	2140	2375	2615	2855
9.5	500	750	1005	1255	1505	1755	2005	2255	2510	2760	3010
10.0	530	790	1055	1320	1585	1845	2110	2375	2640	2900	3165
10.5	555	830	1105	1385	1660	1940	2215	2490	2770	3045	3320
11.0	580	870	1160	1450	1740	2030	2320	2610	2900	3190	3480
11.5	605	910	1210	1515	1820	2120	2425	2725	3030	3335	3635
12.0	630	945	1260	1575	1890	2205	2520	2835	3150	3465	3780

Figure 10-16. NACO descent rate table

you are below the glide slope, or if your speed is low and you are above the glide slope, a pitch change will solve both problems. If you are high and fast or low and slow, it will take a power change to solve your problem.

You can get a handle on wind shear by estimating the correct descent rate on the glide slope. If you are indicating 100 knots with the glide slope needle centered, your no-wind descent rate is pretty close to 500 feet per minute. If the vertical speed indicator shows a descent of only 300 feet per minute with the glide slope centered you have a strong headwind, and if the reported wind at the surface is light and variable you have a surprise in store as you descend through the shear layer; the airspeed will decrease and the airplane will sink below the glide slope if you are not right there with some power. An on-glideslope descent with a vertical speed greater than that estimated by the rule above means that you have a tailwind; if the surface wind is blowing right down the runway,

that tailwind is going to change to a headwind as you descend, and as you pass through the shear zone the airspeed will increase and you will balloon above the glide slope.

Interpreting and holding the glide slope is made easier by knowing some important numbers for your airplane. First, determine what airspeed you want to maintain during the final approach segment and the associated vertical speed. Next, determine the power setting necessary to maintain that airspeed in level flight. Pilots of retractable gear airplanes might want to make this determination with the wheels up and the flaps in the approach configuration.

If your wheels are welded in place and your propeller is a solid piece of metal, you can approximate the desired rate of descent without changing airspeed by reducing the throttle 50 rpm for each 100 feet per minute. If you have selected 100 knots as final approach speed and 500 feet per minute as the rate of descent, a power reduction of 250 rpm should put you in the ballpark. Not right on, of course, because the glide slope is affected by ground speed, not airspeed. If the airplane is pulled through the air by a constant-speed propeller, make the power reduction one inch of manifold pressure for every 100 feet per minute of target descent rate.

As the pilot of a retractable, you must take one additional step: after learning what it takes to maintain approach speed in level flight with the wheels up, hang them out and descend to maintain the same indicated airspeed.

Note the vertical speed; it will take a few seconds for the vertical speed to stabilize. Let's say that 20 inches of manifold pressure will maintain 100 knots with the gear up and that you descend at 350 feet per minute while maintaining 100 knots with the gear down. You need an additional power reduction of about an inch and a half, right?

The glide slope follows the rule that 1° equals 100 feet one mile from the antenna (look back at Figure 10-9). A typical glide slope is 1.4° thick, according to the AIM, so at a distance of one mile from the antenna full-scale deflection is 70 feet up and 70 feet down.

In the latter stages of an ILS approach it is all too easy to react to a "fly up" indication with back pressure and throttle, only to fly right through the top of the glide slope and into a missed approach. As you near the threshold, remember that full-scale deflection is only a matter of a few feet, and limit your corrections accordingly. How do you know how far out you are? If the glide slope descends 300 feet per mile, as almost all of them do, you will be 300 feet above touchdown zone elevation when you are a mile out, 600 feet AGL when you are two miles out, etc. This has to be an approximation because the glide slope antenna is not right at the threshold.

Because the ILS is a precision approach with vertical guidance (Figure 10-17), you may descend to a published decision height, and Part 91 says that when you reach that altitude you have a clear-cut decision to make; either land or begin the missed approach. *Do not begin to level off as you approach decision height for fear of descending beneath it.* Part 91 says that you cannot *continue* beneath decision height, not that you can't descend through that altitude while transitioning to the missed approach. If you are in position to make a normal landing and have sighted lights or markings associated with the runway (91.175 lists the alternatives), go ahead and land—but if you are still in the clouds at decision height you have no alternative but to add go-around power and pitch up to climb attitude. If you catch a glimpse of the runway during the transition process you can only add the experience to your collection of flying stories—you can't change your mind and land anyway because you are no longer in position to make a normal landing. Look back at Figure 6-13; if you have to circle, staying on the glide slope until you reach circling MDA avoids the obstructions on either side close to the localizer.

The real limiting factor in IFR minimums is flight visibility, and your approach plate tells you just how much visibility is required in order for you to land legally. Flight visibility is determined in the cockpit, not by a controller in the tower. The distance from the middle marker to the threshold is printed on the approach plate. If the distance from the middle marker to the threshold is ½ mile and ½ mile visibility is required, you had better be able to see the approach lights or threshold when the middle marker light starts blinking. Note that in Figure 10-17 the approach path starts upward before it crosses the middle marker.

If the wind is blowing out of the north during an approach in a category A airplane at Bremerton, Washington (Figure 10-17), but you elect to shoot the ILS approach to runway 19, you will have to circle to land on runway 1. In this situation you would ride the glide slope down to circling minimums (1,180 feet), then break off to the right or left and fly a downwind. The approach becomes nonprecision as soon as you leave the glide slope. I hope you marked the time at the OM so you'll know when to execute the missed approach if you can't see the runway to circle. Be sure to keep the runway in sight throughout the circling maneuver. If the weather permits, you can fly straight down runway 19 and make a course reversal in visual conditions. Circling can be a pretty shaky maneuver, especially at night, so if you can accept a little tailwind it might be best to complete the ILS.

Missed Approach Procedures

For every instrument approach procedure there is a missed approach procedure, and you should be aware of what that procedure requires before you initiate the approach.

You can remember the elements of the missed approach procedure with the memory aid MARTHA:

M Missed
A Approach
R Radio/Radial/Route
T Time
H Heading
A Altitude

The time to study the missed approach procedure is when you know which approach you are going to use. Don't wait until you have passed the final approach fix to look at the plate for instructions. At the very least you should know the initial missed approach heading and altitude before you get to the FAF.

You shouldn't necessarily resign yourself to performing the published missed approach procedure, however. If you are in a radar environment, the controller will probably have other plans for you, most likely vectors for another approach. If the controller does not issue specific missed approach instructions, ask "Do you want me to do the published miss?" That request may shake out something

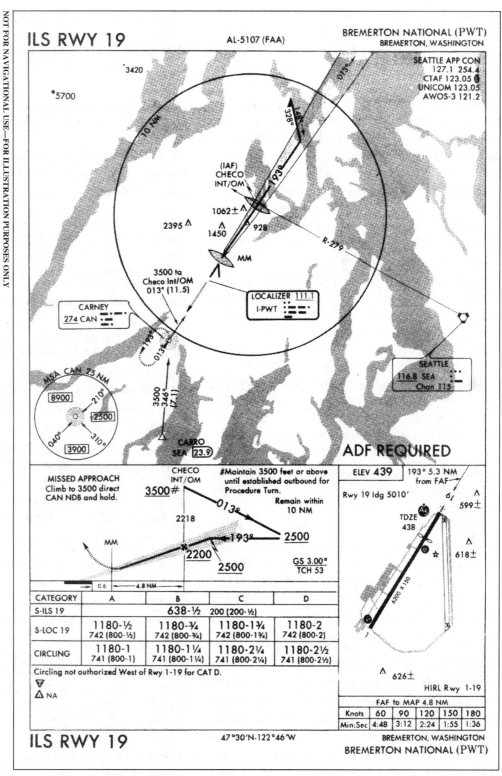

Figure 10-17. ILS RWY 19, Bremerton, WA

less onerous than holding at a fix 15 miles from the airport. If you do receive specific instructions from ATC, they supersede the instructions on the approach plate.

If your instructions involve proceeding to a navaid and you can tune it without reducing your capabilities for the approach itself, by all means select, tune, and identify that aid well in advance. Do not, however, sacrifice the ability to use your #2 radio as a backup to the #1 just so that you can tune it to the missed approach aid. Having a backup might ensure a successful approach! Both Jeppesen and NACO plates identify the missed approach point unmistakably. Each provides a note giving the distance from the final approach fix to the MAP, and each changes the representation of the procedural track as it turns into a missed approach track.

In its design of an instrument approach procedure, the FAA begins with the missed approach segment. After all, if a pilot can't execute the missed approach safely, why start the approach in the first place? Quite often, published minimums don't make sense at first glance—why should an approach over water call for five miles visibility and an MDA more than 1,700 feet AGL (South Lake Tahoe, California)? Because the missed approach path heads straight for some pretty tall mountains, that's why. This not an uncommon situation in the high country. That's why you must begin the missed approach at the MAP as closely as you can determine it—not before you get there or after you have flown along at MDA for a few moments in the hope that something long and flat will appear in the windshield.

That may seem like a simplistic statement, but think about what you should do if you are halfway between the final approach fix and the runway and your course guidance needles are pegged—you know that you are irretrievably off course. If the missed approach procedure calls for a turn, do you turn as soon as you realize that you will have to declare a missed approach?

No, because the missed approach airspace is not protected for an early turning maneuver; you must proceed to the MAP and then initiate the missed approach procedure to ensure that you remain in protected airspace.

If you can't turn early, can you turn late? Again, no. The designers provide a reasonable amount of latitude in maneuvering and must ensure that the procedure is safe for airplanes much faster than yours. Still, you cannot forge ahead hoping that something good will happen while delaying the initiation of the miss.

Can you initiate the missed approach climb early? Absolutely—just don't go above the published altitude for the miss.

Nothing is more valuable than altitude when your position is uncertain. Tell the controller what you are doing, of course. Any turning maneuvers must wait until you have reached the MAP, however.

For precision approaches, there should be no doubt about where the missed approach is to be initiated: if you descend to decision height and do not have the threshold or markings associated with the threshold in sight, you must add pitch and power and get out of there. If you have drifted off of the localizer due to wind or poor technique, you know that a climb straight ahead on the localizer course will take you to the airport, where there are no tall obstructions. Because you can't use the glide slope to determine DH under these conditions you can't continue your descent if you are off the localizer; you must use the published MAP for the localizer-only approach.

Figure 10-18 illustrates a situation where the approach is not authorized if the glide slope is unusable but has circling authorization. The only way you can identify the missed approach point if you drift off the localizer is by timing.

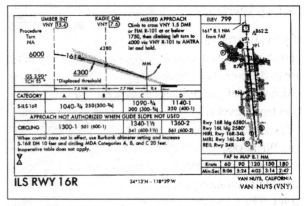

Figure 10-18. Glide slope unusable

The localizer-only is a nonprecision approach, and for most such approaches the missed approach point is determined by timing from the final approach fix or from a fix specified on the approach plate. In the discussion of straight-in nonprecision approaches, I showed you how to calculate a decision window by shortening the time given on the plate. This has no bearing on the execution of the missed approach, which must begin at the expiration of the published time to MAP (unless the approach navaid is on the field and no timing is required).

Because timing is required for most nonprecision approaches, you should make a habit of starting your timer at the FAF, even when flying an ILS (although timing an ILS is not required by the FAA); a glideslope failure or drifting away from the localizer centerline may make timing critically important.

But what if you forget to start your watch at the FAF? You certainly won't be the first pilot to forget. The answer lies in research and planning. Look at *all* the approach plates for the destination airport. Is there a navaid depicted on one that is not shown on another? The middle marker for runway 4 shown on the ILS plate will be there when you are shooting the NDB approach to runway 4, even if it's not on the NDB approach plate, and you can use it to help identify the MAP. Is there a VOR radial that crosses near the runway threshold? I know, it hasn't been flight tested, but all you want is to avoid inadvertent overflight of the MAP. The A/FD might contain a radial and distance from a nearby VORTAC that identifies the airport reference point—it's better than nothing. And of course if RNAV (to be defined later), LORAN, or GPS are available they can be used to back up your timer.

If you do remember to start the timer at the FAF, as you should, how accurate will your timing be? There are two elements to the answer: airspeed control and estimation of ground speed. Unless you can transition from level flight at 90 knots (for example) into a descent at 600 feet per minute while still maintaining 90 knots, you will have trouble with timing nonprecision approaches. Airspeed control is paramount in validating the time to the missed approach point. Then you must adjust for the reported wind, because the table on the approach plate is based on ground speed, not airspeed. Unless you have DME,

LORAN, or GPS to supply a groundspeed readout, your estimate of ground speed will be only as good as the information you have available.

A surface wind report from a tower or FSS may bear little relation to the changing winds you will encounter in the descent on final approach. I have no magic formulas. I do suggest that you adjust your indicated airspeed on final to make your ground speed agree with a tabulated time, however. If you anticipate a seven knot headwind and want to use the time for 90 knots, fly an indicated airspeed on 97 knots. Don't try to interpolate between tabulated figures while on final—you have more important things to do.

At airports that have radar available, the missed approach procedure may call for you to climb and fly to a fix, without holding instructions. In these situations it is anticipated that you will be in radar contact after the miss and that the controller will provide further instructions.

But what happens if communications are lost? The controller may volunteer this information in advance: "In the event of lost communications, cross GOOFI intersection at 4,000 feet, proceed direct to the NORML locator outer marker and perform the ILS approach to runway 6." If you do not know what you are expected to do if communications fail after the approach is initiated, ask the controller. Before accepting any clearance, ask yourself what you would do if the radios fail and have a plan in mind.

Other Types of Approaches

We've discussed the most common precision and nonprecision approaches. Now let's take a look at other types of approaches you may encounter.

The LOC and BC-LOC are nonprecision approaches with no vertical guidance, but with the same lateral guidance accuracy as the full ILS (except for the SDF).

A localizer approach (LOC) is simply an ILS with no glide slope. It is adjusted full-scale needle deflection approximately 700 feet wide at the runway threshold, regardless of runway length, so the localizer signal for a long runway will be narrower than the signal for a short runway. This type of approach will always have a final approach fix (the Maltese cross on the profile portion of the approach plate), and determining the missed approach point will usually require timing. Where distance measuring equipment is colocated with the LOC transmitter, DME readings can be used to identify stepdown fixes and the missed approach point. Note that in Figure 10-19 the title of the approach indicates that you must have DME equipment in order to fly the approach, while at Arlington, Washington (Figure 10-20) no DME is required.

Take a look at the 80-foot penalty imposed if you can't get a local altimeter setting at Glasgow, Kentucky, and also note that the approach is not authorized if no altimeter setting is available (Figure 10-19). There are lots of restrictions at places like Glasgow—read those notes long before you get there.

Glide Slope Inoperative

An ILS with an inoperative glideslope transmitter (or an inoperative GS receiver in your airplane) turns into a localizer approach. Almost all ILS approach charts accommodate these situations or those pilots who do not have glideslope receivers by publishing approach paths, procedure altitudes, and minimum descent altitudes. Where the existence of obstacles makes vertical guidance necessary, no LOC ONLY minimums are published (Figure 10-18) and the straight-in approach is out-of-bounds for the pilot without glideslope capability. Take a look back at Figure 10-17, though; in the event of glideslope failure, straight-in localizer minimums are 1,180 feet and $\frac{1}{2}$-mile for category A and B.

Back-Course Approaches

A back-course approach (Figure 10-21) utilizes the signal transmitted "behind" the ILS localizer transmitter. Unless it has been physically blocked off, every localizer transmits a back-course signal, but only those which have been approved and published may be used for navigation.

When you are flying an LOC-BC procedure using a standard VOR indicator the needle will have reverse sensing; that is, you will fly away from the needle. This is true whether you are flying toward the airport on the approach or away from the airport on the missed approach (that would be called "flying outbound on the front course"). With an HSI, you just turn the course arrow to the front course and fly the

needle normally. That is, if you are flying the front course ILS to runway 31 at Salem, OR, you would set the arrowhead to 310° and fly toward the deflected needle. If the wind shifted and you wanted to fly the back course at Salem (Figure 10-21) you would still have the arrowhead on 310°, but your heading would be close to 130° and the tail of the needle would be on 130°; your heading would be approximately 130°, depending on the wind, and you would fly toward the deflected needle. The TO/FROM flag never changes when a localizer frequency is selected—it always points to the front course. Again, there is no reverse sensing with an HSI.

On a normal (front course) ILS approach, the localizer antenna is at the far end of the runway and the signal is 700 feet wide at the threshold; on a back-course approach, the antenna lies between you and the runway and the localizer needle becomes extremely sensitive as you approach the antenna. The FAA makes sure that the missed approach point is reached well before you pass over the antenna, but the difference in sensitivity between a front course and a back course can be disconcerting.

You will probably receive glideslope indications while flying a back course approach, but they are to be disregarded except at those few locations in the world with a back-course ILS. There are none in the United States.

Some back-course approaches, like Salem, Oregon, have back-course markers which are identified by the white light on the panel and which send two dots (·· ··) modulated at 3,000 Hz.

SDF and LDA

A simplified directional facility (SDF) is a localizer-type navaid which is much less sensitive than a normal localizer. Its course width is either 6° or 12° wide and its final approach course may not be aligned with the runway (although the offset should not exceed 3°). *See* Figure 10-22.

Continued on Page 10-29

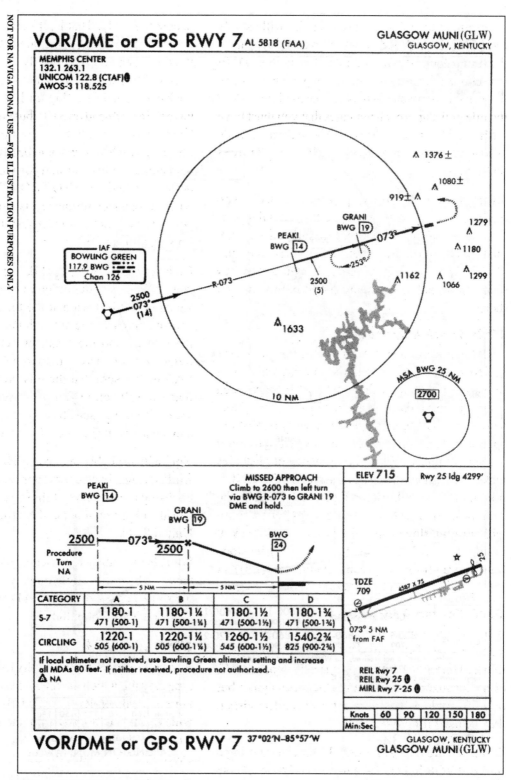

Figure 10-19. *Glasgow, Kentucky*

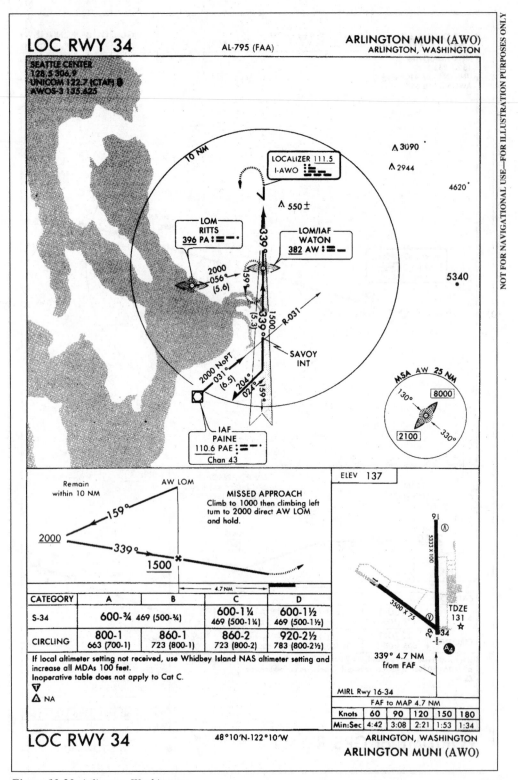

Figure 10-20. *Arlington, Washington*

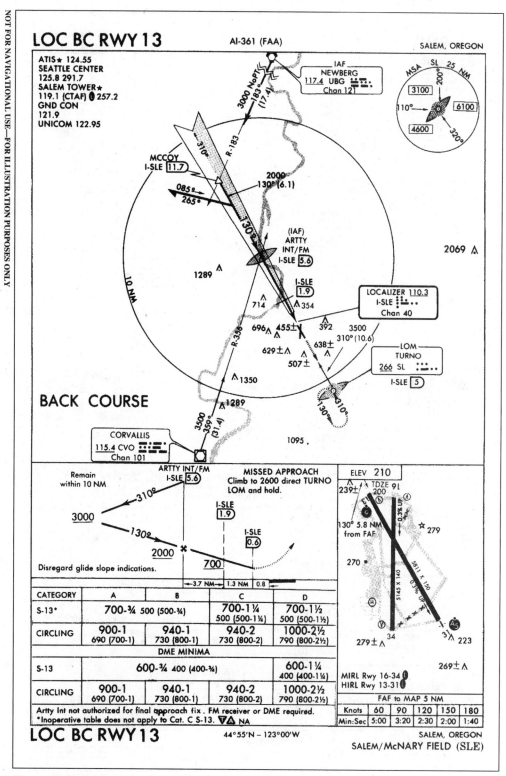

Figure 10-21. Back-course approach

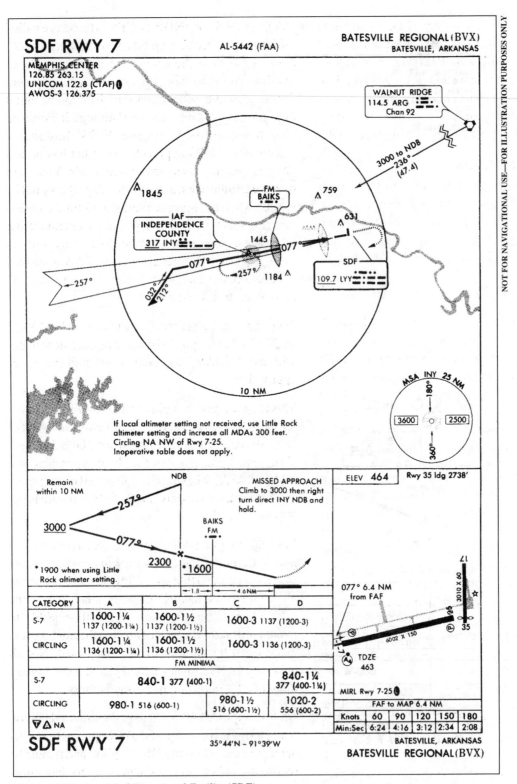

Figure 10-22. Simplified Directional Facility (SDF)

A Localizer-type Directional Aid (LDA) compares in sensitivity to a standard localizer but is not aligned with the runway. The LDA/DME-D approach to Petersburg, Alaska, is an example (Figure 10-23 on the next page). When the final approach course is more than 30° out of alignment with the runway, only circling minimums are published for the approach.

RNAV Approaches

At the end of a flight using RNAV (not GPS) such as that described in Chapter 8, you might want to shoot an RNAV approach. These approaches are disappearing rapidly, but the one at Emporia, Kansas (Figure 10-24) is still valid—and the approach illustrated back in Figure 8-11 has been converted to a GPS approach.

In Chapter 8, you flew from waypoint to waypoint, finally arriving at an initial approach fix waypoint. Let's assume that you have arrived over HEYDN waypoint on your way into Emporia. Your RNAV stores at least four waypoints, so you will have already entered the EMP 350.6 radial at 12.6 miles (QWAKI), the EMP 342 radial at 7.9 miles (GRIZY), and the EMP 311.8 radial at 3.7 miles (FREMO) into the equipment, ready to be called up as needed.

Outbound from HEYDN you will have selected the QWAKI waypoint and will keep the OBS needle centered while the DME counts down. With 26 miles to go you have plenty of time to enter the missed approach waypoint, KEEGA, to be used if needed. No procedure turn is required if you transition from HEYDN or POMON; the one-minute holding pattern course reversal would be used only if you arrived at QWAKI from the EMP VORTAC (VORs that form part of the enroute structure are automatically IAFs).

With course guidance taken care of, your next concern is altitude. Cross QWAKI at or above 2,900, and the 2.2-mile fix at 1,960 on the way down to an MDA of 1,560, for a straight-in to runway 19. One mile flight visibility is required. Execute the missed approach procedure at MAP when the TO-FROM flag flips.

GPS Approaches

There is no doubt that the Global Positioning System (GPS) represents the future of navigation on land, sea, and air—and the future is now. Throughout this chapter you have seen approach plates that said "VOR or GPS" or "NDB or GPS." These are called GPS overlays, because a pilot can use either an FAA-approved GPS or the underlying navaid. To fly an overlay, you must have the appropriate equipment for the ground-based approach in the airplane, but it does not have to be turned on (although it would be foolish not to use it). Figure 10-25 illustrates a "stand-alone" GPS approach—one that has no underlying ground-based navigational aids. Your path over the ground when using GPS will probably not be exactly what the approach plate shows for the underlying approach. Once again, you must remember that all of these approaches can be flown *only* with an FAA-approved GPS receiver in an FAA-approved installation. No handhelds—and you can't file "/I" en route with a handheld.

Note: Approach plate procedure names such as "VOR or GPS" are being phased out; the replacement plates will use "RNAV" to identify all point-in-space approaches.

This is a good place to point out that an IFR-approved GPS can be used as a substitute for either an NDB or DME if those facilities are named in the GPS database. That means you can shoot an NDB approach or a DME arc without having an ADF or DME equipment in your airplane, but only if your GPS software is up-to-date.

My goal in writing this chapter has been to show you how different kinds of instrument approaches are flown—I can't do that with GPS, because just about all the decision-making has been taken out of the pilot's hands. Unfortunately it is still possible to make a mistake, but chances are that the mistake was made when the equipment was purchased. Not all approved GPS receivers are alike, and some impose more of a workload on pilots than others.

An IFR-approved GPS receiver contains a database with all of the fixes required to fly approaches. This database cannot be edited by the pilot, and it must be renewed regularly so that the most up-to-date information is available. The FAA requires that when a specific approach has been selected from the database and activated, the GPS equipment automatically sequences through the fixes—the pilot just

Continued on Page 10-33

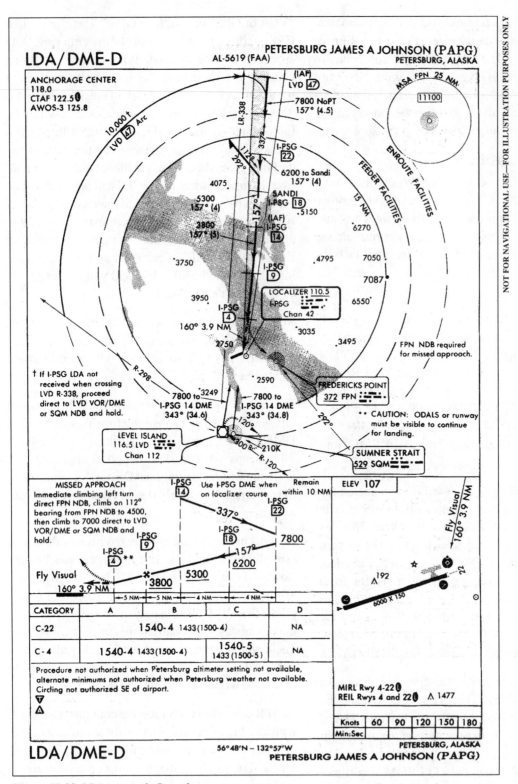

Figure 10-23. LDA approach, Petersburg

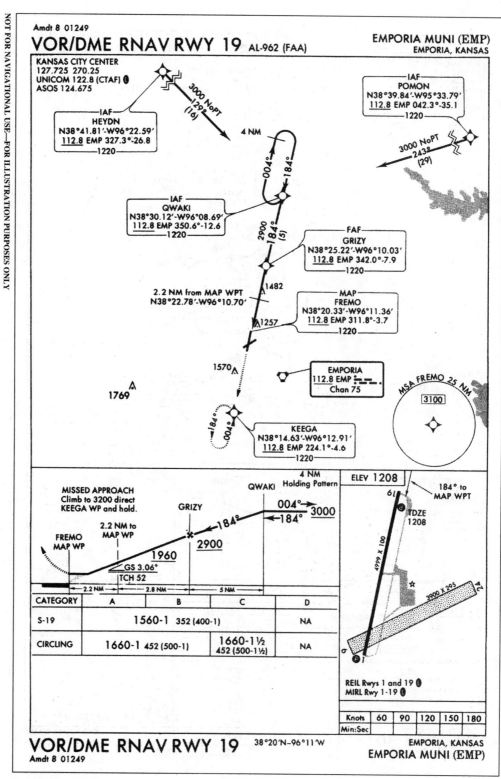

Amdt 8 01249

VOR/DME RNAV RWY 19 AL-962 (FAA)

EMPORIA MUNI (EMP)
EMPORIA, KANSAS

KANSAS CITY CENTER
127.725 270.25
UNICOM 122.8 (CTAF) ⓞ
ASOS 124.675

—IAF—
HEYDN
N38°41.81'-W96°22.59'
112.8 EMP 327.3°-26.8
—1220—

3000 NoPT
129°
(16)

4 NM

—IAF—
POMON
N38°39.84'-W95°33.79'
112.8 EMP 042.3°-35.1
—1220—

3000 NoPT
243°
(29)

004°
184°

—IAF—
QWAKI
N38°30.12'-W96°08.69'
112.8 EMP 350.6°-12.6
—1220—

2900 184° (5)

—FAF—
GRIZY
N38°25.22'-W96°10.03'
112.8 EMP 342.0°-7.9
—1220—

2.2 NM from MAP WPT
N38°22.78'-W96°10.70'

△ 1482

△ 1257

—MAP—
FREMO
N38°20.33'-W96°11.36'
112.8 EMP 311.8°-3.7
—1220—

1570 △

EMPORIA
112.8 EMP ▄▄▄ ▄ .
Chan 75

MSA FREMO 25 NM
3100

△ 1769

184°
004°

KEEGA
N38°14.63'-W96°12.91'
112.8 EMP 224.1°-4.6
—1220—

MISSED APPROACH
Climb to 3200 direct
KEEGA WP and hold.

4 NM
QWAKI   Holding Pattern

ELEV 1208

184° to
MAP WPT

GRIZY

004°
3000
184°

TDZE
1208

2.2 NM to
MAP WP

FREMO
MAP WP

184°

1960

2900

GS 3.06°
TCH 52

	2.2 NM	2.8 NM	5 NM

CATEGORY	A	B	C	D
S-19	1560-1 352 (400-1)			NA
CIRCLING	1660-1 452 (500-1)		1660-1½ 452 (500-1½)	NA

REIL Rwys 1 and 19 ⓞ
MIRL Rwy 1-19 ⓞ

Knots	60	90	120	150	180
Min:Sec					

4999 X 100
3900 X 295

VOR/DME RNAV RWY 19   38°20'N-96°11'W

EMPORIA, KANSAS
EMPORIA MUNI (EMP)

Amdt 8 01249

Figure 10-24. Emporia, Kansas

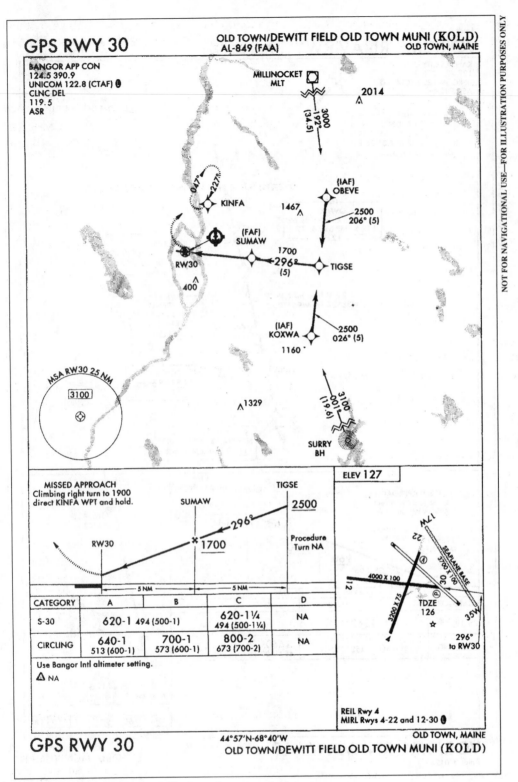

Figure 10-25. *"Stand-alone" GPS approach*

keeps the needle centered. The equipment provides advance warning of proximity to waypoints such as TURTL (look back at Figure 9-17).

Receiver sensitivity increases as the airplane nears the airport, again without any pilot input. The approach to Westheimer Airport at Norman, Oklahoma is a good example of the FAA's "basic T" method of approach design. Pilots flying in the enroute structure will transition from waypoints such as SUZET to the initial approach fixes, TURTL, TTURN, or FIRST. As they near the IAFs, the pilots will arm (enable) the approach mode on their GPS equipment. This sets the stage for receiver sensitivity to increase to 1 NM either side of centerline when the airplane is within 30 NM of the IAF. At a distance of 2 NM to the FAF, receiver sensitivity increases to .3 NM either side of centerline. At the missed approach point, the pilot must manually select the missed approach fix, BOBLO. And remember, *GPS altitude is not as accurate as your barometric altimeter!*

Looking back at the GPS overlay approaches in this chapter, you can see that they do not follow the "basic T" design. Many will require procedure turns, even with GPS, and this is where your purchasing decision comes into play. The FAA tells the avionics manufacturers that an approved GPS receiver must perform certain functions and lets each manufacturer decide how those functions should be accomplished. Compare two sets from different manufacturers and where one has knobs the other will have buttons. Compare two models from one manufacturer and you will find operational differences between them. Unless you are fortunate enough to find two airplanes with identical GPS installations you will have to sit down with the approved flight manual supplement and learn the procedures for each type and model you encounter. And then sit in the cockpit and practice.

Depending on the manufacturer and model GPS you are using, you might have to shift to "manual" mode to fly outbound and reverse course, re-activating the approach function when you turn inbound, or the whole process might be done for you. Things change rapidly in the world of GPS avionics. When the Wide Area Augmentation System and Local Area Augmentation System (*see* Figures 8-12, 8-13 on Page 8-17) are in place around 2005, your GPS will have

to be modified or replaced if you are to enjoy their greater accuracy. There will be no GPS precision approaches until those systems have been installed and tested.

That's why there is no "how to" for GPS approaches in this book. ASA's *GPS Trainer* software program will give you some insight into how different products work.

Stand-Alone GPS Approaches

Look back at Figure 9-17 (Chapter 9, Page 9-19); it also illustrates the new charting format for GPS approaches and introduces some new symbols. The procedure name "RNAV RWY 17" is the first time in this text that RNAV has applied to GPS. Notice the "pilot briefing" section across the top; it contains information on frequencies, restrictions, the missed approach procedure, and the approach lighting system. The "channel number" provides a means of identifying the approach in certain models of GPS; most units use menus for this purpose. The temperature restriction applies to barometric altitudes in extremely cold weather.

The symbols in the elevation view offer a quick review of the missed approach procedure. Reading from left to right, they read "173° to 5000, BOBLO, left to 083° SUZET and hold." The symbol for BOBLO is the "fly-by" waypoint symbol; the symbol for SUZET is the "fly-over" symbol. These symbols are new to instrument pilots. The GPS equipment is programmed to lead the turn at fly-by waypoints and to not turn until a fly-over waypoint has been passed. This symbology is provided so that pilots will know what to expect when an autopilot is flying the airplane, and for guidance when hand-flying.

The minimums box provides for a number of capabilities and eventualities. Like the minimums presentation on "old" plates, the lowest minimums are at the top. "WAAS PA DA" indicates that when the Wide Area Augmentation System is working, all of the elements of a precision system are met, and that the minimum is a decision altitude, just like an ILS. Obstacle clearance provision has been made for a momentary descent below DA during the transition to the missed approach procedure. WAAS PA minimums can be as low as 200 feet and ½ statute mile. If PA is missing, minimums will be no lower than 300 feet and ¾.

RADAR MINS

RADAR INSTRUMENT APPROACH MINIMUMS

BATTLE CREEK, MI Amdt. 2, DEC 13,1990 ELEV **952**
W. K. KELLOGG
RADAR - 121.2 340.9

	RWY GS/TCH/RPI	CAT	DH/ MDA-VIS	HAT/ HAA	CEIL-VIS	CAT	DH/ MDA-VIS	HAT/ HAA	CEIL-VIS
CIRCLING		A	**1420**-1	468	(500-1)	B	**1440**-1	488	(500-1)
		C	**1480**-1½	528	(600-1½)	D	**1520**-2	568	(600-2)
		E	**1740**-2¾	788	(800-2¾)				

When Kalamazoo control tower closed, procedure not authorized.
When Battle Creek control tower closed, use Kalamazoo altimeter setting and increase all MDA's 60 feet and Category E visibility ¼ mile.

FLINT, MI Amdt. 7, NOV 16,1989 ELEV **782**
BISHOP INTL
RADAR - 128.55 257.9

	RWY GS/TCH/RPI	CAT	DH/ MDA-VIS	HAT/ HAA	CEIL-VIS	CAT	DH/ MDA-VIS	HAT/ HAA	CEIL-VIS
ASR	36	AB	**1260**-1	478	(500-1)	C	**1260**-1¼	478	(500-1¼)
		D	**1260**-1½	478	(500-1½)				
	18	AB	**1260**-1	481	(500-1)	C	**1260**-1¼	481	(500-1¼)
		D	**1260**-1½	481	(500-1½)				
	27	AB	**1340**-½	570	(600-½)	C	**1340**-1	570	(600-1)
		D	**1340**-1¼	570	(600-1¼)				
CIRCLING		AB	**1340**-1	558	(600-1)	C	**1340**-1½	558	(600-1½)
		D	**1340**-2	558	(600-2)				

CAUTION: Brightly lighted parking lot 4000' E of approach end of rwy 27 can easily be confused for rwy 27.

GRAND RAPIDS, MI Amdt. 10, FEB 29, 1996 ELEV **794**
KENT COUNTY INTL
RADAR - 128.4 257.6

	RWY GS/TCH/RPI	CAT	DH/ MDA-VIS	HAT/ HAA	CEIL-VIS	CAT	DH/ MDA-VIS	HAT/ HAA	CEIL-VIS
ASR	26L	ABC	**1100**/24	310	(400-½)	D	**1100**/50	310	(400-1)
	26R	ABC	**1140**-1	353	(400-1)	D	**1140**-1¼	353	(400-1¼)
	8L	ABC	**1180**-1	393	(400-1)	D	**1180**-1¼	393	(400-1¼)
	8R	AB	**1200**-½	406	(500-½)	C	**1200**-¾	406	(500-¾)
		D	**1200**-1	406	(500-1)				
CIRCLING		AB	**1260**-1	466	(500-1)	C	**1260**-1½	466	(500-1½)
		D	**1360**-2	566	(600-2)				

When control tower closed, ASR not authorized.

Figure 10-26. NACO radar minimums from instrument approach plate book

Poor GPS satellite geometry or atmospheric interference may cause the GPS equipment to annunciate LNAV/VNAV instead of WAAS. When this occurs, the LNAV/VNAV minimums must be observed. Note that this is also a decision altitude.

The LNAV minimums are to be used when only lateral guidance is available and barometric altitude must be relied on. This is a minimum descent altitude (MDA).

Surveillance or Precision Radar Approaches

A discussion of precision radar approaches probably does not belong in a section on nonprecision approaches; however, when radar is available you will look to the same sources for information regardless of which type of approach service is provided. NACO prints *Radar Instrument Approach Minimums* on page N1 of each volume of instrument approach plates (*see* an example in Figure 10-26), and Jeppesen provides a radar approach plate wherever such an approach exists.

By FAA definition, a "ground controlled approach" is any procedure in which the pilot follows instructions from the ground. When the term "GCA" is used, the reference is to a military procedure. Civilian radar approaches are either airport surveillance radar (ASR), or precision approach radar (PAR). There is only one published PAR approach in the continental United States; there are three at joint-use airports in Alaska. Most are at airports which are either military/civilian joint-use airports or which have heavy military traffic. Your only source of information on the availability of military ground controlled approaches (GCA) is local knowledge; military fields are not listed in the A/FD or in approach plate booklets.

The precision radar controller has both azimuth and altitude information available and is able to guide you to the threshold with accuracy approaching that of an ILS. The controller will provide you with continuous information on your position in relation to the final approach course and glide path, and will inform you of your distance from the touchdown point at least once each mile. A PAR has a decision height (DH) and you are expected to execute a missed approach if the runway is not in sight when you reach that altitude. The controller will direct you to execute a missed approach if you deviate beyond safe limits in azimuth or elevation during the approach.

Although PAR or GCA approaches are few and far between, learn where they are available in your area of operation. When you are tired and your confidence is low because you have missed several approaches, a precision radar approach will get you on the ground to think it over. Landing at a military field involves some hassle and paperwork but it is worth it in a tight situation.

A surveillance approach is one which provides only azimuth information on the final approach course. Its accuracy is not as great as that of a PAR, and the minimums are accordingly higher. No altitude information is available, but the controller will tell you when to begin your descent to the MDA. At your request, the controller will tell you what your altitude should be each mile on final, based on the descent gradient established for the procedure. You will be advised of the location of the missed approach point and of the missed approach procedure.

If your gyro instruments have failed or if you question their accuracy, the radar controller can provide a no-gyro approach procedure. While vectoring you to the final approach course, the controller will tell you to "START TURN" and "STOP TURN," anticipating that you will turn at a standard rate of 3° per second and evaluating the result of each instruction on the radar scope before commanding another turn. When you are established on the final approach course you should respond to turn commands with one-half standard rate turns.

Loss of your gyroscopically stabilized instruments warrants declaring an emergency and requesting a radar approach. Unless you make the controller aware of the problem you will be vectored and sequenced normally.

Visual Descent Point

Optical illusions have played a part in many IFR accidents and incidents; the pilots involved misinterpreted visual clues and descended into the terrain while on the approach. The FAA has established visual descent points (VDPs) at many airports to aid you in determining when it is safe to descend under visual conditions. The VDP is indicated by a "V" on the profile view of both NACO and Jeppesen approach plates, and is located at the point where a 300-400 foot per nautical mile glide path intercepts the minimum descent altitude (see Figure 9-17). The VDP may be a DME indication, a cross-radial from a VOR, a marker beacon, or a radar fix. If your equipment cannot identify the VDP, just ignore it and fly the approach normally.

If you spot the runway while still outside of the VDP, stay at the MDA until you have passed the VDP. If the runway is equipped with a visual approach slope indicator you should get an "on glide path" indication at the visual descent point.

Contact and Visual Approaches

Contact approaches and visual approaches allow you to proceed to the airport without following a specific printed approach procedure, and without giving up all of the protection provided by being in the IFR system. Both have advantages, and both carry responsibilities which you must be aware of before accepting a visual or contact approach clearance.

Visual approaches are the most common, and can be either requested by the pilot ("Speedwing 35Z has the field in sight; request a visual") or offered by the controller ("Speedwing 35Z, do you have the field in sight? Cleared for a visual approach to runway..."). VFR weather conditions must exist for a visual approach. If there is no weather reporting service available at the airport, ATC may initiate a visual approach if area weather reports indicate that the airport is VFR; the pilot's acceptance of the clearance indicates that the approach can be conducted in VFR conditions—don't accept the clearance if it can't.

"Speedwing 35Z, you are following a Jetbird on 5 mile final—report that aircraft in sight." "Maintain visual separation, cleared for the visual approach to runway...". That is another way of getting a visual—and the pilot of the Jetbird may be following yet another aircraft. Yes, you can be cleared for a visual approach when you can't see the airport but can see an airplane whose pilot can either see the airport or is following another airplane whose pilot can either see the airport...etc.

Unless you are ready and willing to accept a visual approach, don't report either the airport or a preceding airplane in sight, because just as soon as you do the controller is going to clear you for the visual approach. Your acceptance means that you agree to take responsibility for maintaining a safe approach interval and wake turbulence separation. You do not have to accept a clearance for a visual approach, but don't open the door for the controller by reporting the field or a preceding airplane in sight and then refuse the clearance.

A visual approach has no missed approach segment, because you shouldn't miss an approach in VFR conditions. If you somehow manage to accomplish this, however, you must maintain VFR conditions while ATC fits you back into the system.

Do not cancel your IFR clearance just because you encounter VFR weather conditions. Stay in the system; once you leave it, returning can be difficult and time consuming. Besides, it's good practice to operate in the system no matter what the weather.

If you can't maintain basic VFR, you may request a contact approach instead of a visual approach—the controller cannot offer it. Only you are in position to know if you have one mile flight visibility and can proceed to the airport while maintaining clearance from all clouds, and you should request a contact approach only when you recognize objects on the ground and know that you can navigate to the airport by ground contact; it is not the thing to do at a strange airport.

You can request a contact approach only to an airport with a published approach procedure, because a published missed approach procedure must be available if things go sour. You cannot use a contact approach clearance as a means of getting to one airport and then, when in visual contact with the ground, proceeding to another airport.

ATC will provide separation between your airplane and other IFR or Special VFR aircraft while you are on a contact approach.

Circling Approaches

Almost any instrument approach, precision or nonprecision, can terminate with a circle-to-land maneuver: the runway may be more than 30° from the final approach course, the wind may favor a runway other than that served by the approach procedure, or there may be only one approach to the airport and you may be flying that approach with a tailwind. An ILS approach changes from a precision to a nonprecision operation just as soon as you are cleared to circle. You will find plenty of examples in this chapter.

The circling MDA is measured above the published airport elevation (HAA), not above the elevation of the touchdown zone; the area protected against obstacles is defined by drawing an arc with a radius which depends on aircraft category (1.3 NM for category A) from the end of each runway and connecting the arcs with straight lines. In this way a larger area is protected for faster airplanes because of their larger turning radius. At Wausau (Figure 10-27), the circling MDA is the same for all categories; this situation does not exist at all airports because obstructions within the turning radius of category C and D aircraft may require a higher MDA for those categories.

Circling is a VFR operation, and the FAA expects you to remain within sight of the airport; they recognize, of course, that during some turning maneuvers the airplane's structure may interfere with a direct view of the runway. However, if you encounter less-than-VFR conditions while circling you are to turn immediately in the direction of the landing runway and execute the published missed approach procedure.

You should not descend below the circling MDA until you are in position to make a *normal descent* for landing. This does not mean that you must be on final before you descend, but when you consider that you are circling at an altitude much lower than a VFR pattern you may not be in a familiar position until you are on final. If you decide to follow your VFR habit and descend from a point opposite the threshold when you are only 400 feet up instead of normal pattern altitude, how high will you be when you turn final?

Circling to land when the weather is at or near minimums is not a good idea. Consider this hypothetical situation: it is dark, the turbulence is moderate, and the visibility is restricted by rain and fog; when you turn final there will be a strong, gusty crosswind from the right. You are flying a high-wing airplane and will circle using a normal left-hand pattern. As you begin the turn to base leg you know that a fairly steep bank angle will be required to avoid being blown too far away from the runway. Will you be in position to land when you roll out of the turn? Will you still be able to see the runway? All too often the answer to both questions is "no," and it's missed approach time.

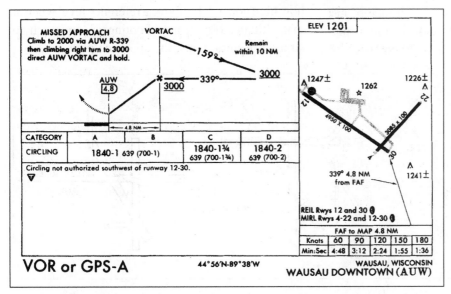

Figure 10-27. *Circling limitation*

Unless there is a restriction on the approach plate (Figure 10-27), you can circle to land using any maneuver of your choice, as long as you maintain an altitude at or above the published circling minimum altitude and stay within the airspace protected for your category of aircraft. Figure 10-28 shows several alternatives. At a controlled airport the tower may ask that you circle in a specific direction, and unless you have a valid objection, that is what you will have to do.

Practice Approaches

As a practical matter, a practice instrument approach is a VFR operation (see AIM 4-3-21); when you ask a controller for a practice approach, "Maintain VFR" will be part of the clearance. Procedures for practice approaches are promulgated at least annually by ATC facilities to all pilots in their regions by Letters to Airmen, and are probably thrown in the trash by most of them.

If you want to shoot some approaches to stay current or stay sharp and want to receive IFR separation services, file an IFR flight plan and either put "multiple approaches" in the remarks section, or tell the controller what you want to do. In this situation, do not use the words "practice approach."

"I've Got the Runway!"

When you approach an airport VFR, just about everything you need to know about that airport (except field elevation) is laid out before your eyes. As an instrument pilot, however, your first glimpse of a strange airport may be from an altitude of just 200 feet, and your pre-flight study of the airport environment will pay dividends. Where will the runway appear, and what markings should you expect? With any wind at all, you will see the runway through one side of the windscreen. If a circling approach is to be attempted, are there any restrictions? Is it safer to circle one way than another? If there are notes on the approach plate restricting maneuvering, why are they required? If your approach will be in darkness, what approach lighting system should you expect? To answer those questions, you need a sectional chart, the approach plate and airport diagram, and the A/FD or equivalent.

You probably thought that you were through with sectional charts, but they are a part of the thinking instrument pilot's equipment. That note that "Circling not authorized SE of runways 6 and 24" might be explained by the sectional's depiction of a bluff rising above the airport on the southeast side. You won't learn from an instrument chart that the airport lies in a valley or sits on top of a plateau (although Jeppesen is providing some terrain features on approach plates), or that it is located just northwest of a major freeway interchange. Sectional charts come in handy if you have to make an unplanned-for stop for fuel or passenger relief. It's embarrassing to have to ask Flight Service for information about an airport when you could have had that information in the cockpit. Don't assume that IFR flights require only IFR charts.

The minimums table on the approach chart tells you the minimum altitude above sea level to which you can descend during an approach, and it also tells you how high you will be above a reference level when at that altitude. If you are shooting an approach to straight-in minimums, the approach plate tells you

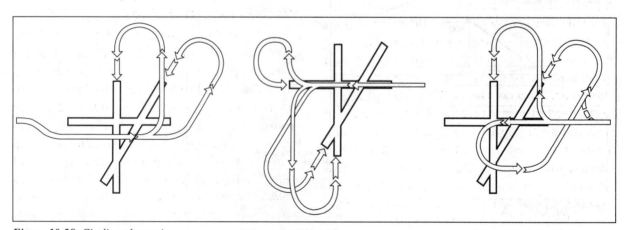

Figure 10-28. Circling alternatives

the height above the touchdown zone elevation (TDZE). The touchdown zone is the first 3,000 feet of runway, and its elevation is not always the same as the published airport elevation. This altitude is called HAT—height above touchdown—and it is shown on NACO plates immediately after the MDA/DH and visibility. In Figure 10-17 the circling HAT is 781 feet for all approach categories. Jeppesen puts HAT in parentheses in the same location.

If your approach has circling minimums only, or if the wind dictates that you circle to land, the minimum descent altitude is given as HAA—height above the airport. At Bremerton, WA (Figure 10-17), HAA is 741 feet. Flight at circling minimums guarantees you only 300 feet of clearance above obstructions, so check the airport diagram and sectional chart to see which direction is safest for circling.

Runway Markings

A runway used for precision instrument approaches is specially marked to help you land safely, as shown in Figure 10-29. The glide slope usually takes you to the fixed-distance markers, the two large rectangles of white paint (slippery when wet) 1,000 feet down the runway. Most light airplanes should be able to land between the touchdown zone markers and the fixed distance markers.

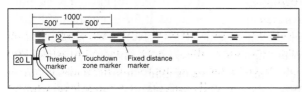

Figure 10-29. *Precision instrument runway*

A runway used for nonprecision approaches will have only threshold markings and a centerline (Figure 10-30) although fixed-distance markings are provided on runways 4,000 feet long or longer used by jet aircraft. Note the double hold line in the illustration; this is a Category II hold line which is to be observed whenever Category II operations are in progress on a runway used for precision approaches. If you taxi beyond these lines, your airplane may interfere with the ILS guidance system. As a practical matter, do you want to take off if the weather is so bad that CAT II procedures are in effect? How would you get back to the airport in an emergency?

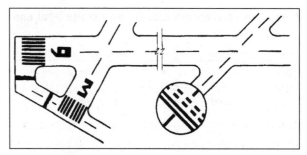

Figure 10-30. *Nonprecision instrument runway*

At night, and in conditions of poor visibility, the approach lighting system will guide you to a safe landing. The NACO airport diagram shows the type of system in use, and there is a description of each system on the inside back cover of the approach plate booklet. The airport diagram portion of a Jeppesen approach plate shows an accurate representation of the lighting system and the airway manual contains a color illustration of each system.

Almost all approach lighting systems include a wide bar comprised of white lights 1,000 feet from the threshold; 14 CFR 91.175 requires that you be at least 100 feet above the touchdown zone as you fly over that bar if you are relying solely on the approach lighting system for guidance to the runway. Check the approach plate for the existence of runway end identifier lights (REIL) and visual approach slope indicators (VASI). At some locations, the flashing REIL is the only thing that enables you to pick the airport out of a sea of background lights, and observing the VASI will ensure that you land on the runway surface. On a dark and rainy night it is all too easy to descend early and land short of the runway when no glide path information is available.

Visual Approach Aids

Figure 10-31 shows typical 2- and 3-bar visual approach slope indicator (VASI) installations found at many airports. With the 3-bar system, the center and most distant bar provide guidance for large aircraft, and the center and nearest bar provide guidance for small aircraft. In each case, an on-glidepath indication is red over white, a too-high indication is all white and a too-low indication is all red. As a pilot of a small airplane, then, you would look for two reds over one white to provide a 3° glide path to the runway. A slightly high or slightly low position is indicated when a white light shades toward red, and in some poor visibility conditions a white light can appear to be colored.

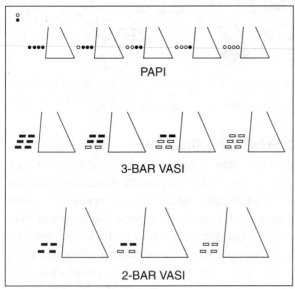

Figure 10-31. Visual descent aids

Figure 10-31 also shows the precision approach path indicator (PAPI) which the FAA has now designated as its standard visual approach system for new installations. The PAPI is designed to provide more accurate glide path information to the pilot. As is the case with the VASI, an all red presentation indicates that the airplane is below the glide path; the PAPI all red indication means that the airplane is beneath a 2.5° glide path. One white and three reds shows that the airplane is on a 2.8° glide path, slightly below the centerline. Two whites and two reds is the on-glidepath indication. If you are slightly above the centerline, descending on a 3.2° slope, you will see three whites and a red, and if your flight path is 3.5° or steeper you will see four white lights. The PAPI provides more accurate small-deviation information than the VASI.

Visual Illusions

Electronic and visual glideslope information is required because the human eye is easily fooled. Anyone who has flown over a sparsely settled area at night knows how easily the stars merge with the scattered lights on the ground, and many pilots have made abrupt maneuvers to avoid collision with the planet Saturn because a fixed source of light appears to move if you look at it long enough (autokinesis).

Take a moonless night, throw in some rain and a strange runway, and a normal landing might turn out to be anything but normal. Haze or mist will make a pilot think that the runway is farther away than it actually is, and a lower than normal approach is flown. A pilot who regularly flies into runways that are 150 feet wide will fly a high approach to a runway that is only 75 feet wide, trying to make the distance between the two rows of lights look "normal." On the other hand, if the runway slopes upward, away from the pilot, it will appear to the pilot that he is too high, and controlled flight into terrain short of the runway is a possibility.

Minimum descent altitude for most nonprecision approaches is 400 to 800 feet above the ground, and in the absence of visual aids a pilot who has ground contact at MDA should not begin descent until the threshold is visible (visibility minimums are never less than a mile). An altitude no lower than 50 feet AGL should be maintained until landing on the runway surface is assured.

General Airport Information

The remarks section of each airport listing in the Airport/Facility Directory is your best source of general information about the airport, such as the prevalence of birds in the vicinity, special local regulations, etc. Always check for current Notices to Airmen and be sure to ask if there are any published Flight Data Center (FDC) NOTAMs applicable to your flight; FDC NOTAMs include changes and amendments to instrument approach procedures. When NOTAMs are published in the bi-weekly Class II NOTAMs book, they are erased from the computer at the flight service station and the briefer may not be aware of their existence.

Airport Signs

It's dark, windy, and raining, and you have just landed at an airport you have never visited before. If it is a large, busy airport the surface is a sea of colored lights. You don't want to taxi onto or across an active runway in error, and the controller is still trying to figure out where you are. Asking for "progressive taxi instructions" will work once the controller has located your airplane, but if the airport's signage meets the requirements of Part 139 you should be able to figure things out on your own. The FAA has implemented standardization of signs marking taxiways, runways, intersections, etc.; Figure 10-32 shows the most important signs, and there is a complete explanation in the AIM.

Mandatory instruction signs have a red background with white letters or numbers; this includes runway holding position signs, runway numbers at the ends of runways and at intersections, ILS critical areas, and "NO ENTRY" signs where aircraft movement is prohibited.

If you were holding at an intersection of runway 15-33 you would see Figure 10-32A; the threshold for runway 15 is to the left and the threshold for runway 33 is to the right. Holding short of runway 33 at the threshold, you would see Figure 10-32B.

Figure 10-32C illustrates a sign for a taxiway that leads to the intersection of two runways. You would find Figure 10-32E at an intersection where taxiing takes you beneath the flight path of a landing runway but does not cross that runway. Figure 10-32D marks an ILS critical area; doing your runup in this area might affect the accuracy of the ILS. Figure 10-32F is the familiar "no entry" sign and might be located where aircraft might conflict with ground vehicles.

Location signs are black with yellow letters or numbers. An example would be a sign off to your right after you taxi into position and hold, confirming that you are on the correct runway. Similar signs are located along taxiways. If you were rolling down runway 15 on takeoff or after landing, Figure 10-32G would assure you that you were on the correct runway.

Black-on-yellow signs are directional, or Destination Signs—they point you toward the runway or taxiway you are looking for or tell you which way to go to get to the ramp, the cargo area, etc. The familiar hold line painted on the taxiway is mirrored by a black on yellow sign facing the runway as you taxi off. The ILS critical area marking on the taxiway is also mirrored by a "railroad track" sign adjacent to the ILS hold line.

Figure 10-32I would be alongside a taxiway leading to the departure end of both runway 27 and 33. At the intersection of two taxiways, Figure 10-32J says that runway 5 is to your left and runway 13 is straight ahead; and if you are looking for taxiway Alfa, Figure 10-32H points the way.

These are just a few of the signs you will encounter; read Chapter 2, Section 3 of the AIM for more details.

Closing Your Flight Plan

How are you going to close your flight plan? If you cancel in flight or land at a controlled airport, that will not be a problem. If you land at an uncontrolled airport, you may have to relay your landing time and cancellation through an FSS or by telephone. The A/FD listing will give you the information you need. You can use your cell phone once the wheels are on the ground.

Getting the Weather

You already know about getting the destination airport weather and runway in use from the ATIS or the controller, but how about a nontower airport with an automated weather reporting device such as an ASOS or AWOS? Yes, that is a legal weather report, and yes, you can make your decision on whether or not to proceed based on an automated report. AWOS and ASOS with broadcast capability are updated every minute, so before you get too involved in the approach itself, check the weather and advise the controller: "Cessna 1357X has the one-minute weather, request VOR runway 16 approach." The ATC controller might be several miles away, so you are in the best position to ascertain the validity of the automated report and advise ATC accordingly.

Microbursts and Wind Shear

The effects of localized thunderstorm activity belong in a discussion of the airport environment, because they have the greatest impact on flight operations close to the ground. You can usually see and avoid a thunderstorm cell when cruising on top of a cloud deck, but it is an entirely different situation when you are in or beneath clouds that hide one.

A. Runway Holding Position Sign

B. Holding Position Sign at beginning of takeoff runway

C. Holding Position Sign for a Taxiway that intersects the intersection of two runways

D. Holding Position Sign for ILS Critical Area

E. Holding Position Sign for a runway approach area

F. Sign Prohibiting Aircraft Entry into an area

G. Runway Location Sign

H. Direction Sign for runway exit

I. Destination Sign for common taxiing route to two runways

J. Destination Sign for different taxiing routes to two runways

K. Runway Distance Remaining Sign indicating 3,000 feet of runway remaining

Figure 10-32. Airport signs (from AIM ¶2-3-8)

Every thunderstorm contains downrushing currents of air, and when these downdrafts hit the ground they spread out in all directions. If they are sufficiently strong, they are called *microbursts* (*see* Figure 10-33). It is this "gust front" that creates problems when you are on final approach. If you are in a stabilized descent at a constant airspeed when you encounter the gust front, the airplane will pitch up and the indicated airspeed will increase (position 1 in the figure). Your natural reaction is to push the nose over and reduce power, but don't do it—recognize what is happening and get out of there. (Note that a rapid change in airspeed without a change in thrust is the first evidence of wind shear.) After you have passed through the area of outflowing air, you will enter the downdraft and encounter a tailwind (positions 3 and 4). Indicated airspeed and pitch angle will decrease and sink rate will increase; you will be low, slow, and underpowered. The best action at position 1 is to add climb power, pitch up to climb attitude, and execute a missed approach. Wait until the storm has moved away before trying again.

Expect your airplane to react similarly to any wind shear situation. If a tailwind component suddenly disappears and you enter an area of calm air, the airplane will pitch up and the indicated airspeed will increase just as if you had encountered a headwind. Similarly, if a headwind shears to calm or to a tailwind component, the airplane will pitch down and the indicated airspeed will decrease.

The best means of preventing wind shear problems is avoidance. Listening to the ATIS, querying Flight Watch, or pilot reports of wind shear should provide notice that thunderstorm activity is present at or near the airport, and you should seriously consider holding or diverting. When you are preparing for takeoff or landing and learn of thunderstorm activity, delay your operation until the threat has passed.

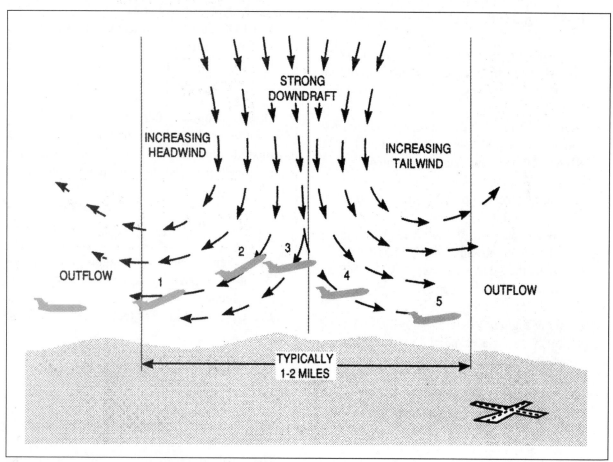

Figure 10-33. Microburst section chart

Chapter 10
Instrument Approaches Review Questions

Another all-instrument review section. Figures referenced in these questions start on the next page.

Instrument Student Questions

1. Assume this clearance is received:

   "CLEARED FOR ILS RUNWAY 07 LEFT APPROACH, SIDE-STEP TO RUNWAY 07 RIGHT."
   When would the pilot be expected to commence the side-step maneuver?

   A—As soon as possible after the runway environment is in sight.
   B—Any time after becoming aligned with the final approach course of Runway 07 left, and after passing the final approach fix.
   C—After reaching the circling minimums for Runway 07 right.

2. (Refer to Figure Q10-1.) Under which condition should the missed approach procedure for the RNAV RWY 33 approach be initiated?

   A—Immediately upon reaching the 5.0 DME from the FAF.
   B—When passage of the MAP waypoint is shown on the ambiguity indicator.
   C—After the MDA is reached and 1.8 DME fix from the MAP waypoint.

3. (Refer to Figure Q10-1.) What is the MDA and visibility criteria respectively for the S-33 approach procedure?

   A—1,240 feet MSL; 1 SM
   B—1,280 feet MSL; 1 and 1/4 SM
   C—1,300 feet MSL; 1 SM

4. (Refer to Figure Q10-1.) What is the minimum number of waypoints required for the complete RNAV RWY 33 approach procedure including the IAF's and missed approach procedure?

   A—One waypoint
   B—Two waypoints
   C—Three waypoints

5. How does a pilot determine if DME is available on an ILS/LOC?

   A—IAP indicates DME\TACAN channel in LOC frequency box.
   B—LOC\DME are indicated on en route low altitude frequency box.
   C—LOC\DME frequencies available in the *Aeronautical Information Manual.*

6. (Refer to Figure Q10-2.) At which indication or occurrence should you initiate the published missed approach procedure for the ILS RWY 6 approach provided the runway environment is not in sight?

   A—When reaching 374 feet MSL indicated altitude.
   B—When 3 minutes (at 90 knots groundspeed) have expired or reaching 374 feet MSL, whichever occurs first.
   C—Upon reaching 374 feet AGL.

7. (Refer to Figure Q10-3.) What are the restrictions regarding circle to land procedures for LDA RWY/GS 6 approach at Roanoke Regional?

   A—Circling to runway 24 not authorized.
   B—Circling not authorized NW of RWY 6-24.
   C—Visibility increased ½ mile for circling approach.

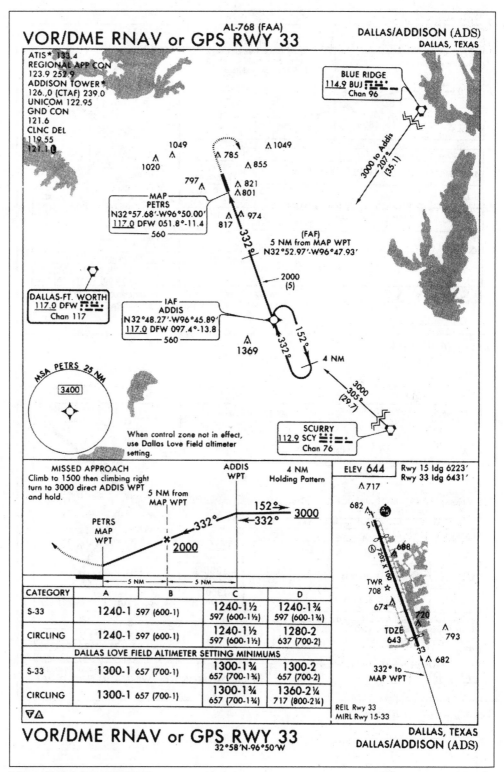

Figure Q10-1. RNAV RWY 33

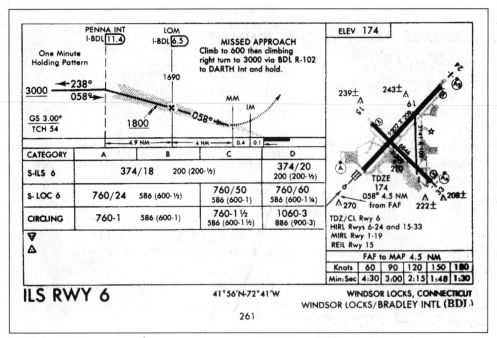

Figure Q10-2. *ILS RWY 6*

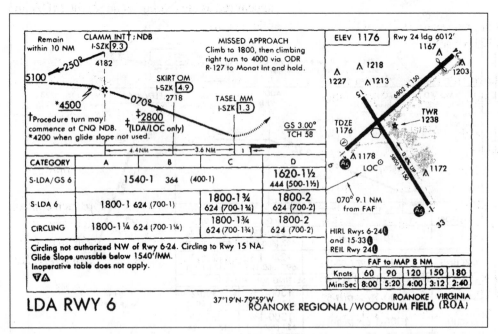

Figure Q10-3. *LDA RWY 6*

8. Immediately after passing the final approach fix inbound during an ILS approach in IFR conditions, the glide slope warning flag appears. The pilot is

A—permitted to continue the approach and descend to the DH.

B—permitted to continue the approach and descend to the localizer MDA.

C—required to immediately begin the prescribed missed approach procedure.

9. (Refer to Figure Q10-4.) If cleared for an S-LOC 17R approach at Lincoln Municipal from over TOUHY, it means the flight should

A—land straight in on runway 17R.

B—comply with straight-in landing minimums.

C—begin final approach without making a procedure turn.

10. What conditions are necessary before ATC can authorize a visual approach?

A—You must have the preceding aircraft in sight, and be able to remain in VFR weather conditions.

B—You must have the airport in sight or the preceding aircraft in sight, and be able to proceed to, and land in IFR conditions.

C—You must have the airport in sight or a preceding aircraft to be followed, and be able to proceed to the airport in VFR conditions.

11. If an early missed approach is initiated before reaching the MAP, the following procedure should be used unless otherwise cleared by ATC.

A—Proceed to the missed approach point at or above the MDA or DH before executing a turning maneuver.

B—Begin a climbing turn immediately and follow missed approach procedures.

C—Maintain altitude and continue past MAP for 1 minute or 1 mile, whichever occurs first.

12. Which of these facilities may be substituted for an MM during a complete ILS IAP?

A—Surveillance and precision radar.

B—Compass locator and precision radar.

C—A VOR/DME fix.

13. While flying a 3° glide slope, a constant tailwind shears to a calm wind. Which conditions should the pilot expect?

A—Airspeed and pitch attitude decrease and there is a tendency to go below glide slope.

B—Airspeed and pitch attitude increase and there is a tendency to go below glide slope.

C—Airspeed and pitch attitude increase and there is a tendency to go above glide slope.

14. If an approach is being made to a runway that has an operating 3-bar VASI and all the VASI lights appear red as the airplane reaches the MDA, the pilot should

A—start a climb to reach the proper glidepath.

B—continue at the same rate of descent if the runway is in sight.

C—level off momentarily to intercept the proper approach path.

15. Where may you use a surveillance approach?

A—At any airport that has an approach control.

B—At any airport which has radar service.

C—At airports for which civil radar instrument approach minimums have been published.

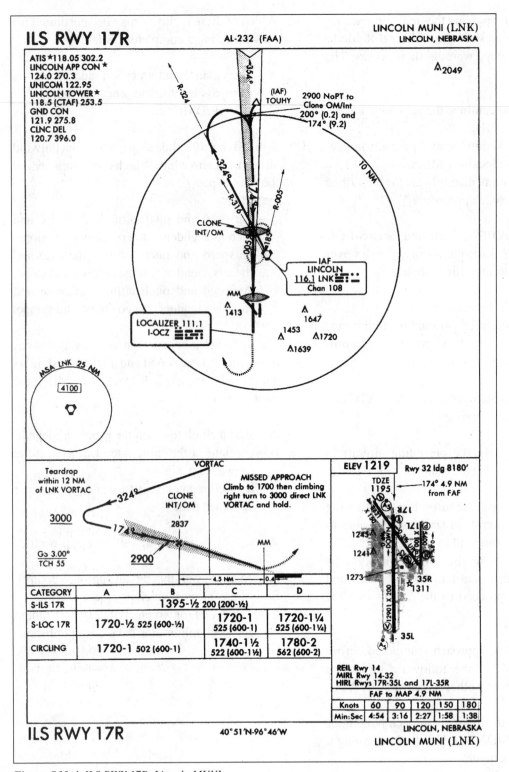

Figure Q10-4. *ILS RWY 17R, Lincoln MUNI*

Cockpit Organization and Procedures

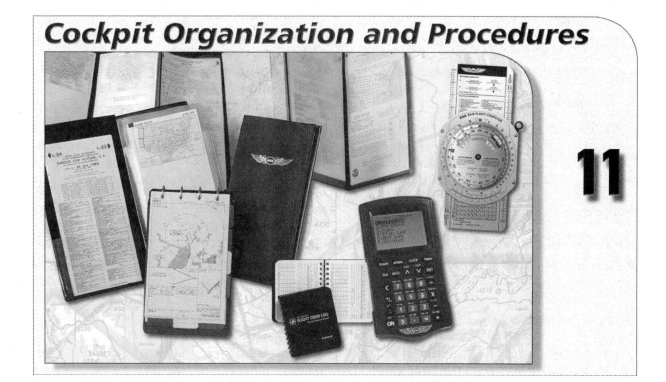

11

Getting Organized

The information in this chapter will be useful to both commercial and instrument students, although it is couched in instrument pilot terms.

Some things about instrument flying defy classification because they apply to all instrument flight and to all kinds of approaches. In this chapter we will discuss such subjects as cockpit organization, radio usage, and thought processes.

First, the hardware. You have spent enough time in pilot supply stores and have read enough catalogs to realize that there is a mini-industry dedicated to solving all your cockpit organization problems. There are kneeboards, clipboards, and yoke clips to ensure that the approach plate you are using is readily visible and that other plates are close at hand.

NACO approach plates are sold in a loose-leaf format or a bound booklet. The loose-leaf packet is four-hole punched, and a four-ring clamp is available, sold separately. The clamp is a bit unwieldy; a better solution is a four-ring binder, such as the one shown in the illustration above.

If you do use loose NACO plates or Jeppesen loose-leaf plates, inserting them in plastic sheet protectors will make them easier to handle—they won't blow off your lap. You can stick several plates in plastic protectors under your right thigh (you do fly from the left seat, don't you?) where they are readily available and won't fall on the floor unless you do a negative-G maneuver. This works best with Jepp plates, because the procedure identification is in the upper right hand corner. NACO puts the procedure identification in the upper and lower left corners, making the under-the-thigh method less practical (unless you are good at reading upside-down.)

Next in importance to keeping the charts from disappearing under the seat is having something to write with that will not hide when it is most critically needed. Hang a pencil around your neck, stick a couple of Velcro-wrapped pencils to a piece of Velcro attached to the sidewall, or buy a couple of self-adhesive ballpoint pens with retractable cords. There is no way you can have too many writing implements available. Try to locate your pencils or pens so that you can reach for them and replace them without looking.

You will need a scratch pad on which to copy clearances and make notes. Many instructors recommend that you lay out your scratch pad in columns headed HEADING, ALTITUDE, FREQ, and SQUAWK. As you receive new assignments, write them in the appropriate column and draw a line through the old assignment. The instructors who advocate this have seen too many students turn to a heading, change to an altitude, or select a transponder code which was written on the scratch pad but was not, unfortunately, the most recent heading, altitude, or squawk.

You don't have to write down everything that is said to you, however. Some instructors advocate using the rotatable azimuth on the ADF as a "scratch pad" for headings, and you can be setting up a new frequency on one radio while acknowledging the change on the other radio. Write down transponder codes, headings, or altitude changes which are to take place at a later time (after a missed approach, for example,) but if the change is to take effect immediately, just do it—don't waste time writing it down.

You absolutely must have some form of timer that can be read quickly and can be set and reset without distraction. There are a variety of panel mounted timers available, some built into ADF receivers; the clock with a sweep second hand has been pretty much replaced by digital devices. A sports-type stopwatch is an excellent timer and is easily mounted or can be hung around your neck on a lanyard. Your many-knobbed wristwatch is great *if* you can set it and reset it without being distracted from your primary duty of aircraft control.

A timer that can be pre-set for a final approach segment and counts down to zero before sounding an alarm is an excellent aid; you might not notice a count-up timer until too late. I have seen a "talking" timer with a computerized voice that counts down the seconds.

When you progress into airplanes with panel space to spare, many of your organizational tasks will be performed by a multifunction display (MFD). GPS receivers with moving map displays are no longer "gee whiz" items in the cockpit, and MFDs are capable of adding radar weather, navigational track, ground features, terrain and special use airspace warnings, and even ATC communications to the display panel. Some will even tune your communications and navigation radios for you. Your airplane's position and the track to your destination will be displayed on the moving map in color, and all you will have to do is stay on the magenta line. While you struggle with holding pattern entries and nonprecision approaches, consider that pilots using multifunction displays complain that they no longer feel challenged by IFR.

Anyone who flies at night without a flashlight should be sent to the funny farm; electrical systems do fail, but the airplane will continue to fly if you can see the instruments. The pilot supply industry has developed a number of methods of mounting lights so that you do not need to hold one in your mouth while trying to talk on the radio. What color flashlight? A red lens has the least effect on night adaptation but distorts colors on charts, so the use of red light should be restricted to those situations where optimum night vision is required; the AIM says that white lighting must be available when needed. There is some sentiment in favor of green light — ASA sells a flashlight with a blue-green lens. In any case, cockpit illumination should be at a minimum level of intensity to preserve as much night adaptation as possible.

You should have the following charts close at hand as you prepare for departure: the plate for the approach in use at your departure airport so that you have all of the frequencies available and can set your radios for a possible emergency return, any DPs that are likely to be assigned, and the area chart or low altitude enroute chart that covers your transition from the terminal environment to the enroute structure folded so that the area of interest is visible. Once en route, you can get out all the approach plates for your destination plus the area chart if there is one.

You can do a lot to prepare yourself for departure by checking with the tower or FSS to learn which departure is in use for your direction of flight. If you can call your local radar facility or Center without spending a fortune, you might call and ask the supervisor what routing would be most efficient for your flight. It's no fun to file a flight plan and have the Center computer reject it. When you copy your clearance, draw it on the area chart or low altitude chart so that the names of those obscure VORs and intersections that the controller wants you to fly over will be easier to understand. From the moment you line up on the runway and apply takeoff power, you should be able to break your IFR flight down into segments, each with a **H**eading, an **A**ltitude, and an appropriate air**S**peed. Each segment will have a **T**ermination point which is the beginning of the next segment, just like a parade of circus elephants following each other trunk to tail.

H-A-S-T is your memory aid, and its use will avoid those embarrassing situations where you find that you have forgotten to turn, descend, or have flown through a desired course. Consider this relatively simple clearance:

"Maintain runway heading, leaving 2,000 feet turn right direct Podunk radiobeacon, cross the beacon at or above 4,000 feet, thence outbound on the 180° bearing to intercept the Podunk 140° radial, climb and maintain 6,000 feet."

For the first segment, the heading is runway heading, the altitude is "climbing to 2,000 feet," the speed is best rate of climb, and the termination point is leaving 2,000 feet. The second segment heading is direct to the radio beacon, the altitude is "climbing to 4,000 feet," the airspeed is cruise climb, and the termination point is at the beacon.

At that point you enter the third segment, which is a heading to track outbound on the 180° bearing, an altitude of "climbing to 6,000 feet," cruise climb airspeed, and this segment terminates when the VOR needle centers, indicating that you have intercepted the 140° radial.

Although it may be difficult to believe in the hectic early days of your instrument training, there will be times during an IFR flight when absolutely nothing is happening. These are the times when you should run H-A-S-T through your head, and also to take time to review your radio panel to ensure that each radio is doing its best for you.

Another virtue of H-A-S-T is that it forces you to establish priorities. If the flight segment you are on terminates with the interception of a radial, don't let yourself become distracted by other cockpit duties when interception is imminent. Avoid performing cockpit duties such as tuning radios and making pre-landing checks when you are approaching a newly assigned altitude, preparing to roll out on a heading, or intercepting a course.

Modern digital radios give you the ability to store more than one frequency for recall when needed, so that when you shift frequencies the one you just left is still available if you can't raise anyone on the new frequency. *See* Figure 11-1. If your airplane has manually tuned radios and you shift from #1 to #2 and back, you should not change #1 radio from the old frequency to the next anticipated frequency until you are talking to ATC on the newly assigned frequency on the #2 radio.

A common communication error is failing to switch transmitters when handed off from one controller to another. You will hear pilots at all levels of experience make this mistake. You can eliminate it by using one radio for all ATC communications and reserving the other one for ATIS, UNICOM, etc.

Each navigation radio should also be set to provide the best information possible, and you should attempt to stay one frequency ahead of the controller if possible. When you are cleared "direct" to a navigational aid you should already have that aid tuned and

Figure 11-1. Typical communication transceiver

identified; if it is a non-directional beacon the needle will point toward the station, and if it is a VOR you should be keeping the needle centered so that you know what the course to the station is.

Most instrument pilots use the #1 omni for course guidance and use the second nav radio for off-course VORs to identify intersections. This practice can pay off some turbulent, rainy night, because if you switch back and forth between nav radios, you may select the wrong one when it really counts. The #2 can also be used to stay constantly aware of your position by keeping it tuned to an off-course VOR. With #1 on the airway and #2 centered, you should be able to put your finger on your location at any time.

When you are established on an approach and the #2 omni head is not needed to identify intersections, select the same frequency and radial that you have selected on the #1 radio. This is especially true of localizer frequencies. *Never* have both nav radios tuned to the same VOR frequency with one OBS set for the outbound radial and the other for the inbound radial. When those needles start moving in opposite directions, you will be momentarily uncertain which one to believe.

Selecting radials can take your attention away from the flight instruments if you don't think before you reach for the knob. For instance, if you know that you are southeast of the station you want to fly toward, it is wasted effort to rotate the OBS to 090° or 240°— reach up and rotate it to a generally northwest setting and you should be sufficiently close that the next time you look at the instrument (you haven't been looking at it all this time, have you?) you can turn the selector slightly right or left to center the needle.

Tuning radios can also be a distraction—but it need not be. You should be able to do most of the knob

twisting without looking, by counting the clicks as you rotate the tuning selector. An occasional glance should suffice to tell you if one click more or less would put the radio on the desired frequency. Looking at the radio during the entire tuning process will result in a change in heading, altitude, or both.

Familiarize yourself with the radios on the ground. Does clockwise rotation increase frequency? In steps of .2, .5, or 1? Will continuous rotation allow you to tune through 136.00 to 118.00 instead of going back? If it is a digital radio, can you select a frequency by turning the knob either clockwise or counter-clockwise?

Setting the transponder should be easy—it has only eight numbers. *See* Figure 11-2.

If one digit is presently on 6 and you want to change it to 1, it only takes three clicks forward instead of five clicks backward to do the job. Emergency transponder codes begin with 7, so don't dawdle when clicking through on your way to 1. Do not turn the transponder to STANDBY when changing codes— that practice, which is mentioned in some older texts, causes modern ATC radar to lose your signal while you are resetting the transponder and it may take several seconds to re-acquire your radar.

Be sure that the transponder is either OFF, in the STANDBY position, or set to code 1200 when you first get into the airplane. If the last person who used the airplane left it on an assigned code and ON, you will begin transmitting that code in error when you turn on the radio master switch. When you have received your IFR clearance with its assigned transponder code, leave the function switch in the STANDBY position until you are ready to turn onto the runway for takeoff.

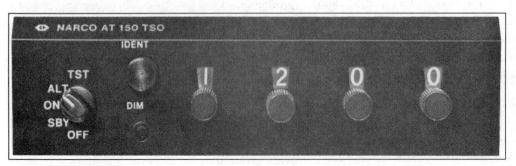

Figure 11-2. Transponder

Radar waves can take some funny bounces, and if the ATC radar somehow interrogates your transponder while you are still on the ramp or in the runup area it will generate a departure slip at the radar facility. You will know that you haven't taken off yet, but the controller will think that you are airborne. Worse, if the transponder is still on the code assigned on the last flight it might tell the ATC radar that United 456 has taken off because UAL 456 has that code today.

If your transponder is not working and you know it before takeoff, give ATC a one-hour advance warning to get a waiver.

Clearance Copying

The format for IFR clearances is fairly straightforward, and you can avoid being totally snowed under with a little advance planning. This is the format:

C Clearance limit. Usually, but not always, your destination airport or a navaid serving that airport.

R Route of flight. May include a DP "and then as filed" or just "cleared as filed."

A Altitude. A complex departure may involve cruise segments at several altitudes before you reach your filed altitude.

F Frequency. This may be departure control or Center.

T Transponder code.

With a little research, you might be able to anticipate just about all of the clearance except for the transponder squawk, and have your best guess written in this format. If what the controller gives you differs in some respect from what you expected, you need only ask for clarification of those portions, rather than subject yourself to the torrent that follows, "Say again all after ATC clears..."

It would be embarrassing to accept a clearance and then find out that one of your navigation radios necessary to carrying out that clearance is inaccurate or inoperative. You should make as many checks as practicable before calling for your clearance.

Checking the ADF receiver may be as simple as tuning and identifying two or more navaids within range of your position on the ramp and assuring yourself that the needle moves to point toward each

station. Most ADF receivers have a TEST function, which "parks" the ADF needle in a specific position on the dial. If the needle swings back to point at the station when the switch is returned to the ADF position, all is well.

If your airplane's VOR log shows that an accuracy test was made within the past 30 days you can legally accept that log entry as evidence that the VORs are ready for use. Wouldn't you feel safer if you made the check yourself, however, right now, before takeoff? The FAA provides several methods for you to use in checking VOR accuracy. Each volume of the Airport/Facility Directory contains a listing of VOR checkpoints in its area of geographic coverage; Figure 11-3 is a typical list.

If you are on the ground at the Amarillo, Texas International Airport and want to check your VOR receivers for accuracy, you should taxi to the east runup pad for runway 22, and when the airplane is in the painted circle you should tune the receiver to 117.2 MHz. The allowable error for this kind of check is plus or minus 4°, and the CDI on each VOR receiver should center with an OBS setting of 206° – 214° FROM or 026° – 034° TO.

You could check your VOR receivers at 1,100 feet over the grain elevator at Corpus Christi International; the allowable error for airborne checks is plus or minus 6°, so readings of 181° – 193° FROM would be acceptable.

The San Antonio International Airport has a VOR test facility (VOT); VOTs are listed after VOR checkpoints in the Airport/Facility Directory. All VOTs transmit just one radial: 360° FROM, and you should be able to check your receivers by tuning to 110.4 MHz from any point on the airport. Acceptable error is plus or minus 4°. This is a ground check only—some VOTs are approved for both air and ground checks; refer to the appropriate A/FD for details.

The FAA even provides for a "roll your own" type of airborne VOR accuracy test. To accomplish this type of test, select a prominent landmark on an airway and center the needle when you are over that landmark at a reasonably low altitude; your OBS should read within 6° of the published radial.

TEXAS

VOR RECEIVER CHECK POINTS

Facility Name (Arpt Name)	Freq/Ident	Type Check Pt. Gnd. AB/ALT	Azimuth from Fac. Mag	Dist. from Fac. NM	Check Point Description
Abilene	113.7/ABI	A/2800	047	10.5	Over silos in center of Ft. Phantom Lake
Alice (Alice International)	114.5/ALI	G	270	0.5	On twy N of hangar
Amarillo (Amarillo International)	117.2/AMA	G	210	4.5	On east runup pad rwy 22
Austin (Robert Mueller Muni)	114.6/AUS	G	118	0.6	On runup area on twy to rwy 31L
Beaumont (Jefferson County)	114.5/BPT	G	310	1.0	On runup area for rwy 12
Big Spring	114.3/BGS	A/3500	106	10.1	Over water tank in Coahama
College Station (Easterwood Field)	113.3/CLL	G	097	3.2	On W edge of parking ramp
Corpus Christi (Corpus Christi Intl)	115.5/CRP	A/1100	187	7.5	Over grain elevator
Corpus Christi (Sinton)	115.5/CRP	A/1100	318	9.5	Over rotating beacon on arpt.

VOR TEST FACILITIES (VOT)

Facility Name (Arpt Name)	Freq	Type VOT Facility
San Antonio International	110.4	G

Figure 11-3. Excerpt from Airport/Facility Directory

If you have two VOR receivers and both use the same antenna, you can check them against each other. Tune both receivers to the same station and select the same bearing on both radios. When the needles are centered, the OBS readings should not differ by more than 4°.

After every test of the VOR system you must log the date, place, type of test, the results of the test, and sign the entry.

Mandatory Reports

The FAA expects some reports from you without prompting from a controller; these reports might be required while you are en route or while you are in the terminal area. Part 91 of the Federal Aviation Regulations requires that you report if you encounter any unforecast weather conditions and anything affecting the safety of flight; 91.187 gets specific and requires a report if any of the following malfunctions occurs while you are IFR in controlled airspace:

1. Loss of VOR, ADF, or low frequency navigation capability.
2. Complete or partial loss of ILS receiver capability.
3. Impairment of air/ground communications capability.

Do not feel limited by this list. If you make ATC aware of anything that might require special han-

dling of your flight, the controllers can plan for you. Don't keep a low fuel situation or a failed vacuum system to yourself; you may limit the controller's ability to help you if you reveal the problem at the last moment.

These are mandatory reports at all times:

1. Vacating an assigned altitude for a newly assigned altitude.
2. Before changing altitudes when operating VFR-On-Top.
3. When you are unable to climb or descend at a rate of at least 500 feet per minute.
4. When you have missed an approach.
5. When your true airspeed varies from the airspeed filed in the flight plan by 5 percent or 10 knots, whichever is greater.
6. The time and altitude of reaching a holding fix or point to which you have been cleared.
7. When leaving any holding fix or point.

When you are not in radar contact, these reports are also mandatory:

1. Leaving the final approach fix inbound on final.
2. A corrected estimate whenever it becomes apparent that an estimate you have made will be in error in excess of 3 minutes.

Communication

Earlier in the book I stated that three essential elements of instrument flying were cross-check, interpretation, and airplane control. Three equally essential skills are understanding the ATC system, visualizing your position in space, and communicating.

Figure 11-4 illustrates a common situation: in the first two exchanges the controller recognizes that the person on the other end knows the importance of saying no more than what needs to be said, and treats that pilot as a professional no matter what his or her credentials might be. The third exchange, if it ever gets straightened out, makes the controller suspicious of the pilot's qualifications, and may result in additional transmissions to that pilot. It would be reasonable for the controller to assume that if the pilot can't communicate properly, there might be doubt about his or her ability to follow instructions. Because of this, the controller might ask this pilot to report reaching new altitudes, to report intercepting radials, or to make similar reports, so that the controller can "keep an eye on" the apparent novice, and pass the word along to other controllers.

You would be surprised how the handling of your flight by ATC is affected by your radio procedure. I do not mean strict adherence to the AIM—you will hear crusty old airline pilots fooling around on the airwaves—but radio transmissions that are concise and accurate.

A communications procedure drummed into your head by your primary instructor may cause some problems in a busy IFR environment: acknowledging every call from a controller. Assume that you are Mooney 75W in this scenario:

"United 340 heavy climb and maintain flight level 350.

"Mooney 75W turn left 100° and proceed on course. Navajo 12S say again your SQUEEEEEEEAL...67C cleared for the approach..."

You know where the squeal came from, don't you? It came when you said, "Roger, 75W, left to 100°" while the controller was still transmitting. This is a judgment call, because the AIM says that you must acknowledge headings and altitudes; however, if

doing so will disrupt communications with others you should think twice before keying the microphone. At some busy airports the controller does not want to hear from you at all.

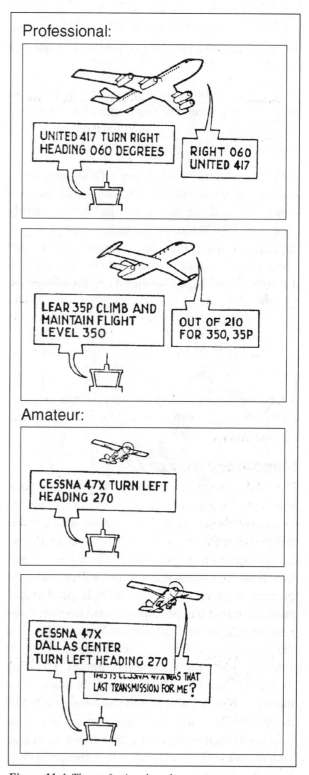

Figure 11-4. The professional vs. the amateur

Much coordination between controllers takes place behind the scenes, leading pilots to take up valuable air time giving controllers information they already have. For example, when your clearance is issued, a "flight strip" is generated at the tower, departure control facility, and Center which will handle your flight (even more facilities might be involved in a busy area).

This strip contains your airplane number, aircraft type and equipment suffix, destination, and final altitude; more data may be supplied if required. They know you are coming and where you are going.

Before one controller hands you off to another, he or she has communicated by telephone with the new controller, and the new controller has positively identified your return on the radar scope. Through this coordination, the new controller knows just about everything about your flight before you pick up the microphone, and you need not repeat any of it.

Figure 11-5. Radar controller

One thing that the new controller will not take for granted, however, is your altitude. If you have an encoding altimeter, the controller will ask you to say your altitude at the first contact. You can short-cut the system by saying to the new controller on your first call, "Fastwing 34X level at eight" or "Fastwing 34X five thousand climbing eight thousand." Although you won't find it in the *Aeronautical Information Manual*, virtually all instrument pilots flying below 18,000 feet report altitude using a decimal system: two point five for 2,500 feet, five point three for 5,300 feet, etc.

The FAA expects you to read changes in heading or altitude back to the controller for verification: "Whizzer 57M, turn left heading 030°" "Left to 030°, 57M." "Fleetwing 23J, turn right heading 090°, climb and maintain 6,000" "Right to 090°, out of 4,000 climbing 6,000, 23J." Controllers are human, and are subject to error. Suppose you are heading 210° and hear this: "Speedy 67R, turn right heading 150°." Would you meekly say, "Right to 150°, 67R," or would you say, "Verify right to 150°, the long way around, for 67R?" Chances are that you caught the controller in a momentary lapse, because when they want you to turn the long way around or to fly through the final approach course they will tell you so: "56T continue heading 100° through the localizer for spacing."

You can limit the length of your exchanges with controllers by reading the approach plate and using common sense. If the plate says that the approach control frequency is 120.4 and you think the Center controller said 126.4, the odds are that you are mistaken. Say "Confirm 120.4" and make sure he confirms it. If your position is southeast of the VOR and you think the controller said to turn to 030° instead of 300°, you are probably wrong again, but this time there is nothing specific on the approach plate. Just say, "Flybird 23 Sierra, say again the heading." Always ask for confirmation of any clearance that seems questionable.

You should also acknowledge approach clearances, which brings up a couple of special cases. When the controller says, "Cleared for the approach," you are to maintain the last assigned altitude until you are on a segment of a published instrument approach procedure (one of the heavy black lines on the plate), and you are to fly at the published altitude for each succeeding segment of the approach.

In a non-radar environment, where you are on your own, the clearance will be to an initial approach fix: "Cleared direct GOONI intersection, cleared for the VOR approach to runway 27 at Hometown Airport, cross the VOR outbound at or above 3,000 feet, contact Hometown Radio over the VOR inbound." This constitutes a clearance to leave your present altitude, fly direct to GOONI, and from that point onward to follow the headings and altitudes on the approach plate. You say, "Direct GOONI, cleared for the approach, out of 5 descending 3, 23 Quebec." You need not report every heading or altitude change after that because they are on the plate and you have acknowledged that you will follow the published procedure. Calling ATC (the FSS in this case) at the final approach fix is a mandatory report—you don't have to tell the controller that you are going to follow the regulations.

You get a special kind of approach clearance when you are in a radar environment and are being vectored to intercept the final approach course—it is not so much a transmission as it is a paragraph, and it almost always begins with a distance: "Fleetbird 1234 Mike, you are 5 miles from NOLLA, turn right heading 100°, intercept the localizer and proceed inbound, cleared for the ILS runway 13 approach, maintain at or above 2,200 feet until on the localizer, contact the tower 120.6 over NOLLA." If you try to remember all that and repeat it back, you will never make it. Weed out the items that are printed on the approach plate or are required by regulation and you will respond, "Right to 100°, cleared for the approach, tower at NOLLA, 34M."

The approach plate would show that the glideslope intercept altitude is 2,200 feet and that the tower frequency is 120.6. If you read back 2,300 feet or 121.6, valuable time would be lost while the controller got you straightened out, and you would probably fly through the localizer during the discussion. That brings up another point about approach clearance transmissions.

When the controller says, "You are 6 miles from GIZMO, turn left heading 260° to intercept—," start turning! The controller began that transmission when your radar echo was positioned so that a normal, standard rate turn to 260° would allow a smooth intercept of the final approach course. If you wait until the whole transmission is complete (or worse, until you have read it back), you will turn too late.

Expectation-of-Landing Syndrome

Expectation-of-landing syndrome is a malady common to instrument pilots. The symptoms develop when every approach ends with a landing, month after month, year after year. The victim soon begins to believe that missed approaches only happen to

other people, and on the fateful day when the weather is a bit worse than forecast, he or she descends blithely below minimums. You can imagine the rest of the story.

You can avoid expectation-of-landing syndrome by assuming that every instrument approach you initiate will be missed. You will have the radios properly set, the first missed approach heading and altitude in mind, and the airplane all ready for the inevitable pull up when the runway fails to appear on schedule. Of course, you will almost always be pleasantly surprised to see the runway in plenty of time to make a normal landing. If, however, the runway does not appear at the appointed time you will be ready.

This philosophy works equally well for multi-engine pilots, by the way. Be ready to lose an engine on every takeoff and maybe it will never happen.

Controllers are subject to expectation of landing syndrome, too.

They fully expect you to shoot the approach, land, and terminate your IFR activities for the day. Once they have issued an approach clearance and received an acknowledgment they pretty much forget about you. They do not expect you to suddenly pop back up on their frequency, declare a missed approach, and ask to be re-inserted into the landing sequence. You can avoid this problem by advising the controller well in advance if there is any possibility that you will miss the approach.

IFR Proficiency

The FAA says that before you can act as pilot-in-command under instrument flight rules, you must have flown six instrument approaches during the preceding six months and have practiced holding patterns and tracked navigational aids. All six approaches can be logged in an approved ground trainer. How about the mysterious workings of "the system," though? This currency regimen doesn't help a bit. If you let your currency lapse, you must take an instrument proficiency check (formerly instrument competency check) with an instrument instructor or examiner.

The other side of the coin is continuous currency: you fly regularly, taking the weather as it comes, and have to fly an approach three or four times a week. You work in the ATC system so much that talking to controllers becomes second nature. This is great: it is why you became instrument rated in the first place. Depending on where you operate, however, your IFR exposure may be limited to being vectored to ILS approaches with nothing out of the ordinary occurring, and your knowledge of holding, procedure turns, and nonprecision approaches may fade away without your realizing it.

To really feel good about your ability to absorb anything that might crop up on an IFR flight, you must make a conscious effort to remain proficient on instruments, not just current. This will require some time under a hood with a safety pilot and some time in a ground trainer, in addition to your regular flying.

Section 4-3-21 of the AIM contains instructions on the conduct of practice approaches.

Under the watchful eye of a safety pilot, you should work on precise airplane control while wearing some type of vision restricting device. Two exercises are especially helpful: horizontal S's and vertical S's.

To perform a horizontal S, stabilize on a heading (I'll use 360° as an example) and trim for straight and level flight. Select headings 60° either side of the airplane's nose—300° and 060° in this example. Your task is to make smooth level turns between these two headings while maintaining altitude and airspeed. Start with a bank angle of 10° and work up to a bank angle of 45°. Lead your rollouts so that you do not overshoot the target headings, and be ready to make elevator and throttle adjustments as the airplane rolls through wings level flight when reversing the direction of turn. Because induced drag increases as bank angle increases, expect to use more throttle movement to maintain airspeed as you bank more and more steeply. If you are feeling really sharp, try a horizontal S with 60° banks; you should never have to bank that steeply in normal IFR flight, but it's encouraging to know that you can do it without changing altitude or airspeed.

The vertical S has direct application to nonprecision approaches and missed approach procedures, and requires that you establish a given vertical speed and airspeed while climbing and descending.

To begin, stabilize the airplane in level flight at the speed you intend to maintain during the exercise. As you pitch up to climb attitude, the airspeed indicator is the primary pitch control, but when the vertical speed needle reaches the desired value the VSI becomes primary pitch while the airspeed indicator reverts to being the primary power instrument. As you approach the top of the climb, lead the reversal by 20 to 30 feet. The primary pitch instrument is that instrument with the indication you want to keep constant, so as you push over at the top of the climb the airspeed indicator becomes primary pitch and the power instrument(s) become primary power as you select the appropriate settings for the descent. Once again, as the VSI reaches the desired value it takes over as the primary pitch instrument. At the bottom of the S, lead the reversal by 40-60 feet—you have the force of gravity working against you and may overshoot the desired altitude.

When working on the vertical S you should use no more than two airspeeds. The manufacturer of your airplane gives you the best rate-of-climb speed, and that should be the speed you use immediately after takeoff and in the initial stages of a missed approach; use that airspeed for some vertical S's while maintaining rates of climb of 500 feet per minute and 700 feet per minute. For the second airspeed, select an approach speed that gives you good stability and control of the airplane in the landing configuration and practice vertical S's at that airspeed and at vertical speeds of 500 feet per minute to 1,000 feet per minute. When descending to the MDA on a nonprecision approach you need good airspeed control to make the time-to-MAP valid, while descending at a rate which will get you to the MDA before you reach the missed approach point. Before you and your safety pilot head back for the airport you should be able to climb and descend at a constant airspeed while nailing the VSI on a given value.

To give yourself a real workout, do some vertical S's combined with standard rate turns. A 500 feet per minute vertical rate and a standard rate turn should result in a 500-foot altitude change during every 180° turn; check both altitude and progress of the turn at the halfway points and make any changes that will result in the new altitude and new heading being reached simultaneously. Do not let your safety pilot get involved in grading your maneuvers—he or she should be looking out the window.

A good simulator instructor will be able to put you into situations not easily duplicated in the airplane. An enroute hold with an expect-further-clearance time followed by loss of two-way communications is an excellent example—it's pretty difficult for the ATC system to accommodate a practice lost communications situation. Your simulator operator should put you through the types of procedures with which you are least familiar; ADF approaches usually fall into that category. If you haven't been forced to execute a missed approach from minimums lately, the instructor should definitely include at least one during your training session.

You won't have to ask the simulator instructor to fail the gyroscopic instruments or the glide slope—those types of things happen with monotonous regularity during simulator training, and without the psychological crutch of having the failed instruments simply covered as is the case in flight. After all, when they fail in flight there will be no neat little device to cover the instruments and warn you of the failure, unless you carry some covers.

Don't confuse currency with proficiency. You can stay IFR current while your skills slowly deteriorate; long hours of simply flying straight and level in the clouds and being vectored to precision approaches may give you a false sense of competency. Staying proficient is your responsibility to yourself, your passengers, and to others who fly in the IFR system.

There are a number of excellent flight simulator programs for home computers. These programs allow you to fine-tune your understanding of navigation and approach procedures and in many cases you can adjust the weather conditions to duplicate almost anything. Up to ten hours of your training for the instrument rating can be logged in an FAA-approved computer-based simulator (called a PCATD) under the watchful eyes of an instrument instructor. You can continue to use these programs to stay sharp (notice that I didn't say "current") after you receive your instrument ticket, and you can do it solo. Don't log the time, though.

Proficiency in General

The behavioral scientists have identified "psychomotor response" as actual changes in brain activity as a result of training. For example, a non-pilot's reaction as an airplane descends is to pull back on the yoke to "hold the airplane up." You know that this will lead to a stall, and that the appropriate response is coordinated use of elevator and throttle, even if it is necessary to lower the nose to decrease angle of attack. As your instructor trained you in stalls and stall recovery, the correct response was "programmed" into your brain. Similarly, a multi-engine pilot must learn to respond with rudder, not aileron, when an engine fails. The muscles do the right thing without conscious thought because the brain has developed shortcuts.

When these skills are not used, the trained reactions (or psychomotor responses) atrophy and pilots revert to their untrained status no matter how many flight hours they have logged.

What I am trying to convey is that recurrent proficiency training is not just a way for flight instructors to make more money—you have to keep those brain-muscle connections fresh.

The Aviation Safety Reporting Program

The FAA has delegated to the National Aeronautics and Space Administration (NASA) responsibility for the Aviation Safety Reporting System (ASRS). Stick with me—this is important.

When you notice something wrong in your operating environment, like a VOR that doesn't work very well or a ditch between the taxiway and the gas pumps, the FAA wants to know about it so that corrections can be made. They want to know about all problems or potential problems, and to get the information the FAA is willing to grant waivers from prosecution to pilots or controllers who report unsafe conditions or operations. Advisory Circular 00-46 contains details about the program.

Reporting forms are available at FAA facilities. Get several and keep them in your flight bag. If you even suspect that you have done anything wrong such as busting an altitude assignment or violating an airspace restriction, file an ASRS form immediately (within ten days, anyway). NASA will tear off the part of the form containing your name and address and return it to you as a receipt; the form itself goes into the system with no identifying information on it. If you receive a letter from the FAA regarding the violation (based on information that they have developed on their own, such as a report from another pilot or an eyewitness), the fact that you have filed the ASRS report will get you off the hook unless they can prove that it was a willful violation. There is no way the ASRS information itself can be used against you.

Chapter 11
Cockpit Organization and Procedures Review Questions

Commercial students will not find any questions on their knowledge exam that are answered by information in this chapter. I have included for commercial students a question that is taken from the instrument rating knowledge test, however, because this information is critical to a commercial pilot.

Instrument Student Questions

1. To meet the minimum instrument experience requirements, within the last 6 calendar months you need

   A—six instrument approaches, holding procedures, and intercepting and tracking courses in the appropriate category of aircraft.
   B—six hours in the same category aircraft.
   C—six hours in the same category aircraft, and at least 3 of the 6 hours in actual IFR conditions.

2. After your recent IFR experience lapses, how much time do you have before you must pass an instrument proficiency check to act as pilot in command under IFR?

   A—6 months.
   B—90 days.
   C—12 months.

3. What minimum conditions are necessary for the instrument approaches required for IFR currency?

   A—The approaches may be made in an aircraft, approved instrument ground trainer, or any combination of these.
   B—At least three approaches must be made in the same category of aircraft to be flown.
   C—At least three approaches must be made in the same category and class of aircraft to be flown.

4. What response is expected when ATC issues an IFR clearance to pilots of airborne aircraft?

   A—Read back the entire clearance as required by regulation.
   B—Read back those parts containing altitude assignments or vectors and any part requiring verification.
   C—Read-back should be unsolicited and spontaneous to confirm that the pilot understands all instructions.

5. Which clearance items are always given in an abbreviated IFR departure clearance? (Assume radar environment.)

   A—Altitude, destination airport, and one or more fixes which identify the initial route of flight.
   B—Destination airport, altitude, and DP Name-Number-Transition, if appropriate.
   C—Clearance limit, and DP Name, Number, and/or Transition, if appropriate.

6. When making an airborne VOR check, what is the maximum allowable tolerance between the two indicators of a dual VOR system (units independent of each other except the antenna)?

   A—4° between the two indicated bearings of a VOR.
   B—Plus or minus 4° when set to identical radials of a VOR.
   C—6° between the two indicated radials of a VOR.

7. What record shall be made in the aircraft log or other permanent record by the pilot making the VOR operational check?

A—The date, place, bearing error, and signature.

B—The date, frequency of VOR or VOT, number of flight hours since last check, and signature.

C—The date, place, bearing error, aircraft total time, and signature.

8. How should the pilot make a VOR receiver check when the aircraft is located on the designated checkpoint on the airport surface?

A—Set the OBS on 180° plus or minus 4°; the CDI should center with a FROM indication.

B—Set the OBS on the designated radial. The CDI must center within plus or minus 4° of that radial with a FROM indication.

C—With the aircraft headed directly toward the VOR and the OBS set to 000°, the CDI should center within plus or minus 4° of that radial with a TO indication.

9. Which report should be made to ATC without a specific request when not in radar contact?

A—Entering instrument meteorological conditions.

B—When leaving final approach fix inbound on final approach.

C—Correcting an E.T.A. any time a previous E.T.A. is in error in excess of 2 minutes.

Commercial Student Question

10. What limitation is imposed on a newly certificated commercial airplane pilot if that person does not hold an instrument pilot rating?

A—The carrying of passengers or property for hire on cross-country flights at night is limited to a radius of 50 nautical miles (NM).

B—The carrying of passengers for hire on cross-country flights is limited to 50 NM for night flights, but not limited for day flights.

C—The carrying of passengers for hire on cross-country flights is limited to 50 NM and the carrying of passengers for hire at night is prohibited.

Regulations

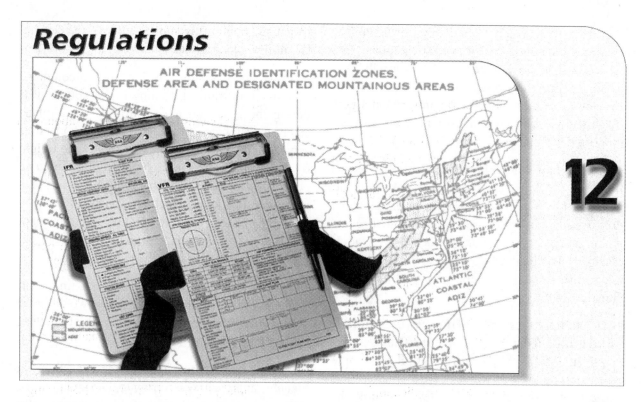

AIR DEFENSE IDENTIFICATION ZONES,
DEFENSE AREA AND DESIGNATED MOUNTAINOUS AREAS

12

This chapter will include information for both commercial and instrument operations. Both knowledge exams will include some very basic questions that go back to your private pilot days, and no trees will die to repeat that information here. As an instrument pilot you will be affected by sections of the Federal Aviation Regulations that you weren't even aware of as a VFR pilot, and in this chapter we will discuss only those regulations which are new to you or which might be of special interest to you when you have the ability to punch up through the clouds and fly in the sunshine. The last half of the chapter is devoted to regulations for commercial pilot operations.

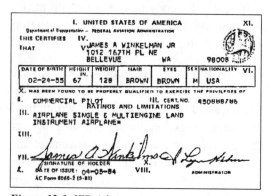

Figure 12-1. IFR ticket

Part 61

14 CFR 61.3: **Requirement for certificates, ratings, and authorizations.** You must hold an instrument rating to act as pilot-in-command under instrument flight rules or in weather conditions less than those required for VFR flight. Even in uncontrolled (Class G) airspace, you must hold an instrument rating if the flight visibility is less than one mile. But how about Special VFR? You have probably flown in weather worse than VFR with a Special VFR clearance. It is possible to fly in controlled airspace (Class E or higher) without an instrument rating when the weather is less than that required for VFR through use of Special VFR, so you can safely say that an IFR ticket is required to fly in the weather when the visibility is less than one mile. *See* Figure 12-1.

You must have an instrument rating to fly in Class A airspace, above 18,000 feet MSL, regardless of weather conditions, because all operations in Class A airspace must be under instrument flight rules.

Must you have an instrument rating to operate an airplane solely by reference to instruments? Of course not—you flew under the hood as a student pilot, didn't you?

As a VFR pilot, you have probably flown above a layer of clouds in excellent VFR conditions. The FAA calls that "VFR over the top." As you will learn when you get to the discussion of Part 91, "VFR-On-Top" is an operation under instrument flight rules, and you must hold an instrument rating to ask for VFR-On-Top.

14 CFR 61.15: Offenses involving alcohol or drugs. If you are convicted on a drug charge, or for a traffic violation for driving while under the influence of drugs or alcohol, you must make a written report within 60 days of conviction to the Civil Aviation Security Division in Oklahoma City. This will have a definite impact on your employability as a commercial pilot.

14 CFR 61.31: Type rating requirements, additional training, and authorization requirements. As a new instrument pilot or a new commercial pilot, you will be stepping up to more sophisticated flying machines. Two logbook endorsements are required (after the appropriate training, of course): A "high performance" endorsement is required if you are to act as PIC of an airplane that has *an engine* with more than 200 horsepower (total HP for a twin doesn't count). Pilots who have flown such an airplane before August 4, 1997 are grandfathered. A "complex" endorsement is required to act as PIC of an airplane with flaps, retractable landing gear, and a controllable pitch prop—but time in such an airplane is required for the commercial pilot certificate anyway. Note that you can *log* PIC time in these airplanes, but you cannot *act as PIC.*

14 CFR 61.51: Pilot logbooks. You may log as "instrument flight time" all time during which you control the airplane solely by reference to the instruments. As an instrument student, that will probably be the time you spend wearing a hood or using an approved ground training device and any time flown in actual instrument meteorological conditions (IMC).

There are other situations, however, which meet the definition of instrument time: flight in the clear on a moonless night with no visible horizon requires that you control the airplane solely by reference to instruments, as does flight between cloud layers or on top of all clouds if the natural horizon is not visible.

(There are opinions from the Office of the General Counsel supporting that statement.)

Note that two persons can log pilot-in-command time on an instrument training flight: you are PIC during the time you are controlling the airplane solely by reference to the instruments (hooded or actual), and your instructor, who carries the weight of responsibility for the flight. Of course, only one person can *act* as PIC, and that is the instructor. This is the sole situation in which you can log PIC time *in instrument weather* before you take the instrument checkride, unless you fly with an instrument-current pilot who agrees to *act* as PIC during the flight.

Do not confuse *logging* of instrument time with *acting* as pilot-in-command. They are two different things, although in most situations the pilot acting as PIC will log the time.

Also, make no attempt to learn what constitutes a loggable approach by referring to the regulations or AIM—no such guidance exists. It is generally accepted that any approach during which instrument conditions are encountered is loggable, even if the encounter is temporary.

14 CFR 61.53: Operation during medical deficiency. Operation during medical deficiency. This regulation catches a lot of pilots who think that just because their medical certificate has not expired, they can continue to fly with a medical problem until it does expire. The fact is that as soon as you are diagnosed with any illness or notice any physical problem that would keep you from passing a physical exam, your medical is invalid. You simply cannot fly with a physical deficiency just because you have a piece of paper saying that you were physically fit at the time of the exam.

14 CFR 61.57: Recent flight experience. To act as pilot-in-command or to fly in weather conditions less than those required for VFR, you must, within the 6 calendar months preceding the date of the proposed flight, have performed at least 6 instrument approaches, practiced holding procedures (or have entered holding as a result of an ATC clearance), and have intercepted and tracked courses through the use of navigation systems in the appropriate category of aircraft for the instrument privileges sought. That last provision is pretty open-ended. Does tracking a localizer during an approach count? It would be in your best interest to make your logbook entries specific as to exactly what you did during an instrument flight or practice session. You are not required to fly in actual IFR weather conditions. All six of the approaches can be performed in an FAA-approved simulator or ground training device and must be signed off by an instructor.

A logbook entry for simulated instrument time (under the hood) must include the place and type of instrument approaches completed and the name of the safety pilot. The safety pilot must be appropriately rated and current in the aircraft flown; if the flight enters instrument meteorological conditions the safety pilot must be instrument rated and current on instruments.

If you allow your instrument currency to lapse, you have a six month period during which you can regain current status by accumulating the required experience and approaches with a CFII or appropriately rated safety pilot, or by taking an instrument competency check from an FAA inspector or an instrument flight instructor. After the expiration of the six-month period you must take an instrument competency check that will make you current for another six months. All or part of the instrument competency check may be performed in a flight training device approved by your local Flight Standards District Office.

The FAA has approved the use of personal computer-based aviation training devices (PCATDs) for credit toward the instrument rating, but only under very strict conditions laid out in Advisory Circular 61-126. These devices are still not approved for meeting the currency requirements, although they are excellent for maintaining proficiency.

14 CFR 61.133: **Aeronautical experience.** A commercial pilot who does not hold an instrument rating is prohibited from carrying passengers for hire at night or on cross country flights of more than 50 nautical miles. Expect a "VFR Only" endorsement on your commercial pilot certificate until you receive the instrument rating.

Part 91

14 CFR 91.117: **Aircraft speed.** Generally, indicated airspeed below 10,000 feet MSL is limited to 250 knots. If you are within 4 nautical miles of the primary airport in Class C or D airspace and are flying at or below 2,500 feet above the airport elevation, your indicated airspeed must not exceed 200 knots—the same limit applies where there is a VFR corridor through Class B airspace.

14 CFR 91.167: **Fuel requirements for flight in IFR conditions.** When operating in IFR conditions, you must have enough fuel on board to fly to your destination, and from there to your alternate (if an alternate is required), plus 45 minutes fuel at normal cruising speed. Don't forget that you might be vectored or delayed at your destination, and carry plenty of fuel. The only time you can have too much fuel is when the airplane is on fire. Do not hesitate to declare "minimum fuel" to ATC if it looks as though you are going to eat into your reserve fuel—declare an emergency if you have to. Don't wait until you have less than 45 minutes fuel on board; the regulation states that you cannot operate the aircraft in IFR conditions without the required reserves on board.

You are not required to file an alternate airport if, for a period of ONE hour before to ONE hour after your estimated time of arrival at your destination airport, weather reports or forecasts indicate that the ceiling at your destination will be at least TWO thousand feet above the airport elevation and that the visibility will be at least THREE miles. This is called the "1-2-3 rule," for obvious reasons. If you will be shooting a GPS approach at your destination, the alternate must have a ground-based approach (ILS, VOR, NDB).

14 CFR 91.215: **ATC transponder and altitude reporting equipment and use.** You must have an altitude-reporting transponder (Mode C) if you operate in controlled airspace above 10,000 feet MSL, in or over Class C airspace or within 30 miles of a Class B airspace airport. The regulation makes an exception for those pilots who may be above 10,000 feet MSL but who are within 2,500 feet of the surface.

14 CFR 91.211: **Supplemental oxygen.** Use of supplemental oxygen. Your new instrument rating may take you to oxygen altitudes, so you should review the oxygen regulations. (*See* Figure 12-2.)

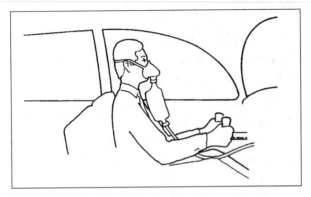

Figure 12-2. Stay sharp–use oxygen

At cabin pressure altitudes between 12,500 feet MSL and 14,000 feet MSL, you must use supplemental oxygen for the duration of time at those altitudes which exceeds 30 minutes.

At cabin pressure altitudes above 14,000 feet MSL, you must use supplemental oxygen continuously.

Above a cabin pressure altitude of 15,000 feet MSL, passengers must also be provided with supplemental oxygen.

(For unpressurized airplanes, the cabin pressure altitude is the same as the indicated altitude.)

14 CFR 91.205: **Instrument and equipment requirements.** For IFR flight, your airplane must have all the equipment and instrumentation required for VFR flight, plus:

- Two-way radio communication system and navigational equipment appropriate to the ground facilities to be used.

- Gyroscopic rate of turn indicator (needle or turn coordinator) and a slip-skid indicator (or ball). These are usually combined in one instrument.

- Sensitive altimeter, adjustable for barometric pressure.

- A clock with a sweep second hand or digital presentation.

- Gyroscopic attitude indicator.

- Gyroscopic heading indicator.

- Distance measuring equipment is required if you plan to fly at or above 24,000 feet MSL and to use VOR airways.

- A generator of sufficient capacity to operate all required equipment.

14 CFR 91.121: **Altimeter settings.** When operating above Flight Level 180 (18,000 feet MSL), your altimeter must be set to 29.92 inches; you should have a descent checklist item to ensure that it is re-set to the local altimeter setting when you descend through 18,000 feet. *See* Figure 12-3.

If you are planning an IFR flight when the local barometric pressure is below 29.91 inches and intend to fly above 18,000 feet, you will run up against the "lowest usable flight level" provisions of this regulation. For instance, if the local altimeter setting is 28.92" through 29.41", you will not be assigned an altitude below 19,000 feet to avoid conflict with aircraft using the local altimeter setting while you are using 29.92".

14 CFR 91.173: **ATC clearance and flight plan required.** No person may operate an aircraft under IFR in controlled airspace unless an IFR flight plan has been filed and an IFR clearance received. Note that you must have an instrument rating to fly in IMC in uncontrolled (Class G) airspace but you need not

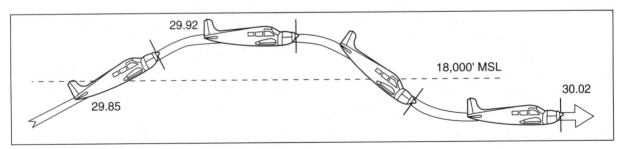

Figure 12-3. Set your altimeter to 29.92 above 18,000 feet MSL

have a clearance. Clearances are required only in controlled airspace (everything except Class G). If you decide to fly IFR in uncontrolled airspace, however, consider that there might be another adventurous soul just a few feet away in the same cloud— and ATC can't help either one of you.

14 CFR 91.175: **Takeoff and landing under IFR.**

When flying an instrument approach, you cannot descend below the minimum descent altitude or *continue* below the decision height, unless at least one of the following visual clues is visible and identifiable:

(1) The approach light system, except that you may not descend below 100 feet above the touchdown zone using the approach lights as a reference unless the red terminating bars or the red side row bars are clearly visible. These red light bars are 1,000 feet before the threshold.

(2) The threshold.

(3) The threshold markings.

(4) The threshold lights.

(5) The runway end identifier lights (REIL).

(6) The visual approach slope indicator.

(7) The touchdown zone or touchdown zone markings.

(8) The touchdown zone lights.

(9) The runway or runway markings.

(10) The runway lights.

The last two items seem to give you the authority to land well down the runway; however, air carriers and air taxis must land in the first 1,500 feet of the runway. Isn't that a good practice for you to follow?

14 CFR 91.177: **Minimum altitudes for IFR operations.**

You must always observe the minimum applicable IFR altitude, but if none is published you must maintain an altitude at least 1,000 feet above the highest obstacle within 5 statute miles of the course to be flown (2,000 feet in mountainous areas). These provisions will apply when you are flying "random routes" using area navigation or LORAN (no domestic enroute flight using GPS unless the equipment meets TSO C-129). *See* Figure 12-4.

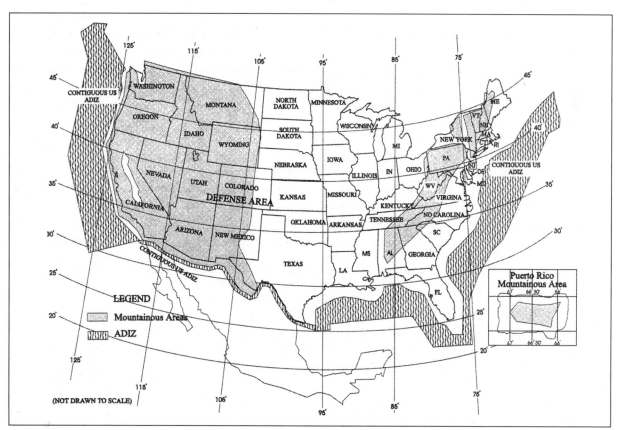

Figure 12-4. Mountainous areas

If both a minimum enroute altitude (MEA) and a minimum obstacle clearance altitude (MOCA) are published and your clearance permits, you may descend from the MEA to the MOCA when you are within 25 statute miles (22 nautical miles) of the VOR concerned.

If you are approaching an intersection beyond which a higher altitude applies, you must start your climb immediately after passing the intersection. If high terrain intervenes, a minimum crossing altitude (MCA) will be published for that intersection, and you must climb to cross the intersection at or above the MCA.

14 CFR 91.179: **IFR cruising altitude or flight level.** When flying IFR you must fly along the centerline of the airway or, if flying off-airways, along the direct route between the fixes defining the off-airway route.

14 CFR 91.183: **IFR radio communications.** You must maintain a continuous listening watch on the appropriate frequency when flying IFR in controlled airspace, and you must report to ATC the time and altitude at which you cross designated reporting points. If you are in radar contact, you need report only those points that ATC specifically requests. You are also required to report unforecast weather conditions and any other information relating to the safety of flight. NOTE: If you encounter icing conditions, don't keep it to yourself; other pilots

need that information and the FAA does not base enforcement action on pilot reports. If you make an icing PIREP you will help the National Weather Service improve its forecasting abilities.

14 CFR 91.209: **Aircraft lights.** Position lights and the anti-collision system must be turned on between sunset and sunrise.

14 CFR 91.411 and 91.413: **Altimeter/transponder tests and inspections.** You cannot file IFR unless your altimeter, static system, and transponder have been tested and inspected within the preceding 24 calendar months. Checking to ensure that these checks have been performed is your responsibility as pilot-in-command. Check the airplane maintenance log-books before you file. Be sure that these checks are current for the airplane in which you take the checkride.

Airspace Review

While you are flying on an IFR clearance and in instrument meteorological conditions, you can almost forget about airspace rules; there is no need to worry about how close the clouds are or how poor the visibility is, and the ATC system is designed to ensure that separation from other IFR traffic is maintained. Restricted areas, Class B, C, or D airspace— why worry? The controller will smooth your path, and you need never know that you have crossed any invisible airspace boundaries.

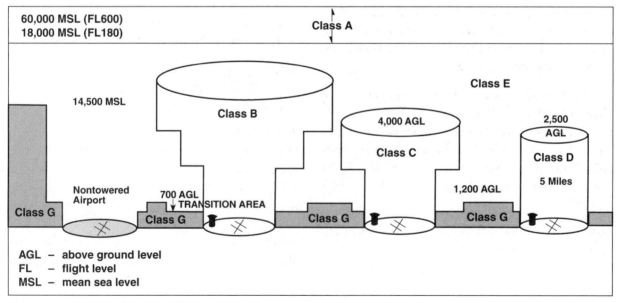

Figure 12-5. Airspace classification

When the weather is not solid IFR, however, it is a different story. When you are rated to fly in the clouds you will exert every effort to stay out of them, and "What are the tops?" will become your favorite question. When you are not actually immersed in the murk, you will be sharing the airspace with VFR pilots who may not be as good at estimating cloud distance and visibility as you are, and you will have to be doubly alert. That is why you need to know which regulations apply to the airspace that you are in. *See* Figure 12-5.

Controlled Airspace (Classes A, B, C, D, and E)

Class A airspace extends from 18,000 feet (Flight Level 180) up to Flight Level 600. Every aircraft in Class A airspace must be on an instrument flight plan and every pilot must have an instrument rating, even if the weather is "severe clear."

Class B airspace exists around major airports; a clearance is required before entry when operating under visual flight rules. VFR pilots in Class B airspace must have 3 miles flight visibility and remain clear of clouds. A transponder with Mode C is required when operating within 30 nautical miles of the primary airport from the surface to 10,000 feet MSL. (Remember that if your transponder is inoperative you can ask for a waiver one hour in advance of entering Class B airspace.)

Note for commercial students: When operating under VFR, always assume that you will be unable to get an expeditious clearance into Class B airspace and be ready to do a 360 well outside of its boundaries (at least one mile). Do not penetrate Class B airspace while waiting for clearance.

Class C airspace requires two-way communication with ATC before entry. Required VFR flight visibility is 3 miles, cloud clearance requirements are 1,000 feet above, 500 feet below, and 2,000 feet horizontally. A transponder with Mode C is required in Class C airspace and in the column of air above it to 10,000 feet MSL.

Instrument pilots on IFR flight plans are not affected by any of these restrictions.

At airports with an operating tower, Class D airspace begins at the surface and extends upward to 2,500 feet AGL or as charted, and Class E begins where Class D ends. You must be in contact with the tower to operate in Class D airspace, whether you are landing, taking off, or just passing through. If you are on an IFR flight plan and your assigned heading and altitude will take you into Class D airspace, the ATC controller handling your flight will take care of coordination with the tower.

Controlled airspace (Class E) extends all the way to the surface at some airports with an instrument approach and no control tower in operation; this is depicted by a magenta dashed line around the airspace on a sectional chart. At some airports which have an instrument approach but no control tower, the airspace above the area depicted on the chart with magenta tint is uncontrolled (Class G) from the surface to 700 feet AGL and controlled (Class E) above that. Everywhere else, Class E airspace has a floor at 700 feet, at 1,200 feet, or at an altitude above mean sea level indicated on navigational charts, or 14,500 feet MSL. For aircraft operating in controlled airspace (Class C, D, or E) under VFR at an altitude less than 10,000 feet MSL, cloud clearance requirements are 1,000 feet above the clouds, 500 feet below them, and a distance of 2,000 feet horizontally. Required flight visibility is 3 statute miles.

If everyone is playing by the rules, then, when you pop up out of the clouds there should be no VFR aircraft within 1,000 feet of the cloud tops, and when you descend below the clouds there should be no VFR aircraft within 500 feet of the cloud bases.

When you penetrate isolated clouds there should be no VFR aircraft lurking within 2,000 feet on the other side (that's 10 seconds at 120 knots).

Transition Area

Controlled airspace exists to protect IFR flights from takeoff to landing. When the floor of Class E airspace is 1,200 feet while en route, some provision has to be made in order to protect the flight as it descends out of 1,200 feet toward the destination airport. You will see this "transition area" depicted on enroute low-altitude charts (and sectionals) as a dashed magenta line where it extends to the surface. The floor of a transition area is at 700 feet within the magenta shading, creating a sort of step-down in the floor of Class E airspace from 1,200 feet to 700 feet, and then to the surface in Class G airspace. The top of a transition area is where it joins the overlying controlled airspace.

Uncontrolled Airspace (Class G)

The airspace between the surface and 700 feet at airports that have an instrument approach but no weather observer and between the surface and 1,200 feet elsewhere is uncontrolled airspace (Class G). As an instrument pilot, you will not be flying that low except during departures and approaches. In Class G airspace less than 1,200 feet (700 feet in transition areas), a VFR pilot only needs to stay clear of the clouds and to have one mile flight visibility to be legal in the daytime (three miles visibility at night). If you are flying an instrument approach to an airport without Class E airspace to the surface, you may find yourself in conflict with a VFR flight operating legally beneath the clouds. In this situation it is wise to announce your position and intentions on the Common Traffic Advisory Frequency for that airport as recommended in the AIM and listed in the A/FD. The fact that you are on an instrument clearance and have been cleared for the approach gives you no special rights once you have broken into VFR conditions. The ATC system has no responsibility for your safety when you are in Class G airspace—you are on your own insofar as separation from other aircraft is concerned.

As stated earlier, your greatest exposure to Class G airspace will be during approaches and departures, and that will only happen at airports without a weather observer or local altimeter setting. There are many such airports, and at those airports you will fly into Class G airspace as you descend within 1,200 feet or 700 feet of the ground, depending on the overlying control area. This situation is not fully understood by the average pilot, VFR or IFR, so be extra careful.

Regulations for the Commercial Pilot

The Commercial Pilot Knowledge Exam is heavy on regulations unrelated to instrument flight, so they will be discussed separately.

Requirements

The requirements for the commercial pilot certificate were revised in August, 1997. The minimum flight time under Part 61 is 250 hours, and the cross-country requirements include a dual instruction day VFR trip of at least two hours with a landing at an airport 100 nautical miles from the point of departure. The applicant must also fly an identical night VFR dual flight. You must also have logged 50 hours of PIC cross-country time, and in this context "cross-country" means a landing at an airport more than 50 nautical miles from the original departure point. Note that the word "leg" is not used in this regulation; if you want to fly a round-robin trip with legs of 40 NM each, that's just fine—as long as one of the landings is at an airport more than 50 straight-line miles from your point of departure on the trip. Military pilots who can substantiate an "out-and-back" flight without a landing are exempt from the landing requirement.

The long cross-country trip is not less than 300 nautical miles total, with landings at a minimum of three points, one of which is at least 250 straight-line miles from the departure airport—and this is *solo* time: No spouse, no kids, no pilot buddies. (The regulation in effect before August 1997 called for the long trip to be as PIC.)

In addition to the long dual cross-country at night, you must have logged at least five hours of night solo time with ten takeoffs and landings at an airport with an operating control tower.

The required ten hours of training and practice in an airplane with a controllable pitch propeller, flaps, and retractable landing gear is all dual time.

What Can a Commercial Pilot Do?

There are no airports set aside for the use of commercial pilots, and no airspace segment is the exclusive province of the commercial pilot; airplanes react to a commercial pilot's control inputs just as they do when a private pilot moves the yoke. What, then, marks the difference between private pilots and those who hold commercial certificates? The answer is: regulations. The Federal Aviation Regulations expect adherence to higher standards when pilots get paid for flying, and those higher standards are laid out in Parts 91, 119, 121, 125, and 135. That's

Figure 12-6. Commercial pilot flying

why a review of the regulations as they apply to for-hire operations comes first. Part 119 governs the operation of air taxi *companies*, so that is where the exemptions are found. Part 135 contains the operating rules.

Ask most commercial pilot aspirants what they will do when they get their ticket and you will hear "Fly charters," or "Fly for an air taxi outfit." Wrong. It's a common misunderstanding, based on reading those private pilot exam questions about it being illegal to fly for compensation or hire without a commercial certificate. Anyone desiring to operate an aircraft as an air carrier or commercial operator must comply with Part 119 and obtain an Air Taxi or Commercial Operator (ATCO) certificate.

There are a few exemptions: Part 119 does not cover student instruction, nonstop sightseeing flights within 25 statute miles of the airport of takeoff, ferry or training flights, aerial work operations such as banner towing, crop dusting, or firefighting, or carrying parachutists (within 25 statute miles of the takeoff airport). Read Part 119 for full details.

A pilot with nothing more than a commercial certificate can fly in any of the capacities listed above—but

how about a flight of less than 25 SM with an enroute stop, or a flight of more than 25 SM, period? The pilot of those flights would have to be qualified under Part 135. There is another bump in the road for the prospective air taxi pilot—the drug testing program. Although Part 119 exempts local sightseeing flights, Part 135 contains a special provision covering such flights for the specific purpose of bringing the pilots into the drug testing program. An "occasional" sightseeing flight is OK, but advertising sightseeing flights or having a regular program such as dinner flights is a red flag to the FAA.

Figure 12-7. Aerial photography and mapping are not Part 135 operations, so this is an option once you have commercial ticket in hand.

What *can* you do with your brand new ticket? Follow the lead of thousands of pilots before you and become a flight instructor, for one thing, but that is certainly not the only avenue available. Look at the list of exemptions in 119.1 again: Agricultural work is a fulfilling career in itself, one that can take you across the country with the seasons; banner towing and aerial photography bring new challenges every day; you will cram a lot of takeoffs and landings into each day that you fly parachute jumpers; and pipeline or powerline patrolling means logging many hours of low altitude flight. With a commercial certificate and a multiengine class rating you can get into the right seat of a borate bomber or similar fire-fighting craft—and that's heavy airplane time.

Flying a corporate turboprop might be a long-term goal, but there are plenty of corporations whose fleets consist of one or more single engine airplanes. In the left seat of Amalgamated Blivet's Bonanza, Centurion, or Saratoga you aren't carrying passengers for hire—you are a company employee whose duties include transporting fellow employees. Choose the right company and you might find yourself flying across the continent just like an airline pilot, only lower and slower.

If you live in a part of the country where gliders and sailplanes probe the skies for lift, you can build time by flying the tow plane. No instrument rating or other special qualification is required, except that your logbook must contain an endorsement by a certified glider instructor to the effect that you have received flight and ground instruction in gliders and that you are familiar with the techniques and procedures essential to the safe towing of gliders.

Many commercial operations require that the airplane be modified in some way that changes its certification status—this might be something as simple as removing a door for aerial photography or parachute jumping. The Approved Flight Manual should contain data on this type of change. You should never do anything on your own that might change an airplane's certification status—check with the FAA. Your insurance agent will be grateful.

Many Normal category airplanes can be operated in the Utility category if certain weight limits are observed and maneuvers are limited to those approved in the Flight Manual. You can carry passengers for hire in such airplanes, but you cannot carry paying passengers if the airplane's certification is Experimental, Restricted, Limited, or Primary.

Instrument Restriction

If you don't have an instrument rating and are operating as a commercial pilot outside of Part 135—as a corporate pilot, for example—remember that your commercial certificate will be endorsed "Carriage of passengers for hire on cross-country flights of more than 50 nautical miles or at night prohibited." An excellent reason to have an instrument rating.

Flight Instructor or Time Builder?

I mentioned earlier that most pilots view a flight instructor's certificate as the quickest and best way to gain experience and hours. Don't take this route unless you feel that you can take your responsibilities seriously. It doesn't take very long for a student to realize that the instructor is just going through the motions at the student's expense. When you move up to that commuter or corporate twin, you want your old students to applaud your success instead of complaining that you used them as stepping-stones while building time.

Part 61 places some restrictions on just how quickly you can accumulate flight hours as an instructor. Although you may want to fly from the crack of dawn until long after sunset, the FAA says that you cannot instruct for more than eight hours in any 24 hour period. Additionally, if you are hired by a Part 135 operator and want to instruct on the side, you should know that 135 pilots are limited to no more than 34 hours of commercial flying (135 and instructing combined) in a seven day period, 120 hours in any calendar month, and 1,200 hours in any calendar year. Staying within these limits is your responsibility, not that of the flight school or Part 135 operator.

Be a "Freight Dog"?

Many new commercial pilots begin their Part 135 careers flying cargo. The regulations are not as strict for cargo flights as they are for those carrying passengers; those differences will be discussed later.

As a Part 135 pilot flying cargo, however, you should know that only a crewmember or other employee of the certificate holder can go along for the ride—you can't take a friend along to keep you company. There are two exceptions: if you are carrying animals, a qualified handler can go along and not be considered a passenger, and if you are carrying hazardous materials any person necessary for their safe handling can be carried.

Part 135 Operations

For those pilots who aspire to a position with a major airline, Part 135 air taxi or commuter experience is an excellent foundation. Let's just touch on a few differences between Part 91 and Part 135. These are differences, remember—it's your responsibility to know the Part 91 regulations.

First, there's a new player in the game. Although you, as pilot-in-command, will continue to be responsible for the safety of each flight, you are now working for a commercial operator. In the eyes of the FAA, the "operator" is that person who, for compensation or hire, engages in the carriage by aircraft in air commerce persons or property for hire (that's the person who has to comply with Part 119). To you, he or she is the boss. The operator is the person who, in the words of the regulation, uses, causes to be used, or authorizes the use of the aircraft, and who exercises authority over initiating, conducting, or terminating a flight. The operator must hold an Air Taxi and Commercial Operator (ATCO) certificate and meet strict federal requirements as to the qualifications and experience of key management personnel. It is the operator who must ensure that required maintenance is performed and the correct records kept, and who keeps track of where you are going and what your cargo is. You still get to do the preflight and the weight and balance calculations, however.

The operator has another distinction: he or she "holds out" to the public the offer of aviation services through advertising or other means. What is "holding out"? Here is an example: If you have a commercial pilot certificate and also have a suitable airplane available, you might place a classified ad stating "Commercial pilot flying to the Rose Bowl, departing 12-29, returning 1-2, $90 per person round trip." If you did so, however, you would be holding yourself out to the public as an air taxi operator, ready to furnish transportation to anyone who wants it. Without an ATCO certificate you would be in a lot of trouble with the FAA. On the other hand, if you went to a local real estate firm and contracted to fly its sales

personnel and clients on property inspection trips for a fixed cost per hour, you would be considered to be a private carrier and no ATCO certificate would be required. You could have several such arrangements and still protect your status as a private carrier; spread the word too widely about your availability, however, and you may be accused of holding yourself out to the public as a common carrier. That's a no-no—unless you hold an air taxi/commercial operator certificate. Before you decide on your own that a proposed operation is private carriage and thus exempt from Part 135, read Advisory Circular 120-12A and talk it over with the FAA—they come down hard on improper 119/135 operations.

You can have it both ways, however. Part 135 provides for single-pilot commercial/air taxi operators, who must meet much less stringent regulatory requirements. First, you must have exclusive use of an aircraft for at least six consecutive months. Exclusive use means you can't use your friend's airplane for Part 135 flights if he or she wants to use it on weekends. If it's not your airplane, the lease agreement with the aircraft owner must specify who is responsible for maintenance. With a single-pilot ATCO certificate you are considered to be both owner and operator, assuming the duties and responsibilities of both; your name goes on the Operations Specifications. Any aircraft used to carry passengers for hire must be certificated in the Normal category, of course; no limited, restricted, or experimental aircraft need apply. You won't need to prepare an operations manual, and you can ignore the Part 135 requirements for flight and ground training, although you will have to seek out an approved Hazardous Materials Handling program for recognition training.

If you have just won the lottery and have purchased a turbojet or a large airplane that requires a second crewmember, you can qualify for Part 135 certification as a Single Pilot-in-Command. Again, your name will appear on the Operations Specifications and no other PIC can fly your airplane, but you can have up to three second-in-command pilots. Don't buy too big an airplane, however; Single PIC operators are limited to nine passenger seats or less. The FAA can authorize a complete waiver of the manual, training, and management requirements for a Single

Pilot-in-Command certificate holder. If you lease a large airplane you must send a copy of the lease to the FAA in Oklahoma City within 24 hours of signing it.

Although the Basic Part 135 Operator certificate dates from 1988, most on-demand charter outfits probably fit the description. A Basic 135 operation can use more than one pilot-in-command, although no more than five pilots (including seconds-in-command) are authorized. No more than five aircraft can be used and not more than three different types of aircraft are authorized. Once again, nine passenger seats is the limit. An operations manual must be prepared, but its content need not be as extensive as that for a full Part 135 operation. Also, training and management requirements can be modified by the local FAA office.

Every Part 135 operation, from a single pilot to a major charter outfit, must have a system for keeping track of its flights if a flight plan is not filed. The obvious solution is to require that a flight plan be filed with the FAA for every trip.

The preceding paragraphs mentioned Operations Specifications for every type of 135 operator. What are they? Upon approval of the application for ATCO status, each commercial operator is issued operational specifications which lay out in detail just what that operator is allowed to do: day or night, IFR or VFR, specific aircraft to be used (by N-number), and geographic area of operation. If flight into a foreign country is authorized by the op specs, it must be with the approval of and in compliance with the regulations of that country. As noted above, some op specs even name the pilots.

Each Part 135 operator, except for single-pilot and single PIC operators, must have an operations manual (approved by the FAA, of course) containing detailed guidance for every conceivable situation an employee might encounter. Each employee must receive a copy of the manual and keep it up to date. If you are employed by an operation that requires an operations manual, it takes much of the decision making out of your hands—you must comply with the manual. In most cases, if you are faced with a situation not covered in the manual you must call your home base for instructions (the manual must contain all of the relevant telephone numbers).

Flightcrew Qualifications

Before you can fly as a member of a Part 135 crew you will have to go through ground and flight training administered by the operator. The initial ground training portion will include the operations manual, hazardous material (HAZMAT) handling, and provisions of Part 135 among other subjects. This training will be repeated at recurrent intervals. If you upgrade from the copilot's seat to pilot-in-command you will receive upgrade training, and if you move from one type of airplane into another you will receive transition training to alert you to any disparity between the two. You will be flight checked by either an FAA inspector or by a company check airman before you can act as a Part 135 crewmember, and you can expect to be flight checked every six months thereafter. If you will be flying both singles and twins, your first checkride will be in a multi-engine aircraft and after that the checks will alternate between classes. If you run your own single-pilot 135 operation, you can forget about the ground training—but you can't escape the checkrides.

Most Part 135 operators expect pilot applicants to have at least 1,000 hours of flight time. The regulations do provide for pilots with only 500 hours of flight experience to act as PIC under visual flight rules (VFR), even if they are instrument rated, but that might not be enough to get hired. Before you can be pilot-in-command under instrument conditions you will have to log at least 1200 hours of flight time including 750 cross-country, 100 at night, and 75 hours of actual or simulated instrument time. If you are a little short in the cross-country column, remember that although the regulations contain specific distance requirements for the private and commercial certificates and the instrument rating, for all other purposes a cross-country is any trip that departs one airport and lands at another. You probably have more cross-country time than you think.

If you plan to apply to a commuter airline, there are additional restrictions to be aware of. If the carrier uses airplanes with a passenger seating capacity of ten or more, a second in command is required—that's a plus for you, because all you need to fill that seat is a commercial certificate with instrument and multiengine ratings. Because of the requirement for two pilots, you can log as second-in-command all time during which you act as SIC. The captain of that over-ten-passenger airplane has to hold an ATP certificate and must have logged 100 hours PIC time in make and model before moving to the left seat for a passenger-carrying flight. If the aircraft seats less than ten passengers, you can (and probably will) be replaced by an autopilot.

You may be wondering how anyone can collect any PIC time while riding the right seat. There are a couple of ways. First, in the typical on-demand air taxi operation where a copilot can be replaced by an autopilot (Seneca, Baron, 310, etc.), it is the PIC's decision whether or not to use the autopilot authorization. There is no requirement that an autopilot be used just because one is installed. In those situations, you can log as PIC all time during which you are sole manipulator of the controls because two pilots are required for passenger-carrying IFR air taxi flights. (61.51(c)(2)(i) and 135.101).

Second, if your carrier flies larger aircraft which require type ratings and you get typed in the aircraft during your initial training, you will be swapping legs with the designated PIC and can, again, log sole manipulator time as PIC. When it is the captain's leg, of course, you will be logging SIC time. When it is time for you to upgrade to captain, your carrier may pair you with a check-airman for the first 100 hours. You don't have to rent a Jetstream or Brasilia, honest.

Those large aircraft have another benefit—if the passenger seating capacity is more than 19, a flight attendant is required. It's nice to have a third person available when you are trying to accomplish all of the preflight tasks that fall to a co-pilot and assist the passengers at the same time.

Although flying larger aircraft is good for the ego and the employment résumé, there is one provision of Part 135 that places special responsibilities on operators of planes with seating capacities of ten or more passengers: a crewmember must determine that a passenger seated next to an emergency exit has the physical size, strength, and dexterity to open the exit and that the passenger is able to understand emergency evacuation instructions.

While you are back in the cabin testing the passengers for strength and dexterity, you might mention that little planes are just like big planes—no smoking is allowed on scheduled flights, regardless of airplane size or seating capacity. "Scheduled" is the key word—the restriction does not apply to on-demand charters.

You can't serve drinks on a Part 135 trip, and you (as pilot-in-command) cannot allow anyone on board who is intoxicated. You also cannot allow anyone to manipulate the controls of the airplane other than an employee of the operator or a representative of the FAA Administrator. I will leave to your imagination the results of having an inebriated passenger with ambitions to be a pilot in the copilot's seat.

Single Pilot Operations

Part 135.101 requires two pilots for all flights carrying passengers under instrument flight rules, subject to the autopilot waiver in 135.105.

Second-In-Command and Autopilot Authorization

14 CFR 135.105: Unless you are assigned to copilot an aircraft which requires two pilots when operating VFR, an aircraft weighing over 12,500 pounds, or a commuter with more than ten passenger seats, you can be replaced by a three-axis autopilot (pitch, roll, and yaw—altitude hold has nothing to do with it). The company's operations specifications must be amended to show that an autopilot can be substituted for a second pilot, and the pilot-in-command must have an autopilot authorization.

You can, of course, log as second-in-command time all time during which you act as SIC of an aircraft requiring two pilots, or any time during which two pilots are required by the regulations for the operation being conducted. Remember 135.101, cited above. Can you log SIC time when the autopilot is inoperative? Sure. Can you log SIC time when the pilot-in-command determines that VFR conditions will not be encountered within 15 minutes flying time and that the whole trip will be IFR? Absolutely—the regulations require two pilots under those conditions.

Using an Autopilot

Before I discuss autopilots, a general caution: You will find an autopilot supplement in your Approved Flight Manual, and included in that supplement you will find a pre-flight test procedure. Do not fail to perform this check before takeoff—if you are going to share piloting duties with a device that might have different ideas than you have about the conduct of the flight, you *must* test all of the means of turning that device off.

Autopilot authorization is a mixed blessing. When an autopilot is used to replace a warm body in the right seat, you must refer to the Approved Flight Manual to see what it says about altitude loss in the event of a malfunction. That information will be provided by the airframe manufacturer based on flight test data.

Unless you are shooting an instrument approach, you can't fly with the autopilot engaged any closer to the terrain than 500 feet or twice the maximum altitude loss in the Flight Manual, whichever is higher. If you are on a non-precision approach with the A/P engaged, you can't go lower than 50 feet below the minimum descent altitude (MDA) for that approach or twice the maximum loss in the book, again choosing whichever is higher. Since you can't descend below MDA until you have the runway environment in sight, the effect of this part of the regulations is that you must disengage the autopilot when you leave the MDA and hand-fly the descent.

On an ILS approach with the autopilot engaged (a "coupled approach"), the minimum altitude to which you can descend before disengaging the autopilot is 50 feet above the ground or the maximum altitude loss provided in the Flight Manual for an autopilot malfunction, whichever is higher. Experience will teach you that glide slopes can do funny things close to the ground, and if the autopilot is flying the airplane you may get an exciting ride. Watch out for notations like "Glideslope unusable inside MM" on approach plates.

Two additional comments on the subject of autopilots: Learn how your airplane reacts when it intercepts the glideslope while the autopilot is engaged. In most cases it will pitch over smoothly and the passengers will never know it. However, you may run across an occasional autopilot installation that pitches down sharply at glideslope intercept, causing the passengers to lift up against their seatbelts. Sometimes it is better to disengage the autopilot and hand-fly the first few seconds of the descent before re-engaging it. Also, learn all the methods available for

disengaging the A/P when it does something unexpected (second warning). Using the electric trim switch will usually shut the autopilot off, but there may be other means available. If all else fails, shut off the master switch. All certificated autopilots can be overpowered by a pilot while the "shut-it-off" switch is being found. *Never* apply pressure to the control yoke when the autopilot is flying the airplane. Imagine that Chuck Yeager is flying from the other seat and imagine his reaction if you applied control pressure in opposition to his inputs.

Part 135 Airspace Regulations

As a pilot operating under Part 91 with either a private or a commercial certificate, you are governed by the airspace regulations that you had to memorize for the private pilot written. When you go to work for a Part 135 operator, or when you become one yourself, the rules change.

You know that when you fly over a congested area as a Part 91 pilot you must maintain an altitude which is 1,000 feet above the highest obstacle within a 2,000 foot radius from your aircraft, that when the area is not congested you can descend to maintain an altitude as low as 500 feet above the surface, and that when you fly over water or sparsely settled areas there is no altitude restriction but you must stay at least 500 feet away from any persons or property. As a Part 135 pilot you have new numbers to remember. The 500 foot altitude restriction applies everywhere during daylight hours, and you must remain at least 500 feet horizontally away from any obstacle. At night, you can't fly lower than 1,000 feet above the highest obstacle within five miles of your courseline; in mountainous areas, that cushion increases to 2,000 feet. In uncontrolled airspace, forget about "one mile visibility and clear of clouds." No scud running allowed under Part 135—if the ceiling is less than 1,000 feet you must have at least two miles visibility. Because Part 91 was changed in 1989 to require three miles visibility in uncontrolled airspace at night, Part 135 may be changed to three miles as well...but it hasn't happened as of this printing.

Night Operations

In addition to the airspace limitations above, there are further limitations on night operations while carrying passengers under Part 135. Basically, your departure and destination airports must have runway lights or boundary markers. Makeshift lights such as automobile headlights or flare pots don't qualify (flare pots are OK if their use is approved by the Administrator, which is kind of tough in an emergency).

Flights operating for hire must have an operating landing light, according to 14 CFR 91.205.

Single-Engine IFR

The FAA has approved the use of single-engine airplanes in passenger-carrying service under instrument flight rules. However, there are specific requirements that must be met. The airplane must have two independent sources of electrical power, either of which can handle the anticipated demand, it must have two independent sources of power for the gyroscopic instruments, with a means of selecting between the two sources, and it must be operated under a maintenance program that provides for trend-monitoring such as spectrographic oil analysis. Every air taxi operator has an FAA Principal Operations Inspector assigned, and that person will decide if the program meets the standards of the regulation.

Also, two pilots are required for single-engine IFR operations unless an autopilot is installed and the PIC has an autopilot authorization letter. The PIC must also have at least 1,200 hours of flight time including 500 hours cross-country, 100 hours of night time, and 75 hours of actual or simulated instrument flight.

Supplemental Oxygen Under Part 135

Regulations requiring the use of supplemental oxygen are a little more strict under Part 135 than they are under Part 91. If you are occupying a pilot seat on a Part 135 flight in an unpressurized aircraft, you must use oxygen continuously when you are above 10,000 feet through 12,000 feet for that part of the flight that is of more than 30 minutes duration, and at all times when above 12,000 feet; it was 12,500 feet and 14,000 when you were a Part 91 pilot, remember? (See Figure 12-8.) Your unpressurized bird must be equipped to provide enough oxygen and dispensers for at least ten percent of the passengers when flying between 10,000 feet and 15,000 feet for flight at those altitudes in excess of 30 minutes, and continuously when above 15,000 feet. Note that the passengers do not have to use oxygen, but it must be made

available. If your flight plan will take you above 10,000 feet for more than 30 minutes, it is a good idea to tell the passengers during the pre-takeoff briefing that Federal regulations require you to wear an oxygen mask above a certain altitude. If you don't, when you put the oxygen mask on they will suspect that something awful has happened and you are keeping it to yourself. It's not a bad idea to brief the passengers on the O$_2$ masks and outlets; they may have never seen a bayonet fitting before and won't know how to use one if the need arises.

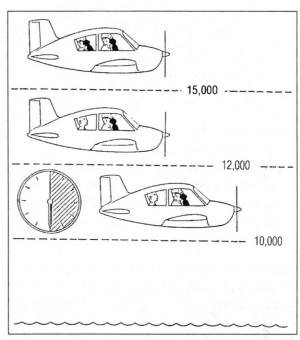

Figure 12-8. Pilot and passenger oxygen regulations under Part 135

Of course, your plans are to fly pressurized airplanes, where oxygen masks are not necessary, right? Part 135 says that when the cabin pressure altitude is above 10,000 feet you will comply with the regulations above. Most pressurization systems will maintain the cabin pressure altitude at something lower than 10,000 feet, making masks unnecessary unless the system springs a leak. At flight altitudes above 25,000 feet through 35,000 feet, each pilot should have available a quick-donning oxygen mask—one that can be put on with one hand. When one pilot goes back into the cabin to make the passengers comfortable (or for physiological reasons), the other pilot must put on a quick-donning mask and wear it until the absent pilot returns to the flight deck. If the boss says that quick-donning masks are too expensive, one pilot will have to wear a mask continuously above 25,000 feet. At flight altitudes above 35,000 feet, at least one pilot must wear oxygen continuously; the time of useful consciousness at those altitudes is too short to rely on both pilots being able to put on masks and handle an explosive decompression simultaneously.

At flight altitudes above 25,000 feet, the folks in the back must have at least a ten-minute supply of supplemental oxygen for use during a descent to more comfortable altitudes in the event of loss of pressurization. There are additional regulations covering passenger oxygen when cabin pressure exceeds 10,000 feet and the airplane is not equipped to meet the requirements already listed, but you won't find many airplanes capable of those altitudes that are not already so equipped.

Formation Flight

Part 135 prohibits airplanes carrying passengers from flying in formation, even if the pilots agree beforehand (that's a Part 91 requirement). If you are wondering how those exciting airborne photographs are taken, go back to 119.1 and note that aerial photography is exempt from the strictures of Part 135.

Carrying Cargo

Chances are that you will begin your Part 135 career hauling packages. Cargo doesn't need oxygen or complain about turbulence. There are a few things you must know about cargo, however. It has to be stowed in an approved cargo rack or bin and be secured by an approved means or, if your airplane doesn't have cargo racks or bins, it must be secured by a safety belt or other tiedown forward of the passengers. It must be packaged or covered to avoid possible injury to the occupants of the airplane—you don't want something heavy to come up and join you in the cockpit in the event of a sudden stop. Cargo must be loaded so that at least one regular or emergency exit is available for all occupants. And, of course, you must observe the load limits on the floor structure of the airplane.

Watch out for cargo items that are packed in dry ice, such as flowers or some medical supplies. You may want to wear oxygen continuously if your cargo is supplying unwanted carbon dioxide.

You may find yourself flying in a combination passenger/cargo operation. In that situation, no cargo can be carried directly above seated passengers, and no normal or emergency exit can be obstructed by packages. You must also keep the aisle between the passenger compartment and the crew compartment unobstructed.

Maintenance Regulations, Parts 91 and 135

As a private pilot, you know that your airplane must be inspected and declared airworthy by a mechanic on an annual basis. Your passengers know you, know that you are not a commercial pilot, and rely on you to ensure that the airplane is kept airworthy between annual inspections. When you start to fly for money, your passengers don't know you or your abilities and rely on your compliance with FAA regulations for a safe flight.

For commercial operations, the FAA tightens up the rules. An airplane used to carry passengers for hire must be inspected every 100 hours. Because an annual inspection is more thorough than a 100 hour inspection, it can substitute for a 100 hour inspection. The regulations permit you to fly ten hours beyond the 100 hour limit if that is necessary to get to a place at which the inspection can be done, but that excess time is subtracted from the next 100 hours. For example, if the tachometer on your airplane read 2341.7 when the last 100 hour was accomplished and you find yourself out in the wilderness when the tach reads 2441.7, you have ten hours to get to a maintenance facility. Not to your home base, by the way, but to a place at which the inspection can be done. If it takes three hours to get to such a place, and the tach reads 2444.7 when the mechanic returns the airplane to service, the next inspection is due at 2541.7—the three hours aren't free.

Airplanes used for flight instruction do not have to be inspected every 100 hours unless they are provided by the instructor, according to 91.409. Most flight schools give their training planes 100 hour inspections anyway.

If any inspection results in work being done on the airplane that might affect its flight characteristics, it must be test flown by at least a private pilot before being returned to service, and that pilot must log the flight in the aircraft records. It is just common sense to fly an airplane under visual flight rules without passengers on board when it has been in the shop. You don't want to be airborne in the dark with paying passengers on board and find out that the intermittent electrical problem that required the shop time has turned into a total loss of electrical power.

Recordkeeping

Records of all maintenance and inspections, including preventive maintenance, must be kept for each airframe, engine, and propeller. Some items are life-limited, and others (such as propellers) must be inspected at specified intervals. The maintenance records must reflect the status of these items so that you can tell at any time just how many hours you have before a propeller inspection is due or before a certain accessory must be replaced. The status of all Airworthiness Directives (ADs) must be made clear in the maintenance records, including the tach time and date when the AD was performed. If the AD requires compliance every 50 hours (for instance), the maintenance logs must show the date and tach time when the next action is required.

Records of inspections and preventive maintenance should be kept until the work is repeated (or superseded—why keep a record of replacing a rotating beacon bulb after you have replaced it with a strobe light?) but in no case less than a year after the work was done. As a commercial pilot, you should be able to look at the airframe and engine logs and determine the airworthiness status of the airplane. Remember that the airplane's Certificate of Airworthiness never expires, but is kept in force by the "return to service" endorsement of the mechanic who does the inspection.

Records containing time-in-service and time-remaining information and records of AD compliance must be retained and transferred with the airplane when it is sold. If you decide to go into aircraft sales you will want to watch this carefully. Watch out for the "zero-time" engine that really isn't; only the original manufacturer or its authorized agent can issue a new maintenance record for a rebuilt engine, including any Airworthiness Directives performed on that engine.

Regulations Specific to Part 135

Chances are that you will not be the Director of Maintenance for your 135 operation. For a full-blown air taxi operation, the maintenance boss must hold an Airframe and Powerplant Mechanic's license and have worked as an aircraft mechanic for at least three years, among other requirements. If yours is a small operation, it's more likely that you will contract for maintenance with a facility acceptable to the local FAA office.

Although you won't get grease under your fingernails, you will have to know more about maintenance and recordkeeping requirements as a Part 135 pilot than you ever needed to know when operating under Part 91.

The primary responsibility for airworthiness of a Part 91 airplane belongs to the owner or operator, but in a Part 135 operation the certificate holder (who might very well be the owner) bears that burden.

Chapter 12
Regulations Review Questions

There are plenty of regulations questions for everyone. The FAA knowledge examinations are heavy on regulations, so be prepared.

Instrument Student Questions

1. The pilot in command of a civil aircraft must have an instrument rating only when operating

   A—under IFR in positive control airspace.
   B—under IFR, in weather conditions less than the minimum for VFR flight, and in Class A airspace.
   C—in weather conditions less than the minimum prescribed for VFR flight.

2. To meet instrument experience requirements of 14 CFR part 61, section 61.57(c), a pilot enters the condition of flight in the pilot logbook as simulated instrument conditions. What qualifying information must also be entered?

   A—Location and type of each instrument approach completed and name of safety pilot.
   B—Number and type of instrument approaches completed and route of flight.
   C—Name and pilot certificate number of safety pilot and type of approaches completed.

3. Which flight time may be logged as instrument time when on an instrument flight plan?

   A—All of the time the aircraft was not controlled by ground references.
   B—Only the time you controlled the aircraft solely by reference to flight instruments.
   C—Only the time you were flying in IFR weather conditions.

4. When is an IFR flight plan required?

   A—When less than VFR conditions exist in either Class E or Class G airspace and in Class A airspace.
   B—In all Class E airspace when conditions are below VFR, in Class A airspace, and in defense zone airspace.
   C—In Class E airspace when IMC exists or in Class A airspace.

For questions 5. through 10., refer to the "Airspace Classifications" figure on Page 12-6 (Figure 12-5).

5. What is the floor of Class E airspace when designated in conjunction with an airway?

   A—700 feet AGL
   B—1,200 feet AGL
   C—1,500 feet AGL

6. Which altitude is the normal upper limit for Class D airspace?

   A—1,000 feet AGL
   B—2,500 feet AGL
   C—4,000 feet AGL

7. Which altitude is the upper limit for Class A airspace?

   A—14,500 feet MSL
   B—18,000 feet MSL
   C—60,000 feet MSL

8. What is the maximum altitude that Class G airspace will exist? (Does not include airspace less than 1,500 feet AGL.)

   A—18,000 feet MSL
   B—14,500 feet MSL
   C—14,000 feet MSL

9. If the aircraft's transponder fails during flight within Class B airspace,

 A— the pilot should immediately request clearance to depart the Class B airspace.
 B— ATC may authorize deviation from the transponder requirement to allow aircraft to continue to the airport of ultimate destination.
 C— the aircraft must immediately descend below 1,200 feet AGL and proceed to destination.

10. What is the floor of Class E airspace when designated in conjunction with an airport which has an approved IAP?

 A— 500 feet AGL
 B— 700 feet AGL
 C— 1,200 feet AGL

11. What are the vertical limits of a transition area that is designated in conjunction with an airport having a prescribed IAP?

 A— Surface to 700 feet AGL.
 B— 1,200 feet AGL to the base of the overlying controlled airspace.
 C— 700 feet AGL or more to the base of the overlying controlled airspace.

12. For aircraft other than helicopters, what minimum conditions must exist at the destination airport to avoid listing an alternate airport on an IFR flight plan when a standard IAP is available?

 A— From 2 hours before to 2 hours after ETA, forecast ceiling 2,000, and visibility 2 and 1/2 miles.
 B— From 2 hours before to 2 hours after ETA, forecast ceiling 3,000, and visibility 3 miles.
 C— From 1 hour before to 1 hour after ETA, forecast ceiling 2,000, and visibility 3 miles.

13. For aircraft other than helicopters, what minimum weather conditions must be forecast for your ETA at an airport that has a precision approach procedure, with standard alternate minimums, in order to list it as an alternate for the IFR flight?

 A— 600-foot ceiling and 2 SM visibility at your ETA.
 B— 600-foot ceiling and 2 SM visibility from 2 hours before to 2 hours after your ETA.
 C— 800-foot ceiling and 2 SM visibility at your ETA.

14. When must a pilot fly at a cardinal altitude plus 500 feet on an IFR flight plan?

 A— When flying above 18,000 feet in VFR conditions.
 B— When flying in VFR conditions above clouds.
 C— When assigned a VFR-On-Top clearance.

15. If all ILS components are operating and the required visual references are not established, the missed approach should be initiated upon

 A— arrival at the DH on the glide slope.
 B— arrival at the middle marker.
 C— expiration of the time listed on the approach chart for missed approach.

16. What are the requirements for a contact approach to an airport that has an approved IAP, if the pilot is on an instrument flight plan and clear of clouds?

 A— The controller must determine that the pilot can see the airport at the altitude flown and can remain clear of clouds.
 B— The pilot must agree to the approach when given by ATC, and the controller must have determined that the visibility was at least 1 mile and be reasonably sure the pilot can remain clear of clouds.
 C— The pilot must request the approach, have at least 1-mile visibility, and be reasonably sure of remaining clear of clouds.

17. Unless otherwise authorized, the pilot in command is required to hold a type rating when operating any

A—aircraft that is certificated for more than one pilot.
B—aircraft of more than 12,500 pounds maximum certificated takeoff weight.
C—multiengine aircraft having a gross weight of more than 12,000 pounds.

18. What flight time may a pilot log as second-in-command?

A—All flight time while acting as second in command in aircraft configured for more than one pilot.
B—All flight time when qualified and occupying a crewmember station in an aircraft that requires more than one pilot.
C—Only that flight time during which the second in command is the sole manipulator of the controls.

19. To act as pilot-in-command of an airplane towing a glider, the tow pilot is required to have

A—a logbook endorsement from an authorized glider instructor certifying receipt of ground and flight training in gliders, and be proficient with techniques and procedures for safe towing of gliders.
B—at least a private pilot certificate with a category rating for powered aircraft, and made and logged at least three flights as pilot or observer in a glider being towed by an airplane.
C—a logbook record of having made at least three flights as sole manipulator of the controls of a glider being towed by an airplane.

20. Portable electronic devices which may cause interference with the navigation or communication system may not be operated on U.S.-registered civil aircraft being operated

A—under IFR.
B—in passenger carrying operations.
C—along Federal airways.

21. In the contiguous U.S., excluding the airspace at and below 2,500 feet AGL, an operable coded transponder equipped with Mode C capability is required in all airspace above

A—10,000 feet MSL.
B—12,500 feet MSL.
C—14,500 feet MSL.

22. In accordance with 14 CFR Part 91, supplemental oxygen must be used by the required minimum flightcrew for that time exceeding 30 minutes while at cabin pressure altitudes of

A—10,500 feet MSL up to and including 12,500 feet MSL.
B—12,000 feet MSL up to and including 18,000 feet MSL.
C—12,500 feet MSL up to and including 14,000 feet MSL.

23. No person may operate a large civil U.S. aircraft which is subject to a lease, unless the lessee has mailed a copy of the lease to the FAA Aircraft Registration Branch, Technical Section, Oklahoma City, OK within how many hours of its execution?

A—24
B—48
C—72

24. Which is true with respect to formation flights? Formation flights are

    A—authorized when carrying passengers for hire with prior arrangement with the pilot in command of each aircraft in the formation.
    B—not authorized when visibilities are less than 3 SM.
    C—not authorized when carrying passengers for hire.

25. Aircraft maintenance records must include the current status of the

    A—applicable airworthiness certificate.
    B—life-limited parts of only the engine and airframe.
    C—life-limited parts of each airframe, engine, propeller, rotor, and appliance.

26. Assuring compliance with an Airworthiness Directive is the responsibility of the

    A—pilot-in-command and the FAA certificated mechanic assigned to that aircraft.
    B—pilot-in-command of that aircraft.
    C—owner or operator of that aircraft.

27. No person may operate an aircraft in simulated instrument flight conditions unless the

    A—other control seat is occupied by at least an appropriately rated commercial pilot.
    B—pilot has filed an IFR flight plan and received an IFR clearance.
    C—other control seat is occupied by a safety pilot, who holds at least a private pilot certificate and is appropriately rated.

28. A second-class medical certificate issued to a commercial pilot on April 10, this year, permits the pilot to exercise which of the following privileges?

    A—Commercial pilot privileges through April 30, next year.
    B—Commercial pilot privileges through April 10, 2 years later.
    C—Private pilot privileges through, but not after, March 31, next year.

29. Regulations that refer to "commercial operators" relate to that person who

    A—is the owner of a small scheduled airline.
    B—for compensation or hire, engages in the carriage by aircraft in air commerce of persons or property, as an air carrier.
    C—for compensation or hire, engages in the carriage by aircraft in air commerce of persons or property, other than as an air carrier.

30. To act as pilot-in-command of an airplane with more than 200 horsepower, a person is required to

    A—receive and log ground and flight training from a qualified pilot in such an airplane.
    B—obtain an endorsement stating that the person is proficient to operate such an airplane.
    C—receive and log ground and flight training from an authorized instructor in such an airplane.

31. If a pilot does not meet the recency of experience requirements for night flight and official sunset is 1900 CST, the latest time passengers should be carried is

    A—1959 CST.
    B—1900 CST.
    C—1800 CST.

32. Pilots who change their permanent mailing address and fail to notify the FAA Airmen Certification Branch of this change, are entitled to exercise the privileges of their pilot certificate for a period of

A—30 days.
B—60 days.
C—90 days.

33. What action must be taken when a pilot in command (PIC) deviates from any rule in 14 CFR Part 91?

A—Upon landing, report the deviation to the FAA Flight Standards District Office.
B—Advise ATC of the pilot-in-command's intentions.
C—Upon the request of the Administrator, send a written report of that deviation to the Administrator.

34. When operating a U.S.-registered civil aircraft, which document is required by regulation to be available in the aircraft?

A—A manufacturer's Operations Manual.
B—A current, approved Airplane Flight Manual.
C—An Owner's Manual.

35. With U.S.-registered civil airplanes, the use of seatbelts is required during movement on the surface, takeoffs, and landings for

A—safe operating practice, but not required by regulations.
B—each person over 2 years of age on board.
C—commercial passenger operations only.

36. If weather conditions are such that it is required to designate an alternate airport on your IFR flight plan, you should plan to carry enough fuel to arrive at the first airport of intended landing, fly from that airport to the alternate airport, and fly thereafter for

A—30 minutes at slow cruising speed.
B—45 minutes at normal cruising speed.
C—1 hour at normal cruising speed.

37. Which is required equipment for powered aircraft during VFR night flights?

A—Flashlight with red lens if the flight is for hire.
B—An electric landing light if the flight is for hire.
C—Sensitive altimeter adjustable for barometric pressure.

38. Which incident would require that the nearest NTSB field office be notified immediately?

A—In-flight fire.
B—Ground fire resulting in fire equipment dispatch.
C—Fire of the primary aircraft while in a hangar which results in damage to other property of more than $25,000.

39. When should notification of an aircraft accident be made to the NTSB if there was substantial damage and no injuries?

A—Immediately.
B—Within 10 days.
C—Within 30 days.

40. The carriage of passengers for hire by a commercial pilot is

A—not authorized in "utility" category aircraft.
B—not authorized in "limited" category aircraft.
C—authorized in "restricted" category aircraft.

41. The maximum cumulative time that an emergency locator transmitter may be operated before the rechargeable battery must be recharged is

A—30 minutes.
B—45 minutes.
C—60 minutes.

42. While in flight a helicopter and an airplane are converging at a 90 degrees angle, and the helicopter is located to the right of the airplane. Which aircraft has the right-of-way, and why?

A—The helicopter, because it is to the right of the airplane.
B—The helicopter, because helicopters have the right-of-way over airplanes.
C—The airplane, because airplanes have the right-of-way over helicopters.

43. What is the maximum indicated airspeed allowed in the airspace underlying Class B airspace?

A—156 knots
B—200 knots
C—230 knots

44. What is the minimum altitude and flight visibility required for acrobatic flight?

A—1,500 feet AGL and 3 miles
B—2,000 feet MSL and 2 miles
C—3,000 feet AGL and 1 mile

45. If not equipped with required position lights, an aircraft must terminate flight

A—at sunset.
B—30 minutes after sunset.
C—1 hour after sunset.

46. Except when necessary for takeoff or landing or unless otherwise authorized by the Administrator, the minimum altitude for IFR flight is

A—3,000 feet over all terrain.
B—3,000 feet over designated mountainous terrain; 2,000 feet over terrain elsewhere.
C—2,000 feet above the highest obstacle over designated mountainous terrain; 1,000 feet above the highest obstacle over terrain elsewhere.

47. If an aircraft's operation in flight was substantially affected by an alteration or repair, the aircraft documents must show that it was test flown and approved for return to service by an appropriately-rated pilot prior to being operated

A—under VFR or IFR rules.
B—with passengers aboard.
C—for compensation or hire.

48. An ATC transponder is not to be used unless it has been tested, inspected, and found to comply with regulations within the preceding

A—30 days.
B—12 calendar months.
C—24 calendar months.

Answers:
1.B, 2.A, 3.B, 4.C, 5.B, 6.B, 7.C, 8.B, 9.B, 10.B, 11.C, 12.C,
13.A, 14.C, 15.A, 16.C, 17.B, 18.B, 19.A, 20.A, 21.A, 22.C,
23.A, 24.C, 25.C, 26.C, 27.C, 28.A, 29.C, 30.C, 31.A, 32.A,
33.C, 34.B, 35.B, 36.B, 37.B, 38.A, 39.A, 40.B, 41.C, 42.A,
43.B, 44.A, 45.A, 46.C, 47.B, 48.C

For Commercial Students

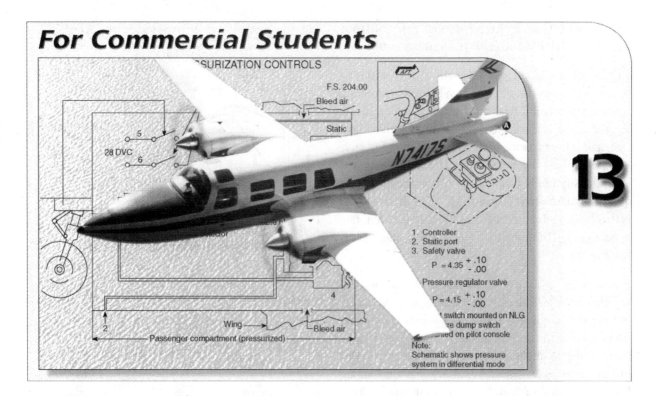

PRESSURIZATION CONTROLS

F.S. 204.00
Bleed air
Static
5
28 DVC
6
4
2
Wing
Bleed air
Passenger compartment (pressurized)

1. Controller
2. Static port
3. Safety valve

$$P = 4.35 \,^{+\,.10}_{-\,.00}$$

Pressure regulator valve

$$P = 4.15 \,^{+\,.10}_{-\,.00}$$

switch mounted on NLG
re dump switch
ed on pilot console

Note:
Schematic shows pressure
system in differential mode

13

Remember when you took your private pilot check-ride? Be honest—how much did you really know about airplane engines and the airplane itself? If your knowledge has increased, it's because you took the initiative to learn on your own, because there is no requirement that you ever open a book after you get your license. Of course, most pilots recognize the limitations of primary training and use it as a foundation for learning as much as they can. But there are a few pilots who struggle through their basic training and quit learning the day they get their licenses. When they have accumulated enough flight hours, however, they want to become commercial pilots. The commercial pilot exam goes into enough detail to separate the serious pilots from the rest; this chapter will touch on a few of the subjects in that exam.

Mixture Control

A surprising number of private pilots misunderstand the purpose of the mixture control. They know that if you pull it back far enough the engine will quit, and they figure that is reason enough to leave it alone. After all, in a trainer-type airplane you can climb to the airplane's service ceiling and fail to lean the mixture and it will not cause the engine to run rough—it will lose power, of course, but the com-

forting roar of rampaging pistons will not be interrupted. These pilots get a real surprise when they apply carburetor heat at altitude, because that *does* cause the engine to run rough. Until that point in their experience, the carburetor heat knob has always been a friend, and now it is apparently an enemy.

This misunderstanding has caused accidents at high altitude airports (and at airports where high temperature has increased the density altitude) when pilots who knew only that the red knob should be all the way in for takeoff failed to lean the mixture for best power and never achieved a safe climb speed. It's a good bet that these pilots experienced engine roughness during the carb heat portion of the preflight runup and didn't realize that the roughness could be eliminated by leaning the mixture.

The mixture control performs only one function: it controls the amount of fuel flow in either carbureted or fuel injected engines. The other side of the fuel/air mixture equation is a function of air density. In airplanes with fuel injected engines, the pilot who wants to maintain a given amount of power gets a clue to the reduction of air density with altitude from the manifold pressure gauge—its reading falls off one inch per thousand feet of altitude and the throttle must be pushed in to compensate. The pilot of an airplane with a carbureted engine gets that clue from a reduction in RPM and feeds in throttle accordingly.

Any reduction in air density with a fixed mixture setting means a loss of power. When the heated air from the carburetor heat muff hits the carburetor, it has the same effect as a climb of several thousand feet, and if the mixture knob has been left at full rich and the airplane is near its altitude limit that decrease in air density might be enough to cause the engine to quit. This is called "loading up." The lesson here is that leaning the mixture is not just a nice idea, but a necessity. Running too rich causes spark plug fouling, too.

When the throttle position is fixed, the density (or weight) of the air entering the carburetor is fixed, and the mixture control is used to establish the proper fuel/air ratio for the job at hand. Your goal would seem to be to make sure that 100 percent of the mixture is burned—that takes about 15 pounds of air for every pound of fuel. Life isn't that simple. You might want the best economy mixture, where you give up some airspeed, or the best power mixture, where you burn more fuel but get the most power for a given throttle setting.

With nothing but basic instrumentation, the best you can do is get close. With a fixed throttle setting, lean the mixture until the engine just begins to run rough (students hate this) and then push in mixture control until the engine smoothes out. This can be done any time that the engine is developing less than 75 percent power; unless the engine is turbocharged, its power output will drop below 75 percent at a density altitude of about 5,000 feet anyway.

With a needle-type exhaust gas temperature gauge (EGT) you should lean the mixture until the needle reaches its peak reading (observe any temperature limitations in the airplane manufacturer's literature) and then richen until the EGT reading goes down 25 degrees for best economy or 100 degrees for best power (see Figure 13-1).

Note: Most engine operating procedures contained in Pilot's Operating Handbooks were written decades ago. New research indicates that operating lean of peak EGT is better for the engine. Check this out with a mechanic who knows the type of engine in

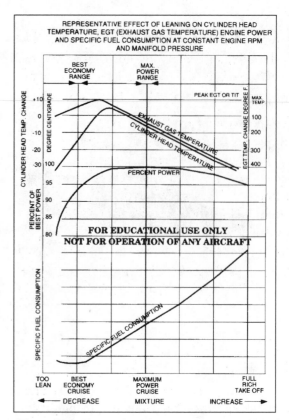

Figure 13-1. Leaning by exhaust gas temperature gauge

question and has the latest information from the manufacturer.

Most EGT installations have a temperature probe for just one cylinder, supposedly the hottest, so that when you have completed your setting the other cylinders should be cooler. An installation with probes for all cylinders, of course, allows you to check all of the temperatures.

You may run across one of the newer electronic EGT indicators, some of which use light-emitting diodes instead of a needle. These may combine cylinder head temperature readings with the exhaust gas temperatures. Other electronic indicators give you a digital temperature readout. Regardless of the type of instrumentation, it is important to your engine's health that you use the mixture control intelligently.

When it is time to start downhill, student pilots are quite often told to place the mixture control in the full rich position, although their Pilot's Operating Handbooks say things like "adjust mixture for smooth operation" or "enrich as required." The best way to handle this to keep the engine toasty warm and the fuel bills low is to leave the mixture at its cruise setting until some roughness develops and then only push the mixture control in enough to make the roughness go away. You don't want to overcool the engine by being too early with a full-rich mixture.

As an air taxi pilot flying into small airports you should be concerned about the availability of the proper grade of fuel for your airplane. Call ahead to be sure—occasionally, they sell the right grade but the pump is broken, or the pump would work if the electricity hadn't failed. Be ready for anything. Don't take a chance with fuel grade—using too low a grade may result in detonation (instantaneous combustion instead of progressive burning). Detonation can also be the result of running too lean in an attempt to avoid a fuel stop (remember that ETE plus 30 or 45 minutes regulation?).

Carburetor Heat

For years, owner's manuals have created uncertainty about the use of carburetor heat through use of terms such as "when necessary" or "when in conditions conducive to induction system icing," and accidents have occurred when pilots either didn't use enough heat or didn't use it in time. The National Transportation Safety Board has recommended that pilots use full carburetor heat whenever power is reduced below the cruise power setting and that it be left full hot until after landing. The major engine manufacturers agree.

Fuel Injection

An injected engine has its fuel delivered in precise amounts directly to the intake manifold, neatly positioned to mix with the incoming air and be vaporized. Starting procedures for Lycomings and Continentals are diametrically opposite insofar as priming the engine is concerned, so follow the manufacturer's starting procedure for your airplane.

Fuel injected engines have a reputation of being hard to start when hot. This problem, when it exists, is usually caused by vapor lock, the result of fuel boiling into vapor in the fuel lines. When you shut down the engine at the completion of a flight the flow of cooling air no longer exists, and the engine must simply radiate its heat to its surroundings. It is inevitable that the fuel lines absorb some of this heat. The manufacturer's approved flight manual will

include a "hot start" procedure. If this doesn't work you may simply have to wait until the fuel cools to a liquid state.

Ignition

It is unlikely that you will be flying an airplane with anything other than magneto ignition anytime soon. Because they rely on nothing more than relative motion between a magnet and a coil of wire, magnetos are far simpler than automotive ignition systems. You may, however, find yourself flying an airplane with pressurized magnetos. In the thin air at high altitude, which has low electrical resistance, voltage can arc between contacts and cause misfiring. As the name implies, pressurized magnetos are sealed and kept under high pressure to avoid this problem.

You probably learned during your student pilot days that a broken "P" lead, or magneto ground wire, makes it dangerous to move the propeller because the engine might start unexpectedly. There have been some instances where a faulty ignition switch had the same result. Because either of these situations is dangerous, manufacturers now suggest that the ignition switch be turned to the OFF position momentarily while the engine is idling before shutdown. They say that no damage will result and, of course, if the engine doesn't shut down you know that there is a problem somewhere. Better to find out while you're in the cockpit than when you are moving the prop to connect the tow bar.

Detuning

No, this section is not misplaced from a chapter on radios or pianos. You are going to be flying airplanes equipped with engines that have crankshaft counterweights, and improper throttle use can cause detuning and potential problems.

An airplane engine is an assemblage of rapidly moving metallic parts, all trying to escape. There is both rotary and reciprocating motion involved, and destructive vibration could occur within certain RPM ranges if the manufacturer had not anticipated the problem. When the manufacturer determines that vibrations are occurring within the normal operating range of the engine, the addition of counterweights to the crankshaft moves the frequency of the vibrations outside of that range to where they can't cause any trouble. It is possible through really gross misuse of the throttle (especially during multi-engine training) to deform the counterweights or the surface on which they ride, defeating their purpose. One of the reasons the FAA made you accumulate so many hours before deeming you qualified to be a commercial pilot is to ensure that you have learned to treat engines gently—but they're going to ask about detuning on the exam anyway.

Propellers

Pilots tend to take propellers for granted, failing to realize the enormous forces they have to withstand. Those blades are developing enough lift (we usually call it thrust, but prop blades are airfoils, and they develop lift) to overcome the parasite drag of the whole airframe. Those pilots unlucky enough to lose a whole propeller can testify that once one gets loose, it accelerates away until it's out of sight. Losing a whole propeller is much better than losing part of one, by the way. When you consider that the force on the back of the propeller disc is measured in tons, and that the outer one-third to one-half of the propeller flexes in flight, those little nicks and scratches take on a new importance. ·

We begin our flying experience with fixed-pitch propellers, which of necessity must compromise between cruise performance and climb performance. A fixed-pitch propeller is most efficient at one combination of airspeed and RPM; change either factor and efficiency is reduced. Engineers measure efficiency as the ratio between thrust horsepower and brake horsepower, or the ratio of what you put in to what you get out. It might be easier for us as pilots to think of it as the difference between how far a given propeller would screw itself forward in a solid medium (Jell-O?) compared to how far it screws itself forward in air. This difference is called slippage.

Prop blades are twisted (vary in pitch) along their length to allow for a relatively constant angle of attack during cruising flight. After all, the inner portion of the blade is moving fairly slowly compared to the tips, which would approach supersonic speed if the manufacturer didn't take steps to prevent it. The noise that the neighbors complain about is caused by the propeller, not the engine. Three-bladed props are quieter than two-bladed props because they don't have to rotate as fast to develop the same amount of lift.

Through the use of a governor, constant-speed props change the pitch of the whole propeller blade to keep engine RPM constant at a pilot-selected speed (Figure 13-2). You want a flat (low) pitch and high RPM for takeoff, to develop maximum thrust. For cruise, you want to select the lowest RPM setting at which the engine runs smoothly and select manifold pressure based on desired true airspeed and fuel economy considerations. At a low RPM setting, the propeller will be taking big bites of the air (high pitch). When you advance the throttle, the governor increases prop pitch, and when you reduce the manifold pressure the governor decreases prop pitch.

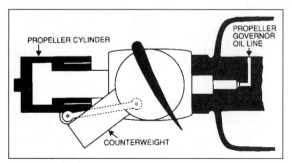

Figure 13-2. Controlling propeller pitch

A constant-speed prop is like a sharp tool—it makes the work easier but can hurt you if not used wisely. There is little that you can do wrong during takeoff, climb, and cruise, but you can cause yourself some real problems on short final. As you reduce the manifold pressure, the governor keeps the RPM constant by flattening the blade pitch. When the pitch is as flat as it can go (we're not talking turboprops here), further throttle reduction has no effect. This usually happens at about 12" of manifold pressure but can vary from one installation to another.

Wait until the manifold pressure is less than 15 inches before pushing the prop control forward (if you do...you certainly don't have to). That will keep the airport neighbors from hearing the annoying br-a-a-a-p-p-p that leads to petitions for airport closure.

When the propeller pitch is at its flattest, it has the effect of a flat metal disk bolted to the propeller hub. The tremendous drag of this disk is called flat plate drag. It can be useful when you need to lose a couple of hundred feet to get on a proper descent path, but can cause hard landings if flat plate drag still exists during the flare. The secret is to keep the manifold pressure in the 11" to 12" range, where the prop is essentially idling and not holding you back. Pulling the throttle back to the stop guarantees that you will have more drag than you plan for when you extend the flaps.

What is Manifold Pressure, Anyway?

A manifold pressure gauge acts like a barometer, measuring the pressure in the intake manifold downstream (on the engine side) of the throttle butterfly. At power settings near idle, when the descending pistons are trying to pull air past the closed throttle butterfly, the manifold pressure is low. As you open the throttle to increase power, the pressure measured in the intake manifold increases as airflow increases. Without turbocharging, manifold pressure will approach but never equal the outside air pressure (unless you shut the engine down, something I don't recommend unless all three wheels are on the ground).

Which Knob When?

The manifold pressure gauge reacts directly to throttle movement. For takeoff, the propeller control (linked to the governor to control RPM) is set full forward for high RPM. After the engine/propeller team have done their work and gotten you into the air in a hurry, leave the throttle alone (for best cooling) and pull the prop control back 100-200 RPM to decrease noise complaints from airport neighbors. This goes against the accepted wisdom (to reduce power use the throttle first, then the prop control, but this is reduced noise, not power). During the climb, because barometric pressure decreases 1 inch per 1,000 feet of altitude, you must adjust the throttle setting to maintain climb power.

At cruise altitude, set cruise power according to the manufacturer's cruise chart for that altitude; a good thumb-rule is the lowest RPM setting that allows smooth engine operation without vibration, and a manifold pressure (throttle) setting that meets your requirements for either speed or economy. As you retard the prop control at altitude, the governor will increase the blade angle to take bigger bites of the air (low RPM): the characteristics of a cruise prop. Once you have set the propeller control to the desired RPM, the governor will change blade angle as required to maintain that RPM.

If you have to add power to climb, or to increase airspeed, always advance the propeller control before the throttle; this will ensure that dangerously high pressures are not developed in the cylinders. Most pre-landing checklists include a reminder to move the propeller control to the high RPM position, to position it properly in case of an aborted landing. Before blindly following this procedure, however, use a little common sense. Is there an airplane at the hold line waiting for takeoff? Is there a child with a bicycle or a loose animal near the runway? In that kind of situation, it is wise to prepare for a go-around. If there is no potential conflict, leave the mixture and prop controls alone until the wheels are on the runway. If you do push the prop control full forward, you have completed the first half of the "increase power" procedure.

Turbine Engines

Turbine engines are so expensive, and the consequences of improper operation so severe, that is it likely that you will be sent to a factory school before your employer's insurance company will allow you to act as PIC of a jet or turboprop. It's even unlikely that you will be given the opportunity to start a turbine engine without a certain amount of training. A moment of brain-fade or indecision and the cost to the airplane owner can approach $100,000. On the other hand, if you exhibit some knowledge of turbines and how they work it may make the difference in a hiring decision.

In a turbine engine, combustion takes place in a combustion chamber (burner can) and the expanding gases resulting from that combustion spin a turbine. Several compressor stages will be included, because the thrust of a gas turbine engine can be increased by increasing the mass flow of air through the engine. No reciprocating motion, as in a turbocharged piston engine—just smooth rotating motion. The turbine may spin a propeller or it may accelerate gases out through a nozzle. Quiet, vibration-free operation and a high power-to-weight ratio make turbines the engines of choice for high-end airplanes.

In a turboprop, the turbine shaft is connected directly or indirectly to a propeller. In a turbofan engine, which is the type of jet engine you are most likely to encounter in general aviation, the exhaust gases drive a fan that is essentially a multi-bladed shrouded propeller and the resulting thrust drives the airplane forward. Because your entry into the world of turbines is most likely to take place in a turboprop rather than a jet, that is where this text will place its emphasis.

Let's get the bad stuff out of the way first. The greatest hazards to the health of a turbine engine exist during starting. The way things are supposed to happen, the starting process gets compressed air flowing through the combustion chamber before fuel is introduced and ignited. If you rush the process and start the fire too early, the result will be a "hot start" or "hung start" and internal temperatures will be higher than the metallurgical limits of the combustion chamber materials. At the very least, this means a complete teardown and inspection of the engine.

This is a good place to mention "hot section" inspections. Turbine engines don't have time-between-overhaul (TBO) limits, they have limits on the number of hours or the number of operating cycles (starts and shutdowns) between inspections of those engine sections exposed to high temperature. This is because metal exposed to high temperature gases and/or centrifugal force tend to "creep," "grow," or erode, so the engine manufacturer tells the operator how often the engine must be opened up and the hot sections inspected.

You'll be dealing with a new kind of electricity source called a starter-generator. Acting as a starter, it uses battery power (*lots* of battery power!) to spin the compressor and turbine up to a specific rotational speed; when that speed is attained the ignition and fuel can come in accelerating the engine further, then the starter-generator puts on its generator hat. With the fire lit, the rotational speed should continue to increase. If the airplane batteries or the external battery cart do not deliver enough electricity (typically 800-1,000 amperes) to make the starter-generator get all that metal spinning fast enough, you will have a hot start. If the rotational speed does not increase but "hangs," a hung start is the result. Instead of a controlled flow of hot gases you have a puddle of fuel just sitting there and burning, with more fuel coming in every second that you delay a shutdown.

Many airplane models automate the starting process so that all you have to do is push a button and then sit back and relax. Ever heard of Murphy's Law? You *must* monitor the engine instruments during any kind of a start, automated or not, alert to abort the start if the exhaust gas temperature does not stabilize or if the compressor speed does not continue to increase after the fire starts.

The most common types of general aviation turboprop engines are Pratt & Whitneys and Garretts. Walking down the ramp, you can pick out the P&W powered airplanes because the props will be feathered and may be tied to prevent them from rotating with the wind. Their propeller shafts are not directly connected to the shaft that drives the compressor and turbine stages, and the pilot can keep the engine running while the propeller is stopped. Garrett engines have solid shafts connecting the compressor and turbine stages with the propeller.

With the P&Ws, you will have two RPM gauges to monitor: one for the gas generator (N1) and one for the propeller (N2), and prop RPM can be controlled independent of engine RPM. Garrett props run at 100-percent of engine RPM continuously (your ears will tell you when a Garrett-powered airplane taxis past).

The control quadrant will have three sets of knobs, like any other twin, but one set will be called "condition levers." The throttle and mixture controls perform their usual functions, while the condition levers are similar but not identical to prop controls.

Another term you can use to show that you know your way around turbines is "flat rated." The maximum power output of turbine engines falls off as altitude increases, just like reciprocating engines. The manufacturer of a turboprop handles this by installing engines with, for example, 700 horsepower capability but limiting the pilot to a flat rating of only 500 horsepower for takeoff and continuous operation. Thus a turbine engine is just loafing at altitude while delivering high true airspeeds and excellent specific fuel consumption. Turboprop engine ratings are stated as shaft horsepower, but the pilot's instrumentation reads torque and/or temperature and the operating restrictions are stated in those terms. When setting takeoff power, the pilot must be sure that the maximum torque or temperature limits are not exceeded. On one of those high, hot, and humid days it is not unusual for a pilot to be unable to get rated torque out of the engines before reaching the temperature limit. Density altitude doesn't care how much the airplane costs.

This is hardly an exhaustive discussion of turbine engines, but it should be basic preparation for the manufacturer's classes. It has been short on specifics because of the many differences between engines and engine models. That's also the reason why no pictures or diagrams have been used.

Winter Operations

As a private pilot, if you didn't want to fly on a cold day you stayed home by the fire. As a commercial pilot you don't have that luxury. It's embarrassing when your passengers are standing around looking at their watches while you handle a problem that could have been avoided. If you operate as a commercial pilot under Part 91, you must observe any restrictions in the Pilot's Operating Handbook (new 91.9). In most cases, this will be something like "flight into icing conditions not authorized." It's up to you to determine whether weather forecasts indicate the possibility of encountering icing conditions and whether they can be avoided. As a Part 135 pilot you are more restricted; you cannot depart under VFR into known or forecast light or moderate icing conditions unless the airplane is fully equipped with prop and wing boots and a hot windshield, or under IFR into known or forecast light or moderate icing conditions no matter how well the airplane is equipped.

Fortunately for all of the Part 135 pilots, there is an out. If current weather reports and briefing information indicate that the icing conditions in the forecast will not be encountered, you are on your own. Be prepared to explain your decision to an Operations Inspector if you are forced to divert or land short because of icing. If you are flying an airplane that is not certificated for flight into icing conditions, do not let that stop you from reporting an icing encounter to ATC. Controllers are not required to know the certification status of either pilots or airplanes, and they have neither the time or the authority to initiate enforcement actions. However, if you report an icing encounter and subsequently have an accident be-

cause you did not take action to get out of the icing conditions, you are in trouble.

Part 135 says that you cannot take off with any frost, snow, or ice adhering to the props, windshield, wings or stabilizing surfaces, or control surfaces. Although it is difficult to imagine why a pilot operating under either Part 135 or 91 would ignore this restriction, every winter someone tries it with disastrous results.

Part 135 makes it the responsibility of the operator to establish deicing procedures with supporting training. You can be pretty sure that an approved procedure will boil down to: "The PIC shall ensure that no ice is adhering to…" as above.

Preheat

You load your passengers, climb into the pilot's seat, and hit the starter. The engine fires a couple of times and quits, and ignores your further efforts while you abuse the starter and battery. If it's a cold day, ice has probably bridged the spark plugs, shorting them out. They will have to be removed and dried before they will fire or, if any type of heater is available, five minutes or so per plug applied with the plugs in place should do the trick. The passengers will be plenty hot by this time.

If the outside air temperature is +20°F or colder, you should apply preheat to the whole engine; not just the top end or the oil pan, but the whole engine. If resources are limited, apply the heat at the bottom of the engine and pile blankets and coats on the cowling to retain the heat. Plug the air intakes temporarily to avoid losing heat. After starting, keep the engine at idle until the oil temperature is $\frac{1}{3}$ of the way into the green. Of course, you would be better off if you did all of this before the passengers showed up.

Don't ignore the cockpit area when you are spreading the heat around, because the flight instruments don't take kindly to operating under frigid conditions. And while you are preflighting the airplane, be sure that the crankcase breather tube is free of ice. When you shut the engine down in cold weather, water vapor is drawn through the breather and may freeze there. If it isn't removed, pressure will build up in the crankcase and may blow out some seals, taking the engine oil with them.

Complex Airplane

You will take all or part of your commercial checkride in a complex airplane, meaning one with flaps, retractable landing gear, and a constant speed propeller. Before your instructor recommends you for the ride, you will have to have at least ten hours of dual instruction in a complex airplane. Flaps should be no mystery, and constant speed propellers have already been discussed, so it's time to discuss retractable gear systems.

Retractable Landing Gear

When drag increases, the horsepower required to overcome that increase is the cube of the added drag, so it takes a lot of horses to pull fixed landing gear through the air. Causing the gear to disappear into the wings or fuselage puts those added horses to work increasing airspeed, climb capability, or both.

When you fly an airplane with fold-up gear, you have two new V-speeds to memorize: V_{LO}, which is the landing gear operating speed, and V_{LE}, which is the maximum speed with the gear extended. You will find many airplanes in which the speeds are identical, because the doors which cover the wheels when retracted are fastened to the wheel assembly. The drag of the extended gear will limit how much you can accelerate, but occasionally you will extend the gear and then the tower will say "Maintain 160 on final, jet traffic to follow." If V_{LE} is less than 160, either retract the gear (bad idea) or tell the tower you will be unable to comply.

When the gear doors must open to allow the landing gear to extend and then close again, as is the case with almost all jets and turboprops (and Cessna Skymasters and some 210s), the V_{LO} speed will be much lower than the V_{LE} speed. While the doors are opening and closing they are vulnerable to excessive speed. You will almost always be ahead of the game if you slow to five knots or so below V_{LO} before reaching for the gear handle—if you overstress anything in the extension/retraction system it may fail on you at the most inopportune time.

Gear extension and retraction systems are either all-electric, electro-hydraulic, or hydraulic. Systems that rely exclusively on hydraulics have fallen out of favor, although you can find them on Aztecs, Apaches, and a few other models. With the exception of the lights that indicate gear down, in transit, or up, there are no electric elements to these systems. In the usual multi-engine installation there is only one engine-driven hydraulic pump, and if that engine becomes inoperative you will have to extend the gear manually using a handpump. These installations usually have a last-ditch extension system that uses carbon-dioxide gas to blow the gear down.

All-electric systems use a reversible electric motor to drive the gear extension and retraction mechanism. They will have circuit breakers to protect the motor against overload, and if the gear fails to extend, the circuit breaker panel is the first place you should look. The emergency extension system is usually a handcrank or similar device. The emergency extension checklist will tell you to pull the circuit breaker before beginning the manual extension procedure, because if a temporary electrical glitch heals itself while you are cranking you are in for a real surprise.

Electro-hydraulic systems utilize an electric motor to drive a hydraulic pump, and hydraulics provide the muscle to move the landing gear and to hold it in the retracted position. It's not unusual to hear the motor go "brrrrp" every now and then to keep the pressure up and the wheels in the wells. Because it is hydraulic pressure that keeps the wheels retracted, the emergency extension procedure usually just releases the pressure and lets the landing gear fall into position through gravity. You want to be flying nice and slow when you do this, so that air loads will not keep the wheels from locking in the down position.

You must become familiar with the emergency extension system of any retractable gear airplane you fly, and it doesn't hurt to go out and try the system occasionally. You should be especially careful after the airplane has had maintenance performed on it; some pilots have learned too late that the emergency crank has been covered by upholstery or made inaccessible in some other way.

When you take your checkride, the examiner will ask you to explain how many ways that you can tell that the gear is down and locked—this may be lights, mirrors, or mechanical indicators. Are you able to tell if the main gear is locked down but the nose gear is unsafe? What do you do if you only get two green lights? And what happens to the gear indicating lights when you turn the panel lights on? You are expected to know the system inside and out.

Do not rush to retract the landing gear after liftoff; there is little to gain and much to lose. Wait until you have a positive rate of climb on the vertical speed indicator and no more usable runway in front of you before you reach for the gear switch. Similarly, don't be in a big hurry to retract the flaps after landing. What does that have to do with retractable gear? If you mistakenly reach for the gear switch instead of the flap handle you will find out. Your system should have a squat switch that opens the retraction circuit when the weight of the airplane is on the wheels, but don't trust that switch to save you if you grab the wrong handle.

Environmental System

Your passengers want to be comfortable while you speed them to their destination. Keeping them from turning blue is part of your responsibility, and you might want to re-read the section on supplemental oxygen in that regard, but in this section the subject is heating and cooling.

As the pilot-in-command of a single-engine Part 135 airplane the environmental system is simple: a heater muff around the exhaust stack provides heated air, controlled by the "CABIN HEAT" knob, and ventilation is provided from the outside by the "CABIN AIR" knob. Used in combination, you can control the temperature and the flow of heated air or provide a flow of cool air. There will be a "DEFROST" knob that will allow you to steal some of that hot air to defrost the windshield. Hard to make a mistake, and the heat is always available.

When you climb into the left seat of a twin, however, things get more complicated. Transporting hot air from the nacelles to the cabin doesn't work too well, so sometimes a fuel-fired internal combustion heater is provided (Figure 13-3). The heater will be located somewhere where you can't get at it in flight. If you're not sure of its location, look for a little stack sticking out through the fuselage with a smudge of dirt aft of it. The heater will have an OFF-FAN-HEATER switch, which will allow you to run the ventilation blower for a few moments to cool things down after the heater is turned off. Placing the switch in the HEATER position will initiate fuel flow and ignite the heater. There will be a cabin temperature lever or knob which will allow you to govern the amount of heat delivered, and there may be controls to allow diversion of heated air to the front and back seats. Before any of this happens, however, there will be a control labeled CABIN AIR or INTAKE AIR which must be partially or fully open. Of course, there will be a defroster control.

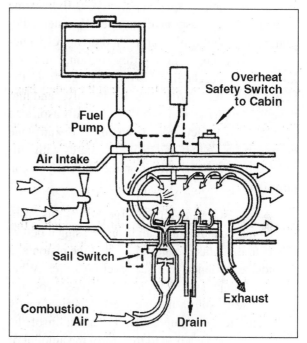

Figure 13-3. Typical combustion heater

Be sure that you know how to operate the heating system! It is relatively easy to mishandle the controls and convince yourself that the heater has failed, while you and your passengers shiver. In a Baron you can do it if you pull the air control out too far, and in a Seneca you can do it if you don't open the air control far enough. Other models have their own idiosyncrasies. With no heat the passengers are complaining, and the last thing you want to do (but should do) is break out the manual to study the system.

The heater has a fail-safe over-temperature reset button which will shut the system down if it gets too hot—this is usually the result of running the heater on the ground without the ventilation fan on (in some systems the fan runs on the ground automatically and is shut off by a squat switch when the airplane lifts off). If the button pops you will have to land to reset it.

Remember that the heater uses fuel (usually from the right tank) and factor that into your fuel planning. It will use about 3 pounds per hour.

If your boss will go along with it and the system will permit it, it's nice to have the cabin warm when the passengers board.

Turbocharging

You have probably spent most of your flying time behind "normally aspirated" engines. Webster's dictionary says that aspiration is "a drawing of something in, out, up, or through by suction," and you know that a descending piston sucks air from the induction system, through the intake valve, and into the cylinder on the intake stroke. Normally aspirated engines start to get short of breath as the airplane climbs, because the air density decreases with altitude, and this places a limit on the altitude you can climb to.

In its simplest form, a turbocharger solves this problem by taking that thin air and compressing it before it gets to the intake manifold, so that the piston and cylinder experience near-sea level pressures. What runs the compressor? Exhaust gases pass through a waste gate to spin a turbine wheel that is directly connected to the compressor. The position of the waste gate can be adjusted to control the amount of gas flowing over the turbine and thus compressor speed. When the waste gate is fully open, all of the exhaust bypasses the turbine and is discharged overboard, and when the waste gate is fully closed, all exhaust gas must pass over the turbine on its way out.

There are many turbocharger systems, and each has its own operating procedure. You must study and understand the systems you use, because misuse of the turbocharger can cause severe engine damage. Manual systems, where you have direct control of the waste gate, offer the greatest potential for mistakes. With such a system, the waste gate is fully open for takeoff, because the air is dense and no "boosting" is required. When increasing altitude causes the engine to lose power, you can gradually close the waste gate to keep the manifold pressure at its sea level climb value. At cruise altitude, the waste gate may be fully closed. If you forget to open the waste gate as you descend, the increasing density of the air coupled with the effect of the compressor may

raise the manifold pressure above the red line (maximum) set by the manufacturer.

Some systems have a fixed waste gate, which limits the amount of manifold pressure that can be delivered by allowing all exhaust gas over a preset value to bypass the turbine. This places a limit on the critical altitude (the altitude at which the turbocharging system is doing as much as it can and any further climb will result in a decrease in manifold pressure). It's a tradeoff between maximum altitude capability and having a safety margin.

Some cabin-class twins have automatic controllers that sense changes in air density and adjust the waste gate accordingly; you can set the throttle for climb power and forget it. Because the systems react to changes in airspeed as well as density (because of varying ram air pressure), these systems require a lot of juggling of throttle and mixture controls for maximum efficiency. Figure 13-4 shows the Seneca II system.

Operating turbocharged engines requires special attention to temperature management; they generate a lot of heat because they can develop sea-level power at altitudes where the cooling effect of air is diminished by lower air density. You must use the throttle, mixture, and cowl flaps singly or in combination to keep the engine operating temperatures within safe limits.

You cannot transfer experience with one turbocharged airplane into another model. Systems change from model to model and sometimes from one model year to another, so you must know the system you are using thoroughly.

Pressurization

Pressurization and turbocharging go together, because the air that it takes to inflate the cabin comes from the turbocharger. Systems and controls vary widely enough that this discussion will deal in generalities (a typical system is shown in Figure 13-5). It is vitally important that you study and understand the system in the airplanes you fly.

If you took some excess air from the turbocharger and piped it to a sealed passenger cabin, you would soon develop a pressure differential between the cabin and the outside atmosphere that would at best

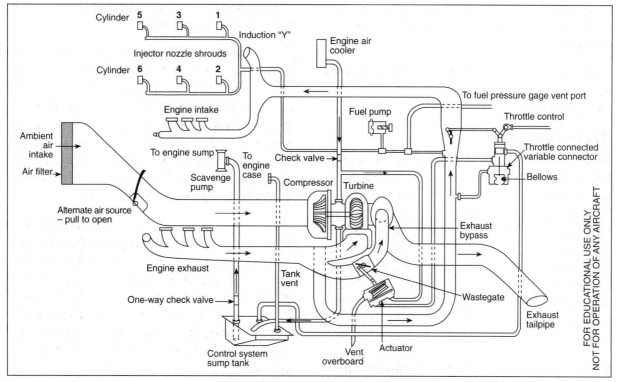

Figure 13-4. Typical turbocharger system

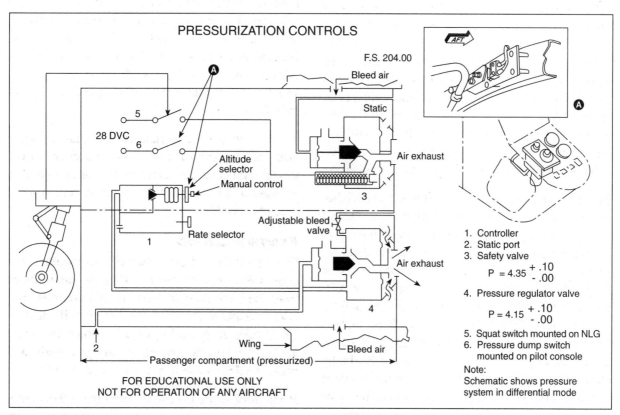

Figure 13-5. Typical pressurization system

overstress the structure and at worst blow out the windows. The maximum operating altitude of a pressurized airplane is determined by the maximum pressure differential that the fuselage and its windows and doors will withstand. At sea level, the pressure both inside and outside the airplane is approximately 14.7 pounds per square inch (psi) and there is no pressure differential (and a squat switch ensures that the airplane cannot be pressurized on the ground!). At 10,000 feet MSL, where atmospheric pressure is 10.1 psi, if the cabin pressure is maintained at the 14.7 sea level figure the differential is 4.6 psi. Take the airplane to 30,000 feet with a sea level cabin and the differential between inside and outside is 10.3 psi. You can see why the fuselage and its fittings have to be stronger as operating altitude increases. The airlines fudge on this a bit by allowing their cabins to climb to about 8,000 feet at cruise altitude, reducing the differential slightly.

If too much pressure differential presents a problem, it is apparent that every pressurized airplane must leak continuously. The calibrated leak is the outflow valve, and its setting is determined by the pressurization controller; by controlling how much cabin air leaks out, the pilot controls the cabin pressure and thereby the cabin altitude. In most systems the controller allows the pilot to set a cruise altitude and the system automatically maintains the desired differential, although the rate at which the cabin climbs can be controlled manually if desired. When the airplane is climbing 1,500 feet per minute it is kind to the passenger's ears to climb the cabin at 500 feet per minute. Typically, the pilot sets the controller 500 or 1,000 feet above the actual cruise altitude so that the outflow valve is not continually opening and closing (and affecting everyone's ears). Figure 13-5 illustrates how a system works.

If the outflow valve should malfunction or stick in the closed position, a cabin safety valve set at the maximum differential will open to avoid structural damage. If smoking is allowed in your airplane, the outflow valve will require regular cleaning and maintenance—all that tar-laden air flows out through it.

Airport Operations

As a commercial pilot you will not have a lot of control over which airports your customers want to fly to, so you may find yourself dealing with a different mix of traffic than you are accustomed to. Many airports serve general aviation and the military as well as the air carriers, so one day you may be asked to keep your speed up to maintain spacing from a following jet and the next day you may be following a flight of National Guard helicopters. The common thread will be wake turbulence avoidance.

To review procedures for avoiding vortices from heavy airplanes, remember that the strength of the vortex is greatest when the generating airplane is heavy, clean, and slow—just after liftoff. If you are in position to take off following a jet at a controlled airport, the tower will impose a delay which you can waive if you so desire; my advice is to sit and wait. At a nontower airport give yourself three or four minutes. If other airplanes want to taxi around you and take off while you're waiting, let them. Have your camera ready—you might have a picture for the 6 o'clock news. If you are going to takeoff after a jet has landed, taxi down the runway or at least delay your rotation until you have passed the point at which the jet's nose wheel touched down. Remember that vortices are generated when the wings are developing lift, and when the airplane's weight has been transferred from the wings to the wheels the vortices go away.

If you are landing behind a jet, stay above its flight path (a dot or two high on the glide slope if you are shooting an approach) and land beyond its touchdown point. On the other hand, if a jet is rolling for takeoff and you are on final, aim for the numbers. It won't start throwing vortices until well into its takeoff run.

Wing-tip vortices do drift with the wind, and that can be both good and bad. Maybe a crosswind will blow the vortices from an airplane taking off on a parallel runway away from the runway you plan to use—and maybe the wind will drift those vortices onto your runway. If you are taking off behind a large airplane, the vortex from its right wing will move to the right—unless there is a crosswind from the right, in which case it will just lie there and wait for you. A light quartering tailwind presents the greatest hazard to lightplane pilots.

Helicopters have their own version of wake vortices. When they are hovering, their downwash strikes the ground and vortices go in all directions. Stay at least three rotor diameters (150 feet?) away from hovering helicopters. As they move forward, helicopters produce vortices similar to those developed by large fixed-wing aircraft; use caution when operating behind landing and departing helicopters, because they are throwing vortices all the time.

Land and Hold Short Operations

You are going to be operating at many airports that have crossing runways and/or taxiways, and you may be instructed to "land and hold short" (LAHSO) of an intersecting runway/taxiway on days when basic VFR minima exist (1,000-foot ceiling, 3 statute miles visibility). You must read back all LAHSO instructions, including the words "hold short of runway__" and you must immediately inform the controller if you will not be able to stop in time. The available landing distance (ALD) is published in the A/FD and on approach plates (or will be provided by ATC on request). It is your responsibility to ensure that you can land and stop within that distance.

Helpful Hints

There is more to being a charter pilot than the ability to fly and obey the regulations. Your passengers quite properly look to you as the solution of their transportation problem, and although you will probably never see a specific passenger more than once, you owe it to them and to your profession to treat all passengers as though they were your full-time employers.

The FAA's standards for airport security have caused confusion and consternation. You may not be able to get from the ramp to the outside world without considerable effort and inconvenience, and your passengers will wonder why you were taken by surprise (it's even more fun when they return to the airport and can't get to the plane). Look in the Airport/Facility Directory for any notes that might alert you to problems. It is also very much worthwhile to telephone an operator at the destination airport and ask about ramp access — they may keep someone on past closing time just to solve your problem. Phone numbers are in the AOPA Aviation USA publication, in addition to other sources.

Before you load your passengers, determine if they will be met at the other end and if the folks at the destination know where on the airport you will be

Figure 13-6. The good old days

arriving. While they are calling the folks at the other end with that information, they might as well tell them the airplane number and model. Nothing is worse than having your passengers sit at one FBO waiting for pickup while their relatives or associates are at another FBO (or the airline terminal!) saying "I don't know — it's a little airplane."

Unless your passengers express a desire to be left alone while in flight, keep them in the loop by explaining what you are going to do: "I'm going to extend the landing gear now; you'll hear a thump and we'll slow down a little." The great majority of charter passengers use that mode of transportation not by choice, but because there is no other means of transportation available that meets their needs, and they are leery of small propeller driven airplanes. It is your job to convince them that light airplane travel is safe, and more fun than the airlines.

Expect your passengers to be apprehensive; many will never have been in a small plane before and will not be too happy about it. That apprehension can lead to hyperventilation, which in turn can lead to unconsciousness. Passengers exhibiting symptoms such as light-headedness and tingling in the fingers and toes are suffering from hyperventilation. The problem is not lack of oxygen but lack of carbon dioxide, because the level of CO_2 in the blood triggers the breathing reflex. Having the passenger breathe into cupped hands or into a paper bag should resolve the situation, and the passenger should be advised to breathe at a slower rate.

If your airplane has a toilet, tell the passengers how to use it during your preflight announcements. Nonflyers have no idea that airplanes smaller than 727s have toilet facilities. It really makes your day when you go back into the cabin and learn what innovative measures your passengers have used while sitting four feet from a functioning potty. If your airplane doesn't have any facilities, make that point clear to everyone before takeoff.

Have plenty of large sick-sacks available and show your passengers where they are.

If there is any way that a passenger could inadvertently hit or obstruct a switch, knob, or handle, point out that possibility and ask that they take special care—the fuel-drain lever on the front surface of the rear passenger seats in Piper PA-32s makes a great footrest until the engine quits, and the emergency gear extension crank in many airplanes can get tangled up with purses and camera straps.

Be sure that your pretakeoff announcement includes instructions for getting out of the airplane if you are "busy handling any possible emergency," which is better than saying unconscious. If there is only one exit door, make certain that everyone on board knows how to open it. Twins, of course, have to have at least two exits and you should identify them both. Of course, preface your announcement by saying that Federal regulations require that you inform the passengers about emergency measures, just as the big iron pilots must (14 CFR 135.117).

Expect surprises, and be ready to exercise your PIC authority.

Don't let your passenger's needs dictate the conduct of the flight. If your passengers bring along some unannounced friends, or baggage which is unusually bulky or heavy, don't take the trip unless the loading meets your personal standards, which should be at least as tough as the regulations.

Don't allow your passenger's agenda to force you to fly into deteriorating weather or into an unsuitable airport. If they have to catch a bus to their destination from the airport at which you land, they will be angry but safe.

Unless your charter is a sightseeing or survey flight from the outset, don't let your passenger's desire to fly over their home or place of business distract you

from completing the flight as filed. An unexpected diversion, especially at night, has the potential for real problems.

Let your passengers listen to the radio, even if you are wearing a headset, and explain briefly what is going on. They will be amazed to learn that you share frequencies with the airlines. But tell them not to ask questions when you are close to the destination airport—you don't want to miss any calls close in.

Doors have been known to pop open just after liftoff, creating noise and confusion in the cabin. One method of forestalling this possibility is to close the door yourself, even if that means leaning across the right seat passenger. If the door does open, however, make no attempt to close it in flight but return to the airport and close it on the ground. Every U.S. certificated airplane can be controlled with a door open, although some models experience buffeting due to the disturbed airflow over the tail surfaces.

Aeronautical Decision Making

Statistics tell us that over eighty percent of all aircraft accidents can be traced to pilot error; running out of fuel, icing up, and entering destructive turbulence are examples of pilot error. Taking passengers on a trip in instrument conditions immediately after an annual or one-hundred hour inspection, or flying an airplane that has been parked for months or years are other examples. Almost every pilot error accident or incident can be traced to a chain of poor decisions— and almost always the final link in the chain is getting into the airplane and taking off.

My personal mantra when faced with an aeronautical decision is "How would a prosecution lawyer in a negligence lawsuit describe my decision to a jury?" That has served me well for over thirty years. The FAA's position is more detailed. They ascribe poor decisions to one of five attitudes: anti-authority ("they can't tell me what to do!"), impulsivity ("do something, even if it's wrong"), invulnerability ("accidents happen to other people"), macho ("I can fly anything"), and resignation ("what's the use — I'm going to crash"). Advisory Circular 60-22, *Aeronautical Decision Making*, contains a Hazardous Attitude Inventory test that all pilots should take to determine if they see any of these attitudes when they look in the mirror. This AC should be in every pilot's library.

Each hazardous attitude has an antidote: a pilot who feels that regulations are for other pilots should think "Just about every regulation was written after an accident. I can't go wrong if I follow the rules." A pilot who is impulsive should think "*Whoa! Slow down! Think before you act!*" A pilot who feels invulnerable need only read the accident reports in aviation magazines (or on the NTSB website at www.ntsb.gov/aviation/Accident.htm).

Macho pilots have to realize that the laws of physics are immutable and that strength and bravado will always fail when pitted against physical laws. Pilots who consider themselves as passengers forced to accept whatever the fates deal out should have a good instructor build their confidence—an intact airplane will go wherever the pilot directs it, but the pilot must take command.

Pilots with poor decision-making skills can fall into one or more of these subtle traps:

Peer pressure—not wanting to look weak or indecisive in front of friends, associates, or other pilots. Trying to show that you have the "right stuff."

Mind set—failure to accept the fact that conditions have changed and modify the planned flight accordingly.

Get-There-Itis—letting the need to meet a scheduled event overcome common sense.

Duck-Under Syndrome—the tendency to descend below minimums on an instrument approach "just to take a look."

Scud Running—the tendency to fly lower and lower to stay out of the clouds.

Continuing VFR into instrument meteorological conditions—the natural result of scud running taken to extremes.

Getting Behind the Aircraft—being surprised by events instead of being ready for them.

Loss of Situational or Positional Awareness—losing track of where you are, or getting so far into a bad situation that you can't get out.

Operating Without Adequate Fuel Reserve—needs no explanation; there is no excuse for running out of fuel.

Descending Below Minimum Enroute Altitude—the duck-under syndrome, applied to cruise flight.

Flying Outside the Envelope—Unjustified reliance on illusory built-in "safety factors" or on the pilot's imagined superhuman skill.

Neglect of Flight Planning, Preflight Inspection, Checklists, etc.—reliance on memory, familiarity with routine, flying a familiar route.

Paradoxically, high-time pilots are the most likely to want to demonstrate that they have the "right stuff," although these traps await pilots at all skill levels.

Risk management begins with recognizing hazardous thoughts and attitudes; it looks at situational awareness, problem recognition, and good judgment. Aeronautical decision making is a systematic approach to the mental process used by pilots to consistently determine the best course of action for a given set of circumstances.

When all is said and done, though, ask yourself how you would defend your decision that the weather was good enough, the fuel supply was adequate, or the runway was long enough when in the witness chair—you'll make the right decision every time. Chicken Little was a survivor.

Chapter 13
Review Questions for Commercial Students

These questions are for commercial pilot students and should, for the most part, be a simple review of private pilot knowledge.

1. Fouling of spark plugs is more apt to occur if the aircraft

   A—gains altitude with no mixture adjustment.
   B—descends from altitude with no mixture adjustment.
   C—throttle is advanced very abruptly.

2. The best power mixture is that fuel/air ratio at which

   A—cylinder head temperatures are the coolest.
   B—the most power can be obtained for any given throttle setting.
   C—a given power can be obtained with the highest manifold pressure or throttle setting.

3. Which statement is true concerning the effect of the application of carburetor heat?

   A—It enriches the fuel/air mixture.
   B—It leans the fuel/air mixture.
   C—It has no effect on the fuel/air mixture.

4. A detuning of engine crankshaft counterweights is a source of overstress that may be caused by

   A—rapid opening and closing of the throttle.
   B—carburetor ice forming on the throttle valve.
   C—operating with an excessively rich fuel/air mixture.

5. Which statement best describes the operating principle of a constant-speed propeller?

   A—As throttle setting is changed by the pilot, the prop governor causes pitch angle of the propeller blades to remain unchanged.
   B—A high blade angle, or increased pitch, reduces the propeller drag and allows more engine power for takeoffs.
   C—The propeller control regulates the engine RPM and in turn the propeller RPM.

6. The reason for variations in geometric pitch (twisting) along a propeller blade is that it

   A—permits a relatively constant angle of incidence along its length when in cruising flight.
   B—prevents the portion of the blade near the hub from stalling during cruising flight.
   C—permits a relatively constant angle of attack along its length when in cruising flight.

7. Which is true regarding preheating an aircraft during cold weather operations?

   A—The cabin area as well as the engine should be preheated.
   B—The cabin area should not be preheated with portable heaters.
   C—Hot air should be blown directly at the engine through the air intakes.

8. Propeller efficiency is the

   A—ratio of thrust horsepower to brake horsepower.
   B—actual distance a propeller advances in one revolution.
   C—ratio of geometric pitch to effective pitch.

9. When landing behind a large aircraft, which procedure should be followed for vortex avoidance?

   A— Stay above its final approach flightpath all the way to touchdown.
   B— Stay below and to one side of its final approach flightpath.
   C— Stay well below its final approach flightpath and land at least 2,000 feet behind.

10. Choose the correct statement regarding wake turbulence.

   A— Vortex generation begins with the initiation of the takeoff roll.
   B— The primary hazard is loss of control because of induced roll.
   C— The greatest vortex strength is produced when the generating airplane is heavy, clean and fast.

11. Aeronautical Decision Making (ADM) is a

   A— systematic approach to the mental process used by pilots to consistently determine the best course of action for a given set of circumstances.
   B— decision making process which relies on good judgment to reduce risks associated with each flight.
   C— mental process of analyzing all information in a particular situation and making a timely decision on what action to take.

12. What is the first step in neutralizing a hazardous attitude in the ADM process?

   A— Recognition of invulnerability in the situation.
   B— Dealing with improper judgment.
   C— Recognition of hazardous thoughts.

13. While on an IFR flight, a pilot emerges from a cloud to find himself within 300 feet of a helicopter. Which of the following alternatives best illustrates the "macho" reaction?

   A— He is not too concerned; everything will be all right.
   B— He flies a little closer, just to show him.
   C— He quickly turns away and dives, to avoid collision.

14. Who has the final authority to accept or decline any "land and hold short" (LAHSO) clearance?

   A— ATC tower controller.
   B— Airplane owner/operator.
   C— Pilot-in-Command.

Preparing for the Practical Tests

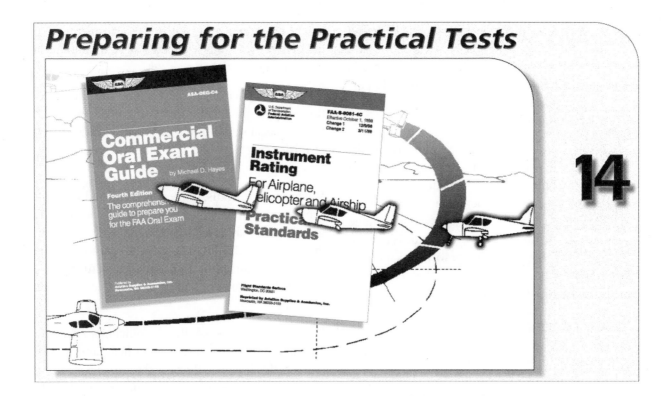

For Instrument Students Only

If the airline transport rating is the Ph.D. of pilot certificates, the instrument rating is the master's degree. When the examiner hands you your temporary certificate, you will be legally qualified to take your loved ones on a cross-country trip at night in instrument conditions while sharing the airspace with air carriers and other IFR old-timers. That's why this is an especially tough checkride. You will improve your chances if you buy a copy of the appropriate Practical Test Standards (PTS) so that you will know what is expected of you and what the standards of performance are. Go through the PTS occasionally during your training to be sure that you are learning the things you need to know. The PTS also contains a checklist of items to bring with you to the checkride.

The examiner will want you to be able to explain every symbol and number on enroute charts and approach plates, and will expect you to know the regulations governing instrument flight without error. While the examiner will not insist that you use government charts, it would be to your advantage to be able to interpret them even if you use Jeppesen. You will be asked to prepare an instrument flight log and flight plan for a cross-country trip, get the

weather and any Notices to Airmen, and explain how the flight will be affected. You should be able to use all of the performance charts in the Pilot's Operating Handbook (POH) to predict your airplane's performance during the flight.

Have the airplane's maintenance logs with you, and be able to show the examiner that it has had all of the tests required to make it legal for instrument flight.

The examiner will ask you to perform at least one instrument approach using partial panel, and your instructor should prepare for this by having you shoot all kinds of approaches with the gyro instruments covered. Don't let success go to your head, however—if you ever actually lose your vacuum system the thing to do is declare an emergency and ask for vectors to an airport that is VFR or has high minimums.

You will be expected to perform one precision and two nonprecision approaches. If your airplane does not have an ADF receiver, and none of the approaches used requires an ADF, you can meet this requirement with one VOR and one localizer approach. If the airplane used for the checkride has an approach-certified GPS, you can perform a GPS overlay or stand-alone approach.

The flight portion of the examination will be an anticlimax, repeating things that you have done with your instructor dozens of times. Trust your instructor's judgment—if he or she didn't think you could perform to the required standards you would not have a signed application to give to the examiner.

Your flight examiner will expect you to fly intelligently and safely, not perfectly—examiners reserve their expectations of perfection for Airline Transport Pilot checkrides. The examiner has no way of knowing what you are thinking, so it is to your advantage to verbalize your thoughts. If your altitude is in error and you say nothing, the examiner will think that you haven't noticed the error, and that will cast doubt on your scanning ability. If you say, "I'm correcting back to 2,000," the examiner will know that you picked up the discrepancy.

If you elect to fly a wind correction heading rather than the course printed on the approach plate, speak up: "I'm going to use 235° outbound to allow for the wind." The examiner will give you brownie points for thinking. If the examiner asks you to shoot an NDB approach to a runway served by a VOR and an ILS, tune in all three. That's what you would do with passengers on board, isn't it? The examiner will "fail" the navigation receivers that he or she doesn't want you to use. If you have a handheld GPS, use it as a backup—but tell the examiner that you know the GPS cannot be used as an "official" navigational aid.

Learn as much as you can about how the checkride is to be conducted before you get into the airplane. Remember, you are the pilot-in-command and the examiner is a passenger. When the controller asks if you want vectors or the full approach, or asks what your intentions are after the approach, you should have the answer ready from your preflight briefing and not have to look to the examiner for guidance. You don't want to say, "I thought you wanted me to…" after the flight.

Preparing for the Multi-Engine Instrument Flight Test

If you already hold a multi-engine rating when you are ready for the instrument rating checkride, you will be required to demonstrate your ability to handle an engine failure or other emergency while flying solely by reference to the flight instruments. The alternative is a "single-engine only" limitation on your instrument ticket.

Your training in instrument scanning and interpretation will be invaluable in the event of an engine failure, because the initial physical sensations may be misleading. And you were taught to ignore everything but the instruments, weren't you?

When an engine fails, the resulting roll and yaw will show up on four flight instruments: the attitude indicator will show a bank toward the dead engine, the heading indicator will show a turn toward the dead engine, and the ball will deflect toward the good engine. The turn coordinator will react to both yaw and roll.

Your primary responsibility is to maintain heading and airspeed. If you are able to maintain or gain altitude, that is a plus. Because the airplane is rolling and yawing toward the dead engine, you must apply full rudder to stop the turn. Step on the ball. Never start a takeoff roll in a twin unless your seat is adjusted so that you can push either rudder pedal to the firewall.

You will be tempted to use full aileron travel to raise the wing—don't do it. That action will cause the aileron on the side of the failed engine to deflect downward, adding induced and parasitic drag to a wing that already has more drag than it can handle. Handle the emergency with your feet plus small aileron inputs. However, don't let anything deter you from doing everything possible to maintain control—if you do have to bank more than 5° and sacrifice altitude it will only be for a few seconds while you are cleaning up the airplane by getting rid of the drag items.

The position of your feet when the airplane is maintaining heading will lead you through the immediate actions required to shut down the failed engine and eliminate the drag of the windmilling propeller. You demonstrated all of the remaining actions when you took the many-motor checkride.

With gear and flaps up and the offending propeller feathered, the optimum bank angle for performance will only be a degree or so toward the good engine, with the ball out of its cage by almost a full diameter. Do whatever it takes to get the best rate-of-climb.

With everything under control, advise ATC of the failure and tell them which engine is out. They will take this information into account when assigning turns, because your turn radius will be larger. As an instrument pilot you will have an assigned altitude, and you may feel constrained to maintain that altitude no matter what. Again—don't do it. Maintaining control of the airplane is more important than maintaining altitude, and it is possible to lose control in an attempt to hold the airplane up in the air.

Give up altitude grudgingly. You have lost 50% of the available power and climb performance will be negligible. You may lose precious altitude every time you bank, so keep bank angles to a minimum. When on a nonprecision approach, descend more gradually than normal, because you may not be able to maintain level flight.

Many pilots have decided to delay landing gear extension under engine-out conditions, planning to hang it out at the last minute. Many of those pilots have added a gear-up landing to their problems as a result. Follow your normal procedure, but retain an altitude and airspeed cushion. Stay a dot or two high on the glide slope and 5 to 10 knots fast until approaching minimums.

If you suspect engine failure while on an approach, add enough power (at least 20" MAP) to get meaningful information from rudder pressure—you can fool your feet with aileron pressure, but you can't fool them when the throttles go forward.

Although I advise retaining an altitude cushion during any type of engine-out IFR approach, squeeze that cushion down to nothing as you near the missed approach point. You do not want to miss the approach on one engine, and if you are 100 feet high at the MAP (with the weather at minimums) you may have to do exactly that.

During an engine-out approach, it is the good engine that causes the problems, not the failed engine, so don't get into a position where you have to add power to the good engine to regain the glide slope or lost airspeed. Adding power will create control problems. Manage the available power by starting out with more than enough and make gradual reductions, always retaining enough power to avoid sinking below MDA or the glide slope.

Most importantly, practice engine-out procedures under the hood as often as possible.

Summarizing the Instrument Checkride

There are books on how to pass the instrument knowledge examination, books on weather, books on aerodynamics and books on IFR procedures. In this book I have tried to touch all the bases without attempting exhaustive coverage of any single area of interest. The world of instrument flight is in constant flux, and technology is moving at a rapid pace. You must stay on top of the procedural changes that each new edition of the *Aeronautical Information Manual* brings, you must read the aviation press to stay abreast of changes in regulations that affect IFR flight, and you must monitor the approach plates, the en route charts, and the A/FD for your area of operation to pick up changes.

You may find things in this book that conflict with what your instructor has told you—that would not be unusual in the rapidly changing world of aviation education. The procedures advocated in this book meet with the requirements of the Federal Aviation Regulations, the AIM, and the Terminal Instrument Procedures Manual.

In researching procedural questions I have relied on the Seattle Flight Safety District Office, personnel from the Seattle ARTCC and Seattle TRACON, the Flight Inspection and Procedures staff of the Northwest/Mountain Region of the FAA, and the editors of the FAA's *General Aviation News*. It is unfortunate, but interpretation of the regulations differs between individuals and between regions. You can get the real "word" only by writing to the Office of the General Counsel at FAA Headquarters. Go with the interpretations of your local FAA office while you wait for a reply.

Preparing for the Commercial Flight Test

Confidence is everything. You are going to present yourself to total strangers as a pilot capable of delivering them safely and comfortably to their destination, and you should exude confidence as you meet them, load them into the airplane, and conduct the flight. You should appear no less confident as you meet the pilot examiner. Making the proper impression on the examiner will have a lot to do with the result of the checkride.

Test Requirements

You must show the examiner a current medical certificate and hand over your knowledge test results and your private pilot certificate.

You will be expected to show up with a complex airplane (retractable landing gear, flaps, and a controllable-pitch propeller) for the takeoff and landing and emergency procedures portions of the practical test. If you want to, you can then perform the rest of the checkride in a more basic airplane. My recommendation is that you plan to take the entire checkride in the complex airplane, although this will probably be more expensive.

Learn the commercial maneuvers in a basic trainer and then finish your training by practicing them in the complex airplane. Its added power will allow you to easily complete maneuvers that would have the basic trainer straining for performance. 14 CFR Part 61 requires that you have ten hours of dual instruction in a complex airplane to qualify for the checkride, and that should allow more than enough time for you to become accustomed to how the throttle response and control pressures vary from those of the basic trainer.

Do not fail to have the POH (and the latest weight and balance information, if it is separate) and the aircraft and engine logbooks with you when you report for the checkride. Be ready to prove to the examiner that the airplane has had all of the inspections required for legal flight. It would be worthwhile to sit down with a mechanic and go over the logbooks before the day of the checkride, so that you will be able to go right to the appropriate page when the examiner asks when the next 100-hour inspection or annual is due.

Airplane Systems

Are your airplane's control surfaces moved over pulleys, by cables, or by pushrods? How is the landing gear extended, and how can it be extended if the primary method fails? How many "gear down" indicators are there? Is the airplane carbureted or fuel injected, and how do the engine instruments work? These are only a few of the type of questions you can be asked by the examiner. Spend some time with the operating handbook and then ask your instructor to give you a closed-book quiz.

Emergency Procedures

Be ready to explain the aerodynamics of spins and how you would recover from an unintentional spin in the airplane you will be flying for the checkride. Demonstration of intentional spins and recoveries is not required.

The examiner will choose from a laundry list of possible emergency conditions and ask you to explain how you would handle each of them. Remember that despite the name, very few emergencies require that you take immediate action based on your memory. In most cases, if the airplane is still flying the correct answer will be "get out the book and follow the checklist."

Of course, if the engine fails or fire is involved, there is no time to read the book and you should have the emergency actions memorized. For systems emergencies, however, you will make more points with the examiner by using checklists than by relying on your memory.

Determining Performance and Limitations

As noted earlier, your passengers rely on you to get them to their destination safely. That means being sure that the airplane is properly loaded and runway lengths at both ends of the trip are adequate for the existing conditions.

The examiner will expect you to be able to use each performance chart with accuracy, speed, confidence and, more importantly, will expect you to explain what would happen if you exceed any of the performance limitations. You will also be asked to explain how seasonal or atmospheric changes affect each performance factor. There is no better way to prepare for this portion of the checkride than to spend a few hours with the performance charts. The examiner will be favorably impressed if you come up with the correct book performance figures and then add a fudge-factor on the side of conservatism.

Visual Inspection

Know the airplane inside and out. Know how to use external power for starting, if that capability is installed. Know where the battery is located and show the examiner where the brake fluid reservoir can be found. As you go through the external preflight examination, be prepared to tell the examiner what you are looking for and what the effect on flight safety any discrepancy might have.

Guidelines for the Commercial Flight Test
Normal Takeoff

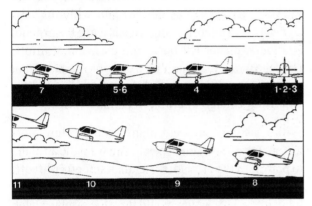

Figure 14-1

1. Pretakeoff checklist complete.
2. Takeoff clearance obtained—visually clear for traffic on final.
3. Taxi into position.
4. Smoothly apply maximum allowable takeoff power.
5. Maintain directional control with rudder.
6. Check engine instruments, especially EGT and fuel flow.
7. Rotate to positive pitch attitude at manufacturer's recommended speed.
8. Adjust pitch attitude to maintain V_Y ±5 knots; trim.
9. Retract landing gear with positive rate of climb.
10. Maintain straight track with takeoff power, V_Y ±5 knots to safe altitude.
11. Comply with noise abatement procedures.
12. Complete after-takeoff checklist.

What is a normal takeoff? It's a takeoff from a long, smooth surface with either no wind or a wind blowing right down the runway. Any other conditions would require special techniques, and those conditions will be discussed later.

For most airplanes, flaps are left up for normal takeoff. There are several models, however, that have a designated takeoff flap setting. You have to know what configuration is appropriate for the checkride airplane.

You should be able to recite the best angle (V_X) and best rate (V_Y) of climb speeds at maximum gross takeoff weight, and you should be able to tell the examiner how these speeds are affected by lighter weights. Hint: reduce these speeds by one-half of the percentage change in weight. If your takeoff weight is 20 percent less than max gross, reduce the climb speeds by 10 percent. Look at the normal takeoff distance chart and use the procedure and rotation speed shown so that you can duplicate book conditions as closely as possible.

Do an Academy Award job of checking for traffic on final before rolling onto the runway, even at a controlled field, and make sure that the transponder is set properly before rolling into position. When you are in the runup area and when holding short, remember to hold the aileron and elevator controls properly to allow for the wind.

If the performance chart says to run the throttle up to takeoff power with the brakes locked, that's the way to do it. In the absence of specific instructions, the throttle should be pushed in smoothly and positively to maximum allowable power. With a turbocharged engine, hesitate briefly at half-power to allow the turbo to kick in, then monitor manifold pressure to avoid overshooting the maximum allowable setting. Maintain directional control with the rudders and don't drag the brakes!

Check the engine instruments before rotation—the exhaust gas temperature and fuel flow gauges (if installed) are your best last-minute indicators of problems. In their absence, rely on the manifold pressure and tachometer.

Start applying back pressure as the airspeed needle approaches rotation speed; if you wait until that speed is attained you will rotate late. Rotate to a pitch attitude that will give you best rate of climb speed; you should have determined that attitude long before checkride day.

First impressions are critical, and during the first few moments of climb you will show the examiner a lot about your flying skills. If you use aileron rather than rudder to offset the left-turning tendency the examiner will wonder what other aerodynamic effects you shrug off. Use your feet!

Don't rush the gear and flaps up—late is better than early—and use an after-takeoff checklist.

Crosswind Takeoff

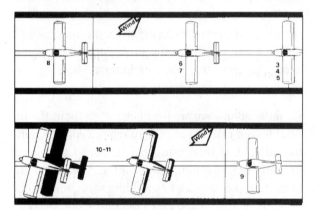

Figure 14-2

1. Pretakeoff checklist complete.
2. Takeoff clearance obtained—visually check for traffic on final.
3. Taxi into position, using flight controls to correct for crosswind.
4. Upwind aileron fully deflected into the wind.
5. Smoothly apply maximum allowable takeoff power.
6. Maintain directional control with rudder; gradually reduce aileron deflection as speed increases and ailerons become effective.
7. Check engine instruments before liftoff.
8. Rotate at manufacturer's recommended speed and accelerate to V_Y ±5 knots.

9. Make a coordinated turn into the wind; the upwind aileron deflection will start the turn for you as soon as the wheels leave the ground.
10. Comply with noise abatement procedures.
11. Establish a crab angle that will allow you to track the extended runway centerline.
12. Complete appropriate checklists.

Everything noted under normal takeoff applies except that you should be holding full aileron into the wind when you begin the takeoff roll. Use rudder as required for directional control. As airspeed builds and the ailerons become more effective, you can relax some of the pressure but you will still have some upwind aileron as the wheels leave the ground, and the airplane will bank into the wind at liftoff; level the wings and establish a crab into the wind that will allow the airplane to track the extended centerline. Not using enough aileron is a common error.

With a gusting crosswind, plan on adding a few knots to your normal rotation speed. You want the airplane to pop off of the ground, rather than smoothly lift off, to eliminate any possibility of having a momentary lull in the wind, which would drop the airplane back onto the runway.

Short-Field Takeoff

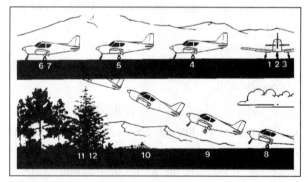

Figure 14-3

1. Complete pretakeoff checklist.
2. Takeoff clearance obtained—check for traffic on final.
3. Taxi into position, using the maximum amount of runway.
4. Extend flaps as recommended by manufacturer.
5. Smoothly apply maximum takeoff power before brake release.

6. Maintain a level pitch attitude; do not apply back pressure.

7. Check engine instruments before liftoff.

8. Rotate at manufacturer's recommended speed.

9. Establish pitch attitude to maintain V_X +5, –0 knots to 50 feet above the surface.

10. Retract landing gear with positive rate of climb.

11. With obstacle cleared, maintain V_Y ±5 knots.

12. Retract flaps, maintain takeoff power to a safe maneuvering altitude, then set climb power.

13. Complete appropriate checklists.

Short-field technique is used when the runway is short or when there are obstacles in the takeoff path. It is imperative that you calculate the airplane's performance based on density altitude and weight before attempting a short-field takeoff. If there is any runway gradient or if the surface is not paved, add at least 50 percent to the calculated takeoff distance.

Be sure that you duplicate the conditions shown on the Maximum Performance Takeoff charts in the performance section of the POH: setting takeoff power with the brakes locked, proper flap setting, mixture leaned as required under high density altitude conditions. Pay special attention to the liftoff and climb speeds. You want to have an indicated airspeed at least 75 percent of rotation speed at the halfway point. Be sure to tell the examiner what you have planned. Use every available inch of runway surface; don't roll out onto the runway and leave 100 feet of surface behind.

During the takeoff roll, any forward or aft control yoke pressure will slow the airplane—let the airplane accelerate without any elevator control input. Begin to apply back pressure when the airspeed needle is two or three knots short of rotation speed so that the wheels leave the surface at rotation speed. Climb at best angle of climb speed (V_X +5, –0 knots) until all obstacles are cleared. Chances are that your checkride will use the FAA standard 50-foot obstacle in the examiner's mind instead of an actual short field, and the examiner will be checking for technique and your altitude as a runway light or other marker is passed.

If flaps are used for a maximum performance takeoff, follow the manufacturer's recommendation with regard to flap retraction. Many airplanes use flaps to shorten the takeoff roll but note that obstacle clearance performance will suffer with flaps extended. When you retract the flaps, do so in increments to avoid sinking or a large pitch change.

Soft-Field Takeoff

Figure 14-4

1. Pretakeoff checklist complete.

2. Takeoff clearance obtained—check for traffic on final.

3. Set flaps as recommended by manufacturer for soft field takeoff.

4. Taxi onto runway surface without stopping. Elevator control fully back.

5. Smoothly apply maximum allowable takeoff power; nose will pitch up—be ready for it. Relax some back pressure.

6. Maintain directional control with rudder; nose-wheel steering will not be effective.

7. Check engine instruments before liftoff.

8. Let airplane fly off at slowest possible airspeed.

9. Apply forward pressure to keep airplane in ground effect while accelerating to V_X or V_Y.

10. Establish pitch attitude to maintain V_Y ±5 knots, trim.

11. Retract gear with positive rate of climb.

12. Retract flaps, maintain V_Y ±5 knots; trim.

13. Maintain V_Y ±5 knots and takeoff power to safe maneuvering altitude, then set climb power.

The goal of soft-field takeoff technique is to transfer the airplane's weight from the wheels to the wings as quickly as possible and, in the case of a tricycle gear airplane, to eliminate the rolling friction or drag of the nose wheel as quickly as possible. This is accomplished with the elevator control all the way back in your lap as power is applied, or as you line up with the runway in the case of a rolling takeoff. This will mean a nose-high attitude and may result in poor visibility of the runway ahead. The airplane will want to fly well before its normal rotation speed, and you should allow it to lift off as soon as possible. When the wheels leave the ground the nose will want to pitch up because induced drag is reduced in ground effect. You must counter this reaction with forward pressure to keep the airplane in ground effect until it has accelerated to the best rate-of-climb speed (V_Y) or the best angle-of-climb speed (V_X) if there are obstacles in the takeoff path. Because you must hold the airplane close to the ground (within ½ wingspan) while accelerating, taking off from a field that is both short and soft is chancy and requires pre-takeoff decision making.

If there is a seaplane operation nearby, it is instructive to watch floatplanes take off. Their procedure to reduce water friction is exactly what you want to follow to reduce ground friction.

Once again, the odds are that the examiner will have you demonstrate your soft-field takeoff technique on a paved runway rather than search out an actual soft field. The most common errors are being surprised by the pitch-up tendency, and failure to hold the airplane within 5 to 10 feet of the surface while accelerating. While you are practicing this maneuver, ask yourself what the outcome would be if the soft field was at a high density altitude, increasing the takeoff run. A grass field at a density altitude of 10,000 feet might require three times as much runway as a paved field at sea level.

Because soft field technique eliminates the directional stability afforded by having three wheels on the ground during the takeoff roll, using this technique in a crosswind can be hazardous—the wind will try to weathervane the airplane while airspeed is too low for rudder effectiveness. When the examiner asks you to demonstrate soft field technique in a crosswind, maybe he or she is looking for you to demonstrate good judgment and say "no."

Slow Flight and Stalls
Maneuvering During Slow Flight

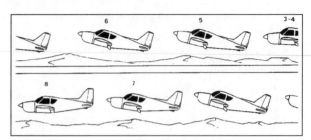

Figure 14-5

1. Select an altitude that will allow the task to be completed no lower than 1,500 feet AGL.

2. Stabilize and maintain the airspeed at an attitude such that an increase in pitch results in a stall.

3. Establish straight-and-level flight and level turns; gear and flaps as specified by the examiner.

4. Maintain altitude ±50 feet.

5. Maintain heading during straight flight ±10°.

6. Maintain specified bank angle ±10° during turning flight.

7. Roll out on examiner-specified heading ±10°.

8. Divide your attention between airplane control and orientation.

Slow flight is a skill that pilots learn for the checkride and then forget to use when it is called for. If you are overtaking another airplane in the pattern or when entering the pattern, use this skill to lose airspeed without losing altitude while the spacing improves. This "Task" on the Practical Test shows the examiner how you perform at the low-speed end of the operational envelope, an area in which you will have to operate during short-field operations. If you are uncomfortable with a ten- or twenty-percent margin over the stall and always add 5 or 10 knots for the wife and kiddies, you will have a hard time when space is restricted.

Don't schedule a checkride unless you can slow from cruise to slow flight and accelerate back to cruise smoothly, without changing heading or altitude.

Power-Off Stalls

1. Choose an altitude that will allow at least 1,500 feet AGL for recovery.

2. Clear the area for traffic.

3. Establish a stabilized descent in the approach or landing configuration as specified by the examiner.

4. Transition smoothly from the approach or landing attitude to an attitude that will produce a stall.

5. Maintain the specified heading ±10° in straight flight; maintain a specified angle of bank +0/–10° in turning flight, while inducing a stall.

6. Recognize and announce the onset of the stall at the first aerodynamic buffeting or decay of control effectiveness (not when the stall warning sounds).

7. Recover promptly as the stall occurs by simultaneously lowering the pitch attitude, increasing power, and leveling the wings with a minimum loss of altitude.

8. Retract flaps to the recommended setting (not all at once) and retract landing gear after a positive rate of climb has been established.

9. Accelerate to V_X or V_Y speed before final flap retraction, as specified by the manufacturer.

10. Return to the heading, altitude, and airspeed specified by the examiner.

Power-On Stalls

1. Select an altitude that will allow the task to be completed no lower than 1,500 feet AGL.

2. Establish takeoff configuration and slows the airplane to normal lift-off speed.

3. Set the power to the manufacturer's recommended power-on stall setting (or no less than 55-60 percent of full power) while establishing a climb attitude.

4. Maintain the specified heading ±10° in straight flight; maintain a specified bank angle (not to exceed 20°) ±10° in turning flight.

5. Recognize and announce the onset of the stall by identifying the first aerodynamic buffeting or decay of control effectiveness.

6. Recover promptly as the stall occurs by lowering the pitch attitude, increasing power, and leveling the wings with minimum altitude loss.

7. Retract flaps and gear after a positive rate of climb has been established.

8. Return to the heading, altitude, and airspeed specified by the examiner.

This Task is meant to replicate a stall entered inadvertently during the first few moments after takeoff. Your attention might be diverted by waving to friends on the ground, the trim might be set nose-up—several things might lead you into allowing the airplane's angle of attack to become excessive. As is the case with all stall recoveries, decreasing the angle of attack is of primary importance. In real life, as distinguished from stall recovery practice, takeoff power would already be set—takeoff power is not used in setting up this situation because the pitch attitude would become excessive.

Spin Awareness

You will not be required to demonstrate a spin entry or recovery, but you will be asked to explain the aerodynamics of spins and the recovery procedure used with the airplane in which you are taking the checkride.

Steep Turns

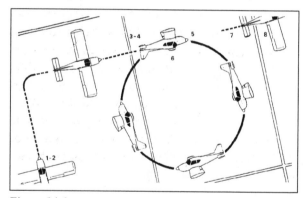

Figure 14-6

1. Choose an altitude that is at least 1,500 feet AGL.

2. Clear the area for traffic.

3. Establish and maintain the manufacturer's recommended entry speed (or the design maneuvering speed, whichever is higher).

4. From straight-and-level flight, roll into a 360° turn with a 50° bank, ±5°, immediately followed by a 360° turn in the opposite direction.

5. Adjust power to maintain altitude and airspeed; trim.

6. Use opposite aileron to correct for overbanking tendency.

7. Roll out on the entry heading ±10° (watch out for ballooning as you go through wings-level).

8. Maintain entry altitude throughout the maneuver, ±100 feet; maintain airspeed within ±10 knots.

This is the maneuver that most instructors use when they want to get a quick handle on a pilot's abilities during rental checkouts or flight reviews. A bank angle of 45° to 55° will cause a steep turn to degenerate into a diving spiral in no time if the pilot is not ahead of the airplane. Take advantage of the 10° allowed change in bank angle to maintain altitude— if you are drifting higher, go to 55°; if you begin to drift lower, go to 45°.

Before you begin practicing this maneuver, get a grease pencil and put a mark on the windshield directly in front of your eyes with your head in its normal position; a line from your eyes to the spot should parallel the airplane's longitudinal axis. You will use this reference point for this and other commercial maneuvers. Do the same thing on the airplane you will take the checkride in, preferably not in the presence of the examiner—good poker players do not show their hole cards. Learn and practice this maneuver with an instructor, of course, and note the power setting required to maintain altitude at these bank angles. For "solo" practice, take a friend along to simulate the examiner's weight.

From the entry heading, with your reference spot on the horizon, roll smoothly to a 45° bank; don't rush the back pressure but start adding it as the bank angle passes through 30°. A common error is adding back pressure immediately and climbing during the initial bank. When you reach 50°, use trim and power to reduce stick pressure and maintain airspeed. Keep your eyes outside of the airplane as much as possible, keeping the reference point on the horizon and scanning the airspace you are turning into (be sure that the examiner is aware that you are looking for traffic), Occasionally move your eyes across the panel and check the vertical speed indicator. Give yourself about 20° of lead on the rollout heading and be ready with forward pressure as you roll the wings through level into the opposite bank. The added power and/

or trim will make the airplane want to balloon as the wings pass through level, yet you don't want to change the trim or throttle setting if they were working for you during the first 360. Use the same lead and forward pressure as you complete the second 360, but this time pull the power back to the setting you had as you entered the maneuver.

Chandelles

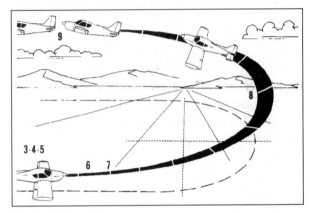

Figure 14-7

1. Choose an altitude that is at least 1,500 feet AGL.

2. Clear the area for traffic.

3. Establish cruise configuration.

4. Establish cruise power.

5. Entry speed is cruise airspeed or V_A, whichever is lower. Reference point off wing tip.

6. Establish a bank angle of not more than 30°, begin climbing turn while increasing power (fixed pitch).

7. Power still increasing to maintain airspeed as pitch attitude increases.

8. At the 90° point, with reference straight ahead, begin a coordinated constant-rate-of-turn rollout with constant pitch attitude that will result in a rollout within ±10° of entry heading within ±5° of power-on stall speed.

9. Reduce pitch attitude to resume straight-and-level flight at the final altitude attained ±50 feet.

A chandelle is a maximum performance 180° climbing turn, ending with the wings level and the airspeed just above the stall. The examiner will be looking at your coordination and planning more than anything else, because weakness in these areas is easily seen.

Find a location where a road or mountain can be used to establish the 90° and 180° points and prepare for a chandelle by establishing cruise power with gear and flaps up. If you are flying a fixed-gear, fixed-pitch propeller airplane, you may want to dive to pick up about 10 knots over cruise speed, but don't bank until your reference point on the windshield is on the horizon. Entry airspeed can be anything slower than maneuvering speed. Note the entry altitude. Roll quickly but smoothly to a 30° bank. Don't take your time, because you are not supposed to apply back pressure until the bank is established. The Practical Test Standards call for a coordinated turn, but applying rudder with the turn will start the turn too soon. I'm reluctant to say "bank and yank" for fear that you will perform the maneuver mechanically, yet that phrase describes what you have to do.

With the 30° bank established, begin smoothly increasing the pitch attitude; maximum pitch must be established by the 90° point. If you pitch up too much during the initial turn you will stall at its completion, and if you don't pitch up enough you will be too fast at the end of the maneuver. You can't fool the examiner either way. With a fixed-pitch prop, you'll be adding power to keep the speed up during the initial turn; you should have full throttle by the 45° point. During practice, note the pitch attitude on the attitude indicator at the 90° point and remember it, because the attitude should stay the same for the rest of the maneuver.

When performing a chandelle to the left, torque will increase the bank angle beyond 30° unless you are alert. In a chandelle to the right, torque will be trying to decrease the bank angle. Because the airspeed will be constantly decreasing, the effect of torque will be more noticeable as the maneuver progresses. Keep the ball centered during practice and you will develop a feel for the pressures required.

At the 90° point, maintain the pitch attitude you have established and begin to roll back toward wings level. The vertical component of lift will be increasing during the rollout and there will be a tendency for the pitch angle to increase—if you let it, you will stall before the turn is completed. Relax some of the back pressure during the last 90° of turn. When rolling out of a chandelle to the left, right rudder will be required because of torque and adverse aileron drag. When rolling out of a chandelle to the right, it's easy to have too much left rudder pressure at a time when torque is doing most of the work.

Ideally, the stall warning will be sounding intermittently as you reach the 180° point. Smoothly lower the nose and return to cruise airspeed. Note the change in altitude; a chandelle is supposed to result in maximum altitude gain, and you should strive for the maximum change, but not at the expense of planning and coordination.

Lazy Eights

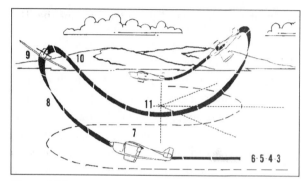

Figure 14-8

1. Choose an altitude at least 1,500 feet AGL.

2. Clear the area for traffic.

3. Enter from cruise configuration.

4. Set cruise power.

5. Set cruise airspeed or V_A, whichever is lower.

6. 90° reference point off a wing tip.

7. Begin climbing turn toward the reference point.

8. At the 45° point; maximum pitch, 15° bank.

9. At the 90° point; level pitch, 30° bank, nose passing through reference point.

10. At the 135° point; maximum pitch, 15° bank.

11. At the 180° point; level pitch, wings level, reference off opposite wing tip, begin climbing turn toward the reference point.

12. Throughout the maneuver, achieve a constant change of pitch, bank, and turn rate; altitude and airspeed should be consistent at the 90° points ±100 feet and ±10 knots; attain the starting altitude and airspeed and the completion of the maneuver to the same degree of precision. Heading tolerance is ±10° at each 180° point.

A properly performed lazy eight is rhythmic and smooth, one turn flowing into another without pause. Your goal is to use the longitudinal axis (your grease spot) to draw a horizontal figure eight on the horizon, with each loop extending the same distance above and below the horizon. There are checkpoints, to be sure, but you must not let them distract you from your goal.

Like a chandelle, a lazy eight is entered with cruise power at an airspeed no higher than maneuvering speed. You should have selected a reference point and maneuvered to place it directly off a wing tip. Imagine that your extended longitudinal axis is a pencil, resting on the horizon directly ahead. Begin a climbing turn toward the reference point, increasing both pitch and bank angle; after 45° of turn the airplane's pitch attitude should be as high as it is going to get and bank angle should be continuing to increase. Be sure that you do not let the rate of roll increase too rapidly—as speed decreases, the rate of turn for a given bank angle increases, and you don't want to reach the 45° point before you reach the highest pitch attitude.

From the 45° point, back pressure is relaxed until the airplane's pitch attitude is level at the 90° point; the bank angle reaches its maximum at that point. The extended longitudinal axis should be on the reference point on the horizon; at that position in the turn, airspeed should be at its minimum. Your "pencil" will have drawn half of a loop on the sky. As the turn continues to the 135° point the aircraft should be pitched down, with pitch attitude reaching its lowest point and airspeed at its maximum after 135° of turn. The nose position below the horizon should be the same as its position above the horizon at the 45° point. As you continue toward the 180° point, pitch attitude is raised so that the airplane reaches level flight attitude as the reference point appears directly off the opposite wing. Bank angle will have been reduced from approximately 30° at the 90° point to wings level at the 180° point. Begin a climbing turn toward the reference point to start the second half of the figure. At the completion of the first half you should be at the original entry altitude and airspeed, but you probably won't be. Adjust the power so that the completion of the second half of the eight will terminate closer to the original entry altitude.

Because pitch attitude, bank angle, and airspeed are continually varying during a lazy eight, control pressures are never constant and you must fly the airplane all the time. If possible, don't practice this maneuver solo, but take someone along to check airspeeds and altitudes while you just try to draw a smooth figure eight on the horizon. The examiner will be looking for coordination and your ability to plan ahead.

You might ask your instructor to let you start out by doing lazy eights with a 45° maximum bank. The maneuver will go more quickly and be more fun. Then, after you get the idea, limit the maximum bank angle to 30°. On their standardization checkrides, examiners are required to perform lazy eights with a maximum bank angle of 15°—that is a challenge!

Eights on Pylons

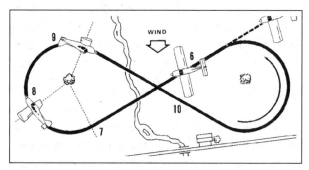

Figure 14-9

1. Select two pylons on a line perpendicular to the wind and at the same elevation.
2. Clear the area for traffic.
3. Establish pivotal altitude on downwind heading; should be predetermined.
4. Establish power at low cruise.
5. Set cruise configuration.
6. Enter diagonally between pylons.
7. When first pylon is abeam, roll into bank to acquire pylon off wing tip reference point.
8. As ground speed decreases, pylon will move ahead; apply forward pressure to move wing tip to pylon, thus increasing ground speed.
9. As ground speed increases, pylon will move aft; apply back pressure to move wing tip to pylon, thus decreasing ground speed.
10. Fly straight leg between pylons, crab as required for straight track.

On-pylon eights require that you keep a wing tip reference point on a pylon while flying around it. The distance from the pylon will increase on the side of the pylon away from the wind and decrease on the windward side as the airplane is drifted toward the pylon, as illustrated. Make sure that you can circle a single pylon while keeping the wingtip on the pylon before adding the second pylon.

Learning this maneuver will be easier if you understand the concept of pivotal altitude. As the name implies, pivotal altitude is that altitude at which you can bank 30° to 40° and keep a wing tip reference point on the pylon. Assuming no wind, so that airspeed is equal to ground speed, pivotal altitude is equal to ground speed squared divided by 11.3 (for knots) or 15 (for miles-per-hour). For example, if your airspeed is 100 knots, pivotal altitude is 100 x 100 = 10,000/11.3 or 909 feet AGL. With a ten knot wind, ground speed when directly downwind will be 110 knots and pivotal altitude will be 1,070 AGL. On the other side of the pylon, ground speed will be 90 knots and pivotal altitude will be 716 feet AGL. You can see how your altitude will vary as you circle the pylon.

I have used the term "wing tip reference point" to give you a general idea of the maneuver. It is very unlikely that your reference point in a given airplane will be the wing tip itself; instead, it should be that point on the wing tip which is directly in line with your eyes and parallel to the lateral axis of the airplane. High wing or low wing, you should be able to look out at either wing tip with your line of sight perpendicular to the lateral axis and pick out the line of rivets or other reference that you will use. There is nothing wrong with sitting in the airplane while someone puts a piece of tape at your reference point.

As you fly around a pylon at pivotal altitude, any small error will be reflected in relative movement between your wing tip reference point and the pylon. If you are too high, for example, you could say that the reference point falls aft of the pylon or you could say with equal validity that the pylon moves ahead of the wing. Too low, and the reverse is true. I would prefer that you think in terms of pylon movement, because that will make your instinctive actions correct.

Again, select two pylons which are at approximately the same height above sea level and oriented perpendicular to the wind. They should be spaced so that there will be a straight leg as you fly from one pylon to the other, and it should go without saying that you will have chosen the pylons and practiced on them many times before checkride day. Remember, the examiner does not select the pylons—you do.

Enter on a diagonal between the pylons at approximately the correct pivotal altitude for your airspeed (at this point you can't be sure about ground speed) and with the wind behind you. When the first pylon is abeam, bank toward it and place your wing tip reference point on it. As your turn continues and you begin to head into the wind, decreasing ground speed will cause the pylon to move ahead of the reference point; apply forward pressure to move the reference point up to the pylon. This will accomplish two thing simultaneously: it will increase airspeed and thus ground speed, and it will decrease your altitude toward the lower pivotal altitude that is appropriate for flight into the wind.

Depart the first pylon in position to fly a diagonal leg and put the second pylon directly off of the opposite wing tip reference point. Crab as required to fly a straight path. As the wind comes around behind you the pylon will appear to drift behind your reference point, and you should react by applying back pressure to bring the wing tip back to the pylon. This will both increase altitude and decrease airspeed and thus ground speed.

Using the airspeed and wind velocity in my example, you will be climbing and descending 354 feet during each turn around a pylon. It is my opinion that a ten-knot wind change gives you about all that you can reasonably handle. Stronger winds call for greater changes in altitude, and you might find yourself making power adjustments which would complicate your life. But try it. During your practice sessions, try on-pylon maneuvers (you don't need two) in stronger winds and see if you can handle the resulting altitude changes.

Do not attempt to change the relationship between the reference point and pylon by using rudder pressure! Use rudder for coordination only (you will be going up and down hill, after all), and elevator pressure to hold the pylon.

Normal Landing

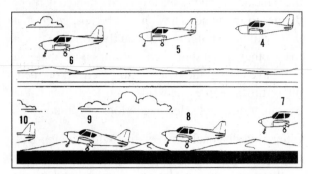

Figure 14-10

1. Follow standard pattern entry procedure. Be at pattern altitude on the 45° entry leg.
2. Turning base to final, plan turn so as to align with runway at completion of turn.
3. On final approach, stabilize airspeed at 1.3 V_{SO}; trim.
4. Control rate of descent with power.
5. Extend landing gear on downwind if not already extended on 45.
6. Set flaps to final setting.
7. Over-the fence, slow to 1.2 V_{SO}.
8. Power to idle, smooth back pressure to establish landing attitude. Maintain attitude as airplane slows.
9. Touch down on main gear, nose slightly high.
10. Lower nosewheel, maintain directional control with rudder.

The PTS combines normal and crosswind approaches and landings, but I am going to treat them separately.

The examiner is going to be looking primarily at speed and glidepath control and secondarily at the effect of configuration changes. You should be able to extend gear and flaps and minimize any resulting pitch change with appropriate use of elevator control pressure and trim. If this is not the case, you are not sufficiently familiar with the airplane.

Fly a rectangular pattern, applying drift correction as necessary. Because the wind is blowing directly down the runway, you should be crabbed toward the runway on base leg. If you are flying a plane with retractable landing gear, you will have lowered the gear and slowed to pattern speed by the time you reach the 45. Under normal conditions—long, smooth, paved runway with no crosswind and no obstructions—you should complete the turn to final with full flaps extended and airspeed trimmed to maintain 1.3 V_{SO} hands-off. Insofar as speed and flap use prior to turning final are concerned, just be consistent. You'll be making more than one approach and landing during your checkride, and you should use the same speeds and flap settings for all of them.

A good normal landing results in the airplane stalling just as the wheels touch the surface and as the power is reduced to idle. No float, just a solid touchdown with no sideways drift. Slowing to 1.2 V_{SO} on short final (over-the-fence speed) will give you a good margin above the stall.

Remember the grease spot you used for steep power turns and lazy eights? I hope you haven't washed it off. On final approach, the point where your grease spot falls on the runway is the spot on which you will crash-land if you don't flare. If the grease spot moves up the runway, you will land long and should reduce power, and if the grease spot moves off of the runway and into the approach lights, you will land short and should add power. If the airplane is properly trimmed, these small power changes will not change the airspeed noticeably.

Practice crosswind landings by finding a nice long runway and flying its length just one foot above the ground while keeping the airplane over the centerline with coordinated aileron and rudder. When you can do that consistently, descending that final foot and landing on the upwind wheel will have become second nature.

After touchdown, maintain directional control with rudder and keep adding aileron into the wind; don't be surprised if you have fully deflected ailerons when the airplane comes to a stop. Perform the After Landing checklist when you have cleared the runway.

Crosswind Landing

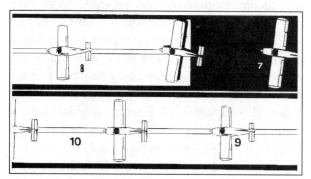

Figure 14-11

1. Follow standard pattern entry procedure. Be at pattern altitude on the 45° entry leg.

2. Turning base to final, plan turn so as to align with runway at completion of turn with crab into the wind established.

3. On final approach, stabilize airspeed at 1.3 V_{SO}; trim. Maintain crab.

4. Control rate of descent with power.

5. Landing gear down if not already extended on the 45.

6. Flaps to final setting (full flaps if crosswind is constant).

7-8. Convert crab into a slip by lowering upwind wing and using rudder to align the airplane with the runway centerline.

9. Maintain the slip, power to idle, touchdown on upwind main gear.

10. Lower nosewheel, increase aileron deflection into the wind, maintain directional control with rudder.

First, be sure that the crosswind is within your airplane's capability. You know and I know that if the crosswind component exceeds the airplane's demonstrated ability you will have canceled the checkride—no one goes out to demonstrate their proficiency and precision on a day when they must exercise all of their skills just to keep the airplane right side up. But be ready to answer the examiner's question: What is the maximum demonstrated crosswind component for this airplane and what does that mean?

Fly a normal rectangular pattern, crabbing as required. However, make your base-to-final turn so that you roll out on the runway's extended centerline with a crab into the wind sufficient to keep the airplane on the centerline. The PTS does not require you to use any particular method of crosswind correction but leaves it up to your judgment. The *Airplane Flying Handbook* recommends the wing-low or slipping method and that is what I suggest that you use.

After a few moments of crabbed flight on the centerline you will have a feel for the amount of crosswind component. Remembering that the reported surface wind has little to do with the wind at 400 feet above the ground on final, use this rule to estimate the crosswind component: at a 90-knot airspeed you will be crabbing ¾ of a degree for each knot of crosswind component. A 10° crab into the wind means the crosswind component is 7.5 knots. At 60 knots the figure is one degree per knot, and at 120 knots it is ½ degree per knot. If you are crabbed 15° into the wind, you probably won't be able to handle the crosswind unless it decreases considerably as you descend toward the runway.

As soon as you have the crosswind component figured out, transition to a wing-low slip by lowering the upwind wing while applying opposite rudder to keep the airplane's longitudinal axis aligned with the runway. Divide your body in half at the waist, assigning the top half the duty of using aileron to offset any drift while the bottom half uses rudder to keep the airplane pointed down the runway. If the wind drift is so great (wind velocity so strong) that the bank angle required to stop the drift calls for full rudder to keep the airplane aligned with the runway, you have reached the airplane's crosswind limit and should abandon the approach and go elsewhere.

Assuming that the required bank angle and rudder pressure are such that the crosswind can be easily handled, maintain the slip all the way to touchdown, landing first on the upwind wheel and rolling on it for a few yards as the downwind wheel comes down. Lower the nosewheel to the surface positively and maintain direction with rudder. Keep the upwind wing lowered with aileron deflection, increasing the amount of aileron as the airplane slows until you have full aileron into the wind as you bring the airplane to a stop.

Practice this maneuver by asking the tower controller to let you make several low approaches (or go to an uncontrolled field) and fly down the center of the runway at an altitude of a foot or so while keeping one of the main landing gears directly over the centerline. Even if there is little or no crosswind, the aileron and rudder pressures you must apply during this practice maneuver will prepare you to make crosswind corrections quickly and smoothly. Try it with different flap settings; unless the wind is gusty, the FAA recommends full flaps for all landings unless the manufacturer recommends otherwise.

Short-Field Landing

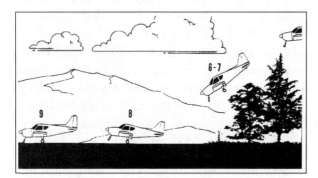

Figure 14-12

1. Follow standard pattern entry procedure. Be at pattern altitude on the 45° entry leg.
2. Turning base to final, plan turn so as to align with runway at completion of turn.
3. On final approach, stabilize airspeed at 1.3 V_{SO} or manufacturer's recommendation; trim.
4. Extend full flaps.
5. Extend landing gear, if not already extended.
6. Keep reference point on landing target, adjusting pitch and power as required.
7. Decrease airspeed to not less than 1.2 V_{SO}, not more than 1.3 V_{SO}.
8. At ground contact, power to idle, lower nosewheel.
9. Apply maximum braking without skidding.

Fly a normal pattern, rolling out on final about 500 feet above the touchdown zone with full flaps extended. The key to a successful short-field landing is

to touch down with minimum forward speed, and you cannot afford to have excess speed on the final approach leg; trim the airplane to maintain an airspeed no faster than 1.3 V_{SO} or the manufacturer's recommended short-field speed. The examiner will allow you to let the airspeed vary by plus or minus five knots, but you should only err on the slow side. After all, you have a 30 percent cushion over the stalling speed. If gusts are present, you can add one-half of the gust factor to your approach speed; that is, if your airspeed is 75 knots and the wind is reported to be right down the runway at 10 knots, gusting to 15, you would adjust your airspeed to 77 knots.

Coordinated use of pitch and power will allow you to maintain the desired descent path and approach speed. Once again, you can use the greasy spot method to control your touchdown point. Place the grease spot on your windshield right at the threshold, not 100 or 200 feet down the runway. If there are no obstructions and you are using this technique simply because the field is short, place your aiming point 50 feet or so before the threshold, counting on the flare to cover that distance with a touchdown right at the threshold. When obstructions make it difficult to see the threshold until you have passed them, this technique won't work. In that situation, you will have to slow to 1.2 V_{SO} as you pass over the obstructions and carry that speed down to the flare.

With the airplane properly trimmed for an airspeed of 1.2 to 1.3 V_{SO}, you can make small power corrections to control rate of descent. Do not let the airplane slow below 1.2 V_{SO}, because if you let the airplane get too slow and it starts to sink into the trees, a large amount of power will be required and that will cause the nose to pitch up, worsening the situation. You must always have an airspeed cushion above stalling speed.

With the flaps fully extended and the airspeed 20 to 30 percent above V_{SO}, raising the nose to flare will quickly bleed off the excess airspeed. The power should be smoothly reduced to idle as the airplane touches down, and back pressure should be maintained to add aerodynamic braking. Wheel brakes should be applied as soon as the airplane is firmly on the ground, and maximum braking (short of skidding) should be used. Be realistic, however. There is nothing to be gained by wearing flat spots on the tires, and the success of the maneuver should be gauged by your airspeed at touchdown. If the runway length is so limited that short-field technique plus panic braking is required, you have probably made a big mistake by attempting the landing.

Soft-Field Landing

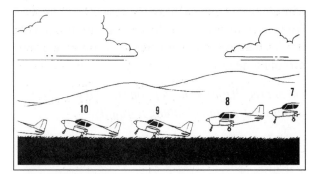

Figure 14-13

1. Follow standard pattern entry procedure. Be at pattern altitude on the 45° entry leg.

2. Turning base to final, plan turn so as to align with runway at completion of turn.

3. On final approach, stabilize airspeed at 1.3 V_{SO} or manufacturer's recommendation; trim.

4. Control rate of descent with coordinated pitch and power.

5. Extend landing gear.

6. Flaps to final setting.

7. Airspeed 1.3 V_{SO}; this is a power-on landing.

8. Allow airplane to settle with power, nose-high.

9. Touch down with full up-elevator; use throttle to keep nosewheel from descending.

10. Keep airplane moving until you reach a firm surface.

To fully appreciate soft-field landing technique you should spend some time watching float plane pilots or waterbirds land. Neither man nor bird can afford to land in too flat an attitude, for fear that the tip of a float or a webbed foot could catch a wave and cause the plane or bird to flop over on its back. When you land a tricycle-gear airplane on a soft surface, you must ensure that the nosewheel does not touch the mud, snow, or foot-tall grass until the airplane has rolled to a virtual standstill.

The approach is flown normally, maintaining an airspeed of 1.3 V_{SO} or the manufacturer's recom-

mended speed on final. You must have sufficient airflow over the horizontal tail surface to keep it effective as long as possible. Flare one to two feet above the surface and keep the nose coming up as the airplane settles. Do not reduce the throttle to idle—you need that airflow over the tail feathers. As the airplane touches down in a nose-high attitude, you may even need to add a little power to "blow the tail down" as the rolling friction with the surface brings the main wheels to a halt.

Practicing soft-field landings is fun. Pick a nice long runway and fly down its centerline maintaining an altitude of a foot or two (get tower permission, if appropriate) at an airspeed just above normal touchdown speed. At first, you will be jockeying the throttle and elevator and may even touch down inadvertently once or twice. Believe me, the nosewheel will be well clear of the runway. As you become more comfortable operating close to the surface, lower your target altitude to six inches. Then reduce power just enough to roll the main landing gear on the runway with the nose well up. The end result will be perfect soft-field technique.

The method described above will obviously not work on a short runway with a soft surface, and the FAA provides no guidance for that condition. You must decide which is the governing factor, length or surface condition, and meld the two techniques as you see fit. If you maintain enough speed to hold the nosewheel off, you may run off the end of a short runway, and if you land slowly enough for a short field you may not have enough elevator authority to keep the plane from tripping over its nosewheel.

Do not attempt to use soft-field technique in a crosswind. You need the friction of the nosewheel on the surface to counter a weathervaning tendency, and if you hold the nosewheel off you are at the mercy of the wind.

Going Around from a Rejected Landing

Although you may feel that failing to land out of every approach might raise questions as to your competence, the reverse is true. You will make more points with those whose opinions count—your customers and the examiner—by going around for a second approach than you will make by forcing the airplane onto the runway at the conclusion of a faulty approach. If the situation presents itself during the checkride, by all means abandon a poor approach and go around. What is more likely is that the examiner will tell you to "go around" when you are about 3 feet up with gear and flaps extended. Your first actions (simultaneous) will be to apply takeoff power with one hand and establish a climb attitude with the other. Leave the gear down until you have a positive climb indication on the altimeter and vertical speed indicator and have reduced the flap setting to half-flaps or the manufacturer's recommended setting. Full flaps create more drag than the landing gear, and if you should inadvertently allow the airplane to settle to the ruway during the transition from landing to going around, having the wheels in place will avoid embarrassment.

At the instant you decide to abort the landing, the airplane will be trimmed for approach speed and the sudden application of takeoff power will create heavy control pressures. You have no option but to overcome those pressures with muscle until your other duties have been taken care of, then make a rough trim change to reduce the pressures before retracting the gear. Because you will be slow with full power, expect the need for right rudder to offset the left-turning tendency.

Do not reach for the microphone until the airplane is under control and climbing normally.

Chapter 14
Instrument Flight Test Review Questions

Instrument Student Questions

The instrument pilot examination contains several sets of problems that involve a specific airplane type on a specific trip. The earlier chapters have contained the information you need to handle this kind of presentation, and this review section will provide two typical sets of questions for you.

1. (Refer to the FD excerpt below, and use the wind entry closest to the flight planned altitude.) Determine the time to be entered in block 10 of the flight plan.
   Route of flight .... Figures Q14-1, Q14-3, Q14-4, Q14-5, Q14-6, Q14-7
   Flight log & MAG VAR .... Figure Q14-3
   GNATS One Departure,
       Excerpt from AFD .... Figure Q14-6

FT	3000	6000	9000
OTH	0507	2006+03	2215-05

   A— 1 hour 10 minutes
   B— 1 hour 15 minutes
   C— 1 hour 20 minutes

2. (Refer to Figures Q14-2, Q14-6.) What is your position relative to GNATS intersection and the instrument departure routing?

   A— On departure course and past GNATS.
   B— Right of departure course and past GNATS.
   C— Left of departure course and have not passed GNATS.

3. (Refer to Figure Q14-6.) During the arc portion of the instrument departure procedure (GNATS1.MOURN), a left crosswind is encountered. Where should the bearing pointer of an RMI be referenced relative to the wingtip to compensate for wind drift and maintain the 15 DME arc?

   A— Behind the right wingtip reference point.
   B— On the right wingtip reference point.
   C— Behind the left wingtip reference point.

4. (Refer to Figures Q14-4, Q14-5.) What is the TDZ elevation for RWY 16 on Eugene/Mahlon Sweet Field?

   A— 363 feet MSL
   B— 365 feet MSL
   C— 396 feet MSL

5. (Refer to Figures Q14-1, Q14-3.) What CAS must be used to maintain the filed TAS at the flight planned altitude if the outside air temperature is -5°C?

   A— 134 KCAS
   B— 139 KCAS
   C— 142 KCAS

6. (Refer to Figures Q14-1 and Q14-6.) To which maximum service volume distance from the OED VORTAC should you expect to receive adequate signal coverage for navigation at the flight planned altitude?

   A— 100 NM
   B— 80 NM
   C— 40 NM

Continued on Page 14-25

U. S. DEPARTMENT OF TRANSPORTATION FEDERAL AVIATION ADMINSTRANTION **FLIGHT PLAN**	(FAA USE ONLY)	☐PILOT BRIEFING ☐ STOPOVER	☐ VNR	TIME STARTED	SPECIALIST INITIALS

1 TYPE	2 AIRCRAFT IDENTIFICATION	3 AIRCRAFT TYPE/ SPECIAL EQUIPMENT	4 TRUE AIRSPEED	5 DEPARTURE POINT	6 DEPARTURE TIME		7 CRUISING ALTITUDE
					PROPOSED (Z)	ACTUAL (Z)	
VFR X IFR DVFR	N132SM	C 182/	155	MFR			8,000

8 ROUTE OF FLIGHT

GNATS 1, MOURN, V121 EUG

9 DESTINATION (Name of airport and city) MAHLON/SWEET FIELD, EUGENE, OR.	10 EST TIME ENROUTE		11 REMARKS
	HOURS	MINUTES	INSTRUMENT TRAINING FLIGHT

12 FUEL ON BOARD		13 ALTERNATE AIRPORT(S)	14 PILOTS NAME, ADDRESS & TELEPHONE NUMBER & AIRCRAFT HOME BASE	15 NUMBER ABOARD
HOURS	MINUTES	N/R	17 DESTINATION CONTACT/TELEPHONE (OPTIONAL)	

16 COLOR OF AIRCRAFT	CIVIL AIRCRAFT PILOTS. FAR Part 91 requires you file an IFR flight plan to operate under instrument flight rules in controlled airspace. Failure to file could result in a civil penalty not to exceed $1,000 for each violation (Section 901 of the Federal Aviation Act of 1958, as amended, Filing of a VFR flight plan is recommended as a good operating practice. See also Part 99 for requirements concerning DVFR flight plans.

FAA Form 7233-1 (8-82)   CLOSE VFR FLIGHT PLAN WITH _____ FSS ON ARRIVAL

AIRCRAFT INFORMATION

MAKE CESSNA   MODEL 182

N 132SM   Vso 57

AIRCRAFT EQUIPMENT/STATUS**

**NOTE: X= OPERATIVE   INOP= INOPERATIVE   N/A= NOT APPLICABLE
TRANSPONDER: X (MODE C) X ILS: (LOCALIZER) X (GLIDE SLOPE) N/A
VOR NO.1 X (NO 2) X ADF: X RNAV: N/A
VERTICAL PATH COMPUTER: NA DME: X
MARKER BEACON: (AUDIO) Inop. (VISUAL) Inop.

Figure Q14-1. Flight plan and aircraft information

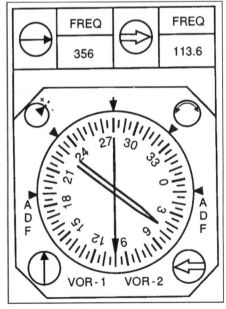

Figure Q14-2. RMI indicator

FLIGHT LOG

MEDFORD - JACKSON CO. AIRPORT TO HAHLON/SWEET FIELD, EUGENE, OR.

CHECK POINTS		ROUTE		WIND	SPEED-KTS		DIST	TIME		FUEL	
FROM	TO	ALTITUDE	COURSE	TEMP	TAS	GS	NM	LEG	TOT	LEG	TOT
MFR	MERLI	GNATS 1 CLIMB	333°		155			:11:0			
	MOURN	V121	287°			AVER. 135					
	RBG	8000 V121	272°								
	OTH	8000 V121	024°								
	EUG	8000 APPROACH									
APPROACH & LANDING		DESCENT						:10:0			
	SWEET FIELD										

OTHER DATA:
NOTE: MAG. VAR. 20° E.
AVERAGE G.S. 135 KTS. FOR GNATS 1
DEPARTURE CLIMB.

FLIGHT SUMMARY

TIME	FUEL (LB)	
		EN ROUTE
		RESERVE
		MISSED APPR.
		TOTAL

Figure Q14-3. Flight planning log

EUGENE

§ **MAHLON SWEET FLD** (EUG) 7 NW GMT-8(-7DT) 44°07′19″N 123°13′03″W   KLAMATH FALLS
365 B S4   FUEL 100LL, JET A OX 1, 2, 3, 4 TPA—1165(800) CFR Index B   H-1A, L-1B
RWY 16-34: H6202X150 (ASPH-PFC)   S-155, D-190, DT-300   HIRL   IAP
RWY 16: MALSR.   RWY 34: ODALS. VASI(V4L)—GA 3.0°TCH 54′
RWY 03-21: H5221X150 (ASPH)   S-60, D-68, DT-105   MIRL
RWY 03: VASI(V4L)—GA 3 0°TCH 50.4′. Trees.   RWY 21: VASI(V4L)—GA 3.0°TCH 53.2′ Trees
AIRPORT REMARKS: Attended continuously, phone 503-687-5431 between 0100-1600Z‡. CAUTION—migratory
waterfowl and other birds in vicinity. ACTIVATE MALSR Rwy 16 and ODALS Rwy 34—118.9. MIRL Rwy 03-21
unavailable when twr clsd. CLOSED to unscheduled air carrier operations with more than 30 passenger seats during
twr closure except PPR call arpt manager 503-687-5430. Taxiways F and G closed to Part 121 opns. Terminal apron
available to scheduled air carriers and flights with prior permission. Control Zone effective continuously
COMMUNICATIONS: CTAF 118.9   ATIS 125.2 (1400-0800Z‡)   UNICOM 122.95
PORTLAND FSS (PDX) LC 688-8411. NOTAM FILE EUG.
EUGENE RCO 122.3 122.1R 112.9T (PORTLAND FSS)
Ⓡ EUGENE APP/DEP CON 119.6 (280°-090°) 120.2 (091°-279°) (1400-0800Z‡)
Ⓡ SEATTLE CENTER APP/DEP CON 125.8 (0800-1400Z‡)
EUGENE TOWER 118.9 (1400-0800Z‡)   GND CON/CLNC DEL 121.7
STAGE II SVC ctc APP CON within 25 NM
RADIO AIDS TO NAVIGATION: NOTAM FILE EUG.
EUGENE (H) ABVORTAC 112.9 ■ EUG Chan 76 44°07′16″N 123°13′18″W at fld. 360/20E
General outlook on TWEB 0600-1300Z‡.
FRAKK NDB (LOM) 260 EU 44°12′47″N 123°13′10″W 179°5.5 NM to fld.
NDB unusable 190°-270°beyond 11 NM.
ILS 109.5 I-EUG RWY 16 LOM FRAKK NDB
ILS unmonitored when tower closed.

Figure Q14-4. Excerpt from Airport/Facility Directory

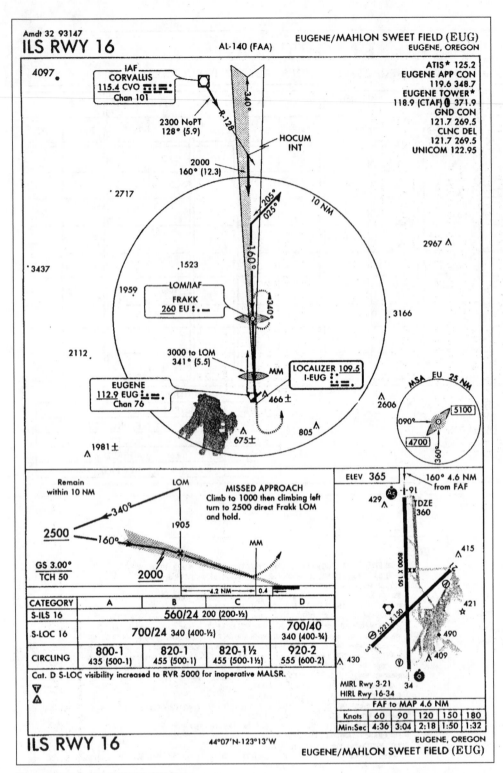

Figure Q14-5. ILS RWY 16 (EUG)

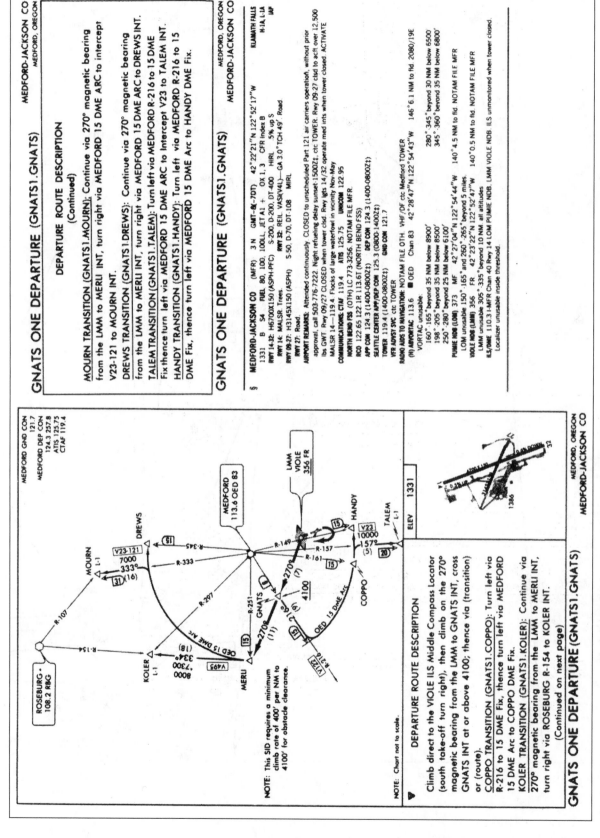

Figure Q14-6. GNATS One Departure, with excerpt from Airport/Facility Directory

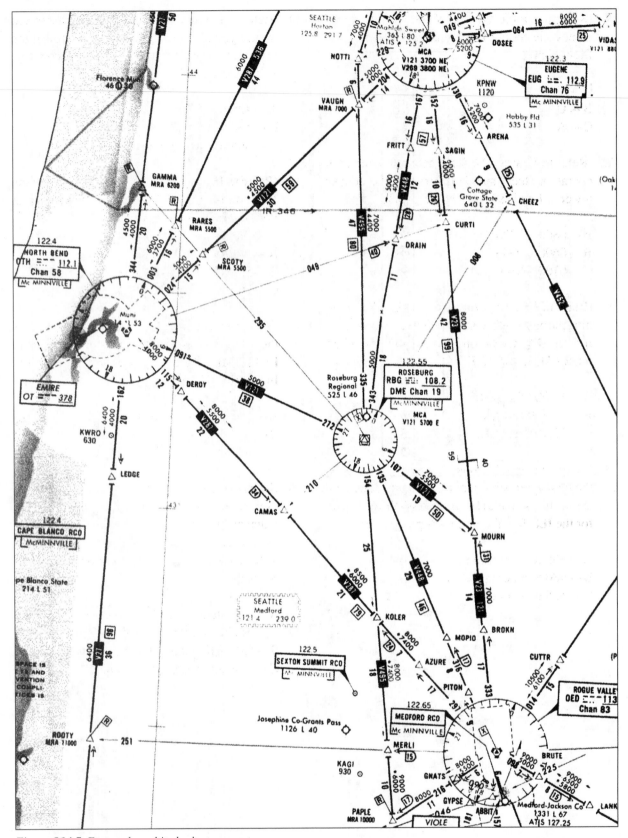

Figure Q14-7. Enroute low-altitude chart segment

7. (Refer to Figure Q14-1.) What aircraft equipment code should be entered in block 3 of the flight plan?

A—T
B—U
C—A

8. (Refer to Figure Q14-4.) What are the hours of operation (local standard time) of the control tower at Eugene/Mahlon Sweet Field?

A—0800 – 2300
B—0600 – 0000
C—0700 – 0100

9. (Refer to Figure Q14-8 on next page.) For planning purposes, what is the highest usable altitude for an IFR flight on V573 from the HOT VORTAC to the TXK VORTAC?

A—16,000 feet MSL
B—14,500 feet MSL
C—13,999 feet MSL

10. Using an average ground speed of 90 knots on the final approach segment, what rate of descent should be used initially to establish the glidepath for the ILS RWY 6 approach procedure?

A—395 feet per minute
B—480 feet per minute
C—555 feet per minute

11. (Refer to Figure Q14-10.) What rate of descent should you plan to use initially to establish the glide path for the ILS RWY 36L approach? (Use 120 knots ground speed.)

A—425 feet per minute
B—530 feet per minute
C—635 feet per minute

12. (Refer to Figure Q14-11.) What determines the MAP on the LOC/DME RWY 21 approach at Portland International Airport?

A—I-GPO 1.2 DME
B—5.8 NM from ROBOT FAF
C—160° radial of BRG VORTAC

13. (Refer to Figures Q14-11 and Q14-12.) What is the MDA and visibility criteria for a straight-in LOC/DME RWY 21 approach at Portland International?

A—1,100 feet MSL; visibility 1 SM
B—680 feet MSL; visibility 1 SM
C—680 feet MSL; visibility 1 NM

14. (Refer to Figure Q14-11.) You have been cleared to the CREAK intersection via the BTG 054° radial at 7,000 feet. Approaching CREAK, you are cleared for the LOC/DME RWY 21 approach to PDX. Descent to procedure turn altitude should not begin prior to

A—completion of the procedure turn, and established on the localizer.
B—CREAK outbound.
C—intercepting the glide slope.

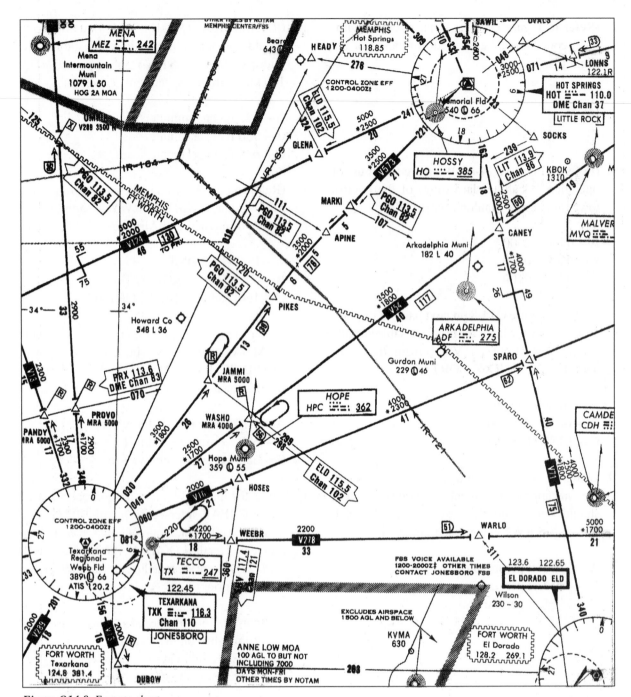

Figure Q14-8. *Enroute chart*

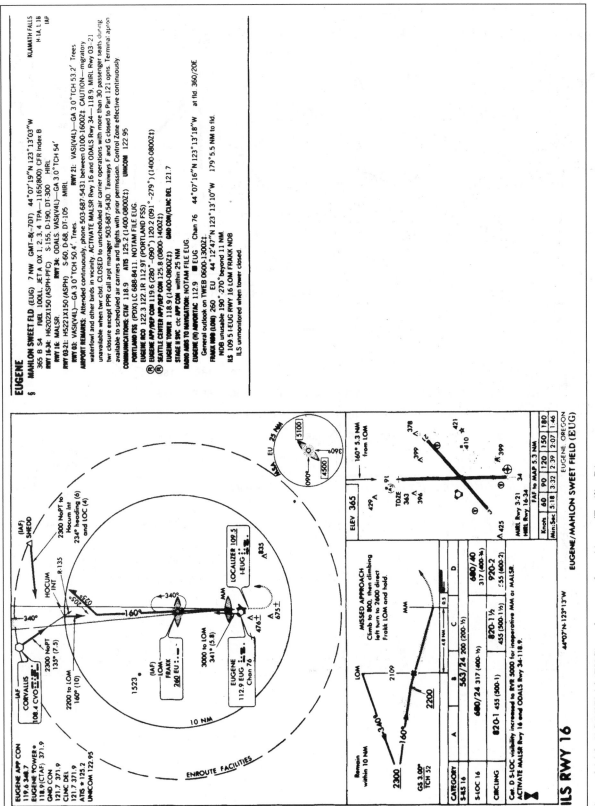

Figure Q14-9. ILS RWY 16 (EUG), and excerpt from Airport/Facility Directory

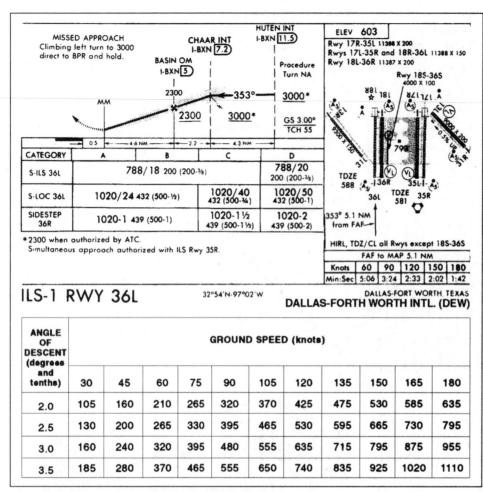

ILS-1 RWY 36L

MISSED APPROACH
Climbing left turn to 3000
direct to BPR and hold.

HUTEN INT
I-BXN 11.5

CHAAR INT
I-BXN 7.2

BASIN OM
I-BXN 5

353°

3000*

Procedure
Turn NA

2300

2300

3000*

GS 3.00°
TCH 55

0.5   4.6 NM   2.2   4.3 NM

ELEV 603
Rwy 17R-35L 11388 X 200
Rwys 17L-35R and 18R-36L 11388 X 150
Rwy 18L-36R 11387 X 200

Rwy 18S-36S
4000 X 100

TDZE
588

TDZE
581

353° 5.1 NM
from FAF

CATEGORY	A	B	C	D
S-ILS 36L	788/18 200 (200-⅜)			788/20 200 (200-⅜)
S-LOC 36L	1020/24 432 (500-½)		1020/40 432 (500-¾)	1020/50 432 (500-1)
SIDESTEP 36R	1020-1 439 (500-1)		1020-1½ 439 (500-1½)	1020-2 439 (500-2)

*2300 when authorized by ATC.
Simultaneous approach authorized with ILS Rwy 35R.

HIRL, TDZ/CL all Rwys except 18S-36S

FAF to MAP 5.1 NM					
Knots	60	90	120	150	180
Min:Sec	5:06	3:24	2:33	2:02	1:42

ILS-1 RWY 36L   32°54'N-97°02'W

DALLAS-FORT WORTH, TEXAS
DALLAS-FORTH WORTH INTL. (DEW)

ANGLE OF DESCENT (degrees and tenths)	GROUND SPEED (knots)										
	30	45	60	75	90	105	120	135	150	165	180
2.0	105	160	210	265	320	370	425	475	530	585	635
2.5	130	200	265	330	395	465	530	595	665	730	795
3.0	160	240	320	395	480	555	635	715	795	875	955
3.5	185	280	370	465	555	650	740	835	925	1020	1110

Figure Q14-10. ILS RWY 36L profile view, and excerpt from rate-of-descent table

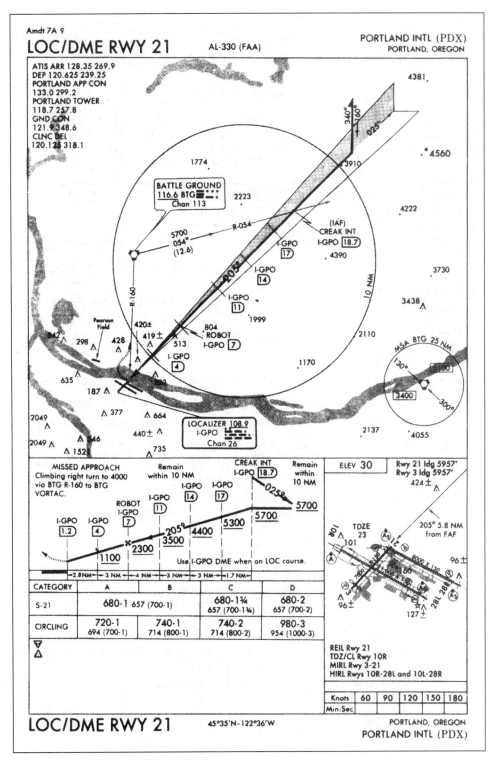

Figure Q14-11. LOC/DME RWY 21 (PDX)

Form Approved: OMB No. 2120-0034

U.S. DEPARTMENT OF TRANSPORTATION FEDERAL AVIATION ADMINISTRATION **FLIGHT PLAN**	(FAA USE ONLY) ☐ PILOT BRIEFING ☐ VNR ☐ STOPOVER	TIME STARTED	SPECIALIST INITIALS

1. TYPE	2. AIRCRAFT IDENTIFICATION	3. AIRCRAFT TYPE/ SPECIAL EQUIPMENT	4. TRUE AIRSPEED	5. DEPARTURE POINT	6. DEPARTURE TIME PROPOSED (Z)	ACTUAL (Z)	7. CRUISING ALTITUDE
VFR X IFR DVFR	N3678A	PA31/	180 KTS	YKM			12000

8. ROUTE OF FLIGHT
GROMO 2, HITCH, V468 BTG, DIRECT

9. DESTINATION (Name of airport and city)	10. EST. TIME ENROUTE HOURS	MINUTES	11. REMARKS
PORTLAND INTL. AIRPORT PDX			INSTRUMENT TRAINING FLIGHT

12. FUEL ON BOARD HOURS	MINUTES	13. ALTERNATE AIRPORT(S)	14. PILOT'S NAME, ADDRESS & TELEPHONE NUMBER & AIRCRAFT HOME BASE 17. DESTINATION CONTACT/TELEPHONE (OPTIONAL)	15. NUMBER ABOARD
		N/A		2

16. COLOR OF AIRCRAFT	
GOLD/WHITE	CIVIL AIRCRAFT PILOTS. FAR Part 91 requires you file an IFR flight plan to operate under instrument flight rules in controlled airspace. Failure to file could result in a civil penalty not to exceed $1,000 for each violation (Section 901 of the Federal Aviation Act of 1958, as amended). Filing of a VFR flight plan is recommended as a good operating practice. See also Part 99 for requirements concerning DVFR flight plans.

FAA Form 7233-1 (8-82) CLOSE VFR FLIGHT PLAN WITH ______________ FSS ON ARRIVAL

AIRCRAFT INFORMATION

MAKE Piper MODEL PA-31

N 3678A Vso 77

AIRCRAFT EQUIPMENT/STATUS**

**NOTE: X= OPERATIVE INOP= INOPERATIVE N/A= NOT APPLICABLE
TRANSPONDER: X (MODE C) X ILS: (LOCALIZER) X (GLIDE SLOPE) X
VOR NO. 1 X (NO. 2) X ADF: X RNAV: X
VERTICAL PATH COMPUTER: N/A DME: X
MARKER BEACON: X (AUDIO) INOP (VISUAL) X

Figure Q14-12. Flight Plan and Aircraft Information

Answers:
1.C, 2.B, 3.A, 4.A, 5.B, 6.C, 7.C, 8.B, 9.A, 10.B, 11.C, 12.A,
13.B, 14.B

This glossary includes terms from the *Aeronautical Information Manual*'s "Pilot/Controller Glossary," which is published by the FAA for the purpose of promoting a common understanding of the terms used in the Air Traffic Control system. *The Complete Advanced Pilot* text contains more aviation-related terms than are covered by the Pilot/Controller Glossary, and these terms have been added and marked with an asterisk (*). *Note:* Some of these additional terms repeat Pilot/Controller Glossary terms—where there are two entries for one term, the asterisked term is defined and stated more in accordance with the text of *The Complete Advanced Pilot*.

Terms used by the International Civil Aviation Organization (ICAO) are also defined; these are marked by the bracketed "[ICAO]" when they differ from the FAA definition of a term. The Pilot/Controller Glossary also makes many references to other government publications, such as the AIM, various regulations, and FAA Order 7110.65, a publication concerning details of the Air Traffic Control system operations. Terms most commonly used in pilot/controller communications are printed in **bold italics**.

AAI. (*See* arrival aircraft interval).

AAR. (*See* airport arrival rate).

abbreviated IFR flight plans. An authorization by ATC requiring pilots to submit only that information needed for the purpose of ATC. It includes only a small portion of the usual IFR flight plan information. In certain instances, this may be only aircraft identification, locations, and pilot request. Other information may be requested if needed by ATC for separation/control purposes. It is frequently used by aircraft which are airborne and desire an instrument approach or by aircraft which are on the ground and desire a climb to VFR on top. (*See* VFR-On-Top) (Refer to AIM).

abeam. An aircraft is "abeam" a fix, point, or object when that fix, point, or object is approximately 90 degrees to the right or left of the aircraft track. Abeam indicates a general position rather than a precise point.

abort. To terminate a preplanned aircraft maneuver; e.g., an aborted takeoff.

ACC. [ICAO] (*See* area control center).

accelerate-stop distance available (ASDA). The runway plus stopway length declared available and suitable for the acceleration and deceleration of an airplane aborting a takeoff. [ICAO] The length of the takeoff run available plus the length of the stopway if provided.

ACDO. (*See* Air Carrier District Office).

acknowledge. Let me know that you have received my message. [ICAO] Let me know that you have received and understood this message.

ACLS. (*See* Automatic Carrier Landing System).

ACLT. (*See* actual calculated landing time).

acrobatic flight. An intentional maneuver involving an abrupt change in an aircraft's attitude, an abnormal attitude, or abnormal acceleration not necessary for normal flight. (Refer to 14 CFR Part 91). [ICAO] Maneuvers intentionally performed by an aircraft involving an abrupt change in its attitude, an abnormal attitude, or an abnormal variation in speed.

active runway. (*See* runway in use/active runway/duty runway).

actual calculated landing time (ACLT). ACLT is a flight's frozen calculated landing time. An actual time determined at freeze calculated landing time (FCLT) or meter list display interval (MLDI) for the adapted vertex for each arrival aircraft based upon runway configuration, airport acceptance rate, airport arrival delay period, and other metered arrival aircraft. This time is either the vertex time of arrival (VTA) of the aircraft or the tentative calculated landing time (TCLT)/ACLT of the previous aircraft plus the arrival aircraft interval (AAI), whichever is later. This time will not be updated in response to the aircraft's progress.

actual navigation performance (ANP). (*See* required navigation performance).

additional services. Advisory information provided by ATC which includes but is not limited to the following:
1. Traffic advisories.
2. Vectors, when requested by the pilot, to assist aircraft receiving traffic advisories to avoid observed traffic.
3. Altitude deviation information of 300 feet or more from an assigned altitude as observed on a verified (reading correctly) automatic altitude readout (Mode C).
4. Advisories that traffic is no longer a factor.

Continued

5. Weather and chaff information.
6. Weather assistance.
7. Bird activity information.
8. Holding pattern surveillance.

Additional services are provided to the extent possible contingent only upon the controller's capability to fit them into the performance of higher priority duties and on the basis of limitations of the radar, volume of traffic, frequency congestions, and controller workload. The controller has complete discretion for determining if he/she is able to provide or continue to provide a service in a particular case. The controller's reason not to provide or continue to provide a service in a particular case is not subject to question by the pilot and need not be made known to him/her. (*See* traffic advisories) (Refer to AIM).

ADF. (*See* automatic direction finder).

*****ADF.** Automatic direction finder; a receiver with an associated indicator which points to the transmitting station.

ADIZ. (*See* Air Defense Identification Zone).

ADLY. (*See* arrival delay).

Administrator. The Federal Aviation Administrator or any person to whom he/she has delegated his/her authority in the matter concerned.

*****advection.** Horizontal movement of air.

advise intentions. Tell me what you plan to do.

advisory. Advice and information provided to assist pilots in the safe conduct of flight and aircraft movement. (*See* advisory service).

advisory frequency. The appropriate frequency to be used for Airport Advisory Service. (*See* Local Airport Advisory, UNICOM). (Refer to AC 90-42 and AIM).

advisory service. Advice and information provided by a facility to assist pilots in the safe conduct of flight and aircraft movement. (*See* Local Airport Advisory, traffic advisories, safety alert, additional services, radar advisory, Enroute Flight Advisory Service) (Refer to AIM).

aerial refueling. A procedure used by the military to transfer fuel from one aircraft to another during flight. (Refer to VFR/IFR wall planning charts).

aerodrome. A defined area on land or water (including any buildings, installations and equipment) intended to be used either wholly or in part for the arrival, departure, and movement of aircraft.

aerodrome beacon. [ICAO] Aeronautical beacon used to indicate the location of an aerodrome from the air.

aerodrome control service. [ICAO] Air traffic control service for aerodrome traffic.

aerodrome control tower. [ICAO] A unit established to provide air traffic control service to aerodrome traffic.

aerodrome elevation. [ICAO] The elevation of the highest point of the landing area.

aerodrome traffic circuit. [ICAO] The specified path to be flown by aircraft operating in the vicinity of an aerodrome.

*****aerodynamics.** The study of the forces acting on bodies moving through the air.

aeronautical beacon. A visual NAVAID displaying flashes of white and/or colored light to indicate the location of an airport, a heliport, a landmark, a certain point of a Federal airway in mountainous terrain, or an obstruction. (*See* airport rotating beacon) (Refer to AIM).

aeronautical chart. A map used in air navigation containing all or part of the following: Topographic features, hazards and obstructions, navigation aids, navigation routes, designated airspace, and airports. Commonly used aeronautical charts are:

1. *Sectional charts* (1:500,000). Designed for visual navigation of slow or medium speed aircraft. Topographic information on these charts features the portrayal of relief and a judicious selection of visual check points for VFR flight. Aeronautical information includes visual and radio aids to navigation, airports, controlled airspace, restricted areas, obstructions, and related data.

2. *VFR terminal area charts* (1:250,000). Depict Class B airspace which provides for the control or segregation of all the aircraft within Class B airspace. The chart depicts topographic information and aeronautical information which includes visual and radio aids to navigation, airports, controlled airspace, restricted areas, obstructions, and related data.

3. *World aeronautical charts* (WAC) (1:1,000,000). Provide a standard series of aeronautical charts, covering land areas of the world at a size and scale convenient for navigation by moderate speed aircraft. Topographic information includes cities and towns, principal roads, railroads, distinctive landmarks, drainage, and relief. Aeronautical information includes visual and radio aids to navigation, airports, airways, restricted areas, obstructions, and other pertinent data.

4. *Enroute low altitude charts*. Provide aeronautical information for enroute instrument navigation (IFR) in the low altitude stratum. Information includes the portrayal of airways, limits of controlled airspace, position identification and frequencies of radio aids, selected airports, minimum enroute and minimum obstruction clearance altitudes, airway distances, reporting points, restricted areas, and related data. Area charts, which are a part of this series, furnish terminal data at a larger scale in congested areas.

5. *Enroute high altitude charts*. Provide aeronautical information for enroute instrument navigation (IFR) in the high altitude stratum. Information includes the portrayal of jet routes, identification and frequencies of radio aids, selected airports, distances, time zones, Special Use airspace, and related information.

6. *Instrument approach procedures (IAP) charts*. Portray the aeronautical data which is required to execute an

instrument approach to an airport. These charts depict the procedures, including all related data, and the airport diagram. Each procedure is designated for use with a specific type of electronic navigation system including NDB, TACAN, VOR, ILS/MLS, and RNAV. These charts are identified by the type of navigational aid(s) which provide final approach guidance.

7. *Instrument departure procedure (DP) charts.* Designed to expedite clearance delivery and to facilitate transition between takeoff and enroute operations. Each DP procedure is presented as a separate chart and may serve a single airport or more than one airport in a given geographical location.

8. *Standard terminal arrival (STAR) charts.* Designed to expedite air traffic control arrival procedures and to facilitate transition between enroute and instrument approach operations. Each STAR procedure is presented as a separate chart and may serve a single airport or more than one airport in a given geographical location.

9. *Airport taxi charts.* Designed to expedite the efficient and safe flow of ground traffic at an airport. These charts are identified by the official airport name; e.g., Washington National Airport.

[ICAO] A representation of a portion of the earth, its culture and relief, specifically designated to meet the requirements of air navigation.

Aeronautical Information Manual (AIM). A primary FAA publication whose purpose is to instruct airmen about operating in the National Airspace System of the U.S. It provides basic flight information, ATC Procedures and general instructional information concerning health, medical facts, factors affecting flight safety, accident and hazard reporting, and types of aeronautical charts and their use.

Aeronautical Information Publication (AIP). [ICAO] A publication issued by or with the authority of a state and containing aeronautical information of a lasting character essential to air navigation.

A/FD. (*See* Airport/Facility Directory).

affirmative. Yes.

*****AGL.** Above Ground Level.

*****agonic line.** The line of zero magnetic variation.

*****ailerons.** Movable control surfaces at the outer trailing edge of each wing. They control the airplane in rolling around the longitudinal axis of the airplane.

AIM. (*See* Aeronautical Information Manual).

AIP. [ICAO] (*See* Aeronautical Information Publication).

airborne delay. Amount of delay to be encountered in airborne holding.

Air Carrier District Office (ACDO). An FAA field office serving an assigned geographical area, staffed with Flight Standards personnel serving the aviation industry and the general public on matters related to the certification and operation of scheduled air carriers and other large aircraft operations.

aircraft. Device(s) that are used or intended to be used for flight in the air, and when used in air traffic control terminology, may include the flight crew. [ICAO] Any machine that can derive support in the atmosphere from the reactions of the air other than the reactions of the air against the earth's surface.

aircraft approach category. A grouping of aircraft based on a speed of 1.3 times the stall speed in the landing configuration at maximum gross landing weight. An aircraft shall fit in only one category. If it is necessary to maneuver at speeds in excess of the upper limit of a speed range for a category, the minimums for the next higher category should be used. For example, an aircraft which falls in Category A, but is circling to land at a speed in excess of 91 knots, should use the approach Category B minimums when circling to land. The categories are as follows:

1. *Category A.* Speed less than 91 knots.
2. *Category B.* Speed 91 knots or more but less than 121 knots.
3. *Category C.* Speed 121 knots or more but less than 141 knots.
4. *Category D.* Speed 141 knots or more but less than 166 knots.
5. *Category E.* Speed 166 knots or more.
   (Refer to 14 CFR Parts 1 and 97).

aircraft classes. For the purposes of Wake Turbulence Separation Minima, ATC classifies aircraft as Heavy, Large, and Small as follows:

1. *Heavy.* Aircraft capable of takeoff weights of more than 255,000 pounds whether or not they are operating at this weight during a particular phase of flight.
2. *Large.* Aircraft of more than 41,000 pounds, maximum certificated takeoff weight, up to 255,000 pounds.
3. *Small.* Aircraft of 41,000 pounds or less maximum certificated takeoff weight.
   (Refer to AIM).

aircraft conflict. Predicted conflict, within URET CCLD, of two aircraft, or between aircraft and airspace. A Red alert is used for conflicts when the predicted minimum separation is 5 nautical miles or less. A Yellow alert is used when the predicted minimum separation is between 5 and approximately 12 nautical miles. A Blue alert is used for conflicts between an aircraft and predefined airspace.

*****aircraft situation display (ASD).** ASD is a computer system that receives radar track data from all 20 CONUS ARTCCs, organizes this data into a mosaic display, and presents it on a computer screen. The display allows the traffic management coordinator multiple methods of selection and highlighting of individual aircraft or groups of aircraft. The user has the option of superimposing these aircraft positions over any number of background displays. These background options include ARTCC boundaries, any stratum of enroute sector boundaries, fixes, airways, military and other special use airspace, airports, and geopolitical boundaries. By using ASD, a coordinator can monitor any number of traffic situations or the entire systemwide traffic flows.

Aircraft Surge Launch and Recovery (ASLAR). Procedures used at USAF bases to provide increased launch and recovery rates instrument flight rules conditions. ASLAR is based on:

1. Reduced separation between aircraft which is based on time or distance. Standard arrival separation applies between participants including multiple flights until the DRAG point. The DRAG point is a published location on an ASLAR approach where aircraft landing second in a formation slows to a predetermined airspeed. The DRAG point is the reference point at which MARSA applies as expanding elements effect separation within a flight or between subsequent participating flights.

2. ASLAR procedures shall be covered in a Letter of Agreement between the responsible USAF military ATC facility and the concerned Federal Aviation Administration facility. Initial Approach Fix spacing requirements are normally addressed as a minimum.

air defense emergency. A military emergency condition declared by a designated authority. This condition exists when an attack upon the continental U.S., Alaska, Canada, or U.S. installations in Greenland by hostile aircraft or missiles is considered probable, is imminent, or is taking place. (Refer to AIM).

Air Defense Identification Zone (ADIZ). The area of airspace over land or water, extending upward from the surface, within which the ready identification, the location, and the control of aircraft are required in the interest of national security.

1. *Domestic Air Defense Identification Zone.* An ADIZ within the United States along an international boundary of the United States.

2. *Coastal Air Defense Identification Zone.* An ADIZ over the coastal waters of the United States.

3. *Distant Early Warning Identification Zone (DEWIZ).* An ADIZ over the coastal waters of the State of Alaska.

ADIZ locations and operating and flight plan requirements for civil aircraft operations are specified in 14 CFR Part 99. (Refer to AIM).

*airfoil. A shape designed to develop lift by accelerating airflow over its surface.

Airman's Meteorological Information. (*See* AIRMET).

AIRMET. In-flight weather advisories issued only to amend the area forecast concerning weather phenomena which are of operational interest to all aircraft and potentially hazardous to aircraft having limited capability because of lack of equipment, instrumentation, or pilot qualifications. AIRMETs concern weather of less severity than that covered by SIGMETs or Convective SIGMETs. AIRMETs cover moderate icing, moderate turbulence, sustained winds of 30 knots or more at the surface, widespread areas of ceilings less than 1,000 feet and/or visibility less than 3 miles, and extensive mountain obscurement. (*See* AWW, SIGMET, Convective SIGMET, and CWA) (Refer to AIM).

*AIRMET. A broadcast of weather hazardous to light aircraft.

air navigation facility. Any facility used in, available for use in or designed for use in, aid of air navigation, including landing areas, lights, any apparatus or equipment for disseminating weather information, for signaling, for radio directional finding, or for radio or other electrical communication, and any other structure or mechanism having a similar purpose for guiding or controlling flight in the air or the landing and takeoff of aircraft. (*See* navigational aid).

airport. An area on land or water that is used or intended to be used for the landing and takeoff of aircraft and includes its buildings and facilities, if any.

*airport acceptance rate (AAR). A dynamic input parameter specifying the number of arriving aircraft which an airport or airspace can accept from the ARTCC per hour. The AAR is used to calculate the desired interval between successive arrival aircraft.

airport advisory area. The area within ten miles of an airport without a control tower or where the tower is not in operation, and on which a Flight Service Station is located. (*See* Local Airport Advisory) (Refer to AIM).

*airport advisory area. An area within 10 miles of an airport with a Flight Service Station.

airport elevation. The highest point of an airport's usable runways measured in feet from mean sea level. (*See* touchdown zone elevation, aerodrome elevation [ICAO]).

Airport/Facility Directory (A/FD). A publication designed primarily as a pilot's operational manual containing all airports, seaplane bases, and heliports open to the public including communications data, navigational facilities, and certain special notices and procedures. This publication is issued in seven volumes according to geographical area.

*Airport/Facility Directory (A/FD). A government publication containing information on all airports including radio frequencies and navigational aids available.

airport information desk. An airport unmanned facility designed for pilot self-service briefing, flight planning, and filing of flight plans. (Refer to AIM).

airport lighting. Various lighting aids that may be installed on an airport. Types of airport lighting include:

1. *Approach Light System (ALS).* An airport lighting facility which provides visual guidance to landing aircraft by radiating light beams in a directional pattern by which the pilot aligns the aircraft with the extended centerline of the runway on his final approach for landing. Capacitor Discharge Sequential Flashing Lights/Sequenced Flashing Lights may be installed in conjunction with the ALS at some airports. Types of Approach Light Systems are:

a. *ALSF-1.* Approach Light System with Sequenced Flashing Lights in ILS Cat I configuration.

b. *ALSF-2.* Approach Light System with Sequenced Flashing Lights in ILS Cat II configuration. The ALSF-2 may operate as an SSALR when weather conditions permit.

c. *SSALF.* Simplified Short Approach Light System with Sequenced Flashing Lights.

d. *SSALR.* Simplified Short Approach Light System with Runway Alignment Indicator Lights.

e. *MALSF.* Medium Intensity Approach Light System with Sequenced Flashing Lights.

f. *MALSR.* Medium Intensity Approach Light System with Runway Alignment Indicator Lights.

g. *LDIN.* Lead In light system: Consists of one or more series of flashing lights installed at or near ground level that provides positive visual guidance along an approach path, either curving or straight, where special problems exist with hazardous terrain, obstructions, or noise abatement procedures.

h. *RAIL.* Runway Alignment Indicator Lights (Sequenced Flashing Lights which are installed only combination with other light systems).

i. *ODALS.* Omnidirectional Approach Lighting System consists of seven omnidirectional flashing lights located in approach area of a nonprecision runway. Five lights are located on the runway centerline extended with the first light located 300 feet from the threshold and extending at equal intervals up to 1,500 feet from the threshold. The other two lights are located, one on each side of the runway threshold, at a lateral distance of 40 feet from the runway edge, or 75 feet from the runway edge when installed on a runway equipped with a VASI. (Refer to Order 6850.2).

2. *Runway lights/runway edge lights.* Lights having a prescribed angle of emission used to define the lateral limits of a runway. Runway lights are uniformly spaced at intervals of approximately 200 feet, and the intensity may be controlled or preset.

3. *Touchdown zone lighting.* Two rows of transverse light bars located symmetrically about the runway centerline normally at 100-foot intervals. The basic system extends 3,000 feet along the runway.

4. *Runway centerline lighting.* Flush centerline lights spaced at 50 foot intervals beginning 75 feet from the landing threshold and extending to within 75 feet of the opposite end of the runway.

5. *Threshold Lights.* Fixed green lights arranged symmetrically left and right of the runway centerline, identifying the runway threshold.

6. *Runway End Identifier Lights (REIL).* Two synchronized flashing lights, one on each side of the runway threshold, which provide rapid and positive identification of the approach end of a particular runway.

7. *Visual Approach Slope Indicator (VASI).* An airport lighting facility providing vertical visual approach slope guidance to aircraft during approach to landing by radiating a directional pattern of high intensity read and white focused light beams which indicate to the pilot that he is "on path" if he sees red/white, "above path" if white/white, and "below path" if red/red. Some airports serving large aircraft have three bar VASIs which provide two visual glidepaths to the same runway.

8. *Boundary lights.* Lights defining the perimeter of an airport or landing area. (Refer to AIM).

airport marking aids. Markings used on runway and taxiway surfaces to identify a specific runway, a runway threshold, a centerline, a hold line, etc. A runway should be marked in accordance with its present usage such as:

1. Visual.

2. Nonprecision instrument.

3. Precision instrument. (Refer to AIM).

airport reference point (ARP). The approximate geometric center of all usable runway surfaces.

Airport Reservation Office (ARO). Office responsible for monitoring the operation of the high density rule. Receives and processes requests for IFR operations at high density traffic airports.

airport rotating beacon. A visual NAVAID operated at many airports. At civil airports, alternating white and green flashes indicate the location of the airport. At military airports, the beacons flash alternately white and green, but are differentiated from civil beacons by dual peaked (two quick) white flashes between the green flashes. (*See* Special VFR operations, instrument flight rules) (Refer to AIM) (*See* aerodrome beacon [ICAO]).

airport surface detection equipment (ASDE). Radar equipment specifically designed to detect all principal features on the surface of an airport, including aircraft and vehicular traffic, and to present the entire image on a radar indicator console in the control tower. Used to augment visual observation by tower personnel of aircraft and/or vehicular movements on runways and taxiways.

airport surveillance radar (ASR). Approach control radar used to detect and display an aircraft's position in the terminal area. ASR provides range and azimuth information but does not provide elevation data. Coverage of the ASR can extend up to 60 miles.

airport taxi charts. (*See* aeronautical chart).

Airport Traffic Control Service. A service provided by a control tower for aircraft operating on the movement area and in the vicinity of an airport. (*See* movement area, tower) (*See* aerodrome control service [ICAO]).

airport traffic control tower. (*See* tower).

air route surveillance radar (ARSR). Air route traffic control center (ARTCC) radar used primarily to detect and display an aircraft's position while enroute between terminal areas. The ARSR enables controllers to provide radar air traffic control service when aircraft are within the ARSR coverage. In some instances, ARSR may enable an ARTCC to provide terminal radar services similar to but usually more limited than those provided by a radar approach control.

air route traffic control center (ARTCC). A facility established to provide air traffic control service to aircraft operating on IFR flight plans within controlled airspace and principally during the enroute phase of light. When equipment capabilities and controller workload permit, certain advisory/assistance services may be provided to VFR aircraft. (*See* NAS Stage A, enroute air traffic control service) (Refer to AIM).

airspace conflict. Predicted conflict of an aircraft and active Special Activity Airspace (SAA).

airspace hierarchy. Within the airspace classes, there is a hierarchy and, in the event of an overlap of airspace: Class A preempts Class B, Class B preempts Class C, Class C preempts Class D, Class D preempts Class E, and Class E preempts Class G.

airspeed. The speed of an aircraft relative to its surrounding air mass. The unqualified term "airspeed" means one of the following:

1. *Indicated airspeed.* The speed shown on the aircraft airspeed indicator. This is the speed used in pilot/controller communications under the general term "airspeed." (Refer to 14 CFR Part 1).

2. *True airspeed.* The airspeed of an aircraft relative to undisturbed air. Used primarily in flight planning and enroute portion of flight. When used in pilot/controller communications, it is referred to as "true airspeed" and not shortened to "airspeed."

*airspeed indicator. An instrument calibrated in speed units that measures the pressure difference between the pitot and static inputs.

airstart. The starting of an aircraft engine while the aircraft is airborne, preceded by engine shutdown during training flights or by actual engine failure.

air taxi. Used to describe a helicopter/VTOL aircraft movement conducted above the surface but normally not above 100 feet AGL. The aircraft may proceed either via hover taxi or flight at speeds more than 20 knots. The pilot is solely responsible for selecting a safe airspeed/altitude for the operation being conducted. (*See* hover taxi) (Refer to AIM).

air traffic. Aircraft operating in the air or on an airport surface, exclusive of loading ramps and parking areas. [ICAO] All aircraft in flight or operating on the maneuvering area of an aerodrome.

air traffic clearance. An authorization by air traffic control, for the purpose of preventing collision between known aircraft, for an aircraft to proceed under specified traffic conditions within controlled airspace. The pilot in command of an aircraft may not deviate from the provisions of a visual flight rules (VFR) or instrument flight rules (IFR) air traffic clearance except in an emergency or unless an amended clearance has been obtained. Additionally, the pilot may request a different clearance from that which has been issued by air

traffic control (ATC) if information available to the pilot makes another course of action more practicable or if aircraft equipment limitations or company procedures forbid compliance with the clearance issued. Pilots may also request clarification or amendment, as appropriate, any time a clearance is not fully understood, or considered unacceptable because of safety of flight. Controllers should, in such instances and to the extent of operational practicality and safety, honor the pilot's request. Part 91.3(a) states: "The pilot-in-command of an aircraft is directly responsible for, and is the final authority as to, the operation of that aircraft." THE PILOT IS RESPONSIBLE TO REQUEST AN AMENDED CLEARANCE if ATC issues a clearance that would cause a pilot to deviate from a rule or regulation, or in the pilot's opinion, would place the aircraft in jeopardy. (*See* ATC instructions) (*See* air traffic control clearance [ICAO]).

air traffic control (ATC). A service operated by appropriate authority to promote the safe, orderly and expeditious flow of air traffic. (*See* air traffic control service [ICAO]).

air traffic control clearance. [ICAO] Authorization for an aircraft to proceed under conditions specified by an air traffic control unit. *Note 1:* For convenience, the term air traffic control clearance is frequently abbreviated to clearance when used in appropriate contexts. *Note 2:* The abbreviated term clearance may be prefixed by the words taxi, takeoff, departure, enroute, approach or landing to indicate the particular portion of flight to which the air traffic control clearance relates.

air traffic control service. (*See* air traffic control).

air traffic control service. [ICAO] A service provided for the purpose of:

1. Preventing collisions:
   a. Between aircraft; and
   b. On the maneuvering area between aircraft and obstructions; and

2. Expediting and maintaining an orderly flow of air traffic.

air traffic control specialist. A person authorized to provide air traffic control service. (*See* air traffic control, Flight Service Station) (*See* controller [ICAO]).

Air Traffic Control System Command Center (ATCSCC). An Air Traffic Operations Service facility consisting of four operational units.

1. *Central Flow Control Function (CFCF).* Responsible for coordination and approval of all major intercenter flow control restrictions on a system basis in order to obtain maximum utilization of the airspace. (*See* quota flow control).

2. *Central Altitude Reservation Function (CARF).* Responsible for coordinating, planning, and approving special user requirements under the Altitude Reservation (ALTRV) concept. (*See* altitude reservation).

3. *Airport Reservation Office (ARO).* Responsible for approving IFR flights at designated high density traffic airports (John F. Kennedy, LaGuardia, O'Hare, and Washington National) during specified hours. (Refer to 14 CFR Part 93 and Airport/Facility Directory).

4. *ATC Contingency Command Post*. A facility which enables the FAA to manage the ATC system when significant portions of the system's capabilities have been lost or are threatened.

air traffic service. A generic term meaning:
1. Flight Information Service,
2. Alerting Service,
3. Air Traffic Advisory Service,
4. Air Traffic Control Service,
   a. Area Control Service,
   b. Approach Control Service, or
   c. Airport Control Service.

airway. A Class E airspace area established in the form of a corridor, the centerline of which is defined by radio navigational aids. (Refer to 14 CFR Part 71, AIM) (*See* federal airways). [ICAO] A control area or portion thereof established in the form of corridor equipped with radio navigational aids.

airway beacon. Used to mark airway segments in remote mountain areas. The light flashes Morse Code to identify the beacon site. (Refer to AIM).

AIT. (*See* automated information transfer).

alerfa (alert phase). [ICAO] The code word used to designate an emergency phase wherein apprehension exists as to the safety of an aircraft and its occupants.

alert area. (*See* Special Use airspace).

alert notice (ALNOT). A request originated by a Flight Service Station (FSS) or an air route traffic control center (ARTCC) for an extensive communication search for overdue, unreported, or missing aircraft.

alerting service. A service provided to notify appropriate organizations regarding aircraft in need of search and rescue aid and assist such organizations as required.

ALNOT. (*See* alert notice).

along track distance (LTD). The distance measured from a point-in-space by systems using area navigation reference capabilities that are not subject to slant range errors.

alphanumeric display. Letters and numerals used to show identification, altitude, beacon code, and other information concerning a target on a radar display. (*See* automated radar terminal systems, NAS Stage A).

alternate aerodrome. [ICAO] An aerodrome specified in the flight plan to which a flight may proceed when it becomes inadvisable to land at the aerodrome of intended landing.
   Note: The aerodrome from which a flight departs may also be an enroute or a destination alternate aerodrome for the flight.

alternate airport. An airport at which an aircraft may land if a landing at the intended airport becomes inadvisable. (*See* FAA term alternate aerodrome [ICAO]).

*__altimeter.__ An instrument that indicates altitude by measuring changes in atmospheric pressure.

altimeter setting. The barometric pressure reading used to adjust a pressure altimeter for variations in existing atmospheric pressure or to the standard altimeter setting (29.92). (Refer to 14 CFR Part 91, AIM).

*__altimeter setting.__ A value received from a ground station to which the altimeter setting window must be adjusted in order to correct for pressure variations.

altitude. The height of a level, point, or object measured in feet Above Ground Level (AGL) or from Mean Sea Level (MSL). (*See* flight level).
1. *MSL Altitude*. Altitude expressed in feet measured from mean sea level.
2. *AGL Altitude*. Altitude expressed in feet measured above ground level.
3. *Indicated Altitude*. The altitude as shown by an altimeter. On a pressure or barometric altimeter it is altitude as shown uncorrected for instrument error and uncompensated for variation from standard atmospheric conditions.
   [ICAO] The vertical distance of a level, a point or an object considered as a point, measured from mean sea level (MSL).

altitude readout. An aircraft's altitude, transmitted via the Mode C transponder feature, that is visually displayed in 100 foot increments on a radar scope having readout capability. (*See* automated radar terminal systems, NAS Stage A, alphanumeric display) (Refer to AIM).

altitude reservation (ALTRV). Airspace utilization under prescribed conditions normally employed for the mass movement of aircraft or other special user requirements which cannot otherwise be accomplished. ALTRVs are approved by the appropriate FAA facility. (*See* Air Traffic Control System Command Center).

altitude restriction. An altitude or altitudes, stated in the order flown, which are to be maintained until reaching a specific point or time. Altitude restrictions may be issued by ATC due to traffic, terrain, or other airspace considerations.

altitude restrictions are canceled. Adherence to previously imposed altitude restrictions is no longer required during a climb or descent.

ALTRV. (*See* altitude reservation).

*__ammeter.__ A meter that indicates the output of the generator or alternator in amperes, the unit of electric current.

*__amphibian.__ An airplane able to land and takeoff on both land and water. Airplanes with boat hulls (and retractable wheels) and float planes (with retractable wheels) are amphibians.

AMVER. (*See* Automated Mutual Assistance Vessel Rescue System).

*__angle of attack.__ The angle between the chord line and the relative wind; the pilot's best means of controlling lift development.

*angle of incidence. The fixed angle at which the wing is attached to the fuselage; the angle between the chord line and the longitudinal axis.

approach clearance. Authorization by ATC for a pilot to conduct an instrument approach. The type of instrument approach for which a clearance and other pertinent information is provided in the approach clearance when required. (*See* instrument approach procedure, cleared for approach) (Refer to AIM and 14 CFR Part 91).

Approach Control Facility. A terminal ATC facility that provides approach control service in a terminal area. (*See* Approach Control Service, radar approach control facility).

Approach Control Service. Air traffic control service provided by an approach control facility for arriving and departing VFR/IFR aircraft and, on occasion, enroute aircraft. At some airports not served by an approach control facility, the ARTCC provides limited approach control service. (Refer to AIM). [ICAO] Air traffic control service for arriving or departing controlled flights.

approach gate. An imaginary point used within ATC as a basis for vectoring aircraft to the final approach course. The gate will be established along the final approach course 1 mile from the outer marker (or the fix used in lieu of the outer marker) on the side away from the airport for precision approaches and 1 mile from the final approach fix on the side away from the airport for nonprecision approaches. In either case when measured along the final approach course, the gate will be no closer than 5 miles from the landing threshold.

approach light system. (*See* airport lighting).

approach sequence. The order in which aircraft are positioned while on approach or awaiting approach clearance. (*See* landing sequence). [ICAO] The order in which two or more aircraft are cleared to approach to land at the aerodrome.

approach speed. The recommended speed contained in aircraft manuals used by pilots when making an approach to landing. This speed will vary for different segments of an approach as well as for aircraft weight and configuration.

appropriate ATS authority. [ICAO] The relevant authority designated by the State responsible for providing air traffic services in the airspace concerned. In the United States, the "appropriate ATS authority" is the Program Director for Air Traffic Operations, ATO-1.

appropriate authority.
1. Regarding flight over the high seas: the relevant authority is the State of Registry.
2. Regarding flight over other than the high seas: the relevant authority is the State having sovereignty over the territory being overflown.

appropriate obstacle clearance minimum altitude. Any of the following:
(*See* minimum IFR altitude (MIA)).
(*See* minimum enroute altitude (MEA)).
(*See* minimum obstruction clearance altitude (MOCA)).
(*See* minimum vectoring altitude (MVA)).

appropriate terrain clearance minimum altitude. Any of the following:
(*See* minimum IFR altitude (MIA)).
(*See* minimum enroute altitude (MEA)).
(*See* minimum obstruction clearance altitude (MOCA)).
(*See* minimum vectoring altitude (MVA)).

apron. A defined area on an airport or heliport intended to accommodate aircraft for purposes of loading or unloading passengers or cargo, refueling, parking, or maintenance. With regard to seaplanes, a ramp is used for access to the apron from the water. [ICAO] A defined area, on a land aerodrome, intended to accommodate aircraft for purposes of loading or unloading passengers, mail or cargo, refueling, parking or maintenance.

arc. The track over the ground of an aircraft flying at a constant distance from a navigational aid by reference to distance measuring equipment (DME).

*area aviation forecast (FA). A forecast of general weather conditions over an area as large as several states.

area control center (ACC). [ICAO] An ICAO term for an air traffic control facility primarily responsible for ATC services being provided IFR aircraft during the enroute phase of flight. The U.S. equivalent facility is an air route traffic control center (ARTCC).

area navigation (RNAV). A method of navigation that permits aircraft operation on any desired course within the coverage of station referenced navigation signals or within the limits of a self-contained system capability. Random area navigation routes are direct routes, based on area navigation capability, between waypoints defined in terms of latitude/longitude coordinates, degree/distance fixes, or offsets from published or established routes/airways at a specified distance and direction. The major types of equipment are:

1. *VORTAC* referenced or Course Line Computer (CLC) systems, which account for the greatest number of RNAV units in use. To function, the CLC must be within the service range of a VORTAC.
2. *OMEGA/VLF,* although two separate systems, can be considered as one operationally. A long range navigation system based upon Very Low Frequency radio signals transmitted from a total of 17 stations worldwide.
3. *Inertial (INS) systems,* which are totally self-contained and require no information from external references. They provide aircraft position and navigation information in response to signals resulting from inertial effects on components within the system.
4. *MLS Area Navigation (MLS/RNAV),* which provides area navigation with reference to an MLS ground facility.
5. *LORAN C* is a long range radio navigation system that uses ground waves transmitted at low frequency to provide user position information at ranges of up to 600 to 1,200 nautical miles at both enroute and approach altitudes. The

useable signal coverage areas are determined by the signal to noise ratio, the envelope to cycle difference, and the geometric relationship between the positions of the user and the transmitting stations.

6. *GPS* is a space-base radio positioning, navigation, and time-transfer system. The system provides highly accurate position and velocity information, and precise time, on a continuous global basis, to an unlimited number of properly equipped users. The system is unaffected by weather, and provides a worldwide common grid reference system.

[ICAO] A method of navigation which permits aircraft operation on any desired flight path within the coverage of station referenced navigation aids or within the limits of the capability of self-contained aids, or a combination of these.

area navigation (RNAV) approach configuration.

1. *Standard T.* An RNAV approach whose design allows direct flight to any one of three initial approach fixes (IAF) and eliminates the need for procedure turns. The standard design is to align the procedure on the extended centerline with the missed approach point (MAP) at the runway threshold, the final approach fix (FAF), and the initial approach/intermediate fix (IAF/IF). The other two IAFs will be established perpendicular to the IF.

2. *Modified T.* An RNAV approach design for single or multiple runways where terrain or operational constraints do not allow for the standard T. The "T" may be modified by increasing or decreasing the angle from the corner IAF(s) to the IF or by eliminating one or both corner IAFs.

3. *Standard I.* An RNAV approach design for a single runway with both corner IAFs eliminated. Course reversal or radar vectoring may be required at busy terminals with multiple runways.

4. *Terminal arrival area (TAA).* The TAA is controlled airspace established in conjunction with the Standard or Modified T and I RNAV approach configurations. In the standard TAA, there are three areas: straight-in, left base, and right base. The arc boundaries of the three areas of the TAA are published portions of the approach and allow aircraft to transition from the en route structure direct to the nearest IAF. TAAs will also eliminate or reduce feeder routes, departure extensions, and procedure turns or course reversal.

   a. *Straight-in area.* A 30 NM arc centered on the IF bounded by a straight line extending through the IF perpendicular to the intermediate course.

   b. *Left base area.* A 30 NM arc centered on the right corner IAF. The area shares a boundary with the straight-in area except that it extends out for 30 NM from the IAF and is bounded on the other side by a line extending from the IF through the FAF to the arc.

   c. *Right base area.* A 30 NM arc centered on the left corner IAF. The area shares a boundary with the straight-in area except that it extends out for 30 NM from the IAF and is bounded on the other side by a line extending from the IF through the FAF to the arc.

ARINC. An acronym for Aeronautical Radio, Inc., a corporation largely owned by a group of airlines. ARINC is licensed by the FCC as an aeronautical station and contracted by the FAA to provide communications support for air traffic control and meteorological services in portions of international airspace.

*arm. The distance a weight is located from a fulcrum or datum point.

Army Aviation Flight Information Bulletin (USAFIB). A bulletin that provides air operation data covering Army, National Guard, and Army Reserve aviation activities.

ARO. (*See* Airport Reservation Office).

arresting system. A safety device consisting of two major components, namely, engaging or catching devices and energy absorption devices for the purpose of arresting both tailhook and/or nontailhook equipped aircraft. It is used to prevent aircraft from overrunning runways when the aircraft cannot be stopped after landing or during aborted takeoff. Arresting systems have various names; e.g., arresting gear, hook device, wire barrier cable. (*See* abort) (Refer to AIM).

arrival aircraft interval (AAI). An internally generated program in hundredths of minutes based upon the AAR. AAI is the desired optimum interval between successive arrival aircraft over the vertex.

arrival center. The ARTCC having jurisdiction for the impacted airport.

arrival delay (ADLY). A parameter which specifies a period of time in which no aircraft will be metered for arrival at the specified airport.

arrival sector. An operational control sector containing one or more meter fixes.

arrival sector advisory list. An ordered list of data on arrivals displayed at the PVD/MDM of the sector which controls the meter fix.

arrival sequencing program (ASP). The automated program designed to assist in sequencing aircraft destined for the same airport.

arrival time. The time an aircraft touches down on arrival.

ARSR. (*See* air route surveillance radar).

ARTCC. (*See* air route traffic control center).

ARTS. (*See* automated radar terminal system).

ASD. (*See* aircraft situation display).

ASDA. (*See* accelerate-stop distance available).

ASDA. [ICAO] (*See* accelerate-stop distance available [ICAO]).

ASDE. (*See* airport surface detection equipment).

ASLAR. (*See* Aircraft Surge Launch and Recovery).

ASP. (*See* arrival sequencing program).

ASR. (*See* airport surveillance radar).

ASR approach. (*See* surveillance approach).

*****ATA.** Actual time of arrival—to be filled in on your flight log and compared with your estimates to determine how the actual flight is progressing.

ATC. (*See* air traffic control).

ATCAA. (*See* ATC assigned airspace).

ATC advises. Used to prefix a message of noncontrol information when it is relayed to an aircraft by other than an air traffic controller. (*See* advisory).

ATC assigned airspace (ATCAA). Airspace of defined vertical/lateral limits, assigned by ATC, for the purpose of providing air traffic segregation between the specified activities being conducted within the assigned airspace and other IFR air traffic. (*See* Special Use airspace).

ATC clearance. (*See* air traffic clearance).

ATC clears. Used to prefix an ATC clearance when it is relayed to an aircraft by other than an air traffic controller.

ATC instructions. Directives issued by air traffic control for the purpose of requiring a pilot to take specific actions; e.g., "Turn left heading two five zero," "Go around," "Clear the runway." (Refer to 14 CFR Part 91).

ATCRBS. (*See* radar).

ATC requests. Used to prefix an ATC request when it is relayed to an aircraft by other than an air traffic controller.

ATCSCC. (*See* Air Traffic Control System Command Center).

ATCSCC delay factor. The amount of delay calculated to be assigned prior to departure.

ATCT. (*See* tower).

*****ATE.** Actual time enroute.

ATIS. (*See* Automatic Terminal Information Service).

*****ATIS.** Automatic Terminal Information Service—a recorded broadcast of noncontrol information at busy airports.

ATS Route. [ICAO] A specified route designed for the flow of traffic as necessary for the provision of air traffic services. *Note:* The term "ATS Route" is used to mean airway, advisory route, controlled or uncontrolled route, arrival or departure, etc.

*****attitude.** The position of the airplane's nose or wings in relation to the natural horizon.

autoland approach. An autoland approach is a precision instrument approach to touchdown and, in some cases, through the landing rollout. An autoland approach is performed by the aircraft autopilot which is receiving position information and/or steering commands from on board navigation equipment. (*See* coupled approach).
Note: Autoland and coupled approaches are flown in VFR and IFR. It is common for carriers to require their crews to fly

coupled approaches and autoland approaches (if certified) when the weather conditions are less than approximately 4,000 RVR.

automated information transfer (AIT). A precoordinated process, specifically defined in facility directives, during which a transfer of altitude control and/or radar identification is accomplished without verbal coordination between controllers using information communicated in a full data block.

Automated Mutual Assistance Vessel Rescue System. A facility which can deliver, in a matter of minutes, a surface picture (SURPIC) of vessels in the area of a potential or actual search and rescue incident, including their predicted positions and their characteristics. (*See* Order 7110.65 Paragraph 10-73, In-flight contingencies).

automated radar terminal systems (ARTS). The generic term for the ultimate in functional capability afforded by several automation systems. Each differs in functional capabilities and equipment. ARTS plus a suffix roman numeral denotes a specific system. A following letter indicates a major modification to that system. In general, an ARTS displays for the terminal controller aircraft identification, flight plan data, other flight associated information; e.g., altitude, speed, and aircraft position symbols in conjunction with his radar presentation. Normal radar coexists with the alphanumeric display. In addition to enhancing visualization of the air traffic situation, ARTS facilitate intrafacility and interfacility transfer and coordination of flight information. These capabilities are enabled by specially designed computers and subsystems tailored to the radar and communications equipments and operational requirements of each automated facility. Modular design permits adoption of improvements in computer software and electronic technologies as they become available while retaining the characteristics unique to each system.

1. *ARTS II.* A programmable nontracking, computer aided display subsystem capable of modular expansion. ARTS II systems provide a level of automated air traffic control capability at terminals having low to medium activity. Flight identification and altitude may be associated with the display of secondary radar targets. The system has the capability of communicating with ARTCCs and other ARTS II, IIA, III, and IIIA facilities.

2. *ARTS IIA.* A programmable radar tracking computer subsystem capable of modular expansion. The ARTS IIA detects, tracks, and predicts secondary radar targets. The targets are displayed by means of computer generated symbols, ground speed, and flight plan data. Although it does not track primary radar targets, they are displayed coincident with the secondary radar as well as the symbols and alphanumerics. The system has the capability of communicating with ARTCCs and other ARTS II, IIA, III, and IIIA facilities.

3. *ARTS III.* The Beacon Tracking Level (BTL) of the modular programmable automated radar terminal system in use at medium to high activity terminals. ARTS III detects, tracks, and predicts secondary radar derived aircraft targets. These are displayed by means of computer

generated symbols and alphanumeric characters depicting flight identification, aircraft altitude, ground speed, and flight plan data. Although it does not track primary targets, they are displayed coincident with the secondary radar as well as the symbols and alphanumerics. The system has the capability of communicating with ARTCCs and other ARTS III facilities.

4. *ARTS IIIA*. The Radar Tracking and Beacon Tracking Level (RT & BTL) of the modular, programmable automated radar terminal system. ARTS IIIA detects, tracks, and predicts primary as well as secondary radar derived aircraft targets. This more sophisticated computer driven system upgrades the existing ARTS III system by providing improved tracking, continuous data recording, and fail-soft capabilities.

automated UNICOM. Provides completely automated weather, radio check capability and airport advisory information on an Automated UNICOM system. These systems offer a variety of features, typically selectable by microphone clicks, on the UNICOM frequency. Availability will be published in the Airport/Facility Directory and approach charts.

automatic altitude report. (*See* altitude readout).

automatic altitude reporting. That function of a transponder which responds to Mode C interrogations by transmitting the aircraft's altitude in 100-foot increments.

Automatic Carrier Landing System (ACLS). U.S. Navy final approach equipment consisting of precision tracking radar coupled to a computer data link to provide continuous information to the aircraft, monitoring capability to the pilot, and a backup approach system.

automatic direction finder (ADF). An aircraft radio navigation system which senses and indicates the direction to a L/MF nondirectional radio beacon (NDB) ground transmitter. Direction is indicated to the pilot as a magnetic bearing or as a relative bearing to the longitudinal axis of the aircraft depending on the type of indicator installed in the aircraft. In certain applications, such as military, ADF operations may be based on airborne and ground transmitters in the VHF/UHF frequency spectrum. (*See* bearing, nondirectional beacon).

Automatic Terminal Information Service (ATIS). The continuous broadcast of recorded noncontrol information in selected terminal areas. Its purpose is to improve controller effectiveness and to relieve frequency congestion by automating the repetitive transmission of essential but routine information; e.g., "Los Angeles information Alfa. One three zero zero Coordinated Universal Time. Weather measured ceiling two thousand overcast, visibility three, haze, smoke, temperature seven one, dew point five seven, wind two five zero at five, altimeter two niner six. ILS Runway Two Five Left approach in use, Runway Two Five Right closed, advise you have Alfa." (Refer to AIM). [ICAO] The provision of current, routine information to arriving and departing aircraft by means of continuous and repetitive broadcasts throughout the day or a specified portion of the day.

autorotation. A rotorcraft flight condition in which the lifting rotor is driven entirely by action of the air when the rotorcraft is in motion.

1. *Autorotative Landing/Touchdown Autorotation*. Used by a pilot to indicate that he will be landing without applying power to the rotor.

2. *Low Level Autorotation*. Commences at an altitude well below the traffic pattern, usually below 100 feet AGL and is used primarily for tactical military training.

3. *180 degrees Autorotation*. Initiated from a downwind heading and is commenced well inside the normal traffic pattern. "Go around" may not be possible during the latter part of this maneuver.

Available Landing Distance (ALD). The portion of a runway available for landing and roll-out for aircraft cleared for LAHSO. This distance is measured from the landing threshold to the hold-short point.

Aviation Weather Service. A service provided by the National Weather Service (NWS) and FAA which collects and disseminates pertinent weather information for pilots, aircraft operators, and ATC. Available aviation weather reports and forecasts are displayed at each NWS office and FAA FSS. (*See* Enroute Flight Advisory Service, Transcribed Weather Broadcast, Weather Advisory, Pilots Automatic Telephone Weather Answering Service) (Refer to AIM).

AWW. (*See* severe weather forecast alerts).

*axis of control. An imaginary line around which the pilot controls the airplane.

azimuth (MLS). A magnetic bearing extending from an MLS navigation facility. *Note:* azimuth bearings are described as magnetic and are referred to as "azimuth" in radio telephone communications.

back-taxi. A term used by air traffic controllers to taxi an aircraft on the runway opposite to the traffic flow. The aircraft may be instructed to back-taxi to the beginning of the runway or at some point before reaching the runway end for the purpose of departure or to exit the runway.

base leg. (*See* traffic pattern).

beacon. (*See* radar, nondirectional beacon, marker beacon, airport rotating beacon, aeronautical beacon, airway beacon).

bearing. The horizontal direction to or from any point, usually measured clockwise from true north, magnetic north, or some other reference point through 360 degrees. (*See* nondirectional beacon).

below minimums. Weather conditions below the minimums prescribed by regulation for the particular action involved; e.g., landing minimums, takeoff minimums.

blast fence. A barrier that is used to divert or dissipate jet or propeller blast.

*bleed air. Compressed air "bled" from the turbocharger to operate pressurization cabin heating and deicing systems.

blind speed. The rate of departure or closing of a target relative to the radar antenna at which cancellation of the primary radar target by moving target indicator (MTI) circuits in the radar equipment causes a reduction or complete loss of signal. (*See* blind velocity [ICAO]).

blind spot. An area from which radio transmissions and/or radar echoes cannot be received. The term is also used to describe portions of the airport not visible from the control tower.

blind transmission. (*See* transmitting in the blind).

blind velocity. [ICAO] The radial velocity of a moving target such that the target is not seen on primary radars fitted with certain forms of fixed echo suppression.

blind zone. (*See* blind spot).

blocked. Phraseology used to indicate that a radio transmission has been distorted or interrupted due to multiple simultaneous radio transmissions.

boundary lights. (*See* airport lighting).

braking action (good, fair, poor, or nil). A report of conditions on the airport movement area providing a pilot with a degree/quality of braking that he might expect. Braking action is reported in terms of good, fair, poor, or nil. (*See* runway condition reading).

braking action advisories. When tower controllers have received runway braking action reports which include the terms "poor" or "nil," or whenever weather conditions are conducive to deteriorating or rapidly changing runway braking conditions, the tower will include on the ATIS broadcast the statement, "BRAKING ACTION ADVISORIES ARE IN EFFECT." During the time braking action advisories are in effect, ATC will issue the latest braking action report for the runway in use to each arriving and departing aircraft. Pilots should be prepared for deteriorating braking conditions and should request current runway condition information if not volunteered by controllers. Pilots should also be prepared to provide a descriptive runway condition report to controllers after landing.

breakout. A technique to direct aircraft out of the approach stream. In the context of close parallel operations, a breakout is used to direct threatened aircraft away from a deviating aircraft.

broadcast. Transmission of information for which an acknowledgment is not expected. [ICAO] A transmission of information relating to air navigation that is not addressed to a specific station or stations.

calculated landing time (CLT). A term that may be used in place of tentative or actual calculated landing time, whichever applies.

calibrated airspeed. The reading of the airspeed indicator corrected for installation or position error.

call up. Initial voice contact between a facility and an aircraft, using the identification of the unit being called and the unit initiating the call. (Refer to AIM).

call for release (CFR). Wherein the overlying ARTCC requires a terminal facility to initiate verbal coordination to secure ARTCC approval for release of a departure into the enroute environment.

camber. The convexity or curvature of an airfoil from its chord.

Canadian Minimum Navigation Performance Specification (CMNPS) airspace. That portion of Canadian domestic airspace within which MNPS separation may be applied.

carburetor. A device that mixes a metered amount of fuel with airflow, atomizing it for combustion.

cardinal altitudes. "Odd" or "Even" thousand foot altitudes or flight levels; e.g., 5,000, 6,000, 7,000, FL 250, FL 260, FL 270. (*See* altitude, flight level).

cardinal flight levels. (*See* cardinal altitudes).

CAT. (*See* clear air turbulence).

CDT programs. (*See* controlled departure time programs).

CDI. Course Deviation Indicator—the "needle" on a VOR display that tells you if you are on the desired radial.

ceiling. The heights above the earth's surface of the lowest layer of clouds or obscuring phenomena that is reported as "broken," "overcast," or "obscuration." [ICAO] The height above the ground or water of the base of the lowest layer of cloud below 6,000 meters (20,000 feet) covering more than half the sky.

CENRAP. (*See* Center Radar ARTS Presentation/processing).

CENRAP-plus. (*See* Center Radar ARTS Presentation/processing-plus).

center. (*See* air route traffic control center).

center's area. The specified airspace within which an air route traffic control center (ARTCC) provides air traffic control and advisory service. (*See* air route traffic control center) (Refer to AIM).

center of gravity (CG). That part of a body (an airplane, in this case) about which all forces are balanced.

center of lift. The single point on the wing where all lifting forces are resolved (concentrated).

Center Radar ARTS Presentation/processing (CENRAP). A computer program developed to provide a backup system for airport surveillance radar in the event of a failure or malfunction. The program uses air route traffic control center radar for the processing and presentation of data on the ARTS IIA or IIIA displays.

Center Radar ARTS Presentation/processing-plus (CENRAP-plus). A computer program developed to provide a backup system for airport surveillance radar in the event of a terminal secondary radar system failure. The program uses a combination of air route traffic control center radar and terminal airport surveillance radar primary targets displayed simultaneously for the processing and presentation of data on the ARTS IIA or IIIA displays.

Center Weather Advisory (CWA). An unscheduled weather advisory issued by Center Weather Service Unit meteorologists for ATC use to alert pilots of existing or anticipated adverse weather conditions within the next 2 hours. A CWA may modify or redefine a SIGMET. (*See* AWW, SIGMET, Convective SIGMET, and AIRMET) (Refer to AIM).

Central East Pacific (CEP). An organized route system between the U.S. West Coast and Hawaii.

CEP. (*See* Central East Pacific).

CERAP. (*See* combined center — RAPCON).

***Certificate of Airworthiness.** A certificate awarded at the time of manufacture and kept current by compliance with maintenance and inspection requirements.

CFR. (*See* call for release).

chaff. Thin, narrow metallic reflectors of various lengths and frequency responses, used to reflect radar energy. These reflectors when dropped from aircraft and allowed to drift downward result in large targets on the radar display.

charted VFR flyways. Charted VFR Flyways are flight paths recommended for use to bypass areas heavily traversed by large turbine powered aircraft. Pilot compliance with recommended flyways and associated altitudes is strictly voluntary. VFR Flyway Planning charts are published on the back of existing VFR Terminal Area charts.

charted visual flight procedure approach. An approach conducted while operating on an instrument flight rules (IFR) flight plan which authorizes the pilot of an aircraft to proceed visually and clear of clouds to the airport via visual landmarks and other information depicted on a charted visual flight procedure. This approach must be authorized and under the control of the appropriate air traffic control facility. Weather minimums required are depicted on the chart.

chase. An aircraft flown in proximity to another aircraft normally to observe its performance during training or testing.

chase aircraft. (*See* chase).

***chord line.** An imaginary line from the leading edge to the trailing edge of an airfoil.

circle-to-land maneuver. A maneuver initiated by the pilot to align the aircraft with a runway for landing when a straight-in landing from an instrument approach is not possible or is not desirable. At tower controlled airports, this maneuver is made only after ATC authorization has been obtained and the pilot has established required visual reference to the airport. (*See* circle to runway, landing minimums) (Refer to AIM).

circle to runway (runway number). Used by ATC to inform the pilot that he must circle to land because the runway in use is other than the runway aligned with the instrument approach procedure. When the direction of the circling maneuver in relation to the airport/runway is required, the controller will state the direction (eight cardinal compass points) and specify a left or right downwind or base leg as appropriate; e.g., "Cleared VOR Runway Three Six Approach circle to Runway Two Two," or "Circle northwest of the airport for a right downwind to Runway Two Two." (*See* circle-to-land maneuver, landing minimums) (Refer to AIM).

circling approach. (*See* circle-to-land maneuver).

circling maneuver. (*See* circle-to-land maneuver).

circling minima. (*See* landing minimums).

Class A airspace. (*See* controlled airspace).

Class B airspace. (*See* controlled airspace).

***Class B airspace.** Airspace division which requires a clearance from ATC for entry.

Class C airspace. (*See* controlled airspace).

***Class C airspace.** A controlled airspace area where pilots must maintain two-way communication with the controlling agency, and where radar service is available to VFR pilots.

Class D airspace. (*See* controlled airspace).

Class E airspace. (*See* controlled airspace).

Class G airspace. That airspace not designated as Class A, B, C, D or E.

clear air turbulence (CAT). Turbulence encountered in air where no clouds are present. This term is commonly applied to high level turbulence associated with windshear. CAT is often encountered in the vicinity of the jet stream. (*See* windshear, jet stream).

clear of the runway.
1. A taxiing aircraft, which is approaching a runway, is clear of the runway when all parts of the aircraft are held short of the applicable holding position marking.
2. A pilot or controller may consider an aircraft, which is exiting or crossing a runway, to be clear of the runway when all parts of the aircraft are beyond the runway edge and there is no ATC restriction to its continued movement beyond the applicable holding position marking.
3. Pilots and controllers shall exercise good judgment to ensure that adequate separation exists between all aircraft on runways and taxiways at airports with inadequate runway edge lines or holding position markings.

clearance. (*See* Air Traffic Clearance).

clearance limit. The fix, point, or location to which an aircraft is cleared when issued an air traffic clearance. [ICAO] The point of which an aircraft is granted an air traffic control clearance.

Clearance void if not off by (time). Used by ATC to advise an aircraft that the departure clearance is automatically canceled if takeoff is not made prior to a specified time. The pilot must obtain a new clearance or cancel his IFR flight plan if not off by the specified time. (*See* clearance void time [ICAO]).

clearance void time. [ICAO] A time specified by an air traffic control unit at which a clearance ceases to be valid unless the aircraft concerned has already taken action to comply therewith.

Cleared as filed. Means the aircraft is cleared to proceed in accordance with the route of flight filed in the flight plan. This clearance does not include the altitude, DP, or DP Transition. (*See* request full route clearance) (Refer to AIM).

Cleared (**type of**) *approach.* ATC authorization for an aircraft to execute a specific instrument approach procedure to an airport; e.g., "Cleared for ILS Runway Three Six Approach." (*See* instrument approach procedure, approach clearance) (Refer to AIM) (Refer to 14 CFR Part 91).

cleared approach. ATC authorization for an aircraft to execute any standard or special instrument approach procedure for that airport. Normally, an aircraft will be cleared for a specific instrument approach procedure. (*See* instrument approach procedure, cleared (type of) approach) (Refer to AIM) (Refer to 14 CFR Part 91).

Cleared for takeoff. ATC authorization for an aircraft to depart. It is predicated on known traffic and known physical airport conditions.

Cleared for the option. ATC authorization for an aircraft to make a touch and go, low approach, missed approach, stop and go, or full stop landing at the discretion of the pilot. It is normally used in training so that an instructor can evaluate a student's performance under changing situations. (*See* option approach) (Refer to AIM).

Cleared through. ATC authorization for an aircraft to make intermediate stops at specified airports without refiling a flight plan while en route to the clearance limit.

Cleared to land. ATC authorization for an aircraft to land. It is predicated on known traffic and known physical airport conditions.

clearway. An area beyond the takeoff runway under the control of airport authorities within which terrain or fixed obstacles may not extend above specified limits. These areas may be required for certain turbine powered operations and the size and upward slope of the clearway will differ depending on when the aircraft was certificated. (Refer to 14 CFR Part 1).

climbout. That portion of flight operation between takeoff and the initial cruising altitude.

Climb to VFR. ATC authorization for an aircraft to climb to VFR conditions within Class B, C, D, and E surface areas when the only weather limitation is restricted visibility. The aircraft must remain clear of clouds while climbing to VFR. (*See* Special VFR) (Refer to AIM).

close parallel runways. Two parallel runways whose extended centerlines are separated by less than 4,300 feet, having a Precision Runway Monitoring (PRM) system that permits simultaneous independent ILS approaches.

closed runway. A runway that is unusable for aircraft operations. Only the airport management/military operations office can close a runway.

closed traffic. Successive operations involving takeoffs and landings or low approaches where the aircraft does not exit the traffic pattern.

cloud. A cloud is a visible accumulation of minute water droplets and/or ice particles in the atmosphere above the Earth's surface. Cloud differs from ground fog, fog, or ice fog only in that the latter are, by definition, in contact with the Earth's surface.

CLT. (*See* calculated landing time).

clutter. In radar operations, clutter refers to the reception and visual display of radar returns caused by precipitation, chaff, terrain, numerous aircraft targets, or other phenomena. Such returns may limit or preclude ATC from providing services based on radar. (*See* ground clutter, chaff, precipitation, target) (*See* radar clutter [ICAO]).

CMNPS. (*See* Canadian Minimum Navigation Performance Specification airspace).

coastal fix. A navigation aid or intersection where an aircraft transitions between the domestic route structure and the oceanic route structure.

codes. The number assigned to a particular multiple pulse reply signal transmitted by a transponder. (*See* discrete code).

*coefficient of lift.** A complex element of the lift formula which includes angle of attack as one component.

combined center — RAPCON (CERAP). An air traffic facility which combines the functions of an ARTCC and a radar approach control facility. (*See* air route traffic control center, radar approach control facility).

common point. A significant point over which two or more aircraft will report passing or have reported passing before proceeding on the same or diverging tracks. To establish/maintain longitudinal separation, a controller may determine a common point not originally in the aircraft's flight plan and then clear the aircraft to fly over the point. (*See* significant point).

common portion. (*See* common route).

common route. That segment of a North American Route between the inland navigation facility and the coastal fix.

Common Traffic Advisory Frequency (CTAF). A frequency designed for the purpose of carrying out airport advisory practices while operating to or from an airport without an operating control tower. The CTAF may be a UNICOM, MULTICOM, FSS, or tower frequency and is identified in appropriate aeronautical publications. (Refer to AC 90-42).

compass locator. A low power, low or medium frequency (L/MF) radio beacon installed at the site of the outer or middle marker of an instrument landing system (ILS). It can be used for navigation at distances of approximately 15 miles or as authorized in the approach procedure.

1. *Outer Compass Locator (LOM).* A compass locator installed at the site of the outer marker of an instrument landing system. (*See* outer marker).
2. *Middle Compass Locator (LMM).* A compass locator installed at the site of the middle marker of an instrument landing system. (*See* middle marker) (*See* locator [ICAO]).

compass rose. A circle, graduated in degrees, printed on some charts or marked on the ground at an airport. It is used as a reference to either true or magnetic direction.

composite flight plan. A flight plan which specifies VFR operation for one portion of flight and IFR for another portion. It is used primarily in military operations. (Refer to AIM).

composite route system. An organized oceanic route structure, incorporating reduced lateral spacing between routes, in which composite separation is authorized.

composite separation. A method of separating aircraft in a composite route system where, by management of route and altitude assignments, a combination of half the lateral minimum specified for the area concerned and half the vertical minimum is applied.

*****compressor discharge temperature gauge.** An instrument that monitors the temperature of the air being discharged from the compressor into the intake manifold of a turbocharged engine.

compulsory reporting points. Reporting points which must be reported to ATC. They are designated on aeronautical charts by solid triangles or filed in a flight plan as fixes selected to define direct routes. These points are geographical locations which are defined by navigation aids/fixes. Pilots should discontinue position reporting over compulsory reporting points when informed by ATC that their aircraft is in "radar contact."

conflict alert. A function of certain air traffic control automated systems designed to alert radar controllers to existing or pending situations between tracked targets (known IFR or VFR aircraft) that require his immediate attention/action. (*See* Mode C intruder alert).

conflict resolution. The resolution of potential conflictions between aircraft that are radar identified and in communication with ATC by ensuring that radar targets do not touch. Pertinent traffic advisories shall be issued when this procedure is applied. *Note:* This procedure shall not be provided utilizing mosaic radar systems.

Consolan. A low frequency, long distance NAVAID used principally for transoceanic navigation.

contact.

1. Establish communication with (followed by the name of the facility and, if appropriate, the frequency to be used).
2. A flight condition wherein the pilot ascertains the attitude of his aircraft and navigates by visual reference to the surface. (*See* contact approach, radar contact).

contact approach. An approach wherein an aircraft on an IFR flight plan, having an air traffic control authorization, operating clear of clouds with at least 1 mile flight visibility and a reasonable expectation of continuing to the destination airport in those conditions, may deviate from the instrument approach procedure and proceed to the destination airport by visual reference to the surface. This approach will only be authorized when requested by the pilot and the reported ground visibility at the destination airport is at least 1 statute mile. (Refer to AIM).

contaminated runway. A runway is considered contaminated whenever standing water, ice, snow, slush, frost in any form, heavy rubber or other substances are present. A runway is contaminated with respect to rubber deposits or other friction-degrading substances when the average friction value for any 500-foot segment of the runway within the ALD falls below the recommended minimum friction level and the average friction value in the adjacent 500-foot segments falls below the maintenance planning friction level.

conterminous U.S. The 48 adjoining States and the District of Columbia.

continental United States. The 49 States located on the continent of North America and the District of Columbia.

continue. When used as a control instruction, should be followed by another word or words clarifying what is expected of the pilot. Example: "continue taxi," "continue descent," "continue inbound" etc.

control area. [ICAO] A controlled airspace extending upwards from a specified limit above the earth.

*****controllable-pitch propeller.** A propeller with two (or more) blades, joined at the hub and capable of having the blade angle changed in flight by a governor to maintain a constant engine speed.

*****controlled airport.** An airport with an operating control tower.

controlled airspace. An airspace of defined dimensions within which air traffic control service is provided to IFR flights and to VFR flights in accordance with the airspace classification. *Note 1.* Controlled airspace is a generic term that covers Class A, Class B, Class C, Class D, and Class E airspace. *Note 2.* Controlled airspace is also that airspace within which all aircraft operators are subject to certain pilot qualifications, operating rules, and equipment requirements in 14 CFR Part 91 (for specific operating requirements, please refer to Part 91). For IFR operations in any class of controlled airspace, a pilot must file an IFR flight plan and receive an appropriate ATC clearance. Each Class B, Class C, and Class D airspace area designated for an airport contains at least one primary airport around which the airspace is designated (for specific designations and descriptions of the airspace classes, please refer to 14 CFR Part 71).

Controlled airspace in the United States is designated as follows:

1. *Class A:* Generally, that airspace from 18,000 feet MSL up to and including FL 600, including the airspace overlying

the waters within 12 nautical miles of the coast of the 48 contiguous States and Alaska. Unless otherwise authorized, all persons must operate their aircraft under IFR.

2. *Class B:* Generally, that airspace from the surface to 10,000 feet MSL surrounding the nation's busiest airports in terms of airport operations or passenger enplanements. The configuration of each Class B airspace area is individually tailored and consists of a surface area and two or more layers (some Class B airspace areas resemble upside down wedding cakes), and is designed to contain all published instrument procedures once an aircraft enters the airspace. An ATC clearance is required for all aircraft to operate in the area, and all aircraft that are so cleared receive separation services within the airspace. The cloud clearance requirement for VFR operations is "clear of clouds."

3. *Class C:* Generally, that airspace from the surface to 4,000 feet above the airport elevation (charted in MSL) surrounding those airports that have an operational control tower, are serviced by a radar approach control, and that have a certain number of IFR operations or passenger enplanements. Although the configuration of each Class C area is individually tailored, the airspace usually consists of a surface area with a 5 nautical mile (NM) radius, an outer circle with a 10 NM radius that extends from 1,200 feet to 4,000 feet above the airport elevation and an outer area. Each person must establish two-way radio communications with the ATC facility providing air traffic services prior to entering the airspace and thereafter maintain those communications while within the airspace. VFR aircraft are only separated from IFR aircraft within the airspace.

4. *Class D:* Generally, that airspace from the surface to 2,500 feet above the airport elevation (charted in MSL) surrounding those airports that have an operational control tower. The configuration of each Class D airspace area is individually tailored and when instrument procedures are published, the airspace will normally be designed to contain the procedures. Arrival extensions for instrument approach procedures may be Class D or Class E airspace. Unless otherwise authorized, each person must establish two-way radio communications with the ATC facility providing air traffic services prior to entering the airspace and thereafter maintain those communications while in the airspace. No separation services are provided to VFR aircraft.

5. *Class E:* Generally, if the airspace is not Class A, Class B, Class C, or Class D, and it is controlled airspace, it is Class E airspace. Class E airspace extends upward from either the surface or a designated altitude to the overlying or adjacent controlled airspace. When designated as a surface area, the airspace will be configured to contain all instrument procedures. Also in this class are Federal airways, airspace beginning at either 700 or 1,200 feet AGL used to transition to/from the terminal or enroute environment, enroute domestic, and offshore airspace areas designated below 18,000 feet MSL. Unless designated at a lower altitude, Class E airspace begins at 14,500 MSL

over the United States, including that airspace overlying the waters within 12 nautical miles of the coast of the 48 contiguous States and Alaska, up to, but not including 18,000 feet MSL, and the airspace above FL 600.

[ICAO] An airspace of defined dimensions within which air traffic control service is provided to IFR flights and to VFR flights in accordance with the airspace classification. *Note:* Controlled airspace is a generic term which covers ATS airspace Classes A, B, C, D, and E.

controlled departure time programs. These programs are the flow control process whereby aircraft are held on the ground at the departure airport when delays are projected to occur in either the enroute system or the terminal of intended landing. The purpose of these programs is to reduce congestion in the air traffic system or to limit the duration of airborne holding in the arrival center or terminal area. A CDT is a specific departure slot shown on the flight plan as an expected departure clearance time (EDCT).

controlled time of arrival (CTA). The original estimated time of arrival adjusted by the ATCSCC ground delay factor.

controller. (*See* air traffic control specialist). [ICAO] A person authorized to provide air traffic control services.

control sector. An airspace area of defined horizontal and vertical dimensions for which a controller or group of controllers has air traffic control responsibility normally within an air route traffic control center or an approach control facility. Sectors are established based on predominant traffic flows, altitude strata, and controller workload. Pilot communications during operations within a sector are normally maintained on discrete frequencies assigned to the sector. (*See* discrete frequency).

control slash. A radar beacon slash representing the actual position of the associated aircraft. Normally, the control slash is the one closest to the interrogating radar beacon site. When ARTCC radar is operating in narrow band (digitized) mode, the control slash is converted to a target symbol.

*****control yoke.** The control the pilot uses to pitch and roll the airplane. Older airplanes used a "stick" and this term continues in use today.

*****convection.** Vertical movement of air.

Convective SIGMET. A weather advisory concerning convective weather significant to the safety of all aircraft. Convective SIGMETs are issued for tornadoes, lines of thunderstorms, embedded thunderstorms of any intensity level, areas of thunderstorms greater than or equal to VIP level 4 with an area coverage of 4/10 (40%) or more, and hail 3/4 inch or greater. (*See* AWW, SIGMET, CWA, and AIRMET) (Refer to AIM).

Convective Significant Meteorological Information. (*See* Convective SIGMET).

coordinates. The intersection of lines of reference, usually expressed in degrees/minutes/seconds of latitude and longitude, used to determine position or location.

coordination fix. The fix in relation to which facilities will handoff, transfer control of an aircraft, or coordinate flight progress data. For terminal facilities, it may also serve as a clearance for arriving aircraft.

copter. (*See* helicopter).

***Coriolis force.** A force generated by the rotation of the earth that deflects the gradient wind to the right in the Northern Hemisphere.

correction. An error has been made in the transmission and the correct version follows.

coupled approach. A coupled approach is an instrument approach performed by the aircraft autopilot which is receiving position information and/or steering commands from on board navigation equipment. In general, coupled nonprecision approaches must be discontinued and flown manually at altitudes lower than 50 feet below the minimum descent altitude, and coupled precision approaches must be flown manually below 50 feet AGL. (*See* autoland approach).

Note: Coupled and autoland approaches are flown in VFR and IFR. It is common for carriers to require their crews to fly coupled approaches and autoland approaches (if certified) when the weather conditions are less than approximately 4,000 RVR.

course.
1. The intended direction of flight in the horizontal plane measured in degrees from north.
2. The ILS localizer signal pattern usually specified as the front course or the back course.
3. The intended track along a straight, curved, or segmented MLS path.
   (*See* bearing, radial, instrument landing system, Micro wave Landing System).

***course.** A line connecting two points on a planned flight.

***cowling.** The smooth metal or fiberglass enclosure surrounding the engine. The cowling streamlines the engine compartment and directs cooling air over the engine.

CPL. [ICAO] (*See* current flight plan).

critical engine. The engine which, upon failure, would most adversely affect the performance or handling qualities of an aircraft.

Cross (fix) at (altitude). Used by ATC when a specific altitude restriction at a specified fix is required.

Cross (fix) at or above (altitude). Used by ATC when an altitude restriction at a specified fix is required. It does not prohibit the aircraft from crossing the fix at a higher altitude than specified; however, the higher altitude may not be one that will violate a succeeding altitude restriction or altitude assignment. (*See* altitude restriction) (Refer to AIM).

Cross (fix) at or below (altitude). Used by ATC when a maximum crossing altitude at a specific fix is required. It does not prohibit the aircraft from crossing the fix at a lower altitude; however, it must be at or above the minimum IFR altitude. (*See* minimum IFR altitude, altitude restriction) (Refer to 14 CFR Part 91).

crosswind.
1. When used concerning the traffic pattern, the word means "crosswind leg." (*See* traffic pattern).
2. When used concerning wind conditions, the word means a wind not parallel to the runway or the path of an aircraft. (*See* crosswind component).

crosswind component. The wind component measured in knots at 90 degrees to the longitudinal axis of the runway.

***crosswind component.** That portion of the total wind which tends to drift the airplane sideways.

cruise. Used in an ATC clearance to authorize a pilot to conduct flight at any altitude from the minimum IFR altitude up to and including the altitude specified in the clearance. The pilot may level off at any intermediate altitude within this block of airspace. Climb/descent within the block is to be made at the discretion of the pilot. However, once the pilot starts descent and verbally reports leaving an altitude in the block, he may not return to that altitude without additional ATC clearance. Further, it is approval for the pilot to proceed to and make an approach at destination airport and can be used in conjunction with:
1. An airport clearance limit at locations with a standard/special instrument approach procedure. The FARs require that if an instrument letdown to an airport is necessary, the pilot shall make the letdown in accordance with a standard/special instrument approach procedure for that airport, or
2. An airport clearance limit at locations that are within/below/outside controlled airspace and without a standard/special instrument approach procedure. Such a clearance is NOT AUTHORIZATION for the pilot to descend under IFR conditions below the applicable minimum IFR altitude nor does it imply that ATC is exercising control over aircraft in Class G airspace; however, it provides a means for the aircraft to proceed to destination airport, descend, and land in accordance with applicable FARs governing VFR flight operations. Also, this provides search and rescue protection until such time as the IFR flight plan is closed. (*See* instrument approach procedure).

cruise climb. A climb technique employed by aircraft, usually at a constant power setting, resulting in an increase of altitude as the aircraft weight decreases.

cruising altitude. An altitude or flight level maintained during enroute level flight. This is a constant altitude and should not be confused with a cruise clearance. (*See* altitude) (*See* cruising level [ICAO]).

cruising level. [ICAO] A level maintained during a significant portion of a flight.

cruising level. (*See* cruising altitude).

CT message. An EDCT time generated by the ATCSCC to regulate traffic at arrival airports. Normally, a CT message is automatically transferred from the Traffic Management System computer to the NAS enroute computer and appears as an EDCT. In the event of a communication failure between the TMS and the NAS, the CT message can be manually entered by the TMC at the enroute facility.

CTA. (*See* controlled time of arrival).

CTA. (*See* control area [ICAO]).

CTAF. (*See* Common Traffic Advisory Frequency).

***CTAF.** Common Traffic Advisory Frequency—used at uncontrolled airports by all airplanes operating at that airport. Also, a frequency to be used at a controlled airport when the tower is not in operation.

current flight plan (CPL). [ICAO] The flight plan, including changes, if any, brought about by subsequent clearances.

CVFP approach. (*See* charted visual flight procedure approach).

CWA. (*See* Center Weather Advisory) (*See* Weather Advisory).

***cylinder head temperature gauge.** An instrument which monitors the temperature of the cylinder head itself. It is a better guide to general engine overheating than is the oil temperature gauge.

DA. [ICAO] (*See* decision altitude/decision height [ICAO]).

DAIR. (*See* direct altitude and identity readout).

danger area. [ICAO] An airspace of defined dimensions within which activities dangerous to the flight of aircraft may exist at specified times. *Note:* The term "Danger Area" is not used in reference to areas within the United States or any of its possessions or territories.

data block. (*See* alphanumeric display).

dead reckoning. Dead reckoning, as applied to flying, is the navigation of an airplane solely by means of computations based on airspeed, course, heading, wind direction, and speed, ground speed, and elapsed time.

decision altitude/decision height. [ICAO] A specified altitude or height (A/H) in the precision approach at which a missed approach must be initiated if the required visual reference to continue the approach has not been established.

Note 1: Decision altitude (DA) is referenced to mean sea level (MSL) and decision height (DH) is referenced to the threshold elevation.

Note 2: The required visual reference means that section of the visual aids or of the approach area which should have been in view for sufficient time for the pilot to have made an assessment of the aircraft position and rate of change of position, in relation to the desired flight path.

decision height (DH). With respect to the operation of aircraft, means the height at which a decision must be made during an ILS, MLS, or PAR instrument approach to either continue the approach or to execute a missed approach. (*See* decision altitude/decision height [ICAO]).

decoder. The device used to decipher signals received from ATCRBS transponders to effect their display as select codes. (*See* codes, radar).

defense visual flight rules (DVFR). Rules applicable to flights within an ADIZ conducted under the visual flight rules in 14 CFR Part 91. (*See* Air Defense Identification Zone) (Refer to 14 CFR Parts 91 and 99).

Delay indefinite (reason if known) expect further clearance (time). Used by ATC to inform a pilot when an accurate estimate of the delay time and the reason for the delay cannot immediately be determined; e.g., a disabled aircraft on the runway, terminal or center area saturation, weather below landing minimums, etc. (*See* expect further clearance (time)).

delay time (DT). The amount of time that the arrival must lose to cross the meter fix at the assigned meter fix time. This is the difference between ACLT and VTA.

***density.** Weight per unit volume. A cubic foot of air that weighs two pounds is more dense than a cubic foot of air that weighs one pound.

Departure Center. The ARTCC having jurisdiction for the airspace that generates a flight to the impacted airport.

departure control. A function of an approach control facility providing air traffic control service for departing IFR and, under certain conditions, VFR aircraft. (*See* Approach Control Facility) (Refer to AIM).

Departure Sequencing Program (DSP). A program designed to assist in achieving a specified interval over a common point for departures.

departure time. The time an aircraft become airborne.

descent speed adjustments. Speed deceleration calculations made to determine an accurate VTA. These calculations start at the transition point and use arrival speed segments to the vertex.

desired course.
1. *True*—A predetermined desired course direction to be followed (measured in degrees from true north).
2. *Magnetic*—A predetermined desired course direction to be followed (measured in degrees from local magnetic north).

desired track. The planned or intended track between two waypoints. It is measured in degrees from either magnetic or true north. The instantaneous angle may change from point to point along the great circle track between waypoints.

***detonation.** The explosive burning of the fuel/air mixture in the cylinder, as opposed to smooth burning. Detonation can result in destructive forces in a matter of seconds.

detresfa (distress phase). [ICAO] The code word used to designate an emergency phase wherein there is reasonable certainty that an aircraft and its occupants are threatened by grave and imminent danger or require immediate assistance.

***deviation.** A compass error caused by magnetic influences within the airplane which varies with magnetic heading.

deviations.

1. A departure from a current clearance, such as an off-course maneuver to avoid weather or turbulence.
2. Where specifically authorized in the Federal Aviation Regulations and requested by the pilot, ATC may permit pilots to deviate from certain regulations. (Refer to AIM.)

*dew point.** The temperature at which an air mass becomes saturated with moisture.

DF. (*See* direction finder).

DF approach procedure. Used under emergency conditions where another instrument approach procedure cannot be executed. DF guidance from an instrument approach is given by ATC facilities with DF capability. (*See* DF guidance, direction finder) (Refer to AIM).

DF fix. The geographical location of an aircraft obtained by one or more direction finders. (*See* direction finder).

DF guidance. Headings provided to aircraft by facilities equipped with direction finding equipment. These headings, if followed, will lead the aircraft to a predetermined point such as the DF station or an airport. DF guidance is given to aircraft in distress or to other aircraft which request the service. Practice DF guidance is provided when workload permits. (*See* direction finder, DF fix) (Refer to AIM).

DF steer. (*See* DF guidance).

DH. (*See* decision height).

DH. [ICAO] (*See* decision altitude/decision height [ICAO]).

direct. Straight line flight between two navigational aids, fixes, points, or any combination thereof. When used by pilots in describing off airway routes, points defining direct route segments become compulsory reporting points unless the aircraft is under radar contact.

direct altitude and identity readout (DAIR). The DAIR system is a modification to the AN/TPX-42 interrogator system. The Navy has two adaptations of the DAIR System. Carrier Air Traffic Control Direct Altitude and Identification Readout System for aircraft carriers and Radar Air Traffic Control Facility Direct Altitude and Identify Readout system for land-based terminal operations. The DAIR detects, tracks, and predicts secondary radar aircraft targets. Targets are displayed by means of computer generated symbols and alphanumeric characters depicting flight identification, altitude, ground speed, and flight plan data. The DAIR system is capable of interfacing with ARTCCs.

direction finder. A radio receiver equipped with a directional sensing antenna used to take bearings on a radio transmitter. Specialized radio direction finders are used in aircraft as air navigation aids. Others are ground based, primarily to obtain a "fix" on a pilot requesting orientation assistance or to locate downed aircraft. A location "fix" is established by the intersection of two or more bearing lines plotted on a navigational chart using either two separately located Direction Finders to obtain a fix on an aircraft or by a pilot plotting the bearing indications of his DF on two

separately located ground based transmitters, both of which can be identified on his chart. UDFs receive signals in the ultra high frequency radio broadcast band; VDFs in the very high frequency band; and UVDFs in both bands. ATC provides DF service at those air traffic control towers and flight service stations listed in the Airport/Facility Directory and the DOD FLIP IFR Enroute Supplement. (*See* DF guidance, DF fix).

discrete beacon code. (*See* discrete code).

discrete code. As used in the Air Traffic Control Radar Beacon System (ATCRBS), any one of the 4096 selectable Mode 3/A aircraft transponder codes except those ending in zero zero; e.g., discrete codes: 0010, 1201, 2317, 7777; nondiscrete codes: 0100, 1200, 7700. Nondiscrete codes are normally reserved for radar facilities that are not equipped with discrete decoding capability and for other purposes such as emergencies (7700), VFR aircraft (1200), etc. (*See* radar) (Refer to AIM).

discrete frequency. A separate radio frequency for use in direct pilot/controller communications in air traffic control which reduces frequency congestion by controlling the number of aircraft operating on a particular frequency at one time. Discrete frequencies are normally designated for each control sector in enroute/terminal ATC facilities. Discrete frequencies are listed in the Airport/Facility Directory and the DOD FLIP IFR Enroute Supplement. (*See* control sector).

displaced threshold. A threshold that is located at a point on the runway other than the designated beginning of the runway. (*See* threshold) (Refer to AIM).

*displaced threshold.** A threshold moved down the runway so that landing aircraft will clear obstructions in the approach path.

distance measuring equipment (DME). Equipment (airborne and ground) used to measure, in nautical miles, the slant range distance of an aircraft from the DME navigational aid. (*See* TACAN, VORTAC, Microwave Landing System).

distress. A condition of being threatened by serious and/or imminent danger and of requiring immediate assistance.

dive brakes. (*See* speed brakes).

diverse vector area (DVA). In a radar environment, that area in which a prescribed departure route is not required as the only suitable route to avoid obstacles. The area in which random radar vectors below the MVA/MIA, established in accordance with the TERPS criteria for diverse departures obstacles and terrain avoidance, may be issued to departing aircraft.

DME. (*See* distance measuring equipment).

*DME.** Distance Measuring Equipment. DME operates in the UHF range and is limited to line-of-sight. It measures slant range between an airplane and a VORTAC or VOR-DME.

DME fix. A geographical position determined by reference to a navigational aid which provides distance and azimuth information. It is defined by a specific distance in nautical miles and a radial, azimuth, or course (i.e. localizer) in degrees magnetic from that aid. (*See* distance measuring equipment (DME), fix, Microwave Landing System).

DME separation. Spacing of aircraft in terms of distances (nautical miles) determined by reference to distance measuring equipment (DME). (*See* distance measuring equipment).

DOD FLIP. Department of Defense Flight Information Publications used for flight planning, en route, and terminal operations. FLIP is produced by the National Imagery and Mapping Agency (NIMA) for world wide use. United States Government Flight Information Publications (enroute charts and instrument approach procedure charts) are incorporated in DOD FLIP for use in the National Airspace System (NAS).

domestic airspace. Airspace which overlies the continental land mass of the United States plus Hawaii and U.S. possessions. Domestic airspace extends to 12 miles offshore.

downburst. A strong downdraft which induces an outburst of damaging winds on or near the ground. Damaging winds, either straight or curved, are highly divergent. The sizes of downbursts vary from 1/2 mile or less to more than 10 miles. An intense down burst often causes widespread damage. Damaging winds, lasting 5 to 30 minutes, could reach speeds as high as 120 knots.

downwind leg. (*See* traffic pattern).

DP. (*See* instrument departure procedure).

drag chute. A parachute device installed on certain aircraft which is deployed on landing roll to assist in deceleration of the aircraft.

DSP. (*See* Departure Sequencing Program).

DT. (*See* delay time).

due regard. A phase of flight wherein an aircraft commander of a State operated aircraft assumes responsibility to separate his aircraft from all other aircraft. (*See* also FAA Order 7110.65, Chapter 1, Word Meanings).

*duplex. Transmitting on one frequency while receiving on another.

duty runway. (*See* runway in use/active runway/duty runway).

DVA. (*See* diverse vector area).

DVFR. (*See* defense visual flight rules).

DVFR flight plan. A flight plan filed for a VFR aircraft which intends to operate in airspace within which the ready identification, location, and control of aircraft are required in the interest of national security.

dynamic. Continuous review, evaluation, and change to meet demands.

dynamic restrictions. Those restrictions imposed by the local facility on an "as needed" basis to manage unpredictable fluctuations in traffic demands.

EDCT. (*See* expected departure clearance time).

*EFAS. Enroute Flight Advisory Service (Flight Watch)— a weather-only position at a Flight Service Station.

EFC. (*See* expect further clearance (time)).

*elevator. A hinged surface at the rear of the horizontal stabilizer with which the pilot controls the airplane around the lateral (pitch) axis.

ELT. (*See* emergency locator transmitter).

*ELT. Emergency Locator Transmitter—a VHF/UHF transmitter designed to be turned on by impact and transmit a signal to searchers.

emergency. A distress or an urgency condition.

emergency locator transmitter (ELT). A radio transmitter attached to the aircraft structure which operates from its own power source on 121.5 MHz and 243.0 MHz. It aids in locating downed aircraft by radiating a downward sweeping audio tone, 2 to 4 times per second. It is designed to function without human action after an accident. (Refer to 14 CFR §91.3, AIM).

*empennage. The horizontal stabilizer, elevator rudder, and vertical fin or any combination thereof to control the airplane in pitch and yaw.

E-MSAW. (*See* enroute minimum safe altitude warning).

engineered performance standards (EPS). A mathematically derived runway capacity standard. EPS's are calculated for each airport on an individual basis and reflect that airport's aircraft mix, operating procedures, runway layout, and specific weather conditions. EPS's do not give consideration to staffing, experience levels, equipment outages, and in-trail restrictions as does the AAR.

enroute air traffic control services. Air traffic control service provided aircraft on IFR flight plans, generally by centers, when these aircraft are operating between departure and destination terminal areas. When equipment, capabilities, and controller workload permit, certain advisory/assistance services may be provided to VFR aircraft. (*See* NAS Stage A, air route traffic control center) (Refer to AIM).

enroute charts. (*See* aeronautical charts).

enroute descent. Descent from the enroute cruising altitude which takes place along the route of flight.

Enroute Flight Advisory Service (EFAS). A service specifically designed to provide, upon pilot request, timely weather information pertinent to his type of flight, intended route of flight, and altitude. The FSS's providing this service are listed in the Airport/Facility Directory. (*See* Flight Watch) (Refer to AIM).

enroute high altitude charts. (*See* aeronautical chart).

enroute low altitude charts. (*See* aeronautical chart).

enroute minimum safe altitude warning (E-MSAW). A function of the NAS Stage A enroute computer that aids the controller by alerting him when a tracked aircraft is below or predicted by the computer to go below a predetermined minimum IFR altitude (MIA).

Enroute Spacing Program (ESP). A program designed to assist the exit sector in achieving the required in-trail spacing.

EPS. (*See* engineered performance standards).

ESP. (*See* Enroute Spacing Program).

established. To be stable or fixed on a route, route segment, altitude, heading, etc.

estimated elapsed time. [ICAO] The estimated time required to proceed from one significant point to another. (*See* total estimated elapsed time [ICAO]).

estimated off block time. [ICAO] The estimated time at which the aircraft will commence movement associated with departure.

estimated position error. (*See* required navigation performance).

estimated time of arrival (ETA). The time the flight is estimated to arrive at the gate (scheduled operators) or the actual runway on times for nonscheduled operators.

estimated time enroute (ETE). The estimated flying time from departure point to destination (liftoff to touchdown).

ETA. (*See* estimated time of arrival).

ETE. (*See* estimated time enroute).

execute missed approach. Instructions issued to a pilot making an instrument approach which means continue inbound to the missed approach point and execute the missed approach procedure as described on the Instrument Approach Procedure Chart or as previously assigned by ATC. The pilot may climb immediately to the altitude specified in the missed approach procedure upon making a missed approach. No turns should be initiated prior to reaching the missed approach point. When conducting an ASR or PAR approach, execute the assigned missed approach procedure immediately upon receiving instructions to "execute missed approach." (Refer to AIM).

*exhaust gas temperature gauge. An instrument used for proper leaning of the mixture. If the mixture contains too much fuel or too much air, the exhaust gas temperature will be lower than peak (use the manufacturer's recommended EGT setting).

Expect (altitude) at (time) or (fix). Used under certain conditions to provide a pilot with an altitude to be used in the event of two-way communications failure. It also provides altitude information to assist the pilot in planning. (Refer to AIM).

expected departure clearance time (EDCT). The runway release time assigned to an aircraft in controlled departure time programs and shown on the flight progress strip as an EDCT.

Expect further clearance (time) (EFC). The time a pilot can expect to receive clearance beyond a clearance limit.

Expect further clearance via (airways, routes or fixes). Used to inform a pilot of the routing he can expect if any part of the route beyond a short range clearance limit differs from that filed.

expedite. Used by ATC when prompt compliance is required to avoid the development of an imminent situation.

FAF. (*See* final approach fix).

*FAR. Federal Aviation Regulations.

fast file. A system whereby a pilot files a flight plan via telephone that is tape recorded and then transcribed for transmission to the appropriate air traffic facility. Locations having a fast file capability are contained in the Airport/Facility Directory. (Refer to AIM).

FAWP. Final approach waypoint.

FCLT. (*See* freeze calculated landing time).

*FD. A winds and temperatures aloft forecast.

feathered propeller. A propeller whose blades have been rotated so that the leading and trailing edges are nearly parallel with the aircraft flight path to stop or minimize drag and engine rotation. Normally used to indicate shutdown of a reciprocating or turboprop engine due to malfunction.

federal airways. (*See* low altitude airway structure).

feeder fix. The fix depicted on Instrument Approach Procedure Charts which establishes the staring point of the feeder route.

feeder route. A route depicted on instrument approach procedure charts to designate routes for aircraft to proceed from the enroute structure to the initial approach fix (IAF). (*See* instrument approach procedure).

ferry flight. A flight for the purpose of:
1. Returning an aircraft to base.
2. Delivering an aircraft from one location to another.
3. Moving an aircraft to and from a maintenance base.

Ferry flights, under certain conditions, may be conducted under terms of a special flight permit.

field elevation. (*See* airport elevation).

filed. Normally used in conjunction with flight plans, meaning a flight plan has been submitted to ATC.

filed enroute delay. Any of the following preplanned delays at points/areas along the route of flight which require special flight plan filing and handling techniques.
1. *Terminal Area Delay.* A delay within a terminal area for touch and go, low approach, or other terminal area activity.
2. *Special Use Airspace Delay.* A delay within a Military Operating Area, Restricted Area, Warning Area, or ATC Assigned Airspace.

Continued

3. *Aerial Refueling Delay*. A delay within an Aerial Refueling Track or Anchor.

filed flight plan. The flight plan as filed with an ATS unit by the pilot or his designated representative without any subsequent changes or clearances.

final. Commonly used to mean that an aircraft is on the final approach course or is aligned with a landing area. (*See* final approach course, final approach—IFR, traffic pattern, segments of an instrument approach procedure).

final approach. [ICAO] The part of an instrument approach procedure which commences at the specified final approach fix, or point, or where such a fix or point is not specified.

1. At the end of the last procedure turn, base turn, or inbound turn of a racetrack procedure, if specified; or

2. At the point of interception of the last track specified in the approach procedure; and ends at a point in the vicinity of an aerodrome from which:

   a. A landing can be made; or

   b. A missed approach procedure is initiated.

final approach course. A bearing/radial/track of an instrument approach landing to a runway or an extended runway centerline all without regard to distance.

final approach fix (FAF). The fix from which the final approach (IFR) to an airport is executed and which identifies the beginning of the final approach segment. It is designated on Government charts by the Maltese Cross symbol for nonprecision approaches and the lightning bolt symbol for precision approaches; or when ATC directs a lower than published Glideslope/Path Intercept Altitude, it is the resultant actual point of the glideslope/path intercept. (*See* final approach point, glideslope intercept altitude, segments of an instrument approach procedure).

final approach—IFR. The flight path of an aircraft which is inbound to an airport on a final instrument approach course, beginning at the final approach fix or point and extending to the airport or the point where a circle-to-land maneuver or a missed approach is executed. (*See* segments of an instrument approach procedure, final approach fix, final approach course, final approach point) (*See* final approach [ICAO]).

final approach point (FAP). The point, applicable only to a nonprecision approach with no depicted FAF (such as an on-airport VOR), where the aircraft is established inbound on the final approach course from the procedure turn and where the final approach descent may be commenced. The FAP serves as the FAF and identifies the beginning of the final approach segment. (*See* final approach fix, segments of an instrument approach procedure).

final approach segment. (*See* segments of an instrument approach procedure). [ICAO] That segment of an instrument approach procedure in which alignment and descent for landing are accomplished.

final controller. The controller providing information and final approach guidance during PAR and ASR approaches utilizing radar equipment. (*See* radar approach).

final monitor aid (FMA). A high resolution color display that is equipped with the controller alert system hardware/software which is used in the precision runway monitor (PRM) system. The display includes alert algorithms providing the target predictors, a color change alert when a target penetrates or is predicted to penetrate the no transgression zone (NTZ), a color change alert if the aircraft transponder becomes inoperative, synthesized voice alerts, digital mapping, and like features contained in the PRM system. (*See* radar approach).

final monitor controller. Air traffic control specialist assigned to radar monitor the flight path of aircraft during simultaneous parallel and simultaneous close parallel ILS approach operations. Each runway is assigned a final monitor controller during simultaneous parallel and simultaneous close parallel ILS approaches. Final monitor controllers shall utilize the precision runway monitor (PRM) system during simultaneous close parallel ILS approaches.

FIR. (*See* flight information region).

first tier center. The ARTCC immediately adjacent to the impacted center.

fix. A geographical position determined by visual reference to the surface, by reference to one or more radio NAVAIDs, by celestial plotting, or by another navigational device.

fix balancing. A process whereby aircraft are evenly distributed over several available arrival fixes reducing delays and controller workload.

*fixed-pitch propeller. A propeller, forged from one solid piece of metal or laminated from several plies of wood, with a fixed pitch or blade angle.

flag. A warning device incorporated in certain airborne navigation and flight instruments indicating that:

1. Instruments are inoperative or otherwise not operating satisfactorily, or

2. Signal strength or quality of the received signal falls below acceptable values.

flag alarm. (*See* flag).

flameout. An emergency condition caused by a loss of engine power.

flameout pattern. An approach normally conducted by a single-engine military aircraft experiencing loss or anticipating loss of engine power or control. The standard overhead approach starts at a relatively high altitude over a runway ("high key") followed by a continuous 180 degree turn to a high, wide position ("low key") followed by a continuous 180 degree turn final. The standard straight-in pattern starts at a point that results in a straight-in approach with a high rate of descent to the runway. Flameout approaches terminate in the type approach requested by the pilot (normally fullstop).

*flaps. Hinged surfaces at the trailing edge of the wing which are deflected symmetrically to lower the stalling speed and allow for a steeper angle of descent while on a landing approach.

flight check. A call sign prefix used by FAA aircraft engaged in flight inspection/certification of navigational aids and flight procedures. The word "recorded" may be added as a suffix; e.g., "Flight Check 320 recorded" to indicate that an automated flight inspection is in progress in terminal areas. (*See* flight inspection) (Refer to AIM).

flight following. (*See* traffic advisories).

***flight following.** A workload-permitting service which ATC radar facilities provide to VFR pilots.

flight information region (FIR). An airspace of defined dimensions within which Flight Information Service and Alerting Service are provided.

1. *Flight Information Service.* A service provided for the purpose of giving advice and information useful for the safe and efficient conduct of flights.
2. *Alerting Service.* A service provided to notify appropriate organizations regarding aircraft in need of search and rescue aid and to assist such organizations as required.

Flight Information Service. A service provided for the purpose of giving advice and information useful for the safe and efficient conduct of flights.

flight inspection. In-flight investigation and evaluation of a navigational aid to determine whether it meets established tolerances. (*See* navigational aid, flight check).

flight level. A level of constant atmospheric pressure related to a reference datum of 29.92 inches of mercury. Each is stated in three digits that represent hundreds of feet. For example, flight level 250 represents a barometric altimeter indication of 25,000 feet; flight level 255, an indication of 25,500 feet.

[ICAO] A surface of constant atmospheric pressure which is related to a specific pressure datum, 1013.2 hPa (1013.2 mb), and is separated from other such surfaces by specific pressure intervals.

Note 1: A pressure type altimeter calibrated in accordance with the standard atmosphere:

1. When set to a QNH altimeter setting, will indicate altitude;
2. When set to a QFE altimeter setting, will indicate height above the QFE reference datum; and
3. When set to a pressure of 1013.2 hPa (1013.2 mb), may be used to indicate flight levels.

Note 2: The terms height and altitude, used in Note 1 above, indicate altimetric rather than geometric heights and altitudes.

flight line. A term used to describe the precise movement of a civil photogrammetric aircraft along a predetermined course(s) at a predetermined altitude during the actual photographic run.

flight management systems (FMS). A computer system that uses a large data base to allow routes to be preprogrammed and fed into the system by means of a data loader. The system is constantly updated with respect to position accuracy by reference to conventional navigation aids. The sophisticated program and its associated data base insures that the most appropriate aids are automatically selected during the information update cycle.

flight management system procedure (FMSP). An arrival, departure, or approach procedure developed for use by aircraft with a slant (/) E or slant (/) F equipment suffix.

flight path. A line, course, or track along which an aircraft is flying or intended to be flown. (*See* track, course).

flight plan. Specified information relating to the intended flight of an aircraft that is filed orally or in writing with an FSS or an ATC facility. (*See* fast file, filed) (Refer to AIM).

flight plan area. The geographical area assigned by regional air traffic divisions to a flight service station for the purpose of search and rescue for VFR aircraft, issuance of NOTAMs, pilot briefing, in-flight services, broadcast, emergency services, flight data processing, international operations, and aviation weather services. Three letter identifiers are assigned to every flight service station and are annotated in AFDs and Order 7350.5 as tie-in facilities. (*See* fast file, filed) (Refer to AIM).

flight recorder. A general term applied to any instrument or device that records information about the performance of an aircraft in flight or about conditions encountered in flight. Flight recorders may make records of airspeed, outside air temperature, vertical acceleration, engine RPM, manifold pressure, and other pertinent variables for a given flight. [ICAO] Any type of recorder installed in the aircraft for the purpose of complementing accident/incident investigation. *Note: See* Annex 6, Part I, for specifications relating to flight recorders.

Flight Service Station (FSS). Air traffic facilities which provide pilot briefing, enroute communications and VFR search and rescue services, assist lost aircraft and aircraft in emergency situations, relay ATC clearances, originate Notices to Airmen, broadcast aviation weather and NAS information, receive and process IFR flight plans, and monitor NAVAIDs. In addition, at selected locations, FSS's provide Enroute Flight Advisory Service (Flight Watch), take weather observations, issue airport advisories, and advise Customs and Immigration of transborder flights. (Refer to AIM).

***Flight Service Station (FSS).** Air traffic facilities which provide pilot briefings, enroute communications, and many other services to pilots.

Flight Standards District Office (FSDO). An FAA field office serving an assigned geographical area and staffed with Flight Standards personnel who serve the aviation industry and the general public on matters relating to the certification and operation of air carrier and general aviation aircraft. Activities include general surveillance of operational safety, certification of airmen and aircraft, accident prevention, investigation, enforcement, etc.

flight test. A flight for the purpose of:

1. Investigating the operation/flight characteristics of an aircraft or aircraft component.
2. Evaluating an applicant for a pilot certificate or rating.

flight visibility. (*See* visibility).

Flight Watch. A shortened term for use in air/ground contacts to identify the flight service station providing Enroute Flight Advisory Service; e.g., "Oakland Flight Watch." (*See* Enroute Flight Advisory Service).

*__Flight Watch.__ Another name for Enroute Flight Advisory Service, a weather-information-only service of the Flight Service Station.

FLIP. (*See* DOD FLIP).

flow control. Measures designed to adjust the flow of traffic into a given airspace, along a given route, or bound for a given aerodrome (airport) so as to ensure the most effective utilization of the airspace. (*See* quota flow control) (Refer to Airport/Facility Directory).

fly-by waypoint. A fly-by waypoint requires the use of turn anticipation to avoid overshoot of the next flight segment.

fly heading (degrees). Informs the pilot of the heading he should fly. The pilot may have to turn to, or continue on, a specific compass direction in order to comply with the instructions. The pilot is expected to turn in the shorter direction to the heading unless otherwise instructed by ATC.

fly-over waypoint. A fly-over waypoint precludes any turn until the waypoint is overflown and is followed by an intercept maneuver of the next flight segment.

FMA. (*See* final monitor aid).

FMS. (*See* flight management system).

FMSP. (*See* flight management system procedure).

formation flight. More than one aircraft which, by prior arrangement between the pilots, operate as a single aircraft with regard to navigation and position reporting. Separation between aircraft within the formation is the responsibility of the flight leader and the pilots of the other aircraft in the flight. This includes transition periods when aircraft within the formation are maneuvering to attain separation from each other to effect individual control and during join-up and breakaway.

1. A standard formation is one in which a proximity of no more than 1 mile laterally or longitudinally and within 100 feet vertically from the flight leader is maintained by each wingman.
2. Nonstandard formations are those operating under any of the following conditions:
   a. When the flight leader has requested and ATC has approved other than standard formation dimensions.
   b. When operating within an authorized altitude reservation (ALTRV) or under the provisions of a letter of agreement.
   c. When the operations are conducted in airspace specifically designed for a special activity.
   (*See* Altitude Reservation) (Refer to 14 CFR Part 91).

FRC. (*See* request full route clearance).

freeze/frozen. Terms used in referring to arrivals which have been assigned ACLTs and to the lists in which they are displayed.

freeze calculated landing time (FCLT). A dynamic parameter number of minutes prior to the meter fix calculated time of arrival for each aircraft when the TCLT is frozen and becomes an ACLT (i.e., the VTA is updated and consequently the TCLT is modified as appropriate until FCLT minutes prior to meter fix calculated time of arrival, at which time updating is suspended and an ACLT and a frozen meter fix crossing time (MFT) is assigned).

freeze speed parameter (FSPD). A speed adapted for each aircraft to determine fast and slow aircraft. Fast aircraft freeze on parameter FCLT and slow aircraft freeze on parameter MLDI.

friction measurement. A measurement of the friction characteristics of the runway pavement surface using continuous self-watering friction measurement equipment in accordance with the specifications, procedures and schedules contained in AC 150/5320-12, *Measurement, Construction, and Maintenance of Skid-Resistant Airport Pavement Surfaces.*

*__front.__ Where two air masses with different properties meet.

FSDO. (*See* Flight Standards District Office).

FSPD. (*See* freeze speed parameter).

FSS. (*See* Flight Service Station).

fuel dumping. Airborne release of usable fuel. This does not include the dropping of fuel tanks. (*See* jettisoning of external stores).

*__fuel injection.__ An induction system which delivers a metered amount of fuel to each cylinder.

fuel remaining. A phrase used by either pilots or controllers when relating to the fuel remaining on board until actual fuel exhaustion. When transmitting such information in response to either a controller question or pilot initiated cautionary advisory to air traffic control, pilots will state the APPROXIMATE NUMBER OF MINUTES the flight can continue with the fuel remaining. All reserve fuel SHOULD BE INCLUDED in the time stated, as should be an allowance for established fuel gauge system error.

fuel siphoning. Unintentional release of fuel caused by overflow, puncture, loose cap, etc.

fuel venting. (*See* fuel siphoning).

*__fuselage.__ The main body of the airplane to which the wings and empennage are attached. Passenger and crew seating is in the fuselage.

*__G.__ The force of gravity: one times the weight of an object.

gate hold procedures. Procedures at selected airports to hold aircraft at the gate or other ground location whenever departure delays exceed or are anticipated to exceed 15 minutes. The sequence for departure will be maintained in accordance with initial call up unless modified by flow control restrictions. Pilots should monitor the ground control/clearance delivery frequency for engine start/taxi advisories or new proposed start/taxi time if the delay changes. (*See* flow control).

GCA. (*See* ground controlled approach).

general aviation. That portion of civil aviation which encompasses all facets of aviation except air carriers holding a certificate of public convenience and necessity from the Civil Aeronautics Board and large aircraft commercial operators. [ICAO] All civil aviation operations other than scheduled air services and nonscheduled air transport operations for renumeration or hire.

geo map. The digitized map markings associated with the ASR-9 Radar System.

glide path. (*See* glide slope).

glidepath intercept altitude. (*See* glideslope intercept altitude).

glide slope. Provides vertical guidance for aircraft during approach and landing. The glideslope/glidepath is based on the following:

1. Electronic components emitting signals which provide vertical guidance by reference to airborne instruments during instrument approaches such as ILS/MLS, or
2. Visual ground aids, such as VASI, which provide vertical guidance for a VFR approach or for the visual portion of an instrument approach and landing.
3. PAR. Used by ATC to inform an aircraft making a PAR approach of its vertical position (elevation) relative to the descent profile.

(*See* glide path [ICAO]).

glide path. [ICAO] A descent profile determined for vertical guidance during a final approach.

glideslope intercept altitude. The minimum altitude to intercept the glide slope/path on a precision approach. The intersection of the published intercept altitude with the glide slope/path, designated on Government charts by the lightning bolt symbol, is the precision FAF; however, when ATC directs a lower altitude, the resultant lower intercept position is then the FAF. (*See* final approach fix, segments of an instrument approach procedure).

global positioning system (GPS). A space-base radio positioning, navigation, and time-transfer system. The system provides highly accurate position and velocity information, and precise time, on a continuous global basis, to an unlimited number of properly equipped users. The system is unaffected by weather, and provides a worldwide common grid reference system. The GPS concept is predicated upon accurate and continuous knowledge of the spatial position of each satellite in the system with respect to time and distance from a transmitting satellite to the user. The GPS receiver automatically selects appropriate signals from the satellites in view and translates these into three-dimensional position, velocity, and time. System accuracy for civil users is normally 100 meters horizontally.

go ahead. Proceed with your message. Not to be used for any other purpose.

go around. Instructions for a pilot to abandon his approach to landing. Additional instructions may follow. Unless otherwise advised by ATC, a VFR aircraft or an aircraft conducting visual approach should overfly the runway while climbing to traffic pattern altitude and enter the traffic pattern via the crosswind leg. A pilot on an IFR flight plan making an instrument approach should execute the published missed approach procedure or proceed as instructed by ATC; e.g., "Go around" (additional instructions if required). (*See* low approach, missed approach).

*GPO.** Government Printing Office.

GPS. (*See* global positioning system).

*gradient wind, gradient force.** The wind (and the force that drives it) caused solely by pressure differences.

*great circle.** An imaginary circle on the face of the earth cut by a plane which passes through the center of the earth. All meridians are Great Circles, and the equator is a Great Circle.

ground clutter. A pattern produced on the radar scope by ground returns which may degrade other radar returns in the affected area. The effect of ground clutter is minimized by the use of moving target indicator (MTI) circuits in the radar equipment resulting in a radar presentation which displays only targets which are in motion. (*See* clutter).

ground communication outlet (GCO). An unstaffed, remotely controlled, ground/ground communications facility. Pilots at uncontrolled airports may contact ATC and FSS via VHF to a telephone connection to obtain an instrument clearance or close a VFR or IFR flight plan. They may also get an updated weather briefing prior to takeoff. Pilots will use four "key clicks" on the VHF radio to contact the appropriate ATC facility or six "key clicks" to contact the FSS. The GCO system is intended to be used only on the ground.

ground controlled approach (GCA). A radar approach system operated from the ground by air traffic control personnel transmitting instructions to the pilot by radio. The approach may be conducted with surveillance radar (ASR) only or with both surveillance and precision approach radar (PAR). Usage of the term "GCA" by pilots is discouraged except when referring to a GCA facility. Pilots should specifically request a "PAR" approach when a precision radar approach is desired or request an "ASR" or "surveillance" approach when a nonprecision radar approach is desired. (*See* radar approach).

*ground controller.** An air traffic control specialist in a control tower who controls operations on the ramps and taxiways of a controlled airport.

ground delay. The amount of delay attributed to ATC, encountered prior to departure, usually associated with a CDT program.

*ground effect.** A reduction in induced drag experienced when the wing is within one-half wing span of the ground.

ground speed. The speed of an aircraft relative to the surface of the earth.

ground stop. Normally, the last initiative to be utilized; this method mandates that the terminal facility will not allow any departures to enter the ARTCC airspace until further notified.

ground visibility. (*See* visibility).

***gyroscopic precession.** A slow movement of the axis of a spinning body, noticeable in gyroscopic heading indicators as a drift away from agreement with the magnetic compass.

HAA. (*See* height above airport).

HAL. (*See* height above landing).

handoff. An action taken to transfer the radar identification of an aircraft from one controller to another if the aircraft will enter the receiving controller's airspace and radio communications with the aircraft will be transferred.

HAT. (*See* height above touchdown).

have numbers. Used by pilots to inform ATC that they have received runway, wind, and altimeter information only.

Hazardous In-Flight Weather Advisory Service (HIWAS). Continuous recorded hazardous in-flight weather forecasts broadcasted to airborne pilots over selected VOR outlets defined as a HIWAS broadcast area.

hazardous weather information. Summary of Significant Meteorological Information (SIGMET/WS), Convective Significant Meteorological Information (Convective SIGMET/WST), urgent pilot weather reports (urgent PIREP/UUA), Center Weather Advisories (CWA), Airmen's Meteorological Information (AIRMET/WA) and any other weather such as isolated thunderstorms that are rapidly developing and increasing in intensity, or low ceilings and visibilities that are becoming widespread which is considered significant and are not included in a current hazardous weather advisory.

***heading.** The direction in which the airplane is pointing. When correcting for wind drift, the heading will differ from the course by several degrees.

***headwind component.** That portion of the reported wind which opposes the forward motion of the airplane.

heavy (aircraft). (*See* aircraft classes).

height above airport (HAA). The height of the minimum descent altitude above the published airport elevation. This is published in conjunction with circling minimums. (*See* minimum descent altitude).

height above landing (HAL). The height above a designated helicopter landing area used for helicopter instrument approach procedures. (Refer to 14 CFR Part 97).

height above touchdown (HAT). The height of the decision height or minimum descent altitude above the highest runway elevation in the touchdown zone (first 3,000 feet of the runway). HAT is published on instrument approach charts in conjunction with all straight-in minimums. (*See* decision height, minimum descent altitude).

helicopter. Rotorcraft that, for its horizontal motion, depends principally on its engine driven rotors. [ICAO] A heavier than air aircraft supported in flight chiefly by the reactions of the air on one or more power driven rotors on substantially vertical axes.

helipad. A small, designated area, usually with a prepared surface, on a heliport, airport, landing/takeoff area, apron/ramp, or movement area used for takeoff, landing, or parking of helicopters.

heliport. An area of land, water, or structure used or intended to be used for the landing and takeoff of helicopters and includes its buildings and facilities if any.

heliport reference point (HRP). The geographic center of a heliport.

hertz (Hz). The standard radio equivalent of frequency in cycles per second of an electromagnetic wave. Kilohertz (kHz) is a frequency of one thousand cycles per second. Megahertz (MHz) is a frequency of one million cycles per second.

HF. (*See* high frequency).

HF communications. (*See* high frequency communications).

high frequency (HF). The frequency band between 3 and 30 MHz. (*See* high frequency communications).

high frequency communications. High radio frequencies (HF) between 3 and 30 MHz used for air-to-ground voice communication in overseas operations.

high speed exit. (*See* high speed taxiway).

high speed taxiway. A long radius taxiway designed and provided with lighting or marking to define the path of aircraft, traveling at high speed (up to 60 knots), from the runway center to a point on the center of a taxiway. Also referred to as long radius exit or turnoff taxiway. The high speed taxiway is designed to expedite aircraft turning off the runway after landing, thus reducing runway occupancy time.

high speed turnoff. (*See* high speed taxiway).

HIWAS. (*See* Hazardous In-flight Weather Advisory Service).

HIWAS area. (*See* Hazardous In-flight Weather Advisory Service).

HIWAS broadcast area. A geographical area of responsibility including one or more HIWAS outlet areas assigned to an AFSS/FSS for hazardous weather advisory broadcasting.

HIWAS outlet area. An area defined as a 150 NM radius of a HIWAS outlet, expanded as necessary to provide coverage.

holding procedure. (*See* hold procedure).

hold procedure. A predetermined maneuver which keeps aircraft within a specified airspace while awaiting further clearance from air traffic control. Also used during ground operations to keep aircraft within a specified area or at a specified point while awaiting further clearance from air traffic control. (*See* holding fix) (Refer to AIM).

holding fix. A specified fix identifiable to a pilot by NAVAIDs or visual reference to the ground used as a reference point in establishing and maintaining the position of an aircraft while holding. (*See* fix, visual holding) (Refer to AIM).

holding point. [ICAO] A specified location, identified by visual or other means, in the vicinity of which the position of an aircraft in flight is maintained in accordance with air traffic control clearances.

hold for release. Used by ATC to delay an aircraft for traffic management reasons; i.e., weather, traffic volume, etc. Hold for release instructions (including departure delay information) are used to inform a pilot or a controller (either directly or through an authorized relay) that an IFR departure clearance is not valid until a release time or additional instructions have been received. (*See* holding point [ICAO]).

hold-short point. A point on the runway beyond which a landing aircraft with a LAHSO clearance is not authorized to proceed. This point may be located prior to an intersecting runway, taxiway, predetermined point, or approach/departure flight path.

hold-short position marking. The painted runway marking located at the hold-short point on all LAHSO runways.

hold-short position lights. Flashing in-pavement white lights located at specified hold-short points.

hold-short position signs. Red and white holding signs located alongside the hold-short point.

homing. Flight toward a NAVAID, without correcting for wind, by adjusting the aircraft heading to maintain a relative bearing of zero degrees. (*See* bearing). [ICAO] The procedure of using the direction finding equipment of one radio station with the emission of another radio station, where at least one of the stations is mobile, and whereby the mobile station proceeds continuously towards the other station.

***homing.** Navigating to a nondirectional beacon by simply keeping the ADF needle pointed directly to the nose of the airplane.

***horizontal situation indicator (HSI).** An instrument that incorporates a heading indicator and an omni-indicator to show the pilot the airplane's position in relation to a VOR radial as seen from a point above the airplane.

***horizontal stabilizer.** An airfoil-shaped surface at the rear of the airplane that develops a negative lift force to balance (stabilize) the airplane's pitch attitude.

hover check. Used to describe when a helicopter/VTOL aircraft requires a stabilized hover to conduct a performance/power check prior to hover taxi, air taxi, or takeoff. Altitude of the hover will vary based on the purpose of the check.

hover taxi. Used to describe a helicopter/VTOL aircraft movement conducted above the surface and in ground effect at airspeeds less than approximately 20 knots. The actual height may vary, and some helicopters may require hover taxi above 25 feet AGL to reduce ground effect turbulence or provide clearance for cargo sling loads. (*See* air taxi, hover check) (Refer to AIM).

How do you hear me? A question relating to the quality of the transmission or to determine how well the transmission is being received.

Hz. (*See* hertz).

IAF. (*See* initial approach fix).

IAP. (*See* instrument approach procedure).

IAWP. Initial approach waypoint.

ICAO. [ICAO] (*See* International Civil Aviation Organization [ICAO]).

icing. The accumulation of airframe ice. Types of icing are:
1. *Rime Ice.* Rough, milky, opaque ice formed by the instantaneous freezing of small supercooled water droplets.
2. *Clear Ice.* A glossy, clear, or translucent ice formed by the relatively slow freezing of large supercooled water droplets.
3. *Mixed.* A mixture of clear ice and rime ice.
   Intensity of icing:
4. *Trace.* Ice becomes perceptible. Rate of accumulation is slightly greater than the rate of sublimation. Deicing/anti-icing equipment is not utilized unless encountered for an extended period of time (over 1 hour).
5. *Light.* The rate of accumulation may create a problem if flight is prolonged in this environment (over 1 hour). Occasional use of deicing/anti-icing equipment removes/prevents accumulation. It does not present a problem if the deicing\anti-icing equipment is used.
6. *Moderate.* The rate of accumulation is such that even short encounters become potentially hazardous and use of deicing\anti-icing or flight diversion is necessary.
7. *Severe.* The rate of accumulation is such that deicing\anti-icing equipment fails to reduce or control the hazard. Immediate flight diversion is necessary.

ident. A request for a pilot to activate the aircraft transponder identification feature. This will help the controller to confirm an aircraft identity or to identify an aircraft. (Refer to AIM).

ident feature. The special feature in the Air Traffic Control Radar Beacon System (ATCRBS) equipment. It is used to immediately distinguish one displayed beacon target from other beacon targets. (*See* ident).

IF. (*See* intermediate fix).

IFIM. (*See* International Flight Information Manual).

If no transmission received for (time). Used by ATC in radar approaches to prefix procedures which should be followed by the pilot in event of lost communications. (*See* lost communications).

IFR. (*See* instrument flight rules).

IFR aircraft. An aircraft conducting flight in accordance with instrument flight rules.

IFR conditions. Weather conditions below the minimum for flight under visual flight rules. (*See* instrument meteorological conditions).

IFR departure procedure. (*See* IFR takeoff minimums and departure procedures) (Refer to AIM).

IFR flight. (*See* IFR aircraft).

IFR landing minimums. (*See* landing minimums).

IFR military training routes (IR). Routes used by the Department of Defense and associated Reserve and Air Guard units for the purpose of conducting low altitude navigation and tactical training in both IFR and VFR weather conditions below 10,000 feet MLS at airspeeds in excess of 250 knots IAS.

IFR takeoff minimums and departure procedures. 14 CFR Part 91, prescribes standard takeoff rules for certain civil users. At some airports, obstructions or other factors require the establishment of nonstandard takeoff minimums, departure procedures, or both to assist pilots in avoiding obstacles during climb to the minimum enroute altitude. Those airports are listed in NOS/DOD Instrument Approach Charts (IAPs) under a section entitled "IFR Takeoff Minimums and Departure Procedures." The NOS/DOD IAP chart legend illustrates the symbol used to alert the pilot to nonstandard takeoff minimums and departure procedures. When departing IFR from such airports or from any airport where there are no departure procedures, DPs, or ATC facilities available, pilots should advise ATC of any departure limitations. Controllers may query a pilot to determine acceptable departure directions, turns, or headings after takeoff. Pilots should be familiar with the departure procedures and must assure that their aircraft can meet or exceed any specified climb gradients.

IFWP. Intermediate Fix Waypoint.

IF/IAWP. Intermediate fix/initial approach waypoint. The waypoint where the final approach course of a T approach meets the crossbar of the T. When designated (in conjunction with a TAA) this waypoint will be used as an IAWP when approaching the airport from certain directions, and as an IFWP when beginning the approach from another IAWP.

ILS. (*See* instrument landing system).

ILS categories.

1. *ILS Category I.* An ILS approach procedure which provides for approach to a height above touchdown of not less than 200 feet and with runway visual range of not less than 1,800 feet.
2. *ILS Category II.* An ILS approach procedure which provides for approach to a height above touchdown of not less than 100 feet and with runway visual range of not less than 1,200 feet.

3. *ILS Category III.*
   a. *IIIA.* An ILS approach procedure which provides for approach without a decision height minimum and with runway visual range of not less than 700 feet.
   b. *IIIB.* An ILS approach procedure which provides for approach without a decision height minimum and with runway visual range of not less than 150 feet.
   c. *IIIC.* An ILS approach procedure which provides for approach without a decision height minimum and without runway visual range minimum.

ILS PRM Approach. An instrument landing system (ILS) approach conducted to parallel runways whose extended centerlines are separated by less than 4,300 feet and the parallel runways have a Precision Runway Monitoring (PRM) system that permits simultaneous independent ILS approaches.

IM. (*See* inner marker).

IMC. (*See* instrument meteorological conditions).

immediately. Used by ATC when such action compliance is required to avoid an imminent situation.

INCERFA (uncertainty phase). [ICAO] The code word used to designate an emergency phase wherein there is concern about the safety of an aircraft or its occupants. In most cases this phase involves an aircraft which is overdue or unreported.

Increase speed to (speed). (*See* speed adjustment).

*****indicated airspeed.** What the airspeed indicator reads, uncorrected for position and installation error. See calibrated airspeed.

*****induced drag.** Drag which is the inevitable result of lift generation. Induced drag increases with increased angle of attack and is greatest at low speeds that require large angles of attack.

inertial navigation system (INS). An RNAV system which is a form of self-contained navigation. (*See* area navigation/RNAV).

in-flight refueling. (*See* aerial refueling).

in-flight weather advisory. (*See* Weather Advisory).

information request (INREQ). A request originated by an FSS for information concerning an overdue VFR aircraft.

initial approach fix (IAF). The fixes depicted on instrument approach procedure charts that identify the beginning of the initial approach segment(s). (*See* fix, segments of an instrument approach procedure).

initial approach segment. (*See* segments of an instrument approach procedure). [ICAO] That segment of an instrument approach procedure between the initial approach fix and the intermediate approach fix or, where applicable, the final approach fix or point.

inland navigation facility. A navigation aid on a North American Route at which the common route and/or the noncommon route begins or ends.

inner marker (IM). A marker beacon used with an ILS (CAT II) precision approach located between the middle marker and the end of the ILS runway, transmitting a radiation pattern keyed at six dots per second and indicating to the pilot, both aurally and visually, that he is at the designated decision height (DH), normally 100 feet above the touchdown zone elevation, on the ILS CAT II approach. It also marks progress during a CAT III approach. (*See* instrument landing system) (Refer to AIM).

inner marker beacon. (*See* inner marker).

INREQ. (*See* information request).

INS. (*See* inertial navigation system).

instrument approach. (*See* instrument approach procedure).

instrument approach procedure (IAP). A series of predetermined maneuvers for the orderly transfer of an aircraft under instrument flight conditions from the beginning of the initial approach to a landing or to a point from which a landing may be made visually. It is prescribed and approved for a specific airport by competent authority. (*See* segments of an instrument approach procedure) (Refer to 14 CFR Part 91, AIM).

1. U.S. civil standard instrument approach procedures are approved by the FAA as prescribed under 14 CFR Part 97 and are available for public use.
2. U.S. military standard instrument approach procedures are approved and published by the Department of Defense.
3. Special instrument approach procedures are approved by the FAA for individual operators but are not published in 14 CFR Part 97 for public use.

[ICAO] A series of predetermined maneuvers by reference to flight instruments with specified protection from obstacles from the initial approach fix, or where applicable, from the beginning of a defined arrival route to a point from which a landing can be completed and thereafter, if a landing is not completed, to a position at which holding or enroute obstacle clearance criteria apply.

instrument approach procedures charts. (*See* aeronautical chart).

instrument departure procedure (DP). A preplanned instrument flight rule (IFR) air traffic control departure procedure printed for pilot use in graphic and/or textual form. DPs provide transition from the terminal to the appropriate enroute structure. (*See* IFR takeoff minimums and departure procedures.) (Refer to AIM.)

instrument departure procedure (DP) charts. (*See* aeronautical chart.)

instrument flight rules (IFR). Rules governing the procedures for conducting instrument flight. Also a term used by pilots and controllers to indicate type of flight plan. (*See* visual flight rules, instrument meteorological conditions, visual meteorological conditions) (Refer to AIM). [ICAO] A set of rules governing the conduct of flight under instrument meteorological conditions.

instrument landing system (ILS). A precision instrument approach system which normally consists of the following electronic components and visual aids:

1. *Localizer.* (*See* localizer).
2. *Glideslope.* (*See* glideslope).
3. *Outer Marker.* (*See* outer marker).
4. *Middle Marker.* (*See* middle marker).
5. *Approach Lights.* (*See* airport lighting).
   (Refer to 14 CFR Part 91, AIM).

instrument meteorological conditions (IMC). Meteorological conditions expressed in terms of visibility, distance from cloud, and ceiling less than the minima specified for visual meteorological conditions. (*See* visual meteorological conditions, instrument flight rules, visual flight rules).

instrument runway. A runway equipped with electronic and visual navigation aids for which a precision or nonprecision approach procedure having straight-in landing minimums has been approved. [ICAO] One of the following types of runways intended for the operation of aircraft using instrument approach procedures:

1. *Nonprecision Approach Runway.* An instrument runway served by visual aids and nonvisual aid providing at least directional guidance adequate for a straight-in approach.
2. *Precision Approach Runway, Category I.* An instrument runway served by ILS and visual aids intended for operations down to 60 m (200 feet) decision height and down to an RVR of the order to 800 m.
3. *Precision Approach Runway, Category II.* An instrument runway served by ILS and visual aids intended for operations down to 30 m (100 feet) decision height and down to an RVR of the order of 400 m.
4. *Precision Approach Runway, Category III.* An instrument runway served by ILS to and along the surface of the runway and:
   a. Intended for operations down to an RVR of the order of 200 m (no decision height being applicable) using visual aids during the final phase of landing;
   b. Intended for operations down to an RVR of the order of 50 m (no decision height being applicable) using visual aids for taxiing;
   c. Intended for operations without reliance on visual reference for landing or taxiing.

Note 1: See Annex 10, Volume I, Part I Chapter 3, for related ILS specifications.

Note 2: Visual aids need not necessarily be matched to the scale of nonvisual aids provided. The criterion for the selection of visual aids is the conditions in which operations are intended to be conducted.

integrity. The ability of a system to provide timely warnings to users when the system should not be used for navigation.

intermediate approach segment. (*See* segments of an instrument approach procedure). [ICAO] That segment of an instrument approach procedure between either the intermediate approach fix and the final approach fix or point, or between the end of a reversal, race track or dead reckoning track procedure and the final approach fix or point, as appropriate.

intermediate fix (IF). The fix that identifies the beginning of the intermediate approach segment of an instrument approach procedure. The fix is not normally identified on the instrument approach chart as an intermediate fix (IF). (*See* segments of an instrument approach procedure).

intermediate landing. On the rare occasion that this option is requested, it should be approved. The departure center, however, must advise the ATCSCC so that the appropriate delay is carried over and assigned at the intermediate airport. An intermediate landing airport within the arrival center will not be accepted without coordination with and the approval of the ATCSCC.

international airport. Relating to international flight, it means:

1. An airport of entry which has been designated by the Secretary of Treasury or Commissioner of Customs as an international airport for customs service.

2. A landing rights airport at which specific permission to land must be obtained from customs authorities in advance of contemplated use.

3. Airports designated under the Convention on International Civil Aviation as an airport for use by international commercial air transport and/or international general aviation.

(Refer to Airport/Facility Directory and IFIM). [ICAO] Any airport designated by the Contracting State in whose territory it is situated as an airport of entry and departure for international air traffic, where the formalities incident to customs, immigration, public health, animal and plant quarantine and similar procedures are carried out.

International Civil Aviation Organization. [ICAO] A specialized agency of the United Nations whose objective is to develop the principles and techniques of international air navigation and to foster planning and development of international civil air transport. ICAO Regions include:

AFI. African-Indian Ocean Region

CAR. Caribbean Region

EUR. European Region

MID/ASIA. Middle East/Asia Region

NAM. North American Region

NAT. North Atlantic Region

PAC. Pacific Region

SAM. South American Region

International Flight Information Manual (IFIM). A publication designed primarily as a pilot's preflight planning guide for flights into foreign airspace and for flights returning to the U.S. from foreign locations.

*international standard atmosphere (ISA). *See* standard day.

interrogator. The ground based surveillance radar beacon transmitter/receiver, which normally scans in synchronism with a primary radar, transmitting discrete radio signals which repetitiously request all transponders on the mode being used to reply. The replies received are mixed with the primary radar returns and displayed on the same plan position indicator (radar scope). Also, applied to the airborne element of the TACAN/DME system. (*See* transponder) (Refer to AIM).

intersecting runways. Two or more runways which cross or meet within their lengths. (*See* intersection).

intersection.

1. A point defined by any combination of courses, radials, or bearings of two or more navigational aids.

2. Used to describe the point where two runways, a runway and a taxiway, or two taxiways cross or meet.

intersection departure. A departure from any runway intersection except the end of the runway. (*See* Intersection).

intersection takeoff. (*See* intersection departure).

*inversion. When warm air overlies cold air; the reverse of a stable condition.

IR. (*See* IFR military training routes).

I say again. The message will be repeated.

*isobars. Lines of equal barometric pressure on a weather map.

*isogonic lines. Lines of equal magnetic variation.

jamming. Electronic or mechanical interference which may disrupt the display of aircraft on radar or the transmission/reception of radio communications/navigation.

jet blast. Jet engine exhaust (thrust stream turbulence). (*See* wake turbulence).

jet route. A route designed to serve aircraft operations from 18,000 feet MSL up to and including flight level 450. The routes are referred to as "J" routes with numbering to identify the designated route; e.g., J105. (*See* Class A airspace) (Refer to 14 CFR Part 71).

jet stream. A migrating stream of high speed winds present at high altitudes.

jettisoning of external stores. Airborne release of external stores; e.g., tiptanks, ordnance. (*See* fuel dumping) (Refer to 14 CFR Part 91).

joint use restricted area. (*See* Restricted Area).

*kHz. Kilohertz (thousands of cycles per second); a measure of radio frequency.

*knot. One nautical mile per hour. (It is redundant to say "90 knots per hour.")

known traffic. With respect to ATC clearances, means aircraft whose altitude, position, and intentions are known to ATC.

*__Kollsman window.__ The altimeter setting window.

LAA. (*See* Local Airport Advisory).

LAAS. (*See* Low Altitude Alert System).

LAHSO. An acronym for "Land and Hold Short Operation." These operations include landing and holding short of an intersecting runway, a taxiway, a predetermined point, or an approach/departure flightpath.

LAHSO. Dry. Land and hold short operation on runways that are dry.

LAHSO. Wet. Land and hold short operations on runways that are wet (but not contaminated).

land and hold short operations (LAHSO). Operations which include simultaneous takeoffs and landings and/or simultaneous landings when a landing aircraft is able and is instructed by the controller to hold-short of the intersecting runway/taxiway or designated hold-short point. Pilots are expected to promptly inform the controller if the hold short clearance cannot be accepted. (*See* parallel runways). (Refer to AIM).

landing area. Any locality either on land, water, or structures, including airports/heliports and intermediate landing fields which is used, or intended to be used, for the landing and takeoff of aircraft whether or not facilities are provided for the shelter, servicing, or for receiving or discharging passengers or cargo. [ICAO] That part of a movement area intended for the landing or takeoff of aircraft.

landing direction indicator. A device which visually indicates the direction in which landings and takeoffs should be made. (*See* tetrahedron) (Refer to AIM).

landing distance available (LDA). [ICAO] The length of runway which is declared available and suitable for the ground run of an aeroplane landing.

*__landing gear.__ The two main wheels and the nosewheel (or tailwheel).

landing minimums. The minimum visibility prescribed for landing a civil aircraft while using an instrument approach procedure. The minimum applies with other limitations set forth in 14 CFR Part 91 with respect to the Minimum Descent Altitude (MDA) or Decision Height (DH) prescribed in the instrument approach procedures as follows:

1. Straight-in landing minimums. A statement of MDA and visibility, or DH and visibility, required for a straight-in landing on a specified runway, or

2. Circling minimums. A statement of MDA and visibility required for the circle-to-land maneuver.

Descent below the established MDA or DH is not authorized during an approach unless the aircraft is in a position from which a normal approach to the runway of intended landing can be made and adequate visual reference to required visual cues is maintained. (*See* straight-in landing, circle-to-land maneuver, decision height, minimum descent altitude, visibility, instrument approach procedure) (Refer to 14 CFR Part 91).

landing roll. The distance from the point of touchdown to the point where the aircraft can be brought to a stop or exit the runway.

landing sequence. The order in which aircraft are positioned for landing (*See* approach sequence).

last assigned altitude. The last altitude/flight level assigned by ATC and acknowledged by the pilot. (*See* maintain) (Refer to 14 CFR Part 91).

*__lateral axis.__ A line drawn from wing tip to wing tip.

lateral separation. The lateral spacing of aircraft at the same altitude by requiring operation on different routes or in different geographical locations. (*See* separation).

LDA. (*See* localizer-type directional aid).

LDA. [ICAO] (*See* landing distance available [ICAO]).

LF. (*See* low frequency).

lighted airport. An airport where runway and obstruction lighting is available. (*See* airport lighting) (Refer to AIM).

light gun. A hand held directional light signaling device which emits a brilliant narrow beam of white, green, or red light as selected by the tower controller. The color and type of light transmitted can be used to approve or disapprove anticipated pilot actions where radio communication is not available. The light gun is used for controlling traffic operating in the vicinity of the airport and on the airport movement area. (Refer to AIM).

*__loadmeter.__ An ammeter which is calibrated to indicate the electrical load on the alternator in amperes.

Local Airport Advisory (LAA). A service provided by flight service stations or the military at airports not serviced by an operating control tower. This service consists of providing information to arriving and departing aircraft concerning wind direction and speed, favored runway, altimeter setting, pertinent known traffic, pertinent known field conditions, airport taxi routes and traffic patterns, and authorized instrument approach procedures. This information is advisory in nature and does not constitute an ATC clearance (*See* airport advisory area).

localizer. The component of an ILS which provides course guidance to the runway. (*See* Instrument Landing System) (Refer to AIM) (*See* localizer course [ICAO]).

localizer course (ILS). [ICAO] The locus of points, in any given horizontal plane, at which the DDM (difference in depth of modulation) is zero.

localizer offset. An angular offset of the localizer from the runway extended centerline in a direction away from the no transgression zone (NTZ) that increases the normal operating zone (NOZ) width. An offset requires a 50 foot increase in DH and is not authorized for CAT II and CAT III approaches.

localizer-type directional aid (LDA). A NAVAID used for nonprecision instrument approaches with utility and accuracy comparable to a localizer but which is not a part of a complete ILS and is not aligned with the runway. (Refer to AIM).

localizer usable distance. The maximum distance from the localizer transmitter at a specified altitude, as verified by flight inspection, at which reliable course information is continuously received. (Refer to AIM).

local traffic. Aircraft operating in the traffic pattern or within sight of the tower, or aircraft known to be departing or arriving from flight in local practice areas, or aircraft executing practice instrument approaches at the airport. (*See* traffic pattern).

locator. [ICAO] An LM/MF NDB used as an aid to final approach. *Note:* A locator usually has an average radius of rated coverage of between 18.5 and 46.3 km (10 and 25 NM).

***longitudinal axis.** An imaginary line from the nose to the tail of the airplane.

longitudinal separation. The longitudinal spacing of aircraft at the same altitude by a minimum distance expressed in units of time or miles. (*See* separation) (Refer to AIM).

long range navigation. (*See* LORAN).

LORAN. An electronic navigational system by which hyperbolic lines of position are determined by measuring the difference in the time of reception of synchronized pulse signals from two fixed transmitters. LORAN A operates in the 1750 to 1950 kHz frequency band. LORAN C and D operate in the 100 to 110 kHz frequency band. (Refer to AIM).

***LORAN-C.** A long-range navigation system using very low frequency transmissions.

lost communications. Loss of the ability to communicate by radio. Aircraft are sometimes referred to as NORDO (No Radio). Standard pilot procedures are specified in 14 CFR Part 91. Radar controllers issue procedures for pilots to follow in the event of lost communications during a radar approach when weather reports indicate that an aircraft will likely encounter IFR weather conditions during the approach. (Refer to 14 CFR Part 91, AIM).

low altitude airway structure. The network of airways serving aircraft operations up to but not including 18,000 feet MSL. (*See* airway) (Refer to AIM).

Low altitude alert, check your altitude immediately. (*See* safety alert).

Low Altitude Alert System (LAAS). An automated function of the TPX-42 that alerts the controller when a Mode C transponder equipped aircraft on an IFR flight plan is below a predetermined minimum safe altitude. If requested by the pilot, LAAS monitoring is also available to VFR Mode C transponder equipped aircraft.

low approach. An approach over an airport or runway following an instrument approach or a VFR approach including the go around maneuver where the pilot intentionally does not make contact with the runway. (Refer to AIM).

low frequency (LF). The frequency band between 30 and 300 kHz. (Refer to AIM).

MAA. (*See* maximum authorized altitude).

Mach number. The ratio of true airspeed to the speed of sound; e.g., Mach 0.82, Mach 1.6. (*See* airspeed).

Mach technique. [ICAO] Describes a control technique used by air traffic control whereby turbojet aircraft operating successively along suitable routes are cleared to maintain appropriate Mach numbers for a relevant portion of the enroute phase of flight. The principle objective is to achieve improved utilization of the airspace and to ensure that separation between successive aircraft does not decrease below the established minima.

***magnetic bearing.** The direction to or from a transmitting station measured in relation to magnetic north.

***magnetic compass.** A direction-indicating device that reacts to the earth's magnetic field.

***magnetic north.** The direction to the magnetic North Pole, located in Northern Canada.

***magneto.** A self-powered source of ignition using fixed magnets.

MAHWP. Missed approach holding waypoint.

maintain.

1. Concerning altitude/flight level, the term means to remain at the altitude/flight level specified. The phrase "climb and" or "descend and" normally precedes "maintain" and the altitude assignment; e.g., "descend and maintain 5,000."

2. Concerning other ATC instructions, the term is used in its literal sense; e.g., maintain VFR.

maintenance planning friction level. The friction level specified in AC 150/5320-12, *Measurement, Construction, and Maintenance of Skid Resistant Airport Pavement Surfaces,* which represents the friction value below which the runway pavement surface remains acceptable for any category or class of aircraft operations but which is beginning to show signs of deterioration. This value will vary depending on the particular friction measurement equipment used.

Make short approach. Used by ATC to inform a pilot to alter his traffic pattern so as to make a short final approach. (*See* traffic pattern).

mandatory altitude. An altitude depicted on an instrument Approach Procedure Chart requiring the aircraft to maintain altitude at the depicted value.

***manifold.** A pipe with several lateral outlets. In an airplane, the intake manifold delivers the fuel/air mixture to the cylinders; the exhaust manifold collects the exhaust from the cylinders, and pipes it overboard or through a turbocharger.

*manifold pressure. An indirect measure of power output obtained by measuring the pressure of the air in the intake manifold. The higher the pressure, the greater the power output of the engine.

MAP. (*See* missed approach point).

marker beacon. An electronic navigation facility transmitting a 75 MHz vertical fan or boneshaped radiation pattern. Marker beacons are identified by their modulation frequency and keying code, and when received by compatible airborne equipment, indicate to the pilot, both aurally and visually, that he is passing over the facility. (*See* outer marker, middle marker, inner marker) (Refer to AIM).

MARSA. (*See* military authority assumes responsibility for separation of aircraft).

MAWP. Missed approach waypoint.

maximum authorized altitude (MAA). A published altitude representing the maximum usable altitude or flight level for an airspace structure or route segment. It is the highest altitude on a Federal airway, jet route, area navigation low or high route, or other direct route for which an MEA is designated in 14 CFR Part 95 at which adequate reception of navigation aid signals is assured.

mayday. The international radio telephony distress signal. When repeated three times, it indicates imminent and grave danger and that immediate assistance is requested. (*See* pan-pan) (Refer to AIM).

*mayday. The voice equivalent of SOS; used to declare an emergency.

MCA. (*See* minimum crossing altitude).

MDA. (*See* minimum descent altitude).

MEA. (*See* minimum enroute IFR altitude).

*meridians. Lines of longitude — running from pole to pole and all the same length. Each degree of latitude measured along a line of longitude equals 60 nautical miles.

*METAR. An hourly weather observation from an accredited observer.

meteorological impact statement (MIS). An unscheduled planning forecast describing conditions expected to begin within 4 to 12 hours which may impact the flow of air traffic in a specific center's (ARTCC) area.

meter fix time (MFT)/slot time. A calculated time to depart the meter fix in order to cross the vertex at the ACLT. This time reflects descent speed adjustment and any applicable time that must be absorbed prior to crossing the meter fix.

meter list display interval (MLDI). A dynamic parameter which controls the number of minutes prior to the flight plan calculated time of arrival at the meter fix for each aircraft, at which time the TCLT is frozen and becomes an ACLT; i.e., the VTA is updated and consequently the TCLT modified as appropriate until frozen at which time updating is suspended and an ACLT is assigned. When frozen, the flight entry is inserted into the arrival sector's meter list for display on the sector PVD/MDM. MLDI is used if filed true airspeed is less than or equal to freeze speed parameters (FSPD).

metering. A method of time regulating arrival traffic flow into a terminal area so as not to exceed a predetermined terminal acceptance rate.

metering airports. Airports adapted for metering and for which optimum flight paths are defined. A maximum of 15 airports may be adapted.

metering fix. A fix along an established route from over which aircraft will be metered prior to entering terminal airspace. Normally, this fix should be established at a distance from the airport which will facilitate a profile descent 10,000 feet above airport elevation (AAE) or above.

metering position(s). Adapted PVDs/MDMs and associated "D" positions eligible for display of a metering position list. A maximum of four PVDs/MDMs may be adapted.

metering position list. An ordered list of data on arrivals for a selected metering airport displayed on a metering position PVD/MDM.

MFT. (*See* meter fix time/slot time).

MHA. (*See* minimum holding altitude).

*MHz. Megahertz (millions of cycles per second); a measure of radio frequency.

MIA. (*See* minimum IFR altitudes).

microburst. A small downburst with outbursts of damaging winds extending 2.5 miles or less. In spite of its small horizontal scale, an intense microburst could induce wind speeds as high as 150 knots. (Refer to AIM).

Microwave Landing System (MLS). A precision instrument approach system operating in the microwave spectrum which normally consists of the following components:
1. Azimuth station.
2. Elevation station.
3. Precision distance measuring equipment.
   (*See* MLS categories).

middle compass locator. (*See* compass locator).

middle marker (MM). A marker beacon that defines a point along the glideslope of an ILS normally located at or near the point of decision height (ILS Category I). It is keyed to transmit alternate dots and dashes, with the alternate dots and dashes keyed at the rate of 95 dot/dash combinations per minute on a 1300 Hz tone, which is received aurally and visually by compatible airborne equipment. (*See* marker beacon, instrument landing system) (Refer to AIM).

mid RVR. (*See* visibility).

miles in trail. A specified distance between aircraft, normally, in the same stratum associated with the same destination or route of flight.

military authority assumes responsibility for separation of aircraft (MARSA). A condition whereby the military services involved assume responsibility for separation between participating military aircraft in the ATC system. It is used only for required IFR operations which are specified in letters of agreement or other appropriate FAA or military documents.

Military Operations Area (MOA). (*See* Special Use airspace).

military training routes (MTR). Airspace of defined vertical and lateral dimensions established for the conduct of military flight training at airspeeds in excess of 250 knots IAS. (*See* IFR military training routes and VFR military training routes).

minima. (*See* minimums).

minimum crossing altitude (MCA). The lowest altitude at certain fixes at which an aircraft must cross when proceeding in the direction of a higher minimum enroute IFR altitude (MEA). (*See* minimum enroute IFR altitude).

minimum descent altitude (MDA). The lowest altitude, expressed in feet above mean sea level, to which descent is authorized on final approach or during circle-to-land maneuvering in execution of a standard instrument approach procedure where no electronic glideslope is provided. (*See* nonprecision approach procedure).

minimum enroute IFR altitude (MEA). The lowest published altitude between radio fixes which assures acceptable navigational signal coverage and meets obstacle clearance requirements between those fixes. The MEA prescribed for a Federal airway or segment thereof, area navigation low or high route or other direct route applies to the entire width of the airway, segment, or route between the radio fixes defining the airway, segment, or route. (Refer to 14 CFR Parts 91 and 95; AIM).

minimum friction level. The friction level specified in AC 150/5320-12, *Measurement, Construction, and Maintenance of Skid Resistant Airport Pavement Surfaces,* that represents the minimum recommended wet pavement surface friction value for any turbojet aircraft engaged in LAHSO. This value will vary with the particular friction measurement equipment used.

minimum fuel. Indicates that an aircraft's fuel supply has reached a state where, upon reaching the destination, it can accept little or no delay. This is not an emergency situation but merely indicates an emergency situation is possible should any undue delay occur. (Refer to AIM).

minimum holding altitude (MHA). The lowest altitude prescribed for a holding pattern which assures navigational signal coverage, communications, and meets obstacle clearance requirements.

minimum IFR altitudes (MIA). Minimum altitudes for IFR operations as prescribed in 14 CFR Part 91. These altitudes are published on aeronautical charts and prescribed in Part 95 for airways and routes, and in Part 97 for standard instrument approach procedures. If no applicable minimum altitude is prescribed in Part 95 or Part 97, the following minimum IFR altitude applies:

1. In designated mountainous areas, 2,000 feet above the highest obstacle within a horizontal distance of 4 nautical miles from the course to be flown; or

2. Other than mountainous areas, 1,000 feet above the highest obstacle within a horizontal distance of 4 nautical miles from the course to be flown; or

3. As otherwise authorized by the Administrator or assigned by ATC.

(*See* minimum enroute IFR altitude, minimum obstruction clearance altitude, minimum crossing altitude, minimum safe altitude, minimum vectoring altitude) (Refer to 14 CFR Part 91).

Minimum Navigation Performance Specification (MNPS). A set of standards which require aircraft to have a minimum navigation performance capability in order to operate in MNPS designated airspace. In addition, aircraft must be certified by their State of Registry for MNPS operation.

Minimum Navigation Performance Specifications Airspace (MNPSA). Designated airspace in which MNPS procedures are applied between MNPS certified and equipped aircraft. Under certain conditions, non-MNPS aircraft can operate in MNPSA. However, standard oceanic separation minima is provided between the non-MNPS aircraft and other traffic. Currently, the only designated MNPSA is described as follows:

1. Between FL 285 and FL 420;

2. Between latitudes 27° N and the North Pole;

3. In the east, the eastern boundaries of the CTA's Santa Maria Oceanic, Shanwick Oceanic, and Reykjavik;

4. In the west, the western boundaries of CTA's Reykjavik and Gander Oceanic and New York Oceanic excluding the area west of 60° W and south of 38°30' N.

minimum obstruction clearance altitude (MOCA). The lowest published altitude in effect between radio fixes on VOR airways, off airway routes, or route segments which meets obstacle clearance requirements for the entire route segment and which assures acceptable navigational signal coverage only within 25 statute (22 nautical) miles of a VOR. (Refer to 14 CFR Parts 91 and 95).

minimum reception altitude (MRA). The lowest altitude at which an intersection can be determined. (Refer to 14 CFR Part 95).

minimum safe altitude (MSA).

1. The minimum altitude specified in 14 CFR Part 91 for various aircraft operations.

2. Altitudes depicted on approach charts which provide at least 1,000 feet of obstacle clearance for emergency use within a specified distance from the navigation facility upon which a procedure is predicated. These altitudes will

be identified as Minimum sector altitudes or emergency safe altitudes and are established as follows:

a. *Minimum sector altitudes.* Altitudes depicted on approach charts which provide at least 1,000 feet of obstacle clearance within a 25 mile radius of the navigation facility upon which the procedure is predicated. Sectors depicted on approach charts must be at least 90 degrees in scope. These altitudes are for emergency use only and do not necessarily assure acceptable navigational signal coverage. (*See* minimum sector altitude [ICAO]).

b. *Emergency safe altitudes.* Altitudes depicted on approach charts which provide at least 1,000 feet of obstacle clearance in nonmountainous areas and 2,000 feet of obstacle clearance in designated mountainous areas within a 100 mile radius of the navigation facility upon which the procedure is predicated and normally used only in military procedures. These altitudes are identified on published procedures as "emergency safe altitudes."

minimum safe altitude warning (MSAW). A function of the ARTS III computer that aids the controller by alerting him when a tracked Mode C equipped aircraft is below or is predicted by the computer to go below a predetermined minimum safe altitude. (Refer to AIM).

minimum sector altitude. [ICAO] The lowest altitude which may be used under emergency conditions which will provide a minimum clearance of 300 m (1,000 feet) above all obstacles located in an area contained within a sector of a circle of 46 km (25 NM) radius centered on a radio aid to navigation.

minimums. Weather condition requirements established for a particular operation or type of operation; e.g., IFR takeoff or landing, alternate airport for IFR flight plans, VFR flight, etc. (*See* landing minimums, IFR takeoff minimums, VFR conditions, IFR conditions) (Refer to 14 CFR Part 91, AIM).

minimum vectoring altitude (MVA). The lowest MSL altitude at which an IFR aircraft will be vectored by a radar controller, except as otherwise authorized for radar approaches, departures, and missed approaches. The altitude meets IFR obstacle clearance criteria. It may be lower than the published MEA along an airway or J-route segment. It may be utilized for radar vectoring only upon the controller's determination that an adequate radar return is being received from the aircraft being controlled. Charts depicting minimum vectoring altitudes are normally available only to the controllers and not to pilots. (Refer to AIM).

minutes in trail. A specified interval between aircraft expressed in time. This method would more likely be utilized regardless of altitude.

MIS. (*See* meteorological impact statement).

missed approach.

1. A maneuver conducted by a pilot when an instrument approach cannot be completed to a landing. The route of flight and altitude are shown on instrument approach procedure charts. A pilot executing a missed approach prior to the Missed Approach Point (MAP) must continue along the final approach to the MAP. The pilot may climb immediately to the altitude specified in the missed approach procedure.

2. A term used by the pilot to inform ATC that he is executing the missed approach.

3. At locations where ATC radar service is provided, the pilot should conform to radar vectors when provided by ATC in lieu of the published missed approach procedure. (*See* missed approach point) (Refer to AIM).

missed approach point (MAP). A point prescribed in each instrument approach procedure at which a missed approach procedure shall be executed if the required visual reference does not exist. (*See* missed approach, segments of an instrument approach procedure).

missed approach procedure. [ICAO] The procedure to be followed if the approach cannot be continued.

missed approach segment. (*See* segments of an instrument approach procedure).

MLDI. (*See* meter list display interval).

MLS. (*See* Microwave Landing System).

MLS categories.

1. *MLS Category I.* An MLS approach procedure which provides for an approach to a height above touchdown of not less than 200 feet and a runway visual range of not less than 1,800 feet.

2. *MLS Category II.* Undefined until data gathering/analysis completion.

3. *MLS Category III.* Undefined until data gathering/analysis completion.

MM. (*See* middle marker).

MNPS. (*See* Minimum Navigation Performance Specification).

MNPSA. (*See* Minimum Navigation Performance Specifications airspace).

MOA. (*See* Military Operations Area).

MOCA. (*See* minimum obstruction clearance altitude).

mode. The letter or number assigned to a specific pulse spacing of radio signals transmitted or received by ground interrogator or airborne transponder components of the Air Traffic Control Radar Beacon System (ATCRBS). Mode A (military Mode 3) and Mode C (altitude reporting) are used in air traffic control. (*See* transponder, interrogator, radar) (Refer to AIM) (*See* mode [ICAO]).

*Mode A. The "location only" mode of a transponder.

*Mode C. The "ALT" position on the transponder function switch. If an encoding altimeter is installed, Mode C will transmit your altitude to the ground radar facility.

mode (SSR Mode). [ICAO] The letter or number assigned to a specific pulse spacing of the interrogation signals transmitted by an interrogator. There are 4 modes, A, B, C and D specified in Annex 10, corresponding to four different interrogation pulse spacings.

Mode C intruder alert. A function of certain air traffic control automated systems designed to alert radar controllers to existing or pending situations between a tracked target (known IFR or VFR aircraft) and an untracked target (unknown IFR or VFR aircraft) that requires immediate attention/action. (*See* conflict alert).

moment. The product of a distance multiplied by a weight; used in loading calculations.

monitor. (When used with communication transfer) listen on a specific frequency and stand by for instructions. Under normal circumstances do not establish communications.

monitor alert (MA). A function of the ETMS that provides traffic management personnel with a tool for predicting potential capacity problems in individual operational sectors. The MA is an indication that traffic management personnel need to analyze a particular sector for actual activity and to determine the required action(s), if any, needed to control the demand.

monitor alert parameter (MAP). The number designated for use in monitor alert processing by the ETMS. The MAP is designated for each operational sector for increments of 15 minutes.

movement area. The runways, taxiways, and other areas an of airport/heliport which are utilized for taxiing/hover taxiing, air taxiing, takeoff, and landing of aircraft, exclusive of loading ramps and parking areas. At those airport/heliports with a tower, specific approval for entry onto the movement area must be obtained from ATC. [ICAO] That part of an aerodrome to be used for the takeoff, landing and taxiing of aircraft, consisting of the maneuvering area and the apron(s).

moving target indicator (MTI). An electronic device which will permit radar scope presentation only from targets which are in motion. A partial remedy for ground clutter.

MRA. (*See* minimum reception altitude).

MSA. (*See* minimum safe altitude).

MSAW. (*See* minimum safe altitude warning).

MTI. (*See* moving target indicator).

MTR. (*See* military training routes).

MULTICOM. A mobile service not open to public correspondence used to provide communications essential to conduct the activities being performed by or directed from private aircraft.

multiple runways. The utilization of a dedicated arrival runway(s) for departures and a dedicated departure runway(s) for arrivals when feasible to reduce delays and enhance capacity.

MVA. (*See* minimum vectoring altitude).

NAS. (*See* National Airspace System).

NAS Stage A. The enroute ATC system's radar, computers and computer programs, controller plan view displays (PVDs/Radar Scopes), input/output devices, and the related communications equipment which are integrated to form the heart of the automated IFR air traffic control system. This equipment performs Flight Data Processing (FDP) and Radar Data Processing (RDP). It interfaces with automated terminal systems and is used in the control of enroute IFR aircraft. (Refer to AIM).

National Airspace System (NAS). The common network of U.S. airspace; air navigation facilities, equipment and services, airports or landing areas; aeronautical charts, information and services; rules, regulations and procedures, technical information, and manpower and material. Included are system components shared jointly with the military.

National Beacon Code Allocation Plan airspace. Airspace over United States territory located within the North American continent between Canada and Mexico, including adjacent territorial waters outward to about boundaries of oceanic control areas (CTA)/Flight Information Regions (FIR). (*See* flight information region).

National Flight Data Center (NFDC). A facility in Washington D.C., established by FAA to operate a central aeronautical information service for the collection, validation, and dissemination of aeronautical data in support of the activities of government, industry, and the aviation community. The information is published in the National Flight Data Digest. (*See* National Flight Data Digest).

National Flight Data Digest (NFDD). A daily (except weekends and Federal holidays) publication of flight information appropriate to aeronautical charts, aeronautical publications, Notices to Airmen, or other media serving the purpose of providing operational flight data essential to safe and efficient aircraft operations.

National Route Program (NRP). The NRP is a set of rules and procedures which are designed to increase the flexibility of user flight planning within published guidelines.

National Search and Rescue Plan. An interagency agreement which provides for the effective utilization of all available facilities in all types of search and rescue missions.

nautical mile. One minute of latitude; 6,080 feet (rounded off to 6,000 feet for convenience).

NAVAID. (*See* navigational aid).

NAVAID classes. VOR, VORTAC, AND TACAN aids are classed according to their operational use. The three classes of NAVAIDs are:

    T — Terminal.

    L — Low altitude.

    H — High altitude.

    The normal service range for T, L, and H class aids is found in the FAAAIMTOC. Certain operational requirements make it necessary to use some of these aids at greater service ranges than specified. Extended range is made possible through flight inspection determinations. Some aids also have lesser service range due to location, terrain, frequency protection, etc. Restrictions to service range are listed in Airport/Facility Directory.

navigable airspace. Airspace at and above the minimum flight altitudes prescribed in the FARs including airspace needed for safe takeoff and landing. (Refer to 14 CFR Part 91).

navigational aid (NAVAID). Any visual or electronic device airborne or on the surface which provides point-to-point guidance information or position data to aircraft in flight. (*See* air navigation facility).

NBCAP airspace. (*See* National Beacon Code Allocation Plan airspace).

NDB. (*See* nondirectional beacon).

*__NDB.__ Nondirectional beacon — used for navigation with an automatic direction finder.

negative. "No," or "permission not granted," or "that is not correct."

negative contact. Used by pilots to inform ATC that:

1. Previously issued traffic is not in sight. It may be followed by the pilot's request for the controller to provide assistance in avoiding the traffic.
2. They were unable to contact ATC on a particular frequency.

NFDC. (*See* National Flight Data Center).

NFDD. (*See* National Flight Data Digest).

night. The time between the end of evening civil twilight and the beginning of morning civil twilight, as published in the American Air Almanac, converted to local time. [ICAO] The hours between the end of evening civil twilight and the beginning of morning civil twilight or such other period between sunset and sunrise as may be specified by the appropriate authority. *Note:* Civil twilight ends in the evening when the center of the sun's disk is 6 degrees below the horizon and begins in the morning when the center of the sun's disk is 6 degrees below the horizon.

no gyro approach. A radar approach/vector provided in case of a malfunctioning gyro compass or directional gyro. Instead of providing the pilot with headings to be flown, the controller observes the radar track and issues control instructions "turn right/left" or "stop turn" as appropriate. (Refer to AIM).

no gyro vector. (*See* no gyro approach).

no transgression zone (NTZ). The NTZ is a 2,000-foot-wide zone, located equidistant between parallel runway final approach courses in which flight is not allowed.

nonapproach control tower. Authorizes aircraft to land or takeoff at the airport controlled by the tower or to transit the Class D airspace. The primary function of a nonapproach control tower is the sequencing of aircraft in the traffic pattern and on the landing area. Nonapproach control towers also separate aircraft operating under instrument flight rules clearances from approach controls and centers. They provide ground control services to aircraft, vehicles, personnel and equipment on the airport movement area.

noncommon route/portion. That segment of a North American Route between the inland navigation facility and a designated North American terminal.

noncomposite separation. Separation in accordance with minima other than the composite separation minimum specified for the area concerned.

nondirectional beacon (NDB). An L/MF or UHF radio beacon transmitting nondirectional signals whereby the pilot of an aircraft equipped with direction finding equipment can determine his bearing to or from the radio beacon and "home" on or track to or from the station. When the radio beacon is installed in conjunction with the Instrument Landing System marker, it is normally called a Compass Locator. (*See* compass locator, automatic direction finder).

nonmovement areas. Taxiways and apron (ramp) areas not under the control of air traffic.

nonprecision approach. (*See* nonprecision approach procedure).

nonprecision approach procedure. A standard instrument approach procedure in which no electronic glide slope is provided; e.g., VOR, TACAN, NDB, LOC, ASR, LDA, or SDF approaches.

nonradar. Precedes other terms and generally means without the use of radar, such as:

1. *Nonradar approach.* Used to describe instrument approaches for which course guidance on final approach is not provided by ground based precision or surveillance radar. Radar vectors to the final approach course may or may not be provided by ATC. Examples of nonradar approaches are VOR, NDB, TACAN, and ILS/MLS approaches. (*See* final approach, IFR, final approach course, radar approach, instrument approach procedure).
2. *Nonradar Approach Control.* An ATC facility providing approach control service without the use of radar. (*See* approach control facility, approach control service).
3. *Nonradar arrival.* An aircraft arriving at an airport without radar service or at an airport served by a radar facility and radar contact has not been established or has been terminated due to a lack of radar service to the airport. (*See* radar arrival, radar service).
4. *Nonradar route.* A flight path or route over which the pilot is performing his own navigation. The pilot may be receiving radar separation, radar monitoring, or other ATC services while on a nonradar route. (*See* radar route).
5. *Nonradar separation.* The spacing of aircraft in accordance with established minima without the use of radar; e.g., vertical, lateral, or longitudinal separation. (*See* radar separation) (*See* nonradar separation [ICAO]).

nonradar separation. [ICAO] The separation used when aircraft position information is derived from sources other than radar.

NOPAC. (*See* North Pacific).

NORDO. (*See* lost communications).

normal operating zone (NOZ). The NOZ is the operating zone within which aircraft flight remains during normal independent simultaneous parallel ILS approaches.

North American route. A numerically coded route preplanned over existing airway and route systems to and from specific coastal fixes serving the North Atlantic. North American Routes consist of the following:

1. *Common route/portion.* That segment of a North American Route between the inland navigation facility and the coastal fix.

2. *Noncommon route/portion.* That segment of a North American Route between the inland navigation facility and a designated North American terminal.

3. *Inland Navigation Facility.* A navigation aid on a North American Route at which the common route and/or the noncommon route begins or ends.

4. *Coastal fix.* A navigation aid or intersection where an aircraft transitions between the domestic route structure and oceanic route structure.

North Mark. A beacon data block sent by the host computer to be displayed by the ARTS on a 360 degree bearing at a locally selected radar azimuth and distance. The North Mark is used to ensure correct range/azimuth orientation during periods of CENRAP.

North Pacific (NOPAC). An organized route system between the Alaskan west coast and Japan.

northerly turning error. An error in the magnetic compass induced by the vertical component of the earth's magnetic field.

NOTAM. (*See* Notice To Airmen).

Notice To Airmen (NOTAM). A notice containing information (not known sufficiently in advance to publicize by other means) concerning the establishment, condition, or change in any component (facility, service, or procedure of, or hazard in the National Airspace System) the timely knowledge of which is essential to personnel concerned with flight operations.

1. *NOTAM(D).* A NOTAM given (in addition to local dissemination) distant dissemination beyond the area of responsibility of the Flight Service Station. These NOTAMs will be stored and available until canceled.

2. *NOTAM(L).* A NOTAM given local dissemination by voice and other means, such as telautograph and telephone, to satisfy local user requirements.

3. *FDC NOTAM.* A NOTAM regulatory in nature, transmitted by USNOF and given system wide dissemination. (*See* NOTAM [ICAO]).

NOTAM. [ICAO] A notice containing information concerning the establishment, condition or change in any aeronautical facility, service procedure or hazard, the timely knowledge of which is essential to personnel concerned with flight operations.

Class I Distribution. Distribution by means of telecommunication.

Class II Distribution. Distribution by means other than telecommunications.

Notices To Airmen Publication. A publication issued every 28 days, designed primarily for the pilot, which contains current NOTAM information considered essential to the safety of flight as well as supplemental data to other aeronautical publications. The contraction NTAP is used in NOTAM text. (*See* Notice To Airmen).

NTAP. (*See* Notices To Airmen Publication).

***NTSB.** National Transportation Safety Board.

Numerous targets vicinity (location). A traffic advisory issued by ATC to advise pilots that targets on the radar scope are too numerous to issue individually. (*See* Traffic Advisories).

***NWS.** National Weather Service, the source of all government weather information.

***OBS.** Omni-bearing selector — used in VOR navigation to select radials.

obstacle. An existing object, object of natural growth, or terrain at a fixed geographical location or which may be expected at a fixed location within a prescribed area with reference to which vertical clearance is or must be provided during flight operation.

obstacle free zone (OFZ). The OFZ is a three dimensional volume of airspace which protects for the transition of aircraft to and from the runway. The OFZ clearing standard precludes taxiing and parked airplanes and object penetrations, except for frangible NAVAID locations that are fixed by function. Additionally, vehicles, equipment, and personnel may be authorized by air traffic control to enter the area using the provisions of FAAO 7110.65, Para. 3-1-5, VEHICLES/EQUIPMENT/PERSONNEL ON RUNWAYS. The runway OFZ and when applicable, the inner-approach OFZ, and the inner-transitional OFZ, comprise the OFZ.

1. *Runway OFZ.* The runway OFZ is a defined volume of airspace centered above the runway. The runway OFZ is the airspace above a surface whose elevation at any point is the same as the elevation of the nearest point on the runway centerline. The runway OFZ extends 200 feet beyond each end of the runway. The width is as follows:

   a. For runways serving large airplanes, the greater of:

      (1) 400 feet, or

      (2) 180 feet, plus the wingspan of the most demanding airplane, plus 20 feet per 1,000 feet of airport elevation.

   b. For runways serving only small airplanes:

      (1) 300 feet for precision instrument runways.

(2) 250 feet for other runways serving small airplanes with approach speeds of 50 knots, or more.

(3) 120 feet for other runways serving small airplanes with approach speeds of less than 50 knots.

2. *Inner-approach OFZ*. The inner-approach OFZ is a defined volume of airspace centered on the approach area. The inner-approach OFZ applies only to runways with an approach lighting system. The inner-approach OFZ begins 200 feet from the runway threshold at the same elevation as the runway threshold and extends 200 feet beyond the last light unit in the approach lighting system. The width of the inner-approach OFZ is the same as the runway OFZ and rises at a slope of 50 (horizontal) to 1 (vertical) from the beginning.

3. *Inner-transitional OFZ*. The inner transitional surface OFZ is a defined volume of airspace along the sides of the runway and inner-approach OFZ and applies only to precision instrument runways. The inner-transitional surface OFZ slopes 3 (horizontal) to 1 (vertical) out from the edges of the runway OFZ and inner-approach OFZ to a height of 150 feet above the established airport elevation.

(Refer to AC 150/5300-13, Chap. 3 and FAAO 7110.65, Para. 3-1-5, VEHICLES/EQUIPMENT/PERSONNEL ON RUNWAYS).

obstruction. Any object/obstacle exceeding the obstruction standards specified by 14 CFR Part 77, Subpart C.

obstruction light. A light or one of a group of lights, usually red or white, frequently mounted on a surface structure or natural terrain to warn pilots of the presence of an obstruction.

*occlusion. A type of weather front formed when a cold front overtakes a warm front.

oceanic airspace. Airspace over the oceans of the world, considered international airspace, where oceanic separation and procedures per the International Civil Aviation Organization are applied. Responsibility for the provisions of air traffic control service in this airspace is delegated to various countries, based generally upon geographic proximity and the availability of the required resources.

Oceanic Display And Planning System (ODAPS). An automated digital display system which provides flight data processing, conflict probe, and situation display for oceanic air traffic control.

oceanic navigational error report (ONER). A report filed when an aircraft exiting oceanic airspace has been observed by radar to be off course. ONER reporting parameters and procedures are contained on Order 7110.82, Monitoring of Navigational Performance In Oceanic Areas.

Oceanic Published Route. A route established in international airspace and charted or described in flight information publications, such as route charts, DOD Enroute Charts, chart supplements, NOTAMs and track messages.

oceanic transition route (OTR). An ATS Route established for the purpose of transitioning aircraft to/from an organized track system.

ODAPS. (*See* Oceanic Display and Planning System).

off course. A term used to describe a situation where an aircraft has reported a position fix or is observed on radar at a point not on the ATC approved route of flight.

offshore control airspace area. That portion of airspace between the U.S. 12 NM limit and the oceanic CTA/FIR boundary within which air traffic control is exercised. These areas are established to provide air traffic control services. Offshore/Control Airspace Areas may be classified as either Class A airspace or Class E airspace.

off route vector. A vector by ATC which takes an aircraft off a previously assigned route. Altitudes assigned by ATC during such vectors provide required obstacle clearance.

offset parallel runways. Staggered runways having centerlines which are parallel.

OFT. (*See* outer fix time).

OFZ. (*See* obstacle free zone).

OM. (*See* outer marker).

Omega. An RNAV system designed for long range navigation based upon ground based electronic navigational aid signals.

*omnidirectional. Visible or usable in all directions.

one-minute weather. The most recent one minute updated weather broadcast received by a pilot from an uncontrolled airport ASOS/AWOS.

ONER. (*See* oceanic navigational error report).

operational. (*See* due regard).

on course.

1. Used to indicate that an aircraft is established on the route centerline.

2. Used by ATC to advise a pilot making a radar approach that his aircraft is lined up on the final approach course.
   (*See* on course indication).

on course indication. An indication on an instrument, which provides the pilot a visual means of determining that the aircraft is located on the centerline of a given navigational track, or an indication on a radar scope that an aircraft is on a given track.

opposite direction aircraft. Aircraft are operating in opposite directions when:

1. They are following the same track in reciprocal directions; or

2. Their tracks are parallel and the aircraft are flying in reciprocal directions; or

3. Their tracks intersect at an angle of more than 135 degrees.

option approach. An approach requested and conducted by a pilot which will result in either a touch and go, missed approach, low approach, stop and go, or full stop landing. (*See* cleared for the option) (Refer to AIM).

organized track system (OTS). A moveable system of oceanic tracks that traverses the North Atlantic between Europe and North America the physical position of which is determined twice daily taking the best advantage of the winds aloft. *Also:* A series of ATS routes which are fixed and charted; i.e., CEP, NOPAC, or flexible and described by NOTAM; i.e., NAT track message.

OROCA. An off-route altitude which provides obstruction clearance with a 1,000-foot buffer in nonmountainous terrain areas and a 2,000 foot buffer in designated mountainous areas within the United States. This altitude may not provide signal coverage from ground-based navigational aids, air traffic control radar, or communications coverage.

*orographic. Induced by the presence of mountains.

OTR. (*See* oceanic transition route).

OTS. (*See* organized track system).

out. The conversation is ended and no response is expected.

outer area (associated with Class C airspace). Non-regulatory airspace surrounding designated Class C airspace airports wherein ATC provides radar vectoring and sequencing on a full-time basis for all IFR and participating VFR aircraft. The service provided in the outer area is called Class C service which includes: IFR/IFR. standard IFR separation; IFR/VFR. traffic advisories and conflict resolution; and VFR/VFR. traffic advisories and, as appropriate, safety alerts. The normal radius will be 20 nautical miles with some variations based on site specific requirements. The outer area extends outward from the primary Class C airspace airport and extends from the lower limits of radar/radio coverage up to the ceiling of the approach control's delegated airspace excluding the Class C charted area and other airspace as appropriate. (*See* controlled airspace, conflict resolution).

outer compass locator. (*See* compass locator).

outer fix. A general term used within ATC to describe fixes in the terminal area, other than the final approach fix. Aircraft are normally cleared to these fixes by an Air Route Traffic Control Center or an Approach Control Facility. Aircraft are normally cleared from these fixes to the final approach fix or final approach course. *Also:* An adapted fix along the converted route of flight, prior to the meter fix, for which crossing times are calculated and displayed in the metering position list.

outer fix time (OFT). A calculated time to depart the outer fix in order to cross the vertex at the ACLT. The time reflects descent speed adjustments and any applicable delay time that must be absorbed prior to crossing the meter fix.

outer marker (OM). A marker beacon at or near the glideslope intercept altitude of an ILS approach. It is keyed to transmit two dashes per second on a 400 Hz tone, which is received aurally and visually by compatible airborne equipment. The OM is normally located four to seven miles from the runway threshold on the extended centerline of the runway. (*See* marker beacon, instrument landing system) (Refer to AIM).

over. My transmission is ended; I expect a response.

overhead maneuver. A series of predetermined maneuvers prescribed for aircraft (often in formation) for entry into the visual flight rules (VFR) traffic pattern and to proceed to a landing. An overhead maneuver is not an instrument flight rules (IFR) approach procedure. An aircraft executing an overhead maneuver is considered VFR and the IFR flight plan is canceled when the aircraft reaches the "initial point" on the initial approach portion of the maneuver. The pattern usually specifies the following:

1. The radio contact required of the pilot.
2. The speed to be maintained.
3. An initial approach 3 to 5 miles in length.
4. An elliptical pattern consisting of two 180 degree turns.
5. A break point at which the first 180 degree turn is started.
6. The direction of turns.
7. Altitude (at least 500 feet above the conventional pattern).
8. A "Roll-out" on final approach not less than 1/4 mile from the landing threshold and not less than 300 feet above the ground.

overlying center. The ARTCC facility that is responsible for arrival/departure operations at a specific terminal.

*overrun. A stabilized area of pavement not used for normal operations at the end of a runway.

*P-factor. A force which causes a left-turning tendency at low speed and high power in airplanes with propellers that turn clockwise.

P time. (*See* proposed departure time).

pan-pan. The international radio telephony urgency signal. When repeated three times, indicates uncertainty or alert followed by the nature of the urgency. (*See* mayday) (Refer to AIM).

PAR. (*See* precision approach radar).

parallel ILS approaches. Approaches to parallel runways by IFR aircraft which, when established inbound toward the airport on the adjacent final approach courses, are radar separated by at least 2 miles. (*See* final approach course, simultaneous ILS approaches).

parallel MLS approaches. (*See* parallel ILS approaches).

parallel offset route. A parallel track to the left or right of the designated or established airway/route. Normally associated with Area Navigation (RNAV) operations. (*See* area navigation).

parallel runways. Two or more runways at the same airport whose centerlines are parallel. In addition to runway number, parallel runways are designated as L (left) and R (right) or, if three parallel runways exist, L (left), C (center), or R (right).

*parallels. Lines of latitude, which are parallel from the equator to the poles.

*parasite drag. Drag that does not contribute to lift generation; drag caused by landing gear struts, cooling intakes, antennas, rivet heads, etc.

PATWAS. (*See* Pilots Automatic Telephone Weather Answering Service).

PBCT. (*See* proposed boundary crossing time).

permanent echo. Radar signals reflected from fixed objects on the earth's surface; e.g., buildings, towers, terrain. Permanent echoes are distinguished from "ground clutter" by being definable locations rather than large areas. Under certain conditions they may be used to check radar alignment.

photo reconnaissance (PR). Military activity that requires locating individual photo targets and navigating to the targets at a preplanned angle and altitude. The activity normally requires a lateral route width of 16 NM and altitude range of 1,500 feet to 10,000 feet AGL.

PIDP. (*See* programmable indicator data processor).

*****pilotage.** Navigation from point to point by ground reference.

pilot briefing. A service provided by the FSS to assist pilots in flight planning. Briefing items may include weather information, NOTAMs, military activities, flow control information, and other items as requested. (Refer to AIM).

pilot in command. The pilot responsible for the operation and safety of an aircraft during flight time. (Refer to 14 CFR Part 91).

Pilots Automatic Telephone Weather Answering Service (PATWAS). A continuous telephone recording containing current and forecast weather information for the pilots. (*See* Flight Service Station) (Refer to AIM).

pilot's discretion. When used in conjunction with altitude assignments, means that ATC has offered the pilot the option of starting climb or descent whenever he wishes and conducting the climb or descent at any rate he wishes. He may temporarily level off at any intermediate altitude. However, once he has vacated an altitude, he may not return to that altitude.

pilot weather report (PIREP). A report of meteorological phenomena encountered by aircraft in flight. (Refer to AIM).

PIREP. (*See* pilot weather report).

*****PIREPs.** Pilot reports of inflight weather.

*****pitch axis.** An imaginary line drawn from wing tip to wing tip; also called lateral axis.

*****pitot-static system.** A pressure-measuring system that provides input to the airspeed indicator, altimeter, and vertical speed indicator.

*****pitot tube.** A forward-facing tube or aperture that measures ram air pressure, then delivers that pressure to the airspeed indicator.

point out. (*See* radar point out).

polar track structure (PTS). A system of organized routes between Iceland and Alaska which overlie Canadian MNPS Airspace.

*****position lights.** The red, green, and white lights required for night flight.

position report. A report over a known location as transmitted by an aircraft to ATC. (Refer to AIM).

position symbol. A computer generated indication shown on a radar display to indicate the mode of tracking.

practice instrument approach. An instrument approach procedure conducted by a VFR or an IFR aircraft for the purpose of pilot training or proficiency demonstrations.

prearranged coordination. A standardized procedure which permits an air traffic controller to enter the airspace assigned to another air traffic controller without verbal coordination. The procedures are defined in a facility directive which ensures standard separation between aircraft.

precipitation. Any or all forms of water particles (rain, sleet, hail, or snow) that fall from the atmosphere and reach the surface.

precision approach. (*See* precision approach procedure).

precision approach procedure. A standard instrument approach procedure in which an electronic glide slope/glide path is provided; e.g., ILS/MLS and PAR. (*See* instrument landing system, Microwave Landing System, precision approach radar).

precision approach radar (PAR). Radar equipment in some ATC facilities operated by the FAA and/or the military services at joint use civil/military locations and separate military installations to detect and display azimuth, elevations, and range of aircraft on the final approach course to a runway. This equipment may be used to monitor certain nonradar approaches, but is primarily used to conduct a precision instrument approach (PAR) wherein the controller issues guidance instructions to the pilot based on the aircraft's position in relation to the final approach course (azimuth), the glide path (elevation), and the distance (range) from the touchdown point on the runway as displayed on the radar scope. (*See* glide path, PAR) (Refer to AIM).

The abbreviation "PAR" is also used to denote preferential arrival routes in ARTCC computers. (*See* preferential routes). [ICAO] Primary radar equipment used to determine the position of an aircraft during final approach, in terms of lateral and vertical deviations relative to a nominal approach path, and in range relative to touchdown. *Note:* Precision approach radars are designed to enable pilots of aircraft to be given guidance by radio communications during the final stages of the approach to land.

precision runway monitor (PRM). Provides air traffic controllers with high precision secondary surveillance data for aircraft on final approach to parallel runways that have centerlines separated by less than 4,300 feet. High resolution color monitoring displays (FMA) are required to present surveillance track data to controllers along with detailed maps depicting approaches and no transgression zone.

preferential routes. Preferential routes (PDRs, PARs, and PDARs) are adapted in ARTCC computers to accomplish inter/intrafacility controller coordination and to assure that flight data is posted at the proper control positions. Locations having a need for these specific inbound and out bound routes normally publish such routes in local facility bulletins, and their use by pilots minimizes flight plan route amendments. When the workload or traffic situation permits, controllers normally provide radar vectors or assign requested routes to minimize circuitous routing. Preferential routes are usually confined to one ARTCC's area and are referred to by the following names or acronyms:

1. *Preferential departure route (PDR).* A specific departure route from an airport or terminal area to an enroute point where there is no further need for flow control. It may be included in a standard instrument departure (DP) or preferred IFR route.

2. *Preferential arrival route (PAR).* A specific arrival route from an appropriate enroute point to an airport or terminal area. It may be included in a standard terminal arrival (STAR) or preferred IFR route. The abbreviation "PAR" is used primarily within the ARTCC and should not be confused with the abbreviation for Precision Approach Radar.

3. *Preferential departure and arrival route (PDAR).* A route between two terminals which are within or immediately adjacent to one ARTCC's area. PDARs are not synonymous with preferred IFR routes but may be listed as such as they do accomplish essentially the same purpose. (*See* preferred IFR routes, NAS Stage A).

preferred IFR routes. Routes established between busier airports to increase system efficiency and capacity. They normally extend through one or more ARTCC areas and are designed to achieve balanced traffic flows among high density terminals. IFR clearances are issued on the basis of these routes except when severe weather avoidance procedures or other factors dictate otherwise. Preferred IFR routes are listed in the Airport/Facility Directory. If a flight is planned to or from an area having such routes but the departure or arrival point is not listed in the Airport/Facility Directory, pilots may use that part of a preferred IFR route which is appropriate for the departure or arrival point that is listed. Preferred IFR routes are correlated with DPs and STARs and may be defined by airways, jet routes, direct routes between NAVAIDs, waypoints, NAVAID radials/DME, or any combinations thereof. (*See* instrument departure procedure, standard terminal arrival, preferential routes, Center's area) (Refer to Airport/Facility Directory and Notices to Airmen Publication).

preflight pilot briefing. (*See* pilot briefing).

prevailing visibility. (*See* visibility).

PRM. (*See* ILS PRM approach and precision runway monitor).

procedure turn (PT). The maneuver prescribed when it is necessary to reverse direction to establish an aircraft on the intermediate approach segment or final approach course. The outbound course, direction of turn, distance within which the turn must be completed, and minimum altitude are specified in the procedure. However, unless otherwise restricted, the point at which the turn may be commenced and the type and rate of turn are left to the discretion of the pilot. [ICAO] A maneuver in which a turn is made away from a designated track followed by a turn in the opposite direction to permit the aircraft to intercept and proceed along the reciprocal of the designated track. *Note 1:* Procedure turns are designated "left" or "right" according to the direction of the initial turn. *Note 2:* Procedure turns may be designated as being made either in level flight or while descending, according to the circumstances of each individual approach procedure.

procedure turn inbound. That point of a procedure turn maneuver where course reversal has been completed and an aircraft is established inbound on the intermediate approach segment or final approach course. A report of "procedure turn inbound" is normally used by ATC as a position report for separation purposes. (*See* final approach course, procedure turn, segments of an instrument approach procedure).

profile descent. An uninterrupted descent (except where level flight is required for speed adjustment; e.g., 250 knots at 10,000 feet MSL) from cruising altitude/level to interception of a glideslope or to a minimum altitude specified for the initial or intermediate approach segment of a nonprecision instrument approach. The profile descent normally terminates at the approach gate or where the glideslope or other appropriate minimum altitude is intercepted.

programmable indicator data processor (PIDP). The PIDP is a modification to the AN/TPX-42 interrogator system currently installed in fixed RAPCONs. The PIDP detects, tracks, and predicts secondary radar aircraft targets. These are displayed by means of computer generated symbols and alphanumeric characters depicting flight identification, aircraft altitude, ground speed, and flight plan data. Although primary radar targets are not tracked, they are displayed coincident with the secondary radar targets as well as with the other symbols and alphanumerics. The system has the capability of interfacing with ARTCCs.

progress report. (*See* position report).

progressive taxi. Precise taxi instructions given to a pilot unfamiliar with the airport or issued in stages as the aircraft proceeds along the taxi route.

Prohibited Area. (*See* Special Use airspace). [ICAO] An airspace of defined dimensions, above the land areas or territorial waters of a State, within which the flight of aircraft is prohibited.

proposed boundary crossing time (PBCT). Each center has a PBCT parameter for each internal airport. Proposed internal flight plans are transmitted to the adjacent center if the flight time along the proposed route from the departure airport to the center boundary is less than or equal to the value of PBCT or if airport adaptation specifies transmission regardless of PBCT.

proposed departure time (P time). The time a scheduled flight will depart the gate (scheduled operators) or the actual runway off time for nonscheduled operators. For EDCT purposes, the ATCSCC adjusts the "P" time for scheduled operators to reflect the runway off times.

protected airspace. The airspace on either side of an oceanic route/track that is equal to one-half the lateral separation minimum except where reduction of protected airspace has been authorized.

PT. (*See* procedure turn).

PTS. (*See* polar track structure).

published route. A route for which an IFR altitude has been established and published; e.g., Federal Airways, Jet Routes, Area Navigation Routes, Specified Direct Routes.

queuing. (*See* staging/queuing).

QNE. The barometric pressure used for the standard altimeter setting (29.92 inches Hg).

QNH. The barometric pressure as reported by a particular station.

quadrant. A quarter part of a circle, centered on a NAVAID, oriented clockwise from magnetic north as follows: NE quadrant 000 to 089, SE quadrant 090 to 179, SW quadrant 180 to 269, NW quadrant 270 to 359.

quick look. A feature of NAS Stage A and ARTS which provides the controller the capability to display full data blocks of tracked aircraft from other control positions.

quota flow control (QFLOW). A flow control procedure by which the Central Flow Control Function (CFCF) restricts traffic to the ARTC Center area having an impacted airport, thereby avoiding sector/area saturation. (*See* Air Traffic Control System Command Center) (Refer to Airport/Facility Directory).

radar. A device which, by measuring the time interval between transmission and reception of radio pulses and correlating the angular orientation of the radiated antenna beam or beams in azimuth and/or elevation, provides information on range, azimuth, and/or elevation of objects in the path of the transmitted pulses.

1. *Primary Radar.* A radar system in which in a minute portion of a radio pulse transmitted from a site is reflected by an object and then received back at that site for processing and display at an air traffic control facility.

2. *Secondary Radar/Radar Beacon (ATCRBS).* A radar system in which the object to be detected is fitted with cooperative equipment in the form of a radio receiver/transmitter (transponder). Radar pulses transmitted from the searching transmitter/receiver (interrogator) site are received in the cooperative equipment and used to trigger a distinctive transmission from the transponder. This reply transmission rather than a reflected signal, is then received back at the transmitter/receiver site for processing and display at an air traffic control facility. (*See* transponder, interrogator) (Refer to AIM). [ICAO] A

radio detection device which provides information on range, azimuth and/or elevation objects.

Primary Radar. [ICAO] A radar system which uses reflected radio signals.

Secondary Radar. [ICAO] A radar system wherein a radio signal transmitted from a radar station initiates the transmission of a radio signal from another station.

radar advisory. The provision of advice and information based on radar observations. (*See* advisory service).

radar altimeter. (*See* radio altimeter).

radar approach. An instrument approach procedure which utilizes Precision Approach Radar (PAR) or Airport Surveillance Radar (ASR). (*See* surveillance approach, airport surveillance radar, precision approach radar, instrument approach procedure) (Refer to AIM). [ICAO] An approach, executed by an aircraft, under the direction of a radar controller.

radar approach control facility. A terminal ATC facility that uses radar and nonradar capabilities to provide approach control services to aircraft arriving, departing, or transiting airspace controlled by the facility. (*See* Approach Control Service).

Provides radar ATC services to aircraft operating in the vicinity of one or more civil and/or military airports in a terminal area. The facility may provide services of a ground controlled approach (GCA); i.e., ASR and PAR approaches. A radar approach control facility may be operated by FAA, USAF, US Army, USN, USMC, or jointly by FAA and a military service. Specific facility nomenclatures are used for administrative purposes only and are related to the physical location of the facility and the operating service generally as follows:

Army Radar Approach Control (ARAC) (Army).

Radar Air Traffic Control Facility (RATCF) (Navy/FAA).

Radar Approach Control (RAPCON) (Air Force/FAA).

Terminal Radar Approach Control (TRACON) (FAA).

Tower/Airport Traffic Control Tower (ATCT) (FAA). (Only those towers delegated approach control authority.).

radar arrival. An aircraft arriving at an airport served by a radar facility and in radar contact with the facility. (*See* nonradar).

radar beacon. (*See* radar).

radar clutter. [ICAO] The visual indication on a radar display of unwanted signals.

radar contact.

1. Used by ATC to inform an aircraft that it is identified on the radar display and radar flight following will be provided until radar identification is terminated. Radar service may also be provided within the limits of necessity and capability. When a pilot is informed of "radar contact," he automatically discontinues reporting over compulsory reporting points. (*See* radar flight following, radar

Continued

contact lost, radar service, radar service terminated) (Refer to AIM).

2. The term used to inform the controller that the aircraft is identified and approval is granted for the aircraft to enter the receiving controllers airspace.

[ICAO] The situation which exists when the radar blip or radar position symbols of a particular aircraft is seen and identified on a radar display.

Radar contact lost. Used by ATC to inform a pilot that radar data used to determine the aircraft's position is no longer being received, or is no longer reliable and radar service is no longer being provided. The loss may be attributed to several factors including the aircraft merging with weather or ground clutter, the aircraft operating below radar line of sight coverage, the aircraft entering an area of poor radar return, failure of the aircraft transponder, or failure of the ground radar equipment. (*See* clutter, radar contact).

radar environment. An area in which radar service may be provided. (*See* radar contact, radar service, additional services, traffic advisories).

radar flight following. The observation of the progress of radar identified aircraft, whose primary navigation is being provided by the pilot, wherein the controller retains and correlates the aircraft identity with the appropriate target or target symbol, displayed on the radar scope. (*See* radar contact, radar service) (Refer to AIM).

radar identification. The process of ascertaining that an observed radar target is the radar return from a particular aircraft. (*See* radar contact, radar service). [ICAO] The process of correlating a particular radar blip or radar position symbol with a specific aircraft.

radar identified aircraft. An aircraft, the position of which has been correlated with an observed target or symbol on the radar display. (*See* radar contact, radar contact lost).

radar monitoring. (*See* radar service).

radar navigational guidance. (*See* radar service).

radar point out. An action taken by a controller to transfer the radar identification of an aircraft to another controller if the aircraft will or may enter the airspace or protected airspace of another controller and radio communications will not be transferred.

radar required. A term displayed on charts and approach plates and included in FDC NOTAMs to alert pilots that segments of either an instrument approach procedure or a route are not navigable because of either the absence or unusability of a NAVAID. The pilot can expect to be provided radar navigational guidance while transiting segments labeled with this term. (*See* radar route, radar service).

radar route. A flight path or route over which an aircraft is vectored. Navigational guidance and altitude assignments are provided by ATC. (*See* flight path, route).

radar separation. (*See* radar service).

radar service. A term which encompasses one or more of the following services based on the use of radar which can be provided by a controller to a pilot of a radar identified aircraft.

1. *Radar monitoring.* The radar flight following of aircraft, whose primary navigation is being performed by the pilot, to observe and note deviations from its authorized flight path, airway, or route. When being applied specifically to radar monitoring of instrument approaches; i.e., with precision approach radar (PAR) or radar monitoring of simultaneous ILS/MLS approaches, it includes advice and instructions whenever an aircraft nears or exceeds the prescribed PAR safety limit or simultaneous ILS/MLS no transgression zone. (*See* additional services, traffic advisories).

2. *Radar navigational guidance.* Vectoring aircraft to provide course guidance.

3. *Radar separation.* Radar spacing of aircraft in accordance with established minima.

[ICAO] Term used to indicate a service provided directly by means of radar.

Radar monitoring. [ICAO] The use of radar for the purpose of providing aircraft with information and advice relative to significant deviations from nominal flight path.

Radar separation. [ICAO] The separation used when aircraft position information is derived from radar sources.

Radar service terminated. Used by ATC to inform a pilot that he will no longer be provided any of the services that could be received while in radar contact. Radar service is automatically terminated, and the pilot is not advised in the following cases:

1. An aircraft cancels its IFR flight plan, except within Class B airspace, Class C airspace, a TRSA, or where Basic Radar service is provided.

2. An aircraft conducting an instrument, visual, or contact approach has landed or has been instructed to change to advisory frequency.

3. An arriving VFR aircraft, receiving radar service to a tower controlled airport within Class B airspace, Class C airspace, a TRSA, or where sequencing service is provided, has landed; or to all other airports, is instructed to change to tower or advisory frequency.

4. An aircraft completes a radar approach.

radar surveillance. The radar observation of a given geographical area for the purpose of performing some radar function.

radar traffic advisories. Advisories issued to alert pilots to known or observed radar traffic which may affect the intended route of flight of their aircraft. (*See* traffic advisories).

radar traffic information service. (*See* traffic advisories).

radar vectoring. [ICAO] Provision of navigational guidance to aircraft in the form of specific headings, based on the use of radar.

radar weather echo intensity levels. Existing radar systems cannot detect turbulence. However, there is a direct correlation between the degree of turbulence and other weather features associated with thunderstorms and the radar weather echo intensity. The National Weather Service has categorized radar weather echo intensity for precipitation into six levels. These levels are sometimes expressed during communications as "VIP LEVEL" 1 through 6 (derived from the component of the radar that produces the information—Video Integrator and Processor). The following list gives the "VIP LEVELS" in relation to the precipitation intensity within a thunderstorm:

Level 1.   WEAK
Level 2.   MODERATE
Level 3.   STRONG
Level 4.   VERY STRONG
Level 5.   INTENSE
Level 6.   EXTREME

(*See* AC 00-45, *Aviation Weather Services*).

radial. A magnetic bearing extending from a VOR/VORTAC/TACAN navigation facility.

*radial. A line FROM a VOR station. Radials used as airways are printed in blue on sectional charts.

radio.
1. A device used for communication.
2. Used to refer to a Flight Service Station; e.g., "Seattle Radio" is used to call Seattle FSS.

radio altimeter. Aircraft equipment which makes use of the reflection of radio waves from the ground to determine the height of the aircraft above the surface.

radio beacon. (*See* nondirectional beacon).

radio detection and ranging. (*See* radar).

radio magnetic indicator (RMI). An aircraft navigational instrument coupled with a gyro compass or similar compass that indicates the direction of a selected NAVAID and indicates bearing with respect to the heading of the aircraft.

ramp. (*See* apron).

random altitude. An altitude inappropriate for direction of flight and/or not in accordance with FAA Order 7110.65, paragraph 4-5-1.

random route. Any route not established or charted/published or not otherwise available to all users.

RC. (*See* road reconnaissance).

RCAG. (*See* remote communication air/ground facility).

RCC. (*See* Rescue Coordination Center).

RCO. (*See* Remote Communications Outlet).

RCR. (*See* runway condition reading).

read back. Repeat my message back to me.

receiver autonomous integrity monitoring (RAIM). A technique whereby a civil GNSS receiver/processor determines the integrity of the GNSS navigation signals without reference to sensors or non-DoD integrity systems other than the receiver itself. This determination is achieved by a consistency check among redundant pseudorange measurements.

receiving controller. A controller/facility receiving control of an aircraft from another controller/facility.

receiving facility. (*See* receiving controller).

Reduce speed to (speed). (*See* speed adjustment).

*region of reversed command. That area in the power/airspeed relationship where it takes more power to go more slowly, and less power to increase speed.

REIL (Runway End Identifier Lights). (*See* airport lighting).

*relative bearing. The direction to a transmitting station measured clockwise from the nose of the airplane.

*relative wind. Wind caused by motion. A moving body experiences relative wind in calm air.

release time. A departure time restriction issued to a pilot by ATC (either directly or through an authorized relay) when necessary to separate a departing aircraft from other traffic. [ICAO] Time prior to which an aircraft should be given further clearance or prior to which it should not proceed in case of radio failure.

remote communications air/ground facility (RCAG). An unmanned VHF/UHF transmitter/receiver facility which is used to expand ARTCC air/ground communications coverage and to facilitate direct contact between pilots and controllers. RCAG facilities are sometimes not equipped with emergency frequencies 121.5 MHz and 243.0 MHz. (Refer to AIM).

Remote Communications Outlet (RCO). An unmanned communications facility remotely controlled by air traffic personnel. RCOs serve FSS's. RTRs serve terminal ATC facilities. An RCO or RTR may be UHF or VHF and will extend the communication range of the air traffic facility. There are several classes of RCOs and RTRs. The class is determined by the number of transmitters or receivers. Class A through G are used primarily for air/ground purposes. RCO and RTR class O facilities are nonprotected outlets subject to undetected and prolonged outages. RCO (O's) and RTR (O's) where established for the express purpose of providing ground to ground communications between air traffic control specialists and pilots located at a satellite airport for delivering enroute clearances, issuing departure authorizations, and acknowledging instrument flight rules cancellations or departure/landing times. As a secondary function, they may be used for advisory purposes whenever the aircraft is below the coverage of the primary air/ground frequency.

remote transmitter/receiver (RTR). (*See* Remote Communications Outlet).

report. Used to instruct pilots to advise ATC of specified information; e.g., "Report passing Hamilton VOR."

reporting point. A geographical location in relation to which the position of an aircraft is reported. (*See* compulsory reporting points) (Refer to AIM). [ICAO] A specified geographical location in relation to which the position of an aircraft can be reported.

Request full route clearance. Used by pilots to request that the entire route of flight be read verbatim in an ATC clearance. Such request should be made to preclude receiving an ATC clearance based on the original filed flight plan when a filed IFR flight plan has been revised by the pilot, company, or operations prior to departure.

required navigation performance (RNP). A statement of the navigational performance necessary for operation within a defined airspace. The following terms are commonly associated with RNP:

1. *Required Navigation Performance Level or Type (RNP-X).* A value, in nautical miles (NM), from the intended horizontal position within which an aircraft would be at least 95 percent of the total flying time.
2. *Required Navigation Performance (RNP) Airspace.* A generic term designating airspace, route(s), leg(s), operation(s), or procedure(s) where minimum required navigational performance (RNP) have been established.
3. *Actual Navigation Performance (ANP).* A measure of the current estimated navigational performance. Also referred to as Estimated Position Error (EPE).
4. *Estimated Position Error (EPE).* A measure of the current estimated navigational performance. Also referred to as Actual Navigation Performance (ANP).
5. *Lateral Navigation (LNAV).* A function of area navigation (RNAV) equipment which calculates, displays, and provides lateral guidance to a profile or path.
6. *Vertical Navigation (VNAV).* A function of area navigation (RNAV) equipment which calculates, displays, and provides vertical guidance to a profile or path.

Rescue Coordination Center (RCC). A Search and Rescue (SAR) facility equipped and manned to coordinate and control SAR operations in an area designated by the SAR plan. The U.S. Coast Guard and the U.S. Air Force have responsibility for the operation of RCCs. (*See* Rescue Coordination Centre [ICAO]).

Rescue Coordination Centre. [ICAO] A unit responsible for promoting efficient organization of search and rescue service and for coordinating the conduct of search and rescue operations within a search and rescue region.

resolution advisory. A display indication given to the pilot by the Traffic Alert And Collision Avoidance Systems (TCAS II) recommending a maneuver to increase vertical separation relative to an intruding aircraft. Positive, negative, and vertical speed limit (VSL) advisories constitute the resolution advisories. A resolution advisory is also classified as corrective or preventive.

Restricted Area. (*See* Special Use airspace). [ICAO] An airspace of defined dimensions, above the land areas or territorial waters of a State, within which the flight of aircraft is restricted in accordance with certain specified conditions.

Resume own navigation. Used by ATC to advise a pilot to resume his own navigational responsibility. It is issued after completion of a radar vector or when radar contact is lost while the aircraft is being radar vectored. (*See* radar contact lost, radar service terminated).

Resume normal speed. Used by ATC to advise that previously issued speed control restrictions are deleted. An instruction to "resume normal speed" does not delete speed restrictions that are applicable to published procedures of upcoming segments of flight, unless specifically stated by ATC. This does not relieve the pilot of those speed restrictions which are applicable to 14 CFR §91.117.

*****rich mixture.** A fuel mixture with more than one part of fuel to fifteen of air.

RMI. (*See* radio magnetic indicator).

*****RMI.** Radio magnetic indicator—a combination heading indicator, VOR indicator and ADF indicator.

RNAV. (*See* area navigation).

*****RNAV.** Area navigation. A random-route method of navigation using VORTACs and VOR-DMEs.

RNAV approach. An instrument approach procedure which relies on aircraft area navigation equipment for navigational guidance. (*See* instrument approach procedure, area navigation).

road reconnaissance (RC). Military activity requiring navigation along roads, railroads, and rivers. Reconnaissance route/route segments are seldom along a straight line and normally require a lateral route width of 10 NM to 30 NM and an altitude range of 500 feet to 10,000 feet AGL.

roger. I have received all of your last transmission. It should not be used to answer a question requiring a yes or a no answer. (*See* affirmative, negative).

*****roll axis.** An imaginary line from nose to tail, also called longitudinal axis.

rollout RVR. (*See* visibility).

route. A defined path, consisting of one or more courses in a horizontal plane, which aircraft traverse over the surface of the earth. (*See* airway, jet route, published route, unpublished route).

route segment. As used in Air Traffic Control, a part of a route that can be defined by two navigational fixes, two NAVAIDs or a fix and a NAVAID. (*See* fix, route). [ICAO] A portion of a route to be flown, as defined by two consecutive significant points specified in a flight plan.

RSA. (*See* runway safety area).

RTR. (*See* remote transmitter/receiver).

*****rudder.** A hinged surface at the rear of the vertical fin with which the pilot controls the airplane around the yaw axis.

runway. A defined rectangular area on a land airport prepared for the landing and takeoff run of aircraft along its length. Runways are normally numbered in relation to their magnetic direction rounded off to the nearest 10 degrees; e.g., Runway 01, Runway 25. (*See* parallel runways). [ICAO] A defined rectangular area on a land aerodrome prepared for the landing and takeoff of aircraft.

runway centerline lighting. (*See* airport lighting).

runway condition reading (RCR). Numerical decelerometer readings relayed by air traffic controllers at USAF and certain civil bases for use by the pilot in determining runway braking action. These readings are routinely relayed only to USAF and Air National Guard Aircraft. (*See* braking action).

Runway End Identifier Lights (REIL). (*See* airport lighting).

runway gradient. The average slope, measured in percent, between two ends or points on a runway. Runway gradient is depicted on government aerodrome sketches when total runway gradient exceeds 0.3%.

runway heading. The magnetic direction that corresponds with the runway centerline extended, not the painted runway number. When cleared to "fly or maintain runway heading," pilots are expected to fly or maintain the heading that corresponds with the extended centerline of the departure runway. Drift correction shall not be applied; e.g., Runway 4, actual magnetic heading of the runway centerline 044, fly 044.

runway in use/active runway/duty runway. Any runway or runways currently being used for takeoff or landing. When multiple runways are used, they are all considered active runways. In the metering sense, a selectable adapted item which specifies the landing runway configuration or direction of traffic flow. The adapted optimum flight plan from each transition fix to the vertex is determined by the runway configuration for arrival metering processing purposes.

runway lights. (*See* airport lighting).

runway markings. (*See* airport marking aids).

runway overrun. In military aviation exclusively, a stabilized or paved area beyond the end of a runway, of the same width as the runway plus shoulders, centered on the extended runway centerline.

runway profile descent. An instrument flight rules (IFR) air traffic control arrival procedure to a runway published for pilot use in graphic and/or textual form and may be associated with a STAR. Runway profile descents provide routing and may depict crossing altitudes, speed restrictions, and headings to be flown from the enroute structure to the point where the pilot will receive clearance for and execute an instrument approach procedure. A runway profile descent may apply to more than one runway if so stated on the chart. (Refer to AIM).

runway safety area (RSA). A defined surface surrounding the runway prepared, or suitable, for reducing the risk of damage to airplanes in the event of an undershoot, overshoot, or excursion from the runway. The dimensions of the RSA vary and can be determined by using the criteria contained within Advisory Circular 150/5300-13, Chapter 3. Figure

3-1 in Advisory Circular 150/5300-13 depicts the RSA. The design standards dictate that the RSA shall be:

1. Cleared, graded, and have no potentially hazardous ruts, humps, depressions, or other surface variations;

2. Drained by grading or storm sewers to prevent water accumulation;

3. Capable, under dry conditions, of supporting snow removal equipment, aircraft rescue and firefighting equipment, and the occasional passage of aircraft without causing structural damage to the aircraft; and,

4. Free of objects, except for objects that need to be located in the runway safety area because of their function. These objects shall be constructed on low impact resistant supports (frangible mounted structures) to the lowest practical height with the frangible point to higher than 3 inches above grade.

(Refer to AC 150/5300-13, Chapter 3.).

Runway Use Program. A noise abatement runway selection plan designed to enhance noise abatement efforts with regard to airport communities for arriving and departing aircraft. These plans are developed into runway use programs and apply to all turbojet aircraft 12,500 pounds or heavier; turbojet aircraft less than 12,500 pounds are included only if the airport proprietor determines that the aircraft creates a noise problem. Runway use programs are coordinated with FAA offices, and safety criteria used in these programs are developed by the Office of Flight Operations. Runway use programs are administered by the Air Traffic Service as "Formal" or "Informal" programs.

1. *Formal Runway Use Program.* An approved noise abatement program which is defined and acknowledged in a Letter of Understanding between Flight Operations, Air Traffic Service, the airport proprietor, and the users. Once established, participation in the program is mandatory for aircraft operators and pilots as provided for in FAR 91.87.

2. *Informal Runway Use Program.* An approved noise abatement program which does not require a Letter of Understanding, and participation in the program is voluntary for aircraft operators/pilots.

runway visibility value. (*See* visibility).

runway visual range. (*See* visibility).

SAA. (*See* special activity airspace).

safety alert. A safety alert issued by ATC to aircraft under their control if ATC is aware the aircraft is at an altitude which, in the controller's judgment, places the aircraft in unsafe proximity to terrain, obstructions, or other aircraft. The controller may discontinue the issuance of further alerts if the pilot advises he is taking action to correct the situation or has the other aircraft in sight.

1. *Terrain/Obstruction Alert.* A safety alert issued by ATC to aircraft under their control if ATC is aware the aircraft is at an altitude which, in the controller's judgment, places the aircraft in unsafe proximity to terrain/obstructions, e.g., "Low Altitude Alert, check your altitude immediately."

Continued

2. *Aircraft Conflict Alert.* A safety alert is issued by ATC to aircraft under their control if ATC is aware of an aircraft that is not under their control at an altitude which, in the controller's judgment, places both aircraft in unsafe proximity to each other. With the alert, ATC will offer the pilot an alternate course of action when feasible; e.g., "Traffic Alert, advise you turn right heading zero niner zero or climb to eight thousand immediately."

The issuance of a safety alert is contingent upon the capability of the controller to have an awareness of an unsafe condition. The course of action provided will be predicated on other traffic under ATC control. Once the alert is issued, it is solely the pilot's prerogative to determine what course of action, if any, he will take.

sail back. A maneuver during high wind conditions (usually with power off) where float plane movement is controlled by water rudders or opening and closing cabin doors.

same direction aircraft. Aircraft are operating in the same direction when:
1. They are following the same track in the same direction; or
2. Their tracks are parallel and the aircraft are flying in the same direction; or
3. Their tracks intersect at an angle of less than 45 degrees.

SAR. (*See* search and rescue).

Say again. Used to request a repeat of the last transmission. Usually specifies transmission or portion thereof not understood or received; e.g., "Say again all after ABRAM VOR."

Say altitude. Used by ATC to ascertain an aircraft's specific altitude/flight level. When the aircraft is climbing or descending, the pilot should state the indicated altitude rounded to the nearest 100 feet.

Say heading. Used by ATC to request an aircraft heading. The pilot should state the actual heading of the aircraft.

SDF. (*See* simplified directional facility).

sea lane. A designated portion of water outlined by visual surface markers for and intended to be used by aircraft designed to operate on water.

Search and Rescue (SAR). A service which seeks missing aircraft and assists those found to be in need of assistance. It is a cooperative effort using the facilities and services of available Federal, state and local agencies. The U.S. Coast Guard is responsible for coordination of search and rescue for the Maritime Region, and the U.S. Air Force is responsible for search and rescue for the Inland Region. Information pertinent to search and rescue should be passed through any air traffic facility or be transmitted directly to the Rescue Coordination Center by telephone. (*See* Flight Service Station, Rescue Coordination Center) (Refer to AIM).

Search and Rescue Facility. A facility responsible for maintaining and operating a search and rescue (SAR) service to render aid to persons and property in distress. It is any SAR unit, station, NET, or other operational activity which can be usefully employed during an SAR Mission; e.g., a Civil Air Patrol Wing, or a Coast Guard Station. (*See* Search and Rescue).

sectional aeronautical charts. (*See* aeronautical chart).

sector list drop interval (SLDI). A parameter number of minutes after the meter fix time when arrival aircraft will be deleted from the arrival sector list.

see and avoid. When weather conditions permit, pilots operating IFR or VFR are required to observe and maneuver to avoid other aircraft. Right-of-way rules are contained in 14 CFR Part 91. *Also:* A visual procedure where in pilots of aircraft flying in visual meteorological conditions (VMC), regardless of type of flight plan, are charged with the responsibility to observe the presence of other aircraft and to maneuver their aircraft as required to avoid the other aircraft. Right of way rules are contained in Part 91. (*See* instrument flight rules, visual flight rules, visual meteorological conditions, instrument meteorological conditions).

segmented circle. A system of visual indicators designed to provide traffic pattern information at airports without operating control towers. (Refer to AIM).

segments of an instrument approach procedure. An instrument approach procedure may have as many as four separate segments depending on how the approach procedure is structured.
1. *Initial approach.* The segment between the initial approach fix and the intermediate fix or the point where the aircraft is established on the intermediate course or final approach course. (*See* initial approach segment [ICAO]).
2. *Intermediate approach.* The segment between the intermediate fix or point and the final approach fix. (*See* intermediate approach segment [ICAO]).
3. *Final approach.* The segment between the final approach fix or point and the runway, airport, or missed approach point. (*See* final approach segment [ICAO]).
4. *Missed approach.* The segment between the missed approach point or the point of arrival at decision height and the missed approach fix at the prescribed altitude. (Refer to 14 CFR Part 97) (*See* missed approach procedure [ICAO]).

selected ground delays. A traffic management procedure whereby selected flights are issued ground delays to better regulate traffic flows over a particular fix or area.

separation. In air traffic control, the spacing of aircraft to achieve their safe and orderly movement in flight and while landing and taking off. (*See* separation minima). [ICAO] Spacing between aircraft, levels or tracks.

separation minima. The minimum longitudinal, lateral, or vertical distances by which aircraft are spaced through the application of air traffic control procedures. (*See* separation).

service. A generic term that designates functions or assistance available from or rendered by air traffic control. For example, Class C service would denote the ATC services provided within a Class C airspace area.

severe weather avoidance plan (SWAP). An approved plan to minimize the affect of severe weather on traffic flows in impacted terminal and/or ARTCC areas. SWAP is normally implemented to provide the least disruption to the ATC system when flight through portions of airspace is difficult or impossible due to severe weather.

severe weather forecast alerts (AWW). Preliminary messages issued in order to alert users that a Severe Weather Watch Bulletin (WW) is being issued. These messages define areas of possible severe thunderstorms or tornado activity. The messages are unscheduled and issued as required by the National Severe Storm Forecast Center at Kansas City, Missouri. (*See* SIGMET, Convective SIGMET, CWA, AIRMET).

SFA. (*See* single frequency approach).

SFO. (*See* simulated flame out).

SHF. (*See* super high frequency).

short range clearance. A clearance issued to a departing IFR flight which authorizes IFR flight to a specific fix short of the destination while air traffic control facilities are coordinating and obtaining the complete clearance.

short takeoff and landing aircraft (STOL). An aircraft which, at some weight within its approved operating weight, is capable of operating from a STOL runway in compliance with the applicable STOL characteristics, airworthiness, operations, noise, and pollution standards. (*See* Vertical Takeoff and Landing Aircraft).

SIAP (standard instrument approach procedure). (*See* instrument approach procedure).

sidestep maneuver. A visual maneuver accomplished by a pilot at the completion of an instrument approach to permit a straight-in landing on a parallel runway not more than 1,200 feet to either side of the runway to which the instrument approach was conducted. (Refer to AIM).

SIGMET. A weather advisory issued concerning weather significant to the safety of all aircraft. SIGMET advisories cover severe and extreme turbulence, severe icing, and widespread dust or sandstorms that reduce visibility to less than 3 miles. (*See* AWW, Convective SIGMET, CWA, and AIRMET) (Refer to AIM) (*See* SIGMET information [ICAO]).

SIGMET information. [ICAO] Information issued by a meteorological watch office concerning the occurrence or expected occurrence of specified enroute weather phenomena which may affect the safety of aircraft operations.

significant meteorological information. (*See* SIGMET).

significant point. A point, whether a named intersection, a NAVAID, a fix derived from a NAVAID(s), or geographical coordinate expressed in degrees of latitude and longitude, which is established for the purpose of providing separation, as a reporting point, or to delineate a route of flight.

*simplexing. Communication where one person must complete a transmission before the other person can begin; transmitting and receiving on the same frequency.

simplified directional facility (SDF). A NAVAID used for nonprecision instrument approaches. The final approach course is similar to that of an ILS localizer except that the SDF course may be offset from the runway, generally not more than 3 degrees, and the course may be wider than the localizer, resulting in a lower degree of accuracy. (Refer to AIM).

simulated flameout. A practice approach by a jet aircraft (normally military) at idle thrust to a runway. The approach may start at a runway (high key) and may continue on a relatively high and wide down wind leg with a continuous turn to final. It terminates in landing or low approach. The purpose of this approach. is to simulate a flameout. (*See* flameout).

simultaneous ILS approaches. An approach system permitting simultaneous ILS/MLS approaches to airports having parallel runways separated by at least 4,300 feet between centerlines. Integral parts of a total system are ILS/MLS, radar, communications. ATC procedures, and appropriate airborne equipment. (*See* parallel runways) (Refer to AIM).

simultaneous MLS approaches. (*See* simultaneous ILS approaches).

simultaneous operations on intersecting runways. Operations which include simultaneous takeoffs and landings and/or simultaneous landings when a landing aircraft is able and is instructed by the controller to hold short of the intersecting runway or designated hold short point. Pilots are expected to promptly inform the controller if the hold short clearance cannot be accepted. (*See* parallel runways) (Refer to AIM).

single direction routes. Preferred IFR Routes which are sometimes depicted on high altitude enroute charts and which are normally flown in one direction only. (*See* preferred IFR routes) (Refer to Airport/Facility Directory).

single frequency approach (SFA). A service provided under a letter of agreement to military single piloted turbojet aircraft which permits use of a single UHF frequency during approach for landing. Pilots will not normally be required to change frequency from the beginning of the approach to touchdown except that pilots conducting an enroute descent are required to change frequency when control is transferred from the air route traffic control center to the terminal facility. The abbreviation "SFA" in the DOD FLIP IFR Supplement under "Communications" indicates this service is available at an aerodrome.

single piloted aircraft. A military turbojet aircraft possessing one set of flight controls, tandem cockpits, or two sets of flight controls but operated by one pilot is considered single piloted by ATC when determining the appropriate air traffic service to be applied. (*See* single frequency approach).

slash. A radar beacon reply displayed as an elongated target.

SLDI. (*See* sector list drop interval).

slot time. (*See* meter fix time/slot time).

slow taxi. To taxi a float plane at low power or low RPM.

SN. (*See* system strategic navigation).

Speak slower. Used in verbal communications as a request to reduce speech rate.

special activity airspace (SAA). Any airspace with defined dimensions within the National Airspace System wherein limitations may be imposed upon aircraft operations. This airspace may be restricted areas, prohibited areas, military operations areas, air ATC assigned airspace, and any other designated airspace areas. The dimensions of this airspace are programmed into URET CCLD and can be designated as either active or inactive by screen entry. Aircraft trajectories are constantly tested against the dimensions of active areas and alerts issued to the applicable sectors when violations are predicted.

special emergency. A condition of air piracy or other hostile act by a person(s) aboard an aircraft which threatens the safety of the aircraft or its passengers.

special instrument approach procedure. (*See* instrument approach procedure).

Special Use airspace. Airspace of defined dimensions identified by an area on the surface of the earth wherein activities must be confined because of their nature and/or wherein limitations may be imposed upon aircraft operations that are not a part of those activities. Types of Special Use airspace are:

1. *Alert Area.* Airspace which may contain a high volume of pilot training activities or an unusual type of aerial activity, neither of which is hazardous to aircraft. Alert Areas are depicted on aeronautical charts for the information of nonparticipating pilots. All activities within an Alert Area are conducted in accordance with Federal Aviation Regulations, and pilots of participating aircraft as well as pilots transiting the area are equally responsible for collision avoidance.

2. *Controlled Firing Area.* Airspace wherein activities are conducted under conditions so controlled as to eliminate hazards to nonparticipating aircraft and to ensure the safety of persons and property on the ground.

3. *Military Operations Area (MOA).* An MOA is airspace established outside of Class A airspace area to separate or segregate certain nonhazardous military activities from IFR traffic and to identify for VFR traffic where these activities are conducted. (Refer to AIM).

4. *Prohibited Area.* Airspace designated under 14 CFR Part 73 within which no person may operate an aircraft without the permission of the using agency. (Refer to enroute charts, AIM).

5. *Restricted Area.* Airspace designated under 14 CFR Part 73, within which the flight of aircraft, while not wholly prohibited, is subject to restriction. Most restricted areas are designated joint use and IFR/VFR operations in the area may be authorized by the controlling ATC facility when it is not being utilized by the using agency. Re-stricted areas are depicted on enroute charts. Where joint use is authorized, the name of the ATC controlling facility is also shown. (Refer to 14 CFR Part 73 and AIM).

6. *Warning Area.* A warning area is airspace of defined dimensions extending from 3 nautical miles outward from the coast of the United States, that contains activity that may be hazardous to nonparticipating aircraft. The purpose of such warning area is to warn nonparticipating pilots of the potential danger. A warning area may be located over domestic or international waters or both.

Special VFR conditions. Meteorological conditions that are less than those required for basic VFR flight in Class B, C, D, or E surface areas and in which some aircraft are permitted flight under visual flight rules. (*See* Special VFR operations) (Refer to 14 CFR Part 91).

Special VFR flight. [ICAO] A VFR flight cleared by air traffic control to operate within Class B, C, D, and E surface areas in meteorological conditions below VMC.

Special VFR operations. Aircraft operating in accordance with clearances within Class B, C, D, and E surface areas in weather conditions less than the basic VFR weather minima. Such operations must be requested by the pilot and approved by ATC. (*See* Special VFR conditions) (*See* Special VFR flight [ICAO]).

speed. (*See* airspeed, ground speed).

speed adjustment. An ATC procedure used to request pilots to adjust aircraft speed to a specific value for the purpose of providing desired spacing. Pilots are expected to maintain a speed of plus or minus 10 knots or 0.02 mach number of the specified speed.

Examples of speed adjustments are:

1. "Increase/reduce speed to mach point (number)."

2. "Increase/reduce speed to (speed in knots)" or "Increase/reduce speed (number of knots) knots."

speed brakes. Moveable aerodynamic devices on aircraft that reduce airspeed during descent and landing.

speed segments. Portions of the arrival route between the transition point and the vertex along the optimum flight path for which speeds and altitudes are specified. There is one set of arrival speed segments adapted from each transition point to each vertex. Each set may contain up to six segments.

squawk (mode, code, function). Activate specific modes/codes/functions on the aircraft transponder, e.g., "Squawk three/alfa, two one zero five, low." (*See* transponder).

staging/queuing. The placement, integration, and segregation of departure aircraft in designated movement areas of an airport by departure fix, EDCT, and/or restriction.

*stall. Loss of lift caused by exceeding the critical angle of attack and destroying the smooth flow of air over an airfoil.

*standard datum plane. A standard of atmospheric pressure measurement that assumes the sea level pressure to be 29.92 inches Hg.

standard day. Sea level altitude, a temperature of 15°C or 59°F and a barometric pressure of 29.92" Hg (1013.2 mb).

standard instrument approach procedure. (*See* instrument approach procedure).

standard rate turn. A turn of three degrees per second.

standard terminal arrival (STAR). A preplanned instrument flight rule (IFR) air traffic control arrival procedure published for pilot use in graphic and/or textual form. STARs provide transition from the enroute structure to an outer fix or an instrument approach fix/arrival waypoint in the terminal area.

standard terminal arrival charts. (*See* aeronautical chart).

stand by. Means the controller or pilot must pause for a few seconds, usually to attend to other duties of a higher priority. Also means to wait as in "stand by for clearance." The caller should reestablish contact if a delay is lengthy. "Stand by" is not an approval or denial.

STAR. (*See* standard terminal arrival).

state aircraft. Aircraft used in military, customs and police service, in the exclusive service of any government, or of any political subdivision, thereof including the government of any state, territory, or possession of the United States or the District of Columbia, but not including any government-owned aircraft engaged in carrying persons or property for commercial purposes.

static. At rest or in equilibrium; not dynamic or moving.

static restrictions. Those restrictions that are usually not subject to change, fixed, in place, and/or published.

static source. A point on the airplane where no air pressure is exerted as a result of movement through the air; a reference input for the airspeed indicator; the source of air pressure change information for the altimeter and vertical speed indicator.

stationary reservations. Altitude reservations which encompass activities in a fixed area. Stationary reservations may include activities, such as special tests of weapons systems or equipment, certain U.S. Navy carrier, fleet, and antisubmarine operations, rocket, missile and drone operations, and certain aerial refueling or similar operations.

statute mile. A 5,280-foot mile.

stepdown fix. A fix permitting additional descent within a segment of an instrument approach procedure by identifying a point at which a controlling obstacle has been safely overflown.

step taxi. To taxi a float plane at full power or high RPM.

step turn. A maneuver used to put a float plane in a planing configuration prior to entering an active sea lane for takeoff. The STEP TURN maneuver should only be used upon pilot request.

stereo route. A routinely used route of flight established by users and ARTCCs identified by a coded name; e.g.,

ALPHA 2. These routes minimize flight plan handling and communications.

STOL aircraft. (*See* short takeoff and landing aircraft).

stop altitude squawk. Used by ATC to inform an aircraft to turn off the automatic altitude reporting feature of its transponder. It is issued when the verbally reported altitude varies 300 feet or more from the automatic altitude report. (*See* altitude readout, transponder).

stop-and-go. A procedure wherein an aircraft will land, make a complete stop on the runway, and then commence a takeoff from that point. (*See* low approach, option approach).

stop burst. (*See* stop stream).

stop buzzer. (*See* stop stream).

stopover flight plan. A flight plan format which permits in a single submission the filing of a sequence of flight plans through interim full stop destinations to a final destination.

stop squawk (mode or code). Used by ATC to tell the pilot to turn specified functions of the aircraft transponder off. (*See* stop altitude squawk, transponder).

stop stream. Used by ATC to request a pilot to suspend electronic countermeasure activity. (*See* jamming).

stopway. An area beyond the takeoff runway no less wide than the runway and centered upon the extended centerline of the runway, able to support the airplane during an aborted takeoff, without causing structural damage to the airplane, and designated by the airport authorities for use in decelerating the airplane during an aborted takeoff.

straight-in approach—IFR. An instrument approach wherein final approach is begun without first having executed a procedure turn, not necessarily completed with a straight-in landing or made to straight-in landing minimums. (*See* landing minimums, straight-in approach—VFR, straight-in landing).

straight-in approach—VFR. Entry into the traffic pattern by interception of the extended runway centerline (final approach course) without executing any other portion of the traffic pattern. (*See* traffic pattern).

straight-in landing. A landing made on a runway aligned within 30 degrees of the final approach course following completion of an instrument approach. (*See* straight-in approach—IFR).

straight-in landing minimums. (*See* landing minimums).

straight-in minimums. (*See* straight-in landing minimums).

strategic planning. Planning whereby solutions are sought to resolve potential conflicts.

struts, supports. The main landing gear and nose wheel have struts to absorb the shock of landing. Wing sets are braced to the fuselage to support the wing and help absorb any wing movement in relation to the fuselage when landing or in turbulence. Low-wing airplanes and some high-wing airplanes have no external bracing.

substitutions. Users are permitted to exchange CTAs. Normally, the airline dispatcher will contact the ATCSCC with this request. The ATCSCC shall forward approved substitutions to the TMUs who will notify the appropriate terminals. Permissible swapping must not change the traffic load for any given hour of an EQF program.

substitute route. A route assigned to pilots when any part of an airway or route is unusable because of NAVAID status. These routes consist of:

1. Substitute routes which are shown on U.S. Government charts.
2. Routes defined by ATC as specific NAVAID radials or courses.
3. Routes defined by ATC as direct to or between NAVAIDs.

sunset and sunrise. The mean solar times of sunset and sunrise as published in the Nautical Almanac, converted to local standard time for the locality concerned. Within Alaska, the end of evening civil twilight and the beginning of morning civil twilight, as defined for each locality.

super high frequency (SHF). The frequency band between 3 and 30 gigahertz (GHz). The elevation and azimuth stations of the Microwave Landing System operate from 5031 MHz to 5091 MHz in this spectrum.

supplemental weather service location. Airport facilities staffed with contract personnel who take weather observations and provide current local weather to pilots via telephone or radio. (All other services are provided by the parent FSS).

SUPPS. Refers to ICAO Document 7030 Regional Supplementary Procedures. SUPPS contain procedures for each ICAO Region which are unique to that Region and are not covered in the worldwide provisions identified in the ICAO Air Navigation Plan. Procedures contained in chapter 8 are based in part on those published in SUPPS.

surface area. The airspace contained by the lateral boundary of the Class B, C, D, or E airspace designated for an airport that begins at the surface and extends upward.

SURPIC (surface picture). A description of surface vessels in the area of a Search and Rescue incident including their predicted positions and their characteristics. (*See* Order 7110.65, Paragraph 10-7-4, In-flight Contingencies).

surveillance approach. An instrument approach wherein the air traffic controller issues instructions, for pilot compliance, based on aircraft position in relation to the final approach course (azimuth), and the distance (range) from the end of the runway as displayed on the controller's radar scope. The controller will provide recommended altitudes on final approach if requested by the pilot. (Refer to AIM).

SWAP. (*See* severe weather avoidance plan).

SWSL. (*See* supplemental weather service location).

system strategic navigation (SN). Military activity accomplished by navigating along a preplanned route using internal aircraft systems to maintain a desired track. This activity normally requires a lateral route width of 10 NM and altitude range of 1,000 feet to 6,000 feet AGL with some route segments that permit terrain following.

TACAN. (*See* tactical air navigation).

TACAN-only aircraft. An aircraft, normally military, possessing TACAN with DME but no VOR navigational system capability. Clearances must specify TACAN or VORTAC fixes and approaches.

*tachometer. An instrument which reads revolutions per minute. Used on bicycles and automobiles as well as airplanes.

tactical air navigation (TACAN). An ultra high frequency electronic rho-theta air navigation aid which provides suitably equipped aircraft a continuous indication of bearing and distance to the TACAN station. (*See* VORTAC) (Refer to AIM).

*TAF. (*See* terminal aerodrome forecast).

tailwind. Any wind more than 90 degrees to the longitudinal axis of the runway. The magnetic direction of the runway shall be used as the basis for determining the longitudinal axis.

takeoff area. (*See* landing area).

takeoff distance available (TODA). [ICAO] The length of the takeoff run available plus the length of the clearway, if provided.

takeoff run available (TORA). [ICAO] The length of runway declared available and suitable for the ground run of an aeroplane takeoff.

target. The indication shown on a radar display resulting from a primary radar return or a radar beacon reply. (*See* radar, target symbol). [ICAO] In radar:

1. Generally, any discrete object which reflects or retransmits energy back to the radar equipment.
2. Specifically, an object of radar search or surveillance.

target resolution. A process to insure that correlated radar targets do not touch. Target resolution shall be applied as follows:

1. Between the edges of two primary targets or the edges of the ASR-9 primary target symbol.
2. Between the end of the beacon control slash and the edge of a primary target.
3. Between the ends of two beacon control slashes.

MANDATORY TRAFFIC ADVISORIES AND SAFETY ALERTS SHALL BE ISSUED WHEN THIS PROCEDURE IS USED.

Note: This procedure shall not be provided utilizing mosaic radar systems.

target symbol. A computer generated indication shown on a radar display resulting from a primary radar return or a radar beacon reply.

taxi. The movement of an airplane under its own power on the surface of an airport. Also, it describes the surface movement of helicopters equipped with wheels. (*See* air taxi, hover taxi) (Refer to AIM).

Taxi into position and hold. Used by ATC to inform a pilot to taxi onto the departure runway in takeoff position and hold. It is not authorization for takeoff. It is used when takeoff clearance cannot immediately be issued because of traffic or other reasons. (*See* cleared for takeoff).

taxi patterns. Patterns established to illustrate the desired flow of ground traffic for the different runways or airport areas available for use.

TCAS. (*See* Traffic Alert and Collision Avoidance System).

TCH. (*See* threshold crossing height).

TCLT. (*See* tentative calculated landing time).

TDZE. (*See* touchdown zone elevation).

Telephone Information Briefing Service (TIBS). A continuous telephone recording of meteorological and/or aeronautical information. (Refer to AIM).

tentative calculated landing time (TCLT). A projected time calculated for adapted vertex for each arrival aircraft based upon runway configuration, airport acceptance rate, airport arrival delay period, and other metered arrival aircraft. This time is either the VTA of the aircraft or the TCLT/ACLT of the previous aircraft plus the AAI, whichever is later. This time will be updated in response to an aircraft's progress and its current relationship to other arrivals.

*Terminal Aerodrome Forecast (TAF). A forecast of weather conditions at a specific airport.

terminal area. A general term used to describe airspace in which approach control service or airport traffic control service is provided.

terminal area facility. A facility providing air traffic control service for arriving and departing IFR, VFR, Special VFR, and on occasion enroute aircraft. (*See* Approach Control Facility, tower).

terminal VFR radar service. A national program instituted to extend the terminal radar services provided instrument flight rules (IFR) aircraft to visual flight rules (VFR) aircraft. The program is divided into four types of service referred to as basic radar service, Terminal Radar Service Area (TRSA) service, Class B service and Class C service. The type of service provided at a particular location is contained in the Airport/Facility Directory.

1. *Basic Radar Service:* These services are provided for VFR aircraft by all commissioned terminal radar facilities. Basic radar service includes safety alerts, traffic advisories, limited radar vectoring when requested by the pilot, and sequencing at locations where procedures have been established for this purpose and/or when covered by a letter of agreement. The purpose of this service is to adjust the flow of arriving IFR and VFR aircraft into the traffic pattern in a safe and orderly manner and to provide traffic advisories to departing VFR aircraft.

2. *TRSA Service:* This service provides, in addition to basic radar service, sequencing of all IFR and participating VFR aircraft to the primary airport and separation between all participating VFR aircraft. The purpose of this service is to provide separation between all participating VFR aircraft and all IFR aircraft operating within the area defined as a TRSA.

3. *Class C Service:* This service provides, in addition to basic radar service, approved separation between IFR and VFR aircraft, and sequencing of VFR aircraft, and sequencing of VFR arrivals to the primary airport.

4. *Class B Service:* This service provides, in addition to basic radar service, approved separation of aircraft based on IFR, VFR, and/or weight, and sequencing of VFR arrivals to the primary airport(s).

(*See* controlled airspace, Terminal Radar Service Area) (Refer to AIM, Airport/Facility Directory).

Terminal Radar Service Area (TRSA). Airspace surrounding designated airports wherein ATC provides radar vectoring, sequencing, and separation on a full-time basis for all IFR and participating VFR aircraft. Service provided in a TRSA is called Stage III Service. The AIM contains an explanation of TRSA. TRSAs are depicted on VFR aeronautical charts. Pilot participation is urged but is not mandatory. (*See* terminal radar program) (Refer to AIM, Airport/Facility Directory).

terminal—very high frequency omnidirectional range station (TVOR). A very high frequency terminal omnirange station located on or near an airport and used as an approach aid. (*See* navigational aid, VOR).

terrain following (TF). The flight of a military aircraft maintaining a constant AGL altitude above the terrain or the highest obstruction. The altitude of the aircraft will constantly change with the varying terrain and/or obstruction.

tetrahedron. A device normally located on uncontrolled airports and used as a landing direction indicator. The small end of a tetrahedron points in the direction of landing. At controlled airports, the tetrahedron, if installed, should be disregarded because tower instructions supersede the indicator. (*See* segmented circle) (Refer to AIM).

TF. (*See* terrain following).

That is correct. The understanding you have is right.

360 overhead. (*See* overhead approach).

threshold. The beginning of that portion of the runway usable for landing. (*See* airport lighting, displaced threshold).

*threshold. The beginning of the landing surface at the approach end of a runway.

threshold crossing height (TCH). The theoretical height above the runway threshold at which the aircraft's glideslope antenna would be if the aircraft maintains the trajectory established by the mean ILS glideslope or MLS glidepath. (*See* glideslope, threshold).

threshold lights. (*See* airport lighting).

TIBS. (*See* Telephone Information Briefing Service).

time group. Four digits representing the hour and minutes from the Coordinated Universal Time (UTC) clock. FAA uses UTC for all operations. The term "Zulu" may be used to denote UTC. The word "local" or the time zone equivalent shall be used to denote local when local time is given during radio and telephone communications. When written, a time zone designator is used to indicate local time; e.g. "0205M" (Mountain). The local time may be based on the 24-hour clock system. The day begins at 0000 and ends at 2359.

TMPA. (*See* traffic management program alert).

TMU. (*See* traffic management unit).

TODA. [ICAO] (*See* takeoff distance available).

***TO-FROM indicator.** Used in VOR navigation to tell the pilot whether the selected radial is the direction TO or FROM the transmitter; also called ambiguity indicator.

TORA. [ICAO] (*See* takeoff run available).

torching. The burning of fuel at the end of an exhaust pipe or stack of a reciprocating aircraft engine, the result of an excessive richness in the fuel air mixture.

***torque.** A twisting force; used as a term of convenience in flight instruction to describe several forces which combine to create a left-turning tendency.

total estimated elapsed time. [ICAO] For IFR flights, the estimated time required from takeoff to arrive over the designated point, defined by reference to navigation aids, from which it is intended that an instrument approach procedure will be commenced, or, if no navigation aid is associated with the destination aerodrome, to arrive over the destination aerodrome. For VFR flights, the estimated time required from takeoff to arrive over the destination aerodrome. (*See* estimated elapsed time).

touch-and-go. An operation by an aircraft that lands and departs on a runway without stopping or exiting the runway.

touch-and-go landing. (*See* touch-and-go).

touchdown.
1. The point at which an aircraft first makes contact with the landing surface.
2. Concerning a precision radar approach (PAR), it is the point where the glidepath intercepts the landing surface. [ICAO] The point where the nominal glidepath intercepts the runway. *Note:* Touchdown as defined above is only a datum and is not necessarily the actual point at which the aircraft will touch the runway.

touchdown RVR. (*See* visibility).

touchdown zone. The first 3,000 feet of the runway beginning at the threshold. The area is used for determination of touchdown zone elevation in the development of straight-in landing minimums for instrument approaches. [ICAO] The portion of a runway, beyond the threshold, where it is intended landing aircraft first contact the runway.

touchdown zone elevation (TDZE). The highest elevation in the first 3,000 feet of the landing surface, TDZE is indicated on the instrument approach procedure chart when straight-in landing minimums are authorized. (*See* touchdown zone).

touchdown zone lighting. (*See* airport lighting).

tower. A terminal facility that uses air/ground communications, visual signaling, and other devices to provide ATC services to aircraft operating in the vicinity of an airport or on the movement area. Authorizes aircraft to land or takeoff at the airport controlled by the tower or to transit the Class D airspace area regardless of flight plan or weather conditions (IFR or VFR). A tower may also provide approach control services (radar or nonradar). (*See* Airport Traffic Control Service, Approach Control Facility, Approach Control Service, movement area, Tower Enroute Control Service) (Refer to AIM) (*See* aerodrome control tower [ICAO]).

***tower controller.** An air traffic control specialist in a control tower who controls operations on the active runway and in the airport traffic area. (Also "local controller.")

Tower Enroute Control Service (TECS). The control of IFR enroute traffic within delegated airspace between two or more adjacent approach control facilities. This service is designed to expedite traffic and reduce control and pilot communication requirements.

tower to tower. (*See* Tower Enroute Control Service).

TPX-42. A numeric beacon decoder equipment/system. It is designed to be added to terminal radar systems for beacon decoding. It provides rapid target identification, reinforcement of the primary radar target, and altitude information from Mode C. (*See* automated radar terminal systems, transponder).

track. The actual flight path of an aircraft over the surface of the earth. (*See* course, route, flight path). [ICAO] The projection on the earth's surface of the path of an aircraft, the direction of which path at any point is usually expressed in degrees from North (True, Magnetic, or Grid).

***track.** The actual path over the ground followed by an airplane.

traffic.
1. A term used by a controller to transfer radar identification of an aircraft to another controller for the purpose of coordinating separation action. Traffic is normally issued:
   a. in response to a handoff or point out,
   b. in anticipation of a handoff or point out, or
   c. in conjunction with a request for control of an aircraft.
2. A term used by ATC to refer to one or more aircraft.

traffic advisories. Advisories issued to alert pilots to other known or observed air traffic which may be in such proximity to the position or intended route of flight of their aircraft to warrant their attention. Such advisories may be based on:

1. Visual observation.
2. Observation of radar identified and nonidentified aircraft targets on an ATC radar display, or
3. Verbal reports from pilots or other facilities.

The word "traffic" followed by additional information, if known, is used to provide such advisories; e.g., "Traffic, 2 o'clock, one zero miles, southbound, eight thousand."

Traffic advisory service will be provided to the extent possible depending on higher priority duties of the controller or other limitations; e.g., radar limitations, volume of traffic, frequency congestion, or controller workload. Radar/nonradar traffic advisories do not relieve the pilot of his responsibility to see and avoid other aircraft. Pilots are cautioned that there are many times when the controller is not able to give traffic advisories concerning all traffic in the aircraft's proximity; in other words, when a pilot requests or is receiving traffic advisories, he should not assume that all traffic will be issued. (Refer to AIM).

Traffic alert (aircraft call sign), turn (left/right) immediately, (climb/descend) and maintain (altitude). (See safety alert).

Traffic Alert and Collision Avoidance System (TCAS). An airborne collision avoidance system based on radar beacon signals which operates independent of ground based equipment. TCAS-I generates traffic advisories only. TCAS-II generates traffic advisories, and resolution (collision avoidance) advisories in the vertical plane.

traffic information. (*See* traffic advisories).

traffic in sight. Used by pilots to inform a controller that previously issued traffic is in sight. (*See* negative contact, traffic advisories).

traffic management program alert (TMPA). A term used in a Notice to Airmen (NOTAM) issued in conjunction with a special traffic management program to alert pilots to the existence of the program and to refer them to either the Notices to Airmen publication or a special traffic management program advisory message for program details. The contraction TMPA is used in NOTAM text.

traffic management unit (TMU). The entity in ARTCCs and designated terminals responsible for direct involvement in the active management of facility traffic. Usually under the direct supervision of an assistant manager for traffic management.

Traffic no factor. Indicates that the traffic described in a previously issued traffic advisory is no factor.

Traffic no longer observed. Indicates that the traffic described in a previously issued traffic advisory is no longer depicted on radar, but may still be a factor.

traffic pattern. The traffic flow that is prescribed for aircraft landing at, taxiing on, or taking off from an airport. The components of a typical traffic pattern are upwind leg, crosswind leg, downwind leg, base leg, and final approach.

1. *Upwind leg.* A flight path parallel to the landing runway in the direction of landing.
2. *Crosswind leg.* A flight path at right angles to the landing runway off its upwind end.
3. *Downwind leg.* A flight path parallel to the landing runway in the direction opposite to landing. The downwind leg normally extends between the crosswind leg and the base leg.
4. *Base leg.* A flight path at right angles to the landing runway off its approach end. The base leg normally extends from the downwind leg to the intersection of the extended runway centerline.
5. *Final approach.* A flight path in the direction of landing along the extended runway centerline. The final approach normally extends from the base leg to the runway. An aircraft making a straight-in approach VFR is also considered to be on final approach.

(*See* straight-in approach — VFR, taxi patterns) (Refer to AIM, 14 CFR Part 91) (*See* aerodrome traffic circuit [ICAO]).

*****trailing edge.** The sharp edge of the wing; flaps and ailerons are hinged at the trailing edge of the wing.

Transcribed Weather Broadcast (TWEB). A continuous recording of meteorological and aeronautical information that is broadcast on L/MF and VOR facilities for pilots. (Refer to AIM).

transfer of control. That action whereby the responsibility for the separation of an aircraft is transferred from one controller to another. [ICAO] Transfer of responsibility for providing air traffic control service.

transferring controller. A controller/facility transferring control of an aircraft to another controller/facility. (*See* transferring unit/controller [ICAO]).

transferring facility. (*See* transferring controller).

transferring unit/controller. [ICAO] Air traffic control unit/air traffic controller in the process of transferring the responsibility for providing air traffic control service to an aircraft to the next air traffic control unit/air traffic controller along the route of flight.

Note: See definition of accepting unit/controller.

transition.

1. The general term that describes the change from one phase of flight or flight condition to another; e.g., transition from enroute flight to the approach or transition from instrument flight to visual flight.
2. A published procedure (SID Transition) used to connect the basic SID to one of several enroute airways/jet routes, or published procedure (STAR Transition) used to connect one of several enroute airways/jet routes to the basic STAR. (Refer to SID/STAR Charts).

transitional airspace. That portion of controlled airspace wherein aircraft change from one phase of flight or flight condition to another.

transition point. A point at an adapted number of miles from the vertex at which an arrival aircraft would normally commence descent from its enroute altitude. This is the first fix adapted on the arrival speed segments.

transmissiometer. An apparatus used to determine visibility by measuring the transmission of light through the atmosphere. It is the measurement source of determining runway visual range (RVR) and runway visibility valve (RVV). (*See* visibility).

transmitting in the blind. A transmission from one station to other stations in circumstances where two-way communication cannot be established, but where it is believed that the called stations may be able to receive the transmission.

transponder. The airborne radar beacon receiver/transmitter portion of the Air Traffic Control Radar Beacon System (ATCRBS) which automatically receives radio signals from interrogators on the ground, and selectively replies with a specific reply pulse or pulse group only to those interrogations being received on the mode to which it is set to respond. (*See* interrogator) (Refer to AIM). [ICAO] A receiver/transmitter which will generate a reply signal upon proper interrogation; the interrogation and reply being on different frequencies.

transponder. A UHF transmitter which replies to coded inquiries from ground radar stations, giving your position and possibly your altitude for identification and traffic separation purposes.

transponder codes. (*See* codes).

trim tabs. Small adjustable tabs on control surfaces (elevator, rudder and ailerons) used by the pilot to relieve control forces. Typically, the tab moves opposite to desired control surface movement deflecting the elevator trim tab downward causes the elevator to move upward.

TRSA. (*See* Terminal Radar Service Area).

TRSA. Terminal Radar Service Area—an area where radar service is available to VFR pilots on a voluntary basis; outlined in black on sectional charts.

true airspeed. Indicated airspeed corrected for temperature and pressure altitude.

true airspeed indicator. An airspeed indicator which allows the pilot to set temperature and altitude values and read true airspeed directly.

true North Pole. The northern extremity of the earth's axis; where all of the lines of longitude meet.

true wind. The actual movement of air over the earth's surface.

turbocharged. An engine with intake air compressed by a turbine-driven compressor.

turbojet aircraft. An aircraft having a jet engine in which the energy of the jet operates a turbine which in turn operates the air compressor.

turboprop aircraft. An aircraft having a jet engine in which the energy of the jet operates a turbine which drives the propeller.

turn anticipation. Maneuver anticipation.

TWEB. (*See* Transcribed Weather Broadcast).

TVOR. (*See* terminal—very high frequency omnidirectional range station).

two-way radio communications failure. (*See* lost communications).

UDF. (*See* direction finder).

UHF. (*See* ultrahigh frequency).

*UHF. Ultrahigh Frequency range, 300 MHz to 3,000 MHz. Used for DME and some radar equipment.

ultrahigh frequency (UHF). The frequency band between 300 and 3,000 MHz. The bank of radio frequencies used for military air/ground voice communications. In some instances this may go as low as 225 MHz and still be referred to as UHF.

ultralight vehicle. An aeronautical vehicle operated for sport or recreational purposes which does not require FAA registration, an airworthiness certificate, nor pilot certification. They are primarily single occupant vehicles, although some two place vehicles are authorized for training purposes. Operation of an ultralight vehicle in certain airspace requires authorization from ATC. (*See* 14 CFR Part 103).

unable. Indicates inability to comply with a specific instruction, request, or clearance.

uncontrolled airport. An airport without a control tower or an airport with a tower outside of the tower's hours of operation.

under the hood. Indicates that the pilot is using a hood to restrict visibility outside the cockpit while simulating instrument flight. An appropriately rated pilot is required in the other control seat while this operation is being conducted. (Refer to 14 CFR Part 91).

UNICOM. A nongovernment communication facility which may provide airport information at certain airports. Locations and frequencies of UNICOMs are shown on aeronautical charts and publications. (Refer to AIM, Airport/Facility Directory).

UNICOM. An acronym for Universal Communications. Also called Aeronautical Advisory Service, a radio service operated by individuals at airports to provide services to pilots. Not used for air traffic control purposes.

unpublished route. A route for which no minimum altitude is published or charted for pilot use. It may include a direct route between NAVAIDs, a radial, a radar vector, or a final approach course beyond the segments of an instrument approach procedure. (*See* published route, route).

upwind leg. (*See* traffic pattern).

urgency. A condition of being concerned about safety and of requiring timely but not immediate assistance; a potential distress condition. [ICAO] A condition concerning the safety of an aircraft or other vehicle, or of person on board or in sight, but which does not require immediate assistance.

USAFIB. (*See* Army Aviation Flight Information Bulletin).

UVDF. (*See* direction finder).

*__variation.__ The angular difference between measurements in relation to true north and magnetic north. Variation is independent of aircraft heading.

VASI. (*See* Visual Approach Slope Indicator).

*__VASI.__ Visual Approach Slope Indicator—a means of providing approach slope guidance to VFR pilots.

VDF. (*See* direction finder).

VDP. (*See* visual descent point).

vector. A heading issued to an aircraft to provide navigational guidance by radar. (*See* radar vectoring [ICAO]).

*__vector.__ A heading to steer, received from a controller.

*__venturi.__ A tube with a restriction which accelerates air and reduces pressure. Venturis are used in carburetors and on older airplanes to provide vacuum to power flight instruments.

verify. Request confirmation of information; e.g., "verify assigned altitude."

verify specific direction of takeoff (or turns after takeoff). Used by ATC to ascertain an aircraft's direction of takeoff and/or direction of turn after takeoff. It is normally used for IFR departures from an airport not having a control tower. When direct communication with the pilot is not possible, the request and information may be relayed through an FSS, dispatcher, or by other means. (*See* IFR takeoff minimums and departure procedures).

vertex. The last fix adapted on the arrival speed segments. Normally, it will be the outer marker of the runway in use. However, it may be the actual threshold or other suitable common point on the approach path for the particular runway configuration.

vertex time of arrival (VTA). A calculated time of aircraft arrival over the adapted vertex for the runway configuration in use. The time is calculated via the optimum flight path using adapted speed segments.

*__vertical axis.__ An imaginary line through the center of gravity which intersects the lateral and longitudinal axes; also called yaw axis.

*__vertical fin.__ A fixed vertical airfoil at the rear of the airplane which stabilizes the airplane in the vertical axis.

vertical navigation (VNAV). A function of area navigation (RNAV) equipment which calculates, displays, and provides vertical guidance to a profile or path.

vertical separation. Separation established by assignment of different altitudes or flight levels. (*See* separation). [ICAO] Separation between aircraft expressed in units of vertical distance.

*__vertical speed indicator.__ An instrument which indicates rate of change in altitude by measuring rate of change of air pressure.

vertical takeoff and landing aircraft (VTOL). Aircraft capable of vertical climbs and/or descents and of using very short runways or small areas for takeoff and landings. These aircraft include, but are not limited to, helicopters. (*See* short takeoff and landing aircraft).

very high frequency (VHF). The frequency band between 30 and 300 MHz. Portions of this band, 108 to 118 MHz, are used for certain NAVAIDs; 118 to 136 MHz are used for civil air/ground voice communications. Other frequencies in this band are used for purposes not related to air traffic control.

very high frequency omnidirectional range station. (*See* VOR).

very low frequency (VLF). The frequency band between 3 and 30 kHz.

VFR. (*See* visual flight rules).

VFR aircraft. An aircraft conducting flight in accordance with visual flight rules. (*See* visual flight rules).

VFR conditions. Weather conditions equal to or better than the minimum for flight under visual flight rules. The term may be used as an ATC clearance/instruction only when:

1. An IFR aircraft requests a climb/descent in VFR conditions.

2. The clearance will result in noise abatement benefits where part of the IFR departure route does not conform to an FAA approved noise abatement route or altitude.

3. A pilot has requested a practice instrument approach and is not on an IFR flight plan.

All pilots receiving this authorization must comply with the VFR visibility and distance from cloud criteria in 14 CFR Part 91. Use of the term does not relieve controllers of their responsibility to separate aircraft in Class B and Class C airspace or TRSAs as required by FAA Order 7110.65. When used as an ATC clearance/instruction the term may be abbreviated "VFR;" e.g., "MAINTAIN VFR," "CLIMB/DESCEND VFR," etc.

VFR flight. (*See* VFR aircraft).

VFR military training routes. Routes used by the Department of Defense and associated Reserve and Air Guard units for the purpose of conducting low altitude navigation and tactical training under VFR below 10,000 feet MSL at airspeeds in excess of 250 knots IAS.

VFR not recommended. An advisory provided by a flight service station to a pilot during a preflight or in-flight weather briefing that flight under visual flight rules is not recommended. To be given when the current and/or forecast weather conditions are at or below VFR minimums. It does not abrogate the pilot's authority to make his own decision.

VFR-On-Top. ATC authorization for an IFR aircraft to operate in VFR conditions at any appropriate VFR altitude (as specified in Federal Aviation Regulations and as restricted by ATC). A pilot receiving this authorization must comply with the VFR visibility, distance from cloud criteria, and the minimum IFR altitudes specified in 14 CFR Part 91. The use of this term does not relieve controllers of their responsibility to separate aircraft in Class B and Class C airspace or TRSAs as required by FAA Order 7110.65.

VFR terminal area charts. (*See* aeronautical chart).

VHF. (*See* very high frequency).

*VHF.** Very High Frequency range. 30 MHz to 300 MHz range, limited to line-of-sight.

*VHF/DF.** Very High Frequency Direction Finding—a service available at some Flight Service Stations to orient lost pilots. No equipment other than a transmitter and a receiver is required in order to use this service.

VHF omnidirectional range/tactical air navigation. (*See* VORTAC).

video map. An electronically displayed map on the radar display that may depict data such as airports, heliports, runway centerline extensions, hospital emergency landing areas, NAVAIDs and fixes, reporting points, airway/route centerlines, boundaries, handoff points, special use tracks, obstructions, prominent geographic features, map alignment indicators, range accuracy marks, minimum vectoring altitudes.

visibility. The ability, as determined by atmospheric conditions and expressed in units of distance, to see and identify prominent unlighted objects by day and prominent lighted objects by night. Visibility is reported as statute miles, hundreds of feet or meters. (Refer to 14 CFR Part 91, AIM).

1. *Flight visibility.* The average forward horizontal distance from the cockpit of an aircraft in flight, at which prominent unlighted objects may be seen and identified by day and prominent lighted objects may be seen and identified by night.

2. *Ground visibility.* Prevailing horizontal visibility near the earth's surface as reported by the United States National Weather Service or an accredited observer.

3. *Prevailing visibility.* The greatest horizontal visibility equaled or exceeded throughout at least half the horizon circle which need not necessarily be continuous.

4. *Runway visibility value (RVV).* The visibility determined for a particular runway by a transmissometer. A meter provides a continuous indication of the visibility (reported in miles or fractions of miles) for the runway. RVV is used in lieu of prevailing visibility in determining minimums for a particular runway.

5. *Runway visual range (RVR).* An instrumentally derived value, based on standard calibrations, that represents the horizontal distance a pilot will see down the runway from the approach end. It is based on the sighting of either high intensity runway lights or on the visual contrast of other targets whichever yields the greater visual range. RVR, in contrast to prevailing or runway visibility, is based on what a pilot in a moving aircraft should see looking down the runway. RVR is horizontal visual range, not slant visual range. It is based on the measurement of a transmissometer made near the touchdown point of the instrument runway and is reported in hundreds of feet. RVR is used in lieu of RVV and/or prevailing visibility in determining minimums for a particular runway.

   a. *Touchdown RVR.* The RVR visibility readout values obtained from RVR equipment serving the runway touchdown zone.

   b. *Mid-RVR.* The RVR readout values obtained from RVR equipment located midfield of the runway.

   c. *Rollout RVR.* The RVR readout values obtained from RVR equipment located nearest the rollout end of the runway.

[ICAO] The ability, as determined by atmospheric conditions and expressed in units of distance, to see and identify prominent unlighted objects by day and prominent lighted objects by night.

Flight visibility. [ICAO] The visibility forward from the cockpit of an aircraft in flight.

Ground visibility. [ICAO] The visibility at an aerodrome as reported by an accredited observer.

Runway visual range (RVR). [ICAO] The range over which the pilot of an aircraft on the centerline of a runway can see the runway surface markings or the lights delineating the runway or identifying its centerline.

visual approach. An approach conducted on an instrument flight rules (IFR) flight plan which authorizes the pilot to proceed visually and clear of clouds to the airport. The pilot must, at all times, have either the airport or the preceding aircraft in sight. This approach must be authorized and under the control of the appropriate air traffic control facility. Reported weather at the airport must be ceiling at or above 1,000 feet and visibility of 3 miles or greater. [ICAO] An approach by an IFR flight when either part or all of an instrument approach procedure is not completed and the approach is executed in visual reference to terrain.

Visual Approach Slope Indicator (VASI). (*See* airport lighting).

visual descent point (VDP). A defined point on the final approach course of a nonprecision straight-in approach procedure from which normal descent from the MDA to the runway touchdown point may be commenced, provided the approach threshold of that runway, or approach lights, or other markings identifiable with the approach end of that runway are clearly visible to the pilot.

visual flight rules (VFR). Rules that govern the procedures for conducting flight under visual conditions. The term "VFR" is also used in the United States to indicate weather conditions that are equal to or greater than minimum VFR requirements. In addition, it is used by pilots and controllers to indicate type of flight plan. (*See* instrument flight rules, instrument meteorological conditions, visual meteorological conditions) (Refer to 14 CFR Part 91 and AIM).

visual holding. The holding of aircraft at selected, prominent geographical fixes which can be easily recognized from the air. (*See* holding fix).

visual meteorological conditions (VMC). Meteorological conditions expressed in terms of visibility, distance from cloud, and ceiling equal to or better than specified minima. (*See* instrument flight rules, instrument meteorological conditions, visual flight rules).

visual separation. A means employed by ATC to separate aircraft in terminal areas and en route airspace in the NAS. There are two ways to effect this separation:

1. The tower controller sees the aircraft involved and issues instructions, as necessary, to ensure that the aircraft avoid each other.

2. A pilot sees the other aircraft involved and upon instructions from the controller provides his own separation by maneuvering his aircraft as necessary to avoid it. This may involve following another aircraft or keeping it in sight until it is no longer a factor. (*See*: see and avoid) (Refer to 14 CFR Part 91).

VLF. (*See* very low frequency).

VMC. (*See* visual meteorological conditions).

VNAV. (*See* vertical navigation).

voice switching and control system (VSCS). The VSCS is a computer controlled switching system that provides air traffic controllers with all voice circuits (air to ground and ground to ground) necessary for air traffic control.

VOR. A ground based electronic navigation aid transmitting very high frequency navigation signals, 360 degrees in azimuth, oriented from magnetic north. Used as the basis for navigation in the National Airspace System. The VOR periodically identifies itself by Morse Code and may have an additional voice identification feature. Voice features may be used by ATC or FSS for transmitting instructions/information to pilots. (*See* navigational aid) (Refer to AIM).

***VOR.** VHF Omnidirectional Range. The basis for the airways system.

***VOR-DME.** The civilian equivalent of a VORTAC, with both navigation and distance measuring signals, under the control of the FAA.

VORTAC. A navigation aid providing VOR azimuth, TACAN azimuth, and TACAN distance measuring equipment (DME) at one site. (*See* distance measuring equipment, navigational aid, TACAN, VOR) (Refer to AIM).

***VORTAC.** A VOR colocated with a military TACAN (tactical aid to navigations) station. Civilians use the navigational signal from the VOR and the distance information from the TACAN.

VOR test signal. (*See* VOT).

***vortex.** A mass of air having a whirling or circular motion. *plural*: vortices.

vortices. Circular patterns of air created by the movement of an airfoil through the air when generating lift. As an airfoil moves through the atmosphere in sustained flight, an area of low pressure is created above it. The air flowing from the high pressure area to the low pressure area around and about the tips of the airfoil tends to roll up into two rapidly rotating vortices, cylindrical in shape. These vortices are the most predominant parts of aircraft wake turbulence and their rotational force is dependent upon the wing loading, gross weight, and speed of the generating aircraft. The vortices from medium to heavy aircraft can be of extremely high velocity and hazardous to smaller aircraft. (*See* aircraft classes, wake turbulence) (Refer to AIM).

VOT. A ground facility which emits a test signal to check VOR receiver accuracy. Some VOTs are available to the user while airborne, and others are limited to ground use only. (Refer to 14 CFR Part 91, AIM, Airport/Facility Directory).

***VOT.** A special transmitter located at major airports to test VOR receivers for accuracy.

VR. (*See* VFR military training route).

VSCS. (*See* voice switching and control system).

VTA. (*See* vertex time of arrival).

VTOL aircraft. (*See* vertical takeoff and landing aircraft).

WA. (*See* AIRMET, Weather Advisory).

WAAS. (*See* wide-area augmentation system).

wake turbulence. Phenomena resulting from the passage of an aircraft through the atmosphere. The term includes vortices, thrust stream turbulence, jet blast, jet wash, propeller wash, and rotor wash both on the ground and in the air. (*See* aircraft classes, jet blast, vortices) (Refer to AIM).

Warning Area. (*See* Special Use airspace).

waypoint. A predetermined geographical position used for route/instrument approach definition, or progress reporting purposes, that is defined relative to a VORTAC station or in terms of latitude/longitude coordinates.

Weather Advisory (WS) (WST) (WA) (CWA). In aviation weather forecast practice, an expression of hazardous weather conditions not predicted in the area forecast, as they affect the operation of air traffic and as prepared by the NWS. (*See* SIGMET, AIRMET).

when able. When used in conjunction with ATC instructions, gives the pilot the latitude to delay compliance until a condition or even has been reconciled. Unlike "pilot discretion," when instructions are prefaced "when able," the pilot is expected to seek the first opportunity to comply. Once a maneuver has been initiated, the pilot is expected to continue until the specifications of the instructions have been met. "When able," should not be used when expeditious compliance is required.

wide-area augmentation system (WAAS). The WAAS is a satellite navigation system consisting of the equipment and software which augments the GPS Standard Positioning Service (SPS). The WAAS provides enhanced integrity, accuracy, availability, and continuity over and above GPS SPS. The differential correction function provides improved accuracy required for precision approach.

wilco. I have received your message, understand it, and will comply with it.

*wind correction angle. The angular difference between course and heading.

*wind drift. The sideways motion over the ground caused by a crosswind.

wind shear. A change in wind speed and/or wind direction in a short distance resulting in a tearing or shearing effect. It can exist in a horizontal or vertical direction and occasionally in both.

*wind triangle. A graphic means of computing wind correction angle and ground speed.

wing-tip vortices. (*See* vortices).

words twice.

1. As a request: "Communication is difficult. Please say every phrase twice."
2. As information: "Since communications are difficult, every phrase in this message will be spoken twice."

world aeronautical charts. (*See* aeronautical chart).

WS. (*See* SIGMET, Weather Advisory).

WST. (*See* Convective SIGMET, Weather Advisory).

*yaw axis. A vertical line through the center of gravity that intersects the longitudinal and lateral axes. The pilot uses rudder to control the airplane around the yaw axis.

*Zulu time (Z). Time in relation to the time at Greenwich, England; also called Greenwich Mean Time.

A Suggested Self-Briefing Format Using Computer Products

If you must self-brief, you may like to use the following format (not all-inclusive).

1. Adverse Conditions

FA	WSTs
SIGMETs	TWEBs
AIRMETs	TAFs
CWAs	FDs
Current charts	

2. Synopsis

FA	Current charts
TWEBs	

3. Current Weather

Surface observation (METAR)

PIREPs

NWS charts

1. Radar	4. Weather depiction
2. Surface analysis	5. Satellite pictures
3. Upper air analysis	

4. Enroute Forecasts

FAs

TWEBs

TAFs

5. Destination Forecasts

FAs

TWEBs

TAFs

6. Winds and Temperatures Aloft

FDs

7. Aeronautical Information

NOTAM

1. Printed
2. FAA FSS
3. DUATs

8. Request for PIREPs

Honor system

9. Closing Statement

A pilot weather briefer will often give you a summary of the briefing. If you are self-briefing, it is a good idea for you to make your own summary. **See that it makes sense to you; if not, then re-evaluate the situation.**

CWA – Center weather advisory

FA – Area forecast

FD – Winds aloft forecast

TAF – Terminal aerodrome forecast

PIREP – pilot report

TWEB – Transcribed weather broadcast

WST – Convective SIGMET

Continued

Some Important Items to Remember

Cloud Heights in Forecasts

1. Given in feet above ground level (AGL):

   a. In surface observations (METARs)

   b. In terminal aerodrome forecasts (TAFs)

2. Given in feet above sea level (MSL):

   a. In aviation area forecasts (FAs)

   b. In transcribed weather broadcasts (TWEBs)

   c. The exception is when the word "CIGS" is used. If "CIGS" is used, the heights following are above ground level.

   d. PIREPs

   e. Winds aloft forecasts (FDs)

AIRMET

1. Covers light to moderate weather phenomena.

2. Mainly intended for General Aviation (light) aircraft.

3. The phenomena must cover 3,000 square miles or more.

4. Items covered—non-convective:

   a. Turbulence

   b. Icing

   c. IFR conditions

SIGMET

1. Covers greater-than-moderate weather phenomena

2. Intended for all aircraft.

3. Items covered—non-convective:

   a. Turbulence

   b. Icing

   c. IFR conditions

   d. Volcanic ash

Convective SIGMET

1. Covers greater-than-moderate weather phenomena.

2. Intended for all aircraft.

3. Items covered—only convective-related:

   a. Turbulence

   b. Icing

   c. Tornado

Terminal Aerodrome Forecast (TAF)

1. Ceiling, visibility, and wind:

   a. A ceiling is when more than 1/2 of the sky is obscured by clouds.

   b. If a forecast is for a BKN ceiling, and OVC occurs instead, it is still considered a good forecast.

   c. All elements remain in the forecast until taken out at a later time. Let the following example explain: 20 SCT 40 OVC 2515 OCNL C20 BKN. When the sky is 20 BKN, the 40 OVC layer still exists, as does the wind.

   d. Visibility will be mentioned when it is less than 6 miles.

   e. Winds will not be mentioned if less than 6 knots.

AFSS Toll-Free Telephone Numbers

Facility	Station Code	Telephone Number	Facility	Station Code	Telephone Number
Albuquerque, NM	ABQ	866-449-5390	Jackson, TN	MKL	866-840-1051
Altoona, PA	AOO	866-708-9987	Jonesboro, AR	JBR	866-520-8890
Anderson, SC	AND	866-225-2172	Juneau, AK	JNU	866-297-2236
Anniston, AL	ANB	866-609-8684	Kankakee, IL	IKK	866-450-6593
Bangor, ME	BGR	866-295-3835	Kenai, AK	ENA	866-864-1737
Boise, ID	BOI	866-258-9068	Lansing, MI	LAN	866-879-4066
Bridgeport, CT	BDR	866-293-5149	Leesburg, VA	DCA	866-225-7410
Buffalo, NY	BUF	866-678-2759	Louisville, KY	LOU	866-412-7968
Burlington, VT	BTV	866-847-1846	Macon, GA	MCN	866-276-0243
Casper, WY	CPR	866-277-7498	McAlester, OK	MLC	866-269-0189
Cedar City, UT	CDC	866-667-3858	McMinnville, OR	MMV	866-833-7631
Cleveland, OH	CLE	866-780-8261	Miami, FL	MIA	866-347-0316
Columbia, MO	COU	866-223-4352	Millville, NJ	MIV	866-225-7620
Columbus, NE	OLU	866-288-3448	Nashville, TN	BNA	866-890-1348
Conroe, TX	CXO	866-689-5992	Oakland, CA	OAK	866-469-7828
Dayton, OH	DAY	866-505-6163	Prescott, AZ	PRC	866-226-3763
Denver, CO	DEN	866-751-7021	Princeton, MN	PMN	866-841-6469
Deridder, LA	DRI	866-401-5659	Raleigh, NC	RDU	866-663-3354
Elkins, WV	EKN	866-656-2661	Rancho Murieta, CA	RIU	866-272-7525
Fairbanks, AK	FAI	866-248-6516	Reno, NV	RNO	866-281-2737
Fort Dodge, IA	FOD	866-300-2858	Riverside, CA	RAL	866-838-2250
Ft. Worth, TX	FTW	866-272-7915	San Angelo, TX	STJ	866-300-3867
Gainesville, FL	GNV	866-523-7229	San Diego, CA	SAN	866-682-2175
Grand Forks, ND	GFK	866-306-6931	San Juan, PR	SJU	866-822-8537
Great Falls, MT	GTF	866-527-7601	Seattle, WA	SEA	866-384-7323
Green Bay, WI	GRB	866-845-4888	St. Louis, MO	STL	866-671-6176
Greenwood, MS	GWO	866-245-6109	St. Petersbrg FL	PIE	866-295-3983
Hawthorne, CA	HHR	866-879-8252	Terre Haute, IN	HUF	866-224-9906
Honolulu, HI	HNL	866-766-0820	Wichita, KS	ICT	866-672-5145
Huron, SD	HON	866-732-1331	Williamsport, PA	IPT	866-655-6434
Islip, NT	ISP	866-365-5019			

Index